ARABS AT WAR

ARABS AT WAR

MILITARY EFFECTIVENESS, 1948–1991

KENNETH M. POLLACK

A Council on Foreign Relations Book

UNIVERSITY OF NEBRASKA PRESS
LINCOLN AND LONDON

Earlier versions of chapters 1, 2, 3, 5, and 6 appeared as Kenneth M. Pollack, "The Influence of Arab Culture on Arab Military Effectiveness, 1948–1991" (Ph.D. diss., MIT, 1996), chapters 2–6.

Library of Congress Cataloging-in-Publication Data

Pollack, Kenneth M. (Kenneth Michael), 1966–
Arabs at war: Military effectiveness, 1948–1991 / Kenneth M. Pollack.
p.cm — (Studies in war, society, and the military)
"A Council on Foreign Relations book"
Based in part on the author's dissertation (doctoral — MIT, 1996) under the title: The influence of Arab culture on Arab military effectiveness, 1948–1991.
Includes bibliographical references and index.
ISBN 0-8032-3733-2 (cl.: alk. paper)
1. Arab countries — History, Military — 20th century. 2. Arab countries — Armed Forces. 3. Arab countries — Military policy. I. Title. II. Series.

UA854.P65 2002
355'.0330174927'09045-dc21   2002022305

For my parents, Ann and Peter,
who made everything possible.

CONTENTS

MAPS

TABLES

PREFACE

This book is intended to serve two purposes. First, it is designed to try to help answer one of the great vexing questions of post–World War II Middle Eastern affairs: what is it that has consistently hindered the Arab armed forces in battle such that they consistently lose wars or win them just barely? This issue is of more than mere historical curiosity. Every six months or so, another crisis with Iraq reminds us that the U.S. armed forces may again be called on to go to war in the Persian Gulf. Meanwhile, the Middle East peace process has slipped into a torpor, and it is far from certain that it will recover promptly, if at all. If it does not, we may not have written the last chapter in the story of the Arab-Israeli wars. In short, it behooves us to develop a better understanding of the driving forces in Middle Eastern conflicts so that we can be better prepared for another round.

The second purpose of this book is to provide a robust assessment of the strengths and weaknesses of Arab militaries. Since the British withdrawal from "East of Suez" in 1971, the United States has found itself increasingly entangled in the Middle East both diplomatically and militarily. This trend accelerated dramatically after the Iraqi invasion of Kuwait and the massive U.S. military deployment it triggered. Today our military commitment to the Middle East is one of the highest American foreign-policy priorities. As our recent war in Afghanistan has demonstrated, there is every reason to expect that in the future, the U.S. military will again be called on to fight in this part of the world. Because of this commitment, the U.S. military constantly plans and trains to fight both alongside, and against, Arab armies. The rogue states of the Middle East are among our most important potential foes, and the moderate Arab states of the region are among our most important allies. It is crucial that we have a thorough understanding of the capabilities and liabilities of these countries. We have to know what we can count on from our Arab allies and in what areas they most need our support. And we have to know the capabilities of our Arab adversaries so that we can exploit their weaknesses and avoid their areas of strength.

When the United States launched Operation Desert Storm, the military establishment had an imperfect knowledge of our Egyptian, Syrian, Kuwaiti, and Saudi allies as well as our Iraqi enemies. We were fortunate that our own strength was so overwhelming and Iraqi weakness so all-encompassing that we did not really pay for this ignorance. We cannot assume we will be so lucky again in the future.

ACKNOWLEDGMENTS

I have a lot of people to thank for assistance in writing this book. Barry Posen deserves pride of place on this list. Barry constantly pushed me to defend my analysis against the toughest arguments and regularly provided me with new insights that I might otherwise have missed altogether. Indeed, probably more than anyone else, Barry taught me how to think about modern militaries. Without his wisdom, this book and its author would have been much the poorer. Likewise, Stephen Van Evera taught me how to ask the right questions and find the right answers. I will be eternally grateful to him for pointing me in the right direction.

Steve Ward, John Wagner, Bruce Pease, Ben Miller, Red Brewer, Ed Pendleton, Hank Malcom, Gene Lodge, and Lt. Gen. Bernard Trainor taught me everything I know about Middle Eastern militaries. Moreover, all of them reviewed sections of the book dealing with the areas of their expertise and furnished more good advice and criticism than I probably deserved. I also must thank Lisa Anderson, Amatzia Baram, Dan Byman, Mike Eisenstadt, Phebe Marr, Tom McNaugher, Brent Sterling, Joshua Teitelbaum, and Judi Yaphe, all of whom shared their great store of learning about the Middle East to help me with any number of chapters.

Andrew Bacevich, Dan Byman, Eliot Cohen, Mike Desch, Mike Eisenstadt, John Lynn, Daryl Press, Stephen P. Rosen, Chris Savos, and Brent Sterling all read part or all of this study and provided invaluable comments. Likewise, Lauren Rossman has my thanks for helping with some key research issues.

I conducted something on the order of two hundred interviews for this book. Many of those interviewed agreed to allow me to quote them on the record. Many others agreed to do so only on condition of anonymity. Typically, they were active U.S., Israeli, European, Egyptian, Jordanian, and Turkish military officers and intelligence analysts whose governments would not approve of their making statements on the record. Others were retired Egyptian or Jordanian military officers who nevertheless felt it impolitic to have themselves quoted. And some were former Iraqi military officers who have fled Saddam Husayn's regime. All who consented to interviews have my deepest thanks. They made this book a far richer work than it otherwise might have been.

A manuscript version of this work was reviewed before publication by both the Central Intelligence Agency and the Defense Intelligence Agency to ensure that it contained no classified material. Neither agency altered the text in any way. I would like to thank Ben Bonk, Bruce Pease, Jack Duggan, Winston Wiley, and Phil Ferguson for helping guide it through the labyrinthine prepublication review process with the minimum of pain.

Dennis Showalter devoted more of his time and labor to see this study published than I could ever have asked. The reason this book is in bookstores at all is because he was determined to see it there. I have tried hard not to rely on the kindness of strangers, but I am entirely indebted to Dennis for his generosity. Likewise, Pete Maslowski of the University of Nebraska has my gratitude for taking on this project and seeing it through to print. Michael Manley provided invaluable assistance at key points in the life of this work, dealing with the legal minutiae for which I am wholly unequipped. Without Mike's help, I might have fallen into any number of legal potholes. Barbara King Bradbury also has my thanks for helping me get through many tough patches in the writing and research process.

Several institutions provided critical support that helped bring this work to fruition. First, Harvey Sapolsky and the Security Studies Program at the Massachusetts Institute of Technology furnished me with the time, resources, and intellectual stimulation to dream up this project and undertake the major part of the research and writing. Since this work began as part of my doctoral thesis, and Harvey and MIT very generously sponsored and supported that effort, they deserve an equally hefty share of the thanks. I also greatly profited from a year at the John M. Olin Institute for National Strategic Studies at Harvard. Not only did this give me access to Harvard's resources and an uninterrupted year to turn my research into a full-fledged manuscript, it also gave me access to Samuel Huntington and Stephen Peter Rosen — the most important of the many benefits I derived from my time there. Finally, I would also like to thank Leslie Gelb and the Council on Foreign Relations, who supplied invaluable material and psychological assistance in the final stages of this project. Without Les and the Council, I would have been typing in the rain.

And last, but never least, is my wife, Andrea, for whom my gratitude could only be boundless.

The reader, and these friends and colleagues who helped bring this work to fruition, should bear in mind that any mistakes contained in the pages of this book are mine and mine alone.

ARABS AT WAR

UNDERSTANDING MODERN ARAB

MILITARY EFFECTIVENESS

In June 1944 the Soviet Union launched Operation Bagration against the German Wehrmacht's Army Group Center in Byelorussia. Although the Germans were a veteran army defending well-fortified lines, the Soviets had tactical surprise and overwhelming material advantages. They had three times as many troops as the Germans, six times as many tanks, and eight times as many artillery pieces. The result was a total rout. Soviet infantry and artillery blasted huge holes in the German lines, and Soviet tanks and cavalry poured through the gaps and drove deep into the German rear, encircling large formations. Two months later the Soviet advance finally came to a halt on the banks of the Vistula River in Poland, almost 1,000 kilometers from their start lines. In that time the Red Army had obliterated Army Group Center, shattering thirty German divisions and capturing or killing nearly 450,000 of Germany's finest soldiers.[1]

Twenty-nine years later, in October 1973, the Syrian army launched a similarly massive offensive against Israeli forces occupying the Golan Heights. Like the Germans, the Israelis were a veteran army defending fortified lines, and like the Soviets, the Syrians had surprise and over-whelming material advantages on their side, having ten times as many troops as the Israelis, eight times as many tanks, and ten times as many artillery pieces.[2] Syria achieved an even greater degree of surprise than had the Soviets because the Israelis, unlike the Germans, were at peace and not expecting a fight. Nevertheless, the Syrian offensive was a fiasco. They were able to break through the Israeli lines in only one of two designated assault sectors. Syrian armored columns got no farther than twenty kilometers before they were stopped by tiny Israeli forces. Within two days the attack had run out of steam without accomplishing any of its objectives. An Israeli counterattack on the third day of the war smashed the Syrian forces and sent them reeling, driving them off the Golan and erasing all of their modest gains. The Israelis then continued on, pushing toward Damascus itself before they were forced to stop because of the unexpected arrival of reinforcements from Jordan and Iraq.

In 1973 the Syrians had all of the advantages that the Soviets had enjoyed in 1944, probably even more. But the Syrians were unable to achieve the same results as the Red Army. Whereas the Russians went on to win one of the most stunning victories in modern history, the Syrians suffered one of their nation's worst defeats. The Soviet success in Byelorussia was so crushing that it paved the way for the final Soviet assault on Germany and ended the threat to Russia from Hitler's Reich. The failed attack on the Golan was equally decisive, persuading Syria that it had no option to regain the area from Israel by conventional assault, a conclusion that has held firm for nearly thirty years.

Comparing Syrian and Soviet fortunes demonstrates that the history of warfare in the Middle East defies understanding by traditional, material measures. Since the end of the European and Ottoman empires, the Middle East has been consumed by conflict. The Arab states have repeatedly gone to war with Israel, with Iran, with indigenous ethnic groups, with Africans, with Europeans, with Americans, and with each other. Yet in each of these wars, the Arabs have fared worse than expected. The Soviet-Syrian comparison demonstrates that when traditional Western (particularly American) methods for assessing military power are applied to the Middle East, they generally fail to explain the actual outcomes. The Soviets prevailed in 1944 because of the advantages of surprise and numbers. Yet the Syrians, with the same advantages, lost badly.

Nor can other conventional measures of military power adequately explain the outcome of modern Middle Eastern wars. In addition to the numeric balance and considerations of surprise, Western military analysts have traditionally explained battlefield outcomes by reference to imbalances in firepower, the quality of weaponry employed by the combatants, air support, foreign intervention, and a variety of lesser factors. However, the history of Arab armies in combat demonstrates that none of these factors could reasonably explain the outcomes. Numerous examples can be found of Arab armies that, like the Syrians in 1973, enjoyed commanding advantages in one or all of these categories yet still lost, often disastrously.

For example, Libyan forces defending Tripoli's conquests in northern Chad in 1987 deployed far more advanced and more powerful weaponry than their Chadian opponents but were crushed nonetheless. The Libyans were armed with Soviet-made T-62 and T-55 tanks, BTR-60 and BTR-70 armored personnel carriers (APCS), D-30 and M-46 artillery pieces, and MiG-21, MiG-23, and Su-22 fighter-bombers. In contrast, Chadian forces possessed nothing more sophisticated than a handful of older Western armored cars and mostly relied on Toyota pick-up trucks mounting crew-served infantry weapons. The Chadians had no tanks, no APCS, no artillery, no air force, no infantry weapons heavier than the Milan antitank guided missile, and only the complicated and ineffectual Redeye shoulder-launched surface-to-air missile (SAM) for air defense. What's more, the Chadians did not operate their weaponry very well. Nevertheless, an army of as many as 20,000 Libyans was demolished by 10,000 Chadian regulars and 20,000 tribal militia during eight months of fighting.[3]

Similarly, against Iran in 1980, Iraqi forces enjoyed a heavy advantage in the firepower they could bring to bear. Iraq boasted 2,750 tanks, 1,040 artillery pieces, 2,500 APCS, and 330 fighter-bombers. Against this, Iran could muster no more than about 500 operational tanks, probably no more than 300 functioning artillery pieces, and less than 100 operable aircraft.[4] In every battle the Iraqis were able to bring enormous firepower to bear against the outgunned Iranians. Despite this advantage, Iraq's invasion of southwestern Iran hardly dented the disorganized and demoralized Iranian military, nor did Baghdad conquer anything of military or economic value in three months of largely unimpeded offensives. By the end of that same war, Iraqi forces not only enjoyed very sizable advantages in numbers of equipment but also possessed an equivalent edge in the sophistication of their weaponry. For instance, Iraqi forces deployed nearly 5,000 tanks compared to the less than 1,000 operable tanks Iran could muster — and most of the Iraqi tanks that saw the brunt of the fighting were advanced T-72s and T-62s, while the Iranians were mostly equipped with miserable Chinese Type-59s. Whereas the Iraqi Air Force had nearly 700 combat aircraft, including new French Mirage F-1s and Soviet MiG-29s, the Iranians had less than 100 flyable U.S. F-14s, F-4s, and F-5s, few of which were fully functional as a result of the U.S. arms embargo. Still, Iraq was able to eke out a win in 1988 only by resorting to liberal doses of chemical warfare and creating local force ratios of 20- or even 30-to-1 in tanks, troops, and guns.

In short, conventional measures cannot explain Arab experiences in battle. Since 1945 the Arab states have experienced problems that have denied their armed forces the success on the battlefield that objective factors suggest should be within their grasp. The source of this problem is what is often referred to as the "human factor" or military effectiveness. Military effectiveness is the ability of an armed service to prosecute military operations and employ weaponry in military operations.[5] It is therefore a measure of the quality of an army's personnel — not the quality of its weaponry or the quantity of its men or materiel. Military effectiveness refers to the ability of soldiers and officers to perform on the battlefield, to accomplish military missions, and to execute the strategies devised by their political-military leaders. If strategy is the military means by which political ends are pursued, military effectiveness refers to the skills that are employed.

Of course, military effectiveness is not the same thing as victory and is only one of many factors that determines victory or defeat. Highly effective armed forces may still lose wars, and highly ineffective militaries may still win them. For example, the Germany army from 1914 to 1945 is widely considered to have been extremely competent in many areas of military operations, yet it ultimately lost both world wars. But George Washington's Continental Army could never match the battlefield proficiency of its British foes, yet it found a way to win the American Revolutionary War.

It is clear from the comparisons above and a raft of other examples that in the Middle East military effectiveness has played the decisive role in determining the outcome of the various wars fought between the Arabs and their foes. Israel's triumphs over larger and better-armed Arab armies have been a clear sign that the military balance in the region has primarily been driven by the military effectiveness of the opposing forces rather than numbers, equipment, or any other material factor. Thus, since 1948, military officers, analysts, politicians, journalists, and historians have all concluded that war in the Middle East has principally been decided by the quality of the combatants, not their numbers or weapons, their industry or technology, their morale or allies.[6]

Explanations for Arab Military Ineffectiveness

Although there is a consensus that the principal culprit hobbling the Arab states in war is the limited effectiveness of their armed forces, there is disagreement over the specific problems they encounter in combat.[7] Over the course of time, different military officers, analysts, and historians have offered divergent assessments of the strengths and weaknesses of Arab armies and air forces.[8] In every case they have identified certain kinds of military operations they believe the Arab armed forces perform poorly and have claimed that it has been these specific problems that have limited Arab victories and exacerbated their defeats.

Unit Cohesion

Among the most well-known arguments regarding Arab military ineffectiveness is the claim that their armies have been plagued by poor unit cohesion, or the willingness of small military formations — platoons, companies, battalions, squadrons, and such — to stick together and continue to fight and act as a team in the stress of combat. Since the Second World War, a number of American authors, particularly the distinguished combat veteran S. L. A. Marshall, have argued that an army's tactical unit cohesion is probably the single most important element of its overall effectiveness.[9] Several months after the Six Day War, Israel's military intelligence chief, Yehoshofat Harkabi, wrote an article arguing that the collapse of the Arab armies during that war and the 1956 Sinai-Suez War derived from poor unit cohesion, which he in turn ascribed to societal influences in Arab interpersonal relations. Harkabi asserted that Israeli victory had been possible — in fact, easy — in these conflicts primarily because the Egyptian, Syrian, and Jordanian units they fought fell apart quickly when attacked by the Israelis. He described the fighting as consisting of sharp blows from Israeli forces that caused the Arab units to dissolve and left every man for himself. Since Arab units fragmented upon contact, the Israeli victories were quick and required little fighting.[10]

Generalship

Another explanation for Arab military ineffectiveness is that Arab armies have regularly been disappointed by the performance of the generals who led them. This argument is frequently heard in the wake of Middle Eastern wars, especially from the Arabs themselves, many of whom claim that their troops fought well but were betrayed by the incompetence or perfidy of their senior leaders. For example, after the Six Day War, the Egyptians blamed Field Marshal 'Amr for the catastrophe; the Jordanians heaped all fault for their defeat on the Egyptian commander of the eastern front, Lt. Gen. 'Abd al-Mun'im Riyad; and the Syrians nearly ousted Hafiz al-Asad from his post as defense minister for losing the Golan Heights.[11] Likewise, the generals who led the Egyptian, Iraqi, and Syrian armies were all held culpable for their defeat at the hands of the Israelis in 1948, and Saddam Husayn purged nearly all of his top army and air force commanders for the poor showing of Iraqi forces during the 1980 invasion of Iran.[12]

Tactical Leadership

Another explanation for the problems of Arab armed forces is that Arab junior officers are unable to conduct modern maneuver warfare. Competent tactical leadership is crucial to contemporary military operations.[13] On land, combat is dominated by infantry, artillery, tanks, and other armored vehicles, often engaging in fluid battles of maneuver. In the air, combat is dominated by nimble fighter and attack aircraft, whose pilots likewise must prevail in chaotic and quickly changing engagements. The fluidity of these battles places a tremendous burden on tactical leadership.

To succeed on the modern battlefield, a military must be able to decentralize command and have the kind of leaders at the scene with the right demeanor to seize fleeting opportunities to defeat the enemy. In a tank battle it is the commander who recognizes a gap opening between two enemy units and plunges in immediately, before his adversary can close it, who usually prevails. It is the same in air combat, in which a pilot must recognize in the midst of a swirling dogfight — or an airstrike against a heavily defended target — when an opportunity arises allowing him to drive home an advantage. Consequently, modern combat demands tactical leaders — platoon, company, battalion, and brigade commanders as well as pilots and squadron leaders — who are aggressive and have the initiative to take immediate, independent action; who are innovative and able to find creative solutions to battlefield problems; who are flexible and can quickly change their actions to adapt to unforeseen circumstances; who realize the importance of maneuvering to gain a spatial advantage over the enemy and constantly search for ways to achieve this; and who understand how their own mission fits into the larger battle so that they can improvise solutions to unexpected problems and help the efforts of their commanders.

Success on the modern battlefield also requires the tactical integration of the various combat arms. Normally, it is the army that can best coordinate the actions of its infantry, armor, mechanized infantry, artillery, antitank units, aircraft, combat engineers, and antiaircraft forces (to name only a few) that prevails. Because the whole of a modern military working as a team is much more powerful than the sum of its parts, it is crucial for any army to demonstrate good combined-arms operations if it is to perform at its peak. This means that tactical commanders must ensure that their armored forces are properly supported by infantry and artillery to suppress enemy antitank teams, that their infantry is able to advance by using armor to punch through enemy lines and air power to silence enemy artillery, that their engineers clear routes for the tanks and infantry over minefields and across water obstacles, and that their air forces are able to fly unhindered by using armored forces to disrupt enemy air defenses in addition to other considerations.

Many Israeli military officers and Western military historians have cited problems in these areas as the greatest failings of Arab armed forces.[14] Israeli field commanders, almost to a man, aver that Arab junior officers are unable to function in the manner required of tactical leaders in the kinds of fluid ground and air battles that frequently prove decisive in modern wars. Indeed, the Israelis have consciously structured their own military doctrine to take advantage of this perceived weakness.[15]

Information Management

Another problem of military effectiveness frequently ascribed to Arab armed forces is poor acquisition and management of information. Knowing more than one's adversary is often a decisive advantage on the battlefield and failing to get the right information into the hands of those who most need it is often a crippling liability. Israelis, Westerners, and even many senior Arab military officers have acknowledged that Arab armed forces have tremendous difficulty handling information. Here the claim is that Arab militaries pay inadequate attention to gathering intelligence — especially at tactical levels — about their adversaries and that Arab soldiers and officers do not properly pass information along the chain of command to ensure that every unit has the information it needs to execute its mission. In particular, these officers state that Arab militaries compartmentalize information, that little information flows from top levels down to field formations, and that lower levels of the chain of command regularly distort or even fabricate information to exaggerate successes and hide failures.[16]

Technical Skills and Weapons Handling

Machines are an integral part of modern warfare. The weapons of modern armed forces — even the simplest ones such as pistols and rifles — are all mechanical devices. Moreover, since World War II, increasingly complex weapons have been added to the national arsenals. The relatively simple antiaircraft guns of 1945 have been superseded by highly complicated SAMs and radar-controlled guns. Even the most complex tanks of World War II are child's play compared to the computer-controlled versions of the Persian Gulf War of 1990–91. Likewise, the propeller-driven airplanes of the 1940s are a different kind of machine altogether from the jets of the 1990s. In short, throughout the last fifty years, technology and machines have been the sinews of war. It is almost inconceivable to make war without them, and the more powerful the machines an army possesses, and the better an army is able to employ the machines at its disposal, the better it is likely to fare on the battlefield.

A charge frequently leveled against Arab armed forces is that they are unable to fully exploit the capabilities of the weapons and other military equipment they possess. On some occasions, they have complained that the equipment they fielded was either inferior to that of their opponents or obsolete altogether. However, the large number of wars the Arabs have waged in which their equipment was equal or even superior to that of their foe undermines this claim. But Western and Israeli military personnel who have faced the Arabs in battle have repeatedly opined that Arab soldiers and officers are rarely able to employ their equipment to the full extent of its capabilities. They argue that Arab personnel are not technically expert enough to handle their weapons in the fashion intended by the manufacturer, and that the more sophisticated the weaponry, the less able are Arab personnel to employ it properly. Thus, Arab armies have fallen victim to their own lack of technical proficiency and their own inability to use their tanks, artillery, aircraft, and other weapons properly.[17]

Logistics and Maintenance

Closely related to these charges is the claim that Arab armies likewise have difficulty sustaining their forces in battle. Logistics has always been the linchpin of military operations, and today, because of the mechanization of armies and the development of air power, supplying military forces has had to become vastly more complex to handle the quantum increase in logistical demands created by mechanization. Quartermasters now have to worry about not only feeding, clothing, and quartering troops but also ensuring an adequate flow of fuel, lubricants, spare parts, ammunition, and other consumables for the vast array of vehicles and weapons a modern army deploys.

Moreover, it is not enough simply to provide supplies for this equipment; it must be maintained as well. This entails both routine preventive maintenance to ensure that the machinery continues to function properly and repair work to fix or replace equipment damaged by movement, weather, neglect, or combat. Just as supplying a modern army demands technically sophisticated personnel who understand the needs of a mechanized force and can see that its supply requirements are met, so maintenance demands large numbers of technically able support personnel who can keep this military hardware functioning.

Morale

Still another explanation offered for Arab military problems is poor morale. Many observers, particularly in the Arab world, have excused the performance of their armed forces by claiming that the soldiers and officers have lacked the will to fight. They often note that a despotic regime fought these conflicts for goals that were less than compelling to their troops. The Iraqi collapse during the Gulf War is often cited as an example of this phenomenon. In other cases, class differences resulting in friction between officers and enlisted men have been cited as the culprit, creating a spirit of ambivalence or even hostility that sapped any commitment to the cause. This charge is often leveled at the Egyptian army during the Six Day War, in which Egyptian officers—having no ties to their men—allegedly abandoned them to their fate as soon as the Israelis attacked, demoralizing the soldiers and leading to the rout of the entire army.[18]

Training

Some scholars of the Middle East have asserted that Arab defeats resulted from misguided or inadequate training and claim that because Arab militaries are often charged with defending their regime against internal threats, their forces are preoccupied with policing the streets to guard against any popular revolt and shielding the palace of the despot to prevent a coup d'état. Proponents of this explanation argue that Arab militaries train and prepare to deal primarily with internal threats—riots, coups, and revolutions—and not for conventional military operations against foreign armies. It is this lack of preparation that has plagued Arab armed forces, they charge, and claim that if the Arabs were ever to dedicate themselves to a training regimen for conventional warfare, they would do just fine.[19]

A few Western military officers and analysts aver that Arab militaries simply do not train "seriously" for modern combat. By this they mean that training is lackadaisical, sporadic, and often entirely neglected. This is not to say that the preparation is "bad" or "misguided," as those who believe Arab training focuses excessively on internal threats argue. Instead, these commentators assert that rather than being *inappropriate*, Arab training is simply *inadequate*. They believe that this lack of attention to training causes poor tactical leadership, poor morale, poor combined arms operations, poor weapons handling, and poor intelligence gathering. Thus, they claim that many, if not all, of the problems diagnosed by other experts are ultimately the result of inadequate training.[20]

Cowardice

Perhaps the most malicious theory offered to account for the failings of Arab armies in combat is that Arab soldiers and officers are simply cowards who break and run at the first sign of danger. Few military experts subscribe to this, but it has been a widely held belief among Western civilians and even a number of Western military officers, including some with considerable experience fighting the Arabs. For example, Winston Churchill once remarked, "It appeared easier to draw sunbeams out of cucumbers than to put courage into the *fellah*," referring to Egyptian peasants.[21] Some Israeli military officers have also suggested this explanation.[22]

Assessing Arab Military Effectiveness

Clearly, there is no shortage of explanations for Arab military ineffectiveness. The goal of this book is to examine these explanations and assess their validity, both in an absolute sense and relative to one another. Thus, the following chapters attempt to answer two questions: first, to what extent did Arab armies and air forces suffer from each of the problems claimed to be the cause of their difficulties in battle? And second, which of these problems was most detrimental to their fortunes in war? After all, it may well be that while the Arabs experienced a range of problems that all contributed to their poor military effectiveness, some problems may have been more harmful than others. By answering these two questions, one can determine both the problems the Arabs experienced in battle since 1945 and the true causes of their defeats and costly victories.

To accomplish this task, this book recounts the post–World War II military history of Egypt, Iraq, Jordan, Libya, Saudi Arabia, and Syria in some detail to allow the reader to observe how each of these armed forces performed a broad range of operations. These six states encompass the lion's share of Arab experience in war since 1945. Moreover, plumbing their military history allows one to examine a range of battles that pitted Arab forces against a variety of different opponents, in a variety of different kinds of terrain, and in a variety of different missions. This spectrum is important to ensure that any conclusions do not depend on who the Arab armies fought, or where they battled, or what they were trying to accomplish.

Warfare is a competitive activity. Consequently, in any particular conflict an army's effectiveness can be measured only in relation to that of its opponent. It may be that against certain adversaries an army will conduct one type of mission well, but against another opponent it will conduct the same type of mission poorly because of unique features of that adversary's forces. To ensure that any conclusions about a military's effectiveness are not warped by who they are fighting, it is important whenever possible to measure them against a number of different opponents. By examining the full military histories of Egypt, Iraq, Jordan, Libya, Saudi Arabia, and Syria since 1945, one can observe these Arab powers in combat against Israelis, Europeans, Americans, Kurds, Persians, Africans, and each other — a wide enough range to ensure that any conclusions do not simply reflect the interaction of Arab forces with one particular adversary.

By the same token, it is important to observe an army in different geographic settings to properly assess its effectiveness. Land warfare is highly dependent on the terrain in which it is conducted. Deserts, mountains, jungles, forests, rivers, swamps, farmland, grassland, and cities all shape military operations in very different ways. Each constrains some types of operations and aids others. For instance, forests impede the movement of armored vehicles and greatly hinder aircraft attempting to locate and attack ground targets. But forests also can conceal the build-up of forces and hamstring a defender from rapidly shifting reserves to a threatened sector. Because of the tremendous effect of topography on ground combat and on the ability of air forces to contribute to the ground battle, it is important to examine military performance in a range of environments. The Egyptians, Iraqis, Jordanians, Libyans, Saudis, and Syrians have fought in almost every kind of terrain imaginable — except for triple-canopy jungle. Arab armies have fought in the mountains of Lebanon, the deserts of the Sinai, the marshes of Khuzestan, the fields of central Iraq, the savannah of East Africa, the hills of the West Bank, and the streets of Khorramshahr, Port Suez, Port Sa'id, and Jerusalem.

Finally, when attempting to assess the effectiveness of a country's military, it is important to examine its execution of a range of different missions. Different political goals and different military strategies tend to demand certain military skills over others. For instance, a purely defensive strategy probably will test an army's ability to perform tactical defensive operations, counterattacks, and defensive counterair missions more than its ability to conduct large-scale assaults and offensive counterair missions. Thus, the performance of the military in such a role will tell somewhat more about its abilities in defensive operations than in offensive operations. Consequently, it is useful to examine the forces in question while attempting to perform various missions. The history of the six Arab armies investigated here includes all-out offensives, limited attacks intended to serve narrow political objectives, protracted attrition battles, border skirmishes, counterinsurgency campaigns, and defensive operations of every stripe.

The History of Arab Military Effectiveness

Each of the following chapters contains a description of the course of the wars fought by Egypt, Iraq, Jordan, Libya, Saudi Arabia, and Syria. These accounts are not so much meticulous lists of details so much as broader analyses of how well the Arab armies and air forces prosecuted their missions in each campaign. Consequently, I have left out much extraneous material — peacetime operations, the army's relationship to its broader society, and even some minor military operations — that might be important for a pure history of the armed forces but is irrelevant to the development of its effectiveness. In addition, in several cases I have glanced over or left out altogether certain minor skirmishes and peripheral operations that shed little light on the question of military effectiveness. For instance, I do not address the remarkable Israeli drive along the eastern coast of the Sinai toward Sharm ash-Shaykh during the Six Day War because this operation offers no insight into Egyptian military effectiveness.

Another important consideration in writing this book was to present the development of Arab military effectiveness in the proper political and strategic setting. As Clausewitz admonished over 150 years ago, war is a political action fought within a political context. It is impossible to judge the competence of an army if one does not know what it is trying to accomplish. Therefore, for each Middle Eastern war examined, I also outline the strategy and goals of both the Arab militaries and their adversaries to provide the political yardstick against which their military performance must be judged. This is particularly important when attempting to assess generalship because the crucial measure of a strategic plan is its ability to translate political objectives into military operations. The overall mission is less important when assessing tactical performance because a battalion can fight just as well trying to secure what ultimately may prove to be a meaningless objective as it can trying to secure what turns out to be a vital one.

Each chapter also addresses the question of why the Arab militaries won or lost each campaign in which they participated. It is critical to know not only the patterns of military effectiveness evinced by Arab militaries but also the *importance* of each pattern. Since I am attempting to identify the greatest problems afflicting the Arab armies since 1945, their patterns of poor performance are only important to the extent that they influenced the outcome of the conflict. For this reason, each chapter not only describes the course of each war but also includes an assessment of the various factors that resulted in victory or defeat.

For the same reason, each chapter also considers a number of other factors that often are important in deciding the outcome of a conflict. It is important to keep these other influences in mind so that the effect of the different aspects of military effectiveness can be placed in the right context. For instance, it may be that an army not only had awful strategic leadership in a given campaign but also was surprised by an enemy with superior weaponry and a huge advantage in numbers. In this case, the army's poor generalship would not loom as large as a source of defeat as it otherwise might. After all, given the huge disparity in numbers and weaponry, as well as the disadvantage of having been surprised, the army might still have lost the battle even if its generals had been more competent. Therefore, for each campaign, I note the quantitative balance of forces, the effect of the terrain, any weapons superiority, and any advantage of surprise. Another factor I consider is which side was on the defensive. In the modern era, there is an inherent advantage to the defense and therefore the attacker must have some kind of an advantage — quantitative or qualitative — to allow him to prevail.[23] In Clausewitz's words, "The defensive form of warfare is intrinsically stronger than the offensive."[24] Finally, for every engagement, I address the capability of the opponent, even if only implicitly, because warfare is always a competitive activity, and one side's skill level can only be judged relative to that of its adversary.

I

EGYPT

The modern Egyptian military was founded by the Khedive Muhammad 'Ali, who ruled Egypt from 1805 to 1848. He sought to carve an independent realm out of the Ottoman Empire, and for this purpose he bought European weaponry and expertise and built an army that he used to defeat the Ottoman sultan and establish sway over Egypt, Syria, and parts of Arabia. European intervention on behalf of the sultan brought Muhammad 'Ali's dreams of an independent kingdom to an end and sharply curbed the size and independence of the Egyptian military. The armed force he had built then languished until Britain took control of Egypt in 1882.

The defense of Egypt, and especially the Suez Canal, was considered a vital imperial interest both in London and Simla, the seat of British colonial government in India. Consequently, there were always significant numbers of British regulars posted to Egypt, which made the development of indigenous Egyptian military forces less important to Britain than in its other Middle Eastern territories such as Transjordan and Iraq. Therefore, the British started their rule over Egypt by crushing the Egyptian officer corps to ensure its loyalty. They ousted most of the Turks who had previously dominated the officer ranks. Although Egyptians from the entire range of society received commissions, the very poorest *fellahin* (peasants) were excluded from officer billets. Nevertheless, the lowest classes of the *fellahin* filled Egypt's enlisted ranks, while most Egyptian officers came from the (slightly) better-off peasantry and the lower middle classes, creating severe social splits between the officers and their troops. Although the British provided the Egyptians with new military equipment and revamped Egypt's military doctrine along British lines, the presence of Imperial regulars made improving the Egyptian military a low priority, and throughout the period of British rule, the Egyptian army was relegated to internal-security duties. Egyptian units were mostly commanded by British officers and many were incorporated into larger British formations. Indeed, even during the most anxious moments of the German threat to Egypt in 1941–42, London drew very little on Egyptian units to defend North Africa.

The War of Israeli Independence, 1947–48

Although Egypt had nominally been independent since 1932, only after World War II did it actually gain its full sovereignty from Great Britain. In 1946, Cairo rid its army of British officers and effectively seized control of Egyptian foreign policy for the first time in many centuries. As one of its first independent acts on the world stage, in April 1948 Egypt joined with its Arab brothers in opposition to the founding of Israel and sent a large expeditionary force to destroy the Jewish state before it could establish itself. Egypt threw its entire military into this effort. However, because 80 percent of Egypt's male population between fifteen and fifty years of age were mentally or physically unfit for military service, and because Egypt's nascent logistics system was extremely limited in its ability to support ground forces beyond its borders, Cairo never succeeded in putting more than 40,000 men into the field.[1]

Expecting a quick victory over the Jews, Egypt initially dispatched about 10,000 men to Palestine. Although they had had little combat experience during World War II, morale was high among the Egyptians because they had little regard for the fighting qualities of their Jewish opponents. Cairo's expeditionary force was commanded by Maj. Gen. Ahmed 'Ali al-Mwawi and consisted of five infantry battalions, an armored battalion with British Mark VI and Matilda tanks, a battalion of sixteen 25-pounder guns, a battery of eight 6-pounder guns, a medium-machine-gun battalion, and supporting troops. In addition, the Egyptian Air Force had over thirty Spitfires and four Hawker Hurricanes operational to support the invasion force in addition to twenty C-47 transports, which Egyptian mechanics had transformed into crude bombers.[2] Opposing them, the Israeli Haganah could field 50,000 highly motivated but woefully underarmed and undertrained troops. About 6,000 of the Israeli soldiers made up the three elite *Palmach* brigades while another 20,000 manned the six Haganah field brigades. The other troops were mostly regional forces that could be called on to defend their locale but little more. At the start of the war, the Israelis did not have enough small arms to equip all of their troops, with only 22,000 rifles, 11,000 (mostly homemade) submachine guns, and 1,500 machine guns. As for heavy weapons, they had fewer than 900 light mortars, 85 antitank weapons, five ancient artillery pieces, four tanks, and 400–500 homemade armored cars.[3] Moreover, the Haganah not only had the Egyptians to deal with but also had to fight invading armies from Lebanon, Syria, Iraq, and Transjordan as well as indigenous Palestinian forces.

The Egyptian offensive began on 14 May 1948, the day Israel declared its independence. Cairo's invasion force was divided into two columns. The stronger arm was to drive up the coast to capture Tel Aviv, while a smaller force, mostly Egyptian irregulars, pushed through the central Negev Desert, through Beersheba and Hebron, toward Jerusalem to stake Cairo's claim to the Holy City and prevent Transjordan's King 'Abdallah from seizing it.

This eastern column, under Lt. Col. 'Abd al-Aziz, advanced fairly quickly because it met little Israeli resistance until it reached the settlement of Ramat Rachel south of Jerusalem. There the Egyptians linked up with elements of Transjordan's Arab Legion. On 21 May the two forces launched a combined assault against the small Israeli force defending the village, driving them out by sheer weight of numbers. However, later that day a company of the Haganah's Etzioni Brigade reinforced the Israelis, who then counterattacked and retook the village. The Egyptians and Jordanians launched repeated attacks for the next four days but were unable to retake Ramat Rachel. The Egyptians dug-in south of the town and never moved farther north.

The route of the main Egyptian column advancing along the coast was far more eventful. A series of Israeli settlements dotted the Gaza area on the coastal route to Tel Aviv. The first two Israeli settlements the Egyptians came upon, Nirim and Kfar Darom, were so tiny that General Mwawi left reinforced companies to deal with them while the main force moved on. In both cases, despite overwhelming advantages in numbers (there were forty Israeli defenders at Nirim and thirty at Kfar Darom) and firepower (the Egyptians had armor, artillery, and even some air support) the Egyptian units were unable to take either settlement in repeated attacks. They conducted slow-moving frontal assaults in line-abreast against the main Israeli defenses. Their artillery fire and airstrikes were inaccurate, and the infantry turned and ran as soon as it became clear that their firepower had not destroyed or cowed the defenders. In addition, during each attack, Egyptian armor failed to support the infantry, turning back the moment it encountered any resistance from Israelis with bazookas or Molotov cocktails, leaving the infantry to carry on alone.

Meanwhile, on 16 May Mwawi's main force reached the Israeli settlement of Yad Mordechai, which was bigger and better defended than Nirim or Kfar Darom. Mwawi decided he could not mask or bypass the position.

The Egyptians took two days to prepare an assault on the settlement and then, on 19 May, threw two battalions of infantry and a battalion of armor supported by an artillery battalion against the Israeli infantry company defending the settlement. The Israelis beat them back after three hours of heavy fighting. The next day, the Egyptians launched four more attacks, all of which were repulsed. In this battle too the Egyptians were hampered by the inaccuracy of their artillery and air support and by difficulties in co-ordinating the operations of their armor and infantry. They then regrouped for several days while Mwawi apparently worked out better coordination between his armor and infantry. When the Egyptians attacked again on 23 May, the armor did a much better job supporting the infantry, and the assault succeeded in taking part of the settlement. That night, the Israeli defenders, who were exhausted and low on ammunition, withdrew, leaving Yad Mordechai to the Egyptians, who sustained 300 casualties in the fighting.[4]

With Yad Mordechai taken, Mwawi pressed on up the coast, masking and bypassing the well-fortified Israeli settlement of Nitzanin. Reinforced by sea at Ashqelon, he detached part of his force and sent it eastward along the Ashqelon-Hebron road to link up with Aziz's force south of Jerusalem. Mwawi once again resumed the march with the rest of his column, now down to about 2,500 men, but was stopped at the Ashdod bridge three kilometers north of the town of Ashdod on 29 May. Here, only about thirty kilometers from Tel Aviv, the Israelis made their stand. They had destroyed the bridge, brought in several battalions from the Givati Brigade to man the river line, deployed another force southeast of Ashdod to menace the right flank of the Egyptian advance, and had even committed their only two 65-mm artillery pieces. When the Egyptians approached, the Israelis fired back with all they had. In addition, four Messerschmitt Me-109 fighters the Israelis had just acquired from Czechoslovakia attacked the Egyptian col-umn as it approached the river. Although the Israeli air attacks were not terribly accurate, their mere appearance in combination with the unex-pected introduction of Israeli artillery (paltry though it was), the strong Israeli defenses, and the threat on his flank convinced Mwawi to halt.

Checked at Ashdod, Mwawi recognized that his forces were over-stretched and that he needed to consolidate his positions. He left Brig. Gen. Muhammad Naguib in command of the forces at Ashdod and ordered them to dig in. On the night of 2–3 June, the Israelis tried to outflank these Egyptian positions and cut their line of communications along the coast. However, the attack was inept and poorly coordinated and ran into the entrenched Egyptians, who broke it fairly easily. Meanwhile, Mwawi dispatched a force to attack the Israeli settlement of Negba, which threatened his line of communications east to 'Aziz's forces north of Hebron. In this operation, the Egyptians used almost a full battalion of armor supported by infantry. But the infantry lagged far behind while the tanks and armored cars surged ahead. Without infantry support and with only very inaccurate artillery fire, the Egyptian attack was stopped by Israeli infantry with Molotov cocktails in a fierce fight. The Egyptians were beaten back after losing four tanks, two armored cars, and over 100 casualties.[5] Finally, Mwawi himself took the remainder of his force to attack the bypassed settlement of Nitzanin and eliminate it as a lingering threat to the rear. Nitzanin was defended by a company of Israelis, and Mwawi hit it with an infantry battalion, a platoon of tanks, a company of armored cars, and his entire battalion of 25-pounders. In addition, he brought in a squadron of Spitfires to provide air support. He took several days to carefully work out the combined-arms preparations and began the attack in the early hours of 7 June with a six-hour artillery bombardment. Despite this, the Israelis beat back the initial assault, prompting Mwawi to call in more air support. Assisted by constant airstrikes, Egyptian armor was able to penetrate the Israeli defenses and eventually forced the defenders to surrender late that same day.

Stalemate

The rebuffs at Ashdod and Negba and the successful capture of Nitzanin brought the initial Egyptian offensive to a close. The United Nations (UN) imposed a ceasefire on the combatants on 11 June, which lasted until 9 July. Of greater importance, the defeats at Ashdod and Negba caused the Egyptians to begin to doubt that the expedition was going to be the cakewalk they had expected. During the ceasefire, both sides augmented their forces — with the Egyptian contingent reaching roughly 18,000 men — and fortified their positions along the truce lines.[6] In addition, both Israel and Egypt planned to attack as soon as the truce ended. The Egyptians hoped to widen and strengthen their east-west lines of communication by capturing a number of Israeli settlements that constricted the Ashqelon-Hebron corridor. On the other side, the Israelis hoped to pierce this corridor, then turn west and cut the Egyptian lines along the coast road to encircle the Egyptian forces in Ashdod and Ashqelon.

The Egyptians became aware of Israeli preparations, and Mwawi decided to preempt them by launching his own attack on 8 July, 36 hours before the official end of the truce. By doing so, the Egyptians surprised the Israelis and succeeded in driving them out of a few minor positions. Meanwhile, the Israelis responded by moving up the start of their own offensive, jumping off after dark on 8 July. They too were able to seize a few minor positions but were defeated by strong fortifications and a determined Egyptian defense at their main objectives — the town of Iraq Suwaydan and its police post. The next day the Egyptians launched their primary attack, once again against Negba. The Egyptians tried a double envelopment of the town, but both thrusts were quickly defeated by the dug-in Israeli defenders. The Egyptians regrouped and attacked again on 12 July. This time, Mwawi employed three infantry battalions, an armored battalion, an artillery battalion, and every available Spitfire. He also conducted diversionary attacks against two nearby points to try to draw off Israeli reserves. Tactically, the Egyptians tried essentially the same approach they had used on 9 July, deploying armor on both flanks to break through the Israeli lines and encircle Negba while infantry pinned the Israeli center. However, the various units were unable to synchronize their actions, Egyptian infantry-armor teams never got their cooperation right, and the air and artillery support had little effect, with the result that the Israelis defeated several piecemeal Egyptian attacks during the course of the day, inflicting over 200 casualties on the Egyptians while suffering only 21 themselves.[7]

There were several other minor clashes between the Egyptians and Israelis before a second UN truce descended on the combatants on 18 July. The Egyptians attempted to reduce the small Israeli settlement of Binat Yitzhak, which they had earlier masked and bypassed, but were bloodily defeated, losing another 200 casualties to the Israelis' 33.[8] Likewise, the Israelis resumed their attacks against Egyptian fortifications all along the Ashqelon-Hebron road, taking some minor positions but failing to seize any of the critical strongpoints. Most of these attacks were poorly executed frontal assaults that were easily stymied by the Egyptians. The few successes the Israelis enjoyed were instances when they were able to outflank or otherwise surprise the Egyptians, who reacted poorly whenever the Israelis employed maneuver or subterfuge.

Once the second truce began, both sides again used the time to reinforce and improve their fortifications. The Egyptian force now boasted over 20,000 troops in thirteen battalions with 135 tanks, 139 Bren gun carriers, and ninety artillery pieces.[9] Despite the size and firepower of this force, Mwawi considered it wholly inadequate to defend his strung-out positions and asked Cairo if he could withdraw to more defensible lines. Having halted or expelled the other Arab armies, the Israelis were slowly building up their strength opposite his lines and had mustered a force somewhat larger than the Egyptians — albeit not nearly as well armed. Moreover,

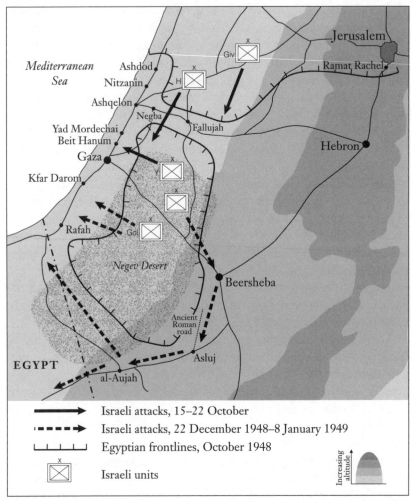

Map 1. Israel's Conquest of the Negev, October 1948–January 1949

although the Egyptians had been able to keep open the Ashqelon-Hebron road, they had never been able to reduce the Israeli settlements south of it between the coastal axis and the Beersheba-Hebron road. As a result, there was a large Israeli-controlled pocket in the northern Negev, and Israeli mobile columns based near the settlements there constantly raided Egyptian lines of communication both in the west, along the coast, and in the east to Beersheba. The Israeli forces in this pocket also constituted a threat to the rear of the positions along the Ashqelon-Hebron road. Nevertheless, Cairo rejected Mwawi's request to pull back.

The Israeli Counteroffensives

On 15 October the Israelis launched Operation Yoav, an offensive designed to drive the Egyptians out of the Negev. The Israelis had concentrated more than three brigades of infantry, a small force of artillery and heavy mortars, and roughly twenty-five fighter aircraft for the operation. They also had infiltrated the fresh Yiftach Brigade into the Negev pocket, withdrawing the exhausted Hanegev Brigade. The Israelis intended to use the Yiftach to drive west from the Negev pocket to cut the Egyptian coastal axis while the Harel and Givati Brigades drove south into the eastern half of the Ashqelon-Hebron road corridor supported by a diversionary attack out of the Negev pocket. The offensive began with a preemptive airstrike by the tiny Israeli Air Force (IAF) against the Egyptian Air Force (EAF) bases in the Sinai. Despite the greater size of the EAF, the Israelis achieved surprise and hit the bases without facing any real resistance. Although the IAF caused only modest physical damage — destroying four Egyptian Spitfires on the ground, shooting down three others in dogfights, cratering a runway, and damaging a few buildings — the shock of the raids kept the EAF on the ground for almost three days, during which the IAF had undisputed control of the air.

The Yiftach Brigade's attack against the coastal axis surprised the Egyptians in a lightly defended sector. Israeli troops infiltrated the Egyptian positions and outflanked and overran several strongpoints. Nearby Egyptian reserves did not move to support the threatened sector, and as a result the Israelis tore a sizable hole in the Egyptian lines. The Israelis were able to cut the coastal road, but fierce resistance by an Egyptian unit well fortified at Bayt Hanun prevented them from reaching the sea and completely cutting off the Egyptian troops in Ashdod and Ashqelon. Mwawi immediately recognized the threat to his forces and began pulling them back. The Bayt Hanun position was able to hold out long enough to allow Egyptian engineers to build an emergency road of wooden logs and wire netting across the beaches of the Gaza Strip over which the forces at Ashdod successfully retreated. Natanel Lorch has remarked about their efforts, "Egyptian engineers demonstrated a degree of initiative and improvising ability completely at variance with that shown by their commanders."[10]

The Egyptian units defending the east-west corridor fared slightly better, at least at first. Here, entrenched Egyptian troops hamstrung the Israelis. Moreover, the Egyptians had occupied a series of British police forts along the route, and these proved virtually impregnable given the limited firepower available to the Israelis. Egyptian soldiers, commanded by the very able Sudanese general Muhammad Sa'id Taha Bey, fought tenaciously. Moreover, they had used the ceasefire to pre-plan artillery fire missions and preregister their guns on key terrain features, with the result that when the Israelis attacked, Egyptian artillery fire proved lethal for the first time. The Israelis made little progress and could not budge the Egyptians from their main defensive positions. After several fruitless attempts to crack the enemy lines, however, the Israeli high command shifted the axis of its attack from the eastern end of the corridor to the western end. Here the attackers took the Egyptians by surprise and were able to find weak points they could penetrate and then flank key positions. There were also fewer strongpoints in the western half of the corridor, and these were not as formidable as those farther east. As a result, in the course of a single night, the Israelis took the three main Egyptian strongpoints in this sector and sliced through most of the corridor. Egyptian tactical reserves did not counterattack to seal the breach, and the Israelis were able to break through and link up with the forces in the Negev pocket. Taking advantage of this development, the Israelis then brought down forces from the Jerusalem area, which attacked and took Beersheba, thereby isolating the Egyptian forces south of Jerusalem as well as those defending the eastern half of what had been the east-west corridor. These isolated forces, amounting to about 5,000 men, concentrated around the Negev town of Fallujah.[11]

In the wake of this defeat, General Mwawi was relieved of his command. His replacement, Major General Sadiq decided to shorten his lines, falling back on Gaza in the west and on Asluj in the east. The Israelis attempted a number of attacks to reduce the Fallujah pocket but, while these succeeded in nibbling away at the Egyptian position, the defenders clung to their fortifications and fought incredibly hard. Outside the pocket, Egyptian forces in the Sinai made several half-hearted attempts to break through the Israeli lines to relieve the trapped forces, but their offensives consisted of small frontal assaults that were quickly halted after meeting strong resistance and quick counterattacks from the Israelis.

In late December 1948, the Israelis launched Operation Horev to clear the Negev of the remaining Egyptian forces. The offensive began on 22 December, with the Israeli Golani Brigade attacking all along the coastal axis as a diversion to draw off Egyptian attention and reserves. Meanwhile, on 23 December, the main attack took place in the east along the Beersheba axis. An Israeli brigade outflanked the Egyptian position at Asluj by following an ancient Roman road that no longer existed on maps but which the Israelis had discovered and had their engineers restore to a usable state. This force then turned south and attacked the Egyptian strongpoint at al-Aujah, the base of the Egyptian salient protruding into the Negev (Asluj was at the top of this salient). Although the defenders of al-Aujah were surprised by this sudden move, they fought very hard, repulsing attacks by the Israelis from all directions over the course of the next two days. Meanwhile, the garrison at Asluj did nothing: they did not send reinforcements to aid the forces at al-Aujah; they did not pull back to avoid being trapped should al-Aujah fall; they did not redeploy forces along the road to the south, either to cut the line of supply of the Israeli units attacking al-Aujah or to prevent additional forces from turning north to hit Asluj from the rear; and they did not even build all-around defenses to protect the rear of their own position. Consequently, on 26 December another Israeli column moved down the old Roman road, turned north, and assaulted the Asluj defensive lines from the rear. The Egyptians fought hard but were quickly defeated. That night, Cairo ordered its troops in al-Aujah to abandon their position and retreat.

Having secured al-Aujah, the Israelis then launched the second part of their plan, pushing west and northwest from al-Aujah into the Sinai to take Qusaymah, Abu Ageilah, B'ir Lafhan, and al-'Arish. The Israelis raced through the Sinai, facing only light resistance, which they brushed aside, and seized the airfield at al-'Arish, capturing several Egyptian aircraft. However, by the time the Israelis reached the fortified positions around the town, they were exhausted, while the Egyptian troops were not only rested but also alerted to the approaching enemy and in their defenses. After a few probing attacks, Israeli commanders decided they did not have the force to take on the garrison and dug in to await the reinforcements then rushing to meet them. Before the Israelis could renew their attack, however, Britain warned Israel to withdraw from the Sinai or the British would invoke their security treaty with Egypt and commit combat forces against the Israelis. To put teeth into these threats, the British began moving troops from their bases in Suez and flying combat aircraft over the Sinai and Negev. These moves prompted Tel Aviv to call off the attack on al-'Arish and pull its troops back to the Negev. For all intents and purposes, the Israeli withdrawal from the Sinai on 4–6 January 1949 ended Egyptian involvement in the first Arab-Israeli war. As part of the eventual ceasefire agreement, the troops trapped with General Taha at Fallujah were allowed to return to Egypt with their arms.

Egyptian Military Effectiveness in the War of Israeli Independence

The performance of Egyptian units during the fighting in 1948 showed some significant strengths as well as some fatal weaknesses. At the tactical level, the Egyptians undoubtedly showed more of the latter than the former. At the strategic level, Egyptian performance was reasonably competent if unspectacular.

TACTICAL PERFORMANCE

To their credit, Egyptian soldiers were quite courageous, conducting repeated frontal assaults into heavy Israeli fire and hanging tough in precarious defensive positions. The conduct of the Egyptian troops in the Fallujah pocket in particular stands out. These forces stuck together, fought ferociously, and would not surrender despite being completely cut off by superior Israeli forces. There were numerous other instances in which Egyptian units stood and fought in the face of heavy odds — Bayt Hanun, Iraq Suwaydan, al-Aujah — and only on a few occasions did Egyptian units break before their position had been compromised. These forces showed somewhat less fortitude when attacking, but in such cases the men only ran when it became clear that their attacks were going to fail. Egyptian forces also did well in set-piece operations, which they had had time to plan and practice beforehand. In these cases, as long as the assaults were kept limited and there were few unforeseen contingencies, the Egyptians did quite well — for example, Nitzanin and the last day of fighting at Yad Mordechai. Egyptian engineers did a very creditable job building effective fortifications and quickly improvising the make-shift road that allowed their comrades trapped at Ashdod to retreat over the beaches of Gaza. Egyptian logistics were unspectacular and did limit the size of Cairo's expeditionary force. But in the final phase of fighting, Egyptian quartermasters were supporting 40,000 troops in Palestine, and logistical breakdowns were never a drag on combat operations. Consequently, one must give Egypt's logisticians a fair degree of credit as well. Last, one must applaud the efforts of their mechanics and maintenance personnel, at least in the EAF. These men kept finicky British aircraft flying throughout the war, improvised bombs and other armaments for their planes, and even performed a number of, admittedly simple, modifications to their aircraft such as turning C-47 transports into crude bombers.

But Egypt's combat forces consistently manifested a number of patterns of behavior in combat that severely hampered their effectiveness. Foremost was the crippling dearth of innovation and initiative among the junior officers. Time and again, Egyptian forces did not react to unexpected Israeli actions, and when they did, their moves were slow and predictable. The situation at Asluj, where the Egyptians sat motionless for two days while the Israelis outflanked them and then attacked al-Aujah to their rear, is only the most egregious example of this behavior. Egyptian commanders rarely tried to employ maneuver, either to outflank Israeli positions or to prevent the Israelis from outflanking their own positions. Egyptian tanks fought as mobile artillery pieces, charging straight at Israeli positions when attacking and sitting motionless in prepared positions when defending, with little effort to maneuver into an advantageous position in either situation.

Egyptian combined arms were largely nonexistent as armor, infantry, and artillery rarely were able to coordinate their efforts effectively even when they actively tried to do so. However, on the few occasions when they made that coordination work, such as at Nitzanin and in the final attack on Yad Mordechai, they achieved decisive results. Egyptian artillery proved very effective when defending fortified lines and had a month or more to carefully site and preregister their guns, but these units were incapable of providing support during the initial Egyptian advance, whenever Israeli attacks penetrated the Egyptian defensive lines, or when the Israelis simply came at them from an unexpected route. Egyptian gunners could not shift fire to deal with fluid situations such as meeting engagements. Israeli general Ariel Sharon summed up his impression of Egyptian tactical performance in the 1948 war by remarking: "Once you allow them to fight a battle they are prepared for, a battle they have rehearsed, they will fight courageously. They are quite capable of dying at their posts, and did exactly that on many occasions. But they don't like to be surprised."[12]

Finally, Egyptian forces evinced debilitating problems handling information. The Israelis found a consistent pattern of Egyptian forces passing along incomplete or misleading information regarding combat operations. As one Israeli veteran of the campaigns in the Negev explained, Egyptian units "would tell their high command that they were attacking and conquering the village, but would not mention the Israeli strongpoint next to it, which they could not take. They just lied to their headquarters."[13] In another example, Israeli signals-intercept units listened for days to Egyptian forces around Beersheba passing reports to their superiors about their desperate attacks on the town when, in actuality, they were not moving at all.[14] The remarkable passivity of Egyptian forces was a product not only of the dearth of initiative among tactical commanders but also the fact that, in most cases, the senior officers were not fully aware of what was happening at the frontlines because of the misinformation they were being fed by their subordinates.

STRATEGIC PERFORMANCE

The Egyptians generally blamed their failure during the 1948 war on poor strategic leadership. This claim is hard to support. First, General Mwawi seems to have done a reasonably good job and in some ways was quite competent. During his initial advance he tried hard to retain the initiative and keep moving no matter what. Although his troops proved incapable of overcoming the tiny Israeli garrisons along his route of advance, Mwawi refused to allow this to slow him down, and so he masked the Israeli settlements and kept moving. His column did move painfully slowly — taking fifteen days to cover the 60–70 kilometers between Rafah and Ashdod against minor resistance. However, the fact that he consistently bypassed settlements along the way rather than get bogged down suggests that the sluggish pace was not his choice but more likely reflected the limitations of the forces under his command. In several instances he tried to maintain his momentum by launching immediate assaults on Israeli positions directly from the route of march, but these all failed. On at least three occasions, Mwawi recognized that his lines were dangerously overextended and had to be tightened up: first at Ashdod in late May, when he reined in his scattered forces after the Israelis concentrated sufficient force to stop his forward progress and threaten his flank; then in October, when he was planning the defense of the Negev and realized his forces were spread too thin to resist the impending Israeli assault; and finally later that month, after the Israelis had broken through his western defenses and were threatening to cut the coastal axis and isolate his forces at Ashdod and Ashqelon. Mwawi also seems to have had a good grasp of combined-arms operations. In fact, the only times the Egyptians were able to effectively coordinate their armor, infantry, and artillery were when General Mwawi was able to spend several days beforehand rehearsing the operation with his troops and then personally directed the assault. In all of the attacks conducted by other commanders, and in all of the attacks led by Mwawi but conducted without several days of preparation, Egyptian forces showed no ability to effectively integrate their various combat arms. Finally, the only time attacking Egyptian forces employed maneuver to strike at the flank of the Israelis was when Mwawi personally directed the assault. His subordinates conducted disjointed, slow-moving frontal assaults that were defeated unless they had overwhelming advantages in numbers and firepower, and often not even then.

Overall, Mwawi appears to have been a competent, although perhaps not brilliant, commander whose greatest problem was the limitations of the forces under his command. The campaign strategy itself was fairly pedestrian, and more creative approaches might have been employed. But if the Egyptians had been able to implement their original plan by driving quickly up the coast to take Tel Aviv and simultaneously driving through Beersheba to Jerusalem, there is no question that this would have been an enormous problem for the Israelis to overcome and could have led to their general defeat. Moreover, there is no evidence that this strategy was inherently flawed: Israeli forces both along the coast and in the central Negev were very weak at the start of the campaign, and the force the Egyptians concentrated should have been able to defeat them fairly handily, given their advantages in numbers and firepower. Thus, the strategy itself was not necessarily the problem; instead, it was the inability of Egypt's armies to execute the strategy.

Another claim offered up by the Egyptians for their defeat in 1948 is the obsolescence and general poor quality of their weaponry. This excuse also rings hollow. The Egyptians consistently had far greater firepower and mobility than the Israelis. In both numbers and quality of operational weapons, there was no time at which Egyptian forces did not have more and better weapons than their opponents, and except during the final Israeli offensives, this superiority was usually very great. It may be that Egypt could have secured even greater force ratios in their favor and employed even more powerful weapons. But the quality and quantity of weapons they actually possessed should have been more than adequate to defeat the Israelis had Egyptian tactical formations performed better.

The Sinai-Suez War, 1956

Defeat at the hands of the Israelis proved to be the death knell for the Egyptian monarchy. The army believed that it had been betrayed by the king and his generals. They felt they had been saddled with inferior and out-of-date equipment and had suffered from poor leadership. In addition, those trapped in the Fallujah pocket were especially bitter that they had fought so stubbornly but had never been relieved. These grievances congealed in the cabal of the Free Officers who, under the leadership of Col. Gamal 'Abd al-Nasser, overthrew the monarchy in 1952.

One of the first acts of the new "Republican" government was to purge many of the colonels and every general officer from the Egyptian armed forces except General Naguib, the figurehead president of the new government, and one brigadier general. Most were simply forced to retire, but some were put on trial for their "crimes" during the War of Israeli Independence.[15] A power struggle then ensued, principally between Nasser's faction and Naguib's faction — supported by the Islamist Muslim Brotherhood — in which Nasser prevailed. By 1954, Nasser was undisputed ruler of Egypt.

Nasser's ascendance and the motivations behind the Free Officers' coup brought about far-reaching changes in the military. At least initially, Nasser recognized that his hold on power derived from his control of the army, and beginning with the purge of the general officers, he moved to ensure its loyalty to him. He appointed many Free Officers to senior positions in the military. In particular, he appointed his close friend Maj. 'Abd al-Hakim 'Amr commander in chief of the armed forces and promoted him to the rank of major general. 'Amr had fought well in 1948, serving as an artillery officer and distinguishing himself in the fighting in the Fallujah pocket. He and Nasser had become close there, and 'Amr had served as Nasser's trusted lieutenant ever since. Once in charge of the armed forces, 'Amr set about appointing Free Officers with kinship or other ties to himself and Nasser to key postings throughout the command structure.

Paradoxically, Nasser and 'Amr also began stressing the professionalization of the officer corps and the rebuilding of Egypt's military power. Although political reliability was an important consideration for promotion to the highest ranks, by choosing competent officers from among those with preexisting ties to himself and Nasser, 'Amr was able to begin improving the overall competence of the Egyptian officer corps while still ensuring its loyalty. Nasser still relied on the army for internal security and to maintain his regime in power, but his determination to avenge 1948 prompted him to simultaneously emphasize the importance of defeating Israel. Nasser also had fairly grandiose ambitions for Egypt on the world stage, and he saw military power as a crucial tool for this task, further stimulating the armed forces to focus on conventional combat with foreign militaries. Under the monarchy, internal security had been the primary mission of the armed forces and external security only a distant second. Although the Egyptian military had prepared somewhat for conventional combat, its training was lackadaisical and reflected the low priority of that mission. Nasser and 'Amr reinvigorated this training, and defeating foreign foes — especially Israel — became at least as important as internal security. Indeed, despite the heavy involvement of the army in politics after 1952, there were no signs that Egyptian officers were neglecting their professional duties. In fact, the opposite was true: these officers generally became more conscientious about preparing their troops for battle.[16]

This change in priorities was manifested in several other ways. First, the government began to commit greater resources toward preparing for war with Israel. Defense spending increased from 3.9 percent of Egyptian GNP in 1950–51 to 8.4 percent in 1955–56.[17] As Michael Barnett notes in his exhaustive study of Egyptian and Israeli military expenditures, "Defense spending climbed over this period [1952–56] as Nasser was intent on creating a modern military that could both confront Egypt's potential enemies and signal to regional and global actors that Egypt had reemerged on the scene and recovered from years of colonial tutelage."[18] Nasser also brought in eighty former Wehrmacht officers to reform the Egyptian army. The mission was led by Col. Gen. Wilhelm Frambecher, one-time inspector general of German artillery. The Germans revised military training, supervised the construction of defenses in the Sinai, drew up plans for a defense against Israel, and outlined changes to armed forces organization and equipment. German officers also were attached as field advisers to major Egyptian combat units. The German influence was less than originally hoped for because the Egyptians rarely adopted their practices in full and sometimes ignored them altogether. Nevertheless, the far-reaching writ of the German advisory mission reflected Cairo's commitment to improving the effectiveness of its forces. The eviction of the British from their bases in Suez in 1955 added impetus to this drive. The move not only deprived Cairo of British protection but also so angered London that it created another powerful enemy threatening to use force against Egypt.

Enter the Soviets

In 1955 Nasser turned to the Soviet Union for the weapons he believed he needed to build a military capable of defeating Israel and asserting Egypt's place on the world stage. Immediately after the War of Israeli Independence, the United States, France, and Britain had agreed to refrain from selling major weapons systems to any of the Middle Eastern states to try to prevent the outbreak of future wars. By turning to the USSR, Nasser was able to circumvent this embargo, and on 27 October 1955, Egypt secured a large order of modern weaponry from the Soviet Union via Czechoslovakia. The "Czech arms deal" was a major boost to Egypt's arsenal and gave it considerable superiority over Israel, at least on paper. By October 1956, Egypt had received 230 tanks (primarily T-34/85s), 200 APCs (mostly

BTRS), 100 Su-100 self-propelled guns, 500 artillery pieces, and 200 jet aircraft (120 MiG-15 fighters, 50 Il-28 bombers, and 20 Il-14 transports) as well as several destroyers, submarines, and motor torpedo boats.[19]

The infusion of Soviet weaponry upset the regional balance. For example, prior to the arms sale, Egypt and Israel had had less than 200 tanks apiece. Moreover, the T-34/85s were superior to any tank then in either arsenal; most of Egypt's tanks were British surplus from the Second World War, while most of the Israeli tanks were M-4 Shermans the Israeli Defense Forces (IDF) had scrounged from postwar scrap yards. Similarly, before the Russian deal, Egypt had 80 old, first-generation British jet aircraft (mostly Vampires), while Israel had only 50 early-model French and British jets (Ouragons and Meteors).[20] Thus, Cairo's new MiGs and Illyushins not only outnumbered the Israelis four-to-one but also were more capable aircraft.

The Armies on the Eve of War

In the fall of 1956, a crisis was clearly brewing in the Middle East, but it was unclear who would be embroiled in the coming war. France chafed at Nasser's support for the Algerian rebels, while Britain was seething over the loss of Suez. London and Paris threatened Egypt with everything from an international "Canal-users" commission to oversee canal operations to direct military action. All of the Arab states regularly proclaimed their intent to destroy the state of Israel, and Egypt, Syria, and Jordan were all permitting—if not supporting and encouraging—Palestinian attacks on Israel from their territory. Israel was fearful of the massive augmentation of the Egyptian military resulting from the Czech arms deal and the efforts of Egypt's German advisers. Eventually, despite Israel's lingering hatred of Britain from their experiences during the mandate era, London and Paris were able to secure secret Israeli participation in a scheme to retake the Suez region. The plan was for Israel to invade the Sinai and threaten Suez, giving Britain and France a pretext to intervene as neutrals to secure the canal and disentangle the combatants. This collusion provided the Europeans with an excuse to retake Suez and gave Tel Aviv the opportunity to crush the Egyptian army with British and French aid before it could fully assimilate the new Soviet weapons.

In the summer of 1956, Egyptian military intelligence concluded that Israel might conduct one or more raids against Palestinian training camps in the Sinai but would not launch a full-scale invasion. The Israelis had carefully created the impression that they were preparing for an invasion of Jordan, going so far as to mass most of their military power along the Jordanian border. Based on this false assessment, Cairo concentrated the majority of its forces in the Nile Delta to guard against a possible British invasion to retake the canal or overthrow Nasser's government. Only about 30,000 of Egypt's 90,000 troops, along with 200 tanks and self-propelled guns, were deployed in the Sinai.[21] This was far less than had been envisioned in Frambecher's scheme for the defense of that region. The Germans had planned a defense-in-depth involving two infantry divisions covering the border area, two more infantry divisions deployed in depth along the major east-west roads of the Sinai, and an armored division in reserve to counterattack the major Israeli attack when it was identified. In addition, several battalions were to cover the crucial Mitla and B'ir Gifgafah Passes as a final line of defense. Instead, Egypt deployed only two infantry divisions (one of them a Palestinian division of dubious reliability), an independent armored battalion, a National Guard brigade, and some miscellaneous units to hold the Sinai.[22] These forces were inadequate to execute Frambecher's plan, so instead both infantry divisions were concentrated in northeastern Sinai — the 3d Division at al-'Arish, Rafah, and Abu Ageilah, and the 8th Palestinian in the Gaza Strip — leaving the National Guard brigade to defend the rest of the border. The armor was parceled out among the infantry units and virtually nothing was left in operational reserve.

Despite this significant change in plans, the Egyptians were hardly defenseless. They had built very extensive fortifications in Sinai, especially at Rafah and Abu Ageilah, where their German advisers had done much of the design and had supervised the construction process. All of the major road junctions, axes of advance, and key communication nodes were prepared with concertina wire, mines and defensive positions, and were either manned or ready to be manned. The Egyptian units had been in their Sinai positions for many months and had repeatedly exercised their defensive plans. Cairo had carefully planned counterattacks for all of its local reserves — often with German assistance — and the troops had rehearsed these moves many times.[23] Moreover, two of Egypt's infantry divisions and its only armored division were deployed just across the canal, in the Ismailia area, and could quickly cross back into the Sinai if necessary. Finally, the EAF had 120 MiG-15s, 50 Il-28s, and 84 Vampires and Meteors on hand to deal with the Israelis' 60 jet-powered Meteors, Ouragons, and Mysteres and 50 propeller-driven Mustangs and Mosquitos.[24]

On the other side, the Israelis had concentrated 45,000 troops in ten brigades — including one armored and three mechanized brigades with about 200–250 tanks — for the invasion of the Sinai. The Israeli plan was to use a force of three brigades in the primary thrust to take the heavily fortified Egyptian positions at Umm Qatef–Abu Ageilah and then push through the central Sinai. The invasion would begin with a secondary thrust, a crucial parachute drop by one battalion of the 202d Parachute Brigade at the Mitla Pass, after which the rest of brigade, led by its commander, Ariel Sharon, would travel overland via al-Kuntillah and Nakhl to link up with the battalion and seize or block the Mitla. Later, another three brigades would take Gaza and the al-'Arish area and then push on along the northern coast to the canal. Another infantry brigade would wind its way down the tortuous mountain path along the Sinai's eastern shore to capture the Egyptian position at Sharm ash-Shaykh, from which the Egyptians had blockaded all maritime traffic heading to the Israeli port of Eilat. The last two brigades would remain in reserve.

The Israeli Offensive

The Israeli invasion began in the evening of 29 October with the parachute drop at the eastern end of the Mitla Pass. The battalion quickly secured the mouth of the pass and dug in for the night. Early the next morning, the rest of Sharon's brigade linked up with the battalion after brushing aside minor Egyptian resistance during the night. Over the next few days, the Israelis attempted to take control of the pass. The Egyptians fought back ferociously, trapping an Israeli unit in the pass below them. Egyptian fighters conducted numerous disruptive airstrikes against the Israeli positions. Eventually, Sharon was forced to clear the eastern end of the pass ledge by ledge and cave by cave and was only able to extract his troops with heavy casualties. Afterward, the Israelis pulled back from the mouth of the Mitla, blocking it but leaving it in Egyptian hands.

Meanwhile, for about twelve hours after the initial airdrop, Egyptian intelligence still had not figured out the size and intent of the Israeli operation.[25] The general staff did not wait for its intelligence service to come up with a conclusion. Based on the initial reports of a paradrop at the Mitla and Sharon's attack across the border at al-Kuntillah, 'Amr, Nasser, and the Sinai front commander all concluded quickly that this was a major Israeli offensive. The Sinai commander had already ordered two infantry brigades in the canal zone to begin heading for the Mitla Pass (the force Sharon encountered was a reinforced battalion from one of these brigades). The general staff then ordered the 4th Armored Division to move immediately to B'ir Gifgafah and counterattack the main Israeli thrust when it was identified.

South of Abu Ageilah on the first night of the war, the Israeli 4th Infantry Brigade overran the Egyptian positions at Qusaymah — where the defenders simply broke and ran without a fight — and then part of this force

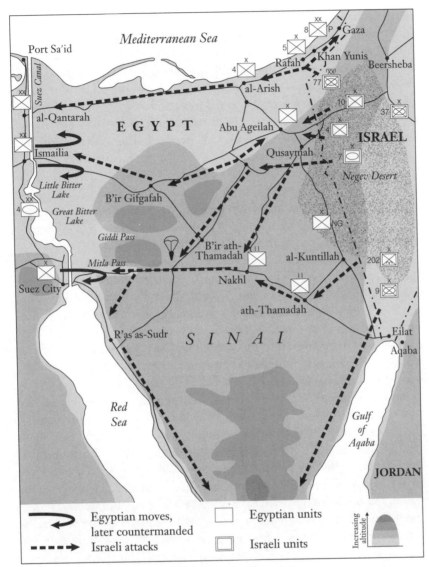

Map 2. The Israeli Conquest of the Sinai, October 1956

continued on into central Sinai to screen the flank of Sharon's advance farther south. With their southern flank secured, the Israelis then assaulted Abu Ageilah itself. During the night of 30–31 October, the Israeli 10th Infantry Brigade attacked the main Egyptian position on the fortified hill of Umm Qatef, which guarded the eastern passage to the town. The Israeli attack was miserable: a slow, disjointed frontal assault against the Egyptian defenses that the Egyptians beat back easily. Meanwhile, an understrength Israeli battalion task force under Lt. Col. Avraham "Bren" Adan, consisting of a company of infantry in halftracks, a company of infantry in trucks, and a company of Sherman tanks, had worked its way into the rear of the Egyptian position and, in conjunction with the infantry assault on the two eastern hills, began attacking from behind. The Abu Ageilah position was too big, intricate, and well manned for Adan's small force to significantly affect the course of the fighting farther east at Umm Qatef.

During the next two days, the Israelis repeatedly assaulted the Umm Qatef positions, first with the 10th Infantry Brigade and elements of the 4th Infantry Brigade, and later added the 37th Mechanized Brigade. However, the Israeli commanders were terribly inept, failing to coordinate the actions of their various units, moving slowly, conducting one frontal assault after another, and frequently attacking without proper combined arms cooperation. The Egyptians fought back hard, would not relinquish their positions, and inflicted heavy casualties.

In the meantime, Adan's tiny detachment fought on in the rear of Abu Ageilah. First, Adan's force secured the vital crossroads, then they turned their attention on the Ruafah Dam position, which guarded the rear of the Umm Qatef defenses. Adan's force again was too small to break through the Egyptian defenses, but the Egyptians could not overwhelm it. They launched several counterattacks in which they neither maneuvered against the tiny Israeli force nor tried to overpower it by weight of numbers; they simply moved up a bit and then opened fire, hoping to destroy the Israelis through firepower. After a few minutes, when it became clear that this tactic was not working, the Egyptians would retreat. Meanwhile, the general staff was concerned by the heavy Israeli pressure on Abu Ageilah and dispatched a battalion of infantry with two companies of tanks from al-ʾArish to reinforce Abu Ageilah. However, the leaders in Cairo had not been informed by their field commanders of the Israeli presence behind Abu Ageilah so that these reinforcements stumbled blindly into Adan's rear guard at the crossroads. Adan quickly disengaged his main body from the Ruafah Dam and hurried back in time to defeat an inept attack on his crossroads position by the two Egyptian battalions. Despite their numeric

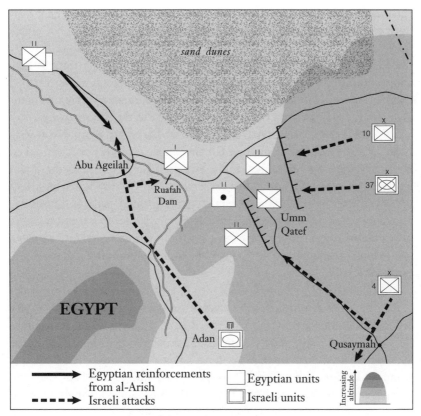

Map 3. The Battle of Abu Ageilah, October 1956

advantage, the Egyptians again would not charge the Israeli positions nor try to outflank them, relying instead on weight of firepower. Eventually, Adan was able to use a small portion of his force to envelop the Egyptians, a maneuver that broke their attack and sent them reeling back toward al-'Arish. The Israelis then turned back and, with the last of their strength, took the Ruafah Dam.[26] Remarkably, despite Adan's heroics in their rear, the Egyptian units at Umm Qatef never wavered, and the Israelis were unable to take the position by force. Ultimately, Umm Qatef fell only after Nasser ordered a general retreat from the Sinai on 1 November and the Egyptians pulled out.

While Adan was fighting for Abu Ageilah, the rest of his parent unit, the 7th Armored Brigade, had pushed on west of Abu Ageilah on the main road to Ismailia. Reports of Israeli armor nearing B'ir Gifgafah prompted the

Egyptian General Staff to order the 4th Armored Division to attack eastward to clear this critical road. However, the division moved extremely
slowly, in part because of repeated raids by the IAF. On 31 October, Tel Aviv
reined in the 7th Armored Brigade because it was suspicious of the British
and wanted to make sure they and the French were going to invade — as
they had agreed — before Israeli ground forces became too deeply entangled in the Sinai. During the early evening of the thirty-first, the British
and French began their airstrikes against EAF bases. Despite the war with
Israel, the EAF was not flying combat air patrol missions nor had it taken
precautions against air raids. Its planes were caught on the ground and
largely in the open. Over the next three days, British and French airstrikes
destroyed over 150 Egyptian aircraft on the ground, facing only minor
resistance from the Egyptians. The EAF did fly about 40 aircraft to bases
in southern Egypt, where they were not only out of range of European
planes but also unable to contribute to the fighting either in the Sinai or the
canal zone.

Nasser and the Egyptian General Headquarters (GHQ) correctly read the
British and French air raids as the prelude to an amphibious assault. Nasser
ordered an immediate retreat from the Sinai to concentrate all of his forces
for a defense of Cairo and the canal. This order reached the troops in the
Sinai at various times on 1 November. Of greatest importance, the 4th
Armored Division immediately turned around and headed back over the
canal, freeing up the central axis through the Sinai and allowing the Israeli
7th Armored Brigade to push ahead without resistance.

With British and French participation now assured, Tel Aviv launched
its assault in the northern Sinai early on 1 November, before Cairo had
ordered its retreat. The Israelis intended to break through the Egyptian
defenses at Rafah at the base of the Gaza Strip, then part of the force would
turn northeast and clear Gaza from behind while the main body headed
west to the Suez Canal via al-'Arish. The positions around Rafah were very
formidable, consisting of at least three belts of mines in front of numerous
reinforcing strongpoints built on a series of hills east of the main roads.
Still, the Israelis punched through these lines at two points — south and east
of Rafah — during the early morning hours. Resistance was spotty. In some
areas the Egyptians fought hard, forcing the Israelis to breach their lines
and reduce their positions before they would retreat or surrender. At other
points, however, the Egyptians simply abandoned their posts after only
perfunctory resistance, sometimes without a fight at all. At no time did the
Egyptians counterattack, nor did their strongpoints coordinate defensive
operations to aid one another against Israeli flank attacks. Egyptian artillery

laid down heavy barrages in front of the defensive lines, but because the Israelis generally were able to find alternative routes of advance that the Egyptian artillery could not shift to cover, the guns caused few casualties. For the most part, the Israelis were able to outmaneuver the Egyptians and defeat them without much difficulty. The two attacking columns turned inward, executing a double envelopment, and then together headed west toward al-'Arish.

By this point, it was about midday, and the various Egyptian units in the Sinai had begun to receive the order that they were to conduct a fighting withdrawal to the canal. In some cases this was impossible; thus, the encircled Egyptian forces at Abu Ageilah abandoned most of their heavy equipment, snuck out of their positions during the night of 1–2 November, and set out across the desert toward B'ir Gifgafah before the Israelis realized what was happening. Elsewhere, Egyptian units executed a fairly effective fighting withdrawal, especially elements of the 3d Infantry Division pulling out of the Rafah–al-'Arish area. Nevertheless, the Israelis pursued the Egyptians and caught up with them at several points in the north, inflicting heavy casualties on them while taking few of their own. In the most important of these, thirty-four Israeli tanks (two companies of Shermans and a company of AMX-13s) caught up with the main body of the Egyptian 1st Armored Brigade of the 4th Armored Division (roughly seventy T-34s) west of B'ir Gifgafah. In a five-hour battle, the Israelis virtually annihilated the Egyptian brigade. In all of these clashes, the Egyptians mostly clung to the roads and failed to put out adequate flank guards so that they were constantly outflanked by the Israelis. They rarely tried to maneuver against the Israelis. Only occasionally did they even try to counterattack when the Israelis caught them; instead, they mostly just stopped and tried to drive off their attackers with firepower or else tried to flee even faster. Moreover, the Israelis proved to be superior marksmen and did considerably more damage to the Egyptians than they suffered in return.

Because of the rapid pace of the Israeli pursuit, the retreat turned into a rout. Egyptian units simply could not withdraw as quickly as the Israelis could pursue, and many were caught from behind or had their lines of retreat blocked by faster Israeli forces. Other Egyptian troops, such as those defending Abu Ageilah, set out across the desert in hope of finding their way back to the canal but either died in the desert or were rounded up by the Israelis. In all, Israel took 6,000 prisoners, the overwhelming majority of whom surrendered during the withdrawal.[27] The IAF flew constant airstrikes against the retreating Egyptians, further slowing them and causing numerous casualties. Many units disintegrated during the course of the retreat, and Cairo's senior leadership panicked when these bedraggled troops began to trickle into the capital in dribs and drabs rather than as organized units.[28] Only one Egyptian battalion returned from the Sinai intact and capable of engaging in combat operations.[29] East of the canal, the fighting was all but over by 3 November, as the Israelis drove to the canal in central Sinai, rolled up the Palestinians in the Gaza Strip, and seized Sharm ash-Shaykh.

The British and French Invasion

The Egyptians had expected the British to land at Alexandria, march down to Cairo to overthrow the government, and then move to secure the Suez Canal. This was, in fact, the original intent of the British and French ground commanders, Gen. Sir Hugh Stockwell and Maj. Gen. André Beaufre, but the political leadership in London decided the British public would not accept such an operation if the ostensible reason for the invasion was the defense of the canal from Egyptian and Israeli forces fighting in Sinai. Consequently, the allied commanders were forced to invade at Port Sa'id and Port Fuad at the northern end of the canal and then try to march south along the narrow causeway to secure the length of the Suez. For this, the British had assembled an infantry division, an airborne brigade, and a Royal Marine commando brigade, while the French committed an airborne division, an independent parachute battalion, and a light mechanized brigade. The British and French also had a huge naval force with six aircraft carriers and hundreds of modern jet fighters and bombers. Against this, the Egyptians had two battalions of reservists at Port Sa'id, which they reinforced with two companies of regulars and another battalion of reservists. The only armor the Egyptians had in the area were four Su-100 self-propelled guns. The one advantage the Egyptians had was the terrain: two cramped Middle Eastern towns stuck out at the end of a narrow causeway.

The Allied fleet moved very slowly, and the initial airborne assault did not begin until the morning of 5 November after heavy carrier airstrikes. The Egyptian defenders fought hard but were slowly reduced by the elite British and French paratroopers. By the end of the day, much of western and southern Port Sa'id was in British hands and the French had taken all of Port Fuad. Of greatest importance, the paratroopers had seized the southern exits to the city — the bridge at Raswah (which the Egyptians failed to destroy), and the road leading down the causeway. Once the bridge fell to the French, the Egyptians counterattacked repeatedly with armor and infantry, but their attacks, while determined, were nothing more than mad charges, which the French beat back with ease.

Early the next morning, the British began amphibious landings along the northern shore of Port Sa'id. Most of the Egyptian defenders were driven off by a forty-five-minute preparatory bombardment, leaving few to oppose the landings. Despite the ease with which the Egyptians could have bottled up the allied forces in Port Sa'id, they failed to do so. Not only had they not blown the bridge at Raswah — the only bridge to the causeway — they had not deployed a force to block the road by 6 November (five days after the GHQ began moving forces to Port Sa'id to counter a British-French landing). As a result, British armor was able to race down the causeway during the night of 6–7 October, getting as far as al-Kap before politics intruded. London buckled under diplomatic pressure — especially from the United States — and agreed to a ceasefire, halting the invasion in its tracks.[30]

As a final reckoning, the Egyptians suffered roughly 1,000 killed, 4,000 wounded, and 6,000 captured. They also lost roughly 215 aircraft, 200 artillery pieces, and at least 100 tanks in the fighting. Against this, the Israelis counted 189 dead, 900 wounded, and only 4 captured. Israel lost 15 aircraft, mostly to antiaircraft artillery (AAA). British and French losses totaled 26 killed and 129 wounded, along with 10 aircraft lost to accidents and Egyptian antiaircraft fire.[31]

The War in the Air

The Egyptian Air Force turned in a mostly mediocre performance during the 1956 fighting. Although on paper the EAF had formidable strength, in reality it was plagued with problems. Of greatest importance, Cairo had few pilots capable of flying the modern jet fighters they had acquired from the Soviet Union. Despite the relative simplicity of these first- and second-generation aircraft, the Egyptians had had difficulty training personnel to fly them, thus, for example, the EAF had only about thirty pilots qualified to fly its 120 MiG-15s.[32] To compensate for this shortage, Marshal 'Amr ordered the EAF to have multiple planes available for each pilot so that after one returned from a mission, he could immediately jump into another fueled and armed plane and take off for another. Obviously, the strain on Egypt's pilots probably would have cut short this practice had the EAF participated in the conflict for longer than two days. To some extent, the pilot shortage was also excused by the limited number of operational planes the Egyptians could put into the air. Because of maintenance and repair problems, the Egyptians had only about 70–80 aircraft operational, including 30–35 of 120 MiG-15s and 12 of 50 Il-28 bombers.[33] Given these numbers, it is not surprising that on 30 October they managed only fifty sorties of all types. On 31 October, 'Amr's decree boosted the number of sorties to about ninety.[34] The next day, British and French airstrikes destroyed most of Egypt's operational planes, and those still flyable withdrew to southern Egypt.

The planes Egypt got airborne and into combat on 30 and 31 October had only a modest effect on the fighting. On the thirtieth, Cairo sent six Illyushins to bomb IAF airbases, but only one actually found its way to Israel, and unable to locate its target, dropped its bombs on a deserted hill south of Jerusalem. The Egyptians flew a considerable number of airstrikes against the Israeli paratroopers at the Mitla Pass and Sharon's column moving through central Sinai, which disrupted their operations only slightly and did only minor physical damage. Only once did Egyptian fighters cause any real harm to the Israelis; at the height of Sharon's battle inside the Mitla Pass, Egyptian air attacks on the Israeli units pinned down on the valley floor caused thirty casualties and knocked out three vehicles.

In air-to-air combat the Egyptians did no better. Their fighters mostly avoided dogfights with the Israelis and did not contest the British and French airstrikes at all. Generally, the Egyptians tried to ambush single Israeli aircraft or pairs returning from strike missions and low on fuel. The Egyptians only willingly engaged when they had an advantage of at least 2 to 1 and preferably 4 to 1. Egyptian fighters did not succeed in shooting down a single IAF jet, downing only a light plane and a P-51. The Israelis aggressively pursued EAF aircraft and shot down eight jets in dogfights (four MiG-15s, four Vampires).[35] In the largest air battle of the war, on 30 October over Kabrit Airfield, sixteen Egyptian MiGs took on eight Israeli Mysteres, but the Israelis prevailed by breaking up the Egyptian formations, disrupting their methodical tactics, and forcing them to improvise. The Egyptians showed little flair for air-combat maneuvering and tried to escape as quickly as they could. Although the Mysteres were terribly low on fuel, they shot down two MiGs before the Egyptians were able to break off the engagement.

Egyptian Military Effectiveness in the Sinai-Suez War

A mediocre Israeli performance, a politically shackled Anglo-French operation, and Cairo's decision to retreat from the Sinai only two days into the war make it somewhat difficult to assess Egyptian military effectiveness in this war.[36] Egyptian forces were not really tested in battle. The initial clashes allowed Egyptian units to remain on the defensive behind their impressive fortifications, and they began to retreat just when their defensive system began to come unglued — and when they would have had to act quickly and decisively if they were to restore the situation. Nevertheless, even from the limited evidence available, Egyptian performance was uneven at best.

TACTICAL PERFORMANCE

The Egyptians showed tremendous tenacity and considerable bravery in defending their fortified positions despite the fact that Tel Aviv so completely duped Egyptian intelligence that the Israelis enjoyed strategic surprise at the outset of the campaign. At Umm Qatef–Abu Ageilah, the Mitla Pass, Port Sa'id, and a number of other places, Egyptian defenders gave their adversaries all they could handle. In each of these battles, Egyptian units remained cohesive and continued to fight long after their positions had become untenable. At the Raswah bridge, Egyptian units counterattacked repeatedly despite taking heavy casualties and accomplishing little. However, there were also a number of occasions when Egyptian troops broke and ran under just slight pressure. At al-Kuntillah, Qusaymah, an-Nakhl, B'ir ath-Thamadah, and the Jiradi Pass, the Egyptians fled from or surrendered in good defensive positions after only a brief battle with the Israelis. Similarly, the Palestinian 8th Infantry Division in the Gaza–Khan Yunis area fought fiercely to defend some locations but disintegrated under Israeli probes in others. At least part of the problem with unit cohesion can be tied to poor officer-soldier relations. In many cases, Egyptian officers fled at the first sign of trouble, and this frequently resulted in their troops surrendering or running when they came under fire from the Israelis.

Unit cohesion, static defense, and personal bravery were the main, and perhaps only, bright spots in Egyptian tactical military performance. Fortunately for the Egyptians, during the first few days of the fighting, this was almost all that was required of their army in the Sinai. Ham-handed Israeli efforts to take Um Qatef–Abu Ageilah and the Mitla Pass by frontal assault played into the Egyptians' hands. The Cairo-ordered retreat began just when the Israelis, particularly the 7th Armored Brigade, had broken through the first line of Egyptian defenses and were beginning to cut into the operational depth of the Sinai defensive system. Nevertheless, significant flaws had begun to manifest themselves even during the initial, static phase of combat. This suggests that even if Nasser had not ordered Egyptian forces to pull back to defend the canal, they still would have been evicted from the Sinai.

The passivity and sluggishness of Egyptian forces were probably the most obvious problems, at least to the Israelis. Every operation initiated by the Egyptians took inordinately long to accomplish. When attacked head on, the Egyptians fought back, but their counterattacks were slow to develop and often were not launched until after the crucial moment in the battle. They frequently did not shift reserves in time to bolster crumbling sectors, and the movement of reserves and reinforcements mostly took too long to contribute to the battle. For example, the 4th Armored Division began moving east the night of 29 October and was across the canal before dawn on 30 October, but it did not muster at B'ir Gifgafah until 1 November. Even taking into account the persistent Israeli air attacks, it is absurd that an Egyptian mechanized formation would need two full days to administrative march less than 90 kilometers. By contrast, Sharon's column traversed over 150 kilometers from al-Kuntillah to the Mitla Pass in one day — also against air interdiction and in an advance-to-contact mode. The quickness of Israeli actions coupled with the sluggishness of Egyptian operations combined to give the Israelis a significant advantage.

Although the Egyptians did quite well in static defensive operations, they performed poorly in more fluid engagements. Junior officers showed little ability to innovate or improvise responses once the course of battle obviated their original orders. Time and again, Egyptian units forced to diverge from their prepared plan of action either did nothing or continued to execute their previous mission even if changed circumstances made this dangerous or counterproductive. Israeli, French, and British officers unanimously observed that the Egyptians fought very hard but showed little imagination, thus they were fairly easily overcome by flanking operations or other unexpected moves. Egyptian local commanders consistently waited for directions from the highest levels before undertaking any actions, a pattern that was a primary culprit in their slow pace of operations. Perhaps the best example of this was the attempt to reinforce Abu Ageilah from al-'Arish; these units were outmaneuvered and defeated by Colonel Adan's handful of Israelis and then never tried another attack eastward to relieve the forces trapped around Abu Ageilah, even while Adan was busy trying to break through the Ruafah Dam position to hit Umm Qatef from behind. Local Egyptian counterattacks were a rarity because the initiative to conduct any offensive movement invariably had to come from very high levels, often the general staff. Moreover, as Gen. Moshe Dayan has observed, because the Egyptian General Staff could provide only the most basic guidance to its field forces in ordering counterattacks and the specifics had to be decided by tactical commanders in the field, these operations invariably came off as slow, frontal assaults conducted with vigor but little skill.[37] On top of all this, Cairo insisted on keeping a tight rein on its field commanders and approving all significant command decisions, further limiting the flexibility and speed of Egyptian tactical operations. The problems of overcentralization and limited tactical initiative were reinforcing: Egyptian GHQ micromanaged many of the battles, but by the same token, Egyptian field commanders went out of their way to refer all decisions back to the general staff.

Egypt failed to take advantage of its considerable superiority in numbers and quality of weapons over Israel. Egyptian tanks and self-propelled guns, in particular, were never used like tanks. Instead, they served primarily as movable pillboxes that remained in their defensive positions regardless of the course of battle. On the few occasions that Egypt threw its armor into counterattacks, the tanks relied solely on their firepower to knock out the enemy, forfeiting their inherent advantages of shock power and maneuver. Tactics such as these allowed the Israelis in Shermans and AMX-13s to defeat Egyptian T-34/85s, Su-100s, and Archers in virtually every armored engagement. Egyptian maintenance practices also were extremely poor. In addition to the only partial use of air force assets, only about half of Egypt's new Soviet tanks were operational at the start of the war.[38] Moreover, the Israelis noted that in all of the Sinai there was not a single Egyptian maintenance workshop.[39]

The Egyptians were further hampered by inadequate attention to combined-arms coordination. For example, at Raswah the Egyptian infantry failed to support their armor, allowing French paratroopers to easily beat back the tanks with antitank weapons and then turn on the infantry. Similarly, in the fighting against Adan's force, the Egyptians never adequately coordinated infantry, armor, and artillery, with the result that the Israelis were able to defeat each element separately.

Another very damaging problem the Egyptians experienced throughout their command structure was a constant distortion and obfuscation of information. Successes were exaggerated, while bad news generally was not passed up the chain of command at all — or if it was, the reported size of the enemy force was greatly increased to make defeat seem more palatable. Dayan noted that the Egyptians routinely reported "the presence of Israelis battalions and brigades even when they are faced only by sections and platoons."[40] Even catastrophic failures were sometimes claimed as great victories, and as these deceptions proliferated over the course of the fighting, GHQ had a less and less accurate picture of what was happening in the Sinai. For example, the Egyptian forces at Abu Ageilah did not alert their superiors that they had lost the crossroads and that Israeli armor and infantry were attacking the Ruafah Dam. Consequently, Egyptian quartermasters continued to send a steady stream of unarmed supply convoys to Abu

Ageilah—which Adan's men destroyed or captured as soon as they appeared.[41] In another case, the early reports from Egyptian forces fleeing al-Kuntillah on 29 October made out Sharon's single airborne brigade to be the entire Israeli army. From these, the general staff concluded that the Israelis were conducting a massive invasion of the Sinai, which was ultimately correct but based on inaccurate information.[42] The Egyptian 1st Armored Brigade (the main force of the 4th Armored Division) tried to excuse its slow progress on 31 October by claiming it was locked in battle with Israeli armor—upon which it was inflicting heavy casualties—although it never actually engaged the Israelis until the next day, when it began retreating and the Israeli 7th Armored Brigade caught and repeatedly mauled its rear guards. Egyptian ground and air forces claimed that so many Israeli aircraft were attacking them that Cairo concluded French and British aircraft were participating in these attacks because the tiny IAF clearly could not have been generating so many sorties. Meanwhile all six of the Egyptian Ilyushin pilots sent to bomb IAF airfields reported having caused serious damage to their targets, although only one could even find Israel itself.

STRATEGIC PERFORMANCE

It is at the strategic-operational level that Egypt's performance in the Sinai-Suez War is most difficult to assess. Very little information is available regarding decision making at the level of the general staff and Cairo's senior field commanders; however, a number of points can be made. First, it is clear that most of Egypt's top military leadership, particularly General 'Amr, did not react well to news of the initial Israeli attack. Having been assured by their intelligence services that Israel would not attack, they were surprised by the invasion and may have panicked to some extent. 'Amr in particular has been criticized by other Egyptian leaders for losing his cool, interfering excessively in tactical decisions, and issuing inappropriate commands. Little information is available regarding his specific actions, but the information that is available suggests that even if the Egyptian high command did panic, this did not have an undue effect on combat units or strategic decision making.[43] It is hard to find problems among Egyptian tactical formations that can be reasonably blamed on panic among the senior ranks: most units fought very hard in static positions, they generally did not crack under even intense Israeli pressure, and what eventually compromised their defensive scheme was their inability to match the Israelis in rapid-maneuver warfare. Indeed, the Egyptian defenses in the Sinai had only just begun to crumble when Cairo ordered a retreat, and even during the fallback, many Egyptian units kept good order and tried to conduct a fighting withdrawal rather than simply rushing madly for the canal (as they would in 1967).

With regard to strategic decisions, the few that we know were made by the general staff appear on closer inspection to have been intelligent moves. Egyptian decision making during the war looks especially competent when one takes into account the thick shroud of illusions and misimpressions spun by the Egyptian field units in the Sinai. The initial decision to concentrate their forces in the delta rather than in the Sinai was entirely sensible given that Egyptian intelligence assured Cairo that Israel would not launch a major attack and a British landing in the Nile Delta and march on Cairo and the canal was a far more dangerous threat than losing the Sinai to Israel. Later, when the GHQ became aware of the Israeli move against the Mitla Pass with no sign of British action — and because they were led to believe that Sharon's column was a much larger force than was actually the case — they ordered an infantry brigade to the Mitla and dispatched their elite armored division to B'ir Gifgafah to counterattack the main Israeli thrust. Meanwhile, they kept their other three infantry divisions in place along the canal and in the delta to guard against the lingering possibility of a British invasion. Regardless of how panicked 'Amr and the general staff may have been, these were very reasonable strategic decisions. In fact, if 4th Armored Division had gotten out to B'ir Gifgafah quicker and been able to counterattack into Sharon's right flank, it might have done serious damage to the Israeli offensive. Indeed, this was one of the IDF's greatest fears on 31 October and one of the main reasons General Dayan ordered the 7th Armored Brigade to press on into central Sinai: to engage Egyptian armor before they could turn on Sharon.[44]

The next major act by the Egyptian leadership was the decision to withdraw from the Sinai during the night of 31 October–1 November to concentrate against the British and French invasion. Here again, it is hard to find fault with Egyptian reasoning. The British threat was definitely the most dangerous because the Egyptians had concluded (correctly) that the Eden government wanted to overthrow Nasser and reassert British control over the canal, whereas there was little reason to believe that Israel would do more than occupy the Sinai. Thus, the 4th Armored Division, as the most capable unit in the Egyptian army and its only real mechanized reserve, had to withdraw west to deal with the British threat. Without this unit, it is extremely doubtful that Egyptian forces in the Sinai could have held back the Israelis, who were already in the process of encircling the major Egyptian troop concentrations at Abu Ageilah, Rafah, and the Gaza

Strip. Indeed, given the poor performance of even 4th Armored Division units in combat, it is unlikely the Egyptians could have held the Sinai even with the 4th Armored there. Consequently, to *not* order a general withdrawal from eastern Sinai when that division returned to the delta would have been foolish.[45]

The one area in which the reported panic in the Egyptian high command seems to have influenced Cairo's strategic thinking was the decision to fall back all the way to the canal. Specifically, Nasser and his generals do not seem to have considered any alternatives to a general retreat to the Suez, thereby relinquishing all of the Sinai. For example, the successful defense of the Mitla Pass against Sharon's force suggests that the Egyptians could have fallen back to the passes in western Sinai and reformed their defensive line there. This might have been Cairo's best course; the forward positions in eastern Sinai were clearly compromised by the flanking move of the Israeli 7th Armored Brigade, but the passes were still in Egyptian hands and could be easily defended. Yet the decision to retreat does not appear to have ever been seriously questioned in Cairo, probably because the sudden British and French airstrikes coming on top of the surprise Israeli invasion had so unnerved Nasser and the GHQ that they simply wanted to pull as much combat power back to defend the canal and the delta as they could and did not think through alternative scenarios.

Overall, the performance of Egypt's generals was not brilliant, but it was certainly adequate. Given the quantitative and qualitative imbalances between Egyptian forces on the one hand and Israeli, British, and French forces on the other, the actions of Egypt's senior commanders were reasonable; it is difficult to blame them for Egypt's defeat. After being misled by their intelligence service into believing Israel would not attack, they concentrated against the British. When the Israelis attacked in force but the British and French did not, they quickly shifted reserves to meet the eastern threat. When the British and French did attack days later, they pulled those same forces back to meet what was clearly the greater menace. Because its forces in the Sinai were in danger of encirclement and all reserves were en route to the delta, Cairo ordered a retreat from the Sinai. In each of these cases, not to have done what the Egyptian GHQ actually did would have been the more foolish course. Even retreating from the Sinai altogether was a better decision than not ordering any withdrawal — even though there may have been better fall-back alternatives.

With regard to each of the strategic decisions made by the Egyptian GHQ, one could attach the postscript "And if only Egyptian tactical formations could have executed this operation better, the war might have turned out differently." The orders of the Egyptian General Staff were adequate at worst, and Egypt's greatest problem was the inability of its battalions, brigades, and divisions to carry out their missions more effectively. The critical variables in Egypt's defeat in 1956 then were: first, the overwhelming advantages of the attackers — especially their ability to attack Egypt on two fronts — and second, the poor performance of Egyptian tactical forces. While Egypt's companies, battalions, and brigades did quite well when conducting static defensive operations from fortified positions, their inability to conduct effective maneuver warfare against the Israelis doomed them. Eventually, the Israelis found ways to penetrate the Egyptians' fortified lines and push into their operational depth, at which point Egyptian units were effectively lost because their own reserves could not contend with the flexible, rapidly maneuvering Israeli units. This allowed the Israelis to break through the forward defensive lines, catch and batter retreating enemy units, and conquer the Sinai. Similarly, critical failings allowed the British and French to overcome all of the advantages the Egyptians gained from the difficult terrain of Port Sa'id, Port Fuad, and the causeway rather easily. Only the diplomatic intervention of the United States prevented the fall of the canal zone to the British and French, and perhaps, the end of Nasser's regime.

Intervention in Yemen, 1962–67

The experience of 1956 had little effect on the Egyptian military. Cairo rationalized its defeat by blaming it on the intervention of Britain and France, two European great powers whom it could not possibly have been expected to defeat. Moreover, the Egyptians tended to believe that the allied decision to suspend operations was as much a result of their resistance as U.S. diplomatic intervention. As for the fighting against the Israelis, the Egyptians fixed on their strong performances at the Mitla Pass and Umm Qatef and convinced themselves that the loss of the Sinai was simply the result of their conscious decision to retreat back to the canal to fight the British and French. Indeed, interviews conducted with Egyptian officers captured by Israel during the Six Day War revealed that they, almost to a man, believed that "if not for western intervention, the Egyptian army would have reached Tel Aviv." One officer even insisted that Gaza had been captured by British forces, not Israelis.[46] Nasser did sack several generals for their poor performance during the war but made little other effort to reform or professionalize the armed forces. All officers from division commanders up were still chosen primarily for their loyalty to the regime rather than any demonstrated ability.[47]

Thus, the major influence on Egyptian military developments after the Suez-Sinai War was not the lessons of that conflict but Nasser's international ambitions and lingering fears. First, Egypt had not yet had its revenge on Israel for the "disaster" of 1948. Second, while the first round had gone to Cairo, it was far from clear to the Egyptian leadership that Britain and France had foregone their claims to the canal or their desires to oust the Egyptian regime. Last, his country's defiance of Britain and France — the old colonial powers — thrust Nasser into the spotlight as a hero of the Third World. This attention prompted Nasser to consider using the Egyptian military to aid the forces of "socialism" and pan-Arabism throughout the Middle East against the forces of "reaction." His military was now expected to serve as a key tool of these goals, leading Cairo to expand and rearm its forces to prepare for future conventional operations. Moreover, according to Field Marshal 'Abd al-Ghani al-Gamasy, Nasser believed his pan-Arab ambitions demanded an "ideologically committed" army rather than a truly professional one.[48]

As part of this effort to enhance Egyptian military power, Cairo drew closer to the Soviets. Egypt procured large amounts of additional Soviet equipment, more Soviet advisers were brought in, and Egyptian officers began attending training courses in the USSR. In addition, Nasser asked the Soviets to take a greater role in training and reforming Egyptian forces. Egypt acquired more advanced weaponry as well, including large numbers of T-55 tanks and MiG-17 and MiG-19 fighters. Nevertheless, the Soviets remained frustrated at the long periods of time required to teach the Egyptians how to operate and maintain this equipment.[49]

Civil War in North Yemen

In September 1962 several factions of Yemeni officers, eventually led by Chief of Staff of the Yemeni Armed Forces Brig. Gen. 'Abdallah as-Sallal, overthrew the monarchy of Imam Muhammad al-Badr and proclaimed the Yemen Arab Republic. Many in the coup d'état were strong supporters of Nasser and pan-Arabism and received aid and pledges of support from the Egyptian government before toppling Muhammad. For Nasser, the coup in the Yemen was the perfect opportunity to demonstrate his commitment to pan-Arabism and use his new military power in the interests of his broader international ambitions. Consequently, within days of the overthrow of Imam Muhammad, 5,000 Egyptian troops, spearheaded by an elite paratrooper brigade, landed in Sanaa to cement the new "Republican" military government's hold on power.

Opposition in Yemen quickly coalesced around Imam Muhammad and members of the royal family who rejected Sallal's government. Moreover, Saudi Arabia—which feared and loathed Nasser and his socialist pretensions—came to the aid of the "Royalists," providing them with money, arms, sanctuary, and provisions. In response, Egypt deployed additional forces to crush these insurgents.

Course of Operations

It is unclear exactly what the Egyptians were trying to do in the beginning. It seems that Cairo did not expect to face a full-blown insurgency (weak, disorganized, and inept though the Royalists were). In the first few months after their intervention, the Egyptians generally concentrated on securing Republican control over Sanaa and a few other major population centers and otherwise blundered around the countryside whenever they received specific reports of opposition activity. By the start of 1963, however, the Egyptians appear to have recognized that they would need to conduct a full-scale counterinsurgency (COIN) campaign to crush the Royalists and began to organize themselves for such an effort. This is not to suggest that the Egyptians had any idea how to conduct a COIN operation, only that they began to consciously plan their military moves and to tie them together toward the general goal of defeating the insurgents. The Egyptian military believed that a systematic campaign against the Royalists would bring a quick victory and secure Yemen in the "progressive camp." In preparation for this effort, Egyptian troop strength in Yemen climbed to about 30,000 men, along with accompanying armor, artillery, and 200 combat aircraft.[50]

EGYPT ASCENDANT

In February 1963 the Egyptians launched the Ramadan offensive. The operation was personally planned and led by now-Field Marshal 'Amr himself. 'Amr's intent was to envelop the insurgent forces in the Jawf region of northeastern Yemen, where they were most active. It was to be a giant pincer movement that would cut the Royalists from their supply lines to Saudi Arabia and hopefully force them to come out and fight to prevent this. 'Amr mustered about 20,000 Egyptian and Republican troops as well as tribal levies for the operation.[51] In many ways the offensive was highly successful: the Royalists scattered before the firepower of the Egyptian forces, who drove deep into northeastern Yemen and captured virtually every population center of any size. At the strategic level, the plan showed a good understanding of maneuver. In one particularly noteworthy operation, an Egyptian thrust eastward from Sanaa took the city of Ma'rib—a major staging area for supplies from Saudi Arabia—by circling around

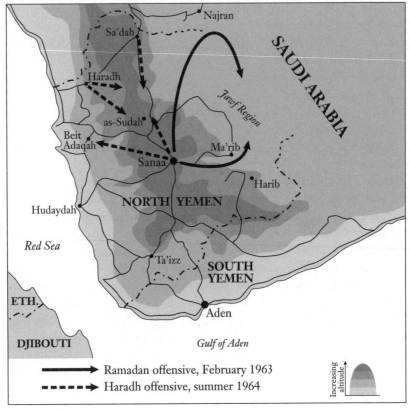

Map 4. Major Egyptian Operations in Yemen, 1962–67

to the eastern side of the city and outflanking its Royalist defenses. Indeed, the Ramadan offensive so disrupted insurgent operations that it forced the Saudis and the Royalists to agree to a ceasefire supervised by a UN observer force.

Although the Ramadan offensive was a well-conceived conventional military campaign and, in the words of Dana Adams Schmidt, "probably the Egyptians' most brilliant operation," its real significance is debatable.[52] First, the offensive was not a true COIN operation, and as the Americans would learn in Vietnam and the Soviets in Afghanistan, successful conventional campaigns count for little against insurgencies. The achievements of the offensive can be mainly attributed to the amateurism of the Royalist forces, who had no sense of how to conduct an insurgency. By employing armor, artillery, and airpower to generate tremendous firepower, the Egyptians succeeded in scattering the Royalist bands, who mostly had not yet successfully adopted guerrilla hit-and-run and ambush tactics. The Egyptians were able to overrun several major supply bases because the Royalists had not learned to locate these in inaccessible locations and then guard their secrecy. The offensive did secure control of many important towns and road junctions in northeastern Yemen but could not win popular support for the Republican cause. Moreover, Egyptian forces moved exceedingly slowly, and tactical commanders showed little willingness to exploit opportunities or aggressively pursue defeated insurgent bands, with the result that most of the damage inflicted was ephemeral. By March, the offensive had ground to a halt without taking the critical Royalist supply route to the Saudi base at Najran, and more important still, the Egyptians had failed to kill many Royalists, for most fled into the mountains and deserts. Consequently, while the effort succeeded in crippling opposition in the northeast for over a year, it did only superficial damage to the insurgency overall. Both sides quickly began cheating on the terms of the ceasefire agreement, and in late 1963 the Royalists began a large-scale campaign of sabotage and hit-and-run attacks in western Yemen. Then, in the spring of 1964, they launched a counteroffensive in the Jawf region, which recouped nearly all of their losses from the Ramadan offensive.

THE TIDE TURNS

In the summer of 1964, responding to the Royalist activity in northwestern Yemen during the winter, the Egyptians mounted a new offensive there in hopes of repeating the success of the Ramadan offensive in the east the year before. 'Amr had relinquished personal control of the operations in Yemen to Lt. Gen. 'Abd al-Majid Kamal Murtagi. Murtagi's Haradh offensive attempted to duplicate many of the aspects of the earlier effort. In some ways it was even more impressive than 'Amr's operation. However, it too was essentially a conventional military campaign and so was doomed to cause only superficial damage at best. Moreover, by 1964, training provided by foreign (mostly European) mercenaries had taught the Royalists guerrilla operations, and arms from the Saudis had given them a bit more punch. Although Egypt bolstered its expeditionary force to about 50,000 men, Royalist forces had also grown.[53]

Much of this expansion can be attributed to the actions of the Egyptian Air Force in Yemen. While the EAF was not terribly attentive in flying missions in support of Egyptian ground forces — and those it did fly had little or no effect on the course of the fighting — it waged a sustained terror-bombing campaign against Yemeni villages to prevent them from being used by the Royalists and to discourage their men from joining the insurgency. The bombing had exactly the opposite effect, and throughout the war it convinced more and more otherwise apathetic Yemeni tribes to throw in their lot with the Imam, if only to get the Egyptians out of the country.

The Haradh offensive began on 12 June 1964 with two thrusts from Sanaa by Egyptian troops and armor supported by Republican and tribal units. One column headed west toward Bayt Adaqah to cut the main north-south road in northwestern Yemen. The other column headed northwest to as-Sudah. Murtagi's intention was to use these forces to drive the Royalist forces operating northwest of Sanaa farther from the capital toward their bases and supply routes from Saudi Arabia. Then on 15 August he unleashed his main attack, consisting of two thrusts: one from Haradh in extreme northwest Yemen that moved southeastward and the other southward from Sa'dah, north of Sanaa. Thus, Murtagi's scheme was to chase the insurgents north and northwest with the two attacks from Sanaa, and then to suddenly hit them from the opposite direction by coming south and southeast from Sa'dah and Haradh. The general hoped that his offensive would not only destroy the insurgency in the northwest but also result in the capture of the Imam himself, whose headquarters were known to be in that area.

The preliminary offensives from Sanaa made good progress. The Imam escaped to Saudi Arabia, but the Egyptians overran the headquarters of Prince 'Abdallah Husayn — one of the Royalists' more effective military commanders — temporarily depriving the insurgents of centralized direction in that part of the country. In addition, they took a number of important towns and road junctions through which the insurgents had been moving troops and supplies. However, the second-phase thrusts in August turned into a disaster. The Egyptian columns failed to conduct adequate reconnaissance or to deploy flank guards. They chose terrible locations to make camp and establish fire bases, usually in valleys surrounded by dominating heights, which they did not picket. In addition, by the time they got going in mid-August, rain had turned the floors of the wadis to mud, but the Egyptian units insisted on trying to drive tanks and other vehicles through them anyway. As a result, at several different points the Egyptian armor got stuck in the mud only to be ambushed by Royalist guerrillas. Despite possessing numerical superiority and huge advantages in firepower, the Egyptians were battered on every occasion. They made no attempts to loop around and clear the ambushes from above or from the side, nor did the Egyptians think to rush the Royalist positions on the wadi banks; instead, their tanks and APCs mostly fired wildly in all directions while the infantry scattered. On a couple of occasions the Egyptians were able to call in air support, but their strikes were so inaccurate that they did little damage to the Royalist forces. Overall, the Egyptian main attacks moved slowly, suffered badly, and produced few tangible gains. Very quickly, these thrusts ground to a halt.

Murtagi was frustrated by the failure of the Haradh offensive, and in late December 1964 he tried another, similar campaign in the northwest. Once again his objectives were to drive the insurgents out of the region and capture the Imam, who had returned to the area. Murtagi employed 7,000 Egyptian troops with another 3,000 Republican soldiers in four separate thrusts designed once again to trap the Royalists in a series of staggered and geographically opposed thrusts. However, the Royalists had become much better at guerrilla warfare, while the Egyptians had not improved their COIN capacity. Egyptian forces again failed to deploy adequate patrols or flank guards, made camp in vulnerable locations, and in battle relied exclusively on their firepower to try to obliterate the guerrillas. This pattern favored the insurgents, who could harass and ambush the Egyptian columns and then slip away before the Egyptians were able to bring their superior weaponry to bear. By February 1965, Murtagi's forces had suffered over 1,000 casualties in ambushes, and the offensive had run out of steam.[54]

Much to the surprise of the Egyptians and the Republican government, the Royalists followed up their success with a major counterattack that retook many positions lost in the previous months as well as other positions lost during the Haradh offensive. In the east the Royalists retook Harib, Sirwan, Qafla, and Ma'rib, which they had lost in the Ramadan offensive. In the northwest they captured the fortress of Jabal Razih, which controlled many of the key lines of communication north of Sanaa. They even succeeded in temporarily closing the road from Sanaa westward to the main port of Hodeidah. Riding their initial successes, the Royalists kept their offensive going throughout the spring and summer of 1965. By the fall of that year, nearly all of north, east, and central Yemen were either in Royalist hands or on the brink of capture. Royalist successes became so threatening that the Egyptians felt it necessary to begin using chemical warfare — mustard gas at first, then nerve gas — to try to stop the insurgents.

The Royalists' 1964–65 offensive marked a turning point in the war because it showcased the dramatic improvement in their capabilities. The European mercenaries training them were beginning to have a considerable influence on their skills as insurgents. The Royalists were never great guerrillas: they were undisciplined and few of their commanders showed a flair for tactics. However, they were brave, hardy, good marksmen, cunning, and bloodthirsty — all traits that the Europeans were able to harness and turn into useful insurgent skills. In addition, the advisors began training a picked force of "semiregular" Royalist guerrillas who were to serve as a cadre around which the Royalists could build a more formidable army and that could be used for particularly important operations. By late 1965, there were 15,000–20,000 Royalist semiregulars plus 200,000 tribesmen who could be called upon for local operations.[55]

Moreover, Egyptian and Republican tactical formations were so limited in their abilities that even a modest improvement in Royalist skills shifted the balance in combat to their favor. Egypt proved incapable of bringing to bear its enormous advantages in firepower over the Royalists. Their airstrikes and artillery bombardments were painfully slow to develop and highly inaccurate. David Smiley, an observer during the war, reported one incident in which an entire Egyptian battery of 105-mm pack howitzers unsuccessfully tried for hours to silence a lone Royalist 75-mm gun that sat immobile on a rock outcropping and fired without stop all day long.[56] Time and again, Europeans observing (or participating in) the war remarked that the Egyptians insisted on doing things "by the book" and seemed incapable of acting effectively when things did not go as they had planned. Specifically, their tactical formations refused to move and fight on their own initiative, and their commanders referred even the most minor decisions back to the highest authorities in Sanaa.

This pattern was especially damaging in Yemen, where the mountainous terrain forced large formations to split into much smaller groups that had to be able to both work independently and coordinate their operations. In other words, the terrain — and the nature of COIN operations — forced the devolution of authority to the lowest levels, but Egyptian squad, platoon, company, and even battalion commanders rarely demonstrated the independent judgment and aggressiveness necessary for success in these circumstances. The result was that Egyptian tactical units were virtually helpless when they had to break up into small teams to try to clear insurgent positions in the severe terrain dominating much of Yemen. The Royalists learned that when they ambushed these small formations, the Egyptians rarely tried anything imaginative or aggressive and simply took cover, fired back, and screamed for aid, which rarely came since the commanders of nearby units would not take the initiative and diverge from their orders. Thus, it generally fell to higher echelons to try to organize a response, which rarely could be effected before the trapped unit either was destroyed or surrendered. The Egyptians compounded these problems by dragging tanks and APCs into the rugged terrain, where, because Egyptian infantry generally did not understand how to operate in conjunction with armor, Royalist guerrillas were able to sneak up on the vehicles and destroy them with satchel charges or light antitank weapons. By 1965, one former U.S. military officer in Yemen estimated that the Egyptians were suffering about ten casualties for every one inflicted on the Royalists.[57]

The battle for Harib in March 1965 was illustrative of the change in fortunes. The Royalists captured the town — which had been taken by the Egyptians during the Ramadan offensive — in a surprise attack. They then rushed in 400 of their newly trained semiregulars, who quickly built defenses and earthworks to hold the town. The Egyptians sent a large armored force to retake the town, but the semiregulars decisively defeated the column at al-Jubah. The Royalists outmaneuvered the Egyptians, and Egyptian infantry failed to coordinate its activity with their armor, leaving the tanks easy marks for Royalist antitank teams.

THE EGYPTIAN DEFEAT

Despite the conventional successes of the 1964–65 offensive, the Royalists returned to a more traditional insurgent strategy. Once the Egyptians had regrouped after the disaster of the Haradh offensive and the shock of the Royalist counterattack, it became increasingly difficult for the Royalists to make further gains. The Egyptians fortified the main towns and cities and could defend them with enough firepower to make any direct Royalist attack very costly. However, because of the growing prowess of the insurgents, the Egyptians and Republicans ventured out into the countryside less and less, concentrating instead on keeping the roads open to their far-flung garrisons. In response, the Royalists turned to cutting the lines of communication and supply linking the Republican-held towns to starve out their garrisons. Because of the growing advantage of the insurgents in conducting ambushes and hit-and-run operations, the Royalist stranglehold over these Egyptian and Republican forces grew tighter and tighter. The Egyptians were forced to commit a considerable percentage of their air-transport capacity to Yemen to airlift — or airdrop, in many cases — supplies to beleaguered strongholds. Cairo's initial reaction was to send additional troops to Yemen to try to keep the roads open, and by late 1965, its force in Yemen had grown to about 70,000 men.[58] However, when it became clear that the additional manpower was not having any real effect on declining Egyptian fortunes, Cairo turned to what Nasser called the "Long Breath Policy."

Similar to what the Nixon administration would call "Vietnamization" a few years later, Nasser concluded that Egypt had squandered enough men and treasure on Yemen and began looking for a way to cut his losses. He decided that his troop levels would be greatly reduced, and by mid-1966, Egyptian strength in Yemen had been cut to 20,000 men.[59] Under the Long Breath Policy, Egyptian forces took responsibility for defending the key cities of Yemen and providing air- and heavy-weapons support to Yemeni units in certain circumstances. Training of Republican forces was increasingly turned over to the Russians (who the Yemenis decided were much better instructors than their fellow Arabs), and the Egyptians increasingly left the conduct of Yemeni field operations in the hands of the Republicans and their ever changing kaleidoscope of tribal allies. In addition, Nasser began lobbying hard for a negotiated settlement so that he could withdraw altogether. However, Nasser was unwilling to simply cut and run, and he demanded concessions from the Royalists and their Saudi backers before he would pull out completely. Nevertheless, Cairo continued to draw down its forces in Yemen. By June 1967, only about 15,000 Egyptian troops and 50 aircraft (mostly transports) remained there, and most of the better combat formations had long been withdrawn.[60] After the Six Day War, the Egyptians reduced their strength even further, and at the Khartoum Summit in August 1967, Nasser agreed to withdraw from Yemen completely in return for massive Saudi financial aid to repair the damage to the Egyptian military caused by the Israelis. All told, Egypt had 26,000 soldiers killed in Yemen.[61]

Egyptian Military Performance in Yemen, 1962–67

The Egyptian performance in Yemen was not without redeeming features, but these were few and far between. In particular, the Egyptian logistical effort merits some praise. Cairo's quartermaster corps moved and maintained a force of as many as 70,000 soldiers in the field over 2,000 miles away. Because of the primitive state of the Yemeni economy, Egypt could not rely on the local infrastructure for anything but the most basic items. Instead, virtually all provisions had to be brought down the Red Sea from Egypt itself. For five years the Egyptians moved and maintained their forces in Arabia without significant problems. Of course, supply eventually became a critical issue in the campaign, but the problem was not the ability of Egyptian logisticians to support their troops but the ability of Egyptian combat forces to keep the interior supply routes open. In other words, the problem was a tactical military failure and not a logistical failure per se.

The constant problems afflicting Egyptian tactical effectiveness are detailed above, but what is worth noting is that, as early as 1964, Cairo recognized that its tactical formations were not getting the job done and took a number of steps to resolve the problem. Egypt kept sending troops to Yemen, eventually bringing the expeditionary force there to over 70,000 men in an effort to use quantity to compensate for the absence of tactical quality. Later, Cairo began recruiting ever larger numbers of university graduates into the army to try to improve the junior officer and noncommissioned officer corps. Chemical warfare was Egypt's final bid, and this too proved inadequate.

Three points need to be made about the effectiveness of Egypt's senior military leadership in Yemen. First, Cairo's senior officers generally performed better than most of its junior officers. Top commanders were far more creative and aggressive in their prosecution of operations than were the brigade, battalion, and company officers in the field. Also, the higher echelons of command paid much greater attention to combined arms and the need to employ maneuver rather than firepower alone. Second, Egypt's major offensives were frequently very impressive *conventional* military operations. In particular, 'Amr's Ramadan offensive and Murtagi's various campaigns deserve high marks. They were well planned, made excellent use of operational maneuver to try to crush the Royalists, effectively concentrated large numbers of troops and heavy weaponry, and were innovative and clever. Against a conventional enemy — and with more competent tactical forces — these operations might have produced decisive results. Third, while the various Egyptian offensives were admirable conventional operations, they were not counterinsurgency operations. This was the crucial failing of the Egyptian effort in Yemen. Egypt's generals apparently never figured out how to defeat a guerrilla force. They seemed to believe that the Royalist insurgency was simply a conventional military problem to which conventional military solutions could be applied. Thus, Egyptian failure in Yemen must be considered a product of both poor tactical performance and poor strategy. As the Americans would later learn in Vietnam, even a tactically competent military cannot defeat a guerrilla force without employing a true COIN strategy.[62] However, one cannot heap all the blame on Cairo's generals because it seems doubtful that the tactically ineffective forces at their disposal would have been able to successfully implement even a very good counterinsurgency strategy. Ultimately, either of these failings would probably have been enough to doom the Egyptian intervention in Yemen alone, and their combination simply made the experience that much more painful.

The Six Day War, 1967

The decade between the Sinai-Suez and Six Day Wars saw the deepening of many of the trends in the Egyptian military inaugurated by the Free Officers after their accession to power in 1952. Field Marshal 'Amr and his cronies turned the Egyptian armed forces into their private fiefdom, systematically replacing all of the top military leaders with men loyal to themselves.[63] Although the Egyptian armed forces continued to have an internal-security role, this mission increasingly gave way to external-security considerations as the involvement in Yemen dragged on and as Nasser shifted his internal power base away from 'Amr's increasingly suspect armed forces. Cairo also accelerated its drive to eliminate any lingering dependence on Britain and the West by purchasing ever larger quantities of arms from the USSR and even establishing the foundations for a domestic arms industry to end its dependence on foreign armaments altogether. But this initiative proved a deep disappointment, and by 1967, Egypt's arms factories could not even meet the needs of the armed forces for small-caliber ammunition.

The Armies on the Eve of War

In the spring of 1967, Egypt again found itself at war with Israel. Essentially, the Six Day War was sparked by the cycle of low-level conflict between Israel and Syria along their mutual border between the Golan Heights and the Huleh Valley. The Syrians armed and encouraged Palestinian terrorists to conduct attacks against military and civilian targets in Israel, while that nation relentlessly encroached on the ceasefire lines and regularly provoked the Syrians through direct military action—to which the Israelis would respond with devastating force. In April and May 1967, a series of incidents between the two led to widespread fears that Israel was preparing a major attack on Syria. These fears were fueled by the Soviets, who mysteriously announced that they had detected a massive buildup of Israeli forces along the Syrian border. Although this was immediately revealed to be false, the Syrians used the reported mobilization to goad Nasser into threatening to attack if Israel struck at Syria. Throughout May 1967, Egypt and Israel traded ever more provocative threats and military maneuvers, ultimately culminating in Israel's decision to smash the Egyptian military and eliminate it as a threat.[64]

When war clouds began to gather in May and June 1967, Egypt concentrated its army against Israel, massing 100,000 of its 160,000 troops in the Sinai. Although about one-third of these men were reservists, at least another third, and possibly many more, were veterans of the conflict in Yemen.[65] The forces in Sinai comprised seven divisions (four infantry, two armored, and one mechanized infantry), four independent infantry brigades, and four independent armored brigades. The Egyptian army in Sinai fielded 950 tanks, 1,100 APCs, and over 1,000 artillery pieces. In addition, the Egyptian Air Force could contribute over 450 combat aircraft, including 200 of the USSR's latest fighter, the MiG-21, and 30 supersonic Tu-16 bombers.[66]

Against the Egyptians, Israel deployed roughly 70,000 men in six armored brigades, an infantry brigade, a mechanized infantry brigade, and three paratroop brigades. Eight of these units were grouped into three divisional task forces — *ugdot* in Hebrew. The Israelis fielded over 700 tanks against the Egyptians. The Israeli Air Force had 207 combat aircraft, of which 72 were advanced French Mirages while the rest were much older Mysteres, Super-Mysteres, Ouragons, and Vautours.[67] However, while the IAF also had to deal with Syria, Jordan, and possibly Iraq, the EAF was free to concentrate fully against Israel.

Thus, Egypt possessed a significant, albeit not overwhelming, numerical advantage over Israeli forces. It also possessed something of an advantage in the quality of its equipment. This, anyway, was the opinion of the Soviets and the Egyptians before the war; afterward — after the opportunity to examine and test captured Egyptian equipment — the Israelis reached the same conclusion. In some categories, such as tanks and fighter aircraft, the two sides were about evenly matched, but in most other areas the Egyptians had a meaningful advantage. The workhorse of Israel's armored corps was the British Centurion, which, although badly underpowered and mechanically unreliable, nevertheless had a powerful gun and decent armor. Still, less than half the tanks Israel deployed to the Sinai were Centurions. By contrast, the majority of Egyptian tanks facing Israel were Soviet T-55s, which most of the Israelis considered an even trade-off with the Centurion.[68] But Egypt's Soviet APCs, artillery, antitank weapons, communications gear, and most of its crew-served infantry weapons were both more modern and more capable than the largely obsolete equipment Israel had scrounged from the West. For instance, the Egyptians relied primarily on Soviet BTR-50s and BTR-60s as their primary APCs, whereas the Israelis relied exclusively on old U.S. M-3 halftracks, which lacked the armament and armor of the BTRs. The Egyptians' Soviet artillery pieces could accurately deliver rounds at considerably greater ranges than the Western guns the Israelis used. In the air, the Israelis — who had obtained a working

MiG-21 from an Iraqi defector — concluded that the Mirage was a somewhat better plane than the new MiG, but the Soviet fighter was clearly superior to the other French planes in Israel's air force.

Another important advantage Egypt possessed was its rebuilt and improved defensive positions in the Sinai. With Soviet aid, the Egyptians had refortified the peninsula to withstand an Israeli offensive. They had done a pretty good job too. First, Cairo recognized the primary avenues of advance and built major defensive positions along all of them. Second, they learned from the experience of 1956 and tried to correct mistakes made then, such as leaving the al-Kuntillah–B'irath-Thamadah–an-Nakhl axis lightly defended and failing to guard the flanks of the Abu Ageilah position. However, the Egyptian defensive scheme was far from perfect. Two problems in particular would loom large during the course of the fighting in 1967. First, the Egyptian fortifications were built "by the book." No modifications were made for the terrain, for the capabilities of the Egyptian defenders, or for the style of Israeli attacks. The Egyptians essentially took the Soviet manuals and carved out the examples found there into from the rock and sand of the Sinai. Second, the Egyptians believed that a great deal of terrain was impassable when, in fact, it could be traversed, albeit with difficulty. In particular, the Egyptians decided that the vast stretch of sand dunes between Umm Qatef and the Gaza Strip was impassable, and they anchored the newly extended lines of the Abu Ageilah and Rafah defensive positions on this terrain.

During the crisis that unfolded in the weeks before the war, Egypt made several significant changes to its military organization, command and control, and deployment schemes. First, 'Amr created an intermediate command echelon between the general staff and the Eastern Military District commander, Lt. Gen. Salah ad-Din Muhsin. This command, the Sinai Front Command, he entrusted to General Murtagi, who had returned from Yemen in May 1967.[69] Second, Cairo replaced the commanders and chiefs of staff of six of its divisions in Sinai (all but the "Palestinian" 20th Infantry Division). It is unclear why Egypt did this, but in some of the few cases where information is available, 'Amr replaced political hacks with veterans of the Yemen campaigns. This suggests that he was trying to undo some of the damage of his politicization of the officer corps by removing his cronies and replacing them with proven soldiers.[70] Third, to beef up the army in the Sinai, the Egyptians recalled to duty tens of thousands of reservists. However, rather than organizing them into totally separate formations, Cairo inserted them throughout the command structure to fill out understrength units or reinforce others charged with critical missions. Thus, some units received reservists to bolster their ranks, while others were merged with existing reserve units.

Probably the most disruptive of Cairo's actions in the weeks prior to the Israeli attack was its constant changes to the mission of the army in the Sinai and the redeployments they entailed. Cairo had moved forces back into the peninsula primarily as a show of force on Syria's behalf. However, Nasser's goals and objectives appear to have run through a gamut of options during the crisis, reflected in his orders to the military. The general staff changed the operational plan four times during May 1967; one even envisioned an offensive into Israel to take the southern port of Eilat.[71] Every time the plan changed, Egyptian forces were uprooted and moved to another location. In some cases the changes were fairly significant, while overall the movement from one place to another exhausted the men and vehicles.

When Cairo finally settled on an operational plan to defend the Sinai, it was not what the Egyptian generals had prepared for. The original plan, entitled "Qahir" (Victory), called for a mobile defense-in-depth. Infantry screening forces were to be deployed in the fortifications of eastern Sinai to delay and disrupt the Israelis, while the bulk of the army and virtually all of its heavy forces would be held back in the B'ir Gifgafah and B'ir ath-Thamadah areas. When the IDF penetrated into central Sinai, these forces would conduct a double envelopment of the Israeli units and obliterate them in a gigantic kill zone. In May 1967, however, Nasser forbade the general staff from proceeding with the Qahir plan and instead ordered a forward defense of the Sinai. The president apparently disliked the fact that, by opting for a defense-in-depth, the Qahir plan meant the virtual abandonment of Gaza, Rafah, and al-Kuntillah as well as the likely loss of the extensive Egyptian defensive positions at al-'Arish and Abu Ageilah. Nasser also may have been concerned that Israel might opt for a limited offensive to seize the Gaza Strip or Rafah and expel the exiled Palestinians and their *fedayeen* bases. In any event, the GHQ duly complied with his wishes and repositioned their forces for a forward defense of the Sinai.

The last piece of the prelude to military operations in June 1967 was the role of surprise. There was a colossal failure on the part of Cairo's intelligence services to provide its military with the information required to fight Israel. The first mistake intelligence analysts made was that they could not decide for themselves whether they actually believed Israel was going to attack and instead issued contradictory reports from one day to the next, depending largely on which way the political wind was blowing in the capital.[72] However, this was not really an egregious lapse because it seems to have had little effect on the Egyptian forces in the Sinai. The crisis itself prompted the general staff to take precautions, and both Anwar as-Sadat and Gamasy note that Nasser was certain by 2 June that Israel would attack and so placed Egyptian forces in the Sinai on alert on 3 June.[73] Far more damaging was Egyptian military intelligence's failure to provide any useful information regarding the size, deployment, training, and doctrine of the IDF or its concept of operations for the impending war. Cairo had little idea where Israeli forces were, and the only formation it was sure about — an armored brigade deployed opposite Qusaymah — turned out to be a ruse. Nevertheless, based on this intelligence, the GHQ shifted some of its forces, in particular the 6th Mechanized Division, to cover the threat from this decoy unit.[74] Egypt had no idea what the Israeli attack would look like, what its objectives would be, or where its major thrusts would come, although the misidentification of the armored brigade at Qusaymah led them to believe it would be a repeat of the 1956 invasion, with the deepest thrusts occurring in south-central Sinai.[75] Finally, Egyptian military intelligence just did not know how the Israeli military fought: they didn't know what its tactics were, and they didn't understand its emphasis on speed and constant forward movement, its decentralized command structure, its emphasis on flexibility and ad hoc operations, its reliance on armor supported by air power, or its commitment to preemptive strikes. Moreover, the little bits of intelligence Cairo did have on the Israelis were consistently evaluated incorrectly, further adding to Egyptian confusion. Consequently, Egyptian forces in the Sinai knew little about their adversary and either assumed the Israeli forces were operationally very much like themselves or did not consider this at all.

The Israeli Airstrikes

As has become legendary, the Israelis began the Six Day War with a massive, surprise airstrike against Egypt that effectively eliminated the Egyptian Air Force as a factor. In late 1965 the Israelis had begun the practice of sending huge flights of aircraft out over the Mediterranean every morning to desensitize Egypt's early warning radar operators. Thus, on the morning of 5 June, when Israel sent virtually its entire air force out over the Mediterranean, the Egyptians thought nothing of it, having seen such operations countless times before. However, on this occasion, the Israelis dove down to near sea level (below Egyptian radar coverage) and turned south to strike airbases throughout the Sinai and northeastern Egypt. Israeli intelligence was outstanding, having pinpointed the location of every Egyptian squadron, revealed the layout of every airbase, and mastered every detail of EAF operational procedure. They timed their attack perfectly, catching the EAF after all of its morning patrols had landed, its senior commanders were fighting Cairo's traffic to get to their offices, and its pilots were eating breakfast with hardly anyone standing strip alert. For three hours, every ten minutes ten flights of four Israeli aircraft attacked airfields and other installations throughout Egypt. As a result of this constant hammering by the skilled Israeli pilots, the EAF was devastated. During the course of the morning, the Israelis struck eighteen of Egypt's airbases, cratering runways, blowing up aircraft, and destroying support facilities. The EAF lost over 300 of 450 combat aircraft and 100 combat pilots.[76]

The lion's share of the credit for the success of the air attack must be granted to the remarkable skill and planning of the Israeli Air Force. However, Egyptian mistakes compounded the dividends of that brilliance. The Israeli airstrikes caught Gen. Mahmud Sidqui Mahmud, commander of the EAF, in the air over the Sinai in an unarmed transport — along with Field Marshal 'Amr. Because the Israelis were attacking every base in the area, there was no way for the plane to land, nor could Mahmud issue orders from the air for fear that the Israelis would realize he was airborne and shoot him down. Thus, Mahmud was effectively taken out of the chain of command. In his absence, the EAF was paralyzed. Without specific authorization, the majority of Egypt's air force officers, from air-sector commanders all the way down to pilots, were unwilling to take even the most obvious emergency procedures. One story recounted by Mohamed Heikal conveys the paralysis that gripped the EAF. According to Heikal, at one Egyptian airbase the initial Israeli airstrike left three Sukhoi attack aircraft intact on the runway. Immediately, the Soviet adviser at the base urged the pilots assembled in the mess hall to quickly fly the planes to safety before the Israelis returned. However, to a man, the Egyptians stated that they had no orders to do so and therefore refused. Less than fifteen minutes later, the second wave of Israeli aircraft appeared and destroyed the three aircraft.[77] Only twelve MiGs rose from the attacked airfields to challenge the Israelis, and ten were shot down — although they did manage to knock down four Israeli Mysteres conducting airstrikes before falling to Mirage escorts. The Israelis generally only attacked the Egyptian bases in the Sinai and Nile Delta areas, thus numerous Egyptian airbases in the rest of the country were completely undamaged and could have sent fighters to intercept the attackers, but only one airbase commander was willing to take the initiative to do so. The commander at Hurghadah dispatched twelve MiG-21s and eight MiG-19s to fight the intruders. Four of these planes were shot down in dogfights without doing any damage to the Israelis; the rest were destroyed when they fled the battle but then could not find an uncratered runway before running out of fuel.

The Israeli Invasion

Soon after the first airstrikes went in against the Egyptian airbases, the Israeli army began its attack into the Sinai. Their plan was essentially to do the opposite of what they had done in 1956. Whereas that year they began the operation with a drive across south-central Sinai and only attacked in the north when the southern attack had unhinged Egypt's defenses, in 1967 their main attack came in the north. Brig. Gen. Israel Tal's ugdah (a divisional task force flexibly composed of at least one combat brigade with other units as determined by the mission and the forces available — plural "ugdot") of two armored brigades and a reinforced paratroop brigade was to take Rafah and then roll westward, overrunning al-ʾArish and securing the northern route to the Suez Canal. Brig. Gen. Ariel Sharon's ugdah of an armored brigade, a paratroop brigade, and an infantry brigade would take Abu Ageilah and then drive westward toward the Mitla Pass. Brig. Gen. Avraham Yoffe's ugdah of two armored brigades would push into the sand dunes, which the Egyptians considered impassable, between Tal and Sharon's sectors. Yoffe would support either or both of the other ugdot with flank attacks as needed and by preventing the Egyptians from themselves launching a flank attack against either Tal or Sharon. As was their custom, the Israelis had only vague guidelines for their drive to the canal because they expected to improvise the operation as the course of battle unfolded.

THE BATTLES OF RAFAH AND AL-ʾARISH

The Rafah–al-ʾArish sector contained multiple lines of defensive earth-works and fortifications manned by the Egyptian 7th Infantry Division supported by an independent armored brigade. The Israeli 7th Armored Brigade, the elite of the IDF's armored corps, led Tal's assault on the Rafah position, by punching through the defenses where the Gaza Strip meets the Egyptian border. Although the Israelis made good progress and effectively destroyed the Egyptian units they faced, they took fairly heavy casualties (by Israeli standards). The Egyptians fought extremely hard from their fixed defenses, and for the most part, no matter how accurate the Israeli fire or how devastating their maneuvers, the Egyptians stayed at their posts and kept firing until they were killed or captured. Egyptian artillery was also quite deadly at first, while the Israelis had to move through the preregistered fire zones guarding the fortifications.

Nevertheless, the Egyptians were badly hampered by inferior marks-

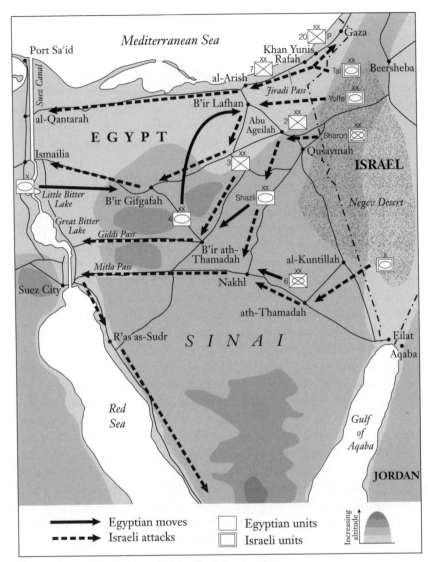

Map 5. The Israeli Conquest of the Sinai, June 1967

manship and a reluctance to maneuver or counterattack the Israelis. Thus the 7th Armored Brigade simply had to weave and push its way through the defensive positions to break through. Once the unit had outflanked or penetrated each defensive line, it was generally free of additional resistance from that position and could either roll up the line or move on to the next one. The Egyptians did a very poor job of maneuvering against the Israelis to prevent them from getting around their flanks. And once into the rear of a position, the Israelis wrought havoc because the Egyptians generally responded either by continuing to fight where they were (rather than regrouping to face the new direction of attack) or by panicking and abandoning their posts. Only once, at Khan Yunis, did the Egyptians counterattack, but this was a clumsy, straightforward charge by a battalion of T-55s — without infantry or artillery support — that ploughed right into the middle of an Israeli double-envelopment and was quickly destroyed. Once the IDF had penetrated the defensive lines and their fluid maneuvers took them onto routes the Egyptians had not anticipated, Egyptian artillery support virtually disappeared since their batteries could not shift fire to keep pace with the fast-moving Israelis. In tank-on-tank duels, the Egyptians were consistently outshot and outmaneuvered by the Israelis, who prevailed in every armor engagement.

By early afternoon, Tal's ugdah had pushed through the defenses around Rafah, seized the crucial road junction there, and was driving westward toward al-'Arish. The Egyptians' last line of defense in this sector was also their strongest: the 6th Infantry Brigade and two battalions of T-55s entrenched in three lines blocking the narrow, thirteen-kilometer-long Jiradi Pass that was the only route between Rafah and al-'Arish. Originally, the Israelis had hoped to outflank this position altogether by sending Tal's other armored brigade, the 60th, through the sand dunes to the south, which the Egyptians believed impassable and so had left undefended. For the only time during this campaign, the Egyptians were proven right about the terrain, and the brigade got stuck in the dunes. Consequently, Tal was forced to commit the 7th Armored Brigade in a frontal assault through the Jiradi Pass. Initially, the Egyptian defenders were surprised by the Israeli assault; the Egyptian units at Rafah had failed to admit that the Israelis were winning and penetrating their lines and instead reported that they had defeated the Israelis and were counterattacking. Thus, the units at Jiradi, several miles behind Rafah, were unprepared when Israeli armor came barreling down on them. This allowed the vanguard of the 7th Brigade to penetrate the entire length of the pass with almost no damage. However, the Egyptians regrouped, and when the main body of the 7th Brigade got to the pass, they ran into a steel wall of Egyptian armor and infantry. This was exactly the sort of battle the Egyptians had hoped for: there was no room for the Israelis to maneuver, and instead they were forced to charge repeatedly into the teeth of dug-in Egyptian troops and tanks. The fighting in the Jiradi Pass was some of the fiercest of the entire war, and the Israelis took very heavy casualties (at least by their standards), including the loss of thirteen tanks. Although it required the entire afternoon of 5 June and much of that night, the Israelis eventually found a way to slip a small force of armor around the edge of the pass to flank the Egyptian lines. The Egyptians again failed to counterattack or even to reorient their defenses to meet the new Israeli attack, and so their defensive line collapsed. Nevertheless, individual Egyptian troops and units continued to resist until that night, when the Israelis brought up their 35th Paratroop Brigade, which, with the tanks of the 7th Brigade, cleared the pass in vicious hand-to-hand fighting.

THE BATTLES OF UMM QATEF AND ABU AGEILAH

The defense of Abu Ageilah and its outlying positions was entrusted to the Egyptian 2d Infantry Division, probably the best infantry unit in the army, bolstered by an independent armored brigade. In 1967 the positions there were even more formidable than they had been in 1956. Thick minefields protected the approaches to Umm Qatef, and multiple, contiguous trench lines stretched from the Jebel Dalfa in the south to the (supposedly impassable) sand dunes to the north. However, the Israelis had also learned from Abu Ageilah. After their inability to reduce the position during the Suez-Sinai War, the Israelis made it a topic of constant scrutiny and, in the years before the Six Day War, their forces had gamed and practiced taking it countless times. Sharon's ugdah basically put into practice what had been learned in these exercises.

In twelve hours, the Israelis captured the entire Egyptian defensive system at Abu Ageilah and effectively destroyed the 2d Infantry Division as a combat unit. In his memoirs, Sharon claims to have structured his plan at Abu Ageilah–Umm Qatef specifically to take advantage of recurrent Arab weaknesses in tactical initiative, improvisation, and adaptation he had observed in his twenty years of fighting Arab armies.[78] The division had two of its infantry brigades and all of its armor support massed to defend the main Abu Ageilah–Umm Qatef positions while its 3d Infantry Brigade was deployed farther southeast at Qusaymah. It was considered common wisdom that Qusaymah had to be taken before Umm Qatef could be attacked, lest the southeastern force hit the attacker in his left flank. Sharon, however,

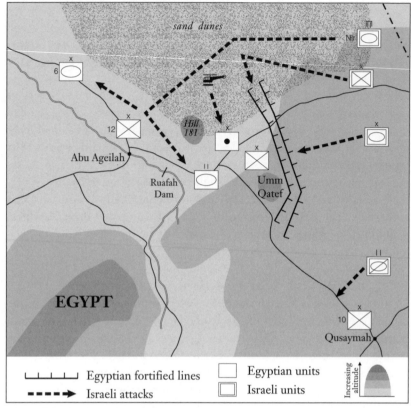

Map 6. The Battle of Abu Ageilah, June 1967

essentially ignored the brigade at Qusaymah, leaving only a small screening force to watch it. Before assaulting the main positions at Umm Qatef, Sharon sent an armored battalion task force, commanded by Lt. Col. Natke Nir, through the supposedly impassable dunes north of Umm Qatef to loop around far to the rear of the Egyptian defense lines, as Adan's battalion had done from the south in 1956. Sharon also landed a battalion of paratroopers by helicopters in the dunes north of the Egyptian artillery park, several kilometers behind the forward trench lines. At 10:30 P.M., Sharon began the attack with an artillery barrage from ninety-six guns (the largest artillery force Israel had ever assembled for an operation). While the artillery and a battalion of tanks pounded the Egyptians in their trenches, Sharon's infantry brigade moved north into the dunes, swung around the northern end of the Egyptian position, and attacked southward down the defensive lines. The paratroopers lurking in the dunes then attacked into the Egyptians' rear, getting in among the artillery batteries and preventing them from supporting the infantry. Finally, Nir's armor, which had also pushed through the sand dunes into the Egyptian rear by this time, charged back through the Abu Ageilah crossroads and attacked the tactical reserve of the Umm Qatef positions — a reinforced Egyptian tank battalion.

The Egyptians were completely surprised by the direction of Sharon's attacks, and while most tried to fight back, their resistance was ineffective. In the trenches the Egyptian infantry fought hard until they were cleared out of every position, but they failed to reorient themselves as units to face northward to block the Israeli advance, instead simply staying in their positions and waiting for the Israelis to come get them. Although it was dangerous work for the Israeli infantry to clear each firing position and trench, the Egyptians' failure to form a new defense line or to counterattack northward to try to halt the flanking forces made their resistance futile. They killed some Israeli soldiers but could not prevent the IDF from clearing the trenches. A greater failure was the passivity of the Egyptian armor behind Umm Qatef, which did not counterattack the Israeli infantry as they flanked the trench lines. Instead, the tanks sat passively until they were eventually hit by Nir's armor from behind. Likewise, the Egyptian operational reserve for Abu Ageilah — an understrength armored brigade deployed west of the crossroads — sat motionless throughout the battle. This unit did nothing to block Nir's armored battalion as it moved to outflank the Egyptian lines nor did it try to counterattack that force once it had turned the northern flank of the Umm Qatef defenses and was threatening to unhinge the entire defensive system. They did not even move to reinforce or counterattack Abu Ageilah and Umm Qatef *after* the main Israeli assault began.

In combat with Israeli armor, Egyptian tanks often sat motionless, turning to fire at the Israelis but rarely maneuvering for a better position. Moreover, the Egyptian crews fought hard as individual tanks, but their commanders failed to form up into larger teams to mount a coordinated defense or to counterattack the Israelis. After losing over half their strength in the fighting, the Egyptian armor bolted. A few groups of Egyptian infantrymen with antitank weapons joined the tank battle toward the end and did some damage, but they were too late and too few to change the outcome. The Israelis brought up mechanized infantry to deal with the antitank teams and secured the position. Finally, as Sharon had expected, the Egyptian infantry brigade at Qusaymah sat motionless throughout the fight, even though they were within earshot of the battle to the north. They did not try to reinforce the Abu Ageilah position, counterattack into the left flank of the Israeli assault, or even provide artillery support.

Egyptian Confusion and Reaction

From the moment the Israeli airstrikes began the fog of war had descended rather heavily on the Egyptian command network. The principal problem was that once the Israelis began smashing various elements of the armed forces, Egyptian personnel at all levels reacted by dissembling, obfuscating, exaggerating, and outright lying to cover their mistakes. The dean of Israeli military correspondents, Ze'ev Schiff, has noted: "From the outset, fictitious reporting, the traditional bugaboo of Arab armies, was rampant. . . . Commanders in the field fabricated successes or, in order to justify failure, exaggerated the size of Israeli forces."[79] First, EAF personnel and Field Marshal 'Amr refused to tell anyone that the Israelis had destroyed the entire air force during the morning of 5 June. Instead, they told Nasser, the general staff, and the Egyptian ground commanders in the Sinai that they had destroyed most of the Israeli aircraft and were in the process of reducing Israeli airbases to rubble. Not until about midday on 5 June would 'Amr and the air force admit the extent of the defeat to Nasser.[80] The army in the Sinai, including General Murtagi, were not told of the true results of the airstrikes until noon on 6 June — twenty-eight hours after the first airstrikes. Meanwhile, Egyptian tactical commanders in the Sinai would not report that they were being overrun and instead claimed that they were winning. Later in the day, however, when many frontline positions had been broken, the reports changed 180 degrees, and dispatches began to pour in of catastrophic defeats at the hands of vast Israeli forces.

These wild and contradictory reports from the top and bottom of the hierarchy produced chaos in the Egyptian chain of command. Based on the initial reports of Egyptian success, Nasser and the Egyptian General Staff told King Hussein and the Jordanian general staff that the EAF had destroyed the IAF and that the Egyptian army was already driving into southern Israel. They asked Jordan to launch an attack into the Negev to link up with this fictitious Egyptian attack. Jordan agreed, began moving its only armored reserves to the Negev, and began to bombard Israeli military installations. Only late in the day, after the IAF began to pound Jordan's airfields and armored columns, did Amman realize that Cairo had been lying.[81] 'Amr himself was catatonic for most of the morning, but in the afternoon he recovered and began issuing orders feverishly, bypassing both Murtagi and Muhsin and speaking directly to division and brigade commanders.[82] In addition, the orders 'Amr issued were often contradictory or misguided because he was indecisive and was relying on inaccurate and contradictory information. Many of the Egyptian units in the Sinai remained motionless for much of 5 June because of the confusion in the general staff and the unwillingness of Egyptian field commanders to act on their own initiative.

One reasonably cogent order 'Amr issued was to have two brigades of the 4th Armored Division move to B'ir Lafhan and counterattack into the left flank of Tal's ugdah as it pushed through Rafah toward al-'Arish. The division's mechanized brigade and one of its armored brigades (both equipped with T-55s) moved out that afternoon, and by nightfall they had arrived at B'ir Lafhan, where they unexpectedly encountered a battalion of Israeli Centurions from the lead armored brigade of Yoffe's ugdah on the wrong side of the supposedly impassable sand dunes south of al-'Arish. After an initial clash in which the Egyptians lost nine tanks while destroying only one Israeli tank, the Egyptians pulled back to await daylight—despite the fact that their night-vision equipment was much better than that of the Israelis. During the night the Egyptians tried harassing the IDF positions with artillery fire, but their shelling was very inaccurate. The next morning the Egyptians realized that they were facing only a small Israeli force and tried a more determined attack to destroy the Israelis and push on to al-'Arish. They launched a frontal assault but never managed to get more than part of their force moving, which was rebuffed by Israeli tank fire and airstrikes. Israeli tank gunners relied on long-range marksmanship to batter the Egyptian formations and then maneuvered from position to position, getting flank shots on Egyptian armor and then darting back behind cover. Finally, a second Israeli tank battalion arrived led by Bren Adan—Yoffe's deputy—which enveloped the Egyptians. This move caved in the flank of the larger force and drove it off. All told, the Egyptians lost somewhere between thirty and eighty tanks (accounts vary), plus large numbers of other armored vehicles, without destroying any Israeli tanks.[83] IAF aircraft continued to harass the Egyptians as they fled westward back to B'ir Gifgafah.[84]

The Egyptian Retreat

The defeat of the 4th Armored Division at B'ir Lafhan appears to have been the last straw for 'Amr. In the afternoon of 6 June, a little more than a day and a half after the first Israeli airstrikes, he ordered a general retreat from the Sinai. The orders went out that all Egyptian units should fall back across the Suez Canal as quickly as possible. 'Amr did not bother to first inform Muhsin or Murtagi to allow them to develop a plan for an orderly withdrawal but called divisions directly and ordered them to retreat west immediately. Consequently, there were no instructions regarding a phased withdrawal or a fighting retreat: units were simply to get out as fast as they could.[85] Later that evening, several senior general-staff officers apparently persuaded 'Amr that the situation was not irretrievable and convinced him to rescind or amend the original order, but by that time the damage was done and the retreat was irreversible.

The Egyptian withdrawal turned into a rout almost from the start. The first problem they encountered was that when many senior field commanders received the order to withdraw, they jumped in their staff cars and fled to Cairo, frequently without issuing any orders to their subordinates as to how to conduct the withdrawal. In most of these cases, no one stepped forward to fill the leadership void, and some units began to fall apart. In some cases the junior officers also decided that it was "every man for himself" and set out on their own. In this chaos, unit cohesion varied widely. Some large formations stuck together despite the desertion of their senior officers, while others disintegrated, prompting soldiers to abandon their equipment and set out across the desert on their own or in small groups to try to make it back to the Suez.

Without direction from the GHQ, most Egyptian forces proved incapable of any action except flight. Only a few units tried to stand and fight to cover the retreat or even deployed rear guards to cover their own withdrawal. For example, Lt. Gen. Sa'd ad-Din Shazli, commanding an armored-division task force southwest of Abu Ageilah, was among the senior officers who fled immediately upon hearing of the retreat. His force was large, intact, and at that point the most powerful Egyptian concentration in the Sinai. However, rather than try to conduct a fighting withdrawal to try to get their armored vehicles and other weaponry out of the Sinai, the unit's junior officers simply set off for the canal without any planning, coordination, or rear guards. Many of Shazli's subordinates abandoned their equipment altogether and tried to make it back to the Suez on foot. Some Egyptian units at least buried their heavy equipment to prevent it from falling into Israeli hands before setting off across the desert, but many others did not.

After 'Amr had come back to his senses, and when it became clear that the Egyptian units in the Sinai were simply retreating pell-mell, the general staff began trying to organize rear guards to slow the Israelis while the rest of the army ran. Elements of the 3d Infantry Division received orders to remain in place in their defensive positions at Jebel Libni, where they put up a stiff fight before they were outflanked and obliterated by Israeli armor. Another brigade of the same division was ordered to make a stand farther west at B'ir Hammah, but in this case the Egyptians put up only perfunctory resistance before fleeing. The remnants of the 4th Armored Division were then ordered to stand and fight at B'ir Gifgafah on 7 June and retreat back across the canal. Although Tal's ugdah destroyed at least a brigade's worth of equipment in a huge tank battle west of B'ir Gifgafah, the 4th executed its mission fairly well, and the remnants of the division (about one-third of its original strength) were able to reach the west side of the Suez as a cohesive force. The general staff then ordered a reserve armored brigade to move east from Ismailia to reinforce the 4th Armored Division at B'ir Gifgafah and cover the withdrawal. GHQ apparently failed to calculate that by the time this force got to B'ir Gifgafah, the 4th would already have fallen back from those positions. Although this brigade passed the remnants of 4th Division retreating westward as it drove eastward to B'ir Gifgafah, without specific orders from the general staff to turn around, the brigade commander kept heading east. When the unit arrived at B'ir Gifgafah, the Israelis had already secured the former Egyptian positions and in a short, sharp battle mauled the brigade. Later the Egyptians conducted several smaller counterattacks near al-Qantarah and the Giddi Pass by units held in GHQ reserve at the canal, but these were easily dispatched by Israeli armor and airstrikes.

Compounding Egyptian problems, the Israelis were now in their element. Having broken through the initial fortified lines and penetrated into the Egyptians' operational depth, Israeli armor now had room to run and cause havoc. The Israelis quickly developed an exploitation strategy by which they sent armored columns deep into central Sinai to seize the Mitla, Giddi, and B'ir Gifgafah Passes before most of the Egyptian army could pass through them. Although some units, like the remnants of the 4th Armored Division, were able to make good their escape because their divisional leadership remained with their command to direct a fighting withdrawal, several did not. Most Egyptian units, including the large and intact 6th Mechanized Division and Shazli Armored Force, were cut off by Israeli armor at the passes and then destroyed by Israeli air and ground forces. In many cases, even this was unnecessary, for large numbers of Egyptians simply abandoned their vehicles and attempted to make it out by foot when they saw the passes were blocked. Although the Israelis spent several weeks rounding up the last of these men, few made it out of the desert alive.

In some cases, the Egyptians tried to fight their way past what were initially very small blocking forces at the various passes. For example, the first Israeli force to arrive at the Mitla Pass was an understrength company of nine tanks (four of which had run out of gas and were being towed) led by Bren Adan, which was left for much of the day on 7 June to contend with most of three Egyptian divisions trying to escape west. Given this absurd force imbalance, it would be quite an understatement to say that the Egyptians fought poorly. At the Mitla and the other defiles, the Egyptians did not attack at all but just kept moving toward the pass or tried to drive off the Israelis with inaccurate tank fire. On the rare occasions when the Egyptians launched a determined attack, it was a clumsy, slow-moving frontal assault that the Israelis had little trouble dispatching with a few quick maneuvers and deft long-range gunnery in every case. Moreover, the Egyptian attacks were conducted only with armor—no effort was made to have infantry sneak up on what were often unsupported Israeli tanks and attack them with antitank weapons. Similarly, the Egyptians directed very little artillery fire against the Israeli blocking forces, and the few barrages they did conduct were inaccurate and caused little damage. Nadav Safran has written, "The Egyptians did indeed fight with skill and courage from prepared positions in the first phase of the battle but once their fixed lines of defense were smashed, they were never able to fight again in any coordinated fashion, and occasional displays of courage by various units notwithstanding, the bulk of the Egyptian troops that had not been affected by the first phase were reduced to a fleeing rabble by the swift Israeli maneuvers."[86]

The Egyptian army was all but obliterated during the Six Day War. They suffered 10,000–15,000 casualties and had 5,500 men captured by the Israelis. The Egyptians left at least 530 tanks in the Sinai, of which about 330 were destroyed in combat. They may have been able to recover as many as another 100 tanks destroyed in combat and withdraw them over the Suez Canal. Nearly 500 artillery pieces were captured as well as 10,000 other vehicles. Nasser reckoned several months later that the Egyptian armed forces had lost 80 percent of their ground equipment in the war.[87] Against this the Israelis suffered about 1,400 casualties and lost 61 tanks.[88]

The War in the Air

The Israeli airstrikes on the morning of 5 June effectively removed the EAF as a potential influence on the course of the war. Thereafter, the Egyptians had few operational aircraft and mustered very few sorties. Even before the decisive Israeli airstrikes, however, the EAF appeared unlikely to have contributed significantly to Cairo's war effort. Egypt continued to experience serious problems assimilating Soviet weaponry, particularly the somewhat more complicated air force equipment. EAF personnel had great difficulty learning to fly and maintain even the relatively simple Soviet MiG-21 fighter. On the first day of the war, 20 percent of the EAF was nonoperational because pilots and flight crews had still not sufficiently mastered their aircraft. Ground crews took excessively long times to repair and prepare aircraft for combat operations. As a result, the EAF had only a 70 percent operational readiness rate, while the MiG-21 squadrons had only a 60–65 percent readiness rate.[89] According to the Israelis, the MiG-21 was a very capable aircraft for its time and in the hands of a good pilot could be very dangerous, but most Egyptian pilots could not approach the full capabilities of their aircraft, were slow to react, unimaginative, and inflexible in combat. Egyptian pilots received far fewer flying hours than their Israeli opponents. And each was trained to fly only one type of mission (air-to-air, ground attack, reconnaissance, or the like), further limiting Egyptian air operations.[90]

As a result, Israeli fighters dominated the EAF in dogfights. The IAF shot down forty-two Egyptian aircraft in air-to-air combat during the war, while losing only a half-dozen of their own to the Egyptians.[91] On the first day of the conflict, the Egyptians lost nineteen planes to Israeli fighters. The following day they lost fourteen planes in dogfights, and on the third day another nine of their planes fell in aerial combat.[92] Nevertheless, the Egyptians did not shy away from the fight. Despite the devastation they suffered in the first hours of the war, throughout the next four days, albeit in ever dwindling numbers, Egyptian fighters came up to do battle with the Israeli interceptors and even mustered 150 attack sorties against Israeli ground formations in the Sinai.[93]

Egyptian Military Effectiveness in the Six Day War

Although the Six Day War was a far greater humiliation than the 1956 Sinai-Suez War, Egyptian combat performance in 1967 was not that much worse than earlier. Tactical performance was equally poor. The performance of Egyptian strategic leadership was worse, though not dramatically so. Although the quantitative balance of forces favored Egypt in 1967 to a much greater extent than in 1956, the quality of Israeli equipment was much closer to that of Egypt than had been the case in 1956. In truth, the major difference between the two wars was the improved effectiveness of the IDF. In 1956 Israeli military performance was fairly mediocre and, in particular, Israel's strategic direction was poor. The plan for the Israeli invasion in 1956 was badly constrained by political considerations and based on a fundamental misunderstanding of Egyptian military effectiveness. By 1967, Israeli tactical proficiency completely outclassed that of the Egyptian armed forces. Israel's generals also devised a much better plan that played to their strengths and Egyptian weaknesses. Moreover, as the campaign unfolded, Israel's generals continued to push the course of operations further and further into those aspects of military operations at which the IDF excelled and the Egyptians had difficulties.

TACTICAL PERFORMANCE

Egyptian tactical performance manifested all of the same patterns of behavior observed in its previous campaigns. On the positive side, Egyptian forces once again demonstrated an impressive ability to conduct static defensive operations. The toughest part of every Israeli attack was breaking through the fixed defenses in eastern Sinai, for the Egyptians fought well from their fortified positions, counterattacked with determination, and clung to their defenses tenaciously. Egyptian gunnery, including artillery fire, was very accurate as long as the Israelis conducted attacks along avenues of approach the Egyptians had recognized and covered with interlocking fire positions and preregistered artillery fire zones. Thus, for example, 153 of the 201 casualties suffered by Israel's 7th Armored Brigade during the war were taken on 5 June in breaking through the Egyptian defenses at Khan Yunis, Rafah, and the Jiradi Pass. Likewise, of the 29 tanks the brigade had damaged or destroyed during the war, 27 of these losses occurred on 5 June.[94]

Egyptian soldiers and airmen also were remarkably brave. Although there were instances of units fleeing without a fight during the opening stages of the war, the Egyptians generally fought very hard when defending their fortified defensive lines. At the Jiradi Pass, Rafah, Abu Ageilah, and Umm Qatef, Egyptian soldiers fought on long after the Israelis had broken through and their positions were untenable. In each of these battles, the Israelis generally had to reduce each strongpoint with infantry because, long after the battle had been decided, the Egyptians kept fighting. This quality was recognized by virtually every Israeli field commander who faced them in 1967. After the war Moshe Dayan commented, "As for the fighting standard of the Arab soldiers, I can sum it up in one sentence: they did not run away."[95]

The cohesion of Egyptian units in the Sinai during the Six Day War was uneven. As long as they were defending fixed positions, most formations hung together superbly. Once again, at the Jiradi Pass, Abu Ageilah, Rafah, Umm Qatef, and Jebel Libni, Egyptian forces fought together until they were physically overpowered by the Israelis. Overall, there were few instances of units disintegrating during the first phase of the war. Conversely, unit cohesion broke down across the board during the retreat beginning the afternoon of 6 June. While the desertion of many senior officers was a contributing factor to that disintegration, it cannot be said to have been decisive. In some cases Egyptian units stuck together even after their commanders had fled, while in other instances they fell apart despite the fact that their senior leadership remained with them.

Likewise, the chaos in the Egyptian command structure also had an effect on Egyptian unit cohesion, but it too was not decisive. If the problem had been the complete breakdown in the Egyptian command and control system, unit disintegration should have occurred when the chaos was greatest: on 6 June immediately after the general retreat order was given, when it was clear that the senior leadership was in a state of panic. While several units did fall apart the moment they received the retreat order, the vast majority hung together and only splintered later, during the retreat, when they realized that the Israelis had blocked the passes.

Finally, more competent Egyptian units did not necessarily display better unit cohesion, nor did less competent units necessarily display worse unit cohesion. For example, the Egyptian 7th Infantry Division, a very mediocre unit, fought just as hard as the 2d Infantry Division, a very competent unit, by Egyptian standards. Likewise, there was no particular congruence in behavior among the best units in the Egyptian army: the 4th Armored Division conducted a very professional fighting withdrawal, while the 6th Mechanized Division bolted en masse after the initial retreat order and disintegrated during the withdrawal.

These patterns — or lack thereof — strongly suggest that it was the process of the retreat itself, or the Israeli actions during the retreat, that triggered the general breakdown in unit cohesion during the withdrawal. Many Egyptian units did not fall apart until they reached the various passes, only to find them blocked by Israeli armor. Even in these cases, many formations retained enough unit integrity to at least try to break through the Israeli blocking positions, and only when it became clear that they could not do so and thus were trapped did they finally collapse. In other instances Egyptian units broke up during the retreat itself before they reached the passes. In these cases their leadership was largely forced to act on its own without guidance from higher command authorities. These ad hoc operations were stilted, simplistic, and poorly thought out. For the most part, commanders simply ordered their men to head for the passes with or without their heavy equipment. Few preparations were made to scout the route, determine the location and direction of Israeli forces, organize the formation for any contingencies along the way, or outline alternative courses of action in case the initial plan became inadequate.

The haphazard conduct of the withdrawal by the Egyptian field officers who had remained in the Sinai seems to have had a profound effect on unit cohesion during the retreat. The results of this can be seen in a comparison of the 4th Armored Division's withdrawal with that of the 125th Mechanized Brigade of the 6th Mechanized Division. In both cases the senior officers remained with the unit — at least initially. However, the 4th Armored Division, which remained in close contact with the general staff, conducted a disciplined and well-prepared fighting withdrawal, whereas the 125th Mechanized Brigade, which was left to its own devices, buried its equipment and simply set out across the desert to find the passes. When it became clear that this plan was not going to work, the brigade's senior leadership abandoned their troops, ordering them to keep heading west while they waited with a good portion of the remaining food and water to be captured by the IDF. As their plight became increasingly desperate, the brigade fell apart, with men and officers scattering across the desert.[96]

The difficulties the Egyptians experienced in conducting an unplanned retreat without the guidance of their senior military leadership were identical to other problems the Egyptians experienced at tactical levels. For the most part, their forces were slow to react to Israeli moves and were inflexible in their actions. They rarely attempted to maneuver and responded poorly to Israeli maneuvers. They conducted few counterattacks, and although those they conducted were often very determined, they were invariably simple frontal assaults, and if the sudden shock was not enough to throw the Israelis back, the counterattack would fail — and the position would fall. The handful of armored counterattacks they conducted — basically just at B'ir Lafhan, B'ir Gifgafah, and the Mitla Pass — were ponderous frontal assaults that relied on firepower rather than maneuver. The Israelis defeated them handily and inflicted heavy losses through superior marksmanship and constant maneuver, both as units and as individual tanks. In most cases Egyptian forces did not counterattack at all but simply sat passively in their defensive positions, firing but not moving, long after their lines had been breached. The inaction of the Egyptian armored reserves at Abu Ageilah–Umm Qatef in particular stand out in this regard.

At the root of these problems were Egypt's junior officers, the commanders from brigade level down. Most of these men displayed little flexibility, initiative, imagination, or ability to react to unforeseen Israeli actions without explicit instructions from higher authorities.[97] After the war General Sharon commented in typically colorful style: "I think the Egyptian soldiers are very good. They are simple and ignorant but they are strong and they are disciplined. They are good gunners, good diggers, and good shooters — but their officers are shit, they can fight only according to what they planned before. Once we had broken through, except for the minefield between Bir Hassneh and Nakhl, which was probably there before the war, the Egyptian officers placed no mines and laid no ambushes to block our line of advance. But some of the soldiers, particularly at the Mitla where we had blocked their line of retreat, fought to the death in an attempt to break westwards to the canal."[98]

These failings undermined the better decisions of Egypt's senior leadership and exacerbated their mistakes. For example, as noted above, Egyptian units changed postings several times during May 1967, and ultimately some units had only been in the positions from which they eventually fought for only a week or so. This was clearly a mistake on the part of the political-military leadership and, to a lesser extent, of the senior military command. However, Egyptian field commanders compounded this problem by failing to have their units dig in when they moved to a new position unless specifically ordered to do so by higher authorities. Thus, in a number of cases, companies, battalions, and brigades did not even take advantage of the limited time they had to prepare their defensive positions because their commanders were unwilling to take even the most obvious precautions on their own initiative.

Another problem for Cairo's forces was that the Egyptians were largely unable to take advantage of the capabilities of the weaponry at their disposal. For instance, after the war the Israelis found that only about 5 percent of all the mines the Egyptians had laid in the Sinai had been properly armed.[99] The equipment itself was not the problem. Most Egyptians concede that the weapons they possessed were as good, if not better than, those of the IDF and were more than adequate for the task at hand.[100] In fact, the Israelis were impressed with the quality of Soviet armored vehicles and reequipped several new brigades with the items they captured — brigades that performed well in the October War six years later.[101] However, Egyptian personnel could not handle these weapons. In the words of Ze'ev Schiff: "For the Egyptians, the great quantity of modern equipment proved to be an impediment. They had a hard time extracting the full benefit the equipment offered."[102]

STRATEGIC PERFORMANCE

Many authors, particularly Egyptian writers, have attempted to lay the blame for the 1967 debacle entirely on the shoulders of Marshal 'Amr and the political hacks he had appointed to many key command positions.[103] While it is certainly true that Cairo bungled many aspects of the campaign, this claim has been exaggerated. First, not all of Egypt's strategic-operational level moves were disastrous, and some were quite creditable.

Second, there is every reason to believe that given the rather severe tactical shortcomings of Egyptian forces, detailed above, and the hypercompetence of Israeli forces at all levels, even very able Egyptian generals would have been hard pressed to salvage victory from the Six Day War.

Egypt's plan for the defense of the Sinai was not that bad, all things considered. The Egyptians once again recognized the primary avenues of advance across the peninsula and built formidable defensive positions to block them. They attached armored brigades to their forward infantry divisions to serve as local counterattack forces and deployed armored and mechanized divisions deeper along the main arteries as operational reserves to block or seal Israeli penetrations. They made three critical, but not unforgivable, mistakes: they failed to properly assess the "traversability" of certain terrain, they assumed that the Israelis would employ the same strategy they used in 1956 (that is, the main thrust would come along the southernmost al-Kuntillah–ath-Thamadah–an-Nakhl axis), and they fell for the Israeli deception scheme that was designed to reinforce this misperception.

Nevertheless, even had they not made these mistakes, it is difficult, if not impossible, to imagine a prewar plan that would have made much of a difference in the final outcome because, at the tactical level, Egyptian forces were no match for the IDF. This point is clearly illustrated by the Israeli assault on Rafah, in which they attacked into the heart of one of Egypt's strongest defensive positions, and yet were able to break through quickly while suffering losses that, though heavier than the Israelis were accustomed to bear, were not debilitating. Thus, even had Egyptian defenses been extended to cover the sand dunes, there is every reason to believe the Israelis still would have broken through — and would have done so relatively quickly and painlessly. Likewise, the major problem with assuming the main Israeli thrust would come in the al-Kuntillah area was that some Egyptian mechanized forces were deployed too far south to quickly react to the Israeli attacks in northern Sinai. However, even had Egyptian armored reserves been better deployed, there is no reason to believe that their counterattacks would have gone any better than the attack by the 4th Armored Division at B'ir Lafhan, in which two intact Egyptian heavy brigades were decisively defeated by two understrength Israeli armored battalions with modest air support. This engagement suggests that had Egyptian armored reserves been positioned farther north, they likely would have been destroyed in counterattacks against the Israeli penetrations rather than in the retreat to the Suez Canal, as was actually the case. Either way, the outcome would likely have been the same.

Some Egyptians contend that had they employed the mobile defense-in-depth strategy envisioned in the Qahir plan, they would have done much better. I disagree. If anything, the Egyptians would have done even worse had they tried to implement Qahir. The plan called for only a light infantry screen in the forward fortifications, while the bulk of the forces, and all of the large mechanized formations, were held back to conduct a massive counterattack against the main Israeli penetration when identified. The problem with this is that it would have demanded that the Egyptians fight and prevail in fluid, meeting engagements with Israeli armor in central Sinai. In the actual course of operations, the Egyptians clearly demonstrated that this kind of warfare was their weakest suit. The fighting at B'ir Lafhan, the performance of Egypt's armored reserves at Abu Ageilah, the tank duels between the IDF and the 4th Armored Division as it retreated from B'ir Gifgafah, and the combat between Adan's tiny force and the elements of the 6th Mechanized Division and Shazli Armored Force at the Mitla Pass all attest to this dramatic imbalance. Based on the actual performance of Egyptian forces during the Six Day War, there is no reason to believe that the Egyptians could have quickly developed an ad hoc plan to conduct a double envelopment of a large Israeli armored force in central Sinai, executed such a maneuver quickly and efficiently, and then defeated the Israelis in tactical armor engagements when the plan was put into effect. This scenario would appear to have been the answer to Tel Aviv's prayers: a massive, swirling maneuver battle in central Sinai where the Israelis' decisive advantages in improvisation, flexibility, and armored combat would have allowed them to obliterate Egypt's armored forces. Add to this Israel's air superiority and the plan could only have turned out as an even worse catastrophe than the actual disastrous course of the war.

With the exception of the politically inconceivable option of simply fortifying and defending the line of the passes in western Sinai, the actual strategy Cairo adopted may have been the best available. By opting to defend forward, Egypt was able to employ a static defense anchored on the imposing fortifications of the eastern Sinai. This allowed Egypt's infantry to do what they did best: defend in place. While Egypt's heavy reserves may not have been ideally deployed, their mission — counterattack or block any Israeli penetration of the forward defensive lines — probably was not only appropriate but also, effectively, all they were capable of doing. If these forces had held better positions and had covered the supposedly impassable gaps in their lines, they would still have lost to the Israelis because of the imbalance in tactical capabilities, but they undoubtedly would have caused greater casualties to the IDF and perhaps held out longer. Thus, the Egyptians probably had the best strategy; they just did not execute it very well.

In contrast, Egyptian senior-level decision making *during* the war was mostly very poor and was a constant detriment to the Egyptian cause. The biggest problem was 'Amr's intermittent inattention and micromanagement of operations as well as his constant flip-flops in thinking and contradictory orders. This behavior contributed to two problems. First, it caused a paralysis at the operational level in the Sinai. That is, with the exception of the order for 4th Armored Division to counterattack into the Tal ugdah's flank, none of the Egyptian heavy divisions made any move in response to the Israeli attacks. (It is noteworthy that no one lower in the chain of command stepped in and took it upon himself to direct the defense of the Sinai. In particular, Shazli's armored task force had the mission of supporting Abu Ageilah, but without explicit orders from GHQ, General Shazli did not lift a finger to help the 2d Infantry Division fighting for its life there.) The second problem caused by the chaos in the general staff was that it unnerved many of the Sinai field commanders, and this demoralization probably trickled down to their subordinates to some extent. Although there is little hard evidence on this point, it seems likely that, as noted above, it contributed to the desertion of so many senior field commanders immediately after the announcement of the withdrawal. The effect of this problem appears to have been mostly concentrated at senior levels, for most Egyptian junior officers remained with their units. This loss of senior leadership in the field was a major reason that Egyptian units fared so poorly during the retreat.

Two other command decisions require discussion: the decision to retreat on 6 June and the issuing of a vague general retreat order rather than a phased fighting withdrawal. As the Egyptians and their advocates point out, 'Amr issued a retreat order while much of the Egyptian army was still intact and after several Egyptian units had fought very hard at Abu Ageilah and Rafah. Similarly, it is also true that 'Amr's simple order to his troops to get out of the Sinai as quickly as possible contributed to the rout, in particular to the desertion by many senior field commanders. However, the effect of these events has been exaggerated, and it is not plausible to contend that they were the *cause* of the Egyptian defeat.

First, although it is true that the Egyptian army was still mostly intact by the afternoon of 6 June, it is also true that the campaign was largely decided by then. With the two strongest Egyptian fortified positions (the Khan Yunis–Rafah and Umm Qatef–Abu Ageilah defense systems) captured, Israeli armor driving deep into the operational depth of the Egyptian army, and the most powerful Egyptian heavy division defeated easily and decisively at B'ir Lafhan, the corner had been turned. By that point, it was highly unlikely that the Egyptians could have mounted a major counter-attack against the Israeli ugdot driving for the passes. Even if the Egyptians had been able to mount a coordinated counterattack with Shazli's armored task force, 6th Mechanized Division, or the remnants of 4th Armored Division, singly or in combination, against one or more of the Israeli ugdot (an extremely unlikely prospect given the inability of much smaller Egyptian forces to coordinate their actions), the experience of the previous thirty-six hours indicated that such a strike would almost certainly have been decisively defeated. Therefore, ordering a general withdrawal on the afternoon of 6 June was a very good decision.

But the manner in which that withdrawal order was issued was clearly inexcusable. The absence of an integrated plan for the Egyptian retreat, coupled with the flight of so many senior field commanders, was disastrous. It is hard to imagine that any army in such a situation could come out intact, but in the case of the Egyptians, it was especially disastrous because it left local commanders to their own devices, and they mostly proved unequal to the task. In addition, the dearth of GHQ guidance meant that Egyptian units could not coordinate their actions beyond the tactical level (although they generally failed to do even this). The result of all this was that the army simply surged back toward the passes in one great, unorganized mass. There were few rear guards deployed, no determination of intermediate fallback positions where hasty defenses and covering positions could be established to deal with Israeli pursuit, and no prioritization among units for withdrawal order. A better organized retreat almost certainly would have succeeded in getting more Egyptian units safely across the Suez.

Some authors have also pointed to the creation of Murtagi's Sinai Front Command as a major cause of the confusion in Egypt's high command and, therefore, a crucial element of Egypt's defeat during the 1967 war.[104] I find little evidence to indicate that this had more than a minor effect on the battle. According to Field Marshal Gamasy, who was Murtagi's chief of staff at that time, the Sinai Front Command was bypassed completely throughout the war. All of the field commanders continued to report to Muhsin, and Muhsin reported directly to 'Amr. Likewise, 'Amr issued orders directly to Muhsin — or to the division commanders, which was a problem in its own right. Murtagi's command was not in the loop at all. In fact, his staff was left so completely out of the chain of command that they did not learn of 'Amr's decision to order a general retreat until they began to see Egyptian units streaming westward toward the canal. While this bypassing of Murtagi may well have been the result of 'Amr's panic on 5 and 6 June, the point is that Murtagi's command organization could not have been a problem for the Egyptians because it played no role in the actual campaign and does not seem to have confused anyone. At both higher and lower echelons, Egyptian officers ignored the new headquarters and acted according to the original command-and-control arrangements.[105]

THE ROLE OF ISRAELI AIR POWER

Many apologists for the Egyptians have blamed their defeat on the destruction of the Egyptian Air Force and Israel's subsequent ability to bring its airpower to bear unhindered against the Egyptian army. This is a considerable exaggeration. There is no question that Israel's command of the air was a significant element of its victory, but this was only one element of Egypt's defeat and probably not the decisive element.

The Israeli Air Force contributed very little to the decisive battles in eastern Sinai in which the IDF broke the Egyptian army and put it to flight. First, with only a few exceptions, the IAF did not participate in the Israeli ground campaign until 6 June. In fact, the IAF did not really bring its full weight to bear against Egyptian ground forces until 7 June. On 5 June most of the IAF's day was taken up in counterair operations, conducting airstrikes against Egyptian, Syrian, Jordanian, and Iraqi airbases. The IAF contributed a relatively small number of airstrikes against Arab ground forces on 5 June, flying only 268 ground-attack sorties on all three fronts (compared to 614 on 6 June and 652 on 7 June). They flew only 170 ground-attack sorties against Sinai on 5 June (compared to 286 on 6 June and 321 on 7 June) and probably destroyed no more than 12–15 Egyptian tanks.[106] On 6 June the IAF focused on ground support, but the Jordanian front took a higher priority than the Sinai. Consequently, more sorties were directed against the Jordanians than against the Egyptians until the course of the battle in the west had already been decided. Moreover, according to Lt. Gen. Mordechai Hod — the IAF commander in 1967 — Israeli airstrikes in Sinai started with the Egyptian forces and infrastructure in the canal zone and then slowly worked their way eastward.[107] As a result, most of the IAF airstrikes flown against Arab ground forces were actually interdiction sorties directed against logistics and rear-area formations rather than the frontline units and operational reserves, whose defeat were the keys to Israeli victory. Even IAF pilot reports claim to have destroyed more trucks and other soft-skinned vehicles than armored vehicles (both as absolute numbers and on a per-sortie basis) on 6 June than they did on 7 June.[108] The IAF only became a significant factor against the Egyptian combat forces on

Table 1. Israeli Air-to-Ground Sorties by Day, by Front, 5–10 June 1967

Front	5 June	6 June	7 June	8 June	9 June	10 June	TOTAL
Egypt	170	286	321	160	20	8	965
Jordan	95	221	233	0	0	0	549
Syria	3	107	98	225	299	345	1,077
TOTAL	268	614	652	385	319	353	2,591

Source: History Branch, IAF, correspondence with author, 10 September 1997.

the Sinai front on 7 June, when Israeli aircraft hammered the masses of Egyptians running helter-skelter back to the canal.

Second, again according to General Hod, the Israelis predominantly flew battlefield interdiction missions, not close-air support, against the Egyptians.[109] The official Israeli survey of battle damage during the war found that nearly all of the Egyptian tanks destroyed by airstrikes in the Sinai were hit during the Egyptian retreat and not during the battles in eastern Sinai that decided the outcome of the war.[110] Third, Israeli and Western damage-assessment teams who canvassed the battlefields in the Sinai concluded that, at most, Israeli airstrikes knocked out less than 100 Egyptian armored vehicles during the entire course of the war.[111] Indeed, the official U.S. survey team found that only 8 percent of Arab tanks captured in the Six Day War (that is, those left on the battlefield either because they were destroyed or abandoned) were even struck by Israeli aerial munitions, and only 2–3 percent were actually destroyed by IAF airstrikes.[112] Even the Israeli survey—which was far more favorable to the IAF—concluded that only 15 percent of Egyptian tank losses were to airstrikes.[113] Clearly then, it was not the Israeli airstrikes that were most destructive of Egyptian ground combat power.[114]

Overall, probably the most important contribution of the IAF was its near perfect counterair effort. The IAF removed the EAF almost completely from the balance of forces. As a result, Israeli ground forces in the Sinai were able to move and fight with almost no interference from Egyptian warplanes. Although Israeli ground forces were so much more competent than their Egyptian counterparts—and in the limited operations they were able to conduct, the EAF revealed itself to be mostly hapless—that they would likely have prevailed even with Egyptian air interference, the campaign would have looked very different. Even inaccurate airstrikes that cause very little damage can be disruptive of ground operations, costing time as the ground forces disperse and then regroup after each attack. Thus, if the IDF had had to fend off Egyptian airstrikes, they almost certainly would have moved slower than was actually the case. Likewise, a few well-timed air attacks (even ineffective ones) could have broken up the Israeli assaults on the Egyptian fortifications centered on Abu Ageilah and Rafah. Last, if the IAF had had to spend its time contesting air superiority with EAF jets rather than striking Egyptian army units, the Egyptian retreat would have looked very different. In short, if the IAF had not smashed the EAF on the first morning of the war, the Israelis probably would have prevailed, but it would have taken them longer, they would have suffered heavier casualties, and far more Egyptian units probably would have been able to escape from the Sinai. Nevertheless, it remains undisputed that the key battles, those that ultimately decided victory or defeat for Egypt and Israel, were won with only the most minimal participation of the IAF. In these contests the only contribution of the IAF was indirect — preventing the EAF from interfering with the work of Israeli armored forces.

THE CAUSES OF EGYPT'S DEFEAT

Overall, blame for the Egyptian collapse must be borne equally by the poor performance of Cairo's tactical and strategic leadership. This assessment is most clearly illustrated by comparing Egyptian military effectiveness in 1956 and 1967. There are both important similarities and important differences in Egyptian performance during these two wars. The similarities exist at the tactical level, where Egyptian forces performed consistently poorly, while the differences lie primarily at the strategic level, where the Egyptians performed adequately in 1956 and poorly in 1967. However, these factors do not fully explain the extent of their defeat. The missing piece of the puzzle is the tremendous gap that had opened between Egyptian and Israeli tactical capabilities.

In both 1956 and 1967, Egyptian units performed quite well when conducting static defensive operations. During both wars, unit cohesion was good initially but broke down during the retreat, particularly when the Israelis were able to cut the Egyptians' escape routes through the passes in western Sinai. Egyptian armored reserves did extremely poorly in combat with Israeli forces during both wars and showed little ability to maneuver, improvise, or act flexibly. There were differences, of course. One key divergence between Egypt's performance in the two wars was that in 1956 its operational reserves were committed much more quickly than in 1967. The panic and confusion in the command structure in 1967 probably were the principal reasons for the inactivity of most of the army's reserves, particularly the Shazli Armored Force and the 6th Mechanized Division. But three additional points are in order. First, in 1967 the general staff did commit 4th Armored Division — the strongest unit in the Egyptian army — at the right time and with the right mission, so they cannot be said to have failed completely on this count. Second, as noted above, none of the commanders further down the chain of command took it upon themselves to execute their missions on their own initiative, even though it was clear that the general staff was no longer functioning effectively. Third, given the actual performance of Egyptian mechanized formations in combat, it is difficult to see how even a timely commitment of Shazli's Armored Force and the 6th Mechanized would have significantly altered the course of the battle. The war would have looked different, but the results almost certainly would have been the same.

Another important difference between Egyptian performance in 1956 and 1967 was the conduct of the retreat. In 1956, Egyptian withdrawal orders were more detailed and an attempt was made to conduct an orderly retreat. This broke down rapidly as Israeli ground units pursued and caught Egyptian units and Israeli airstrikes harassed them, but the Egyptians were able to get far more of their combat power out of the Sinai than was the case in 1967. It is also noteworthy that in 1956, as in 1967, Egyptian unit cohesion disintegrated during the retreat because of the constant IDF pressure and the need for Egyptian junior officers to act largely on their own. While it is doubtful that more competent senior commanders could have prevented the fall of the Sinai to the Israelis (or at least the peninsula east of the passes) in 1967, there is no question that better generalship could have resulted in more Egyptian forces making it across the Suez intact. In particular, had the Egyptian General Staff moved to immediately secure control of the passes with some of the armored reserves in the Sinai and units in strategic reserve in the canal zone, they almost certainly would have gotten far more men and materiel out. In addition, Cairo might have opted for other operational moves that could have contributed to a more successful retreat. For example, they might have tried to use their armored reserves to establish blocking positions on the main north-south roads south of Abu Ageilah (the Israeli breakthrough occurred north of Abu Ageilah, so blocking these roads might have prevented the Israelis from pushing southwest to the passes). Conversely, Cairo might have ordered a counterattack northward with one or more heavy divisions. Such a strike undoubtedly would have failed and resulted in the destruction of the assault force, but it might have kept the Israelis occupied long enough to allow other units in south-central Sinai to get through the passes.

These additional Egyptian failings aside, the primary difference between the two wars was not Egypt's military effectiveness but that of Israel. While the Egyptians performed in about the same manner and at about the same level of competence as they had in 1956, the Israelis performed far better than they had previously. Israel's armored corps was not only dramatically larger than it had been in 1956 but also far more capable, having been made the cornerstone of Israeli ground operations. Its generals designed the entire campaign so that IDF mechanized units would have maximum freedom to maneuver and conduct operations as they saw fit. In 1956 the IAF was tiny and really did not enjoy air superiority until the French and British obliterated the EAF on 1–3 November. In 1967, although the IAF's participation may not have been decisive, it did take out the EAF in one fell swoop and then had sufficient strength to make significant contributions to the ground war in the Sinai. In particular, Israeli airstrikes took a fair toll of the Egyptians during the retreat after the IAF's counterair responsibilities had largely been fulfilled and they could turn their attention to interdiction missions.

During the 1956 war, Israel's campaign plan had to be rewritten at the last minute to conform to the various political considerations introduced by Tel Aviv's collusion with the British and French and Pres. David Ben-Gurion's extreme distrust of the British. Also, the IDF plan labored under General Dayan's false impressions of Egyptian military ineffectiveness. Before the 1956 fighting, Dayan believed that the Egyptians would simply collapse if their positions were outflanked or otherwise compromised. Indeed, there is even some reason to believe that Dayan suspected that the Egyptian units would shatter under any sort of sharp assault. This assumption underlay the entire Israeli plan for the 1956 Sinai campaign, and for this reason, the Israelis got badly hung up when the Egyptians did not collapse at Abu Ageilah as expected.[115] By contrast, Israel's 1967 plan recognized that the Egyptians would fight fiercely, especially from fixed defenses, and so was designed to minimize the importance of Egyptian fortifications and instead place the burden of defense on Egypt's armored and mechanized reserves. The Israelis correctly assessed that their own armored forces could swiftly defeat their Egyptian counterparts, and by shaping the course of operations to ensure that it was these battles that were decisive, the Israelis won one of the most incredible victories in modern history.[116]

The War of Attrition, 1967–70

The Six Day War was a traumatic experience for Egypt. Nasser, upon realizing the extent of the disaster, attempted to resign as president on

9 June 1967. 'Amr and his cronies in the military were also involved in this, seeing the defeat as an opportunity to force out the president. However, the Egyptian people poured into the streets to protest Nasser's resignation and demanded he resume the presidency. Nasser withdrew his resignation, and an internal battle developed in which 'Amr and his loyalists were ousted on 19 June. In August 'Amr committed suicide, and many of his followers were later put on trial and convicted of conspiracy.

After the June catastrophe and 'Amr's failed coup, Nasser decided that he had to professionalize the officer corps and reorient the military so that its sole task was defeating Israel — believing that only in this way would he be safe from a coup and would Egypt be able to regain the Sinai. Nasser weeded out 'Amr's cronies and anyone else who had attained high rank for reasons other than ability. All of Egypt's full generals and most of its lieutenant generals and major generals were ousted. In all, as many as 800 Egyptian officers, most of the rank of colonel or higher, were cashiered.[117] Nasser then promoted the best officers he could find to the newly opened positions. Throughout the military, the promotion process was reoriented to focus on merit rather than political ties. Indeed, Nasser even recalled to service competent officers that 'Amr had previously dismissed for suspected disloyalty.[118] In addition, the president recognized that the military's preoccupation with politics had distracted it and greatly contributed to the 1967 debacle. As he had started to do after 1956, Nasser shifted the regime's domestic base of power farther away from the armed forces and relieved the military of its internal-security responsibilities.[119]

To oversee the rebuilding of his shattered army, Nasser called on four of Egypt's most respected military officers. Gen. Muhammad Fawzi, the former chief of staff of the armed forces, became commander in chief and minister of war. Fawzi was a thoroughly professional soldier and a harsh disciplinarian, a quality that proved invaluable in rebuilding Egyptian morale after the defeats in Yemen and the Sinai. Lt. Gen. 'Abd al-Mun'im Riyad became chief of staff of the armed forces. Riyad was a superb officer who had distinguished himself in Yemen before appointment to oversee the Jordanian armed forces on behalf of the United Arab Command, established before the Six Day War. Riyad was unfairly blamed by the Jordanians for their defeat in that conflict, and Cairo was only too happy to have him back in Egypt. Indeed, Nasser intended to have Fawzi lead the rebuilding of the military but hoped to have Riyad actually plan and direct the eventual offensive to retake the Sinai from Israel. Nasser selected Maj. Gen. Ahmed Isma'il 'Ali to replace Muhsin as eastern district commander, Egypt's most important field command because it controlled the units facing the IDF across the Suez Canal. Isma'il too was considered a highly competent and thoroughly apolitical officer. When Riyad was killed in March 1969 during an Israeli artillery barrage along the canal, Nasser immediately chose Isma'il as the new armed forces chief of staff. Finally, Maj. Gen. Muhammad 'Abd al-Ghani al-Gamasy was made Isma'il 'Ali's chief of staff. Gamasy too was a highly respected and highly intelligent officer who had risen to flag rank by ability, not politicking. Mohammed Heikal remarked of General Gamasy, "Arab politics shocked him to his bones."[120]

Fawzi, Riyad, and their staff got to work immediately reorganizing Egypt's command-and-control structure to eradicate the failings they saw in 1967. The Sinai Front Command was abolished, as was the separate ground forces administrative command, and authority concentrated in the general staff in Cairo and the Eastern District Military Command. A new Air Defense Command was created as the equal of the other three services. This headquarters was given the specific mission of defending Egypt against air attack to prevent a repeat of 1956 and 1967 (and 1948 for that matter). Likewise, Egyptian military intelligence was reformed. Instead of watching the Egyptian officer corps full time and casting an eye toward Israel every once in a while, as it had under 'Amr, Fawzi redirected its efforts fully against Israel. The internal monitoring function was transferred to the security services, freeing military intelligence to fill the needs of the armed forces for tactical information on their adversary across the canal.

The Attrition Strategy

By September 1968, Nasser had completed most of his immediate reforms and had set in motion most of the longer term programs. He was anxious to resume the war against Israel. The destruction of the Egyptian army and Israel's occupation of the Sinai cost Nasser much of his international prestige, and he was eager to regain it. Rekindling the conflict with Israel was crucial to the Egyptian president in order to allow him to recapture the attention of the Arab masses and perhaps their governments as well. However, Egypt was far from ready to try to retake the peninsula. Although the Soviets — who had also been deeply embarrassed by the poor performance of one of their most prominent clients — quickly replaced virtually all of Egypt's lost equipment, the armed forces needed more than new tanks and planes. Egypt's military was thoroughly demoralized. The command structure had been turned inside out during the postwar purges. Cairo recognized that its doctrine had proven empty against the Israelis, and other problems hampered the military from top to bottom. Consequently, Egypt could not contemplate all-out war just yet.

The new general staff also realized that Israel had certain vulnerabilities, however, and that Egypt had certain strengths that could be employed to advantage. First, there was the huge disparity in population, with Egypt boasting over 30 million people, while Israel contained less than 2 million. In addition to this, there was Israel's absolute obsession with minimizing casualties, in part a product of the small size of the country. Finally, there was Israel's heavy reliance on reserves and the severe economic burden of keeping its reserves mobilized. Drawing on these Israeli weaknesses, Cairo formulated a strategy of attrition. Rather than attempting a major military showdown for which Egypt was unready, the Egyptians would harass and attack the Israelis along the canal, low-intensity strikes but on a constant basis. Cairo believed that in this way they could kill Israelis and perhaps force Tel Aviv to keep large numbers of men mobilized and deployed to the Sinai. Egypt hoped that this kind of constant economic and psychological pressure might force Israel to withdraw from part or all of the peninsula. While this was considered a long shot, the campaign had the more tangible benefits of projecting an appearance of Egyptian action against Israel (which was important for Nasser's domestic and international image), re-building the morale of the Egyptian armed forces, and slowly grating on the Israelis and perhaps wearing down their finely honed combat edge. Later, it came to have the added advantage of allowing the Egyptians the opportunity to give commanders combat experience and to try out schemes that they would later employ during the October War of 1973.

Course of Operations

This highly rational approach to the war was still in the future when fighting between Egypt and Israel resumed on 8 September 1968. On that day, the Egyptians bombarded Israeli positions on the east bank of the Suez, firing 10,000 rounds from hundreds of artillery pieces over the course of several hours.[121] At the time, Nasser simply wanted to lash out at the Israelis and played the only cards remaining to him. In coming months, these artillery barrages became more common, and the Israelis responded with artillery fire of their own — pummeling valuable Egyptian economic targets along the canal such as the Suez oil refineries and the cities of al-Qantarah and Ismailia.

Israel's ability to prevail in these artillery exchanges was limited, prompting Tel Aviv to escalate. The Egyptians kept over 100,000 men with 1,000 artillery pieces along the canal, while the IDF deployed less than 10,000 troops in the canal zone, usually with no more than 18–24 artillery pieces.[122] Consequently, Israel began to conduct commando operations deep into Egypt to try to persuade Cairo to cease its shelling. The first of these was a raid against the Naj Hammadi Dam in Upper Egypt. In addition to damaging the dam, the Israelis destroyed the two Nile River bridges there and blew up a power transformer on the high voltage line between Cairo and the Aswan Dam. This raid frightened the Egyptians, causing Cairo to suspend the artillery bombardments for almost five months and redeploy troops to defend key transportation, communications, and industrial targets throughout the country. Another Israeli response to the Egyptian bombardments was to begin construction of the Bar-Lev line, a series of thirty small, fortified strongpoints along the east bank of the canal to provide shelter for Israeli troops watching the canal. Although the Bar-Lev fortifications were never meant to stop a major Egyptian assault by themselves, they were intended to mitigate the damage of the Egyptian shelling, and in this role they performed quite well.

On 8 March 1969, the Egyptians resumed their artillery assault by unleashing a massive barrage against the new Bar-Lev forts. Nasser inaugurated this new phase by proclaiming this bombardment to be the opening of the "War of Attrition." Thereafter, Egyptian and Israeli artillery exchanges became the norm along the canal line. In April, Egypt attempted to escalate the conflict further by conducting its own raids across the canal. Egyptian commando teams began infiltrating across the Suez at night at points distant from Bar-Lev forts. They would then ambush Israeli patrols, attack supply convoys, and harass the forts themselves. The Israelis responded by conducting commando raids of their own, usually much deeper into Egypt and that frequently did far more significant damage than the Egyptian operations. For example, on the night of 19–20 July, Israeli commandos landed on Green Island in the northern Gulf of Suez and destroyed an Egyptian radar located there. Months later, on the night of 25–26 December, Israeli commandos landed at R'as al-Gharib, overpowered the Egyptian garrison, and dismantled and took back with them one of the USSR's newest P-12 (Bar Lock) air defense radars that had recently been sold to Egypt. In another famous episode, on the night of 8 September, Israeli frogmen sank the only two Egyptian missile boats in the northern Gulf of Suez. The next day, Egypt's constant nemesis, Bren Adan, landed on the Egyptian coast of the Gulf of Suez with a company-sized force dressed and equipped entirely in Egyptian style, complete with Soviet tanks and APCs captured during the Six Day War. Adan's force then drove forty-five kilometers along the Egyptian coast, destroying surface-to-air-missile (SAM) and radar sites, killing Egyptian troops, and even capturing one of five new Soviet T-62 tanks in Egypt for trials and evaluation. Ten hours later, the Israelis returned to the Sinai with their booty. Nasser was so furious after this episode that he sacked the armed forces chief of staff, Lieutenant General Isma'il.

Nevertheless, the Egyptian artillery and commando attacks did not cease, and so in July 1969 Israel decided to escalate by committing its vaunted air force to try to force the Egyptians to cease their attacks. Initially, the IAF concentrated its airstrikes on the Egyptian military bases and SAM sites along the canal. The Egyptians responded with airstrikes of their own, but in their first raid, Israeli fighters shot down eleven EAF aircraft for only one IAF plane lost. After that, the EAF mostly stuck to air defense missions and left the offensive part of the war to their artillery batteries. The Israelis increasingly went after the SA-2 SAM sites along the canal and enjoyed great success in these strikes. By October 1969, Egypt's SA-2 belt had been dismantled by Israeli airstrikes. In the first two months of the air campaign, the IAF flew 1,000 sorties against Egypt, while the EAF managed less than 100 against Israeli positions. During this period, Egypt lost twenty-one planes, nearly all in air-to-air combat, while the Israelis lost only three, all to SAMS and AAA.[123]

Yet the Egyptians still kept up their intermittent shelling and commando raids. The Israelis grew increasingly frustrated, and in January 1970 they escalated the conflict again in hopes of persuading Cairo to cease the attacks on the Bar-Lev line. Their strategy this time was to begin deep bombing raids throughout Egypt but especially against military and industrial targets in the Cairo area. The Israelis felt that by concentrating their efforts against the Egyptian military units in the canal zone, they had left the Egyptian people and government untouched by the fighting, the more so because Nasser's tight control over information made sure that only good news was reported to the populace. The Israelis hoped that by hitting targets in and around Egypt's cities they could drive home to the Egyptian people that Israel retained complete dominance over the Egyptian military and so undermine the regime's credibility. Between the start of the deep penetration campaign on 1 January 1970 and its end on 18 April, the IAF flew 3,300 sorties against Egypt and dropped 8,000 tons of munitions.[124]

The Israeli deep penetration raids caused considerable damage and further mauled Egypt's already tattered SA-2 network. Nasser's reaction, however, was wholly unexpected. Rather than throw in the towel, Cairo asked the USSR to take over the defense of Egyptian airspace. The Soviets complied and, beginning in March 1970, set up an entirely new, mostly Soviet-manned air defense system employing the latest Russian hardware. The Soviets installed a new early warning and air-control radar system. They deployed about eighty batteries of the newer SA-3 SAMS, thousands of SA-7 shoulder-launched SAMS, as well as large numbers of new radar-guided AAA pieces. In addition, the Soviets deployed over 100 of the latest model MiG-21 Fishbed-J interceptors with Russian pilots.[125] In mid-April, when the IAF first encountered some of the new Soviet-piloted fighters, Tel Aviv decided not to risk a clash with the USSR and so suspended its deep bombing campaign. However, the Israelis reiterated that they would take whatever means necessary to prevent an extension of the SAM belt within thirty kilometers of the canal.

In the spring the Egyptians and Russians began pushing their air defenses closer to the canal. On 30 June two Israeli aircraft were shot down by missile batteries located within thirty kilometers of the Suez. These new missile sites began taking a heavy toll on Israeli planes, and Soviet-piloted MiGs began flying combat air patrols along the canal, whereas previously they had only operated over the Nile Delta region. Israeli frustration with the Soviets grew, and on 30 July the IAF set up an aerial ambush in which twelve Israeli Phantoms and Mirages shot down five of sixteen Soviet-piloted MiGs (with no losses) in a matter of minutes before the others fled.[126] Within a week after this first Israeli-Soviet clash, the United States stepped in and brokered a ceasefire, bringing the war of attrition to an end.

Egyptian Military Effectiveness during the War of Attrition

At the tactical level, only four elements of the Egyptian armed forces really participated in the conflict. First was Egypt's artillery corps, which carried the brunt of Cairo's offensive action against the Israelis. Unfortunately, details on the performance of Egyptian artillery are sketchy; however, some aspects are discernable. The Egyptians did a good job pummeling the Bar-Lev line fortifications, but this does not say very much. These forts were fixed positions within view of Egyptian artillery spotters on the west bank of the canal, and so it was not terribly difficult to shell them accurately. By the same token, the Egyptians never really found a way to penetrate these forts or otherwise get at the Israeli soldiers who manned the line. About the best the Egyptians did was to eventually adopt a policy of randomly firing shells into the vehicle parks and other exterior spaces of the forts in hope of catching Israeli soldiers outside. There appear to have been few counter-battery duels along the canal, probably because the Egyptians' Soviet-built guns had greater ranges than the Israeli artillery pieces, and so Cairo could deploy them in positions well away from the canal, where they could still hit the Bar-Lev forts along the water but were out of range of Israeli artillery.

Egypt's commandos performed their missions adequately but not spectacularly. Cairo did not try any particularly risky operations, even after some of the more daring Israeli attacks. This suggests that the Egyptian high command had relatively limited confidence in their abilities. The most celebrated raids were an operation on 10 July 1969 in which Egyptian commandos successfully ambushed a small Israeli armored patrol along the canal, destroyed two tanks, and killed seven soldiers; and a raid on 16 November 1969 in which Egyptian frogmen sank three Israeli landing craft in Eilat harbor. However, against these rather modest accomplishments, the Egyptian commandos suffered numerous failures. For example, in one of their more ambitious operations, a commando platoon attempted to penetrate to the Mitla Pass in February 1970 to set up an ambush there, but the unit was discovered and the entire force was either captured or killed. Similarly, during the construction of the Bar-Lev line, Egyptian commandos attempted to capture one of the new Israeli forts, but they were beaten back with heavy losses. In addition, Ariel Sharon, the commander of Israeli forces in Sinai (1970–73), noted that most of the Egyptian commando operations were conducted close enough to the canal so they could be monitored by senior Egyptian officers across the Suez, indicating that Cairo had little confidence in the ability of its commandos to perform their missions without close supervision from higher authority.[127] In confirmation of Sharon's point, Egypt's most successful commando operations were carried out close to the canal and, with the exception of the frogman attack on Eilat, most of Egypt's deeper commando raids achieved little or failed altogether.

The last two Egyptian elements participating in the War of Attrition were its air and air defense forces, which largely bore the brunt of the Israeli air campaign. The EAF primarily flew interception missions against Israeli airstrikes. The Egyptians conducted a few air-to-ground missions, but these had little effect. Moreover, after 11 September 1969, when an Egyptian airstrike of sixteen aircraft lost eight MiGs to Israeli Mirages and three Su-7s to Israeli AAA and Homing-All-the-Way-Killer (HAWK) SAMs, the Egyptians further curtailed their air-to-ground operations.[128]

In air-to-air combat the Egyptians did poorly. First, they were hampered by poor maintenance, which limited the number of aircraft they could put into the air at any time, and poor reaction times, which meant that Egyptian aircraft were often just getting airborne while Israeli aircraft were either already in position overhead or headed home after a successful strike.[129]

Second, and of far greater importance, Egypt's pilots were very mediocre and had great difficulty taking full advantage of the capabilities of their Soviet fighters. The Soviets washed out huge numbers of Egyptians sent for pilot training to the USSR each year. Eventually, the EAF reconciled itself to the fact that, despite a population of over 30 million, they could only produce about thirty qualified fighter pilots each year.[130] In combat, the Israelis found the Egyptian fighter pilots to be slow to react, rigid in their flight patterns, unwilling to improvise or seize fleeting opportunities, and easily duped. As a result, the Egyptians were consistently beaten by the Israelis, even though in dogfights they frequently had twice as many fighters engaged. While accounts vary, it appears that the Egyptians wound up on the short end of at least a 10 to 1 kill ratio in air-to-air combat with the Israelis. U.S. military intelligence estimated that between July 1967 and August 1970, Egypt lost 109 aircraft in combat, most to Israeli fighters. In contrast, the Israelis lost only 16 aircraft, most to Egyptian SAMs and AAA. Additionally, the Egyptians lost another 45–50 aircraft in training accidents — a high number for an air force with only about 400 planes.[131] The ultimate verdict on Egyptian air-to-air performance was rendered by Cairo itself, which first grounded its air force when the IAF began aggressive fighter patrols over Egypt in July 1969 and then simply turned over its air defenses to the Soviets in March 1970.

In ground-based air defense, the Egyptians do not appear to have done much better, although there were some mitigating circumstances. The Israelis consistently won the battles against Egyptian ground-based air defenses until the Soviets arrived in 1970, but this cannot be blamed entirely on Egyptian failings. First, the only SAMs the Egyptians possessed were the old, slow SA-2s, which the Israelis had learned how to defeat. In addition, Egypt had few advanced AAA pieces, particularly ones with advanced tracking and guidance systems. Thus, when the Soviets arrived, they brought with them an entirely new array of equipment, and to some extent it was the weapons themselves that the Israelis had difficulty countering, not the Russian personnel manning them. Nevertheless, it still should be noted that in 1970 the Soviet rule of thumb was that 3–4 SA-2s fired at a target had a very high probability of destroying it, but with the Egyptians, 6–10 SA-2s had only a slightly better than even probability of killing the target.[132]

Despite their constant defeats, the Egyptians were remarkably courageous. Egyptian soldiers, pilots, missileers, gunners, and commandos executed their missions with enthusiasm and determination throughout the war. Indeed, Egypt's fighter pilots staged a sit-down strike to protest being grounded after the heavy losses sustained in aerial engagements with the

IAF during the summer of 1970. Edgar O'Ballance has also noted the bravery of Egypt's military during the War of Attrition: "It should be mentioned that the outfought, inexperienced Egyptian pilots constantly had a go at Israeli aircraft despite casualties and losses, that gunners in positions along the canal stood by their guns despite almost constant aerial and artillery assaults, and personnel working frantically to restore the SAM box as it was shattered nightly showed courage and persistence of a high order."[133]

In contrast to the bravery of Egypt's forces were the problems they displayed handling information. First, Egypt's intelligence effort was abysmal. The air force did not conduct enough reconnaissance missions, and the information they collected was frequently misinterpreted. In particular, Egyptian intelligence continued to report whatever they believed Nasser wanted to hear. Thus, in 1969, Egyptian intelligence assessed that 65–80 percent of the Bar-Lev line had been destroyed, when, in fact, Egyptian artillery barrages had done relatively little damage to the Israeli fortifications. Similarly, Cairo's forces continued to dissemble, exaggerate, and withhold bad information. For example, when Adan's faux Egyptian armored force drove along the Egyptian coast, destroying every military facility it encountered, the armed forces sent a stream of misleading information up the chain of command. Nasser was infuriated by his inability to find out exactly what was happening, and Mohamed Heikal later claimed that Nasser accused the military of "behaving in the 1967 way."[134]

At the strategic level, it is hard to find fault with Cairo's generalship. Fawzi, Riyad, Isma'il, Gamasy, and the other members of Egypt's high command developed a reasonable method of implementing the political directive to resume the conflict with Israel. They correctly identified key Israeli vulnerabilities, as well as certain Egyptian strengths, and then developed an efficient method of employing those strengths to strike at the Israeli vulnerabilities. Indeed, the success of the general staff's methods in the War of Attrition is demonstrated by Israel's repeated escalations of the fighting. While Egypt made the first move — launching the artillery attacks and commando raids against the Israeli side of the canal — Israel initiated most of the steps after that: deep commando raids against Egyptian industrial targets, commitment of the IAF, and then the deep bombing missions against targets in the Nile Delta. In each of these cases, the Israelis escalated the level or extent of the violence they employed to try to force the Egyptians to cease their attacks on the Bar-Lev line. The Egyptians' success can be seen in Israel's frustration in not being able to accomplish this goal.

Ultimately, the general staff did miscalculate. Apparently, the Israeli deep bombing missions touched a nerve with the Egyptian leadership.

Gamasy states that Nasser was genuinely concerned that these attacks would prompt the Egyptian populace to move against the regime, although there was little actual evidence of popular unrest.[135] Nasser's decision to turn Egypt's air defense over to the Soviets was certainly a slap in the face to the Egyptian military — but not necessarily to its generals. Nasser's move was a recognition that at the tactical level, Egypt lacked the weapons and the skill to defeat the Israelis. However, it said nothing about Egyptian strategy or the conduct of the conflict by the general staff. This is demonstrated by the fact that Egypt retained the same strategy and Nasser did not replace any of his senior military commanders.

This is not to suggest that Egypt's strategic conduct of the War of Attrition was flawless. Almost certainly there were actions the Egyptians could have taken that they did not, and missions that they should not have tried but did. However, in the end the Egyptians accomplished many of their goals, and this was primarily the result of good generalship that recognized the job at hand and the tools available and developed a practical approach by which the means employed attained the ends desired. In particular, Egypt's generals recognized the tactical limitations of their troops and tailored a strategy that allowed them to achieve their goals with the forces available. Overall, their performance was inelegant but effective.

The October War, 1973

Gamal 'Abd al-Nasser died in 1970, shortly after the conclusion of the ceasefire that ended the War of Attrition. In the power struggle that followed, Anwar as-Sadat, Nasser's vice president, surprised everyone and emerged as his successor. For domestic political reasons, Sadat was anxious to resolve the Egyptian-Israeli conflict. Initially, he tried to reach a negotiated settlement with Tel Aviv and actually offered fairly generous terms; ultimately, the Camp David Accords were quite similar to his proposals. However, in 1971, Tel Aviv was still flush with its victory in the Six Day War and enjoying the security brought by its huge buffer zone in the Sinai. Consequently, Sadat's diplomatic efforts came to naught, and he turned to the military option to try to solve his problem.

Sadat continued, and in some ways even reinforced, Nasser's policies toward the Egyptian military. He reaffirmed Nasser's decree that promotions be determined by merit rather than loyalty and generally distanced himself from the military rebuilding and planning processes. Like Nasser in his final years, Sadat appointed only competent, professional officers to the senior command slots and sacked those who showed an inclination to dabble in politics.[136]

As a result, Sadat assembled a first-rate team of generals to plan and lead the attack he intended to launch against Israel. Sadat called General Isma'il 'Ali out of retirement to head the intelligence effort against Israel that would serve as the foundation for Egyptian military rebuilding and planning. Then in 1972, Sadat named Isma'il war minister, replacing Gen. Muhammad Ahmed Sadiq, who had intervened in political matters that Sadat believed were not the military's concern. In addition to Isma'il 'Ali's excellent reputation as a commander, Sadat recognized that he was valuable because of his intuitive understanding of the abilities and limitations of the Egyptian soldier. Sadat appointed Lt. Gen. Sa'd ad-Din Shazli as armed forces chief of staff. While Shazli had an excellent military education and a good theoretical understanding of military operations, his service record was rather checkered: he was one of the few Egyptian officers to surrender to the Israelis while a company commander at Fallujah in 1948; he retreated ahead of the Israeli attack as a battalion commander in 1956; he did poorly in Yemen; and he was among the first senior officers to flee the Sinai in 1967 — abandoning his armored division at the height of the Israeli offensive. Shazli's continued rise through the ranks appears mostly the result of his appearance and demeanor: he reportedly was a dashing, handsome paratrooper; a braggart; and enormously charismatic. Sadat picked him to be chief of staff because of Shazli's excellent rapport with Egypt's soldiery, believing he could heal the rift between Egypt's officers and enlisted personnel and would inspire Egyptian troops in the fight against Israel. Moreover, Sadat believed he could count on Isma'il 'Ali to watch Shazli and prevent him from becoming a problem.[137] To oversee the detailed planning and day-to-day operations of the war, Sadat made General Gamasy the deputy chief of staff for operations, the second-most important slot on the Egyptian General Staff. Finally, Sadat picked Air Vice Marshal Muhammad Husni Mubarak to head the Egyptian Air Force. Mubarak had earned high marks in Yemen and had not tarnished his image in 1967, a feat in itself for an EAF officer. He had the reputation of being a sober thinker who would not push his forces beyond their limits, an important quality given the restricted role the EAF was expected to play against Israel.

Egyptian Planning

After the Six Day War, Cairo began to think about going to war with Israel in a way it never had previously. Led by Isma'il 'Ali, in his capacity first as chief of staff under Nasser and later as director of military intelligence, Egypt attempted an objective assessment of Israeli and Egyptian strengths and weaknesses. In particular, the Egyptians studied the enormous number of public interviews Israeli commanders gave after the Six Day War to develop a sense of how the Israelis thought and fought and their impressions of Egyptian qualities. They encouraged their own officers to study the Israeli military, Israeli society, and even to learn Hebrew, which previously had been prohibited. Egyptian intelligence prepared detailed studies of Israeli strategy; the geography, topography, and meteorology of the Sinai; Israeli "psychological temperament"; Israeli order of battle; and the Bar-Lev fortifications. Cairo concluded that the IDF's greatest advantages were its tremendous flexibility and ability to maneuver in battle, which contributed to "outstanding" capabilities in armored warfare and air combat. At the same time they recognized weaknesses in Israel's extreme aversion to casualties, its inability to remain mobilized for more than a few weeks, and its overconfidence resulting from the victory of 1967.[138]

Cairo performed the same sort of analysis on its own forces and capabilities. According to General Gamasy, Isma'il 'Ali "had developed the conviction that the human element — the quality of the fighter — and not the weapon was what counted in victory."[139] The Egyptians concluded that their troops performed poorly in mobile warfare, combined-arms operations, dogfights, and whenever they were outflanked or encircled. They admitted that their forces did poorly in maneuver battles because this form of warfare required initiative, improvisation, and flexibility — all of which their junior officers lacked. However, they also recognized that their troops were relatively successful when fighting from fixed defenses and that, ultimately, Egypt could keep a far larger army in the field longer than the Israelis. In addition, the Egyptians recognized that their strength was really in their infantry, who bore the brunt of the defensive burden, and not in their armor, which the Israelis had consistently manhandled in combat.

An important conclusion of this analysis was that many of the problems that had proven detrimental in past wars were a product of Egyptian culture and thus could not be changed quickly or easily but had to be worked around. For example, the Egyptians reasoned that the constant deception, prevarication, and distortion of information they had experienced at all levels in all of their wars was derived from Arab cultural traits. Mohamed Heikal went so far as to write in his column in *Al-Ahram* that Israel had benefited from certain "behavioral flaws" that resulted in delays in reporting "unpleasant truths."[140] Cairo's response was to try to skirt the problem altogether by building a large signals-intercept site on Jebel Ataqah, a hill west of the Suez Canal. The Israelis were notorious for broadcasting even the most sensitive information in the clear in battle, and Egypt reasoned that it could get accurate reports on the situation at the front by intercepting Israeli situation reports rather than relying on their own troops for such information.

Isma'il 'Ali and Gamasy then developed an operational concept for an offensive across the Suez derived from these assessments of Egyptian and Israeli capabilities. They consciously tailored their planned operations to the actual capabilities of their forces. First, the offensive would have very limited goals. Sadat needed to be able to cross the Suez, which was what he ordered Isma'il 'Ali to do. If the army could liberate all of the Sinai, so much the better, but all Sadat required for his diplomatic gambit was for Egyptian troops to get across the canal and establish a bridgehead on the east bank. To his mind, all that was needed was "the canal crossing and ten centimeters of Sinai."[141] Nevertheless, there was pressure from within the military and elsewhere in the government to liberate all of the Sinai, or at least regain the line of passes.[142] Indeed, these more ambitious goals were embodied in the preexisting "Granite" plans for a crosscanal offensive, which called for a three-phased advance: phase one would be the crossing of the canal and establishment of a bridgehead; in phase two the Egyptians would break out to the line of the passes; and phase three would be a general offensive across the Sinai and possibly into Israel.

Isma'il 'Ali, however, was dead set against attempting any operation that was beyond the capabilities of his forces, and he considered these latter phases very dangerous. Although believing it well within the capabilities of a rebuilt Egyptian army to cross the canal and gain a foothold there, he felt that even a drive to the passes was beyond Egypt's military power at that time. In response to "Granite," Isma'il 'Ali paid lip-service to the original plan but ordered Gamasy to concentrate all his attention on phase one of the operation, the canal crossing and establishment of a bridgehead in the Sinai. In the new Egyptian operational plan, called "High Minarets," the phase one offensive was planned down to the last detail: every contingency was examined, all equipment and capabilities needed for its success were procured, and all of Egypt's training and exercises were geared toward executing this mission. The other phases—the breakout to the passes and the reoccupation of eastern Sinai—were completely ignored; planning never progressed beyond the vaguest outlines, and Egyptian forces never trained to execute them.[143]

For the crossing of the canal and securing of a bridgehead in the Sinai, no expense was spared and no task left undone. The operation would be a set-piece offensive beginning with a surprise attack. Surprise was crucial to Isma'il 'Ali because Israel's heavy reliance on reservists meant that if the Egyptians could attack before the Israelis were mobilized, they would face only a small IDF force in the Sinai. Of greater importance, by surprising Tel Aviv, Isma'il 'Ali hoped to be able to seize and hold the initiative and thus dictate the terms of battle to the Israelis. By forcing them back onto the defensive, Isma'il 'Ali would be able to shape operations in the direction of greatest Egyptian strength and avoid those areas of greatest Egyptian weakness.

The offensive would rely on attrition rather than maneuver to defeat the IDF. The Egyptians would employ a strategic offensive coupled with a tactical defensive: they would surprise the Israelis, cross the canal, push 5–10 miles into the Sinai, and then dig in. They would then let the Israeli armor crash against their defensive lines, wearing the Israeli forces down in bloody attacks against entrenched infantry rather than attempting decisive maneuvers of their own, which Isma'il 'Ali concluded the Israelis would quickly defeat and then exploit. In addition, to neutralize Israel's two great advantages in armored warfare and airpower, the Egyptians deployed enormous numbers of early generation Soviet antitank guided missiles (ATGMs), rocket-propelled grenades (RPGs), mobile AAA systems, and SAMs.

To compensate for past difficulties with combined arms, initiative, and improvisation at tactical levels, the Egyptian high command came up with a novel approach. First, the general staff scripted the entire operation down to the last detail. Every action of every squad and every platoon in the Egyptian army was detailed at every stage of the operation by GHQ planners. The Egyptian script for the canal crossing and securing of a bridgehead was a monumental achievement, reflecting a superb understanding of military operations, but it was up to Egyptian soldiers and field officers to make it work. Consequently, the general staff went to great lengths to make sure their forces could execute this plan. Isma'il 'Ali and Shazli decreed that every Egyptian soldier should have only one mission and that he should learn to perform that mission by heart. Full-scale mockups of the Israeli fortifications, the terrain on the east bank of the Suez, and the canal itself were constructed and used by the Egyptian units to learn their missions. Operations were rehearsed incessantly until every member of every unit knew exactly what he was supposed to do at every step of the operation. The entire offensive was rehearsed as a whole thirty-five times before the actual attack, according to General Shazli.[144] Egyptian soldiers and officers were encouraged to memorize a series of programmed steps, and during the actual canal-crossing operation, junior officers were expressly forbidden from taking actions that were not specifically ordered by the general staff plan.[145] Chaim Herzog provides a good description of this process:

For years the individual soldier was trained in his particular role in war: each unit dealt with its own problem and nothing else. One unit did nothing for three years but train in passing across a water barrier a pipe for transporting fuel; while every single day for three years bridging units would train in backing up trucks to a water barrier, stopping abruptly at the water's edge, causing the elements of the PMP heavy folding pontoon bridge on the truck to slide by momentum into the water, before they bolted together the two elements of the bridge and drove off. Twice a day during four years these units assembled and dismantled the bridge. Similarly, every day for years all operators of Sagger anti-tank missiles lined up outside vans containing simulators and went through half an hour's exercise in tracking enemy tanks with their missile. . . . This system was repeated right down the line in the army until every action became a reflex action.[146]

Eighty Egyptian engineering units practiced blasting down sand ramparts such as those Israel had constructed on the east bank twice a day and twice more every night for two years. Because of this detailed scripting and rote memorization of tasks, the general staff planners were able to write combined-arms coordination, tactical maneuver, and synchronized movement into the operations order, thereby obviating the need for tactical commanders to innovate or act on their own initiative — at least as long as things went according to plan. Thus, it was vital for Egypt to gain surprise and dictate the course of battle to the Israelis so that they could prevent the Israelis from excessively unraveling their intricate plans.

To ensure surprise, Egypt undertook a vast and highly sophisticated deception and camouflage campaign. First, draconian secrecy veiled the entire operation, which worked quite well, especially in keeping secret the timing of the attack. Indeed, even the Egyptian foreign minister was not told of the planned attack until it had begun. The Egyptians built huge sand ramparts on the west bank so Israeli forces on the east bank could not easily monitor their activities. Beginning in 1968, Cairo began staging frequent, large-scale exercises depicting a canal-crossing operation so that over time Israel became accustomed to them. From January to October 1973 alone, Egypt mobilized its reserves and practiced such maneuvers twenty-two times. Eventually, the actual build-up for the real attack was carried out as if it were one of these drills, and Tel Aviv bought the ruse right up until the day of the attack. Under the cover of an exercise, the Egyptians mobilized their forces and brought them up to the canal banks but then sent back only part of each unit, keeping the rest in secret bunkers. Equipment was transported to the canal at night and then buried in place before dawn. The Egyptians even allowed the details of the "exercise" to leak to Israeli intelligence to further convince the IDF that this was nothing more than yet another in a long series of dress rehearsals. To further lull the Israelis into a false sense of security, Cairo leaked information that Egyptian equipment was in terrible condition and that the Egyptian air defense system had been largely destroyed during the War of Attrition and had not been rebuilt.

Rebuilding the Egyptian Military

Cairo simultaneously made a major effort to increase the quality of its tactical formations. First, the Egyptians recognized that their greatest problems in past conflicts had been in tactical leadership, so they focused their efforts on the junior officers. Previously, college students and college graduates had been exempt from military service. After 1967 that exemption was revoked and enormous numbers of college graduates were drafted into the military — most as junior officers — for indefinite periods of time. In 1967 less than 2 percent of Egyptian officers had university degrees, but by 1973 over 60 percent were university graduates.[147] Overall, 110,000 of 800,000 men in the Egyptian army had university degrees in 1973, an unusual proportion for any army.[148] In 1967, 25 percent of Egyptian enlisted personnel had a high school degree or better, but by 1973 this figure had risen to 51 percent.[149] In addition, the military heavily recruited technically skilled men to make up for prior deficiencies. Before his death, Nasser decreed that every tank commander or officer responsible for electronic equipment had to be a graduate of either an engineering or technical school. By the start of the October War, half of all the engineers in Egypt were serving in the armed forces, most in the air force and air defense force.[150] Egyptian officer training also was revamped to reflect the lessons of the 1967 war. In particular, the senior leadership tried to encourage adaptability, improvisation, and independent action throughout the command structure. Likewise, they urged Egyptian field commanders to report all information with 100 percent accuracy, regardless of how bad or embarrassing the truth was.

Determined that this time their air force would not be destroyed on the ground at the start of the war, the Egyptians took steps to improve the survivability of EAF assets. Cairo built hardened aircraft bunkers (HABS) at all of its airbases. A HAB was built for every aircraft in the air force to ensure that it could be protected against airstrikes. Egypt attempted to increase the quantity and quality of its pilot training. Its pilots received more flying time than ever before (although they still lagged behind NATO or Israeli standards), and authorities authorized live-fire practice for the planned airstrikes. In addition, just as they did with the ground forces, the EAF built mock-ups in the desert of Israeli facilities slated to be hit by airstrikes during the initial assault. The Egyptians built these reproductions at the exact distance from the Egyptian airbase that would launch the attack as the actual target. Egyptian pilots then practiced their missions repeatedly, just like their counterparts in the army.

The Egyptians made other changes as well. For example, Cairo went to great lengths to try to overcome the split between officers and enlisted men that had festered since Ottoman times. As noted above, this was one of Shazli's most important tasks as chief of staff. Cairo began recruiting more enlisted personnel from the urban middle and even upper classes to soften the class divide between the two groups. Officers now had to participate in training and exercises with their troops and were denied the overly liberal leave they had previously enjoyed, forcing them to spend more time with their men. Shazli devised a program whereby units were assigned simple (and often recreational) teamwork exercises that built cohesion, trust, and a sense of accomplishment. Simultaneously, he also began to encourage Egyptian soldiers and officers to be more willing to risk casualties to achieve a goal. Previously, Egyptian commanders had been very loathe to do this and would abort an operation when losses began to mount, but Shazli urged them to give completion of the mission precedence over avoiding losses.

The Soviet Role

The USSR played a very significant part in this rebuilding effort. After the Six Day War, Nasser turned to Moscow and asked the Soviets to help him repair and reform his army. They agreed. Soviet advisers were immediately attached to every Egyptian field unit down to brigades. By December 1967, the Soviet presence in Egypt had grown from 500 men to 15,000 men.[151] Eventually, advisers were attached to every Egyptian combat unit down to battalion or squadron level. Indeed, in artillery and armor units, where the Soviets felt the Egyptians were weakest, there were ten advisers per battalion: two with the battalion headquarters and two more with each company. Soviet officers directed the Egyptian military academy and all major training facilities, and thousands of Egyptian personnel were sent to the USSR for training. They further pushed the Egyptians in the direction of mimicking Soviet methods, especially in the areas of tank assaults and anti-tank defenses.

The Egyptians also relied on the Soviets for their weaponry and other military equipment, and it was this dependence that caused their relations with the Russians to oscillate wildly. The Soviets were beginning the period of detente with the United States, and they feared that an Egyptian attack on Israel would ruin this process. Consequently, Moscow refused to sell certain weapons it considered destabilizing to the Egyptians (like the newest MiG-23 fighter), sold only small numbers of other systems (like the ss-1 Scud surface-to-surface missile), and extended the delivery of other items (such as new T-62 tanks) to try to prevent the Egyptians from going to war. Eventually, Cairo's frustration with Moscow prompted Sadat to "throw out" the Russians in July 1972. In actuality, Sadat did not evict the entire Soviet military presence. He kept all of the Soviet technical and training instructors as well as those Soviet personnel manning the most sophisticated electronic warfare and radar equipment, which the Egyptians could not handle themselves. Essentially, the men he expelled were the operational advisers and most of the Soviet combat units that had arrived during the War of Attrition. These were personnel whose services Egypt no longer required: the army and air force largely had been retrained and there were sufficient Egyptian personnel available to take over most of the other tasks. By early 1973, however, Cairo and Moscow had patched up relations, with the result that a slew of long-promised Soviet weapons poured into Egypt; Soviet advisors also crept back in.

The Balance of Forces

When the Egyptians attacked on the afternoon of 6 October 1973, the Israelis were woefully unprepared for war. Tel Aviv had been completely duped by the Egyptian deception scheme and had only barely begun to mobilize before the onslaught began. Normally, the Bar-Lev line forts were manned by a regular army unit that was reinforced in times of tension so that each fort had nearly 100 men. Because it was Yom Kippur, the holiest day of the Jewish year, a reserve battalion was holding the forts to allow the regular-army soldiers to go home for religious services, and only about 30 reservists were holding each fort. Moreover, during Ariel Sharon's tenure as commander of Israel's southern command, he had closed many of the Bar-Lev forts so that now only sixteen were actively manned. Still, the infantry in the Bar-Lev line were never meant to stop an invasion but simply to serve as a trip wire and a delaying force. Behind the canal, the Israelis had the 252d Armored Division of three brigades, which was intended to serve as the major defensive force until the rest of the army could be mobilized and sent south (this was expected to take 48–72 hours). A bit more than a brigade's worth of infantry were also scattered at various locations in the Sinai. In all, the Israelis had about 18,000 men, 300 tanks, and

80–100 artillery pieces available in the Sinai when the war began, with the nearest significant reinforcements about 24 hours away.[152]

One additional comment regarding Israeli forces must be made. After the 1967 war, the Israelis drew the wrong lesson from the performance of their armored forces. They came to the conclusion that the tank-airplane team was all-powerful and needed little support from other combat arms. In particular, they believed that infantry and artillery were not major contributors to modern mechanized warfare. As a result, the Israelis neglected their artillery and infantry forces. In particular, they grossly underestimated the need for armored units to have mechanized infantry and self-propelled artillery support in combat operations. Thus, Israeli armored formations frequently had little or no organic infantry or artillery support at the start of the October War.[153]

For the crosscanal assault, the Egyptians had concentrated two armies west of the Suez: the Second Army, under Lt. Gen. Sa'd ad-Din Ma'mun, and the Third Army, under Lt. Gen. 'Abd al-Mun'im Wasil. The Second was the stronger of the two, with three infantry divisions, a mechanized division, a commando brigade, an amphibious assault brigade, and an independent armored brigade. It had the task of assaulting across the canal north of the Bitter Lakes. The Third Army had only two infantry divisions plus a mechanized division, a commando brigade, and an independent armored brigade, but it had the narrower of the two assault sectors, that south of the Bitter Lakes. These armies were even stronger than they appear on paper, for most had been reinforced for the assault. In particular, the infantry divisions, which normally comprised two infantry brigades and a mechanized infantry brigade, were each reinforced with an armored brigade, boosting their manpower strength to 14,000 and their tank strength to 200. The general staff held another mechanized division, two armored divisions, a paratrooper brigade, an infantry brigade, and miscellaneous other forces in reserve. In all, the Egyptians massed about 300,000 men, over 2,400 tanks, and 2,300 artillery pieces for the war, of which about 200,000 men, 1,600 tanks, and 2,000 artillery pieces were concentrated in the Second and Third Armies for the initial assault.[154]

Cairo had likewise put together a sizable force to wage the air war against Israel. The EAF had been augmented to a strength of 435 combat aircraft, including 210 late-model MiG-21s. Moreover, 55 Algerian MiGs, 20 Iraqi Hawker Hunters, and 30 Libyan Mirages were deployed to Egypt and had been under Egyptian command for over a year. Finally, the Egyptians had concentrated an enormous SAM force to cover the invasion. In addition to 135 SA-2 and SA-3 batteries, the Egyptians had received 20–40 batteries of the new SA-6 (which had never before been used in combat) as well as 2,100 antiaircraft guns and 5,000 shoulder-launched SA-7s. Overall, the Egyptians deployed more SAMs against Israel than the United States then had in its entire arsenal.[155] To oppose Egypt's air and air defense forces, the IAF mustered 366 aircraft: 120 F-4 Phantoms, 160 A-4 Sky-hawks, 70 Mirages, and 16 Super-Mysteres.[156]

Although Cairo's quantitative advantage was staggering, unlike in previous wars with Israel, this time Egypt did not necessarily have a qualitative advantage in weaponry. In the net, the Egyptians and Israelis were about evenly matched. The Centurion was still the favorite tank of the Israeli armored force, but they had been receiving sizable numbers of the new American M-60, which was a tremendous improvement over Tel Aviv's obsolete Shermans. The Egyptians took delivery of the new Soviet T-62 — which the IDF concluded was, on the whole, at least the equal of the Centurion and the M-60 — but their armored corps was still mostly comprised of older T-55s. Egypt again possessed superior Soviet artillery and armored personnel carriers, but Tel Aviv fielded better electronic-warfare equipment, and the IAF — with its new American F-4 Phantoms, A-4 Skyhawks, and advanced air-to-air missiles — far outclassed the Soviet MiG-21s and Su-20s of the EAF.

The Egyptian Assault, 6 October

The Egyptian attack across the Suez began at 2:00 P.M. on 6 October with a thunderous bombardment from 2,000 artillery pieces and 1,900 direct-fire weapons combined with 250–300 sorties by the EAF against Israeli airbases and command-and-control facilities in the Sinai. The Egyptian artillery barrage dropped 10,500 shells on the startled Israelis in just the first minute of the war, suppressing most fire from the Bar-Lev forts during the initial crossing. The airstrikes did little damage to the Israeli airbases and command facilities, but their attacks against Israeli artillery batteries were accurate enough to silence the guns during the canal crossing. However, when IAF fighters arrived over the Sinai, they quickly shot down eighteen Egyptian planes with no losses, prompting Cairo to cancel a planned second wave of airstrikes.[157] After about an hour of shelling, the first wave of 8,000 Egyptian assault troops began crossing the canal. Battalions of Egyptian commandos led the way, picked soldiers who had received the most rigorous training Egypt had to offer. Although intended for special forces missions, because they were considered the best infantry in the Egyptian army, a brigade of commandos was assigned to each of the assaulting armies to spearhead the attack. The commandos' mission was to scale the Israeli sand

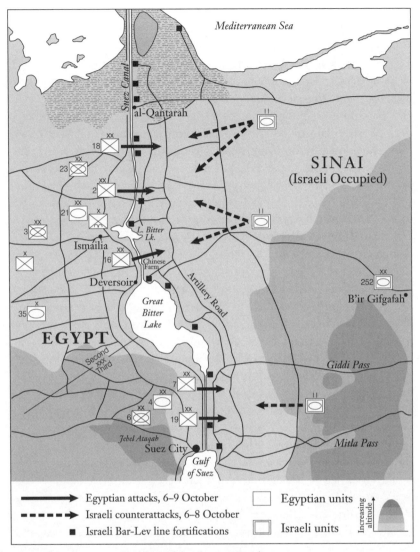

Map 7. The Egyptian Crossing of the Suez, 6 October 1973

ramparts, bypass the Bar-Lev forts, and begin setting up antitank defenses about two kilometers from the canal to provide cover until heavier forces could get across.

Two more brigades of commandos were helicopter-lifted into the Sinai in company- and battalion-sized forces to block Israeli reinforcements heading toward the canal, disrupt Israeli command and control, and generally sow confusion in the rear areas. For the most part, these units inflicted little physical damage on the Israelis. Large numbers of the helicopters were shot down before they were able to land their commando teams. Other teams got lost in the Sinai and failed to carry out their missions. In a couple of cases, the commandos got through and found their targets but still did little damage to the Israelis and usually were wiped out in the fighting. Nevertheless, the Egyptian commandos fought exceptionally hard and created considerable panic, prompting the Israelis to take precautions that hindered their ability to concentrate on stopping the assault across the canal.

General Isma'il 'Ali's plan was to launch all five infantry divisions of the Second and Third Armies across the canal simultaneously. He purposely dispersed his effort all along the front rather than massing against one point so that the Israelis would not be able to identify a main thrust and throw all of their available forces against it. He hoped that the Israelis would either waste time holding back their meager forces to try to identify a main effort that did not exist or else be forced to disperse their assets across the front, where they could be chewed up piecemeal by the much larger Egyptian forces. Isma'il 'Ali knew that the Israelis would respond immediately by counterattacking with their armored forces and their air force. Isma'il 'Ali's antitank teams and SAMs would be ready for them. He hoped the Israelis would suffer heavy casualties beating their heads against his missile shield, would conclude that their attacks were fruitless, and would then be amenable to a negotiated settlement.

The canal crossing went precisely according to plan, largely because of the outstanding efforts of Egypt's combat engineers. The first wave of troops went across in assault boats and rafts, and immediately afterward forty combat engineer battalions began building two heavy-vehicle bridges, one light-vehicle bridge, and two pontoon bridges in each division sector. The IAF furiously attacked these spans and despite taking heavy losses from Egyptian air defenses—especially the SA-6–ZSU-23 combination—repeatedly hit them. However, the Soviet-designed bridges were sectional, and the engineers worked miracles by quickly replacing the damaged sections to minimize the disruption of movement across the canal. To overcome the Israeli sand ramparts, the Egyptians had developed the novel idea of using high-pressure water pumps to blast their way through. Egyptian engineers had repeatedly practiced this operation, and on 6 October the first breaches were cut in the sand barriers in under an hour.[158]

The assault went exactly as Cairo had hoped and far better than it had expected. As Shazli described it, "The whole operation was a magnificent symphony played by tens of thousands of men."[159] During the first eighteen hours, the Egyptians put 90,000 men, 850 tanks, and 11,000 other vehicles across the Suez.[160] Although they had anticipated losses of as many as 10,000 killed just crossing the canal, the Egyptians suffered only 208 dead.[161] Every unit executed its assigned task as it had rehearsed countless times in the past. The operation was directed entirely by the general staff, with every decision referred back up the chain of command to the GHQ headquarters bunker. The Cairo correspondent of *The New York Times* reported: "The Egyptian Army has doggedly adhered to a comprehensive, preconceived strategic and tactical plan. Military spokesmen insist that there have been no departures from the plan, no improvisations and no unauthorized initiatives by local commanders."[162] Of course this had its downside, even during the canal crossing. For example, the Third Army had difficulty bridging the canal and then cutting through the sand barriers because of unforeseen terrain problems. Because the lower-ranking officers had been ordered not to deviate from the detailed plan during the crossing, and because no one higher in the chain of command was willing to take the initiative to make decisions, Isma'il 'Ali was forced to send a senior representative of GHQ to select new locations for several of the Third Army breaches, ultimately delaying their crossing by twelve hours.

The Fight for the Bridgeheads, 7–13 October

As soon as the Egyptian forces crossed the canal, they began consolidating and expanding their bridgeheads. Units tasked to deal with the Bar-Lev forts first isolated and then assaulted these positions. In a few cases, the Israelis were quickly overpowered, but for the most part, the forts only fell to repeated assaults by superior forces or prolonged sieges over many days. Meanwhile, the bulk of the Egyptian infantry divisions began pushing into the hills east of the canal. They established intricate semicircular defensive positions several kilometers wide with minefields; interlocking fields of fire from tanks, ATGMs, antitank guns, and automatic weapons; and supported by mortars and artillery on both sides of the canal. Once a defensive position was set, the Egyptians began slowly expanding outward by creeping forward in a 180-degree arc. Every advance and attack was conducted in exactly the same manner without variation for the terrain or the Israeli defenders present: Egyptian infantry would push forward, infiltrate any IDF positions, and set up their antitank and other heavy weapons. Then Egyptian artillery would lay down a time-phased artillery barrage behind which Egyptian armor and mechanized infantry would advance to link up with the infantry. Any resistance not driven off by the artillery was dispersed by massive doses of firepower from the forward infantry and the advancing armor. In this way the Egyptian defensive positions slowly knitted together into divisional and then armywide bridgeheads.

The Israelis were not idle during this period. Immediately after the first artillery shells began falling, Israeli tanks and aircraft began racing to the canal, only to hit Isma'il 'Ali's missile shield head on. Israeli aircraft began taking heavy losses to the Egyptian SAMs and AAA. In particular, the Israelis found that to avoid the SA-2s, SA-3s, and especially the unexpected SA-6s, they had to stay close to the ground, where they fell prey to antiaircraft guns. The Israelis lost 14 warplanes during the first two days of the conflict and had many others damaged, at which point Tel Aviv ordered the IAF to stay clear of the canal for fear of needlessly depleting its air force. For the next several days, Israeli planes played little role in the fighting because of this edict and because they were desperately needed to deal with the simultaneous (and ultimately more threatening) Syrian invasion of the Golan Heights.

Israel's armored forces did no better. The 252d Armored Division began the war with its 14th Armored Brigade close to the canal, another brigade at about the line of the passes, and the third brigade in central Sinai. Rather than waiting to concentrate the division, all three brigades simply raced to the canal and attacked piecemeal. In addition, as Isma'il 'Ali had hoped, because the Egyptian assault came all across the front and no main effort could be identified, the Israelis dispersed their armor to all points. Consequently, for the first two days, the Israeli counterattacks were conducted by penny packets of Israeli tanks generally unsupported by infantry, artillery, or even air power. The Egyptians fought off these counterattacks extremely well. Their tanks, antitank teams, and artillery all coordinated their efforts beautifully. Egyptian artillery fire was extremely accurate. Infantry equipped with AT-3 Sagger ATGMs and RPGs camouflaged themselves among the dunes and allowed the Israeli tanks to charge through their positions unhindered, only to attack the tanks from the rear once they had gone by. Additional antitank teams plus armor, APCs, mortars, and artillery would then open up on the Israeli tanks from their main lines, catching the Israelis in fire-sacks and hitting them from all sides. Although the Egyptian tank and ATGM fire was actually quite inaccurate, the sheer volume eventually resulted in kills. The Israelis suffered horrendous losses in these attacks: according to the commander of the Israeli 14th Armored Brigade, all but 14 of his 100 tanks were put out of action by the end of the first day, and the entire 252d Armored Division lost 200 of its 300 tanks in the first two days of the war.[163]

On 8 October the Israelis attempted a larger counterattack involving two newly arrived armored divisions — Maj. Gen. Bren Adan's 162d and Maj. Gen. Ariel Sharon's 143d. This attack failed just as miserably as the smaller assaults of the 252d Division the previous two days. The assault was poorly planned and organized, commanders throughout the hierarchy made bad decisions during the attack, and it suffered greatly from the fact that the Israelis still had not figured out how to cope with the new Egyptian tactics. The Egyptians fought fiercely, inflicting heavy casualties on Adan's division while Sharon never even bothered to attack.

Throughout this period, the moment an Israeli counterattack was beaten back, the Egyptians would resume their creeping advance. Once the divisional bridgeheads had been locked together into army bridgeheads, the Egyptians began heading eastward, slowly pushing forward into the hills and sand dunes between the canal and the mountains of western Sinai. However, the offensive soon slowed to a crawl and then to a full halt. The constant Israeli counterattacks did little damage to the Egyptian formations, but by forcing them to halt their advance and defend in place, they cost the Egyptians precious time. By 9 October, Israeli forces had built up to roughly three full armored divisions against the Egyptians. Of equal importance, individual Israeli commanders had begun to find solutions to the Egyptian tactics. To deal with the Saggers and RPGs, for example, Adan deployed M-113 APCs with machine guns in support of his tanks to suppress the Egyptian antitank fire. Other divisions employed artillery to keep the heads of the Egyptian infantrymen down or smoke to hide Israeli armored vehicles from the Sagger teams. Moreover, the Israelis began to counterattack into the flanks of Egyptian units the moment they started moving forward. Because the Egyptians attacked schematically and advanced brigade by brigade or division by division, the Israelis found that gaps would usually open up between these units as they advanced — gaps into which the Israelis could push armor. Egyptian units almost never countered the Israeli moves with maneuvers of their own and proved incapable of reorienting their forces to deal with these flanking attacks. Instead, the advancing force could only stop and try to return fire until its neighboring unit could be brought forward to drive off the Israelis. Consequently, Egyptian units began to suffer heavier casualties and to advance less and less. In addition, as the Egyptians drove farther into the Sinai, their artillery fire became progressively less accurate.[164] They also began losing counterbattery duels to Israeli artillery units, which had redeployed from their prewar positions to new locations. By 9 or 10 October, the Israelis had brought the Egyptian advance to a halt short of Isma'il 'Ali's goal of the so-called "Artillery Road," which paralleled the canal 10–15 kilometers to the east.

The reasons for this halt were not apparent to everyone in Cairo. On 9 and 10 October, many Egyptian leaders were still intoxicated by their astonishing victories during the previous days and tended to attribute the slowing of their advance to the friction endemic to all military operations and eventually brings even the most successful offensives to a halt. Consequently, some generals began agitating for a renewed offensive to seize the line of the passes. Shazli and Gamasy apparently both favored such an offensive, even though both knew that plans for such a move (phase two of the original "Granite" plan) had never made it off the drawing board. Isma'il 'Ali, however, was adamantly opposed to it. He had recognized that Egypt's initial success was due to four crucial factors—surprise, the dramatic imbalance of forces on 6 October, Israeli unpreparedness for Egyptian antitank and antiaircraft tactics, and the brilliant, all-encompassing script of the general staff. By 9 October, all four of these advantages were slipping away: the Israelis had recovered from their surprise, they were concentrating forces in the Sinai, they were figuring out ways to defeat the Egyptian defensive tactics, and the course of operations was diverging further and further from the plan, forcing field officers to shoulder more of the burden of command. What's more, there were no detailed GHQ plans for an attack to the passes. For all of these reasons, despite constant entreaties from Shazli, Gamasy, and others, Isma'il 'Ali refused to order a new, large-scale offensive but instead ordered his troops to continue consolidating their positions and bracing themselves for renewed Israeli attacks.[165]

The Egyptian Offensive of 14 October

While Isma'il 'Ali was able to withstand his subordinates' cries for implementation of the apocryphal "phase two" offensive, he was unable to overcome pressure from Syria. On 6 and 7 October ,the Israelis had fought the Syrians to a standstill on the Golan, and on the morning of 10 October, they launched a major offensive on the Damascus Plain. The Israelis made rapid progress and threatened the Syrian capital itself. The Syrians pleaded with the Egyptians to launch a major attack to force the Israelis to shift forces from the Golan to the Sinai front. Sadat, who also appears to have

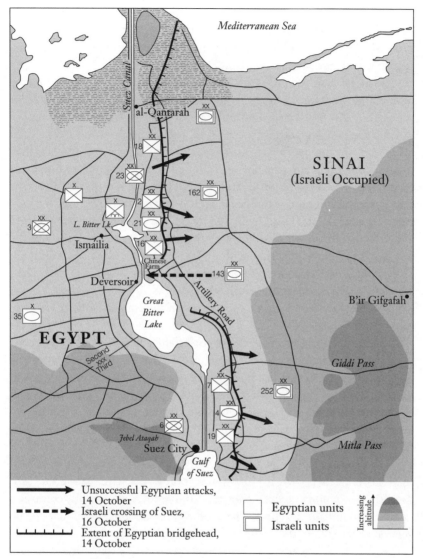

Map 8. Egypt's Offensive and Israel's Attack toward the Suez, 14 and 16 October 1973

been affected by Egyptian success on 6–9 October, agreed to help his Syrian counterpart, Pres. Hafiz al-Asad, and — despite Isma'il 'Ali's protests — ordered the general staff to launch a major attack to the Sinai passes to force the Israelis to ease their pressure on Damascus.

The attack was set for 14 October, and the Egyptians transferred armored and mechanized forces from the GHQ reserve to the east bank for the assault. The offensive would employ Egypt's two armored divisions, the 4th and the 21st, supported by several additional armored and mechanized brigades from the two field armies and the GHQ reserve. Altogether, they massed 800–1,000 tanks for the operation. The offensive was to be a giant pincer move converging on B'ir Gifgafah. The Second Army, led by the 21st Armored Division, would strike out eastward and force the B'ir Gifgafah Pass, while the Third Army, led by the 4th Armored Division, would attack to the northeast, drive through the Mitla Pass, and link up with the Second Army on the far side of the B'ir Gifgafah Pass. In addition, each army would conduct a supporting attack — the Second Army's north toward Romani, the Third Army's south toward R'as as-Sudr — and the Third would also deploy a blocking force to prevent the Israelis from striking out of the Giddi Pass.[166]

The attack was a catastrophe. Egyptian field commanders failed to conduct adequate reconnaissance. Consequently, they had only the information provided by senior headquarters regarding Israeli deployments and locations to use, and they were frequently surprised by unknown Israeli defensive positions. Early on 14 October, Israeli commandos landed on Jebel Ataqah and destroyed most of the sophisticated signals-intercept equipment the Egyptians had been using to monitor Israeli reporting. With this source of intelligence gone, the general staff was forced to rely on the reports of their own troops, and as soon as the battle started to turn sour, these accounts quickly diverged from reality. As a result, confusion spread through the Egyptian chain of command, and the ability of the general staff to direct the battle rapidly diminished.[167]

Another problem the Egyptians encountered was that command and control quickly broke down among operational commanders in the field. The Egyptian formations could not keep together and coordinate their operations. Thus, what should have been two divisional thrusts with three supporting attacks turned into nine brigade-sized attacks scattered all across the front. The Egyptian columns got so spread out that they could not come to each other's aid as each came under attack from quick, maneuvering Israeli armor. Instead of two reinforced armored-division fists, the Israelis were hit almost randomly by piecemeal tank attacks that they pinned, out-flanked, and crushed.

At the tactical level, Egyptian performance was even worse. First, company, battalion, and brigade commanders failed to conduct proper combined-arms operations. For the most part, mechanized infantry went into battle close behind the tanks but never dismounted, and large number of troops were killed without making any contribution to the attack when Israeli tank rounds destroyed their APCs. In particular, the Egyptians did not have their infantry dismount, push ahead of the tanks, and break up the Israeli armor concentrations with their ATGMs and RPGs as they had done so effectively on 6–10 October. Egyptian artillery tried to lay down a covering barrage and also tried to provide fire support to units in trouble, but they simply could not. The artillery barrage covering the attack was huge, employing at least 500 guns, but completely ineffective. As Trevor Dupuy has observed, "Without detailed, prearranged fire plans, such as those they had employed on October 6, the Egyptian artillery concentrations fell largely on empty rock and sand dunes."[168] Egyptian armor attacked Soviet-style in waves, but unlike the Soviets, the Egyptians made no effort to maneuver in battle. Their T-55s and T-62s literally drove straight at the Israelis and tried simply to overwhelm them with firepower. In the words of one Israeli brigade commander, "they just waddled forward like ducks."[169] Israeli armor outmaneuvered the Egyptians effortlessly and inflicted terrible damage on them. Overall, General Adan assessed the 14 October offensive as "a very poor, and a very simple attack, that was broken right from the start."[170] Brig. Gen. S. A. El-Edroos, himself no critic of the Arab militaries, has remarked, "The catastrophic defeat suffered by the Egyptian tank corps reflected the inability of Egyptian commanders, from divisional to troop [company] level, to conduct mobile, flexible, and fluid armored operations."[171]

Soon after it began, the Egyptian offensive came to a halt only a few miles from its initial lines. Against Adan's 162d Armored Division, the Egyptians attacked through a wadi but did not cover the heights on either side. Thus, it was simple for Adan's troops to catch the Egyptians in a fire-trap and smash their attack. Similarly, the Egyptians drove straight at Sharon's brigades without guarding their flanks, so again the Israelis flanked them, pummeled them, and drove them back. As a result, the Egyptians lost 265 tanks and roughly 200 other armored vehicles in the battle.[172] The Israelis took only minor casualties and had less than 40 tanks damaged, of which only 6 could not be quickly repaired and returned to battle.[173]

The Israeli Counteroffensive

The Israelis immediately followed up their success on 14 October with a major counteroffensive. The Second Army had failed to secure its right flank on the Great Bitter Lake, opening a gap near Deversoir between its lines and the Great Bitter Lake. The Israelis had discovered this weakness several days before, and on the night of 15 October, they launched a multi-division operation to push though this seam and cross over to the west bank of the canal, where they intended to drive south into the rear of the Third Army. Sharon's 143d Division (reinforced with a brigade of paratroopers) attacked into the breach. His forces were to drive the Egyptian forces northward to widen the corridor to the canal, then cross over and secure a bridgehead on the west bank, at which point the 162d and the reconstituted 252d Armored Divisions—under Brigadier Generals Adan and Kalman Magen respectively—would cross over and drive south.

The southern flank of the Second Army was anchored on extensive defensive positions built in and around the "Chinese Farm."[174] When Sharon's forces pushed up from Deversoir on the night of 15–16 October, they encountered little resistance since the Egyptians had not placed observation posts between the Chinese Farm and the Great Bitter Lake. As a result, Sharon's paratrooper brigade crossed easily and dug in on the west bank of the Suez. Similarly, when Sharon sent Col. Amnon Reshef's reconstituted 14th Armored Brigade north along the east bank of the canal, they did not encounter any Egyptian flank guards and were able to turn east and attack into the rear of the Chinese Farm defenses. Indeed, Reshef's armor was able to attack into the midst of the headquarters and vehicle park of the Egyptian 16th Infantry Division. Much of the Egyptian 21st Armored Division also was in this area, regrouping and licking their wounds after the failed offensive of 14 October. The Egyptians were completely surprised by the sudden appearance of Israeli armor in their rear, but there were huge numbers of Egyptian troops and armored vehicles everywhere that soon overcame the shock and began to fight back furiously.

Over the next four days, a fierce battle raged around the Chinese Farm position. Most of the Israeli commanders wanted to widen their corridor to the canal and so fought to push the Egyptians out of their fortified defensive positions. General Sharon, however, believed it far more important to expand the bridgehead on the west bank and seemingly wanted the glory of leading the breakout on that side rather than the crucial—but less flashy—task of holding open the bridgehead on both sides of the canal. As a result, Sharon never committed all of his forces in a determined attack to push the Egyptians out of the Chinese Farm. The Egyptian defense was still very creditable. They fought extremely hard to hold on to their positions and caused significant casualties every time the Israelis attacked. However, they made no effort to organize a coherent defensive plan. Instead, the Egyptians simply opened fire and fought from wherever they were. Their forces were only willing to launch small counterattacks to retake specific positions recently lost to the Israelis but were not willing or able to counterattack to improve their position overall, to unhinge the Israeli offensive more broadly, or to relieve the constant pressure on their positions. Moreover, despite the concentration of combat power in the area, none of Cairo's field commanders on the scene acted to form up the mass of vehicles and men into cohesive units and conduct an operational-level counterattack to try to cut the narrow Israeli corridor to the canal. Meanwhile, Egyptian commanders on the west bank misled Cairo as to the size of the Israeli force that had crossed the Suez. Throughout 16 and 17 October, as the Israelis expanded their bridgehead and built up their strength on the west bank to several brigades, Egyptian officers reported to GHQ that the Israelis on the west bank were no more than a raiding force of less than a company.

Based on these misleading reports, the general staff concluded that the forces on the west bank were a diversion and the Israelis' real objective was to take Chinese Farm and then roll up the Second Army's lines on the east bank from south to north. They regarded this as a serious threat, and so on 16 October, Isma'il 'Ali ordered a major counterattack on the east bank by the Second and Third Armies to try to crush the Israeli force that had gotten around the right flank of the Second Army (part of Sharon's ugdah). He ordered the 21st Armored Division to counterattack southward while the T-62-equipped 25th Independent Armored Brigade of the Third Army drove north along the Bitter Lakes to hit the Israelis from the rear.

The counterattack was launched on 17 October, and its execution left much to be desired. First, the Egyptian field commanders again failed to adequately scout their attack and so were not aware that Adan's 162d Division had been brought down to clear the Chinese Farm position and then cross the canal. Second, the 21st Armored Division and 25th Armored Brigade could not coordinate their attacks so that Adan was able to defeat the 21st's attack and then hurry south to deal with the 25th. Third, the Egyptian armored units showed the same problems they had manifested on 14 October: they launched clumsy frontal assaults, failed to maneuver, showed no imagination or flexibility when Israeli units caught them from the flank or rear, and totally neglected combined-arms operations. The 21st Armored Division's attack quickly went nowhere, and after losing 50–60 tanks to the Israelis, they retired. Adan then turned south to deal with the 25th Armored Brigade. This unit was driving north along the Great Bitter Lake in an administrative-march formation without flank guards. Adan set up an ambush with his tanks in front and along the right flank of the advancing Egyptians and then hit them with his entire division. The Egyptian tanks that were not obliterated by Israeli long-range gunnery in the first few moments were quickly dispatched when Israeli tanks moved down and engaged them at close quarters. Of 96 T-62s in the brigade, all but 10 were destroyed; it also lost all of its APCs. Only three Israeli tanks were knocked out in the fighting, and two of these were destroyed when they blundered into an old Israeli minefield.[175]

After the failure of the 17 October counterattacks, the Egyptian General Staff slowly became aware of the true size of the Israeli force on the west bank and concluded that this was a full-scale counteroffensive rather than a mere raid. Soviet Premier Alexei Kosygin arrived in Cairo on 17 October and, either late that night or early on 18 October, showed Sadat Russian satellite imagery of the Israeli units operating on the west side of the Suez. Isma'il 'Ali was apparently livid when he learned of the actual size of this IDF force. He decided he could not trust his field commanders, and he and Sadat dispatched Shazli to the front to find out what was going on. By the early hours of the nineteenth, Shazli confirmed that the Israelis had crossed at least a division to the west bank and were about to launch a major offensive. Isma'il 'Ali ordered two armored brigades — one from each field army — to return to the west bank to help contain the Israeli bridgehead.[176] After Shazli returned from the front on 20 October, the general staff debated about what course of action they should adopt. Shazli recommended withdrawing most of the remaining armor from the east bank and then counterattacking the Israeli force to destroy it. Isma'il 'Ali, however, argued that Egypt should accept an immediate ceasefire to freeze the Israeli force politically before it pushed any further into Egypt. He specifically argued against any withdrawal of forces from the east bank because he feared it would cause a collapse of Egyptian morale and lead to the loss of the hard-won and politically crucial bridgeheads on the east bank. Sadat was persuaded by Isma'il 'Ali and launched efforts to work out a ceasefire with Syria and Russia in the United Nations.

Meanwhile, the Israelis began their offensive on the west bank of the canal. Sharon finally received permission to try to move north to threaten or even cut off the Second Army, but although he was able to push to the outskirts of Ismailia, his division was stopped cold by Egyptian commandos and infantry dug in around the city. Adan, however, beat back several determined but very inept counterattacks by Egyptian armored and mechanized

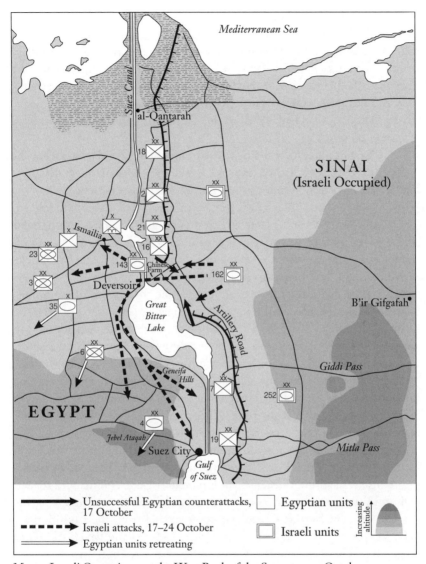

Map 9. Israeli Operations on the West Bank of the Suez, 17–24 October 1973

reserves on the west bank before punching through their hastily formed lines and driving south into the Geneifah Hills. Initially, the Israelis had only Adan's one understrength division with about 200 tanks for the drive south (Adan was joined later by Magen's even smaller ugdah) while the Egyptians had close to four mostly fresh heavy divisions to oppose them. Nevertheless, the Israelis beat them decisively in a series of engagements. By 22 October, Adan had encircled the Third Army and his forces stood at the gates of Suez City.

The Israelis noted that the Egyptians fought considerably worse on the west bank than they had on the east bank. In particular, their defensive battles were not as determined or as skillful and they experienced all of the same problems with inflexibility, lack of initiative, and inability to maneuver in tank battles with the Israelis. Essentially, once Adan was able to break through the ring of Egyptian divisions dug in around Deversoir and his armor suddenly had room to maneuver, the Egyptians found themselves forced to fight fluid meeting engagements against the Israelis. The Egyptian armored divisions simply could not handle these kinds of battles and were smashed one after another by Adan's brigades, leading to a progressive disintegration of Cairo's forces west of the Suez. As these defenses collapsed, the levels of deception and obfuscation from Egyptian tactical formations increased dramatically, and the Egyptian forces on the west bank quickly descended into confusion and paralysis. Egypt's senior leadership scrambled to try to patch together some kind of defense to stop the Israeli advance, but they were hamstrung by the passivity and dissembling of their subordinates. On one occasion, the commander of the Egyptian 4th Armored Division would not accept an order from the Third Army commander to counterattack the Israelis; the order had to be reissued by Isma'il 'Ali himself. In another instance, an Egyptian brigade commander repeatedly told the Third Army commander that he was counterattacking the Israelis when in fact his forces had never moved from their positions.[177] The Egyptians also were hampered by the fact that the Israeli Air Force finally was able to commit itself fully in these battles. First, with the Syrian front largely quiescent, the IAF could concentrate on the Suez front. Second, as the Israeli ground forces moved on the west bank, they went out of their way to overrun Egyptian SAM sites, creating a gap in the Egyptian air defenses in which the IAF could operate freely. Cairo desperately threw in its air force to seal this breach and to stop the Israeli armor, flying as many as 2,500 sorties in less than a week. But Israeli fighters made short work of the Egyptians in several major air-to-air engagements, shooting down over 100 Egyptian aircraft for the loss of only 3 of their own.[178]

In the early morning hours of 24 October, Adan sent part of his division to try to take Suez City. Many troops and even whole units of the Egyptian Third Army had retreated there, and when the Israelis drove in, they were met with a sharp rebuff. The Egyptians fought desperately, cutting off one small Israeli unit that got separated from the main body and nearly destroying it. The Israelis decided that taking the city would entail significant losses and was unnecessary, given that the Third Army already was cut off. At that point, Israel finally bowed to heavy superpower pressure and, on 28 October, gave the Egyptians the ceasefire they had been seeking since the twentieth.

The War in the Air

Sadat, Isma'il 'Ali, and Mubarak all concluded long before 6 October 1973 that the Egyptian Air Force was no match for the IAF and would not be for the foreseeable future. Egyptian air strategy for the October War was built around this central assumption. First, the EAF was almost completely relieved of counterair missions. With the exception of the airstrikes against a few Israeli airfields in the Sinai, there would be no Egyptian offensive counterair effort. In particular, Cairo ruled out offensive fighter sweeps over Israeli lines. Similarly, the defensive counterair mission would be left mostly in the hands of Egypt's ground-based air defenses. Cairo did establish some combat air patrols deeper in Egypt, but these were all either in unimportant sectors or else set as final lines of defense behind the SAM belts. Wherever it was important for the Egyptians to repulse the IAF, the mission fell to the SAMs and AAA. The ground-based air defenses provided all air defense coverage over Egyptian ground forces on both sides of the canal as well as the barrier defenses to prevent Israel from conducting deep penetration raids against strategic targets such as Cairo. In addition, the Egyptian generals concluded that they could expect only very limited support to their ground forces in the form of close air support (CAS) or battlefield air interdiction missions and so instead planned to rely on artillery, mortars, and rocket fire.

While the EAF's role was to be very restricted, it would not be completely inactive. Isma'il 'Ali, Gamasy, and Mubarak assigned Egypt's pilots limited tasks that would be well within their capabilities and that would give them the greatest chance of successfully conducting their mission and then escaping before they could be intercepted by IAF fighters. Thus, Egyptian aircraft would conduct quick hit-and-run raids against specific Israeli targets near the canal zone and then immediately return to base. This effectively ruled out both CAS missions—which require aircraft to loiter over-

head until they are called on by the ground commander — and any interdiction missions deeper than the forward enemy positions.

Even with such minimal goals, EAF performance can hardly be described
as anything more than mediocre. As noted above, the initial airstrikes
against the Sinai facilities caused little damage and the planes were quickly
intercepted by Israeli fighters, resulting in the rapid loss of 5–10 percent of
the attacking force and prompting Cairo to abort the planned second wave.
For the next ten to fourteen days of the war, the EAF did not hinder the war
effort, but neither did it contribute very much. The Egyptians staged quick
hit-and-run strikes against well-identified Israeli positions. These attacks
were annoying to the frontline Israeli forces but did little damage. Egyptian
air-to-ground missions were very uneven. During the first few days, when
the Israeli Army expected the IAF to have air superiority and so did not take
even routine precautions to defend against air attacks, some Egyptian airstrikes caused some damage to IDF field units. But overall, Egyptian air-to-
ground skills were poor and, as soon as Israeli ground forces began to
disperse and pay more attention to air defense, even the minimal effectiveness of Egyptian airstrikes evaporated. Air force command and control was
rigid and highly compartmentalized with the result that Egyptian air power
was not very flexible or responsive to changing battle conditions. In particular, because the EAF refused to loiter over the battlefield, they could not
come to the aid of Egyptian troops meeting Israeli resistance. In fact, airstrikes really could only be conducted against targets that were in place and
identified by the Egyptians at least 24 hours ahead of time, which was about
how long it took for the strike request to filter up through the chain of
command and then the orders to filter back down to the squadron.

Egyptian air-to-air performance was no better. There were fifty-two
major dogfights between the Egyptians and Israelis. In all, the Egyptians
succeeded in shooting down 5–8 Israeli aircraft while losing 172 of their
own to Israeli fighters.[179] As these figures imply, the Egyptians were completely outclassed by the Israelis. While it is true that the Israelis possessed the state-of-the-art Phantom F-4E, which was a generation ahead of
Egypt's MiG-21s, it is also the case that the Israelis generally reserved the
Phantoms for strike missions, and the older Mirages flew the lion's share of
counterair missions (65–70 percent of all counterair sorties). Thus, the
majority of air-to-air battles involved the same combination of planes as in
1967, although both models had been upgraded in the interim. Nevertheless, the modest change in the technological balance cannot account for the
dramatic change in air-to-air outcomes. The Egyptians did much worse in
1973 than they had in 1967, demonstrating that pilot skill was the dominant

factor, not technology. In 1967 the Egyptians had suffered about a 1 to 7 kill ratio to the Israelis, but in 1973 this ratio fell to somewhere between 1 to 20 and 1 to 35 and probably was right around 1 to 25. While IAF pilot skills continued to develop, the Israelis found little improvement among their Egyptian counterparts. As in 1967, Egyptian pilots were inflexible, dogmatic, and slow to react in combat. They stuck closely to doctrinal maneuvers, were heavily reliant on their ground controllers, and panicked when Israeli pilots took unexpected actions or busted up their textbook formations. As a result, when Israeli and Egyptian fighters did tangle, the Egyptians were virtual sitting ducks for the Israelis. For example, in one battle on the first day of the war, 2 Phantoms took on a strike package of 28 MiG-21s and MiG-17s near Sharm ash-Shaykh, and in a few minutes of dogfighting the Israeli planes shot down 8 MiGs and chased off the other 20 with no losses.

The Egyptians again suffered from a low operational readiness rate that diminished their ability to put aircraft in the air. Because of poor maintenance and repair practices, only about 65 percent of the Egyptian fighter force was operationally ready for combat. Overall, the Egyptians managed 6,815 sorties from 540 combat aircraft, or about 0.6 sorties per day per aircraft. By contrast, the Israelis averaged nearly 4 sorties per day per aircraft.[180]

Egypt's ground-based air defenses were highly effective in keeping the IAF from seriously disrupting Egyptian ground operations until late in the war. However, they were terribly inefficient in doing so. Specifically, Egyptian forces probably should have caused far more harm to the Israelis than they actually did. Egyptian SAM and AAA operators had only a limited understanding of their weapons, and their marksmanship was often abysmal. Ultimately, the Egyptians attempted to compensate for their inefficiency by launching masses of SAMs and concentrating entire battalions of antiaircraft guns on Israeli aircraft. The Egyptians probably shot down 20–25 Israeli aircraft with SAMs and another 15–20 with AAA.[181] Given that the Israelis flew about 6,000 sorties against the Egyptians, this translates into a loss rate of only 0.006–0.0075 per sortie — a very poor attrition rate from the Egyptian perspective. The Egyptians fired about 1,000 heavy SAMs of all types plus another 4,000–8,000 SA-7s. Thus, on average, they expended about 40 heavy SAMs and 150 SA-7s for every aircraft shot down.[182] Again, this is a very poor ratio, given that Soviet metrics predicted that downing an enemy aircraft should have required the expenditure of only 5–10 SAMs. Egyptian air defenses apparently shot down more of their own planes than Israelis. Estimates vary, but Egyptian SAMs and AAA brought down somewhere between 45 and 60 EAF aircraft during the war.[183]

Egyptian Military Effectiveness during the October War

The first four days of the October War undoubtedly witnessed Egypt's finest performance in combat in the modern era. However, this sudden effectiveness was largely the result of six years of painstaking preparation during which time Cairo's generals devised a method by which they could avoid the areas of military performance which had been so problematic for Egyptian forces over the previous twenty-five years. When the Israelis forced them to diverge from their carefully laid plans, Egyptian forces reverted to their old patterns of behavior and were once again routed.

The striking feature of Egyptian combat performance in the October War was the dramatic difference between the skill of their operations during the first three or four days of the campaign and the ineptitude of their efforts thereafter. During the initial Egyptian offensive, the IDF was amazed at their performance and believed that the Egyptians had somehow completely reformed their army so that all of the old problems had been extirpated. Egyptian operations were crisp and determined. Combined-arms cooperation was superb. Tactics were clever and effective, and each attack followed quickly on the heels of the last. It was as if the Israelis were fighting a completely different enemy.

By the fourth or fifth day of the war, however, this facade had begun to crumble. The old patterns of behavior began to reemerge. Actions became sluggish and tentative. Golden opportunities were repeatedly squandered by field commanders. Tactical maneuver and creativity vanished. Officers at division level and lower failed to continue employing the highly effective tactics that had brought such success during the first days of the war, reverting instead to simplistic practices that the Israelis defeated easily. Especially after the loss of the Jebel Ataqah signals-intercept site, confusion mounted throughout the chain of command as field officers increasingly misled their superiors about their actual situations. Combined-arms cooperation broke down completely, so much so that on 14 October Egyptian commanders failed to properly employ infantry to support their armored assaults despite having repeatedly witnessed the destruction their own combined-arms operations had inflicted on Israeli tanks when IDF armor had attacked without infantry support during the previous eight days.

STRATEGIC COMPETENCE

This remarkable contrast in performance reflects the importance of both the general staff's planning and the constant rehearsal of the initial Egyptian offensive. The depoliticization of the military enforced by Nasser and Sadat and their conscious effort to promote the most competent officers regardless of political sentiments resulted in very capable leadership at the senior levels of the Egyptian military. The plans drawn up by Isma'il 'Ali, Shazli, Gamasy, and their subordinates on the GHQ were superb. It is difficult to find fault with any part of the canal-crossing operation or the push to consolidate the bridgeheads. This is especially true when one recognizes the limited materials with which the Egyptian high command had to work.

Most other Egyptian strategic decisions were similarly commendable. First, the decision to stop the advance short of the passes clearly was the right one. This is demonstrated by the disastrous failure of the 14 October attack after Sadat overruled Isma'il 'Ali's plea not to advance beyond the initial bridgeheads. Second, when the Israelis launched their counteroffensive and the false reports from the field led Cairo to believe that this was an operation to roll up the Second Army positions along the east bank, the general staff put together a major counterattack to catch the Israelis between two powerful armored forces and seal the breach in their lines. Finally, when the Egyptian high command realized that the Israelis actually were across the canal in force and were threatening to completely outflank one or both of Egypt's field armies, both of the positions advanced in the general staff debate — withdraw armor from the east bank and counterattack or work for a political settlement — were entirely reasonable alternative courses of action. Isma'il 'Ali appears to have ultimately been correct that once the Israelis had broken out on the west bank, Egypt's best course of action was a diplomatic ceasefire. Although this led to some anxious moments in Cairo while the Third Army became surrounded and it was unclear that Israel would abide by the terms of the truce, in the end the gamble paid off, and the Israelis withdrew from the Sinai. Given Isma'il 'Ali's uncanny understanding of his troops, it seems reasonable to accept his opinion that a return of the armor to the west bank would have resulted in a collapse on the east bank as he predicted. Moreover, since the Israelis almost certainly would have defeated an Egyptian counterattack on the west bank just as they had repeatedly crushed armored attacks on the east bank, the Egyptians would have been worse off than they had been before 6 October if they had withdrawn their forces to fight the Israelis on the west bank. In short, Cairo appears to have opted for the better of two reasonable strategic choices.

TACTICAL INCOMPETENCE

The ineptness of Egyptian tactical operations after about 10 October indicates that Egypt's early successes were the product of the general staff's planning and the constant practicing of that plan rather than any newly developed skills among the junior-officer corps. The fact that combined-arms coordination disappeared after about 10 October and that Egyptian field commanders suddenly stopped employing the tactics that had given the Israelis fits for the previous five days indicates that the Egyptians had not internalized these concepts but were simply implementing well-rehearsed operations. The Egyptians displayed good combined-arms operations, clever tactical approaches, crisp timing, and effective maneuver at first because all of these elements had been written into the elaborate orders prepared by the general staff for every unit. These orders were transmitted to the army in the form of simple, straightforward tasks that did the work of integrating the combat arms without any conscious thought required on the part of those executing the plan. But no such planning had been possible for the offensive of 14 October or for the counterattacks on the east bank on 17 October and on the west bank thereafter, and Egyptian units reverted to form: attacking without combined-arms cooperation in direct frontal assaults that were quickly outflanked and smashed by the Israelis. Without the detailed plans of the general staff, the burden of command fell back on the company, battalion, brigade, and division commanders, who demonstrated that they had learned little or nothing from their constant training and earlier successes. In the words of one Israeli brigade commander, after about 10 October, "There was almost no improvisation at all" among Egyptian forces.[184]

In a similar vein, Egyptian artillery fire was deadly during the initial days of the war only because the batteries had had ample time to preregister their guns, detail the location of every Israeli prewar position, and draw up elaborate fire missions. However, after the success of the initial attack, when Israeli units were thrown back into new locations and Egyptian forces were fighting in unexpected areas, Egyptian artillery fire diminished to the point of uselessness. Also, once the Israelis brought up their own artillery, they began making short work of the Egyptians in counterbattery duels. After the Israelis broke out on the west bank, Egyptian artillery was hardly a factor at all.

Egypt likewise enjoyed more efficient information management than ever before during the first days of the war only to have things disintegrate into lies and confusion beginning on 14 October. Prior to that date, Egyptian commanders at all levels, and particularly the high command, appear to have had a good grasp of the situation of their own forces and a reasonable picture of the deployment and actions of Israeli forces. Two sources appear to have contributed to this efficient flow of information along the Egyptian chain of command. First, because the Egyptians were mostly winning before 14 October, there was less reason for field commanders to obfuscate to cover defeats. Second, the general staff's scheme to get information from the Israelis by monitoring their tactical communications appears to have been very successful. On 14 October this situation changed completely after the Israelis destroyed the main signals-intercept site on Jebel Ataqah and the Egyptians began losing tactical engagements. The destruction of their signals-intercept capability also deprived the Egyptians of their primary means of keeping track of Israeli forces because their own field commanders did not send out regular, aggressive patrols but passively waited for information to come to them from higher authority.

Starting on 14 October, the combat reports that began coming in from Egyptian tactical commanders spiraled off into fantasy. The constant deception as to the size of the Israeli force on the west bank is only the best known — and probably most damaging — example of this problem. Egyptian senior commanders were equally bad about keeping their subordinates abreast of important information. For example, an Egyptian pilot shot down on 19 October during the air battles over the Israeli bridgehead on the west bank and captured was shocked to find out that there were Israeli forces on the west side of the canal. As the Insight Team of the *London Sunday Times* concluded, Egyptian communications all along the chain of command were "perverted by lies."[185] They continued: "At the most basic level, the Egyptians simply did not tell each other what they were doing, radios and field telephones were rarely used. Junior commanders simply fought the Israelis as and when the Israelis presented themselves, and gave no priority at all to making combat reports."[186]

BRIGHT SPOTS IN EGYPTIAN MILITARY EFFECTIVENESS

There were, of course, areas in which the Egyptians performed well throughout the campaign with no real fall-off in effectiveness despite the 14 October watershed. One was the engineering effort, which was most impressive during the initial canal-crossing operation but continued to meet all demands thereafter. Egyptian combat engineers did a first-rate job keeping their Suez bridges open and building defensive positions for the forces on the east bank of the canal. Similarly, Egyptian logistics was more than adequate for the entire campaign. This too was a very creditable performance because the obstacle of the canal, the size of the invasion force, and the Israeli operations on the west bank all could easily have caused major snares in logistical distribution, but this was never the case. Even after the first few days, Egyptian forces never complained of a lack of supplies — until, of course, the IDF encircled the Third Army. However, this was a failing of the combat forces, not their logistical support services. Indeed, even the Israelis were impressed with the logistical effort.[187] Egyptian forces conducting static defense operations also did very well throughout the conflict. While counterattacks were often slow to develop and rarely skillful, the Egyptians had no problem building and defending fixed positions. The best example of this was the tremendous fight they waged to hold the Chinese Farm, but even at the end of the war, Egyptian troops were still beating back Israeli assaults on Ismailia and Suez City.

Unit cohesion and personal bravery also were high points for the Egyptians during the October War. Egyptian units hung together under extremely adverse conditions. Once again, the battle of the Chinese Farm is the most obvious illustration of this point. The Egyptians were surprised and outflanked by the Israelis — so much so that Israeli tanks were in the 16th Infantry Division's headquarters compound when they started firing — yet the Egyptians recovered and eventually fought the Israelis to a standstill. Egyptian soldiers consistently sacrificed themselves for the sake of their comrades and their missions. Even by 20–24 October, when the Israelis had broken out and were running amuck on the west bank, they still encountered pockets of Egyptian troops that fought hard and had to be physically overcome even after their positions had long since been rendered untenable by flanking maneuvers. Overall, there were relatively few instances when Egyptian units disintegrated in combat, and most of these came toward the end of the war as Adan and Magen's ugdot swept aside the Egyptian forces on the west bank and eventually cut off the Third Army. At that point, units of Third Army began falling apart little by little, as did some units of the mechanized and armored divisions fighting to hold back the Israeli advance.

OVERALL ASSESSMENT

Although the Egyptians continue to tout the October War as a great victory, in truth their successes were modest and their failures equal or greater than their achievements. The canal crossing and consolidation of the bridgeheads were exceptionally well conceived, well planned, and very competently executed. However, this was hardly the invasion of Normandy. Indeed, what is noteworthy is the amount of effort required to pull off these attacks — operations that never penetrated more than ten or fifteen kilometers into the Sinai. The labor required of the Egyptian General Staff is reminiscent of the planning of such major World War II offensives as the German invasions of France and Russia or the Allied invasion of France and the breakout from Normandy, while the training imposed on Egyptian troops probably was without parallel in modern history. Nevertheless, the successes the Egyptians squeezed from this labor were negligible compared to the success of those German and Allied offensives. As Trevor Dupuy and others have argued, given the enormous advantages the Egyptians enjoyed in force ratios and strategic surprise, they should have been expected to do far better than they did in their initial offensive.[188] Moreover, by 10 October the Egyptians had shot their bolt, and without the detailed operational plans of the general staff, Egyptian forces proved to be as ineffective as in the past.

Thus, the great lesson of the October War was the tremendous restrictions imposed on Egyptian military operations by the limitations of Egyptian tactical formations. While Egypt's generalship may not have been perfect, it was well above average. Generals Isma'il 'Ali and Gamasy, the two field army commanders — Wasil and Ma'mun — and the other members of the general staff performed very well throughout the war. Even though General Shazli acted as if he were commanding a different military, Isma'il 'Ali consistently minimized his influence on Egyptian operations. This level of performance should have produced greater accomplishments, but it did not because the GHQ had few useful tools to work with.

When comparing Egyptian military effectiveness in 1967 and 1973, what stands out is that it was this improvement in Egyptian strategic leadership that was responsible for the improvement in Egyptian fortunes on the battlefield. However, it required a *major* improvement in Egyptian strategic leadership to produce only a *modest* improvement in battlefield fortunes. The great weight holding Egypt back from greater success in 1973 was the ineffectiveness of Egyptian tactical formations resulting from the limitations of Egypt's junior officer corps. This problem was clearly demonstrated in the sudden reversal in Egyptian effectiveness between the first four days of the offensive and the rest of the war. As long as Egyptian tactical formations could follow the superb plans of the general staff they did well, but as soon as those plans ran out and the direction of operations devolved to the tactical commanders, Egyptian operations quickly returned to previous patterns of incompetence.

Border Clashes with Libya, 1977

Although Cairo's forces were ultimately defeated, the shock that the initial Egyptian successes during the October War wrought on the Israeli psyche, coupled with Sadat's deft diplomatic maneuvering to produce a ceasefire before the Israelis had erased all of the gains of 6–10 October, allowed him to pull victory at the bargaining table from the jaws of battlefield defeat. As Sadat had hoped, the October War forced Israel to negotiate the return of the Sinai in return for peace. The ceasefire and disengagement talks that ended the war grew eventually into peace negotiations between Cairo and Jerusalem.

But Sadat's success in wringing political victory from the military defeat of the October War nearly embroiled Egypt in another war, this time with Libya. The mercurial Libyan strongman, Col. Muammar al-Qadhafi, branded Sadat's peacemaking a betrayal of the Arab cause. In trying to dissuade Sadat from negotiating with Israel, Qadhafi began with rhetorical broadsides and then quickly climbed the escalatory ladder to support for Egyptian dissidents — including the Islamic fundamentalists of the Muslim Brotherhood — to arming and training Egyptian insurgents, to actively plotting to assassinate Sadat. Finally, in early 1976, Qadhafi began using his conventional military forces to harass Cairo's units along their common border. Egypt responded in kind, supporting Libyan dissidents, aiding Chadian forces opposed to Libya, possibly encouraging would-be assassins of Qadhafi, and skirmishing with the Libyans along the border.

Sadat had long considered Qadhafi unstable and irritating, and he chafed under the Libyan provocations. When his own efforts to oust Qadhafi through covert action bore no fruit, he began to contemplate an overt military move. Consequently, in the summer of 1976, in response to Libya's provocations along the border, Sadat suddenly moved two Egyptian mechanized divisions from the Suez and Nile Delta areas to the Libyan border and stationed an additional 80 combat aircraft, including several squadrons of its newest MiG-23s, to Marsa Matruh Airbase, Egypt's westernmost airfield. Previously, Egypt had maintained only lightly armed border guards along the frontier with Libya, and this sudden increase of forces alarmed the Libyans. The 25,000–30,000 Egyptians headed toward the Libyan border were roughly the size of Tripoli's entire army at the time. Nevertheless, Qadhafi dispatched 3,000–5,000 of his own troops with 150 tanks to the border to meet the Egyptian build-up. For a brief period there was a tense stand-off, and it appeared Egypt was about to invade Libya. However, after several weeks the Egyptians still had not made a move, and the Libyans and others began to believe that Cairo would not attack. Most observers argued that Sadat had chosen not to invade because a war could only further burden Egypt's already hobbled economy and deepen its estrangement both from the USSR and the Persian Gulf oil monarchies, who publicly condemned Sadat's flirtations with the United States and Israel. However, in retrospect it appears more likely that Sadat refrained from attacking Libya because the Egyptian military was unprepared for it. Several well-informed diplomatic sources have argued that Sadat was determined to march on Tripoli to oust Qadhafi.[189] Thus, it seems that he was only prevented from attacking by the unpreparedness of his army. The Egyptian military had neither planned nor rehearsed a major offensive against Libya, and they lacked the logistical, transportation, and communications infrastructure in the western desert to support a full-scale invasion. The Egyptian General Staff apparently began work on contingency plans for a full-scale assault into Libya at that time.

The sudden build-up of large Egyptian forces along his frontier in 1976 had little discernible effect on Qadhafi. Indeed, he appears to have taken Egypt's failure to attack as a sign of weakness, and so Tripoli increased its pressure — rhetorical, subversive, and martial — on Egypt. Meanwhile, the Egyptians continued to enhance their combat forces and logistical stockpiles near Libya while the general staff honed its plan for an invasion. By the spring of 1977, the Soviets either received information from their own intelligence sources in Egypt that Sadat intended to invade Libya or became convinced from watching the Egyptian preparations in the western desert that Cairo was serious this time. Either way, in May 1977 the Russians warned Libya and other friendly Arab regimes that they had reliable evidence that the Egyptians were planning a full-scale invasion of Libya. The Libyans ignored these warnings, leaving most of their armed forces at low levels of readiness while continuing crossborder raids and artillery duels with the Egyptians. Heavy skirmishes occurred on 12 and 16 July 1977, leading to a four-hour firefight between battalion-sized forces on 19 July 1977. Two days later, Egypt attacked.

The Balance of Forces

Sadat had continued to reinforce his western border after the false-start of the previous summer, and when he finally attacked had developed a considerable advantage. In early July 1977, the two mechanized divisions that had redeployed there in 1976 were now at full strength, dug in, and ready for action. The Egyptians had reinforced these formations with several battalions of commandos, extra combat-support units, and other forces. Moreover, the Egyptians had planned and prepared for the rapid movement of a third heavy division from the Cairo area as well as additional commando battalions, and in the four days of clashes in 1977, they were able to quickly increase their ground strength facing the Libyans to over 40,000 troops in three heavy divisions and twelve commando battalions. To challenge these forces, in July 1977, the entire Libyan army consisted of only 32,000 men.

Moreover, Tripoli had only seven or eight battalions (roughly 5,000 troops) organized into three brigade-sized formations to defend against an Egyptian attack.[190]

Egypt had a number of other advantages over Libya. First, all of the Egyptian formations had participated in the October War just four years before and, despite retirements and demobilization, all (especially the elite commando battalions) had large numbers of veterans who had seen combat against the Israelis. By contrast, none of the Libyan ground forces had had any real experience of battle. Second, although the Egyptians had serious problems both in manning their weapons with technically skilled personnel and maintaining their equipment on a consistent basis, Cairo's problems paled beside those of Tripoli. For example, in 1977 Libya had trained crews for only about 200–300 tanks and no more than 150 trained pilots for its air force. Libyan maintenance practices were appalling and their units — even elite formations — rarely had operational readiness rates in excess of 50 percent.

The Egyptians also had a considerable advantage from the high degree of professionalism still evident among the officer corps. The Egyptian armed forces still enjoyed the various practices that had allowed it to improve so considerably prior to the October War: officers were chosen largely for their competence rather than political connections, the military was focused entirely on preparing for conventional operations against foreign armies, units trained for war with great purpose, and the armed forces were led by a superb group of generals and staff officers in the GHQ. On the other side, the Libyan military was a thoroughly politicized and unprofessional lot. Qadhafi refused to allow standing formations larger than battalions; he placed loyalists in key command billets regardless of their actual qualifications; he frequently and suddenly rotated senior officers to prevent them from developing a rapport with the troops under their command; and he inserted informants and "people's commissars" into the military to keep an eye on the army. Perhaps the one thing the Libyan military had going for it was that morale among its forces was high because the troops believed that the Egyptians had betrayed all of the Arab world by seeking peace with Israel. In contrast, Egyptian morale was uneven: many viewed the Libyans as Arab brothers and considered fighting them as a distressing outgrowth of Sadat's decision to make peace with the Zionist enemy.

Course of Operations

On 21 July Sadat got the provocation he had been looking for. Libyan forces conducted another battalion-sized harassing raid against the Egyptian border town of as-Sallum near the Mediterranean coast similar to the previous operation on 19 July. The Libyan 9th Tank Battalion stumbled into an ambush there, which triggered a well-planned and well-rehearsed counterattack by at least one Egyptian mechanized division. The Egyptians inflicted 50 percent casualties on the 9th Battalion before it stumbled back across the border. A small number of Libyan Mirages also took part in the raid, bombing several nearby Egyptians villages, but they did little damage; the Egyptians claimed to have shot two down with AAA.

After only a few hours to regroup, the Egyptians launched their coun-teroffensive. They began with airstrikes by Su-20s and MiG-21s against Libya's Gamal 'Abd al-Nasser Airbase at al-Adam, the main interceptor field in eastern Libya. The Egyptians caught the Libyans completely by surprise with all of their Mirages and MiGs parked out in the open. But the EAF botched the raid, causing almost no damage to the prostrate Libyans. The Egyptians hit a few radars but do not appear to have inflicted more than minor damage on a few of the parked jets. Then, an Egyptian mecha-nized force, possibly as large as two full divisions, drove into Libya along the coast toward the town of Musa'ad. Libyan forces mostly fled in front of the Egyptians, although there were some desultory tank battles. The opera-tion seems to have been just a reconnaissance-in-force to determine the extent of the Libyan defenses, and at the end of the day the Egyptians retired back across the border, having penetrated fifteen miles into Libya and destroyed around 60 Libyan tanks and APCs in the battles at as-Sallum and Musa'ad.[191]

The next two days saw heavy exchanges across the border but little decisive action. Libyan and Egyptian artillery batteries traded fire without causing much damage. The Libyan Air Force conducted very modest raids (probably no more than 10–20 sorties total) against the Egyptian mecha-nized formations continuing to mass around as-Sallum. The Egyptians claimed to have shot down two Libyan fighters, while Tripoli admitted to the loss of the jets but claimed that one had been shot down by Libyan AAA gunners and the other had crashed into the ground on a reconnaissance mission. Meanwhile, the EAF again struck at Nasser and al-Kufrah Airbases and other Libyan towns and military bases in the border area. Against Nasser Airbase, the Egyptians conducted much larger strikes (three squad-rons of Su-20s and MiGs were involved) but again succeeded in doing only light damage to Libyan aircraft, radars, and ground installations — even though the Libyans still had not bothered to disperse or otherwise protect their aircraft after the raids on the twenty-first. Egyptian jets also con-ducted low-level, high-speed passes over villages throughout eastern Libya as a not-so-subtle display of their freedom to operate in Libyan airspace. Meanwhile, the Egyptian commando battalions began conducting airborne raids against Libyan radar sites, terrorist camps, and military facilities at al-Kufrah Oasis, al-Jaghbub Oasis, al-Adam, Tobruk, and other locations along the border.

On 24 July the Egyptians again escalated the fighting, probably as the opening of their planned invasion. First, they launched the largest raid to date against Nasser Airbase. This time, Egyptian aircraft attacked in concert with helicopter-borne Egyptian commandos. Despite the constant Egyptian attacks over three days, the Libyans had still not dispersed, removed, concealed, or otherwise protected the aircraft at the base. This time, the Egyptians were somewhat more successful, cratering the runway, destroying several armored vehicles and 6–12 Libyan Mirages on the ground, obliterating several early-warning radars, and damaging several SAM sites. However, the Libyans did shoot down at least two Egyptian Su-20s with AAA. The Egyptians also struck al-Kufrah Airbase once again but did little significant damage. Helicopter-borne raids by Egyptian commandos did considerable damage to Libyan forward logistics depots at al-Jaghbub and al-Adam.

Despite the wider scope and greater success of Egyptian operations on 24 July, at the end of the day — while Egyptian commandos were still in action at al-Jaghbub — President Sadat unexpectedly announced an immediate ceasefire. Most outside observers found this perplexing, for Egyptian officials had privately been telling diplomats in Cairo since the first day of the fighting that Egypt intended to conduct a full-scale invasion of Libya to oust Qadhafi.[192] According to a number of diplomatic sources, however, the United States had weighed in heavily with the Egyptian government to prevent an invasion. The Americans knew that the Egyptians intended to drive into Libya in force to try to unseat Qadhafi — probably because Cairo warned the U.S. government that this was its intention, believing that Washington would be equally pleased to see him gone. However, the Americans objected strenuously. Apparently, the U.S. military and intelligence communities had concluded that, based on Egyptian performance during the October War and the far more limited logistical infrastructure in Egypt's western desert, that an Egyptian invasion stood a real risk of failing. They feared that an Egyptian invasion would fall flat on its face, not because the Egyptians could not defeat the Libyans but because Egyptian tactical and logistical capabilities were inadequate to sustain an advance over the 1,000 kilometers from the Libyan border to Tripoli. While they expected the Egyptians to defeat Libyan forces along the border, they seriously doubted that Cairo could adequately direct and supply its forces for the weeks it would take to reach Tripoli, given how badly Egyptian operations ground to a halt after only four days of fighting the Israelis. Moreover, they feared that even if the Egyptians were able to drive several hundred kilometers, say to Benghazi in Cyrenaica, this might not be enough to oust Qadhafi, and the Egyptians would be forced to withdraw in humiliation. Washington regarded this prospect as potentially disastrous: Sadat was crucial to the budding peace between Egypt and Israel, and his hold on power and ability to make peace with the Israelis were derived from the glory he had won in the "victory" of October 1973. Thus, the Americans feared that a failed Egyptian invasion of Libya could undermine Sadat's freedom of action or even lead to his downfall. According to the same diplomatic sources, Washington consequently exerted tremendous diplomatic pressure on Sadat not to continue with his planned invasion. As a result, Egypt's attacks ceased as suddenly and unexpectedly as they had begun.[193]

Some residual fighting between Egyptian commandos and Libyan forces continued over the next two days as the Egyptians pulled back across the border, but Sadat's declaration effectively ended the conflict. Although there was never a formal ceasefire, armistice, or peace treaty, the two sides informally held to a truce and all combat operations halted. Eventually, both sides reduced their military forces along the border, for the limited infrastructure in the area made it difficult for either side to maintain such large formations in the area for long periods of time. All told, the Libyans lost at least ten and possibly as many as twenty Mirages, nearly all of which were destroyed on the ground, in addition to thirty tanks, thirty APCs, and 400 dead and wounded. The Libyans had also sustained minor damage to some of their main eastern airfields and more substantial damage to their air defense network along the Egyptian border. For their part, the Egyptians probably lost as many as four aircraft and took about 100 casualties.[194]

The Gulf War, 1990–91

Ultimately, the political fallout from the October War would have far-reaching consequences for the Egyptian military. Despite Libyan protests, Egypt made peace with Israel in 1978 and recovered the Sinai. At that time, Cairo also severed its twenty-year relationship with the USSR and turned to the United States for military aid, training, and equipment. Peace with Israel made possible numerous changes in Egypt's military posture. For instance, the reduced sense of threat allowed Cairo to begin using the army as a sort of social-welfare program, inducting far more young men than necessary to keep civilian unemployment under control. Most of the college graduates in the armed forces during the October War were demobilized and the caliber of Egyptian military manpower declined thereafter. By the late 1980s, the vast bulk of Egyptian conscripts were uneducated *fellahin*, most of whom had virtually no exposure to sophisticated machinery. The result of these trends was that Egyptian military manpower was even less capable than in the past. U.S. Department of Defense officials and U.S. military officers who have worked in Egypt and trained with the Egyptian armed forces unanimously agree that Egyptian enlisted personnel are incapable of performing military tasks requiring the use of equipment more sophisticated than a rifle or a shovel. Similarly, while most Egyptian junior officers are able to perform tasks reserved for enlisted personnel in the West, they are unable to perform the work normally assigned to junior officers in Western armies. One Defense official with experience in the Middle East, East Asia, and Europe commented that in Egypt he invariably worked with colonels and brigadiers on tasks that normally employed sergeants, lieutenants, and captains in Western and East Asian militaries.[195]

Probably the greatest change for the Egyptian armed forces after Camp David was the abandonment of Soviet equipment, organization, and practices. Beginning in 1978, Egypt began purchasing large quantities of American military equipment and procuring American military assistance in reorganizing and reforming their armed forces. Eventually, the United States became Egypt's primary security benefactor and undertook a complete overhaul of Egyptian forces. The Egyptians had so much Soviet equipment — and American equipment was so expensive — that they could not simply junk all of their older hardware and adopt an American force structure, although Soviet equipment increasingly was shunted off onto secondrate formations. Large numbers of U.S. military advisers went to Egypt to provide weapons instruction and operational training, and Egyptian officers began attending U.S. training courses in droves. By the mid-1980s, the core of the Egyptian military had shed the Soviet practices they had acquired between 1955 and 1973.

After the October War, Sadat and then Mubarak both attempted to maintain the professionalism that had been achieved before the war, though with mixed results. Cairo's desire to have a force capable of fighting foreign adversaries beyond Egypt's borders led to the retention of many measures adopted in the wake of the Six Day War. However, although Cairo still emphasized merit over loyalty to the regime, in recent years political connections have increasingly determined who holds senior command billets in the armed forces. U.S. Defense officials working in Egypt and U.S. military officers who have served there report that advancement more often goes to those with political clout—especially those with close ties to Pres. Husni Mubarak—rather than to competence or experience.[196] Also, knowledge is seen as power, and controlling information is seen as increasing an individual's power. U.S. Defense officials note that in the higher echelons of the chain of command, information is jealously guarded among the senior officers in an effort to secure advantages over one another.[197]

Egyptian Operations in Desert Storm, 1990–91

Egyptian participation in the Gulf War was limited but still significant. The nation initially deployed forces to Saudi Arabia as part of Operation Desert Shield, the defense of the kingdom against a feared Iraqi invasion. Eventually, Cairo agreed to participate in Operation Desert Storm, the offensive into Kuwait and southern Iraq to drive the Iraqis from Kuwait. Egypt sent the second-largest Arab contingent to the war effort and one of the largest contingents overall. Cairo dispatched two divisions—the 3d Mechanized and 4th Armored—as well as the 20th Commando Regiment (brigade), an airborne brigade, and supporting units. All of these formations had been converted over to American equipment and doctrine and were specifically sent because they were considered the best in the Egyptian army. All told, the Egyptian force consisted of over 40,000 troops and about 400 tanks.[198]

The Egyptians were made the centerpiece of the Joint Forces Command–North (JFC–N). The JFC–N was one of two major Arab formations in Desert Storm. (The other was the Joint Forces Command–East, centered on Saudi, Kuwaiti, and Qatari forces that operated along the coast of Kuwait.) In addition to the Egyptians, the JFC–N included two Saudi heavy brigades, two Kuwaiti brigades, a Syrian armored division, and a Syrian commando brigade. Nevertheless, the Egyptians were considered the heart of the JFC–N not only because they had the largest force but also because U.S. military planners expected them to be the most capable and reliable. There was great uncertainty as to whether the Syrians would participate in the offensive at all, and because their Soviet equipment was virtually identical to that of the Iraqis, they were to be kept in reserve to avoid friendly fire problems. The Saudis and Kuwaitis were simply not considered serious combat units by the U.S. personnel assigned to them. Thus, planners decided that the Egyptian 3d Mechanized Division would spearhead the attack, the 4th Armored Division would serve as an exploitation force, the Kuwaiti and Saudi units would conduct supporting attacks on the Egyptians' right flank, and the Syrians would serve as a corps reserve to be called upon only if the other units encountered serious problems. Although U.S. military planners had more confidence in the Egyptians than other Arab contingents of the multinational force, this was entirely relative. In fact, U.S. Central Command (CENTCOM) held the U.S. 1st Cavalry (Armored) Division in theater reserve behind the JFC–N attack so a heavy U.S. force would be available to rescue the JFC–N if they ran into trouble.[199]

CENTCOM assigned the sector between the U.S. Marine Corps' I Marine Expeditionary Force (I MEF) and the U.S. Army's VII Corps to the JFC–N. The I MEF was the primary diversionary force, tasked with attacking into the "heel" of southeastern Kuwait to draw Iraqi attention and reserves from the main Coalition effort. The U.S. VII Corps would be the main effort of the offensive and would attack into southern Iraq west of Kuwait and then turn east to crush the Iraqi Republican Guard. The JFC–N, sandwiched between these two powerful American forces, was given western Kuwait as its operational sector and assigned the task of penetrating into Kuwait itself and then turning east to cut off an Iraqi retreat from southeastern Kuwait by seizing the important al-Basrah–al-Jahrah highway, along which Iraqi forces in southern Kuwait had to travel to escape. An important aspect of the JFC–N's mission was to protect the flanks of the two American forces from a counterattack by Iraqi armor deployed in central Kuwait. Thus, CENTCOM also felt it necessary to have the 1st Cavalry Division available to prevent an Iraqi counterattack into the flanks of the I MEF or VII Corps if the JFC–N were defeated.

The JFC–N attack was originally slated to kick-off at first light on the second day of the ground war, 25 February 1991. However, the I MEF offensive into southeastern Kuwait went so well that the CENTCOM commander, Gen. H. Norman Schwarzkopf, decided to advance the timing of both the U.S. VII Corps attack and the JFC–N attack. Of all the various units that were affected by this decision, only the Egyptian commander of the JFC–N said that he could not comply. General Schwarzkopf did his best to persuade, cajole, and even threaten the Egyptians to get them to move up the start time, but they simply refused. Eventually, the general had to have Cairo order the Egyptian commander to advance the launch of his attack, but even then the Egyptians were not able to attack until 3:00 P.M., well after CENTCOM's preferred time.[200]

When the Egyptians finally did get moving, their operations were mediocre, and they advanced at a glacial pace against almost no Iraqi resistance. They attacked into the sectors of the Iraqi 20th and 30th Infantry Divisions, both of which had been heavily depleted by desertions during the six-week Coalition air campaign. In addition, these units had been repeatedly worked over by Coalition strike aircraft, especially A-10 attack planes, which had destroyed most of their supporting armor and artillery. The U.S. deputy theater commander, Gen. Calvin Waller, remarked in typically colorful fashion, "what the Egyptians are facing, two sick prostitutes could handle."[201] The Egyptians' mission for the first day was to breach the Iraqi defensive lines and seize the al-Abraq barracks about twenty miles into Kuwait. However, when the Egyptians reached the flame trenches the Iraqis had dug in front of their defense lines, the Iraqis lit the trenches. The Egyptians stopped, apparently having not thought through the problem of how to cross flaming trenches. Rather than improvising a solution on the spot, they simply sat and waited for the fires to burn out—which took ten hours. By the end of the first day, they had not even crossed the flame trench, let alone breached the main Iraqi defensive lines.

On the second day, the Iraqi units in front of the Egyptians began deserting en masse, a process that accelerated even further when Baghdad announced a general retreat from Kuwait late that day. The Egyptians kicked off their main attack at 7 o'clock that morning, led by the 3d Mechanized Division. Because of the disintegration and retreat of the Iraqi forces in their sector, the Egyptians encountered almost no resistance in penetrating the Iraqi defensive lines. Egyptian artillery unleashed a massive barrage to cover the advance, but this did little damage since the Egyptians insisted on firing on locations that U.S. intelligence revealed the Iraqis had already abandoned. Because these targets were in the Egyptian artillery fire plan, however, the battery commanders insisted on hitting them. Soon after getting underway, the 3d Mechanized Division came under desultory fire from a couple of Iraqi artillery batteries. Although, as a U.S. liaison officer later reported, "at no time did [the Iraqi artillery fire] ever jeopardize the attack," the Egyptians again halted.[202] They requested U.S. air support, but inclement weather prevented this. When their American advisors suggested they silence the Iraqis with counterbattery fire, the Egyptian officers refused: their artillery had exceeded its ammunition expenditure allocation for the breaching operation and would not allocate any additional rounds to silence the Iraqi artillery. So the Egyptians decided to stop and simply wait until the Iraqis stopped firing, which they did around 10:00 A.M.

When the Egyptians finally got going again, the remaining Iraqi infantry manning the frontline defenses mostly either fled or surrendered. Nevertheless, the Egyptians moved painfully slowly in breaching the essentially undefended Iraqi fortifications. As late as 1:00 P.M., they still had not finished their breaching operations, causing great distress among CENTCOM personnel who wanted the Egyptians to move quicker to cut off the Iraqi withdrawal from southern Kuwait. An Arab journalist accompanying the Egyptians reported that they encountered few Iraqi tanks of any kind for the first two days of the ground war. Nevertheless, they maintained their creeping advance and would not speed up their movements to try to catch the Iraqi forces as they retreated. Eventually, CENTCOM became so concerned about the gap opening up between the rapidly advancing Marines and the floundering Egyptians that they reoriented several American units to cover the I MEF flank.

By the morning of the third day of the ground war, the Egyptians still had not taken their first day's objective of al-Abraq, and CENTCOM ordered them to forego al-Abraq and instead turn east and move to al-Jahrah immediately. Once again, the Egyptian command refused to deviate from their plan unless they received a formal order from the Coalition political leadership. When confirmation of the CENTCOM orders finally arrived, the Egyptians swung part of the force east to creep toward al-Jahrah, but CENTCOM found it necessary to give this task instead to the U.S. Army's 1st Armored "Tiger" Brigade of the 2d Armored Division because the Egyptians were moving so slowly. Meanwhile, officials decided that both Arab commands would enter Kuwait City together as a show of Arab solidarity. By 26 February, the Iraqis had retreated from Kuwait City and the JFC-E was sitting south of the city, waiting to make its triumphal entry, but the JFC-N was nowhere near the capital. Ultimately, selected units of the JFC-N were simply sent to Kuwait City to accompany the JFC-E, while the rest of the Arab force plodded on. However, the Egyptian commander again objected. He had no specific orders to send units to enter Kuwait City, and he refused to comply until Schwarzkopf reached Mubarak himself and had the president order the Egyptian commander to do so. By the end of the war, the Egyptians had taken nearly a hundred casualties but had little to show for the effort.[203]

Egyptian Military Effectiveness 1973-91

The Gulf War revealed what U.S. military personnel had privately admitted for years: that despite fifteen years of American aid, advice, and training, Egyptian military effectiveness had improved little, if any, since the Arab-Israeli wars. While numerous Westerners who have had contact with the Egyptian military claim that most of Cairo's generals are as competent as their U.S., Russian, or Israeli counterparts, tactical performance remains extremely limited.

Egyptian junior officers still tend to show little innovation and initiative in combat. The halting movement of Egyptian units during the Gulf War, their unwillingness to adapt to opportunities presented by the course of battle, and their inability to solve unforeseen tactical problems were indistinguishable from the problems Egyptian units suffered in 1948–73. Egyptian combat operations in the Gulf War and in training exercises have been set-piece operations in both offensive and defensive warfare. According to one U.S. military officer very familiar with the Egyptian military, "The Egyptians would make the simple complicated; something had to be done the way it was always done because they were so inflexible."[204] Overcentralization remains the rule throughout the Egyptian armed forces. One Western military officer observed, "There are few observable signs of real change in the centralized command and control system in either the Army or the Air Force" despite constant U.S. efforts to encourage the Egyptians to decentralize authority.[205] Other sources have commented that virtually all decisions must be made by a general officer, and it is nearly impossible to reverse a decision, even when it is no longer applicable because of changed circumstances — such as the insistence on executing every preplanned artillery fire mission during Desert Storm even when positions were known to be deserted. At times, initiative among junior officers is purposely suppressed, but few tactical commanders display the willingness or ability to act aggressively whenever they are delegated decision-making authority. One U.S. military officer with extensive knowledge of the Egyptian armed forces remarked, "the lower you get in the chain of command the less initiative and creativity you see," while a U.S. Defense official who has worked with the Egyptian military stated simply, "there is no initiative at all" among lower echelons of the armed forces.[206]

Egyptian forces continue to show little understanding of combined-arms operations. In most military exercises there remains a complete separation of the combat arms and little effort to teach their proper integration. Even the most sensationalist Israeli analyses of the Egyptian military have conceded that rather than improving their ability to integrate air and ground forces, the Egyptians actually may be regressing farther from this.[207] According to U.S. military officers and Defense officials familiar with the Egyptian military, training rarely takes place above the battalion level, and infantry, armor, and artillery almost never train together. These same officials unanimously aver that Egyptian infantrymen have little or no understanding of armor operations and vice versa.[208] American personnel suggest that part of this problem may be related to a persistent inability or unwillingness to integrate details into a coherent whole. For example, one U.S. official remarked that tasks are kept so discrete that Egyptian personnel rarely see how they relate to the functioning of an entire machine or unit: "This guy does not *repair* tanks, he puts *this part* on to a tank and that's all he knows how to do."[209] Similarly, Egyptian training continues to focus on set-piece operations with little emphasis on maneuver to gain an advantage over an opponent. This tendency was displayed in the Gulf War when Egyptian armor formations charged ahead in frontal assaults rather than attempting to outflank or envelop Iraqi defensive positions.

As was the case in 1973, Egyptian operations are scripted in minute detail, even for routine training missions, and no deviation is allowed. One U.S. military officer quipped, "Egyptian exercises are totally canned: they aren't for training, they're for show."[210] Another U.S. officer remarked, "The Egyptians put an inordinate effort into tremendously detailed planning, and if the situation changes, don't expect the plan to change: they're sticking with the plan."[211] The efforts of American advisers and training personnel to convince the Egyptians to improvise operations or to issue only broad guidelines and allow subordinates to fill in the details regularly fall on deaf ears. Even the operations and training flights of the elite F-16 squadrons are completely scripted. As one U.S. Defense official observed, "They know where to turn, and where to pretend to fire munitions, and who is going to win" before a training flight even begins.[212] Moreover, the Egyptian pilots get extremely upset when someone does something he is not supposed to do. For this reason there apparently is widespread dislike of joint-training exercises with U.S. forces because the Americans constantly and deliberately improvise rather than stick to an agreed-upon script. As another example, the Egyptians were very impressed with American all-arms coordination, maneuver warfare, and the ability of U.S. forces to carry the battle throughout the depth of the enemy's defense during the Gulf War. However, they argued that the best way to do this is with a highly detailed operational plan that determines objectives, assigns maneuvers to the forces, allocates all air missions beforehand, and details the administrative and logistical support at all levels. In other words, they appear willing to accept U.S. AirLand Battle doctrine, but only if it is conducted in a rigid, scripted, Egyptian fashion.

Manipulation of information throughout the chain of command also remains a major problem. During Operation Desert Storm, CENTCOM assigned U.S. personnel to all Arab Coalition forces before the start of the ground war for the specific purpose of ensuring that what the Arab units reported was actually happening. Regardless of the presence of U.S. military personnel or journalists, Egyptian units still consistently reported fierce battles even though they actually encountered very little resistance at all.[213] U.S. military personnel assigned as liaison to the Egyptian corps reported a pronounced "lack of inter-staff coordination and information sharing within the Egyptian corps staff."[214] Egyptian forces continue to suffer from fabricated reporting — sometimes even directed by superiors to disguise problems from higher echelons. U.S. military officers and Defense officials report that most senior Egyptian military commanders have little idea what is going on in their subordinate commands because they are constantly misled. These same personnel also report that compartmental-ization in Egypt is so severe that, before even the most minor decisions can be taken, all officers with knowledge bearing on the issue must be brought together because no one individual has sufficient knowledge of the entire situation to make an appropriate decision on his own.[215]

Maintenance continues to be another source of problems for the Egyp-tians. U.S. personnel unanimously observe that Egyptian mechanics daily do a remarkable job patching up the more simple and rugged pieces of machinery to make them work well enough to serve their function. How-ever, they have little capacity to handle more sophisticated machinery or more complicated tasks, nor do most Egyptian military personnel under-stand the functioning of their equipment well enough to fix and maintain it properly. For example, Egypt required a large U.S. presence for many years after receiving the F-4E Phantom II, and as late as 1989 its operational readiness rates for the aircraft were still low. In the mid-1980s, the Egyp-tians decided that they could handle the F-4s on their own and canceled the U.S. maintenance contracts for these aircraft. However, the Phan-tom squadrons immediately went "down the tubes" because the Egyptians rarely performed preventive maintenance and could not make proper re-pairs. Consequently, Cairo had to reverse itself and still must have depot-level maintenance performed in the United States.[216] The Egyptians have encountered similar problems with the F-16.

As this last point suggests, many of Egypt's most debilitating problems remain in the air force. The EAF has probably received the most extensive and constant attention from U.S. advisers, it has the most advanced U.S. equipment (including F-16 fighters), and large numbers of Egyptian pilots have had at least some U.S. training. Nevertheless, the EAF remains mori-bund. F-4 pilots generally do not like to fly their planes because they have difficulty operating and maintaining the aircraft and an accident would look bad for the unit. More remarkable still, despite American pleading, they usually succeed in avoiding flying. According to U.S. Defense personnel, virtually none of the Egyptian pilots use the avionics on their U.S.-built aircraft — even the F-16 pilots. They report that even if the radar is on while they are in the air (which is not always the case), the pilots rely on visual sighting and ignore it. Fortunately for them, because exercises are scripted, there is no reason to use the radar or other avionics: every pilot knows exactly where everyone else will be, how they will maneuver, and who will "win."[217] As one U.S. military official put it, "They fly our planes and use our tactics, but you'd never know it."[218] Some U.S. military personnel suspect that Cairo chose not to send any air force units to participate in the Gulf War for fear they would do poorly in combat.

Overall, the changes of the 1980s can be said to have done little to improve Egyptian military effectiveness. Despite abandoning the Soviet model of operations and adopting the American style, Egyptian forces continued to manifest the same patterns of strengths and weaknesses they displayed at the height of their reliance on the Soviets. Indeed, some U.S. personnel continue to mistakenly ascribe Egyptian problems to things they learned from the Russians. Perhaps more accurately, one U.S. military officer highly familiar with the Egyptian military argued, "all that the Russians did was to add science to what the Egyptians have always done anyway."[219] Indeed, Egyptian military effectiveness has resisted change to a remarkable degree throughout the period 1948–91.

Summary: Egyptian Military Effectiveness 1948–91

Egyptian forces demonstrated remarkably persistent patterns of behavior in combat between 1948 and 1991. This is particularly true at the tactical level, where Egyptian formations performed in an almost identical fashion in virtually every war they fought. Their junior officers consistently demonstrated an unwillingness to maneuver, innovate, improvise, take initiative, or act independently. Egypt's forces have suffered from the constant manipulation of information and an inattention to intelligence gathering and objective analysis. The military's command structure has remained heavily centralized, with all decisions referred to the highest levels of authority, contributing to a persistent inability of Egyptian forces to maintain a fast tempo of operations. Egyptian forces have shown little ability to conduct armor, artillery, air-to-air, or air-to-ground operations. Moreover, their combined-arms operations have regularly been very poor, with the important exception of the first four days of the October War. Categories of military effectiveness related to handling military equipment were also areas of weakness for the Egyptians; their units had little maintenance capability, required long periods of time to assimilate new weapons, and rarely were able to take full advantage of the capabilities of their equipment.

The Egyptians also have shown areas of consistently competent performance. The bravery of the individual soldier is beyond question. Similarly, unit cohesion has been inconsistent, though tending more toward the positive side of the spectrum. In general, one is struck by the fact that Egyptian forces regularly have fought tenaciously in impossible situations. On many occasions units fought on long after they had been encircled or otherwise defeated until they were physically overcome in hand-to-hand combat. Egyptian logistics and combat engineering were also areas of real strength.

Egyptian strategic leadership fluctuated considerably during this period. On the one hand, there was the dismal performance turned in by Field Marshal 'Amr and his cronies during the Six Day War. On the other hand, there was the highly commendable direction of the War of Attrition and the October War by Fawzi, Isma'il 'Ali, Gamasy, and their colleagues. Additionally, in most of Egypt's other wars, Cairo's generals mostly performed quite adequately, if not fairly well. Mwawi in Palestine in 1948; 'Amr and Murtagi in Yemen in the 1960s; and Nasser, 'Amr, and their staff in the Sinai in 1956 all did a reasonable job. They may never have been able to secure victory through sheer genius, but neither can they be blamed for losing it out of incompetence.

Overall, Egyptian forces fought well in set-piece offensives and static defensive battles but fell down when forced to conduct unplanned, ad hoc operations or fight fluid battles of maneuver. Ultimately, it was these problems that proved most damaging to Egypt's military fortunes over the years. Because its forces were incapable of anything more than set-piece operations and static defense, against an opponent with any skill, it was simply a matter of time before the adversary was able to take the initiative and force the Egyptians to fight in a manner they could not handle. In the final analysis, every Egyptian campaign ended having achieved less than Cairo had hoped — if not in outright disaster — because of the limitations of Egypt's tactical forces.

2

IRAQ

The modern Iraqi military was established by the British during their mandate over Iraq after World War I. Initially, the British created a formation known as the Iraq Levies, comprising several battalions of troops whose primary responsibility was to garrison the Royal Air Force (RAF) bases with which the British controlled Iraq. Although the Levies were adequate for the defense of the airfields, the threat of war with Turkey forced the British to expand Iraq's indigenous military forces. The Turks claimed the former Ottoman *vilayet* of Mosul as a part of their country. This province consisted of what is today the northern third of Iraq, mainly Iraqi Kurdistan, including the vast Kirkuk oilfields. In 1920, Turkish troops crept into Iraqi Kurdistan, forcing the small British garrisons out of as-Sulaymaniyyah and Rawanduz in eastern Kurdistan. To help deal with this threat, the British founded the Iraqi army in 1921 and six years later added an air force. The British recruited former Ottoman officers to man the junior and middle ranks of the new Iraqi officer corps; however, British officers occupied the senior commands and most of the training positions. In addition, the British provided the new army with weapons and training to defeat the anticipated Turkish invasion of northern Iraq.

By the late 1920s, the threat of a Turkish attack had abated, but there were still potential missions for the Iraqi army. The Iraqis, and their British masters, continued to fret over Turkish or Persian encroachment on their territory. Both of these states were considerably more cohesive than Iraq, possessed superior armies, and had dynamic leaders and territorial claims. There were also frequent internal threats to the integrity of the state from separatist revolts, not only by the Kurds but also by the powerful Arab tribes of western and southern Iraq. However, the British eventually concluded that the Iraqi army was simply not capable of handling either the Turks or the Persians and that the RAF, supported by the Iraq Levies, should assume full responsibility for external defense. Instead, the British increasingly relegated the Iraqi army to internal-security duties. Nevertheless, the army enjoyed considerable prestige. The country's elites saw it as critical for three reasons: first, a strong army ensured Sunni dominance over the Shi'ite majority; second, a strong army would allow Baghdad to control the independent tribes who resisted centralization; and third, a strong army could serve as a modernizing and socializing force that could help knit the backward Ottoman *vilayets* into a modern, unified Iraqi nation.[1]

There was some question as to whether the Iraqi army was capable of even this role. In 1928, London found it necessary to increase the number of British officers commanding units in the Iraqi army because indigenous officers were slow to adapt modern modes of warfare.[2] In 1931, Kurdish unrest broke out into outright revolt, and Iraqi army units were badly punished by tribesmen under Shaykhs Mahmud and Ahmad Barzani, requiring British intervention to restore order. Overall, the new army showed little promise.

In 1932 Great Britain granted Iraq its independence. However, the new state was weak, and in 1936 the regime was effectively removed from power in a coup led by Gen. Bakr Sidqi. The Bakr Sidqi coup ushered in a long period of military rule that ended only in 1941, when the military high command attempted to distance Iraq from Britain at the nadir of British fortunes during World War II. Although Iraq was nominally independent, Britain effectively still governed the country, exercising a veto over Iraqi foreign and national security policy. The Iraqi high command saw the prospect of Britain's defeat at the hands of Nazi Germany as an opportunity to rid themselves of their colonial masters. Britain pulled together a small force from its armies in the Levant, which handily defeated the much larger but thoroughly incompetent Iraqi army and air force; ousted the military commanders and their prime minister, Rashid 'Ali al-Kaylani; and installed pro-British Nuri as-Sa'id in his place.

The War of Israeli Independence, 1948

After the Second World War, the first combat independent Iraqi forces saw was in Palestine. Iraq joined with the other Arab states in opposing the creation of a Jewish national homeland in Palestine and in May 1948 sent a sizable force to help crush the newborn state of Israel. The Iraqi army had grown considerably since its modest beginnings. In 1948 it boasted 21,000 men in twelve brigades and an air force of 100 aircraft, mostly British.[3] This force allowed Baghdad to contribute a large contingent to the war in Palestine. Initially, the Iraqis sent 5,000 men, including four infantry brigades, an armored battalion, and support personnel, plus another 2,500 "volunteers" to serve with the former Ottoman army officer Fawzi al-Kaukji, a Syrian then commanding the Arab Liberation Army (ALA).[4] Iraq continuously sent reinforcements, and at its peak, the Iraqi expeditionary force mustered some 15,000–18,000 men.

Iraqi Operations with the Arab Liberation Army

Iraqi forces received their baptism of fire under Kaukji defending Zefat in April and May 1948. A force of 600 Syrian and Iraqi ALA irregulars were sent to defend this key town, which controlled access between the Huleh Valley and the Sea of Galilee. Located in very difficult terrain, Zefat at that time was protected by two police forts built into the rock of the hills. It was an extremely formidable position. Because of its importance, Zefat was one of the first towns targeted for capture by the Israeli Haganah. In April 1948 the strength of the natural defensive positions allowed the ALA and some local Arab militiamen to defeat two Israeli attacks by elements of the Golani Brigade. However, in May Israel's Col. Yigal Allon returned to Zefat with a fresh battalion and immediately seized one of the two police posts. Allon was then reinforced with another battalion and attacked the Arab forces in the town itself. Despite heavy Israeli mortar fire, the Arabs successfully turned back repeated assaults. Finally, four days after Allon's first attack on the town, the Israelis attacked again at night in a rainstorm and surprised the defenders. The Arabs resisted fiercely and forced the Israelis to fight house to house but were knocked out of the town. After this defeat, the Arabs gave up the last police post without a fight and withdrew.

On April 25, the Israeli Irgun Zvi Leumi (the freelance militia-terrorist group then headed by Menachem Begin) assaulted the Arab town of Jaffa with 600 men. Jaffa was defended by a similar-sized force of Iraqi ALA irregulars. Although the Irgun claimed to specialize in urban warfare, they were stopped cold by the Iraqis in house-to-house combat. At the end of two days of fighting, the Irgun leadership was forced to ask for help from the Haganah. Jaffa fell to the Israelis several days later in a massive brawl that included the intervention of several British units still trying to maintain control before the end of its mandate government on 14 May.

On 29 April units of the Israeli Palmach assaulted positions on the Katamon Ridge south of Jerusalem held by Iraqi ALA irregulars. The Palmach secured a foothold with a surprise night attack that took the monastery dominating the ridge. However, in the morning the Iraqis launched a series of vicious counterattacks. The fighting was extremely tough, but eventually the Iraqis called off their attack to regroup, and at noon the Israelis were reinforced by another battalion. The Iraqis were exhausted and bloodied and decided that they did not have the strength to take on the now-reinforced Israelis. Instead, they retired from the field. After these initial defeats, the ALA was inactive for several months, and when they resumed operations, most of its Iraqi contingent had joined the main Iraqi expeditionary force that had arrived in northern Samaria.

Iraqi Army Operations on the West Bank

When the Iraqi army expeditionary force first arrived in Transjordan in early April 1948, it consisted of one infantry brigade and a supporting armored battalion commanded by Gen. Nur ad-Din Mahmud. On 15 May Iraqi engineers built a pontoon bridge across the Jordan River. The combat units crossed into Palestine and launched a frontal assault against the nearby Israeli settlement of Gesher, only to be quickly driven back. The next day the Iraqis tried again, but this time their armor attacked from the south and their infantry attacked from the north. Although this double envelopment could have put the Israelis in a difficult position, the Iraqi infantry and armor failed to properly coordinate their attacks, allowing the Israelis to redeploy their small force along internal lines and defeat each attack in turn. Both Iraqi forces launched clumsy frontal assaults, and the lack of infantry support for the armor left their tanks and armored cars easy prey for Israeli antitank teams. Several days later, the Iraqis tried to attack another Jewish settlement in the same area but failed to scout their route adequately and fell victim to an Israeli ambush before they could even reach the targeted settlement. These defeats convinced the Iraqis to abandon this sector of the front and try their luck elsewhere.

In late May 1948 the Iraqi expeditionary force moved into the West Bank region of northern Samaria and occupied the "strategic triangle" bounded by the Arab towns of Nablus, Janin, and Tulkarm. This was a key sector for the Arabs because it was the ideal launching pad for an attack westward against Haifa to split the narrow Israeli corridor along the Mediterranean coast and it guarded the right flank of Transjordan's Arab Legion, which was concentrated to the south around the Jerusalem corridor. Previously, this sector had been held by elements of the ALA that were too weak

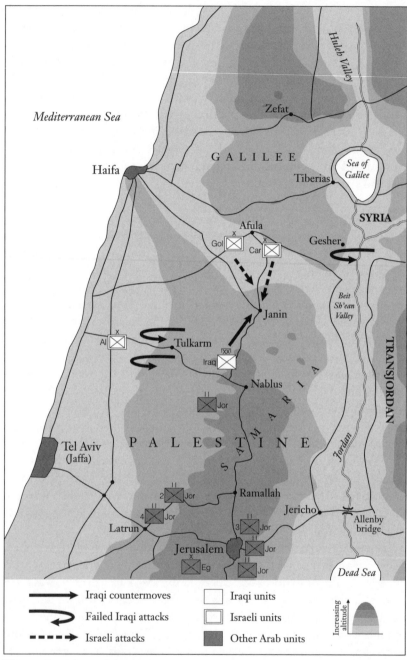

Map 10. Iraqi Army Operations, 1948

to pose much of a threat to the Israelis, but with the arrival of the powerful Iraqi force, the Arabs were hopeful that they could now cut Israel in two. As the Iraqis assembled in this area, they received reinforcements in the form of another infantry brigade and another armored battalion. Additional reinforcements followed, bringing the Iraqi contingent up to seven or eight infantry brigades, an armored brigade, and three air force squadrons.[5]

In late May the Haganah tried to relieve the Arab Legion's stranglehold on Jerusalem with a major assault against the Latrun police fort on the Jerusalem–Tel Aviv road (see chapter 3). Israeli attacks were extremely heavy, and the Jordanians pleaded with the Iraqis to attack either northwest toward Haifa or north into Galilee to draw off Israeli forces from Latrun. The Iraqis were slow to respond and only launched two half-hearted attacks that were easily defeated by local Israeli forces. Nevertheless, Haganah commanders recognized that the size of the Iraqi force and its location in northern Samaria made it a dangerous threat. Rather than wait for the Iraqis to begin an offensive, the Israelis decided to launch a preemptive attack south from Galilee to take Janin, and possibly Nablus, and cut the Iraqi supply lines across the Jordan.

The Israelis kicked off their offensive by sending three brigades against the Iraqis. The plan was to have their Alexandroni Brigade make a diversionary attack against Tulkarm while the Golani Brigade drove south toward Janin. After the Golanis secured the high ground north of Janin, the Carmeli Brigade would pass through its lines and seize the town. The offensive began on the night of 28 May, although for some reason the Alexandronis failed to conduct their feint. The northern attack still made good progress initially, however. The Golanis were able to take a series of hills, villages, and police posts on the route to Nablus. Iraqi defenders were slow off the mark, and their armored-car battalions were repeatedly beaten to important positions by Israeli infantry. In a series of skirmishes, the Golanis outmaneuvered the Iraqi forces, catching them in their flank and mauling them before they could retreat on multiple occasions. In several instances, the Iraqis launched determined attacks against positions to which the Israelis had beaten them, but in every case the Israelis had already dug in by the time the assault arrived and had little trouble throwing back the Iraqis.

Nevertheless, throughout this period the Iraqis sent a steady stream of reinforcements north to stop the Haganah advance. When the Carmeli Brigade took over the spearhead of the Israeli attack, it began to run into these Iraqi units. By the time the Israelis reached Janin on 3 June, an Iraqi brigade had fortified inside the town and on the two key hills that dominated it from the south. The Carmelis launched a clumsy frontal assault during the night but still pushed the Iraqis off both hills in a protracted battle. The next morning the Iraqis brought up fresh forces and counter-attacked with a reinforced battalion, all supported by artillery and some inaccurate but still helpful airstrikes, that eventually retook the southwestern hill from the exhausted Israelis. A fierce battle then developed for control of Janin itself, and although the lines did not change much, the Iraqi commander kept feeding fresh troops into the fight until the Israelis concluded that holding the town was not worth the price in casualties and pulled back to the hills north of Janin.

At this point, Iraq's contribution to the Arab war effort effectively ended. The Israelis had suffered heavy casualties in the fighting for Janin, and although the Iraqis had suffered even worse, they had far more troop strength available. Lt. Gen. John Bagot Glubb, commander of the Arab Legion, urged the Iraqi commanders to immediately pursue the withdrawing Israelis with fresh units in hope of inflicting greater damage and possibly even overrunning eastern Galilee. But the Iraqis would not budge. In the following weeks the Israelis made a series of spoiling attacks against Iraqi positions in the Samarian triangle out of fear that the Iraqis were intending just such an offensive. The Iraqis defended when attacked but made no aggressive moves of their own, ending the war holding these same positions. On the passivity of Iraqi forces, Edgar O'Ballance remarked:

> One can only wonder at the general inaction of such a large body of troops. They merely stepped into positions vacated by Glubb Pasha's troops and Kaukji's men who were pushed out to make way for them, and they made no attempt to extend their territory. Their one clash was that at Janin, which resulted in an Israeli defeat but as they held all the aces and the Israelis walked into their fields of fire and generally used little tactical common sense, they could hardly claim that it was the result of any particular skill on their part. Their brief counterattack, their only offensive movement, was successful, but it was extremely limited and was not followed up. . . . It was a case of a golden opportunity lost merely for the lack of aggressive spirit and energy.[6]

Apparently, the reason for this inaction was that the Iraqi commanders were not given any explicit orders by the military command in Baghdad. They arrived in Palestine with orders to aid the Arab cause but with no specific instructions as to how to do so. The initial attacks on Gesher were General Mahmud's idea, but their failure seems to have squelched his initiative. Afterward, the Iraqi troops simply sat passively, waiting for directions from Baghdad that never came.

Iraqi Military Performance in the War of Israeli Independence

Overall, the Iraqis fought very poorly in 1948. General Mahmud's leadership was at best mediocre, showing little creativity or determination even within the fairly circumscribed limits on his freedom of action. But he cannot be held solely responsible for Iraq's failures. In particular, he met the Israeli thrust into Samaria with real energy, rushing forces north as quickly as possible and counterattacking vigorously to stop the Israelis and prevent them from consolidating their gains. At the tactical level, the Iraqis had little to brag about. Their soldiers demonstrated almost no skill in handling their weapons, poor discipline, and (with the notable exception of the ALA volunteers) a dearth of commitment to the cause. Of greatest importance, Iraqi junior officers were unaggressive, unimaginative, and uninspiring. Their shortcomings were the principal reason for the consistent tactical failure of Iraqi operations. For example, Iraqi armored-car companies repeatedly failed to arrive at key positions before the Israeli infantry because their commanders were slow to move and act, and when faced with problems — in terms of vehicle breakdowns, terrain problems, or unexpected Israeli moves — either continued according to the original plan, regardless of how irrelevant it had become, or else did nothing until higher echelons intervened to tell them what to do.

The only categories of military effectiveness in which the Iraqis showed any cause for praise were unit cohesion and, possibly, logistics. Iraqi forces hung together in battle and fought hard. Their units took very severe casualties, but the soldiers continued to hold their positions in defense and launched repeated attacks on offense. The Iraqi irregulars attached to the ALA, in particular, demonstrated superb cohesion in the fighting for Zefat and the Katamon Ridge.

Iraq's logistical performance is more difficult to assess. We have no direct information relating to the operations of Iraq's quartermaster corps in 1948, but circumstantial evidence suggests it did its job adequately, if not well. At the most obvious level, the Iraqis were able to support a division-sized force in the field, across the Syrian Desert, and over 1,000 kilometers from their depots around Baghdad. There is no evidence that Iraqi forces suffered from any supply problems, and their profligate expenditure of ammunition and gasoline in the West Bank suggests just the opposite. Moreover, it seems highly likely that the Iraqis themselves provided all of these items and that little came from the Jordanians, for the Jordanians were themselves short on military consummables.[7] All in all, such circumstances suggest the Iraqis did a creditable job when it came to supporting their forces in Palestine.

The First Kurdish War, 1961–70

The Iraqi army did not see combat again until the early 1960s, when Kurdish nationalists attempted to break away from the Baghdad regime. In the 1950s the Iraqi monarchy was replaced by a military dictatorship, ushering in a period of sustained political instability. In 1958 Brig. Gen. 'Abd al-Karim Qasim, commander of the 20th Infantry Brigade and leader of a group of disgruntled officers, overthrew the government. The coup was actually executed by Lt. Col. 'Abd as-Salem Arif, commander of a battalion of the 19th Infantry Brigade (a brigade in the same division as Qasim's 20th), who persuaded the other battalion commanders to seize control of the brigade as it moved through the Baghdad area on its way to support the Hashimite monarchy of Jordan, then threatened by Nasserist elements and Palestinian refugees. The coup was quick but bloody, resulting in the deaths of King Faysal II, the regent, and Nuri as-Sa'id. Once in power, Qasim moved to ensure his grip by a series of purges against the monarchists, then the Nasserists, and finally the communists. Qasim's purges ignited smoldering ethnic and tribal rivalries, leading to unrest and several open revolts that Qasim brutally crushed. In several of these uprisings, different army units were pitted against each other in combat, which in turn sparked further purges of the armed forces.

In the midst of this political turmoil, the army struggled to turn itself into a modern force capable of giving a better account of itself than it had in 1948. New brigades were created and grouped into four (later five) divisions. By 1956, the army had 60,000 men and the air force fielded 250 aircraft, mostly British, some of which were modern jet fighters.[8] With Qasim's accession to power, Iraq was able to open a military relationship with the Soviets, which gave Iraq access to their weaponry. The first Soviet arms began to arrive at the end of 1958. The first delivery consisted of a squadron of MiG-15s, which were later followed by MiG-17s, MiG-21s, transport aircraft, and helicopters. In February 1959 about 150 Soviet tanks (mostly T-34/85s) were delivered to the Iraqi army. Meantime, small numbers of Soviet advisers began to arrive, primarily to teach the Iraqis how to operate Soviet hardware, although some were set to work analyzing problems in the Iraqi Air Force.

The Course of the Revolt

When Qasim seized power, the Kurds rallied to his side and helped him consolidate his position, hoping that in return he would grant them autonomy or even independence. However, they were quickly disappointed. Qasim not only refused Kurdish independence but also instituted a series of decrees that threatened Kurdish tribal leaders economically and politically. In September 1961 the charismatic Kurdish leader Mustafah Barzani, the younger brother of Shaykh Ahmad, openly revolted against Baghdad. Starting with a force of 600 loyal followers, Barzani was able to convince a number of other Kurdish tribes to join him, and by spring 1962 he had 5,000 full-time guerrillas and another 5,000–15,000 partisans who could be called up to participate in specific operations for short periods of time. His first offensive in the fall of 1961 caught the Iraqi government by surprise. Barzani's forces moved with great speed and recruited volunteers as they advanced, with the result that within two weeks the Kurds had overrun virtually all of Iraqi Kurdistan and were at the gates of the great northern cities of Mosul, Kirkuk, and Arbil.[9]

Iraq maintained one of its five infantry divisions — the 2d Division — in Kurdistan, and although this unit had sat passively while the Kurds advanced, when their offensive had run its course, Qasim ordered his troops to counterattack. Qasim also bribed a number of Kurdish tribes to turn against Barzani. It is testimony to the weakness of the Kurds at this point that this one Iraqi division was able to reverse most of the gains of the first Kurdish offensive. The 2d Division counterattacked across Kurdistan, with its battalions pushing out along the major roads. But its operations were clumsy: battalions stuck to the roads and rarely put out flank guards or even patrolled territory ahead of them; they consistently kept to the low ground, launched frontal attacks when faced with resistance, and employed their armor largely as moveable canon. Nevertheless, the Kurds were unprepared for serious combat, and they retreated quickly before the Iraqi army.

Barzani was forced to withdraw into the mountains for the winter. However, his cause was greatly helped by the beginnings of large-scale desertions from the Iraqi army. Most of the Kurds in the army were townsmen from the major cities, not tribesmen from the mountains. Thus at first, when as many tribes opposed Barzani as supported him and the revolt seemed to be as much a tribal struggle as anything else, the number of deserters was small. However, as time passed and more and more tribes cast their lot with Barzani, the revolt took on the character of a true nationalist uprising, and then urban Kurds began to desert the army in droves. These defections not only served to sap army strength and morale (the 2d Division was largely Kurdish) but also brought much-needed training and weaponry to the Kurdish guerrillas.

In March 1962 Barzani launched another offensive well before Baghdad believed he could, catching the army by surprise. The Kurds inflicted heavy casualties on government units in Kurdistan but were unable to take the

towns of Zakhu and Dahuk in western Kurdistan, the primary objectives of
the offensive. Barzani did, however, succeed in mauling several of the major
tribes arrayed against him, which was an important victory. Within a few
weeks, this campaign petered out, but the government was content to remain on the defensive, holding the towns and main roads but doing little
else. Thus, the war settled into a stalemate.

OPPOSING STRATEGIES

After the first Iraqi counteroffensive in 1961 failed to crush the Kurds,
Qasim adopted a strategy of remaining on the defensive and hoping that
the revolt would collapse from attrition, tribal infighting, and the difficulty
of supplying guerrilla forces in the mountains. Baghdad reinforced its units
in Kurdistan, redeploying the 1st Infantry Division from ad-Diwaniyah in
Mesopotamia to the Mosul sector, thereby allowing the 2d Infantry Division to concentrate its forces in eastern Kurdistan. Additional reinforcements continued to flow north so that, by May 1963, three-quarters of the
Iraqi army were facing the Kurdish guerrillas. The army maintained garrisons in the various towns of Kurdistan, and to keep these troops supplied
(and to try to prevent supplies from reaching the Kurds), they patrolled the
major roads during the day. Every morning the various Iraqi bases would
send out infantry columns led by tanks and supported by artillery to clear
the roads and disperse Kurdish ambushes. These troops tended to open fire
indiscriminately and massively and routinely looted Kurdish villages they
passed through. In addition, Baghdad began a large-scale air campaign of
terror bombing Kurdish civilians. Iraqi aircraft conducted incessant airstrikes against Kurdish villages — including napalm strikes — in the hope of
convincing Barzani's men to put down their weapons. This strategy did
nothing to advance Baghdad's aims. However, because Iraqi intelligence
was thoroughly politicized and consistently told Qasim what he wanted to
hear — namely that the Kurds were on the verge of collapse — the government persisted in this approach.[10]

If the Iraqis had tried, it is unlikely that they could have come up with a
worse strategy. The government's inactivity gave the Kurds the breathing
space they desperately needed to regroup and train. The Kurds adopted a
similar strategy to that of the regime: they too decided to starve out their
adversary. However, they planned to isolate the scattered Iraqi garrisons
gradually by blocking the roads, ambushing supply convoys, and constantly
raiding and harassing Iraqi camps. The Kurds had the advantage of being at
home in the mountains, and as long as they could get supplies from their
brethren in Iran and Turkey, there was no limit to how long they could hold

out. They were aided in this by Qasim's confused foreign policy, which succeeded in alienating the shah of Iran, who responded by establishing a covert supply line to Barzani. Thus, by taking control of the major roads at night and using secondary routes that the army did not patrol during the day, the Kurds had plenty of access to the supplies they needed. Meanwhile, the systematic destruction of Kurdish villages by Iraqi air and ground forces ensured a steady flow of new recruits and Kurdish deserters from the army to Barzani's camp. Perhaps of greatest importance, the Kurds used this time to turn their men into a true guerrilla army instead of a loose affiliation of roving bandits. Kurdish leaders (particularly Jalal Talabani) used the Kurdish deserters from the army as a cadre around which they built a full-time guerrilla force known as the Peshmerga. By spring 1963, the Kurds fielded 15,000 Peshmerga and another 10,000 irregulars.[11]

IRAQ ON THE OFFENSIVE

Ultimately, the Kurds proved correct in their strategy, and it was the Iraqi garrisons that began to starve. Baghdad increasingly had to resupply different bases with airdrops and even had to withdraw some garrisons altogether. Meanwhile, Qasim's passive strategy galled the Iraqi high command, who recognized that it could not succeed and wanted to go on the offensive. Army discontent with his conduct of the Kurdish campaign contributed to Qasim's overthrow by his former brother-in-arms, 'Abd as-Salem Arif, and the Iraqi Ba'th Party in February 1963. The Ba'th too tried to reach an understanding with the Kurds, but their positions were incompatible, and so the fighting resumed.

With Qasim gone, Baghdad's generals threw away the old starvation strategy and began planning for a major offensive. In June 1963 the Iraqis struck, attacking all across Kurdistan. The army massed three division-sized task forces, each with four infantry brigades and supported by armor and air power, against western, central, and eastern Kurdistan. The Iraqis made greatest progress in western Kurdistan, where they secured the areas around Zakhu, Dahuk, and Aqrah; razed numerous Kurdish villages; and drove deep into the mountains. However, the Kurds simply retreated farther into the mountains, and by September this Iraqi push had run out of steam. The central thrust turned into a near catastrophe as the main brigade-column became trapped in Rawanduz Gorge by Peshmerga under Omar Mustafah. At first, the Iraqis tried to relieve this brigade through concentrated airstrikes against the besieging guerrillas, but their attacks were inaccurate and failed to have any effect on the Kurdish forces. Consequently, the Iraqis had to divert all three other brigades in this sector from

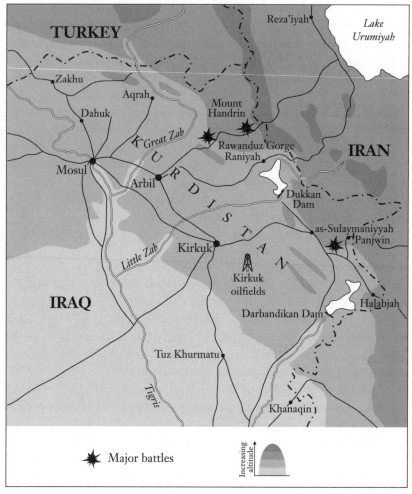

Map 11. Major Battles of the First Kurdish War

their assigned objectives to save the surrounded force, taking eight weeks before the brigade could be extracted from the gorge. The mission of the eastern thrust was to clear the major road from Kirkuk to as-Sulaymaniyyah and then block the routes to Iran. However, it took two brigades two months to secure the road because of stubborn resistance and constant ambushes by the Kurds. The length of time required to accomplish the initial task effectively brought this campaign to a halt as well.

By September, the situation had returned to a stalemate. The failure of the 1963 offensive was largely tactical. While the Kurds had become quite proficient at conducting ambushes, they were incapable of anything else, having failed to develop any tactics that would allow them to follow up and capitalize on the temporary successes of their ambushes. Despite the great improvements in their guerrilla skills, the Kurds had great difficulty operating in units larger than the *Sar Pel*, a battalion-sized force of about 200–250 men. In addition, Kurdish troops had only light weapons — basically nothing heavier than 60-mm mortars — and handled what they had poorly, even rifles and pistols. But the Iraqis more than made up for these shortfalls with limitations of their own. In particular, Iraqi units insisted on conducting frontal assaults against defended Kurdish positions. With the exception of several of the brigades employed in western Kurdistan, they rarely conducted reconnaissance or deployed flank guards while they moved, with the result that they were regularly surprised and ambushed by the Peshmerga. Although the Iraqi Air Force was busy bombing Kurdish civilians, they rarely provided air support to ground forces, and when they did — such as at Rawanduz Gorge — their aim was so bad it was a virtual toss-up as to which side would take casualties. Finally, army communications security was nonexistent, while the Kurds acquired several Iraqi field radios and signals personnel among their army defectors were able to monitor troop movements for the guerrillas.[12]

THE FALL OF THE BA'TH AND THE 1965 IRAQI OFFENSIVE
The debacle in Kurdistan was just one of several disasters the Ba'th regime racked up in its early days in power. This string of misfortune resulted in a relatively bloodless coup by 'Abd as-Salem Arif, who ousted his Ba'th partners and seized full power in November 1963. The abject failure of the 1963 campaign plus internal unrest in Baghdad in the wake of the coup prompted the Arif regime to begin negotiations with the Kurds. These talks broke down in the winter of 1964–65, and in March 1965 the Iraqi army tried another offensive. This time the principal strategic innovation the regime brought to bear was its having secured the cooperation of the

Turkish and Iranian governments, both of whom also had longstanding problems with their own Kurdish populations. The Turks agreed to launch an offensive into Turkish Kurdistan simultaneous with Arif's attack, while Iran agreed to cease support for the Iraqi Kurds and prevent them from retreating into Iran.

This campaign followed the path of previous Iraqi efforts and, if anything, went worse. Poor maintenance and faulty repair work had become a serious problem for the Iraqis; less than half of their relatively new Soviet armored vehicles were operational and only 30 of 140 MiG-17s were flyable.[13] Consequently, Baghdad could only muster about 40,000 troops in only nine combat brigades. Yet once again, the Iraqis attacked all across Kurdistan, dispersing their forces and diluting the strength of their attacks. Once again they advanced along the roads with armor out in front; once again the Kurds ambushed and harassed them all the way; and once again the Iraqis retaliated for these attacks by burning and bombing nearby Kurdish villages. When government columns attacked the towns of Panjwin, Chwarta, and Mahut in eastern Kurdistan, the Peshmerga dug in and fought hard, stopping the army in its tracks. As had become the norm, the government attack was finished with little to show by September.

THE SPRING 1966 OFFENSIVE

Looking to break out of this operational rut, the Iraqi high command decided to try a limited offensive during the winter to try to block the routes to Iran. In the winter the snows closed many of the mountain passes, limiting the number of routes available to the Kurds to move men and supplies back and forth from Iran. So in January 1966 the Iraqis attacked from the Khanaqin area, driving north toward Panjwin. The Iraqis had become so formulaic in their operations that this sudden departure from their routine took the Kurds at unawares. The Iraqis profited from this surprise, capturing Panjwin against only light opposition. The Kurds quickly regrouped, however, and counterattacked hard against the Iraqis in and around the town. The fighting grew increasingly fierce, as did the weather, which threatened the army's supply lines and eventually forced the Iraqi commanders to pull back. Although they accomplished little in terms of securing territory, the Iraqis were greatly heartened by their winter offensive. In particular, they concluded that the supply lines to Iran were both the most valuable to the Kurds (the Iranian government had resumed covert arms supplies to them in late 1965) and the most vulnerable and made plans for a much more ambitious operation in the spring.

The long-awaited Iraqi spring offensive commenced on 4 May 1966.

Baghdad again assembled nine brigades with 40,000 men, but this time they concentrated nearly all of them in the narrow eastern sector of Kurdistan, where they faced only about 3,500 Peshmerga. The Iraqi operation was to be a pincer movement to sever eastern Kurdistan from western Kurdistan and to block the vital supply routes from Iran. The southern pincer would follow largely the same route used during the winter offensive, pushing north in the direction of Panjwin and as-Sulaymaniyyah, while the northern pincer would drive north and east from Arbil to Raniyah and Qal'at Dizah. The northern force initially made good progress, securing Rawanduz Gorge and then pressing on to take Mt. Handrin and Mt. Zozik. However, the Iraqis then made the crucial mistake of building their camp in the valley between these mountains while leaving the surrounding heights undefended. Barzani immediately recognized this golden opportunity and called his forces to Mt. Handrin as quickly as possible. On 11 May Barzani fell on the Iraqi forces in the valley and butchered them. In two days of fighting, the Iraqis suffered 2,000 killed, and those who escaped were forced to leave their heavy equipment behind and make their way out over the mountains. Some Iraqi units surrendered en masse to the Kurds, and many survivors deserted as soon as they reached safety.

The Mt. Handrin disaster brought the 1966 offensive to an abrupt halt. Moreover, it so completely demoralized the army that Baghdad once again resumed negotiations with the Kurds. These talks were suspended on several occasions while domestic politics took center stage in Baghdad. 'Abd as-Salem Arif had died in April 1966 only to be succeeded by his brother, 'Abd ar-Rahman Arif. 'Abd ar-Rahman hung on for another two years before being overthrown by a second coalition of Ba'thists and military officers on 17 July 1968. Having learned its lesson from its experience with the Arifs, the Ba'th immediately moved against its erstwhile allies in the army, and on 30 July they ousted the senior military officers with whom they had colluded only two weeks before.

IRAQ'S FINAL OFFENSIVES

Once the Ba'th Party had consolidated its hold on power in 1969, it returned to the bargaining table with the Kurds. However, the talks again quickly dissolved, and the new regime opted for a military solution to the impasse. The Iraqi high command decided upon an offensive plan similar to the one employed in the disastrous 1966 campaign, but this time they were determined to do it right. They assembled a force of 60,000 men — nearly the entire Iraqi field army — and concentrated it against eastern Kurdistan.[14] Once again, the Iraqi blueprint was to drive north from the

Khanaqin area to seal the border with Iran, while another force drove east from Arbil to split Kurdistan in half. Remembering the success of the first winter offensive, Baghdad attacked in January and again caught the Kurds off guard. Surprise and the sheer size of the Iraqi force allowed the government to throw the Kurds back in several areas and to occupy the key towns of Panjwin and Qal'at Dizah. However, true to form, the Kurds regrouped and fought ferociously as a winter storm descended on Kurdistan. These factors — plus constant ambushes against the Iraqi supply lines — forced the government to pull back and relinquish many of its gains yet again.

The fighting for the rest of the year was no more decisive. On 1 March Barzani counterattacked and drove the Iraqis back to their January start line. In August the army regrouped and launched a ten-brigade offensive into the same area of eastern Kurdistan. However, Barzani had concentrated 15,000 Peshmerga in the region by this time, and they stopped the offensive almost as soon as it began. Specifically, Iraqi units suffered near disasters around Dukan and Arbil, and the specter of another Mt. Handrin convinced Baghdad to bring the operation to a halt. The Ba'th regime also was feeling pressure as a result of several provocative foreign-policy gambits that sparked crises with Israel, Syria, and Iran. These international tensions forced Baghdad to redeploy units from Kurdistan to its external borders. Eventually, the Ba'thists concluded that they had to end the Kurdish revolt, and so in March 1970 the regime published a manifesto granting autonomy and other key concessions to the Kurds.

Iraqi Military Performance against the Kurds, 1961–70

Counterinsurgency (COIN) campaigns are rarely easy for any military, and there is a long list of insurgencies that prevailed or just survived for many years despite the best efforts of very competent armies. For example, Greek and Yugoslav partisans defied the German Wehrmacht for four years, while the Viet Cong and Afghan Mujaheddin eventually outlasted the two superpowers. However, such was not the case with the Kurds. The COIN campaign against the Iraqi Kurds was eminently winnable.

First, the Kurds were lousy insurgents. While they eventually learned how to execute an ambush and quickly disengage in the face of superior numbers or firepower, that was the limit of their abilities. In particular, they never learned to convert the temporary success of an ambush into a more meaningful military defeat for the government. Even after the Mt. Handrin disaster, the Iraqi forces that escaped from the valley were not pursued, nor did the Kurds use the momentum they had gained to overrun additional nearby garrisons — all of which were thoroughly demoralized by the defeat. The Kurds rarely had enough rifles to arm all of their men (who rarely exceeded 15,000–25,000 in number) and did not possess any weapons heavier than light mortars until Iran provided 140 artillery pieces in 1969.[15] Despite the fact that Kurdish men handle weapons from childhood, they were mostly poor marksmen and had awful fire discipline, with the result that they usually were desperately short of ammunition.[16] Kurdish leadership was mediocre at best. Mustafah Barzani was tremendously charismatic but not a particularly good general — his recognition of the opportunity at Mt. Handrin being a notable exception.

Second, the mountains of Kurdistan are not all that unfavorable to a COIN operation, as the Turks and Iranians discovered. While it is difficult for a modern army to bring its war machine fully to bear in such terrain, the mountains do have several advantages for COIN operations. It is difficult to grow food in the elevations of Kurdistan, thus insurgents must have access to the towns and major valleys where food is available, and controlling these areas is not difficult. As the Iraqis eventually figured out, the mountains channel the movement of supplies for the insurgents. There are only a limited number of routes that a cart, a mule, or even a man carrying a pack can take in the mountains, and the Kurds were never willing to employ the kind of human convoys the Viet Cong used to keep their troops supplied over the Ho Chi Minh Trail. In winter the number of routes available for movement of supplies by any means drops precipitously. The Kurds also were heavily dependent on supplies provided by the Kurds of Turkey and, especially, Iran (and later on supplies from the Iranian government). Thus, as the Iraqis finally discovered, cutting the Kurdish supply routes from Iran would cripple their operations.

Finally, it is worth noting that the Iranian and Turkish militaries have both effectively crushed their own Kurdish insurgencies — repeatedly — indicating that Baghdad almost certainly could have done the same. The fact that the Kurds seem to launch an all-out revolt against Turkey and Iran every decade or two does not undermine the point that both Ankara and Tehran have figured out how to defeat these uprisings whenever they occur. The problem Iran and Turkey face is that they consistently fail to address the underlying political problems that give rise to these insurgencies, and so it is only a matter of time before the Kurds revolt again, only to be crushed in yet another COIN campaign. The important point is that there is no particular reason why the Iraqis could not have done the same in 1961–70.

So why is it that the Iraqis not only failed to crush the Peshmerga but were so regularly humiliated in their attempts as well? Baghdad's strategic and operational leadership must be assigned some portion of the blame but cannot be held responsible for the ultimate failure. The Iraqis did not think through how to conduct a counterinsurgency campaign but instead appear to have considered it the same as conventional military operations.[17] In addition, the Iraqi high command seems to have only attempted to formulate a theory of victory over the Kurds twice. The first occasion was under Qasim, and at that time they came up with the wrong answer (the starvation strategy). On the second occasion, in 1965–66, the Iraqis hit upon the dependence of the Peshmerga on the supply lines to Iran. This turns out to have been the right answer: it was the central component of the strategy the Iraqis employed to successfully defeat the Kurds in 1975 and again in 1989. Thus, there is no particular reason this strategy should not have worked in 1966 or 1969. Furthermore, the two offensives the Iraqis launched in 1966 and 1969 to try to implement this strategy were well planned and entirely feasible: the Iraqis concentrated overwhelming force against a vulnerable sector; the mission, to block the passes into Iran and those connecting eastern and western Kurdistan, should have been well within the capabilities of the forces employed; and the campaigns were very competently planned. So why did they fail?

The problem was Iraq's tactical performance. Its tactical units were inept and inflexible. They moved slowly and rarely ventured off the roads. Most units did not bother to deploy flank, rear, or advance guards, and patrolling was virtually unheard of. Iraqi tactical commanders insisted on sticking to the low ground when marching or in camp, thereby forfeiting the high ground to the insurgents. Iraqi units failed to integrate the various combat arms into combined-arms teams and could not coordinate the actions of units as small as platoons and companies. As a result, Iraqi formations were regularly ambushed by the Kurds and in several cases were virtually annihilated by Kurdish traps. Iraqi commanders relied on frontal assaults lacking any subtlety or subterfuge and relying on firepower or pure élan to carry the attack to victory. Despite their control of the skies and the absence of even light antiaircraft weapons in Kurdish hands until the very end of the war, the Iraqis were never able to make their air force count. The Iraqi Air Force generally was used only to bomb defenseless Kurdish villages (constantly replenishing Barzani's ranks), and when committed to direct support of ground operations, it proved useless. Iraqi pilots could not hit anything small enough to have tactical value; they were painfully slow to respond to the needs of ground commanders; and they were frightened off by the slightest resistance from the target.

After several initial miscues, Iraq's generals eventually came up with a good strategy and adequate plans to accomplish that strategy. However,

Iraq's tactical formations proved incapable of executing this strategy, and so the Iraqi military went from failure to failure, and ultimately, the regime was forced to compromise.

The October War, 1973

The Iraqis basically missed the 1967 Arab-Israeli war. A number of factors conspired to prevent them from participating. Although the Iraqi 3d Armored Division was deployed in eastern Jordan, the Israeli attack against the West Bank unfolded so quickly that they could not organize themselves and reach the front lines before Jordan ceased operations. Iraqi forces suffered from severe readiness deficiencies — one-third of their tanks were inoperable because of maintenance problems — that would have required weeks if not months to address. Finally, when the Iraqis did finally get part of their force moving, the Israelis blasted it with heavy airstrikes that essentially stopped the unit in its tracks. Moreover, after the Mt. Handrin disaster, the army was in poor shape and may have been reluctant to take on another conventional army, given their problems with guerrillas.

Iraqi participation during the war was limited to modest air operations.[18] On 5 June two Iraqi Tu-16 bombers tried to bomb Israel but could not locate either Ramat David Airbase or Tel Aviv and so dropped their ordnance on Israeli farmland. Later that day and the next, Israeli planes attacked Iraq's H-3 (al-Walid) Airbase near ar-Rutbah, and Iraqi fighters rose to protect it. According to most Israeli accounts, the Iraqi Hawker Hunters gave the Israelis a very tough time. Some accounts report that many of the Hunters were flown by British-trained Jordanian pilots whose aircraft had been destroyed on the ground and so had been dispatched to fly the Iraqi planes. Nevertheless, even if Jordanian pilots did fly some of the warplanes, the Iraqis still had twenty-one aircraft shot down by the Israelis and probably shot down no more than three Israeli planes in return.[19]

In part to make up for missing out on the Six Day War, Baghdad was determined to contribute a significant force to the Arab cause in the October War. By the end of that conflict, the Iraqi expeditionary force operating with the Syrians southwest of Damascus amounted to 60,000 men, 700 tanks (all T-55s), 500 APCs (mostly Topaz and M-113s), and over 200 artillery pieces. This force comprised two armored divisions, two infantry brigades, twelve artillery battalions, and a special forces brigade.[20] Moreover, the two armored divisions, the 3d and the 6th, were unquestionably the best formations in the Iraqi army. Indeed, the 3d Armored Division, the Salah ad-Din forces, was the elite unit of the army, and Iraqi officers avidly competed to be assigned to it.

The Logistical Effort

To preserve the security of their plans, Egypt and Syria did not inform Iraq of the impending attack. The Iraqis found out about the war the way the rest of the world did, by hearing about it on the radio on 6 October; their logisticians had to start from a standing stop. Moreover, the units the Iraqi General Staff chose to form an expeditionary force to aid the Syrians were deployed all over Iraq while their potential battlefield was 1,000–1,200 kilometers away on the Golan Heights. Iraq's deployment was further hindered by a number of factors. At that time, Iraq had a limited road network, preventing many units from moving directly to Syria. The country had only a small number of heavy-equipment transporters, so many Iraqi armored vehicles had to drive to Syria on their own tracks, resulting in frequent breakdowns that slowed the deployment. Because of negligent maintenance practices, Iraqi units had poor operational readiness rates. Therefore, to bring the various units slated to go to Syria up to full strength, Baghdad had to strip other units of operational equipment and transport it to the earmarked units before they departed. Finally, Syria claimed that it could not provide logistical support for these units, so Iraq not only had to move a corps-sized force 1,000 km in days but also had to keep that force supplied from depots in Iraq for several weeks.

The Iraqis proved more than equal to the task. They named a senior quartermaster officer as overall coordinator of the logistics effort with authority to make all decisions and override all orders regarding the movement of units and supplies to Syria.[21] Iraqi units began moving west immediately, and the first combat formation, the 8th Mechanized Brigade of the 3d Armored Division, arrived south of Sa'sa six days later on 12 October, having driven on its own treads from its training grounds at ar-Ramadi 950 kilometers away. In addition to meeting all of the needs of their corps-sized formation deployed 1,000 kilometers from Baghdad, Iraq's logisticians also managed to transfer to Syria 15,000 tons of jet fuel and 10,000 tons of diesel fuel to replace Syrian losses from Israeli airstrikes.[22] One Syrian officer observed, "Not one of the Iraqi officers I spoke to mentioned that he had faced a logistics problem while moving to the front, whether relating to food, water, fuel, ammunition, repairs or evacuation of damaged equipment or of the wounded."[23]

Combat Operations

Iraq's most important contribution to the Arab war effort was simply being in the right place at the right time.[24] When the 3d Armored Division arrived in Syria, their route of march took them northwestward up through the al-Hara–Kfar Shams area southwest of Damascus. By this time, Israel had retaken the Golan Heights and had launched an assault of its own to threaten the Syrian capital. Iraq's route of march unexpectedly placed them on the right flank of the Israeli counteroffensive. Moreover, by sheer co-incidence, they arrived at the critical moment when the two Israeli ugdot conducting the offensive had begun to wheel to the northeast, exposing an open flank to the arriving Iraqis. Thus, on the morning of 12 October 1973, Israeli general Dan Laner peered through his binoculars to scan the area to the south and saw the lead elements of the Iraqi 3d Armored Division driving cross-country toward his wide-open flank — just when his tanks had broken through the Syrian defenses and were building up momentum to turn the line anchored on the town of Sa'sa. Laner immediately reined in his armor — much to the dismay of his troops — and redeployed them on a group of hills that formed an inverted V facing south. The sudden diversion of Laner's ugdah forced the Israelis to call off their offensive.

The Iraqis had two brigades of the 3d Armored Division present when they first met the Israelis on 12 October: the 8th Mechanized and the 12th Armored. For reasons unknown, the Iraqis only committed the 12th Armored to attack the Israelis, and this they were unable to do until late in the afternoon. By that time, Laner's four understrength and thoroughly exhausted armored brigades (about 200 tanks in all, mostly Super-Shermans) had taken up fighting positions on the hills and were waiting for the Iraqi assault.[25] The 12th deployed about 100 T-55s for the attack (one of its tank battalions had not arrived yet) and an equal number of APCs. The brigade did not attempt to maneuver or outflank the Israelis but drove slowly into the mouth of the inverted-V of hills, walking right into Laner's trap. When the Iraqis were 200 yards away from the forwardmost Israeli tanks, Laner opened fire. The brigade was butchered in the ensuing melee, as Israeli tanks either picked off the T-55s from hull-down positions on the hills or maneuvered onto their flanks to get shots at the more vulnerable side and rear armor of the Iraqi tanks. The Iraqi tankers fired madly in every direction before eventually turning and running off the battlefield. The 12th Armored Brigade lost about 50 tanks in the battle.[26]

The Iraqis remained in contact with the Israeli forces for the next several days but chose to forgo another assault until they could concentrate additional forces for the effort. Nevertheless, by 15 October, the 12th Armored Brigade had lost nearly 80 percent of its tank strength as a result of their earlier attack and subsequent skirmishes with the Israelis. The brigade was pulled off the line and did not return to combat during the war. The rest of 3d Armored Division had arrived by that time; of greatest importance,

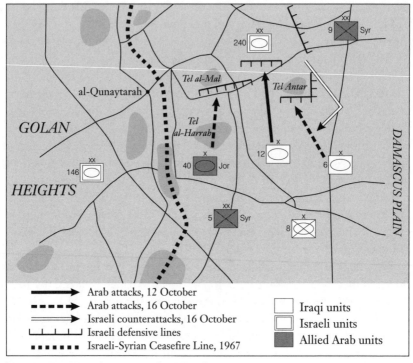

Map 12. Iraqi Attacks on 12 and 16 October 1973

the 6th Armored Brigade took the place of 12th Armored. In addition, the Jordanian 40th Armored Brigade had also arrived to bolster Syria's defenses, and it was placed under Iraqi command and deployed on their left flank.

On 16 October the Iraqis took another crack at the Israeli positions. The Jordanians began moving forward at dawn, as ordered, but the Iraqis did not, with the result that the Israelis easily dealt with the 40th Armored Brigade, sending it reeling with considerable losses. Finally, at about 10:00 A.M., the Iraqis got going. The main unit in the attack was the fresh 6th Armored Brigade with 130 tanks, which was ordered to drive one of Laner's brigades (about 30–40 tanks) off Tel Antar, a commanding hill anchoring the extreme left (east) of the Israeli line. The 8th Mechanized Brigade was also available and in reasonably good shape but was not employed in the attack. Once again, Iraqi armor moved at a ponderous pace and drove straight at the Israeli positions behind a massive but inaccurate artillery bombardment from nine artillery and two multiple-rocket-launcher battalions. Despite accurate Israeli fire, the Iraqis were determined and pressed forward oblivious to their losses. A fierce fight developed at the base of the hill between the Iraqi and Israeli tanks, but Laner detached another of his brigades to loop around behind the Iraqis and caught them in their flank. The 6th Armored Brigade was now in a tight spot, and the Iraqi division commander responded by dispatching part of the idle 8th Mechanized Brigade to help extricate the 6th Armored. The Israelis immediately pinned the Iraqi relieving force and drove it back with accurate, long-range tank gunnery. Eventually, the 6th Armored Brigade was able to disentangle itself from combat but only after losing about 60 tanks.[27]

The Iraqis licked their wounds for three days before having another go at the Israelis. The Israelis used this lull to pull Laner's battered ugdah back to the Golan Heights, relieving it with Maj. Gen. Moshe "Musa" Peled's better rested, though far from fresh, troops. The Iraqi effort was once again directed at Tel Antar and again was to be coordinated with a Jordanian attack farther west, but the Iraqi plan was better this time. They intended to use their special forces brigade to make a night attack against the western flank of Tel Antar, hoping these men could sneak in among the Israeli tanks and knock many of them out with rocket-propelled grenades. This attack would be supported by a mechanized infantry battalion from the 8th Mechanized Brigade to provide additional infantrymen as well as some heavy-weapons support for the attack. Then, while the Israeli armor was fully engaged trying to fend off the Iraqi special forces, the 6th Armored Brigade (replenished with tanks from 12th Armored Brigade and some from the 8th Mechanized) would hit the eastern flank of the Israeli positions under cover of an enormous artillery barrage.

The attack began well. Iraqi special forces successfully infiltrated the Israeli lines and began pushing up the lightly held western slope of the hill. At 2:00 A.M., they were joined by the mechanized infantry battalion. They encountered a small Israeli covering force, which they surprised and easily pushed back. In the confusion and darkness, the Israelis failed to recognize the size of the force on their right flank. At dawn, the 6th Armored Brigade began its attack. The brigade was back up to around its authorized strength of 130 tanks, while the Israeli unit defending the hill was the 205th Armored Brigade, by then down to 50–55 tanks.[28] Almost immediately, though, things began to fall apart for the Iraqis. The artillery bombardment, although heavy, was extremely inaccurate and not timed well with the Iraqi armored attack. Likewise, the special forces troops and mechanized infantry failed to coordinate their attack on the Israeli positions on Tel Antar with the armor assault, allowing the Israelis to concen-

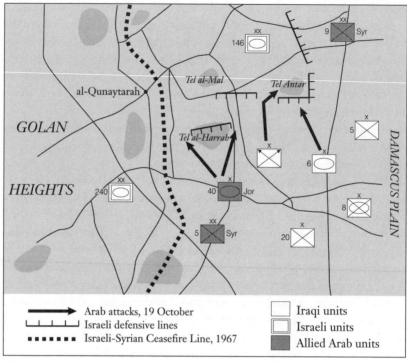

Map 13. Iraqi Attacks on 19 October 1973

trate their full attention on the armor. Finally, rather than trying to swing around the hill as originally intended, the 6th Armored Brigade once again attacked directly into the teeth of the Israeli defenses.

Iraqi tanks and APCs charged straight at the Israeli lines without stopping to dismount the infantry from their vehicles. Having been virtually untouched by the Iraqi artillery barrage, Israeli infantry began picking off Iraqi tanks with French SS-11 antitank guided missiles (ATGMs). The Iraqis still did not dismount any of their infantry to deal with the Israeli ATGM teams but kept pressing forward, with the tanks in the lead, until Israeli artillery got their range and began to bust up their formations. Between the missiles and the artillery fire, the 6th Armored began taking heavy casualties and retreated back to their lines. In so doing, however, they left the special forces brigade and the mechanized infantry battalion stranded on the west side of Tel Antar. The Israelis quickly turned their full attention on these units and drove them off the hill with a combined force of armor and infantry, inflicting heavy losses.

Remarkably, the Iraqis continued the attack. At 10:00 A.M., the 6th Armored again formed up and headed north toward Tel Antar. This time, the Jordanian 40th Armored Brigade also began moving against the right flank of Peled's division. Moreover, in this attack the mechanized infantry led the Iraqi assault supported by inaccurate but heavy covering fire from their armor. Nevertheless, the Iraqis insisted on once again charging directly at the strongest point of the Israeli lines. Their attack succeeded in reaching the Israeli positions out of sheer determination, but in two hours of close combat, they were again thrown back.

At 2:00 P.M., the Iraqis launched a third and final assault on Tel Antar. Once again, the attack was conducted by the 6th Armored Brigade, but for some reason the Iraqis reverted to leading with their tanks while the infantry followed despite their greater success in the second attack when they had done the reverse. For their part, the Israeli brigade was badly worn down and low on ammunition from the previous attacks, and to conserve ammunition they allowed the Iraqi forces to approach much closer before opening fire. Once again, a ferocious fight developed between the Iraqis and Israelis, but again, the tactical skills of the Israelis quickly gave them the upper hand. At the height of the battle, an Israeli company commander of the hard-pressed 205th Brigade was able to maneuver a platoon of tanks around the Iraqis' left flank and begin to roll up their lines. This tiny Israeli counterattack routed the Iraqis, sending them back south for the last time. Altogether, the 6th Armored Brigade lost 70 tanks and a large number of infantry in the day's fighting.[29]

Iraqi Military Performance during the October War

Of the four Arab armies whose forces saw the lion's share of combat during the October War, Iraq's almost certainly performed worst. Trevor Dupuy concluded that Iraqi performance was not only worse than that of any of the other Arab armies participating in the October War, but it was also considerably worse the performance of any of the Arab armies that participated in the even more lopsided Israeli victory in the Six Day War of 1967.[30] In fact, Iraq's operations were so badly conducted that after the attacks on 16 October, the Jordanians demanded that their 40th Armored Brigade be resubordinated to the Syrian 5th Infantry Division (holding the other side of the Jordanian sector) because they were afraid of operating with the Iraqis any longer. The official Israeli assessment concluded that Baghdad's forces proved so incapable of conducting a competent offensive that, "in effect, the Iraqis were banging their heads against a wall."[31]

The performance of Iraq's tactical forces was awful in virtually every category of military effectiveness. Iraqi intelligence was nonexistent. At no point during the battle did they possess a reasonable understanding of the size or disposition of the Israeli forces in front of them because they consistently failed to reconnoiter or probe Israeli lines. For the most part, the Iraqis only initiated contact with Israeli forces during their major attacks, being content to sit in their defensive positions at other times. Their officers occasionally performed commanders' reconnaissances, though always from a great distance. Those Iraqi artillery units that did fire rarely struck Israeli targets, generally because they had not correctly located the Israeli positions. Indeed, Iraqi intelligence was so poor that entire Iraqi formations never fired on the Israelis during two weeks of combat — even with mortars or artillery — because they did not know where the Israelis were. The one time the Iraqis succeeded in attacking an exposed Israeli flank (the special forces attack on the night of 18–19 October), they stumbled on to this sector by accident and then squandered their good fortune by failing to aggressively attack into the flanks of the main Israeli positions defending the southern face of the hill.

Iraqi division and brigade commanders consistently failed to make use of the various advantages they possessed. In particular, they were never able to mass all of their forces for an assault against the Israelis. In every attack they launched, they did not concentrate more than a reinforced brigade for the operation; this despite the fact that plenty of other units were available. On 12 October they employed only the 12th Armored Brigade when the 8th Mechanized Brigade was also available. On 16 October they employed only the 6th Armored Brigade when the 8th Mechanized and the 20th Infantry Brigade were also available. On 19 October the Iraqis primarily employed the 6th Armored (although the special forces brigade participated in the first attack on that day), but again the 8th Mechanized, 20th Infantry, and the 30th Armored Brigade of the 6th Armored Division were also available. Moreover, in those attacks in which more than one brigade was attacking under Iraqi command (primarily when the Jordanian 40th Armored joined in but also when the special forces brigade participated), the Iraqis could not coordinate the timing of their movements to execute an effective strike.

Even with these various problems, the Iraqi attacking forces invariably outnumbered the Israeli defenders in their attack sector, usually by a wide margin. Despite this advantage, Iraq's combat forces achieved little or nothing. Iraqi junior officers showed no initiative, consistently letting slip golden opportunities to hammer the Israelis or take important terrain features. Iraqi tank crews were incapable of independent action, for the death of their unit commander would either paralyze them or send them scurrying in all directions. In the words of one Israeli soldier, "Once you destroyed the leader of the herd, they didn't even know what hit them."[32] Iraqi tactics were rigid and unimaginative, relying on frontal assaults and never attempting to defeat an Israeli foe by outmaneuvering them. Even on those few occasions when Iraq's higher commanders devised a battle plan that involved some effort to outflank Israeli positions, the poor execution by their forces turned the operations back into frontal assaults. Although Iraq relied on British doctrine and attempted to employ typical British bounding-overwatch movements, their forces so badly mangled the implementation that instead they just drove straight at the Israeli lines in two uncoordinated groupings. As a result, Israeli tanks were able to pick off the Iraqis at long ranges without having to worry about covering fire from overwatch elements.[33] Iraqi tank and APC crews showed little ability to properly handle their equipment, regularly getting hung up on difficult terrain and showing little marksmanship with their weaponry. Along similar lines, Iraqi fighter aircraft fared poorly in air-to-air combat, losing 26 of the 110 aircraft sent to Syria without downing any Israeli jets.[34]

Combined-arms operations were an interesting problem for the Iraqis. In general, they seemed to recognize the need to integrate armor, infantry, artillery, and other supporting forces into combined-arms teams but lacked any sense of how to do so. Iraqi commanders switched off between having infantry lead and armor lead on 19 October almost at random. The Iraqis did not seem to realize that they had gotten it right during their second attack—when the infantry led so they could close with the Israeli antitank teams before these cut Iraqi armor to pieces—because two hours later they switched back to having the armor lead. Iraqi infantry units generally failed to provide adequate support to tank units. Iraqi armor did somewhat better supporting infantry operations, but given their poor understanding of tank tactics and operations in general, it is doubtful that this reflected any actual understanding on the part of Iraqi tank crews or their tactical commanders. Finally, Iraq's artillery seemed to be fighting its own war altogether. As noted above, some of the blame for this must be attributed to the lack of reconnaissance and other intelligence operations. However, there were plenty of occasions when Iraqi artillery fired at targets they had fired at many times before and that their maneuver units had attacked on multiple occasions, yet they still could provide only very inaccurate fire support, although only as part of a preplanned bombardment. On those rare occasions when Iraqi artillery tried to provide on-call fire support, their rounds landed everywhere but rarely on the Israelis. Indeed, several sources contend that Iraqi artillery caused more casualties to their own troops and their Jordanian and Syrian allies than to their Israeli foes.[35]

There were, however, a few bright spots in Iraq's performance. The first was the logistical effort, which although not flawless, was extremely impressive. The second was the tenacity and cohesion of the Iraqi units. Iraqi units fought very poorly but very fiercely. The Israelis noted that the Iraqis were far more motivated than the Jordanians and remained so despite appalling losses.[36] In many assaults the Iraqis just kept attacking regardless of how intense or accurate the Israeli defensive fire. Eventually, the Iraqis were able to inflict considerable casualties (by Israeli standards) on several Israeli brigades by attacking repeatedly and by simply refusing to give up. The fight put up by 6th Armored Brigade on 19 October is probably the best example of this. The Israelis were simply amazed that after being beaten back with heavy losses twice that day, the brigade remained cohesive and motivated and launched yet another attack with as much determination as the first. Given this tenacity and their quantitative advantages, it is clear that if the Iraqis had had any tactical skill whatsoever, they might have done substantial damage to the Israelis.

The Second Kurdish War, 1974–75

After four years of broken promises, the Kurds resumed their war against Iraq's Ba'th government.[37] The Kurds had not been idle during that period, suspecting that the Iraqis would not carry through on their part of the agreement. Barzani had diligently recruited and trained additional men so that, by the spring of 1974, he commanded 50,000–60,000 Peshmerga and another 50,000 irregulars. Barzani's forces were now at least three times stronger than they had ever been before. This new strength, plus the memory of their victories in 1966 and 1969, led Barzani to begin to convert the Peshmerga into a conventional army, and they spent much of this time learning conventional military operations. In addition, Barzani had assiduously cultivated ties to Iran, the United States, and Israel, none of whom were particularly fond of the Iraqi regime and who stepped up arms deliveries to the Kurds after Baghdad signed a treaty of friendship with Russia in 1972. With his huge new army and powerful new friends, Barzani was practically itching for a fight by 1974.

Baghdad had also made use of the four-year lull. It is fairly clear that Saddam Husayn, who increasingly supplanted the figurehead ruler, Hasan al-Bakr, as the major force in Iraqi politics, had never intended to abide by the agreements of 1970 and capitulated to the Kurds only as a tactical move to allow the Iraqi army to recover from the defeats of 1966 and 1969. The Iraqis had gradually built up their strength opposite the Kurds and by 1974 had massed 90,000 men, 1,200 tanks and APCs, and 200 combat aircraft in and around Kurdistan.[38] Moreover, Baghdad's commanders had learned several lessons from their first round with the Kurds, and while their experience in the October War was even more painful, they learned from that conflict as well.

The first thing that the Iraqi military learned was that Soviet equipment and methods did not suit their needs. The Ba'thists had always had a stormy relationship with Moscow, and between frequent Soviet attempts to influence Iraqi policy by holding up arms deliveries and the Iraqis' conclusion that Soviet weaponry was inferior to Western equipment, Baghdad consciously began to distance itself from the USSR. Trade with the Soviet bloc dropped from 13 percent of total Iraqi trade to 7 percent in 1975 to under 3 percent in 1980.[39] The Iraqis also tried aggressively to obtain Western military material. In 1976, Baghdad bought 64 Mirage F-1s, and in 1977 it bought 200 AMX-30 tanks from France. In 1978, Iraq bought 200 Cascavel APCs from Britain and ordered ten frigates and corvettes from Italy.[40] The Iraqis wanted to buy even more than this — many generals wanted to abandon the Soviets altogether and make a wholesale changeover to Western arms — but several factors conspired to prevent it. First, Iraq was the constant enemy of two of America's staunchest allies, Israel and Iran, and this limited the amount and quality of weapons that any Western country, even France, was willing to sell. Second, Western weapons were considerably more expensive than Soviet arms and took far longer for Iraqi personnel to learn to use. Third, Iraq regularly went to war during this period, and they were unwilling to risk such a large-scale change in the midst of combat operations.

Although they had never adopted Soviet practices to the same extent as the Syrians and Egyptians, the Iraqis had made a number of changes in accord with Soviet doctrine, particularly in the air force. After the October War, Iraq abandoned many of the Soviet methods it had acquired. Baghdad never had Soviet advisers attached to its operational units in the manner of Egypt and Syria, but there were instructors who trained Iraqi personnel in certain operations. These men were sent home, and only those Soviets needed to teach weapons instruction and technical subjects were retained.[41] In most cases the Iraqis went back to their original British-based doctrine; in other areas — such as unit organization, air defense, and logistics — the

Iraqis welded together Soviet and British practices. Finally, in several important categories they developed their own tactics based on their experiences against the Kurds and the Israelis.

The most important of these indigenous developments was the change in their offensive doctrine. The consistent fiascoes they had undergone with headlong frontal attacks finally convinced them to abandon this as an assault tactic. Instead, they adopted a doctrine of overwhelming firepower. Rather than charging a position as had been their previous practice, Iraqi forces were trained not to assault a well-defended objective at all, but to dig in immediately and then call in massive firepower from tanks, artillery, mortars, multiple-rocket launchers, and close-support aircraft to obliterate the source of resistance.

The Iraqis had also made several other changes based on their experience with the Kurds. Iraq had improved its logistics capability to prevent the Kurds from successfully implementing the isolation strategy that had worked so well for them in 1962–70. To some extent, Iraq's logistical feats during the October War were the product of these reforms. Also, the experience of 1973 pointed out shortfalls in Iraq's mobility assets, which Baghdad moved to correct by buying nearly 2,000 heavy-equipment transporters. Their defeat at the hands of the Israelis and Kurds had also taught Iraqi generals to concentrate overwhelming numerical superiority against a specific sector rather than dissipating their strength across the front. Thus, when war broke out again in Kurdistan, they had massed virtually the entire Iraqi army in the north with the weight of their force deployed against the vital eastern sector. They also had quietly built 700 miles of new roads in Kurdistan, mostly under the pretense of showing their goodwill to the Kurds by helping improve their rudimentary infrastructure. These new roads allowed the Iraqi military rapid entry into formerly inaccessible regions of Kurdistan. Finally, the Iraqis learned to be remorselessly brutal toward the Kurds. While their past treatment had been far from humane, the Iraqi military prepared to wage a vicious scorched-earth campaign against the entire Kurdish population.

Course of Operations

The Kurds moved first, launching attacks throughout Kurdistan against government-held towns and military bases in April 1974. The Iraqis were taken by surprise and had to fall back in many places, but the Kurds still lacked the heavy weapons to force the Iraqis out of their fortified bases. As a result, their campaign quickly petered out. During the summer, the Iraqi army counterattacked, setting in motion its long-planned offensive.

While Iraq's strategy was similar to those it employed in 1966 and 1969, the change in their tactics coupled with the change in Kurdish tactics produced a very different result. Instead of walking blindly into ambushes and charging madly at heavily defended positions, the Iraqis inched forward and, whenever they encountered resistance, called in devastating firepower to level whatever lay in front of them. Of crucial importance to the success of this doctrine, however, was that instead of retreating back into the mountains after contacting a superior Iraqi force, the Kurds now tried to stand and slug it out with the army. Tactically, the Kurds were no better than the government troops (not surprising since they were being trained mostly by deserters from the Iraqi army), but they could not match the firepower the army could bring to bear. Consequently, Kurdish units stood, fought, and were blown to bits. The Iraqi tactics were hardly elegant, but with the cooperation of the Peshmerga, they got the job done.

By early 1975, Iraq was threatening to annihilate the Kurdish resistance. Its forces had cleared the areas around Kirkuk, Arbil, al-Ahmadiyah, and as-Sulaymaniyyah. The Iraqis had used the new road network to push deep into Kurdistan toward the Iranian border, capturing Rawanduz, Raniyah, and even Qal'at Dizah, effectively splitting Kurdistan in half—a goal they had been unable to accomplish in 1966 or 1969. Furthermore, rather than retreating south when the snow began to fall, the Iraqis settled down to maintain their positions throughout the winter. The Peshmerga had suffered heavy casualties and, with the army remaining in Kurdistan, they were in danger of losing their supply links to Iran. Kurdish civilians were also suffering mightily since the Iraqis were equally willing to use their new affectation for firepower against Kurdish villages as well as Peshmerga defensive positions.

This turn of events brought a sharp response from Iran. The Iraqi Kurds were a useful tool for Tehran: they kept the Iraqi army occupied and were a thorn in Baghdad's side that the shah could press whenever he pleased. Iran was not about to forfeit these advantages and cranked up its military aid to the Kurds. Iran began supplying the Peshmerga with antiaircraft weapons, modern artillery pieces, antitank weapons, and more powerful infantry weapons such as heavy machine guns and heavy mortars. At Tehran's urging, the United States and Israel also provided weapons and intelligence to the Kurds.[42] When even this seemed inadequate, the shah began dispatching Iranian soldiers to fight with the Peshmerga, supporting Kurdish forces with Iranian artillery and SAM units, and provoking clashes with the Iraqi military elsewhere along their border to draw off Iraqi forces from the north. These measures finally stalemated the war in the spring of 1975.

Although the Iraqis were furious with Iran's "meddling," they decided to cut a deal. Iraq's successes against the Kurds notwithstanding, Baghdad recognized that its military was no match for the shah's armed forces. The Iranian army was more than twice the size of the Iraqi military, and it was supplied with the latest American weaponry—the very weapons Iraq coveted. Moreover, Saddam Husayn had concluded that it was only Iranian support that had saved the Kurds, and if he could strike a deal with Iran that would dry up their aid, he was certain he could finish off the Kurds once and for all. In the Algiers Accord of 6 March 1975, negotiated by Saddam Husayn, Iraq agreed to a number of territorial concessions to Iran in return for the shah's agreement to cease supporting the Iraqi Kurds.

In the words of Phebe Marr, "The Algiers settlement was little short of a disaster" for the Peshmerga.[43] Within hours of the signing of the agreement, Iranian soldiers began taking back the heavy weapons they had provided to the Kurds and withdrawing behind the Iranian frontier. The Iraqi offensive began the next day, and between the actual loss of their heavy equipment and the psychological devastation of their sudden abandonment, the Kurds collapsed quickly. By 2 April, the Iraqi army had sealed off the borders of Kurdistan, effectively ending that chapter of the Kurdish revolt. Under an amnesty plan, 70 percent of the Peshmerga gave themselves up to the government, while another 30,000 fled to Iran to join the estimated 200,000 refugees already there.[44] To prevent future recurrences, Baghdad embarked on a brutal campaign against the Kurdish population. The Iraqis resettled over a quarter-million Kurds in western and central Iraq. They also depopulated a six-kilometer-wide strip all along the borders with Turkey and Kurdish Iran, razing the villages and forcing out (or killing) the villagers.

Iraqi Military Performance against the Kurds, 1974–75

The most important lesson of Iraqi military effectiveness during the Second Kurdish War is the light it sheds on Iraqi performance in 1961–70. In particular, it highlights the crucial role of Iraqi tactical incompetence during the First Kurdish War. The strategy the Iraqis implemented in 1974 was virtually identical to the strategy they tried in 1966 and again in 1969. The strategy worked in 1974, although it had not in 1966 and 1969. As noted earlier, the strategy itself was a good one, and when successfully implemented it worked—for the Iraqis in 1975 and 1989 and for the Turks and Iranians on several occasions. The principal reason it was successful in 1974–75 had little to do with the Iraqis but was mostly a product of the change in Kurdish tactics. In 1966 and again in 1969, the Iraqis had the right idea, but their units were incapable of executing the strategy and were humiliated by Peshmerga employing traditional guerrilla tactics — and not employing them terribly well, either. In 1974 the Iraqis were on the brink of victory not because the change in their tactics was an improvement but because the change in Kurdish tactics was a catastrophe.

It is highly unlikely that, had Barzani not made the decision to try to fight a conventional war, the Iraqis would have been able to effectively implement their strategy in 1974. Iraq's change to reliance on massive firepower was unlikely to have had any effect on the Kurds had the Peshmerga continued to operate as guerrillas. There are at least two arguments that support this judgment. First, reliance on overwhelming firepower against a guerrilla force was exactly the strategy employed by the U.S. military in Vietnam, and it proved to be a very poor approach. Relying on firepower means destroying one's enemy at a distance rather than grappling with him in close combat. However, to destroy an enemy through firepower one must fix him in place, and the only way to fix a guerrilla force in place is either to trap it in a confined area or to engage it in close combat. Thus, using firepower against guerrillas suffers from an inherent flaw: the guerrillas are too mobile and elusive to be pinned down and destroyed this way. It seems highly likely that the Iraqis would have had roughly the same results as the Americans had — expending a lot of ordnance without doing much damage to the guerrillas and becoming increasingly frustrated at their inability to really hurt the insurgents.[45]

Second, setting aside the various logistical reforms they had conducted, the only significant change the Iraqis had made in their combat operations was the shift in offensive doctrine to reliance on overwhelming firepower. They still had not learned to put out flank guards, carry out regular reconnaissance, outflank ambushes, or otherwise maneuver against Kurdish forces. Nor had they learned to properly integrate their forces into combined-arms teams, properly employ their air power in support of ground operations, coordinate the operations of their units, or conduct aggressive intelligence gathering operations. In short, the Iraqis had done little to correct the problems they had suffered from during the first round of combat with the Kurds, and the only change they had made probably would only have further diminished their ability to defeat Kurdish *guerrilla* tactics. Consequently, there is every reason to believe that if the Peshmerga had continued to employ guerrilla tactics, they would have continued to enjoy success against the Iraqis. It seems almost inevitable that one or more

Iraqi units would have found themselves trapped and mauled by Peshmerga as had happened at Rawanduz Gorge, Mt. Handrin, and numerous other occasions between 1965 and 1970.

Ultimately, the Iraqis prevailed in 1975 despite their tactical incompetence. They eventually figured out the Kurds' vulnerability and developed a strategy that would allow them to exploit that weakness. However, their forces proved so inept that they only succeeded in implementing this strategy when Barzani did the one thing that could possibly have brought the Peshmerga under Baghdad's control: ordering them to stand and fight like a conventional army when they lacked the weapons and training to do so.

The Iran-Iraq War, 1980–88

At the end of the October War, Baghdad inaugurated a major military build up. The Iraqis recognized that they had not performed particularly well against the Israelis and concluded that they needed to improve and expand their armed forces. This desire received considerable impetus from the events of 1974–75. First, the defeat of the Kurdish insurgency taught the Ba'thists that they could achieve policy goals with military operations. Second, the humiliation of having to agree to the conditions of the Algiers Accord in the face of Iranian military superiority convinced Baghdad that, in the Middle East, only the strong prosper. Thus, between 1973 and 1980, Iraq doubled the size of its army both in terms of active-duty manpower and the number of divisions — from six to twelve — of which four were now armored and two mechanized infantry. Iraq bought 1,600 new tanks and APCs, including the USSR's most modern T-72s and BMP-1s, as well as over 200 new combat aircraft, including MiG-23s and Su-22s. In addition, Iraq made a determined effort to improve its training, placing particular stress on combined-arms operations and mechanized warfare.[46]

Baghdad accomplished two other important goals for its military between 1973 and 1980. First, Saddam largely relieved the Iraqi armed forces of their lingering internal-security functions by creating new paramilitary arms such as the 150,000 strong Popular Army specifically to enforce domestic repression while the army was redirected toward a potential war with Israel or Iran. Second, the Ba'thists all but guaranteed the military's loyalty to the regime by purging senior officers of questionable reliability, promoting loyalty to Saddam ahead of military competence, frequently rotating key senior officer billets to prevent generals from developing personal ties to their men, creating multiple security services to watch over the military, and micromanaging military operations and exercises to ensure that the armed forces carried out Saddam's orders.[47] There was only one problem: in so doing, they packed the senior officer ranks with incompetents. Few if any of the generals leading the army and air force had any combat experience, and all were chosen for their loyalty rather than their abilities. Indeed, in a number of cases, Baghdad cashiered aggressive officers rather than promote them to general-officer rank for fear they would attempt to move against the regime. In Edgar O'Balance's pithy description, the Iraqi officer corps above the rank of colonel "lacked the vision, flair, and imagination necessary to execute their responsibilities adequately, let alone with brilliance."[48]

The Invasion of Iran, 1980

Given the limitations of its top military commanders, it should have come as no surprise that Iraq's blueprint for its invasion of Iran was poorly conceived and inadequately prepared. Baghdad's strategy was to seize Khuzestan province in southwestern Iran just across the Shatt al-Arab from Iraq. Khuzestan contained the bulk of Iran's oil-industry, and a significant percentage of its population were Arab Shi'ah, whom Saddam believed he could appeal to on ethnic grounds to rise up and aid the invading Iraqi armies as their savior from Persian oppression. Baghdad labored under several other false assumptions. First, the Iraqis were convinced by dissident Iranian military officers and their own politicized intelligence services that the Iranian army had been so debilitated by desertions and purges resulting from that country's Islamic revolution that Iraq's armed forces would be able to sweep them aside with little effort. Baghdad was equally convinced that the Iranian people despised Ayatollah Ruhollah Khomeini and the mullahs (Shi'ite clerics) who had ousted the shah and would overthrow them if given the opportunity. Numerous Iranian officials, including former prime minister Shapour Bakhtiar and the former commander of Iranian ground forces, Gen. Gholam-'Ali Oveisi, had fled to Iraq after the revolution and filled Saddam's head with visions of a weak fundamentalist regime that would collapse if given a shove but that otherwise would subvert Iraq's oppressed Shi'ah population if not stopped immediately. Saddam intended Iraq's seizure of Khuzestan province to be the spark that would ignite a new revolution in Iran, one that would oust Khomeini and replace him with a government more amenable to Iraqi interests.[49]

Aside from the fact that the Iraqi plan contained no actions designed to specifically bring about this revolution and instead simply assumed that it would occur, in a purely military sense, the plan, broadly considered, should have been adequate to conquer and hold Khuzestan. Baghdad's design called for the invasion of Iran with nine divisions. Three armored divisions and two mechanized divisions would drive into Khuzestan itself, securing the major cities, the major roads, and most important, the Zagros mountain passes through which Iranian forces would have to move to reinforce or retake the province. Farther north, three infantry divisions and another armored division would seize the northern passes through the Zagros, which the Iranians would have to use if they wanted to try to launch a counteroffensive against Baghdad. According to several former Iraqi generals, the whole operation was to be completed in two weeks.[50]

In general terms the Iraqis had identified the right objectives and probably had allocated adequate forces to take them, but the plan fell apart in the details — specifically, that it lacked any details. The final invasion plan was a hasty rewrite of a 1941 British staff exercise of a hypothetical attack to seize Khuzestan and its oil fields with one British division. Iraq's general staff updated the forces involved and laid out the basics of the air support, logistics, engineering, and other necessary support functions, but they did so haphazardly and provided only the most general guidance. Planners relied heavily on the calculations of the British exercise, which was a training document developed at a different time, for different forces, and with different assumptions regarding the political context.[51] Even eighteen years later, a former Iraqi general seethed: "Our troops were just lined up on the border and told to drive into Iran. They had an objective, but no idea how to get there or what they were doing, or how their mission fit the plan, or who would be supporting them."[52]

THE IRAQI PREEMPTIVE AIRSTRIKES

The British were not the only ones the Iraqis borrowed from. Iraq began the war on 22 September with a preemptive airstrike against the Islamic Republic of Iran Air Force (IRIAF) modeled on Israel's 1967 airstrikes. However, the Iraqi leadership had no idea how to conduct such an operation. For starters, their intelligence picture of the IRIAF was negligent to the point of absurdity because they did not conduct any reconnaissance missions or otherwise obtain recent information on their targets before launching the attack. Consequently, the Iraqis had to rely on Iranian defectors to tell them which Iranian aircraft were deployed to which airbases and the location and capabilities of Iranian air defenses. The defectors' information was often out of date, and they deliberately downplayed Iranian capabilities to try to goad the Iraqis to attack. The Iraqis had neglected to study Iranian air force doctrine altogether and simply assumed it was similar to their own, despite the fact that the shah's air force had been trained by the United States, whereas the Iraqis had an awkward mélange of British,

Russian, and even some French doctrine. The Iraqis also were unaware that Iran had built hardened aircraft bunkers (HABS) to protect their combat aircraft from enemy air attack.

Beyond these failings, Iraq's air forces lacked the capability to execute a large-scale air offensive even had the air force leadership between able to plan one properly. Few of Iraq's most modern MiG-23, Su-20, and Su-22 squadrons were operationally ready because their personnel still had not learned to fly and maintain the aircraft. Against the Kurds, the Iraqis had rarely tried to hit targets of military size and had not trained to do so. Instead, the air force had concentrated on high-altitude bombing of fairly large targets, like villages, and they showed little concern for where the bombs fell. Based on their actual performance, the Iraqi Air Force seems to have had a sustained sortie-generation capability of about 40–70 per day, with a surge capability of about 100–120.[53] The Israelis, with incomparably better pilots and against an air force that was about the same size as the IRIAF but that was neither dispersed nor protected by HABS, required close to 700 sorties in one morning to accomplish their feat.[54] The Iraqis attempted to do the same with 100 sorties spread out over an entire day.

The airstrikes on 22 September were pitiful. The first wave struck every major airbase in western Iran, including Mehrabad Air Force Base outside of Tehran. A smaller second wave then struck the five airfields in and around Khuzestan and several key Iranian radars. General Oveisi and some of the other Iranian expatriates had provided the Iraqis with considerable information regarding when and how best to strike. However, Iraq failed to concentrate adequate assets against any of these targets to cause serious damage. Iraqi aircraft frequently were equipped with the wrong ordnance for their assigned mission, minimizing the effectiveness of their attacks. Moreover, Iraqi airstrikes were highly inaccurate; in many cases bombs fell so far from any nearby military facility that the Iranians could not determine what the Iraqis had been trying to hit. In other cases Iraqi aircraft left untouched Iranian military aircraft sitting out in the open, instead sticking to their assigned missions of cratering runways or bombing support buildings. And these Iraqi aircraft made no effort to strafe the parked planes after they had completed their bombing runs, nor apparently did they even alert their superiors to these golden opportunities, for no additional aircraft were directed to the airbases to hit the parked Iranian planes. Iraqi pilots were extremely timid, generally conducting their attacks from high altitudes and aborting their missions in the face of rather slight resistance. To make matters worse, the air force failed to follow up its initial attacks with poststrike reconnaissance and restrikes against targets insufficiently damaged during the first attacks. By the end of the first day, Baghdad's surprise attacks had inflicted negligible damage on a handful of Iranian facilities and overall had no effect on Iranian military capabilities. Iran lost no more than two or three combat aircraft and one transport. Iraq had a bomber and two attack aircraft shot down by Iranian air defenses, and not one of the Iranian airbases was put out of action.[55]

To add insult to injury, the next day Iraq lost air superiority to the crippled IRIAF. The shah's air force had suffered greatly from the revolution. The purges of the Iranian military had fallen most heavily on the air force because of its close ties to the United States. Iran's brand-new computerized logistics system was rendered inoperable by departing U.S. personnel, paralyzing maintenance and repair work on Iran's sophisticated fighters. In the chaos of the revolution, the air force suffered heavy desertions, and there was little training and maintenance work. On 22 September the IRIAF had been surprised by the Iraqi airstrikes and was able to mount only minor resistance. Nevertheless, the next day Iran generated roughly 160 combat sorties and nearly swept the skies clear of Iraqi aircraft. Iraq was able to conduct only a few scattered attacks, largely on Iranian targets close to the border. Although Iraq's operational fighter strength was three to four times that of Iran, Iraqi pilots generally aborted their missions the moment they detected Iranian fighters, and in those instances when the Iraqis either accidentally or purposefully engaged in air-to-air combat, the Iranians prevailed quickly. Iran also conducted airstrikes against Iraqi military, industrial, and oil facilities. Iran's logistical problems prevented it from conducting more than sporadic raids with pairs of F-4s that did little damage to their targets, but the Iraqis were stunned that Iran could even mount such operations. Baghdad reacted by dispersing most of its commercial and military aircraft (including many fighters) to bases in western Iraq and to foreign countries such as Jordan and Kuwait, where they were beyond Iran's reach.

THE INVASION OF KHUZESTAN

Iraq's ground assault was no better. Its greatest problem was that Iraqi forces moved at a snail's pace against meager Iranian resistance. Overall, the balance of forces heavily favored Iraq because the desertions, demoralization, purges, and other distractions attending the Iranian revolution had left few operationally ready military forces. Iraq deployed 2,750 tanks, 1,400 artillery pieces, 4,000 APCs, and 340 fighter-bombers. Against this, Iran could muster no more than about 500 operational tanks, probably no more than 300 functioning artillery pieces, and less than 100 operable aircraft.[56] Iran had close to 100,000 troops in the Islamic Revolutionary Guards Corps (IRGC), or Revolutionary Guard, but at the time these were little more than militant students and street thugs who had secured the revolution but had no formal military training. Roughly one-quarter of Iran's army was tied down fighting a Kurdish revolt, and Iran had only two badly depleted divisions, two equally reduced brigades, and some lightly armed security forces along the border to contend with the nine well-armed divisions that Iraq committed to the invasion.

The local balance of forces in Khuzestan was even more favorable to the Iraqis. The 92d Armored Division at Ahvaz was the only major Iranian formation in the area, and it took several days before it could deploy even company-sized formations let alone the entire division. Otherwise, the Iraqis faced small platoon- and company-sized elements from the Iranian army, Revolutionary Guards, and Iranian gendarmerie fighting mostly with small arms and without any central direction. Most of the Iranian forces did not even try to delay the Iraqi invasion but retreated to the cities and other defensible positions. Nevertheless, two weeks into the campaign, the deepest Iraqi penetrations were only 65 kilometers into Iran, and in most sectors the Iraqis had gone no more than 20–30 kilometers. Whether in the mountains of the Zagros or the dry, open terrain of Khuzestan, the quickest Iraqi units advanced only an average of 5–6 kilometers per day, facing only scattered bands of lightly armed and, in the case of the gendarmerie and Revolutionary Guards, essentially untrained Iranian defenders.

The primary reason for this glacial advance was Iraq's tactical doctrine. As they had done against the Kurds, Iraqi units relied on overwhelming firepower as their method of attack. Iraqi armored and mechanized formations would not advance until the area in front of them had been saturated with tank and artillery fire. They would then advance a short distance and dig in to wait for the next round of bombardment. On those occasions when they encountered Iranian resistance — no matter how light — Iraq's armor would halt, bring up engineers to build defensive positions, and then lay down a massive barrage of fire from tanks, mortars, artillery, multiple-rocket launchers, FROG rockets, airstrikes, and anything else available. When the Iranian position was a smoldering ruin, they would resume their advance only to halt again at the next sign of resistance. Likewise, when Iraqi maneuver units began to approach the maximum range of their artillery support, they would stop, fortify, and wait for the artillery to redeploy before they would resume creeping forward. In the central Zagros Mountains, Iraqi infantry units even added volleys of Sagger ATGMs to their barrages against Iranian roadblocks, which were often undefended. In a few

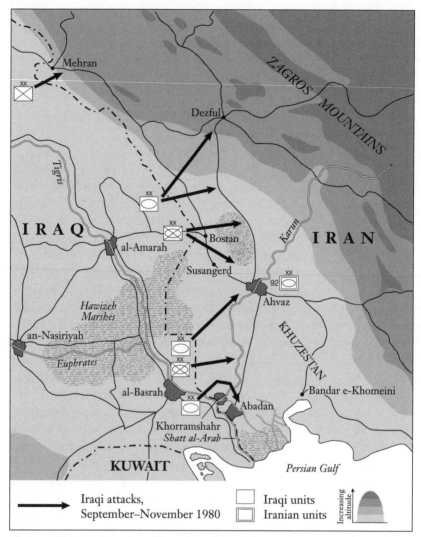

Map 14. The Iraqi Invasion of Iran, September 1980

instances, notably outside of Dezful during the first week of the war, Iraqi forces did employ a sort of flanking attack; the Iranians lacked the troops to form a continuous frontline, and after several days' bombardment, Iraqi forces would take up a position on one of the Iranian wings — threatening to outflank the Iranian lines but not actually conducting a flanking attack — which would cause the outgunned Iranians to pull back.

Even as they fell further and further behind schedule, Iraqi frontline commanders never varied from these tactics. Iraq's tactical leadership simply refused to show any creativity or initiative. Iraqi armored and mechanized formations never used their mobility to bypass Iranian positions, nor did they envelop Iranian defensive positions, nor did they use their shock power to simply overrun what were usually small numbers of ill-trained Iranian infantry with little or no antitank weaponry. John Wagner, a leading expert on the Iran-Iraq War, marvels that "no attempt was made to use fast-moving armored columns to penetrate and disrupt Iranian rear areas and to capture key objectives before the Iranians could react."[57] The Iraqis never tried to seize key terrain to cut off Iranian lines of communication and retreat. Iraq did not once employ airborne or helicopter-borne troops to conduct a vertical envelopment of Iranian positions to speed the passage of their mechanized forces. Iraqi commanders were painfully slow to commit their reserves to overpower Iranian resistance, to meet the few Iranian counterattacks, or to maintain the momentum of an advance when the lead units got bogged down or disorganized. They showed little or no aggressiveness, consistently failing to pursue defeated Iranian units, to quickly overrun undefended territory, or to otherwise exploit sudden opportunities. At Dezful, Khorramshahr, Ahvaz, Abadan, and a host of smaller towns in Khuzestan, large Iraqi mechanized formations reached the outskirts of the town before the Iranians had the chance to bring in reinforcements and heavy weapons, build fortifications, or otherwise organize themselves for defense. In every case, rather than immediately assaulting the town, bypassing it and driving on toward the passes, or even encircling the town to properly besiege it, the Iraqi units dug in and waited for artillery fire to soften up the defenses. When the Iraqis finally launched their attack days later, the Iranians invariably had reinforced the garrison, created a local force of Revolutionary Guards, and built hasty defensive positions. In virtually all of these cases, when Iranian resistance made it clear that bombardment had failed to persuade them to flee, the Iraqis would call off the attack and fortify once again.

The one exception to this rule was Khorramshahr, where the Iraqis were determined to take the city. They eventually did so, but it took four weeks of combat, 8,000 casualties, and the loss of over 100 tanks and APCs to Iranian infantry equipped with small arms, light antitank weapons, and Molotov cocktails.[58] As a result, Khorramshahr was the only city Iraq captured while it failed to secure any number of other towns and cities that were critical communications nodes, transportation junctions, population centers, garrisons, or defensive positions.

Part of the problem can be traced to the dearth of Iraqi tactical intelligence-gathering operations. Iraq's ground units just did not perform reconnaissance. Even on their numerous halts, Iraqi commanders rarely sent out patrols to scout the territory ahead. Apparently, most of the information they did receive from patrols was inaccurate. R. D. McLaurin has commented: "contradictory reporting on locations, activities, and accomplishments from various elements of the Iraqi command appears to reflect communications and control problems as well as willful deception attempts. Some observers commented that lying was endemic throughout the command structure."[59] Nor could such failings be compensated by intelligence provided by higher echelons. Baghdad's senior leadership similarly neglected intelligence gathering. The air force had few reconnaissance aircraft and rarely used those it had. Iraq's ability to exploit photo-reconnaissance missions was poor and subject to severe distortion because Iraq's senior military intelligence officers reported whatever Saddam wanted to hear. Moreover, even this information was rarely disseminated to Iraq's field commanders because the senior leadership saw restricting information as a way of keeping control over their subordinates. Consequently, Iraqi tactical commanders rarely knew what was in front of them and were repeatedly caught off-guard by Iranian deployments and counterattacks.

Despite their reliance on tanks and artillery fire, the Iraqis showed little ability to properly handle either. Iraq employed its tanks as mobile artillery and little more. Its tank crews could not fire on the move and had very poor marksmanship even when stopped. Iraqi tank commanders did not use the mobility of their vehicles to maneuver against their enemy. In armor duels small numbers of Iranian tanks regularly outfought larger Iraqi units. For instance, the Iraqis were ultimately prevented from taking the key Iranian town of Dezful in northern Khuzestan because their vaunted 3d Armored Division was stopped cold by an understrength Iranian tank battalion reinforced by several hundred Revolutionary Guards at the Kharkeh River. In these fights the Iraqi tanks would quickly move into hull-down positions and remain there. By contrast, many Iranian tanks would at least try to stalk their adversary in hopes of getting a flank shot. Because the Iraqis would not move from their initial positions, the Iranians often were able to maneuver for a better shot, and because the Iranians also were usually better marksmen, they scored more kills.

Iraqi artillery was the mainstay of the invasion, but it proved extremely limited in its capabilities. Gunners generally set up firing positions and then stayed for as long as they could rather than relocating after a few rounds to prevent Iranian shell-tracking radars from fixing on them. As a result, the Iraqis suffered in counterbattery engagements with the Iranians. They did well when massing their fire against a designated position if given the time to properly register their guns. But they frequently had difficulty conducting creeping barrages to eliminate opposition (and suppress antitank teams) in front of slowly advancing armor or infantry. Moreover, they simply could not rapidly shift fire nor could they provide quick-fire support to deal with unexpected developments. Finally, *every* Iraqi artillery operation required a great deal of time, a problem that eventually led Baghdad to invest heavily in multiple-rocket launchers, which at least could saturate an area with fire quickly.

Nor could the Iraqis compensate for these problems in their individual combat arms by effectively combining them into integrated teams. As noted above, Iraqi artillery was only capable of supporting maneuvering units under certain very specific conditions. Iraq also continued to experience problems coordinating the operations of infantry and armor. Tanks regularly operated without infantry support and vice versa. These problems resulted in the Iraqis losing a significant number of tanks to ambushes. In the most notorious example of this problem, the Iraqis not only employed an armored division to assault the city of Khorramshahr (built on a marshy island, as if urban terrain were not bad enough for armor), but they even stripped it of its organic infantry elements before sending it in. After the tanks were thrown back by the Iranians, Iraq was forced to airlift in brigades of special forces and Republican Guards, give them a hasty course in urban warfare, and then send them in to take the city.

Air support of ground forces was similarly poor. The Iraqi Air Force performed close air support (CAS) missions infrequently, basically just contributing to the massive-fire plans laid down on particularly well-defended Iranian positions. In these cases, the airstrikes had to be requested well in advance and generally could only be called in on large targets such as towns because the Iraqi pilots lacked the accuracy to hit anything smaller. For the most part, only senior field officers could request air support; all missions had to be approved by Baghdad; and the entire process was conducted through an elaborate command-and-control system. Thus, air support was unresponsive to the needs of commanders on the ground. Although the air force provided sporadic and ineffective CAS, it performed virtually no battlefield air interdiction (BAI) missions, hardly ever trying to disrupt Iranian units regrouping in the rear or to prevent reinforcements and supplies from reaching the front lines.

Although the Iraqi invasion was disastrous, it was not without some redeeming features. First, as always for Iraq, were the logisticians, who accomplished every task required of them. The various lessons learned from previous conflicts paid handsome dividends in 1980. Wary of Soviet machinations, Iraq had built an enormous stockpile of ammunition, spare parts, and other military consumables so that when the USSR slapped an embargo on the country during the first eight months of the war, it had little effect on Iraqi forces in the field.[60] The one exception to this rule was artillery shells, which Iraq expended in such profligate numbers during their "advance by firepower" invasion that they began to run low, forcing Iraqi batteries to conserve their rounds for a few weeks in late October and early November. After the October War, Iraq had developed a hybrid logistics system that relied on British "pull" down to divisional level, but a Soviet "push" system below the division level.[61] This system proved quite efficient, and the Iraqis showed considerable flexibility in adapting it to the needs of the moment. The movement of troops, weaponry, and supplies prior to the invasion were conducted smoothly and efficiently. Supply and transport units kept the combat units well supplied throughout the invasion, although the pace of the advance made this considerably less challenging. Nevertheless, Iraq's logistical system kept nine divisions plus support troops (a force of over 150,000 men) well supplied for over a year in Iran without any glaring mistakes — a considerable achievement by any measure.

The other aspect of military effectiveness in which Iraqi forces really excelled during the initial invasion was combat engineering. During the advance into Iran, Iraqi engineers performed well in overcoming obstacles to the movement of ground forces. In particular, their river-crossing operations were very efficient. The best known of these operations was the crossing of the Karun River on 24 September as part of the advance on Khorramshahr, during which the Iraqis crossed an armored division in a single night. Later in the year, engineers began a prodigious road-building effort to link their supply centers around al-Basrah with the combat units forward in Iran. These roads became crucial in keeping Iraq's forces supplied after the rains came in the late fall and turned Khuzestan into a sea of mud.

Finally, the Iraqi army held together and fought with an unexpected degree of commitment. Many foreign observers admitted being surprised that Iraqi units had not disintegrated when the first shots were fired. Prior to the invasion, the consensus among experts was that Iraq's military had been so thoroughly demoralized by Saddam's purges that it would fall apart under the slightest pressure. However, Iraqi units hung together and remained cohesive even in tough fights such as the house-to-house combat for Khorramshahr. Moreover, Iraqi soldiers often showed tenacity, courage, and endurance in combat. Once again, Khorramshahr is the best example, as Iraqi soldiers determinedly slugged it out with the Revolutionary Guards in the rubble of the city and eventually cleared it. Their operations were rarely elegant but also rarely craven.

The Iranian Counteroffensives, 1981–82

Less than two weeks into the invasion, signs began to emerge that Baghdad was unhappy with the course of its campaign. On 2 October 1980, Iraq announced that its forces had achieved all of their objectives and would only defend their gains. Three days later they announced a unilateral cease-fire. Former Iraqi generals who have since fled the country have confirmed that this was intended only to allow Iraqi forces to regroup, reorganize, and hopefully be able to resume their advance with greater gusto. It was *not* meant as an end to the fighting.[62] Indeed, the day after they declared the ceasefire, the Iraqis launched another major effort to try to capture Khorramshahr (which only fell on 24 October).

By November 1980 the momentum of the Iraqi invasion was over. Iranian resistance was only marginally responsible for this. Iraqi forces had outnumbered the Iranians six to one in the theater of operations at the start of the campaign, and Iranian units had generally opted not to try to defend Khuzestan's open terrain, instead retreating back to the major towns and cities. Essentially, the Iraqis stopped themselves through their slow, bumbling advance. After two months (not the fourteen days originally planned), the Iraqis had failed to secure the major roads in Khuzestan, the only city they had taken was Khorramshahr (although they briefly overran Susangerd but then lost it again when they failed to garrison it and had Iranian units walk back in), and of greatest importance, they had failed to seal the passes through the Zagros. By early December, Iran had brought in reinforcements from all over the country and cut Iraq's numerical advantage to two to one.[63] In addition, in late November the rains arrived in Khuzestan and turned its relatively open terrain — crisscrossed by countless water barriers — into mud. Iraqi forces, which were heavily reliant on their vehicles, became hopelessly road-bound by the mud, making Iranian defensive efforts much easier.

In January 1981 the Iranians were ready to go on the offensive. Their first attack, motivated to a certain extent by domestic political maneuverings, was an attempt to push the Iraqis back from the main city of Ahvaz in central Khuzestan. It was a haphazardly planned operation intended to use the 16th and 92d Armored Divisions to conduct a double envelopment of three or four Iraqi brigades on the outskirts of Susangerd, west of Ahvaz. However, according to former Iraqi generals, Iraqi signals intercepts had picked up all of the details of the Iranian plan, and Baghdad had moved strong forces from the 6th Armored and 5th Mechanized Divisions plus the elite 10th Armored Brigade of Iraq's Republican Guard into the area.[64]

The Iranians attacked during the night of 4–5 January and made good progress at first. During the invasion, they had recognized that the Iraqis fought very poorly at night, generally going into bivouac without posting adequate security or even setting up adequate fighting positions. As a result, the first Iranian attacks overran an Iraqi infantry brigade and routed an armored brigade of the 10th Armored Division. However, a supporting attack by Iran's 77th Infantry Division was stopped cold when it unexpectedly ran into the Iraqi 5th Mechanized Division southwest of Ahvaz. Then, on 7 January, as the Iranian 16th Armored Division drove southeast as the right wing of their double envelopment, the Iranians suddenly found themselves being counterattacked from three sides by the Iraqi 6th Armored Division and Republican Guard 10th Armored Brigade, which were deployed in hull-down positions along their route of march. The brigades of the 16th Armored Division had to drive forward along a single road hemmed in by the Iraqi armor. When the Iraqis opened fire, the Iranians tried to get off the road and maneuver, but many got stuck in the mud, making them sitting ducks for the Iraqis. In all, the Iranians lost 200 of 300 tanks. From the Iraqi perspective, what is interesting is not that they mauled the 16th Armored but that they had so much difficulty doing it. Despite having the Iranians caught in a perfect trap, Iraq still lost nearly 100 of the 350 tanks it committed to the battle, mostly to Iranian fire. As had been the case during the invasion, Iraqi armor would not maneuver — or even change positions on the firmer ground of the surrounding hills — and Iraqi gunners displayed poor marksmanship. Although Iranian tankers were mediocre by Western standards, they were still better than the Iraqis in terms of their accuracy, aggressiveness, and skill.

Rather than exploit their success to turn a tactical victory into an operational achievement, Iraq's field commanders rested on their laurels. Baghdad immediately ordered the 5th Mechanized and 6th Armored Divisions to take Susangerd and several other nearby towns to prepare a renewed drive on Ahvaz. However, the divisions took a week to regroup and reorganize themselves before launching a typically slow, frontal assault that relied entirely on firepower to drive the Iranians out. The Iranian formations had recovered from their defeat by then and were able to stymie the Iraqi attack within a few days, it having advanced only ten kilometers.

For the Iranians, Susangerd was only a temporary setback. In April they launched an attack on Iraqi forces near Qasr-e Shirin in the northern sector of the front. For the first time, Iran employed large numbers of Revolutionary Guards (filled out by the ubiquitous *Basij*, or "mobilization battalions") to spearhead its attack. The Iraqis were surprised and several brigades were overwhelmed. The Iranian assault was a small operation and only gained a few hills for Tehran, but its success convinced the mullahs in Tehran that large-scale infantry assaults relying on the Islamic fervor of the Revolutionary Guards and the Basij were their ace in the hole. During the summer of 1981, the Iranians launched a series of similar operations on Iraq along the front, including several larger attacks that pushed the Iraqis out of key positions around Khorramshahr and Abadan in the far south.

The Iranians used these smaller operations to hone their tactics in preparation for a campaign to reclaim their lost territory. Tehran kicked off this counteroffensive in September 1981, launching a major attack that lifted the siege of Abadan and drove the Iraqis back across the Karun River. After conquering Khorramshahr in October 1980, the Iraqis had driven across the Karun hoping to encircle and take Abadan as well, but they had been stopped by fierce Iranian resistance, leaving their forces in a salient across the river. At midnight on 26 September 1981, The Iranians launched their counteroffensive by hitting this salient from three directions. The Iraqis were surprised and overwhelmed, and their lines began crumbling almost immediately. Baghdad responded by ordering the Republican Guard's 10th Armored Brigade to counterattack. The brigade launched a slow-moving frontal assault at one of the Iranian columns and was easily beaten back with the loss of over one-third of its tanks, allowing Iranian forces to capture the Iraqi bridges over the Karun and trapping several battalions before they could flee.

In late November Iran shifted the focus of its counteroffensive to northern Khuzestan to clear Iraqi forces from the Bostan area that threatened Susangerd and Ahvaz from the northwest. Iranian reconnaissance had discovered that the Iraqis believed the sand dunes north of Susangerd were impassable and so had left their northeastern flank open, believing them anchored on the dunes. During the night of 28–29 November, the Iranians launched an attack with the 16th and 92d Armored Divisions (heavily reinforced by Revolutionary Guards and Basij) against the Iraqi 5th Mechanized and 6th Armored Divisions, catching the Iraqis by surprise. The 16th Armored fixed the 6th Armored in place, while the 92d Armored and a large force of Revolutionary Guards attacked the 5th Mechanized both frontally, concentrating against two weak sectors of the Iraqi line held by battalions from Iraq's Popular Army, and in flank through the supposedly impassable sand dunes. Over the course of the next four days, the Iranians crushed the flank of the 5th Mechanized and then continued rolling south, doing the same to the 6th Armored Division and routing both Iraqi formations.

Iran's victory at Bostan left the Iraqi forces around Dezful farther north in a salient that both sides recognized as vulnerable to an offensive. Iran and Iraq spent the next four months building up their forces in this area. Shortly after midnight on 22 March, the Iranians attacked with at least four divisions from their regular army (about 60,000 troops with fewer than 200 tanks and about 150 artillery pieces) and close to 80,000 Revolutionary Guards and Basijis. The Iraqis had concentrated three infantry divisions along with the 1st Mechanized and the 3d and 10th Armored Divisions, the Republican Guard 10th Armored Brigade, and a number of independent formations and Popular Army units in the area. The first Iranian attacks were on the northern flank of the salient, where the 84th and 21st Infantry Divisions along with large numbers of Revolutionary Guards overran several Iraqi infantry and armored brigades defending the front lines and then penetrated to hit some of the Iraqi armored reserves. The Iraqi IV Corps commander, Maj. Gen. Hisham Sabah al-Fakhri, panicked and ordered the entire 10th Armored Division plus the Republican Guard 10th Armored Brigade to counterattack one Iranian penetration while the 3d Armored Division was sent to counterattack another. Both efforts were slow to develop and hit the Iranians in head-on frontal assaults that were easily stopped. Meanwhile, during the night of 24–25 March, the Iranians unleashed the second part of their double envelopment, launching the 92d and 88th Armored Divisions, along with the elite 55th Airborne Brigade and large numbers of Revolutionary Guards, against the southern flank of the Iraqi line. The attack penetrated through several sectors manned by Iraqi Popular Army units, turned their flanks, and rolled up the lines of the 5th Mechanized Division. With all of their reserves committed in the north (and badly bogged down there), the Iraqi position began to crumble. Over the next four days, the two Iranian pincers pushed forward, grinding up Iraqi armored and mechanized formations. The two arms linked up on 30 March, trapping several Iraqi brigades while the rest of the army fled in disarray. Although there are no reliable numbers available, at least two former Iraqi generals believe the formations at Dezful may have lost close

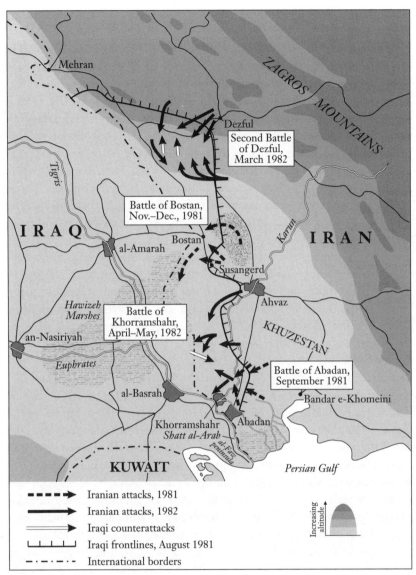

Map 15. Iran's Counteroffensives, 1981–82

to half their effective strength in killed, wounded, and captured during the battle.[65]

The crushing defeat at the second battle of Dezful forced Baghdad to evacuate most of Khuzestan. By the end of April, Iraqi forces held only a salient in extreme southwestern Khuzestan, with its southern flank resting on the Karun River north of Khorramshahr. Iran launched its next offensive there just after midnight on 30 April. Again, the Iranians hit the Iraqi salient on all three sides. In the north the 16th Armored Division launched a fixing attack against the reconstituted Iraqi 5th Mechanized and 6th Armored Divisions. In the south the 21st Infantry Division and large numbers of Revolutionary Guards assaulted across the Karun and overwhelmed the Iraqi reserve and Popular Army formations holding that sector of the front. Meanwhile, the 92d Armored Division and more Revolutionary Guard formations struck the eastern front of the Iraqi line, punching through several infantry brigades holding the line there. This time the Iraqis were slow to commit their main counterattack force (the 3d Armored Division), and by the time it got moving, the Iranians had penetrated across the front and routed most of the Iraqi frontline formations. Moreover, the 3d Armored conducted a very poor counterattack that was easily parried by the badly understrength 92d Armored Division. Iraq then tried to use its air force to stop the Iranians, flying several hundred ground-attack sorties. However, these strikes had no effect on the Iranians and cost Saddam precious planes and pilots, prompting Baghdad to call off the air campaign. By 6 May, with its frontline units in retreat across much of the front, Iraq had regrouped the 3d Armored Division and also brought up the 9th Armored Division. These two units then counterattacked to try to reach the bridges across the Karun to stem the flow of Iranian forces in this sector and stabilize the Iraqi southern flank. Although the 9th Armored initially made some progress through the ranks of lightly armed Revolutionary Guards and Basij, the 3d Armored was stopped by Iranian army units. Then the Iranians again counterattacked with the 92d Armored, sending it into the left flank of the 3d Armored, routing it, and forcing the 9th Armored to pull back or risk being cut off. The 92d kept moving westward and reached the Iran-Iraq border before running out of steam. This trapped a number of Iraqi units against the Karun River, unhinged the southern flank of the entire Iraqi position, and prompted Baghdad to vacate all of Khuzestan except for Khorramshahr, which Saddam bizarrely chose to defend.

The denouement came on the night of 22–23 May, when Iran assaulted Khorramshahr itself and retook the city in twenty-four hours, killing or capturing roughly 15,000 Iraqi troops. Altogether, in the four major Iranian offensives from September 1981 through May 1982, the Iranians regained effectively all of the territory they had lost to the invasion. In these battles Iran inflicted heavy casualties on the Iraqis, including the loss of 600–700 tanks and APCs and over 300 artillery pieces, despite their superior numbers, firepower, and field defenses.[66]

EXPLAINING THE IRAQI DEFEAT

Part of the credit for these impressive operations must go to the Iranians. After the initial shock of the invasion, Iran pulled its military forces together and reorganized them to stop the Iraqi offensive. Former junior officers of the shah's army were recalled to service and sent to the front to take charge of the scattered Iranian units resisting the Iraqi advance. The Islamic Revolutionary Guards Corps (IRGC), which previously had been used by the regime for security and to intimidate internal opposition, was converted into full-fledged military units, given cursory training in basic military operations, and thrown into the fight. Prior to the Iraqi invasion, the Revolutionary Guards and the regular army detested each other: the zealots of the IRGC considered the soldiers and pilots of the armed forces to be agents of the shah and the United States, while the army hated the IRGC for their role in the bloody purges after the revolution. After the invasion, the two organizations hammered out a rough working-relationship between them and even managed to integrate their forces sufficiently to allow them to perform joint operations.

Iran also found a way to defeat the Iraqis on the battlefield despite the damage of the Iranian revolution. The purge of the officer corps, the deliberate sabotage of equipment, the shortage of spare parts because of the U.S. embargo, and the lack of maintenance on most Iranian vehicles drastically reduced both the firepower and the mobility of Iranian forces. Nevertheless, the Iranians learned to work around these problems by conducting offensive operations using massed Revolutionary Guards and Basijis to assault Iraqi positions with fire-support from Iranian army armor and artillery formations. Once the IRGC had punched through the Iraqi lines, mobile army detachments would exploit the breakthrough. This combination allowed the Iranians to conserve their limited numbers of operational tanks, APCs, artillery, and other heavy weapons and employ them only when they could be decisive.

Iran further developed a series of tactics that allowed them to smash even well-entrenched Iraqi units. The Iranians learned to use infiltration tactics to get in among the Iraqi defenders and sow havoc before the main attack.

Eventually, they began complementing their infiltrations with human-wave assaults that, while horribly wasteful of manpower, frequently swamped the defenses or panicked the Iraqi soldiers into abandoning their positions. Through patrols and probing attacks, the Iranians identified the weakest Iraqi units and concentrated overwhelming force against them. Indeed, the Iranians conducted very thorough reconnaissance and mapped Iraqi static positions in great detail prior to each attack. Iranian units, especially the Revolutionary Guards, fought with great ferocity, and their zeal alone often overcame terrified Iraqi units. Moreover, Iran's leadership proved fairly aggressive and imaginative from top to bottom, taking advantage of opportunities as they presented themselves and confounding the Iraqis with unexpected, and frequently unorthodox, approaches. Iranian units constantly searched for flaws in the Iraqi lines and moved immediately to exploit them, turning minor gaps into massive holes. Once into the Iraqi rear, they moved quickly (as quickly as they could, given their very limited mobility) and conducted deep maneuvers that frequently resulted in large-scale envelopements.[67]

Although the Iranians fought well and their offensives were well conceived, they were hardly a juggernaut, and the results of these battles in 1981–82 are as much attributable to Iraqi weakness as to Iranian strength. Essentially, all of the problems Iraq had experienced in its initial invasion reasserted themselves in far more pernicious forms when Iran took the offensive. As long as Iraq held the initiative in 1980 and Iranian forces were crippled and disorganized, Iraq's failings were not so obvious. But when Iran had reinforced and reorganized its army in Khuzestan and then began attacking the Iraqis in full force, these problems became readily apparent.

Iraqi forces were often surprised by Iranian attacks, primarily because the Iraqis never performed adequate reconnaissance, even though in some cases the Iraqis apparently had picked up indications of the attack from signals intercepts.[68] Iraqi tactical formations rarely sent out patrols to see what was happening in the sector immediately in front of them, let alone long-range patrols to try to determine where Iran was massing forces for an attack. In many cases any information that was collected at tactical levels was distorted when conveyed to higher echelons, if it was passed on at all. Nor was this compensated for by strategic assets. The Iraqi Air Force continued to fly only occasional reconnaissance missions, and the reports from these flights hardly ever made it down to the field commanders. Iraq was so negligent in its intelligence-gathering operations that during the offensive to relieve Abadan in September 1981, Iran was able to move a force of 15,000–20,000 troops down the east bank of the Karun, directly in front of Iraqi positions on the same side of the river, without the Iraqis becoming aware of the movement.[69]

The Iraqis also made it relatively easy for the Iranians to break through their defenses. Their failure to develop effective night-fighting capabilities, or even to take adequate security precautions at night, regularly gave the Iranians a key advantage in every breakthrough battle. Saddam decreed that Iraqi units could not voluntarily surrender any Iranian territory, thus Baghdad's commanders were prevented from deploying in the most defensible terrain if it meant giving up conquered territory or from retreating in combat when their positions became untenable.[70] Far more damaging to Baghdad's fortunes, however, was the failure of Iraqi units to guard their flanks, even when deployed in a contiguous line. To make matters worse, Baghdad frequently deployed Popular Army formations to hold the seams between combat divisions. These units — poorly trained and armed — proved incapable of standing up to the Iranians and were the favorite targets of Iranian assaults. As a result, the Iranians usually were able to push through gaps or around the flanks of Iraqi defensive lines.

The relative ease with which Iranian attacks were able to penetrate Iraq's frontlines was particularly problematic because the Iraqis had great difficulty reacting quickly to unexpected developments. Iraq often put its armored and mechanized formations on the forward defensive lines rather than holding them back, leaving few operational reserves available to block Iranian penetrations. The reserves they did maintain took inordinately long periods of time to reinforce a threatened sector or counterattack an Iranian penetration. When counterattacks finally did materialize, they were cumbersome frontal assaults. This despite the fact that the unwieldy masses of Iranian infantry were highly vulnerable to armored attacks against their flanks. If the Iraqis could have swung even battalion-sized armored units into the flanks of an Iranian human-wave attack, the Iranians would have been cut to shreds. These failings were further compounded by the inability of Iraqi units to reorient themselves to deal with any Iranians who penetrated their lines.[71] Indeed, throughout the Iranian offensives, Iraqi forces generally would not reposition or maneuver at all, stubbornly remaining in their prepared defensive positions even after they had been outflanked or enveloped. While they frequently had plentiful artillery support, Iraqi batteries could not redirect fire rapidly to keep pace with the changing flow of the battle and could not shift fire to cover sectors that had not been assigned preplanned fire missions before the start of the attack.

Thus, once the Iranians had penetrated an Iraqi position at one point, it became relatively easy for them to roll up the entire line.

Iraq also could not show the same adaptability or flare for innovation that the Iranians wielded to advantage. Iraqi formations faced with novel Iranian approaches to combat situations normally failed to develop effective countermoves. If the Iranians did not fight "by the book" (that is, the *Iraqi* "book"), the Iraqis did not know what to do and usually either continued trying to overcome the Iranian stratagems with ever greater doses of firepower or would panic and run. Overall, the Iraqis simply did not learn from one battle to the next. Each time they committed the same errors they had the last time. For example, it took years before the Iraqis finally developed even a crude method of handling the human-wave attacks of the Basij and Revolutionary Guards.

Thus, the Iranian offensives of 1981–82 followed an almost formulaic course. The Iranians would mass a large force of Basij and Revolutionary Guards, supported by whatever mechanized forces and artillery the Iranian army could scrape together, against weak sectors of the Iraqi lines — often sectors held by Popular Army units sandwiched between Iraqi field divisions. The Iranians would launch massive human-wave assaults against the Popular Army units, causing them to break and run. Iraqi commanders would take too long forming up and committing their inadequate local reserves — if they moved at all — and the Iranians would punch holes in the line. Iranian heavy forces would then pass through these gaps and into the operational depth of the Iraqi formations, conducting deep encirclements that frequently isolated entire Iraqi combat units. The limitations on Iranian mobility and the fact that they too were not the greatest fighting force in the world meant that these exploitations generally moved slowly and awkwardly. However, Iraqi commanders generally would fail to commit their operational reserves quickly enough, and in those cases where they did muster a counterattack, Iraqi forces invariably launched a frontal assault without adequate infantry or artillery support that would be stopped by Iranian tanks, artillery, and hordes of infantry with light antitank weapons. Meanwhile, the Iraqi units on the frontline that were in the process of being encircled — which often were Iraq's best combat divisions — would frequently sit in their entrenched positions, defending when attacked but unwilling to reorient their lines or counterattack the main Iranian threat, which was now behind them. The result was that fairly slow-moving Iranian infantry attacks supported by small amounts of armor and artillery were able to consistently break through Iraqi defensive lines and encircle their units, often including large mechanized formations.

The Iranian Invasion of Iraq, 1982–86

By 24 May 1982, Iran had evicted the Iraqi forces from Khuzestan. Galvanized by these victories, Ayatollah Khomeini decided to press on to try to overthrow the Ba'thist regime and liberate the Shi'ite holy cities of Karbala and an-Najaf. In mid-July 1982 Iran launched Operation Blessed Ramadan, a major offensive to take al-Basrah, the second city of Iraq. For the next four years, Iranian forces would hammer away at Iraq's defenses. Iran launched one or two major offensives every year between 1982 and 1986 along with as many as a half-dozen lesser attacks. They conducted these offensives in the south against al-Basrah; in the marshes north of al-Basrah, where it was difficult for Iraqi armor to operate; and in the mountains of Kurdistan, where they were aided by the Peshmerga, reborn thanks to revived Iranian support. While the Iranians did make gains here and there, they were slight and never of any real significance to the course of the war. This long period of stalemate was the product of a variety of factors.

THE FIRST BATTLE OF AL-BASRAH

Iran decided to launch its first campaign against Iraq to take al-Basrah, Iraq's second largest city. Tehran saw southern Iraq's heavily Shi'ah population as a natural constituency. The Iranians, knowing that the Shi'ah chafed under Sunni rule and hated Saddam in particular, assumed that if they could take al-Basrah, it would spark a Shi'ite revolt that would at least secure all of Mesopotamia in a new, Iranian-dominated Iraqi state, if not sweep Saddam Husayn and his Sunni supporters from power altogether. In addition, al-Basrah was conveniently located within striking distance of Khuzestan, where Iran now had a large, well-developed military infrastructure that could support large-scale operations into Iraq.

After being thrown out of Khuzestan, the Iraqi military scrambled to regroup. Their first priority was the construction of fortifications to defeat what they believed was an inevitable Iranian invasion. While the rest of the world may have wondered as to Tehran's designs, Baghdad appeared certain that Iran would invade Iraq. With this in mind, engineers labored all through the summer of 1982 to build fortifications around al-Basrah, the obvious first objective of an Iranian invasion. They built two lines of defense, a forward screening line and a main line of fortifications several kilometers behind the first. They laid mines, strung concertina wire, built berms and defensive positions, constructed firing ramps for tanks, built bunkers, and dug artillery pits. In addition, Iraq greatly expanded "Fish Lake," a small fishery east of al-Basrah, which it turned into an enormous artificial pond to bar any approach across the solid, open terrain of the

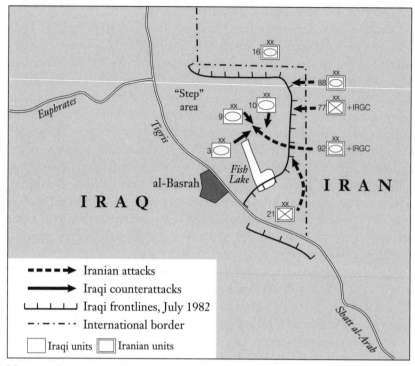

Map 16. The First Battle of al-Basrah, July 1982

step region. They then packed Fish Lake with mines, concertina wire, and power lines that could electrocute anyone in certain sections of the lake.

In July 1982 the Iranians hurled 90,000 Revolutionary Guards and Basij, backed by at least six (badly understrength) army divisions with about 200 tanks, 200 APCs, and 300 artillery pieces, at the step region of Iraq. Operation Blessed Ramadan called for two divisions to conduct a diversionary attack along the northern flank of the step, while two mixed army-IRGC task forces punched through the eastern flank of the defensive lines and then linked up to encircle the Iraqi frontline troops between them. In addition, the 21st Infantry Division and large numbers of Revolutionary Guards would swing south of Fish Lake and try to flank the entire Iraqi position. Waiting to meet the Iranian attack were five reinforced Iraqi divisions manning well-fortified lines, with the 3d, 9th, and 10th Armored Divisions waiting in reserve.

Iran attacked during the night of 13–14 June. Its forces had not faced such heavy Iraqi defenses before, and the diversionary attack in the north and the one of the two pincer thrusts against the eastern flank were stopped in their tracks by the Iraqi frontline formations. However, the southernmost of the two pincers, led by the 92d Armored Division, broke through the Iraqi lines and began pushing westward to try to swing around the northern end of Fish Lake. After the success of the 92d Armored and the failure of the other attacks, Tehran decided to call off the attack by the 21st Infantry Division and send it north to reinforce the 92d's breakthrough. However, that division and its various IRGC formations had effectively walked into a trap, having driven into the space between the three Iraqi armored divisions waiting in reserve. On 15 July all three divisions attacked the Iranian penetration, hitting them on three sides as they had at Susangerd in January 1981. By this point, the Iranians were down to an estimated 100 operational tanks, while the Iraqis struck with over 700, and the overwhelming force routed the 92d Armored and butchered many of the Revolutionary Guard formations.[72] Because the Iraqi mechanized formations continued to show little ability to maneuver in battle, operate as combined-arms teams, or act flexibly, the three divisions still suffered heavy losses, particularly the 9th Armored. Nevertheless, by 17 July, the Iranians had been thrown back just about to their start lines.

The Iranians did not allow one rebuff to stop them, however. Starting on 19 July, they resumed their offensive, launching repeated efforts to break through the Iraqi lines. During the night of 21 July, a Revolutionary Guard assault broke through the Iraqi defenses east of Fish Lake but was driven back the following day by furious tank, helicopter, and artillery fire. On 28 July the 92d Armored Division, the 77th Infantry Division, and IRGC formations again attempted a double envelopment north of Fish Lake, and again the 92d's task force broke through while the 77th's was stopped. Again, the Iraqis counterattacked with three armored divisions and beat the Iranians back with heavy losses. By the beginning of August, both sides were exhausted and bled out. The Iraqis had prevailed, stopping an Iranian offensive for the first time since Susangerd in 1981. However, it had come at a very heavy price. Indeed, the Iraqi 9th Armored Division took such heavy losses that it was disbanded and never reformed—the only Iraqi division to suffer this fate during the war.

IRAQI DEFENSIVE SKILLS

Just as Iran's victories in 1981–82 derived from a series of reinforcing Iraqi weaknesses and Iranian strengths, so too Iraq's victory at al-Basrah was the product of certain Iraqi capabilities reinforced by Iranian weaknesses. Over the next four years, Iraq continued to build on these strengths, while Iran never really found a solution to its weaknesses. The result was four years of stalemate as Iran beat its fists against Iraq's fortified lines without making any meaningful gains.

The victory at al-Basrah convinced the Iraqis of the criticality of their heavily fortified defensive lines. Over the years, Baghdad constantly improved on these defenses, eventually building a formidable line of earthworks and fortifications along nearly the entire length of its border with Iran. The Iraqis made extensive use of flooding and water barriers to channel Iranian attacks and deter assaults on particularly vulnerable sectors, Fish Lake being the best example. They built an extensive new road network that allowed them to rapidly shift mechanized reserves to meet Iranian offensives anywhere along the front. Engineers also built multiple lines of fortifications so that when an Iranian attack broke through one line, it would be confronted with another a few kilometers to the rear. By 1987, al-Basrah was ringed by no less than six concentric circles of fortifications. Indeed, in the latter half of the war, Iraqi engineers routinely began building additional lines of defense behind a sector the moment the Iranians launched an offensive there. Thus, from 1982 to 1986, when Iran attacked using the same tactics it had employed with such success in 1981–82, the Revolutionary Guards and Basij often broke through the first line of defense only to be stopped by a secondary line or by hastily constructed reserve lines behind even that.

Similarly, Iraqi defenses themselves improved slowly over time. For example, initially, Iraqi defensive lines consisted primarily of belts of triangle-shaped company strongpoints, providing all-around protection, deployed in depth and separated by anywhere from several hundred meters to several kilometers, depending on the terrain. This strongpoint system would have been useful against mechanized attacks, but against Iran's massed infantry, the relatively distant strongpoints were quickly isolated and overwhelmed. In response, the Iraqis switched to building lines of raised sand berms as the main fighting positions for their troops. These were large enough to drive a truck across and had predug positions for tanks, APCs, and antiaircraft guns (to "hose down" Iranian human wave attacks, not to defend against air attack). The berms, which stretched for dozens, even hundreds, of kilometers, proved far more effective than the triangular strongpoints, which were mostly discontinued.

While its engineers were fortifying the borders, Baghdad began to try to rebuild its army. Iraq began to conscript increasingly larger percentages of the fit male population, constantly expanding the number of men under arms and the number of combat formations available at any given time.

They purchased more — and more modern — tanks, APCs, artillery pieces, antiaircraft guns, mortars, and anything else they could get their hands on that would allow them to pour fire into the Iranian human-wave attacks. By 1986, Iraq had expanded its army to 700,000 men in forty divisions, with 4,000 tanks, 3,800 other armored vehicles, 3,500 artillery pieces, and nearly 600 combat aircraft.[73] In addition, Baghdad resubordinated the Popular Army brigades to the regular army and began to deploy them only in good defensive terrain in quiet sectors. Finally, Iraq undertook a major expansion of its ground-lift capability, increasing its fleet of heavy-equipment transporters to 3,000 to be able to rapidly shift mechanized formations along the front with Iran. Iraqi transport companies became highly proficient at moving combat formations, and by 1986, Iraq regularly demonstrated the ability to move up to four heavy divisions over hundreds of kilometers in a matter of days.

Baghdad was also aided by the fact that it was now defending its own soil. Most Iraqi soldiers had little love for Iran but even less enthusiasm for Saddam's conquest of Khuzestan. Although many had fought steadfastly in Iran, they never could muster the same passion as Khomeini's "martyr battalions." However, once they had been evicted from Iranian territory and were fighting to prevent the hated Persians from conquering their own land, they suddenly were inspired to remarkable tenacity. Just as Saddam was disappointed that the Arabs of Khuzestan did not rise up to welcome their Iraqi brethren, so too was the ayatollah when the Shi'ah of southern Iraq did not rise up against their Sunni oppressors. Instead, Iraq's largely Shi'ite infantry formations fought hard to defend their country. Unit cohesion similarly improved. While it had been uneven in Iran, with some units hanging together under tremendous pressure and others — particularly Popular Army brigades — disintegrating on first contact with the enemy, once the venue shifted to Iraq itself, Iraqi unit cohesion hardened.

Finally, the Iraqis had embarked on a major expansion of their army that allowed them to generally match the Iranians in numbers of troops (in addition to their advantages in weaponry) despite Tehran's much greater population base — Iraq had only 13.5 million people to Iran's roughly 40 million. When Iraq invaded Iran, it had twelve divisions and a small number of independent brigades and battalions. Soon after the first defeats in early 1981, Iraq began forming new brigades (largely from reservists and Popular Army personnel) to try to fill out their long defensive lines inside Iran. In 1981 Iraq began adding entire new divisions to its order of battle, converting the 11th and 12th Border Guard Divisions to line-infantry formations and adding the 14th Infantry Division to the rolls, followed by the

15th and 16th Divisions in early 1982. This pace continued so that by late 1985, Iraq boasted approximately forty divisional commands and by the end of the war had fifty-five divisions in the field. These numbers are actually misleading, for during the Iran-Iraq War, Iraqi divisions basically abandoned a standard organization with organic brigades. Instead, divisional headquarters were assigned missions (usually to defend a sector or serve as a reserve counterattack force) and were then assigned brigades of various types as needed to perform the mission. Most Iraqi divisions commanded more than the canonical three brigades at any given time, and some commanded as many as eight to ten brigades on occasion. Moreover, nominal "armored" or "mechanized" divisions often might command more infantry formations than anything else.

DEPOLITICIZATION

Perhaps the most important and far reaching move Baghdad made in 1982 was to begin a lengthy process of depoliticization of its officer corps. The defeats in Iran apparently convinced Saddam that his micromanagement of the armed forces had hampered their effectiveness, and with Iran's victorious armies beating down the doors of his realm, it was time to put military effectiveness ahead of political reliability. Thus, beginning in 1982, Saddam began to undo this damage, starting with the characteristically dramatic gesture of dismissing (and in a number of cases executing) between 200 and 300 mostly senior officers who had performed poorly in 1980–82. Moreover, in their place, rather than appointing still more of his cronies, Saddam began promoting officers who had fought well in the first two years of the war.[74]

Depoliticization did not come quickly. The process took several years to show results, but as soon as Saddam began to depoliticize, the Iraqis began to experience greater success, and over time the trend picked up speed. The emphasis on leadership and demonstrated performance over loyalty and personal ties increased until it became the rule rather than the exception.[75] Saddam went so far as to recall to service hundreds of competent junior officers formerly dismissed for suspected disloyalty. Baghdad did away with the political officers formerly assigned to all Iraqi units above battalion-strength and ceased the practice of frequently rotating the commanders of divisions and corps. Instead, Saddam weeded out incompetent commanders (many of whom were friends, loyal supporters, and even relatives), and when he found competent commanders he stuck with them. Over time, this allowed for the emergence of a core of competent senior field commanders such as Generals Hisham Sabah al-Fakhri (whose performance improved markedly over the course of the war), Salim Husayn 'Ali, Saadi Tuma Abbas al-Jabburi, Maher 'Abd al-Rashid, Iyad Futah ar-Rawi, and Salah Abud Mahmud, as well as an efficient general staff under Iraq's capable deputy chief of staff for operations, Gen. Husayn Rashid Muhammad at-Tikriti. Perhaps most difficult of all for Saddam, he slowly relinquished control over military operations and began to give greater latitude to his generals. In turn, his generals thoroughly revamped Iraq's training practices. They began to try to teach combined-arms tactics to their troops in a more comprehensive and systematic fashion, and recognizing their problems in Iran, they began to try to encourage junior commanders to be aggressive and innovative in combat and to react more quickly and effectively to enemy moves.[76]

Depoliticization, and the rise of the competent senior officers it allowed, quickly led to a noticeable improvement in Iraqi defensive strategy. Iraq abandoned its previous reliance on forward defenses, which had been so detrimental during the fighting in Iran. Instead, Baghdad deployed infantry well supported by area-fire weapons along heavily fortified lines along the border. Increasingly, the Iraqis concentrated their armored and mechanized infantry units into reserves that could be quickly shifted around the country by the newly expanded transport battalions to wherever Iran happened to be attacking. These heavy units, supported by artillery, were used to counterattack Iranian assaults and drive them back to their start lines.

IRANIAN PROBLEMS

These various improvements on the Iraqi side were complemented by problems on the Iranian side that increasingly hindered Tehran's military operations. Iran's Achilles' heel continued to be its lack of mechanized formations and motor transport with which to exploit success. During the counteroffensives that drove the Iraqis out of Iran, the Iranians still had enough operational tanks, APCs, self-propelled artillery pieces, and trucks to allow certain units a degree of mobility. These were then able to pass through the Revolutionary Guard breakthroughs, exploit into the operational depth of the Iraqi positions, and encircle the forward-deployed Iraqi forces. However, as the war dragged on, the arms embargo — as well as the oil embargo, which made it difficult for Iran to raise hard currency for arms purchases — began to pinch tighter, and Iran's inventory of operational tanks, APCs, and trucks diminished.

The declining mobility of Iranian formations was also a function of their logistical problems. Tehran never fully sorted out its computerized logistics system after the controlling software was wrecked during the revolution, and throughout the war, teams had to pick through the massive warehouses by hand to find the parts and equipment they needed. With the exception of the arms transfers from the United States as part of the Iran-Contra Affair, the Iranians had lost the source of their major weapons systems and were forced to scour the world for others who had American military equipment comparable to their own and were willing to sell it. Ultimately, Iran was forced to buy large amounts of Soviet-style equipment, mostly from China and North Korea. These weapons were inferior to Iran's American arms to begin with, and the Chinese and North Korean versions generally were poor copies that became maintenance headaches in their own right. Moreover, the proliferation of different types of weapons systems only added to the burden on the already badly strained logistical system.

The rivalry between the IRGC and the Iranian army also played a role in eroding Tehran's offensive capabilities over the course of time. Soon after the last Iraqis had been thrown off Iranian soil in 1982, friction between the army and the IRGC bubbled back to the surface. Many of Tehran's mullahs were still suspicious of the army and on several occasions tried to have it disbanded in favor of the Revolutionary Guards. The mullahs mostly believed that faith in God—the primary "weapon" of the IRGC and the Basijis—was more important in battle than the military skills of the army. For these reasons, plus the dwindling firepower of the army, Iranian offensives tended to rely increasingly on the human-wave attacks of the IRGC and less on the conventional operations of the army. While these mass assaults generally were able to penetrate Iraqi defensive lines, they were slow and cumbersome and could not follow up their penetrations with swift exploitations. Moreover, once sent forward into battle, they became extremely difficult to control. Therefore, even when Iranian commanders recognized an unforeseen opportunity, it often proved impossible to redirect the hordes of Basij to take advantage of it.

As the war plodded on, these mounting problems resulted in Iran's attacks making less and less progress against the Iraqis. The expansion of the Iraqi army and the construction of increasingly formidable fortifications made it harder and harder for Iranian assaults to even penetrate the Iraqi defensive lines. The slow erosion of Iranian mobility assets made it increasingly difficult for its generals to exploit the breakthroughs their assaults created. The ever larger armored forces Iraq had learned to hold back, and the improvement in Iraq's strategic mobility, meant that Iraqi reserves were able to counterattack sooner after an Iranian attack and in greater force. Each Iranian attack seemed to make less progress and suffer more casualties than the last. By 1986, the lines had changed little since

1982, and the Iranian offensives seemed to have passed the point of diminishing returns.

RESILIENT IRAQI TACTICAL PROBLEMS

Of course, it is important not to lose sight of the large number of continuing problems in the Iraqi forces despite their increasing success in stopping the Iranians. After all, the Iraqis were employing all the weaponry available to a modern army to fight what was basically a light infantry force. They generally outnumbered the Iranians, except temporarily at the point of attack, where the Iranians might muster an advantage in manpower for their human-wave assaults. The Iraqis could bring to bear vastly greater firepower than the Iranians and were considerably more mobile than the Iranians. Still, Iraq felt compelled to resort to chemical warfare to break up Iranian attacks as early as October 1983. Indeed, especially in 1982 and 1983, many of the Iraqi victories were very close-run affairs, and there were a number of occasions where the Iranians looked like they were on the verge of a major breakthrough. Given Iraq's daunting advantages in technology, firepower, fortifications, and eventually weapons of mass destruction, the question is not why Iraq was able to stalemate the Iranians, but why it was so difficult for them to do so.

Iraqi intelligence improved in some areas, though not in others. Tactical units still paid inadequate attention to reconnaissance, particularly to longer-range reconnaissance missions that might have given a better sense of Iranian intentions. Iraq's senior commanders began to demand more air force reconnaissance missions, but this seems to have helped only marginally. The Iraqis did not do a very good job analyzing the information collected by reconnaissance flights, nor did much of the information make its way down to the field commanders. Iraqi signals-intercept capabilities were quite good and often provided a tip-off of an Iranian offensive, according to former Iraqi generals.[77] An even greater contribution to Iraqi intelligence came from the "finished intelligence" — that is, information that had been thoroughly analyzed, evaluated, and crosschecked with other sources — on Iranian preparations that Iran began receiving from the United States in the middle of this period.[78] However, even this new source seems to have had limited effect on Iraqi fortunes because Iraqi soldiers and officers continued to distort information being passed up, down, and across the chain of command. Consequently, Iraqi tactical commanders rarely understood the full picture of Iranian activities in their sector and were constantly surprised by Iranian attacks. Similarly, lower echelons regularly claimed either that they had defeated Iranian attacks when they had not or that they were being attacked by far greater forces than was actually the case (to justify having been defeated). Given the behavior of their subordinates, it is not surprising that Iraq's generals were constantly overreacting to some threats and underreacting to others.

Other Iraqi problems continued to manifest themselves acutely at tactical command levels. Although Saddam's grudging depoliticization led to a marked improvement in Iraqi operations at higher levels, Iraq's tactical formations still could not effectively implement the operations devised by their generals. Moreover, this came despite the conscious efforts of both the regime and the senior officer corps to stimulate initiative, creativity, and independent action among their subordinates. For example, the Iraqi General Staff and Baghdad's corps commanders got very good at shifting their mechanized reserves, concentrating them against an Iranian offensive and then using them to counterattack an Iranian penetration. However, Iraqi forces themselves continued to conduct these counterattacks abysmally. Tactical commanders doggedly relied on firepower rather than maneuver, and their counterattacks were too often frontal assaults in which Iraqi armor simply collided head-on with the Iranian forces. Even within these attacks, lower-level Iraqi formations rarely maneuvered in combat and instead tended to simply line up and roll straight at the Iranians, trying to drive off the enemy with sheer firepower. On those (increasingly rare) occasions when they encountered Iranian armor, they tended to prevail only because of overwhelming numerical superiority. When defending a sector of the front, Iraqi mechanized forces sat passively despite the glaring vulnerability of the Iranians to flanking armor attacks. Consistently, the Iraqis preferred to remain in their defensive positions and blast away. This unwillingness to maneuver resulted in battlefields strewn with Iraqi tanks and APCs destroyed by Iranian antitank teams who swarmed over a position or infiltrated the Iraqi lines and then attacked the armor from the rear.

As the war progressed, Iraq's senior officers, despairing that their subordinates would ever learn to use tactical maneuver, began to plan counterattacks more carefully to employ maneuver at an operational level. Previously, a corps commander might order an armored division to deal with an Iranian assault in his corps sector and then leave it up to the division commander to decide how best to conduct the attack. However, later in the war, the corps commanders began to consciously position their reserves on the flanks of Iranian penetrations and then direct specific routes of counterattack, essentially as they had done (largely by accident) at Susangerd in 1981 and al-Basrah in 1982. Thus, even though the company, battalion, and brigade commanders would likely resort to a headlong charge, they would at least be doing it into the flank of the Iranian force. Only by means of such close attention were Iraq's senior military officers able to employ even a limited form of maneuver warfare to defeat Iranian attacks.[79]

There was a limit to how much even the constant scrutiny of the general staff and corps commanders could do to improve Iraqi military effectiveness. For example, the general staff and their corps headquarters got very good at reacting to Iranian assaults, quickly beginning the laborious effort of shifting strategic reserves from elsewhere along the front. However, Iraq's tactical leadership reacted frustratingly slowly. Iraqi junior officers showed little initiative in moving tactical reserves to block or counterattack Iranian assaults, and it invariably required the intervention of higher authority to get the reserves moving. Even then, these units generally executed their tasks sluggishly. This tardiness led to numerous Iraqi positions being overrun before help could arrive and Iraqi counterattacks that came well after a battle had been decided.

Similarly, no matter how hard Iraqi training stressed the integration of the various combat arms, Iraqi tactical formations simply could not fight as combined-arms teams. Corps and division commanders came to deploy their forces along defensive lines so that armor, artillery, infantry, antitank teams, and other supporting formations *had* to support each other simply by having been sited in an integrated fire scheme. Similarly, they increasingly crossattached various combat elements to form combined-arms task forces at lower and lower echelons in hopes that this would improve unit coordination, but it rarely did. Especially in their counterattacks, when the maelstrom of combat forced the devolution of authority to the tactical commanders on the spot, these task forces would regularly disintegrate into their separate elements, with tanks rolling off in one direction, infantry in another, and artillery firing in a third. Ultimately, the Iraqis simply compensated for these failings by concentrating ever greater volumes of fire, including heavy doses of chemical warfare, against the Iranians to break their attacks.

THE WAR IN THE AIR

The Iraqi Air Force had not improved much either. By about 1983, Iraq had won air superiority almost by default. Spare parts shortages had crippled the IRIAF to the point where it could only generate about 10–15 sorties per day on a sustained basis, and though it could probably surge to 70–90 sorties if necessary, doing so invariably hurt the IRIAF's ability to sustain a modest sortie rate thereafter. In addition, Iraq's ground-based air defenses took a heavy toll of Iranian strike aircraft. In late 1981 the IRIAF was forced to shift to high-altitude bombing simply to avoid further losses.

The declining numbers of operational Iranian planes ultimately proved decisive in the battle for air superiority because the Iraqis could not make their numerical advantage count in the air-to-air war. Iraqi pilots were extremely timid and frequently aborted their missions when they detected Iranian fighters. They remained very skittish about air-to-air engagements with the Iranians, often declining combat even at the expense of critical missions. In late 1980, Baghdad began to try to compel its fighter pilots to be more aggressive about challenging the Iranians in the air. A big help came from France, which began providing Iraq with the Mirage F-1 fighters Baghdad had purchased in 1981 (and the training to fly and fight them, more importantly). In November an Iraqi Mirage shot down an Iranian F-14 — the first of the war — and over the next few months shot down several more. This gave the Iraqi Mirage pilots a greater degree of confidence to challenge the Iranians and their colleagues more confidence to execute their missions when they had Mirage escorts. Nevertheless, it was still more often the case that Iraqi jets would lose in air-to-air combat to the Iranians unless they had a significant numerical advantage.

Throughout the war, the Iraqi Air Force devoted relatively few assets to close support of ground operations, insisted on conducting these missions from high altitudes, and would not or could not decrease the long delays and intricate procedures required for ground commanders to receive CAS. Indeed, during the first five years of the war, the army devoted ample resources to helicopter acquisition as a substitute for fixed-wing CAS. Unfortunately, Iraq's helicopters were no more useful than the air force in providing such support. Iraqi helicopter gunship tactics consisted of flying out to a point about a kilometer or so behind Iraqi lines, pointing the helicopter toward the Iranians, firing off all of the munitions on the helicopter, and then returning to base. Needless to say, these helicopters had little effect except when firing into Iranian infantry massed for an assault, when their firepower did prove quite deadly.[80]

The Iraqi Air Force ultimately had a greater effect on the war through its attacks on Iranian strategic and economic targets, but even in this area its achievements were modest and its performance mediocre. At various points during the war, Iraq attempted to use air and missile strikes against Iranian cities as a way of pressuring Iran into a compromise solution. Until 1988, however, Iraq was at a decided disadvantage. Although Iran had fewer operational strike aircraft than Iraq, those it had could carry heavier bombloads, and their pilots were generally more proficient than their Iraqi counterparts. Moreover, Iraq suffered from the distinct disadvantage that Iraq's major cities were generally much closer to the Iranian border than were Iran's largest cities. For example, Baghdad is only 150 kilometers from the Iranian border, while Tehran is 600 kilometers from Iraq. This meant that most of Iran's cities were beyond the range of Iraq's 300-kilometer-range ss-1 Scud surface-to-surface missiles and effectively beyond the range of Iraqi aircraft, for the air force shied away from such long-range missions and was terrified of Iranian air defenses. The Iranians were much more willing to undertake airstrikes, and later, when Iran purchased Scuds from North Korea and Libya, Baghdad and Iraq's other major cities were well within Iran's missile range. Thus for most of the war, Iran could do more damage to Iraqi cities than Iraq could to Iranian cities, and this imbalance often forced Baghdad to scale back or cease its attacks on Iranian cities in hope that the Iranians would follow suit — which they usually did.

Iran and Iraq began attacking each other's oil facilities from the start of the war, and the dimensions of this campaign gradually escalated over time as each side grew more desperate. Initially, both Iraq and Iran tried to strike each other's oil installations — refineries, terminals, and such. However, neither side was able to do much damage. The Iranians had few planes available and great difficulty contending with Iraqi air defenses, while the Iraqis could not effectively plan or execute strike missions against targets even as "small" as an oil refinery and would not press home their attacks in the face of Iranian air defenses. The Iraqis flew few reconnaissance missions before or after their airstrikes and did a very poor job of trying to objectively assess the results of their attacks, preferring instead to simply claim that the target had been destroyed. Initially, Iraqi airstrikes were very inaccurate, in part because the Iraqis insisted on attacking only from high altitude. In 1984 Iraq began to receive the strike version of the Mirage F-1 and advanced AS-30L laser-guided bombs. Iraq had sent its best pilots to France to train on the Mirage, and the combination of its best pilots with good training, a capable plane, and an excellent weapons system made a small but noticeable difference. By the latter half of the war, Iraq had learned to employ the Mirages to take out important targets at key Iranian industrial and oil facilities. However, even with the Mirage F-1s, Iraqi airstrikes were always inadequate, never committing enough sorties to really put Iran's facilities out of action. Thus, while Iraq was able to take a number of Iranian facilities off-line at different times, they never did enough damage to prevent Iran from repairing the facility and bringing it back to operation in a matter of weeks or days.

Because of Iraq's early difficulties targeting Iranian oil facilities, in 1983 the Iraqis shifted gears and launched a determined campaign against Iranian oil tankers in the Persian Gulf. Initially, Iraqi efforts to attack Iranian tankers enjoyed only modest success because the only platform Baghdad used to attack ships at sea were Super Frelon helicopters with Exocet missiles. The Super Frelons had a limited range and could only reach tankers in the northernmost reaches of the Gulf. The Exocet also had a very small warhead that did little damage to most tankers. At first, these attacks were useful to Iraq because they scared off foreign-flagged tankers from putting in to Iranian ports. However, the Iranians simply increased the rewards for tanker captains, moved their export terminals farther south along the coast, and — especially since the Exocets could not actually sink the tankers — Iranian oil exports picked up again. In 1983 Iraq leased from France five Super Etendard attack jets, which had a longer range than the helicopters but still could not reach all of the various ports and oil facilities along Iran's lengthy coastline. Moreover, the Iraqis did not do well identifying targets for their airstrikes, still relied on the Exocet, and with only five aircraft, they could do little damage anyway. The arrival of the Mirages helped matters to a certain extent. Not only did the Mirages have a longer range than the Super Etendards but the Mirages could also refuel each other in flight, thus allowing for considerably longer strike missions. The high-quality training the Mirage pilots had received from the French also paid off in better results. Nevertheless, the Iraqis still suffered from their insistence on using the Exocet missile (rather than more powerful ordnance) as well as their incapacity to properly identify targets ahead of time. On most missions a Mirage would fly at medium altitude along the Saudi coastline, turn into the center of the Persian Gulf, flip on its fire-control radar and fire at the largest ship it detected. Clearly, this was no way to run an antishipping campaign, and it produced very middling results — aside from the embarrassing hit on the USS *Stark*. However, the most important problem with Iraq's air campaign against Iran's oil exports was that Baghdad never made a determined effort to sink large numbers of tankers exporting Iranian oil or to sustain this effort over a long period of time. Instead, Iraqi attacks were sporadic and random, serving more as an annoyance than a real problem for Tehran. Iraqi airstrikes may have reduced Iranian oil exports but could never really cripple the Iranian economy as Baghdad hoped.

Breaking the Deadlock, 1986–87

At the beginning of 1986 the Iran-Iraq War was mired in stalemate, and Iraq believed that its fortifications and tremendous investment in additional firepower had given it the key to thwarting Iran's offensives. At that point, Baghdad sought only to minimize its losses in the ceaseless combat in southern Iraq and Kurdistan and hoped that its pressure on Iran's oil economy and the stalemate on the ground would force Tehran to recognize the fruitlessness of continued fighting. For their part, the Iranians had come to realize both that their manpower was not inexhaustible and that Iraqi firepower could be devastating, but the Ayatollah Khomeini had not concluded that Iran's invasion attempts were in vain. Consequently, Iran kept pounding away at Iraq's defenses, albeit with greater caution than before.

THE FIRST BATTLE OF AL-FAW

What appeared to be an interminable deadlock ended abruptly on the night of 10–11 February 1986. In a rainstorm Iranian forces crossed the Shatt al-Arab at its mouth and overran the al-Faw peninsula, the southeasternmost tip of Iraq. The Iraqis had assumed that Iran lacked the amphibious equipment to cross the Shatt at al-Faw, one of the widest parts of the river. Consequently, the peninsula was held by Popular Army forces, which collapsed with the first Iranian attacks. The Iranians quickly poured troops into al-Faw and began pushing northwest toward al-Basrah and the port of Umm Qasr.

In a panic Baghdad began hurrying units south as fast as it could. Several hastily organized Iraqi counterattacks failed miserably. Although the extremely marshy peninsula made it unsuitable terrain for mechanized forces, Iraq lacked well-trained infantry units and so had to rely mostly on heavy formations. Iraqi tanks counterattacked with minimal infantry support, and even these failed to support the armor, allowing Iranian Cobra attack helicopters and the picked Iranian units who had made the crossing to repulse the counterattacks with ease. In desperation Baghdad committed its air force to the battle. The Iraqi aircraft had little effect on the Iranian forces, which were mostly infantry and therefore presented few high-value targets. The Iraqis also tried to attack the bridges Iran had erected across the Shatt and even tried to interdict Iranian units moving down the roads in Khuzestan toward al-Faw. However, between the rain, Iran's practice of moving mainly at night, and poor piloting skills, the Iraqis did only minor damage and lost 20–25 aircraft for the effort. When the initial counterattacks failed, Iraq rushed its best infantry south to al-Faw — special forces and Republican Guards — for another round of counterattacks, which succeeded in halting the Iranian advance just short of Umm Qasr but could not push them back.[81]

On February 22 Iraq launched a major counterattack to try to expel the

Iranians from al-Faw, mustering three division-strength columns, each commanded by one of Iraq's best corps commanders — Hisham Sabah al-Fakhri, Maher 'Abd al-Rashid, and Sa'adi Tuma 'Abbas al-Jabburi. The Iraqis threw everything they had at the Iranians. They committed the air force in full, flying as many as 200 CAS or BAI sorties per day, in addition to enormous quantities of artillery and heavy doses of chemical agents. However, after three weeks of constant attacks, the Iraqis had made little progress. Iraqi infantry — even the elite units — continued to perform poorly and had to rely heavily on the firepower of their tanks and artillery. Iraqi armor generally had to stick to the roads because of the soft terrain, and even where the ground was firmer, they refused to maneuver against the Iranians. Instead, the tanks tried to just force their way south against the dug-in Iranian infantry, who were well armed with antitank weapons. Iraq was unable to suppress or defeat Iranian antitank teams either with artillery fire — slow to respond and inaccurate as ever — or with infantry, who simply did not understand how to cooperate with the tanks. The Iraqis suffered heavy losses, taking 8,000–10,000 casualties, losing another 20–25 aircraft to Iranian F-14s and air defenses, and sustaining 30 percent casualties among the Republican Guards.[82]

BUILDING A NEW MODEL ARMY

The invasion of al-Faw and the dramatic failure of Iraq's counterattacks jarred Baghdad out of its complacency. In particular it seems to have had three effects. First, it convinced Saddam to remove the remaining shackles on Iraq's generals and allow them to run military operations as they saw fit. Baghdad had been moving inexorably in this direction since 1982, and even before al-Faw, Iraqi senior commanders were mostly free to make all but the most important decisions on their own. After al-Faw, however, the last vestiges of Saddam's Stalinist system were removed from them. Second, the battle convinced Iraq's general staff that their troops lacked the ability to conduct effective offensive operations. Once again, Iraqi forces had possessed every advantage in terms of firepower, technology, air power, and numbers but had failed, and failed badly. Third, the loss of al-Faw convinced the political leadership that Iraq could not simply remain on the defensive and hope that at some point Iran would agree to a ceasefire out of exhaustion or frustration. Baghdad's initial reaction to the loss of al-Faw was to seize the lightly defended town of Mehran just across the border in central Iran and then try to exchange it for al-Faw, but the Iranians quickly retook Mehran. Baghdad then tried to step up its attacks on Iranian tankers and oil facilities, but this had no effect on Tehran, which was concentrating on preparations for a renewed assault on al-Basrah. Thus, eventually, the general staff was able to persuade Saddam that he could not find a clever, low-cost way to bring the war to a close: the only way to end the war was to actually defeat the Iranian army on the ground.

Having won Saddam's consent to build an army capable of defeating the Iranians, the general staff's first move was to create a force able to execute offensive operations. For this purpose, they secured Saddam's approval to dramatically expand the Republican Guard. At the beginning of the war, this force consisted of two brigades that served as the garrison of Baghdad and as Saddam's household troops. Because the Republican Guard was intended to defend the regime against a potential army coup, they were given the best equipment and training Iraq could provide. These units were drawn overwhelmingly from Saddam's hometown of Tikrit and other nearby Sunni cities, such as Samarra, to help ensure its loyalty. Between the Guard's equipment, training, and high esprit de corps, it was considered one of Iraq's elite forces, and throughout the war it was committed to battle whenever the situation looked particularly bleak, such as at the first battle of al-Basrah in 1982. Because it was increasingly called upon to participate in combat operations, the Republican Guard gradually expanded to six brigades in late 1985.

A year after the Iranian seizure of al-Faw, the general staff had expanded the Republican Guards into the new Republican Guard Forces Command (RGFC) — signifying that it was now a corps formation — with eighteen brigades under three divisional commands. During 1987 and early 1988, three more divisional commands were created (including the Special Forces Division), and the Guard's brigade count rose to twenty-eight. Of greatest importance, the general staff also won Saddam's consent to stress proficiency over loyalty in recruiting new members for the RGFC. While its units remained overwhelmingly Sunni and still possessed a higher percentage of Tikritis than the rest of the army, the general staff received permission to expand the RGFC by taking the best personnel rather than the most loyal. As Nasser had done in Egypt after the Six Day War, Saddam repealed the draft exemption for college students, conscripting some of them to fill out the new Republican Guard ranks. Far more of the new RGFC slots, however, were filled out with the best soldiers and officers from regular army units. Many of these new personnel were volunteers, but many more were competent soldiers and officers who were simply assigned to the RGFC for their demonstrated abilities. (Although a heavy preference was still shown to Sunnis over Shi'ahs or Kurds). Their loyalty was then secured by giving them lavish pay and other perquisites as well as the prestige attached to being a member of Iraq's elite force. In addition, as mostly Sunni Arabs, the RGFC had an important tie to the regime and would support it if only because Saddam was a bulwark against a possible Shi'ite or Kurdish take-over. While these measures did buy a considerable degree of loyalty from new members of the RGFC, Saddam's paranoia was not fully assuaged, so he created a new force, the Special Republican Guard, made up mostly of members of the original Republican Guard to handle the mission of gar-risoning Baghdad and defending the regime.[83]

The general staff then took the RGFC out of combat and retrained them, along with a small number of the best regular army divisions (basically the 3d, 6th, and 10th Armored Divisions and the 1st and 5th Mechanized Infantry Divisions). These units received extensive training in combined-arms operations and offensive tactics. They practiced constantly and began conducting large, corps-level maneuvers. These units were lavishly be-decked with combat support and combat-service support units and had first call on supplies and equipment. The RGFC also were provided with the best weaponry in the Iraqi arsenal, including Soviet T-72 tanks and BMP-1 in-fantry fighting vehicles, French GCT self-propelled howitzers, Austrian GHN-45 and South African G-5 artillery pieces, and Soviet SA-13 and SA-14 surface-to-air missiles. Although by stripping the rest of the army of the best soldiers, officers, and equipment Baghdad deprived most Iraqi units of any combat power they previously possessed, it gave the general staff a hard core of about eleven divisions with a modest offensive capability.

Along with its new offensive arm, the Iraqi General Staff developed a new approach to operations, basically extrapolating from lessons learned earlier in the war. The most important element of this new approach was detailed scripting of military operations. The General Staff, led by its deputy chief of staff for operations, Gen. Husayn Rashid Muhammad at-Tikriti, concluded that attempts to train Iraqi tactical formations to con-duct combined-arms operations, employ tactical maneuver, act creatively, and aggressively seize battlefield opportunities had consistently failed. In-stead, they decided that, just as Iraqi operations improved when senior field officers began micromanaging operations, the general staff would begin extensively scripting major offensive operations. Husayn Rashid gathered a group of Iraq's most talented staff officers and began planning both coun-terattack and offensive operations in minute detail. Since they could not count on their field commanders to properly coordinate combined-arms operations, the general staff would do it for them by writing it into the script. Since they could not count on their field commanders to employ tactical maneuver, the general staff would write maneuver into the script as well. Since they could not count on their field commanders to innovate in battle, they wrote innovative approaches into the script of the operation. In short, they tried to overcome all of the failings of Iraqi junior officers by writing operations orders so detailed that, simply by following this guidance, Iraqi field commanders would do everything they needed to win.[84]

These detailed plans were then given to the Republican Guard and the handful of competent regular-army divisions to learn backward and forward. For months beforehand, the RGFC and regular-army units would practice executing these operations. The Iraqis built vast, full-size mock-ups of the relevant terrain and practiced executing their scripted operations on them. The units designated to take part in these offensives would rehearse their specific missions repeatedly. According to the commander of the Hammurabi Armored Division, the RGFC regularly trained for ten to fourteen hours without pause, day after day.[85] Units were trained to perform specific tasks and nothing else, and these tasks they repeated again and again. Initially, units would practice their missions on their own. Then later they would be integrated into larger exercises in which they could practice their tasks in conjunction with supporting forces and adjacent units until the entire operation could be practiced as a whole. Eventually, they reached the point where each plan could be performed from memory.[86]

THE SECOND BATTLE OF AL-BASRAH, 1987

In early January 1987, Iran tried to follow up its success at al-Faw with a major assault against al-Basrah (an operation called "Karbala V"), the largest and most dangerous offensive against the city since 1982. The Iraqis were fixated on the Iranian positions on al-Faw, primarily because it was the only point where Iranian forces were already across the Shatt al-Arab and feared that they would use this bridgehead to launch an offensive to encircle al-Basrah from the southeast. The Iranians played on this fear by launching a diversionary assault across the Shatt just north of the al-Faw position — as if to turn the flank of the Iraqi defensive lines facing the Iranian bridgehead. Iraqi intelligence again failed to uncover Iran's true intentions (although they did detect preparations for an offensive), and the Iraqis bought the Iranian ruse. When the real assault came to the east and northeast of al-Basrah, the Iraqis were caught by surprise. Tehran had concentrated a very large force for the operation, probably between 150,000 and 200,000 men, and more importantly had brought in its most experienced Revolutionary Guard and army divisions for the attack.[87] The Iranians attacked both north and south of Fish Lake, and with the benefits of surprise and the number and quality of forces they had mustered, they quickly punched through the

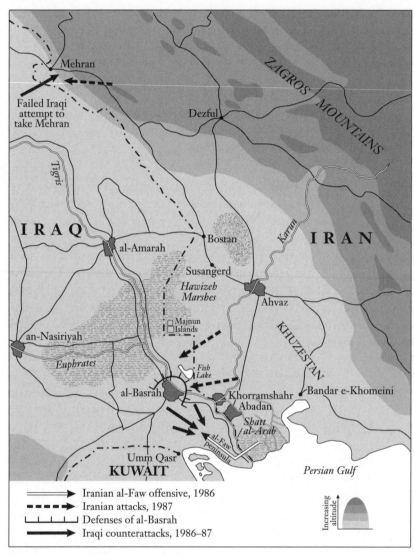

Map 17. Iranian Offensives, 1986–87

first two Iraqi defense lines ringing al-Basrah. However, at this point the attack ground to a halt because of Iran's chronic shortage of mobility assets and the difficulty of sustaining offensive operations reliant on human-wave attacks against rank after rank of Iraqi fortifications.

Both sides then raced to pour reinforcements into the area. Baghdad in particular began committing its best units, including large numbers of RGFC formations, to the defense of al-Basrah. Iraq used enormous amounts of artillery and chemical weapons against the massed Iranian formations. Iraq even unleashed its air force — conducting as many as 500 sorties on some days — in an all-out effort to halt the Iranians. At the end of January, Iraq launched a major counterattack, using local reserves to try to drive in the northern flank of the southern Iranian salient. The plan was to drive south from behind Fish Lake and sever the Iranian penetration at its shoulder. But the operation went nowhere. Although the counterattacking force began as a combined-arms team, it almost immediately separated into its different components, with the infantry veering off to the southwest, the armor veering off to the southeast, and the artillery failing to effectively support either. Moreover, although at an operational level the counterattack took the Iranians in the flank, it moved so slowly that Iran was able to shift forces to block it. Meanwhile, at the tactical level, Iraqi forces simply charged straight at the Iranians, launching frontal assaults against dug-in Iranian infantry that barely dented the enemy lines but led to heavy Iraqi casualties.

For the next month, the Iranians kept up the pressure on al-Basrah, feeding in more and more units to launch one human-wave assault after another. Through sheer determination they continued to inch forward. A major problem for the Iraqis was that under the relentless Iranian pressure, some of their infantry formations inevitably disintegrated, allowing the Iranians to penetrate each line of fortifications. Iraq's air effort made little impression on the Iranians — and resulted in the loss of about 50 Iraqi aircraft, mostly to Iranian tactical air defenses. By late February, however, Iraq had redeployed sufficient numbers of Republican Guard units and special forces to their fortified lines to put up a stout defense along the entire front. Meanwhile, the Iranians had lost so many men to Iraqi firepower and earthworks in its human-wave attacks (probably on the order of 70,000–80,000 casualties) that the offensive ground to a halt — though not before piercing five of the six Iraqi defensive rings and penetrating to within a few kilometers of al-Basrah.[88]

At the beginning of March, Iraq tried another counterattack against the Iranian penetration, again attacking from the Fish Lake area to try to envelop the southern Iranian salient. Again, the Iraqis were hindered by a major breakdown in combined-arms cooperation and the determination of Iraqi mechanized forces to conduct simplistic frontal assaults rather than maneuvering for advantage. In addition, while Baghdad committed heavy air support to the counterattack, the Iraqi Air Force contributed little because its airstrikes were not provided in a timely fashion, were not delivered in sufficient strength to have a substantial effect, and Iraqi pilots were incapable of accurately targeting tactical military targets. Once again the counterattack quickly sputtered to a halt with little to show.

Ultimately, the Iranians were defeated by two forces at second al-Basrah. The first was the skill of Iraq's general staff, which, freed from Saddam's fetters, had concentrated enormous force — including much of the revamped Republican Guard — to hold the lines and had ably employed Iraq's lopsided advantage in firepower against the waves of Iranian infantry. Second was the Iranians' own shortcomings in mobility and supply. The dog that did not bark in this instance was Iraqi tactical effectiveness. Despite the Herculean labors of Iraq's general staff to improve their army, there was little or no discernible enhancement in tactical competence. Iraqi units continued to perform well when sitting behind their impressive fortifications and blasting away at the Iranians, but — as the failure of both of their operational-level counteroffensives demonstrated — they remained hapless at basically all other operations. Iraqi tactical commanders had displayed all of the recurrent problems of passivity, inflexibility, dogmatism, poor combined-arms integration, unwillingness to maneuver, and mismanagement of information. Ultimately, Iraq's generals prevailed at al-Basrah in spite of the forces under their command rather than because of them.

Iraq Goes on the Offensive, 1988

When the Karbala V offensive against al-Basrah failed, Iran finally recognized that its chances of bringing the war to a successful conclusion through a decisive military blow had all but evaporated. Tehran began to talk increasingly of attrition strategies and triumphing by stirring revolution in Iraq. For its part, Iraq was relieved by its successful defense of al-Basrah, but it was committed to bringing the war to a more rapid close by defeating the Iranians on the battlefield. Beginning in April 1988, the Iraqis conducted a series of five major offensives led by the new Republican Guard and employing the new approach developed by the general staff after the Iranian invasion of al-Faw.

The first offensive, "Ramadan Mubarak" (Blessed Ramadan), kicked off on April 17 at al-Faw. The Iraqis conducted an effective deception campaign and exercised tight operational security beforehand. As a result, the sudden Iraqi offensive — the first major attack they had conducted since 1980 — caught the Iranians off-guard. The general staff concentrated 100,000 men of the Republican Guard and the Iraqi VII Corps against the 15,000 second-rate Iranian troops manning the positions on al-Faw. The 26th Naval Infantry Brigade of the RGFC conducted an amphibious assault against the southern coast of the peninsula, flanking the Iranian lines. The Iranians had little artillery support and even less armor, while the Iraqis were plentifully disposed of both. In addition, the attack received over 300 sorties of air support from the Iraqi Air Force. Iraq began the assault with an enormous artillery bombardment that included a heavy chemical-warfare component and simply overwhelmed the Iranian defenders. The Republican Guards, led by their Madinah Munawrah Armored Division and Baghdad Infantry Division, assaulted the southern end of the line. They quickly bowled over the startled Iranian defenders, at which point the RGFC's Hammurabi Armored Division conducted a smooth passage of lines and exploited along the southern coast of the peninsula and into al-Faw itself. Meanwhile, the regular army's VII Corps attacked the northern end of the Iranian line with the veteran 7th Infantry and 6th Armored Divisions. Although the 7th Infantry's attack on the left flank of the VII Corps became bogged down because of bad terrain, unexpectedly heavy fire from Iranian units on the east side of the Shatt al-Arab, and several unaggressive brigade commanders who could not handle these problems, the 6th Armored broke through the Iranian lines and the 1st Mechanized Division pushed through the breach to exploit it, linking up with the Guard units outside of al-Faw. In thirty-five hours, the Iraqis had secured the peninsula and captured much of the Iranian equipment intact.[89]

By 25 May, the Iraqis had regrouped and were ready for another offensive. This attack was the first of a series of four Iraqi offensives known collectively as the "Tawakalnah 'alla Allah" (Trust in God) campaign, specifically designed to smash Iran's ground forces and end the war. In the first of these operations, the Iraqis attacked the Iranian salient south of Fish Lake created during the second battle of al-Basrah. The Iraqis convinced the Iranians that the attack was going to take place farther north and so caught them with their reserves out of place and their units around al-Basrah unprepared. Once again, the Iraqis employed two corps to conduct the attack — the RGFC and the III Corps. Iraq's assaulting formations probably outnumbered the Iranian defenders by five or six to one in manpower and as much as fifteen or twenty to one in tanks and APCs. The artillery attack that preceded this assault was even more massive than that employed

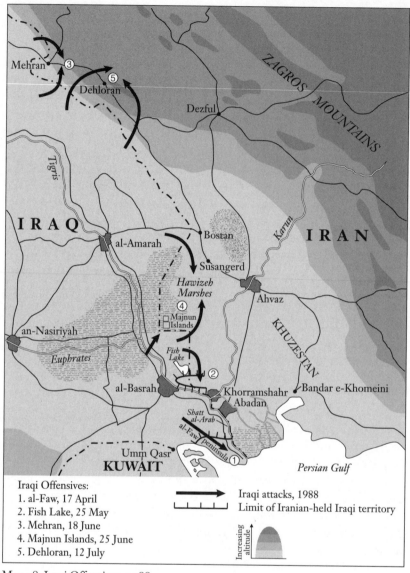

Map 18. Iraqi Offensives, 1988

at al-Faw, and the Iraqis again liberally used mustard gas and nerve agents on Iranian units throughout the battle. The Iraqis employed hordes of armor supported by mechanized infantry in a series of flanking maneuvers that broke through and then rolled up the extensive Iranian fortifications in this sector. An Iranian counterattack temporarily snarled the Iraqi operations, but it was dispersed by sheer firepower, and the attack continued. Although initially the Iranians fought hard, after their counterattack failed, many units broke, leaving their weapons behind. The entire operation took twelve hours to complete, during which time Iraq reduced the Iranian salient and captured about 150 artillery pieces and 100 of Iran's precious supply of operable tanks.

The next attack was a somewhat smaller affair against the Iranian city of Mehran in the central sector of the front. The Iraqis deployed several divisions of their own troops along with a force from the Mujahideen e-Khalq, an Iranian dissident group that Iraq had trained and equipped to oppose Khomeini's regime. Again the Iraqis laid on a huge artillery barrage that included vast quantities of chemical weapons. They followed this with a massed armor assault that overwhelmed the Revolutionary Guard units defending the town and secured the heights to the east. The Iranian defenses again were shattered by the artillery, especially the chemical agents used, and then were swept aside by the Iraqi armor. Anthony Cordesman and Abraham Wagner have estimated that the Iranians lost the equipment of at least two Revolutionary Guard divisions in the attack.[90]

A week later, Iraq launched its next offensive against the Majnun Islands and the surrounding Hawizeh Marshes. The islands were two small, man-made patches of solid ground in the midst of the marshes that were built to help exploit the Majnun oilfields. Iran had taken the islands in 1984 and had held them against several Iraqi counterattacks. On 25 June 1988, Iraq executed its most ambitious offensive to date. Baghdad concentrated over 600 artillery pieces for the attack that commenced with the usual enormous conventional–chemical warfare barrage. Then, the RGFC's 26th Naval Infantry Brigade conducted an amphibious assault against the islands. Once these troops had gained control of the islands, engineers quickly constructed pontoon bridges and earthen causeways, which the Iraqis used to move tanks onto the Majnuns to defend them against a possible Iranian counterattack. Having secured the islands, the Iraqis launched a double envelopment of the Iranian positions in the southern marshes. The RGFC's Hammurabi and Madinah Armored Divisions, supported by the Nebuchadnezzar Infantry Division, swung around to the north and linked up with mechanized formations from the III Corps that had looped around to the south thirty kilometers into Iran. The Iranian forces in the area comprised 50–60 tanks, while the Iraqis packed over 1,500 tanks into their two pincers. Against such firepower, the Iranians were simply obliterated. The Iraqis mauled six to eight army and Revolutionary Guard divisions in their envelopment, seizing all of their weapons before pulling back across the border.[91]

The final Iraqi offensive was conducted near the Iranian city of Dehloran on 12 July. As had become the norm, Iraq began the attack with an artillery bombardment mixed with large quantities of chemical-warfare agents. For this attack, Iraq relied on the RGFC in conjunction with mechanized elements of the IV Corps operating along a 130-kilometer-long front. Again the Iraqis conducted a double envelopment, with the Republican Guard forming one prong and the IV Corps forming the other. At this point, Iranian ground forces were thoroughly demoralized by the string of ever greater and ever easier Iraqi victories. They also were terrified of the Iraqi artillery barrages including chemical agents. Consequently, the Iraqis met little resistance and drove 40 kilometers into Iran, encircling and routing a number of enemy formations. The Iraqis then retired back across the border with the equipment and prisoners they had captured.

IRAN THROWS IN THE TOWEL

These five offensives effectively destroyed Iran's remaining ground power, leaving the country defenseless and forcing Tehran to accept a ceasefire. All told, the Iraqis captured about 600 tanks, 400 other armored vehicles, and 400 artillery pieces in these battles. The remaining Iranian units in the Khuzestan province were broken, demoralized, and down to less than 200 operable tanks to oppose the thousands Iraq could muster for a single operation.[92] The Iraqis could have driven into the province as easily as they had in 1980, but this time their military operations were decisive and efficient, and the Iranians had no interest in gambling on Iraqi intentions. On 8 August 1988 both sides announced an immediate end to the fighting.

The destruction of its ground forces at the hands of the Iraqi army was the most important factor that compelled Iran to accept a ceasefire, but it was certainly not the only one.[93] An important secondary motive was Iran's fear that the United States had actively entered the war on the Iraqi side. On 18 April 1988, the day after Iraq's unexpected victory at al-Faw, the U.S. Navy conducted Operation Praying Mantis, crippling much of the Iranian navy in a series of skirmishes in the Strait of Hormuz. Praying Mantis was meant as a retaliation for Iran's mining of the Persian Gulf and was the culmination of America's growing involvement in the war, beginning after

Iran's attacks on Persian Gulf oil tankers in 1980–81 and growing incrementally ever since. Then, on 3 July, Iranian gunboats attacked two U.S. warships in the Strait of Hormuz. In the ensuing skirmish, one of the U.S. ships, the USS *Vincennes*, accidentally shot down an Iranian commercial airliner, Iran Air flight 655, which had strayed into the battle area.[94] Although Praying Mantis was intended to punish Iran for its previous attacks on shipping, and the destruction of Iran Air 655 was the result of human error, in Tehran these attacks assumed sinister proportions. Iran saw Praying Mantis as a sign that the United States had moved from tacit support of Iraq to open participation in the war. What's more, the Iranians believed the *Vincennes* had purposely shot down their civilian airliner as a warning that the United States would stop at nothing to destroy Iran. Thus, as far as Tehran was concerned, America could be expected to use its full military might against Iran if the fighting continued — which even Ayatollah Khomeini was eventually persuaded would be disastrous.[95]

A further influence on Iran's decision to agree to a ceasefire was the Iraqi missile campaign against Iran's cities. In early 1988 Iraq first deployed its al-Husayn modified Scud missiles. The al-Husayn carried a smaller warhead than the Scud but had a range of over 600 kilometers. This meant that, for the first time, Iraq could hit Tehran with missiles. Between February and August, Baghdad fired over 200 al-Husayns at Iranian cities, mostly Tehran and Qom. Iraq's missile campaign had a far reaching effect on the Iranian population. The citizens of Tehran and other eastern Iranian cities had never been exposed to a sustained missile bombardment, having suffered only sporadic Iraqi airstrikes in the past. Moreover, rumors began to circulate that the Iraqis had developed chemical-warfare warheads for the al-Husayn, news that turned widespread anxiety into mass panic. In the final months of the war, Iranian civilians fled the cities in droves: over one million people deserted Tehran in the first month of the Iraqi missile strikes, and millions more fled before the ceasefire agreement in August. Here as well, the Iraqis had found a way to make the situation intolerable for the Iranians and forced them to accept an end to the fighting.

ASSESSING IRAQ'S 1988 OFFENSIVES

The five offensives Baghdad conducted in the spring and summer of 1988 demonstrated a higher degree of effectiveness than the Iraqi military had ever hinted at previously. Its forces penetrated Iranian defensive positions quickly and usually with a minimum of casualties. Once through the front-lines, Iraqi armored columns operating in conjunction with mechanized infantry and combat engineers — and provided with plentiful artillery and air support — conducted fairly deep maneuvers that led to the encirclement of sizable Iranian forces. The offensives were preceded by highly effective deception operations and benefited from excellent intelligence regarding the disposition of Iranian forces at the start of the battle. What's more, all of the Iraqi operations moved crisply and efficiently, proceeding from one phase to the next with little delay and featuring relatively rapid movement throughout.

It is not the case, however, that the Iraqi victories in 1988 reflected an across-the-board improvement in Iraqi military effectiveness. The five offensives were primarily a testimony to the improvement in Iraq's strategic-level military leadership since the beginning of the war. In particular, the critical element in each of Iraq's victories was the detailed planning by the general staff. The high command was able to rely on its strategic intelligence assets (primarily photo-reconnaissance aircraft, signals intercepts, and information provided by the United States) to put together an accurate picture of Iranian deployments.[96] They then used this information to develop a highly detailed plan to rip apart Iran's frontline defenses, encircle large formations, and defeat its operational reserves. They carefully concentrated overwhelming force against a given sector and convinced Tehran that each attack would come somewhere else so that the Iranians were surprised and misdeployed. Moreover, the general staff wrote into these plans combined-arms coordination, airstrikes and artillery fire-support missions, operational-level maneuver, and the timing and distance of each part of the operation. Finally, the general staff was careful to undertake only limited, short-duration attacks that could be planned in detail in advance because the limited scope of the operations would keep unforeseen events to a minimum. In short, the planning and preparation for each operation were first rate.

The execution of these operations, however, did not live up to the standards set by their planning. At a tactical level, the Iraqis exhibited the same problems that had plagued them throughout the war. While the RGFC and the best regular-army units performed better than the rest of the armed forces, their improvement can only be said to have been relative. In particular, the same old problems could be seen when, for one reason or another, the situation did not develop as anticipated by Baghdad's plan. Whereas combined-arms integration generally was stilted but adequate in most of the assaults, on numerous occasions when Iraqi tactical units were caught off-guard by an Iranian ambush or an unexpected defensive position, this cooperation disintegrated, leading to losses in infantry and tanks. Unforeseen Iranian counterattacks continued to take a disproportionate toll on

Iraqi forces: the Iraqis were slow to react, and in every case their only response was to try to beat back the Iranians with overwhelming firepower. Fortunately for them, their advantage in this area was so enormous (and the Iranian forces were so weak) that it usually worked. Overall, Iraqi tanks continued to rely on massed firepower and the shock effect of frontal assaults rather than maneuver. Although the initial phases of an attack often featured tactical maneuver by tanks and APCs, once the armor broke free and were exploiting, this kind of maneuver became increasingly rare. In those few instances when the Iraqis faced Iranian mobile reserves, they generally reverted to their previous practice of charging the Iranians with guns blazing and tended to defeat the Iranians through sheer weight of numbers rather than any skill in handling a tank or tank formations. Commanders of Iraqi armored and mechanized platoons, companies, and battalions demonstrated little ability to organize and employ their forces as teams. Similarly, Iraqi artillery fire was devastating primarily because of its volume and heavy reliance on chemical warfare. Iraqi artillery batteries only fired preregistered, preplanned fire missions — even in support of the exploitation operations — and as a result, they rarely could contribute if the armored columns took a wrong turn or encountered Iranian resistance where it was not expected. For this reason, Iraqi artillery generally had little effect after the initial breakthrough battle.[97]

These various problems indicate that whatever tactical success Iraq enjoyed was primarily a function of the detailed and well-conceived planning plus the extensive rehearsal on the part of the RGFC and other participating units. The Iraqis built full-scale mock-ups of the terrain, and the units slated for the assaults practiced their tasks until they could be performed flawlessly; however, they did not internalize any of the concepts that lay behind these carefully orchestrated moves. Thus, whenever the plan went awry and local commanders were left to their own devices, the offensives began to unravel. Whenever it fell to the tactical commanders to conduct an operation — such as when Iraqi forces encountered unexpected Iranian ambushes or counterattacks — they demonstrated that they did not understand combined-arms cooperation or maneuver, could not respond or adapt quickly, and were largely incapable of independent initiative or improvisation. Their responses were slow, predictable, and costly. But by keeping most of the operations to only one or two days in duration, Baghdad minimized the extent to which events could develop in an unexpected manner and maximized the extent to which operations could be planned in detail and learned by heart ahead of time.

Overall, Iraq's achievements in 1988 were actually quite modest, given the enormous imbalances between it and Iran. By early 1988, the Iraqi military outnumbered Iran in every category of military manpower and hardware: Iraq boasted roughly 1,000,000 men under arms, while Iran could field only about 600,000; Iraq had over 4,000 functional tanks, while Iran had less than 1,000; Iraq had over 600 combat aircraft, while Iran could surge less than 50.[98] At the point of attack, Iraqi advantages were even greater, with force ratios of ten to one, twenty to one, and even fifty to one in certain categories not uncommon. On top of this, Iraq relied on massive doses of chemical agents to overwhelm Iranian defenders. Given these disparities, what is surprising is that the Iraqis could not do more. In particular, the Iraqis never pushed more than forty kilometers beyond the frontlines and never let their offensives run for longer than thirty-six hours—about as far and as long as the general staff felt they could go without reality diverging so far from the plan that the entire operation came apart.

Additional Observations on Iraqi Military Performance during the Iran-Iraq War

Several additional areas of Iraqi military effectiveness during the Iran-Iraq war bear discussion. First is the issue of the Iraqi Air Force's performance. Iraqi pilots were very poor by Western standards. The French washed out 80 percent of all Iraqi pilots sent to France for training on the Mirage F-1. Likewise, the Soviets estimated that less than half of the Iraqi pilots they trained would have been accepted for duty in Soviet line-fighter regiments.[99] Iraq recognized that only about one-quarter of all its combat pilots were actually qualified to perform combat operations (most were in the Mirage squadrons) and relied heavily on those men for virtually all of their air operations.

Throughout the war, Iraqi fighters were regularly defeated by the Iranians. While neither side scored many kills, most of them went to the Iranians. A principal reason that so few kills were converted was that the Iraqis generally avoided engaging Iranian fighters for fear of being shot down. Only toward the end of the war, when Iraq began staging aerial ambushes employing their elite Mirage F-1s to secure advantages of three to one or four to one, would the Iraqis actively seek air-to-air combat. Iraqi pilots rarely displayed any aggressiveness, imagination, improvisation, or flexibility in dogfights despite their Western air-to-air combat doctrine, which stressed such skills. Moreover, they were heavily reliant on a Soviet-style ground-controlled intercept system, whereby most Iraqi air-to-air engagements were directed from the ground. Indeed, the Iraqis were considered rigid even by Soviet standards.[100]

Iraq's air-to-ground (and air-to-sea) operations were better, but not dramatically so. At a tactical level, the Iraqis eventually learned to do quite well in attacks against Iranian tankers and economic facilities — primarily oil installations. But Iraqi aircraft conducting CAS, BAI, deep interdiction, and strategic bombing missions fared extremely poorly with little change throughout the war. In these missions Iraqi pilots were unwilling to press their attacks home, insisted on delivering their payloads from high or medium altitudes, and had terrible aim. This split appears to be the result of the difference between the Mirage squadrons — with their high-performance aircraft, precision-guided munitions, and better pilots with French training — which were mainly used to attack Iranian tankers and oil facilities, and the rest of the air force.

In contrast to the improvement in their planning and direction of ground operations, the Iraqis never got much better when it came to the strategic direction of air operations. They constantly failed to perform prestrike reconnaissance, air missions were planned rigidly and unrealistically, ordnance frequently was inappropriate to the target being struck, training in air-to-ground operations was poor, and practice was infrequent. Likewise, Iraq never learned to conduct poststrike reconnaissance to accurately assess damage, nor did it ever commit sufficient sorties to a target to either destroy it or suppress it for any length of time. Instead, Iraqi airstrikes were small and sporadic, and their inability to conduct a sustained campaign against any particular target set minimized the effectiveness of even the well-executed Mirage attacks.

The difficulties of the Iraqi Air Force point to the larger problem Iraq had in effectively handling the modern weaponry it received during the war. The Iraqis failed to take full advantage of the weapons they employed and typically never approached their maximum capabilities. Iraqi personnel took an inordinately long time to learn to use new weapons systems. For example, four years after their initial delivery, none of Iraq's Su-24 attack aircraft were fully operational. By 1983, of the approximately 200 aircraft Iraq had lost, many, and possibly most, of these casualties were due to accidents and maintenance problems. Iraqi forces were rarely able to employ the more sophisticated aspects of the weapons in their inventory. More often than not, Iraq employed highly sophisticated weapons systems in highly unsophisticated manners. For example, Iraqi tank crews rarely ever used the night vision equipment or lead computing sights on their later model Soviet tanks because they did not understand them.[101] Similarly, because Iraqi antiaircraft gunners could not work the Gun Dish radars on their ZSU-23-4s, they instead employed a barrage fire system, thereby relieving them of the need to track enemy aircraft.

Iraq's maintenance and repair practices were poor throughout the war. Iraqi combat units paid little attention to day-to-day maintenance, which generally had to be performed by a small group of technicians assigned to every unit of battalion strength and greater. More serious maintenance and virtually all repair work could only be performed at a small number of large depots concentrated around Baghdad and al-Basrah. Moreover, many of the technicians employed in these depots were foreigners, mainly Russians and other Soviet-bloc nationals familiar with Soviet weaponry. Repairs that would routinely be handled by vehicle crews in Western armies had to be performed at battalion or division level, while repairs that would routinely be taken care of at battalion level in Western armies had to be performed at depot level. Lt. Gen. Bernard Trainor, who served as a military correspondent during the war, reported that in most Iraqi armored and mechanized units, a 50 percent operational readiness rate was considered good.[102] Iraqi crews frequently abandoned tanks, APCs, and other heavy equipment on the battlefield because they required minor repairs, and recovery of damaged vehicles could only be performed by corps-level assets.

Finally, Iraq got very little technical support for its military despite the focus of national resources on the war effort. Iraq had a small number of very competent technical personnel, and these Baghdad assigned to a few high-priority projects such as ballistic-missile modification, chemical and biological warfare, and nuclear weapons. In these areas the Iraqis enjoyed some noteworthy success. The al-Husayn missile was inelegant, perhaps not a terribly impressive technical feat, but it got the job done and solved an important military problem for Baghdad — its inability to strike Tehran and other distant Iranian cities on a sustained basis. Similarly, developing most chemical warfare agents is not difficult, but the Iraqis still did it quickly and efficiently. Beyond these narrow successes, however, Iraq had little to show for its efforts. The Iraqi arms industry was never able to supply the armed forces with much more than ammunition and some small arms. Although Iraq claimed to have made numerous modifications to existing weapons systems and even to have developed some of its own, these were mostly shams. The vast majority of the weapons Iraq claimed to have developed were either foreign weapons systems that Iraq had poorly disguised and renamed — for instance, Iraq repainted an Italian drone and called it a new cruise missile — or else remained on paper. The modifications Iraq made to many existing weapons systems largely proved to be either minor — such as adding mine ploughs to Soviet tanks — or disabling — such as mounting the 125-mm smoothbore cannon of the T-72 on the T-55, which made it impossible to fire the gun without the recoil punching the breech through the back of the turret. Moreover, few of these modified weapons ever made it into combat.

The Gulf War, 1990–91

The Persian Gulf War demonstrated just how modest Iraq's improvements in military effectiveness really were. At the time of the Gulf War, Baghdad's military remained largely depoliticized because Saddam had not felt a need to reimpose draconian controls after the end of the Iran-Iraq War. Baghdad retained most of the competent generals who had led its armies to victory over Iran and in many cases promoted them to positions of greater responsibility. Training continued to stress conventional military operations against conventional military threats, and merit continued to be at least as important as loyalty, if not more so, for promotions.[103] Nevertheless, the Iraqis were humiliated by the American-led multinational coalition during the Gulf War. This change in fortunes can be attributed partly to the huge advantages the Coalition enjoyed in numbers, technology, and air power. However, this defeat also reflected just how little Iraqi tactical effectiveness had improved over the years. Without the advantages in numbers and firepower they had enjoyed over the Iranians, without the advantage of chemical warfare, and without the ability to conduct operations the only way they knew how, Iraq's combat formations proved virtually helpless against the Coalition onslaught.

The Invasion of Kuwait

A bit more than two years after the end of the war with Iran, Iraq began another conflict. At 1:00 A.M. on 2 August 1990, Iraq invaded Kuwait and set in motion a train of events that would lead to the destruction of most of its military at the hands of a multinational coalition led by the United States. The entire RGFC, expanded to eight divisions by the formation of the Tawakalnah 'alla Allah Mechanized Division and the Adnan Infantry Division after the Iran-Iraq War, conducted the invasion. The Republican Guard's Hammurabi Armored Division, which roared down the main al-Basrah–al-Jahrah highway, led the way, brushing aside Kuwaiti resistance at the Matlah Pass. Behind the Hammurabi followed the Tawakalnah. The Madinah Munawrah Armored Division pushed into northwestern Kuwait and swung around the Matlah Ridge. Kuwait's plan to resist an Iraqi attack called for a defensive line along the ridge, thus the Madinah's route of advance would have flanked the main defenses if the Kuwaitis had deployed as they had planned. In fact, only a small Kuwaiti force made it to the ridge to stop the Iraqis, and these were overrun by the Hammurabi. Meanwhile, two brigades of the RGFC's Special Forces Division conducted a helicopter-borne assault on Kuwait International Airport and then moved to secure the amir's palace and other key government facilities. These lead units were followed quickly by the four RGFC infantry divisions. By 8:00 A.M., the Hammurabi and Special Forces Divisions had secured the capital. Elements of several Kuwaiti brigades put up a brief resistance south of Kuwait City but were overwhelmed by the Tawakalnah and Madinah Divisions. The Iraqi Air Force had negligible influence on the operation: it conducted airstrikes on Kuwait's two major airbases that failed to hit anything of value and flew combat air patrols over Kuwait that neglected to intercept any of the Kuwaiti planes that flew airstrikes against the Republican Guard before fleeing to Saudi Arabia. Mopping-up operations were over in less than two days.

Like the 1988 offensives against Iran, the invasion of Kuwait was a very competent operation. The Iraqis had employed a corps-level attack over multiple axes of advance. They had employed maneuver — at least at the operational level — and had moved extremely quickly, pushing three heavy divisions 80 kilometers in about ten hours and then driving another 75 or so kilometers in the next twenty-four hours. Although the four infantry divisions followed the lead armor formations at a necessarily slower pace, within twenty-four hours they too were taking up positions throughout Kuwait. Baghdad had staged a large-scale helicopter-borne assault that achieved surprise and, while not without problems, achieved most of its objectives. Of course, the Iraqis were greatly helped by the small size and limited combat capabilities of the Kuwaiti forces and dealt with those units that resisted by applying overwhelming firepower. Perhaps the only mistake one can point to in the planning of the operation was the decision to move two heavy divisions (Hammurabi and Tawakalnah) through Kuwait City, where they got jammed up in the narrow streets and suffered some losses to Kuwaiti units. When one compares the invasion of Kuwait to that of Iran ten years before, the growth in Iraqi capabilities is obvious. Khuzestan and Kuwait are regions of comparable size and were defended by similar sized military contingents, although the Iranians were considerably more competent. Whereas the invasion of Iran was painfully slow, uncoordinated, and meandering, the invasion of Kuwait was rapid, well integrated, and deliberate.

The invasion of Kuwait was also reflective of the 1988 offensives through all of the lessons Iraq employed. The Kuwait operation was meticulously planned months in advance. It relied only on the RGFC, the most competent force in the Iraqi military. The Republican Guard rehearsed the entire operation repeatedly during the summer of 1990 until they could perform their tasks like clockwork. Finally, the invasion, like the 1988 offensives, was conducted strictly by the book. It was a set-piece operation executed very well, and the only times it showed any signs of stress were when reality diverged from the plan — for instance when the Kuwaiti Air Force was able to conduct a few airstrikes against Iraq's armor or when Kuwaiti ground units briefly resisted south of Kuwait City. In those situations the Iraqi response showed far less elegance than the rest of the campaign: they ignored the airstrikes and simply bludgeoned the Kuwaiti army units into surrender.

Iraqi Strategy for the War against the Coalition

When it became clear that Iraq's invasion would not go unopposed, Baghdad developed a grand strategy that it believed would allow it to "win" the war against the Coalition of Western and Arab states that united to oppose Saddam's attack. At the purely military level, this plan consisted not so much of defeating the Coalition forces but merely of gaining a bloody stalemate that would force the Coalition to negotiations.[104] As indicated by the public and private statements of its leaders, the strategy Iraq adopted rested on the key assumption that the Western powers, especially the United States, would be unwilling to tolerate heavy casualties to liberate Kuwait. Baghdad believed that the United States would be unwilling to sacrifice American lives for Kuwaiti oil. The U.S. retreats from Vietnam and Lebanon further convinced Saddam and his advisers that the American public did not have the stomach to slug it out with them over something so inconsequential as Kuwait.[105]

Iraq apparently recognized that the Coalition would begin any attack on the Iraqi forces in Kuwait with an air campaign. In truth, the Iraqis never intended to fight for air superiority against Coalition forces; they actually believed that this would be unnecessary. They expected the air campaign to last from three to seven days — ten days at most — and that they would suffer only limited damage to their military and infrastructure during this time. The Iraqis believed they could weather this brief squall.[106] Thus, Baghdad's primary objective during the Coalition air campaign was just to get through it and get to the ground war. As Michael Gordon and Bernard Trainor have put it, "Iraq's plan was to endure the bombardment, not defeat the allies in the sky."[107] Iraq was convinced it could prevail in the ground war (by stalemating a Coalition offensive with heavy casualties, not necessarily "defeating" Coalition ground forces), so Baghdad hoped only to ride out the air campaign with as little damage as possible.[108]

As a result, the Iraqi air strategy relegated wearing down Coalition air forces to a secondary objective and instead focused on minimizing the damage Coalition planes could do to Iraq's strategic facilities and ground forces in the Kuwaiti Theater of Operations (KTO). Iraq's high command planned to use its fighters to pick off stray or damaged Coalition aircraft, especially after they had conducted their strikes and were returning to base low on fuel. The burden of actively confronting Coalition aircraft instead was placed on the shoulders of Iraq's SAM and antiaircraft artillery (AAA) batteries. During the Iran-Iraq War, the Iraqis had built up a formidable arsenal of Soviet and European SAM systems and had purchased over 7,500 antiaircraft guns of all types. Baghdad hoped the enormous amount of flak and missiles these forces could put up would hinder Coalition pilots and inflict a heavy price on those that tried to press home their attacks. Iraq had also learned from the war with Iran that bunkering a target can significantly reduce its vulnerability to enemy airstrikes, and the Iraqis had built impressive passive defenses around many of their most important military facilities to guard against air attack. The Iraqi warplanes were kept in hardened bomb shelters, many strategic weapons facilities were protected by massive earthen berms, and most of Baghdad's high-level command-and-control facilities were located in deep underground bunkers.[109] During the fall of 1990, Iraq embarked on a countrywide effort to expand these defenses by berming, bunkering, dispersing, camouflaging, and sandbagging virtually everything of military value. In the KTO, Iraqi troops built bunkers for themselves and their command units, bermed and dispersed their tanks and other equipment, and built revetments for their supplies. In addition, as UN inspection teams later discovered, the Iraqis began a large-scale program to secretly remove much of the equipment from key strategic-weapons facilities and move them to hidden or bunkered storage sites.

For the ground war, Iraq put together a strategy derived from its experiences against Iran, particularly the methods it had employed to stop the offensives against al-Basrah in 1987. Iraq would deploy a line of infantry behind earthworks and fortifications to absorb the brunt of the Coalition attack. Behind the infantry, Iraq stationed a series of armored and mechanized reserves that would launch counterattacks to support the infantry and stop or seal any breakthrough. Meanwhile, the Republican Guard was held as a strategic reserve to launch a major counterattack against the main

Coalition effort. As had been the case against Iran, the general staff expected little maneuver or creativity from its tactical commanders, thus the counterattacks by the local mechanized reserves were to be frontal assaults designed to halt the Coalition by simply throwing masses of armor at any penetration. The RGFC units would be employed in an operational-level maneuver to envelop the major Coalition thrust, which hopefully would have been bloodied and slowed, if not halted, by the frontline infantry and the counterattacks of the army heavy divisions. Once again, superior mass was a major element of the Iraqi plan. Baghdad concentrated 51 of its 66 divisions in the KTO, with over 500,000 troops, 3,475 tanks, 3,080 APCs, and 2,475 artillery pieces, to have available the mass necessary to defeat the Coalition.[110]

One significant flaw in Iraq's strategy was that the main Iraqi defensive line in the KTO ended roughly 100 kilometers west of where the Iraq, Kuwait, and Saudi borders met. The Iraqis did not believe that the Coalition would be able to mount a major mechanized offensive in this area and so deployed only a very thin screening force along this flank. Iraqi forces had always had great difficulty navigating in the trackless desert of southwestern Iraq and did not understand that, equipped with the Global Positioning System — which allows a person to determine geographic location down to a few meters via satellites — Coalition forces would have no problem navigating without roads or other geographic features. Perhaps of greater importance, the Iraqis discounted the logistical capabilities of the Coalition, believing that they would never be able to sustain thousands of armored vehicles and tens of thousands of troops across hundreds of kilometers of barren desert.[111] Ultimately, these assumptions proved to be part of Iraq's undoing, for the main Coalition assault was launched through this undefended sector.

Although Iraq generally planned to fight the Coalition as it had fought Iran, it apparently recognized that the Coalition could field a far more powerful armored force than Iran. One noticeable modification Iraq made to accommodate this difference was the creation of two armored corps to serve as theater reserves. Iraqi corps previously had always been geographic organizational entities assigned a sector of the front, responsible for all operations in that sector, and given forces to accomplish the corps' mission, whatever it might be. In the fall of 1990, Iraq redesignated its II Corps as an armored corps, commanding only the 17th Armored and 51st Mechanized Divisions. Likewise, Baghdad created another corps-level formation called the Jihad Forces and assigned it the 10th and 12th Armored Divisions. The Iraqi General Staff then positioned these two forces along the major north-

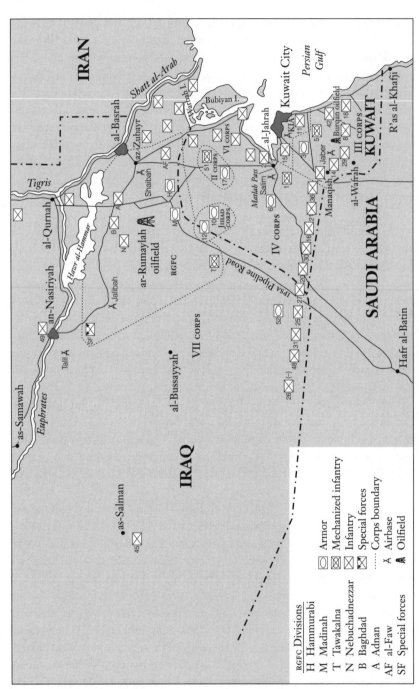

Map 19. Iraqi Divisions in the Kuwaiti Theater of Operations, 24 February 1991

IRAN

IRAQ

KUWAIT

SAUDI ARABIA

Shatt al-Arab

Tigris

Euphrates

Hawr al-Hammar

Persian Gulf

Kuwait City

al-Basrah

az-Zubayr

al-Qurnah

an-Nasiriyah

as-Samawah

as-Salman

al-Bussayyah

al-Jahrah

al-Wafrah

Hafr al-Batin

R'as al-Khafji

Bubiyan I.

Warbah I.

Shaibah

Salim

Jaber

Manaqish

Burqan oilfield

ar-Rumaylah oilfield

Talil

Jalibah

Jihad

Matlab Pass

IPSA Pipeline Road

II CORPS

VI CORPS

IV CORPS

III CORPS

VII CORPS

RGFC

RGFC Divisions
H Hammurabi
M Madinah
T Tawakalna
N Nebuchadnezzar
B Baghdad
A Adnan
AF al-Faw
SF Special forces

⊡ Armor
⊠ Mechanized infantry
⊠ Infantry
⊠ Special forces
····· Corps boundary
⚓ Airbase
⚓ Oilfield

south avenues of advance from Saudi Arabia into the KTO. These two corps had no geographic responsibilities but instead were to be used as armored fists to stun the main Coalition attack and set it up for the decisive counterattack by the Republican Guard.

The Air War, 17 January–24 February 1991

Iraq's prewar strategy for coping with the Coalition air campaign fell apart quickly in the face of Operation Desert Storm. The first casualty of the air campaign was Iraq's integrated air defense network — the French-designed Kari system — which was built to handle small air raids from Israel or Iran and was completely overwhelmed by the thousands of sorties the Coalition threw at it.[112] Within the first two days of the air campaign, the Kari system was essentially shut down as an effective network. This loss deprived Iraqi SAMs, AAA batteries, and interceptors of advance warning of Coalition airstrikes and prevented Baghdad from coordinating its air defense efforts. This loss of central direction also degraded Iraq's barrage-fire AAA system because gunners failed to stick to their assigned fields of fire. Many Iraqi antiaircraft batteries did not open fire on Coalition aircraft until after the planes had finished their attacks and were headed home because the degraded communications network made it difficult to get approval to open fire from Baghdad and battery commanders would not take the initiative to do so on their own.[113] Moreover, Coalition aircraft conducted their strike missions from above 10,000 feet, which rendered the vast majority of Iraq's AAA harmless since it could not reach that altitude.

Iraq's SAM batteries also were quickly neutralized by U.S. F-4G Wild Weasels armed with high-speed antiradiation missiles (HARMs) that homed in on the signals from SAM targeting radars. In the first days of the war, the F-4G–HARM combination wrought havoc with Iraqi SAM batteries. By the third day of the air campaign, Iraqi SAM crews refused to turn on their radars for fear of HARM attack. Some of the braver missileers attempted to turn on their radars for only a few seconds, hoping to illuminate a target before they were locked on by a HARM. Other units simply launched their missiles ballistically without any radar guidance, hoping their weapons would get close enough to a Coalition jet for the terminal guidance system to lock in on it. None of these tactics enjoyed any success.

Baghdad's interceptors encountered similar problems. Iraq was unable to implement its strategy of picking off Coalition aircraft when they were disabled or at a disadvantage because there were too many Coalition fighters around. Iraqi fighter pilots found that whenever they thought they had ambushed a group of Coalition aircraft, they themselves were instead intercepted by U.S. F-14s or F-15s. As if the numeric disadvantage were not enough, Iraqi pilots performed extremely poorly in air-to-air combat. Deprived of ground-controlled intercept guidance, Iraqi pilots were like sitting ducks: incapable of dogfighting or even fleeing effectively, they showed no aggressiveness, imagination, or capacity for independent action. As the U.S. Air Force's *Gulf War Air Power Survey* concluded:

> The consistent and overriding pattern evident in debriefs of engagements by Coalition pilots was the evident lack of situational awareness by their Iraqi adversaries. Accustomed to relying heavily on direction from controllers on the ground, Iraqi interceptor pilots showed little capacity to adjust to dynamic engagements or to exercise much initiative. Those shot down during Desert Storm generally did not react to radar lock-on by Coalition fighters and, for the most part, performed little effective maneuvering, either offensive or defensive; time and again, the principal defensive reaction by Iraqi pilots subjected to attack by Coalition fighters was to descend to low altitude in the apparent belief that the pulse-Doppler radars of Coalition fighters could not lock onto them there.[114]

As a result, Iraqi losses in air-to-air combat mounted quickly, and their pilots had little effect on the Coalition air offensive.

Baghdad did try to strike back at the Coalition, primarily by launching its modified Scuds at Israel and Saudi Arabia, but this effort also went awry. Although Iraq was able to hit Israel with about forty al-Husayn missiles during the course of the war, the United States and its allies were able to convince Tel Aviv to refrain from retaliating. Thus, Israel remained on the sidelines, and the Coalition remained intact. Iraqi Scud attacks on Saudi Arabia also failed to have their desired effect; the presence of the U.S. Patriot SAM system and its *apparent* ability to intercept the Scuds reassured the Saudi government and the international financial community that there was little threat to Saudi oil facilities.[115] Finally, Iraq's only ship-attack mission was thwarted by Coalition air defenses when a Saudi F-15 shot down the two Iraqi Mirage F-1s attempting to launch Exocet missiles at the Coalition fleet in the Persian Gulf.

By the end of the first week of the war, Iraq's air strategy was in shambles. Baghdad reacted to this situation in several ways, all of which may have been plausible, but none of which worked as intended. Iraq's first response was to ground its fighter squadrons, believing they could safely ride out the Coalition air campaign in their hardened bunkers. However, within days, U.S. aircraft began employing superpenetrator munitions to destroy the aircraft inside their shelters. This threw the Iraqis onto the horns of a dilemma: either they could lose their air force in the air to Coalition fighters, or they could lose them on the ground to Coalition bombers. Saddam picked a third option: fly the air force to Iran.[116] Thus, beginning on 24 January, Iraqi aircraft began dashing to airfields in Iran, sometimes escorted by Iraqi fighters but entirely unexpected by the Iranians. Eventually, 115 Iraqi combat aircraft, including all of Baghdad's Su-24s and many of its Mirage F-1s, were flown to Iran, although some were shot down or crashed on the way.[117]

The Battle of R'as al-Khafji, 29–31 January

The other major Iraqi response to the Coalition air campaign was the operation that culminated with the battle of R'as al-Khafji. Baghdad decided it had to take action to try to compel the Coalition leadership to curtail the air campaign and launch its ground offensive. As Gordon and Trainor describe it:

> Convinced that the Americans would not tolerate heavy casualties, the Iraqis' hope had been to force a stalemate on the battlefield in which the Americans took steady losses, which would stir up political opposition to the war at home. But two weeks into the war, there were no signs of an allied ground offensive and Iraq was taking a one-sided pounding from the air. For Iraq's strategy to work it needed the ground war soon. If the Americans would not march north to fight, the Iraqi army would go south and make them fight. By launching an attack, Saddam Hussein could deliver a humiliating defeat on the Saudi forces guarding the border and inflict casualties on any American units coming to their aid. Once his offensive had spurred the Coalition into a ground war, the Iraqis could withdraw behind their defenses, pulling the Americans after them and grinding them down.[118]

The R'as al-Khafji operation was designed to trap a small Coalition force south of the "heel" of Kuwait. The attack was to be conducted by the 5th Mechanized and 3d Armored Divisions, the corps reserve of Iraq's III Corps, which had responsibility for the defense of southeastern Kuwait's border with Saudi Arabia. The III Corps was commanded by Maj. Gen. Salah Abud Mahmud, Iraq's ablest corps commander. Moreover, the 3d and 5th Mechanized Divisions were probably the most competent divisions in Iraq's regular army: they had been among those retrained in 1986–87 and had participated in many of the 1988 offensives. The plan called for elements of the 5th Mechanized to conduct probing attacks along the southern border of Kuwait's heel from al-Wafrah to the coastal highway. The 5th Mechanized was to push into Saudi Arabia where its probing attacks met the least resistance and pin the weak Coalition Arab units deployed in this area. Meanwhile, the 3d Armored would sweep around their left flank and envelop them, crushing them between the two Iraqi heavy divisions and the sea. Having badly bloodied the Coalition, the Iraqi forces would then retire across the Saudi-Kuwaiti border.

Initially, the Iraqis held the advantage of surprise when they attacked on the night of 29–30 January because they had been able to move the 5th Mechanized (reinforced with a number of independent armored units) and part of the 3d Armored to the Kuwaiti-Saudi border largely undetected. Three of four battalion-sized probes conducted by the 5th Mechanized between al-Wafrah and the coast were chased back to Iraqi lines by U.S. Marine covering forces, but the battalion task force moving along the coastal highway stumbled into the deserted Saudi town of R'as al-Khafji. Mahmud immediately reinforced his troops in R'as al-Khafji and began mustering the bulk of his armored forces along the Saudi-Kuwaiti border for the main attack. However, by that time, the Coalition had recovered from its initial surprise, and its air power began to pound the Iraqi units.

During the day on 30 January, the full weight of Coalition air power descended on the Iraqi armored forces as they moved out to execute the primary phase of the operation. Iraqi armored and mechanized formations were attacked relentlessly by Coalition strike aircraft and attack helicopters. The 26th Armored Brigade of the 5th Mechanized Division was caught moving through a narrow lane in one of the Iraqi minefields when its lead tank was destroyed by a lucky shot from a Saudi multiple-rocket launcher. Coalition aircraft quickly descended on the hapless brigade and pummeled it. One survivor from the 26th Armored told his U.S. captors that he had fought with the brigade in every major engagement of the Iran-Iraq War and that all of the damage his unit had sustained in all of those battles combined did not equal the damage they had taken during the thirty minutes they were trapped in that minefield.[119] General Mahmud quickly realized that his armor was being mauled by the Coalition air forces. He concluded that it was impossible for his men to execute the plan and that his two best divisions would be wrecked if the offensive were not canceled immediately. Consequently, the attack was called off, and the two heavy divisions returned to their bivouac areas to escape the Coalition airstrikes. Later, on 1 February, Saudi forces finally recaptured R'as al-Khafji, with considerable support from U.S. air and ground forces.

A few comments can be offered about Iraqi combat performance at R'as al-Khafji. It was planned less than a week before its start date, and the forces that participated were unable to rehearse for the operation because of constant Coalition airstrikes. As could only be expected from Iraqi forces in such circumstances, problems outweighed successes. On the positive side, the Iraqi concealment efforts and operational security achieved surprise for the offensive. On the negative side, Iraqi ground forces fought poorly in the limited clashes that occurred. Against the various U.S. Marine outposts, Iraqi armor essentially just blundered into the Americans. Not only were they not aware that the Marines were there, but when contact was made, they conducted fumbling frontal assaults. In these attacks the Iraqis fought hard initially but retreated after brief firefights that convinced them that the Marines were not going to run from an Iraqi armored charge. As a result, the Iraqis took significant casualties without causing any real damage — indeed, the Marines took far more damage from friendly fire than from the Iraqis.[120] The Iraqi units in the town of R'as al-Khafji itself successfully resisted several inept Saudi attacks before eventually surrendering when their larger operation was aborted and after the Saudis and Americans concentrated unprecedented levels of firepower against them. However, the defense they put up was haphazard and unimpressive. They simply sat behind positions in the town and blazed away at Saudi forces, who crawled forward in a disjointed fashion, refused to support one another, and insisted on conducting frontal assaults even though the Iraqis had failed to adequately protect their flanks. As had been the case against Iran, a small flanking maneuver could have routed the Saudis, but the Iraqis would not move, and thanks to their poor marksmanship, they did little damage to the Saudis. Unable to rely on preregistered fire missions, Iraqi artillery support was miserable, constantly lagging well behind the changing situation on the ground and largely unable to provide supporting fire to the Iraqi defenders.

After R'as al-Khafji failed, the Iraqis did not try another ground offensive or otherwise move to try to force the Coalition's hand. For the most part, Iraqi troops hunkered down in the KTO and tried to make it through the constant aerial bombardment. There was a flurry of diplomatic activity between 12 and 23 February after Baghdad finally concluded its military was being battered too hard by the Coalition air campaign and would not be able to stand up to a ground offensive. For over a week, the Iraqis and the Soviets tried to hammer out an arrangement that would allow the Iraqis to withdraw from Kuwait with their army intact. As a sign of Saddam's real anxiety over the looming ground battle, Iraqi negotiators were willing to make far greater concessions than they ever had previously. However, Saddam would not go so far as to unconditionally accept all of the UN resolutions, and so he eventually abandoned the negotiations.[121]

The Iraqi Army on the Eve of the Ground War

The lengthy Coalition air campaign devastated the Iraqi ground forces entrenched in the KTO. Six weeks of relentless aerial attack destroyed the morale of many of the Iraqi units. Although these forces experienced problems with desertions even before the beginning of Operation Desert Storm, the Coalition air campaign turned a trickle of deserters into a torrent. By the end of February, some Iraqi units had been reduced to less than 50 percent of their deployed strength, and overall Iraqi troop strength in the KTO had fallen to 325,000–350,000 men.[122] The air war was especially effective against the poorly trained and supplied infantry divisions defending Iraq's frontlines. These units were mostly manned with Shi'ite conscripts who had little love for Saddam or his war for Kuwait.

Supply problems caused by the air campaign also increased the misery the average Iraqi soldier had to endure. Many Iraqi generals captured during the war opined that if the air campaign had been allowed to continue for another two or three weeks, the Iraqi army would have been forced to withdraw from Kuwait as a result of logistical strangulation.[123] Although Coalition airstrikes destroyed only a very small percentage of the supplies Iraq had stockpiled inside the KTO, the air campaign shut down Iraq's logistical distribution network within the theater. By mid-February, Iraq found itself virtually incapable of getting supplies to its frontline units: Coalition fighter-bombers prevented its trucks from using the roads to the front; losses to airstrikes had significantly reduced the size of the Iraqi truck fleet; and few Iraqi drivers were willing to make the trip. According to the division commander of the Iraqi 27th Infantry Division, his unit deployed with only eighty trucks, and all but ten were destroyed by the Coalition airstrikes.[124]

These problems were not felt uniformly by the units in the KTO. The Republican Guard units were closest to the Iraqi supply depots and farthest from Coalition airbases, making their supply situation much easier. Moreover, their importance to the regime ensured that Baghdad would spare no effort to keep them provisioned. The heavy divisions of the regular army were a bit farther from the Iraqi depots and a bit closer to Coalition airbases, but they too generally did not suffer from supply problems. Again, it was the largely Shi'ite infantry divisions along the frontlines that bore the brunt of Iraq's supply problems. These units were well within range of Coalition airbases—allowing allied aircraft long loiter times over their positions—and far from the Iraqi depots—making these supply runs the most dangerous. The infantry divisions also had the lowest priority for supplies, and Baghdad grew reluctant to squander its transport assets to supply these troops.

Coalition airstrikes also destroyed a large number of Iraqi weapons and equipment. According to CIA estimates conducted after the war, Coalition air attacks probably destroyed or crippled 20–30 percent of the tanks, APCs, and artillery of the Iraqi heavy divisions in the KTO and may have rendered inoperable more than one-third of all the tanks, APCs, and artillery in the theater.[125] The loss of Iraqi equipment, especially armor and artillery, was heaviest among the frontline infantry units and lightest among the RGFC and several regular-army heavy divisions deployed far from the frontlines, with most of the other army heavy divisions falling somewhere between these two extremes.[126] Damage was kept to this level only because Iraq's passive defenses—berming, camouflaging, and other measures—proved highly effective against airstrikes. Generally, only precision-guided munitions were able to destroy Iraqi armored vehicles with any high rate of success, but these munitions made up only a small proportion of the ordnance dropped in the KTO.[127]

The predicament of Iraqi ground forces in the KTO was compounded by a variety of other problems. When the Coalition finally launched its ground offensive on 24 February 1991, their forces were superior to the Iraqi army in the KTO in virtually every quantitative and qualitative category. After nearly six weeks of airstrikes, Coalition forces exceeded the Iraqi units in the KTO in numbers of troops, tanks, APCs, and most everything else. Moreover, Coalition equipment generally was far superior to Iraqi equipment. For example, the Coalition fielded about 2,200 top-of-the-line battle tanks such as the American M1A1 Abrams and the British Challenger, while the Iraqis had less than 1,000 of their best tanks in the KTO, the older and less capable T-72.

Another major problem for the Iraqis was their lack of intelligence regarding Coalition forces, deployment, or strategy. Iraqi tactical intelligence once again produced little or nothing of value, primarily because the Iraqi army in Kuwait did little patrolling and no long-range reconnaissance.[128] In addition, Iraq had lost the strategic assets it previously had used to compensate for its tactical shortcomings. The Coalition controlled the skies and would not allow the Iraqis to fly reconnaissance aircraft. Iraq was at war with the United States, and Russia was attempting to remain neutral, so two of the best sources of information Iraq had relied on at the end of the war with Iran were lost to it. All in all, Iraqi field commanders went into battle with little idea of how their enemy fought, where his forces were deployed, or what he intended to do.

The Ground War, 24–28 February 1991

When the Coalition finally launched its long-awaited ground offensive, Iraq's frontline infantry divisions collapsed in a mass of desertions and surrenders. Between the six weeks of constant bombardment and the resulting supply shortages, Baghdad's infantry had no interest in a fight and surrendered in the tens of thousands. This completely unhinged Iraq's defensive scheme. The infantry divisions were supposed to delay and disrupt the Coalition advance, and their disintegration meant that Coalition units frequently were on top of Iraqi reserves before the latter had a chance to form up for battle.

On the first day of the ground campaign, the U.S. 1st and 2d Marine Divisions drove into the western side of the "heel" of Kuwait, breaching the Iraqi lines at several points between al-Wafrah and al-Manaqish. The Iraqi III Corps infantry divisions defending this sector disintegrated, surrendering in droves to the United States, and only an immediate counterattack by the 8th Mechanized Brigade of the 3d Armored Division—and the laborious process of wading through Iraqi POWs—slowed the Marines on the first day.[129] Although some Iraqi units resisted, they were quickly and almost effortlessly outflanked and overwhelmed by the Americans. In the far west of the KTO, the French 6th Light Armored Division and the U.S. 82d Airborne Division attacked and easily overpowered the Iraqi 45th Infantry Division defending as-Salman in southern Iraq. Most elements of the 45th put up only perfunctory fire before surrendering. Meanwhile, the Coalition attack was proceeding so smoothly that its high command sped up the timetable of the operation and began the main U.S. VII Corps attack that afternoon rather than the next morning as planned. The U.S. 2d Armored Cavalry Regiment, leading the U.S. 1st and 3d Armored Divisions, swung around the open right flank of the Iraqi 26th Infantry Division at the end of the Iraqi VII Corps line (the westernmost of Iraq's corps in the KTO). Farther east, the U.S. 1st Mechanized Division of the U.S. VII Corps attacked the two forward brigades of the 26th Infantry Division. This division was unable to offer any effective resistance to the U.S. forces, and most of its troops surrendered after a brief fight.[130]

At the end of the first day of the ground war, the Iraqis were almost certainly concerned by the situation but probably did not believe that the battle had been lost. In the east the U.S. Marine Corps attack had overwhelmed the Iraqi frontline infantry. However, the Iraqis still had three of their best army heavy divisions (1st Mechanized, 3d Armored, and 5th Mechanized) in reserve, largely unengaged and intact, in this sector. In the west the situation probably looked even better to the Iraqis. The frontline commanders at that end of the Iraqi VII Corps line had failed to report that the 26th Infantry Division had been overrun by U.S. armored and mechanized forces. Instead, they told Lt. Gen. Ahmad Ibrahim Hammash, the VII Corps commander, only that a small force of eight French tanks and four APCs had skirted the flank of 26th Infantry Division and was making its way toward al-Busayyah. Meanwhile, the Iraqi 27th Infantry Division defending the Wadi al-Batin had rebuffed a diversionary attack by the U.S. 1st Cavalry (Armored) Division. This was where the Iraqis were expecting the main U.S. VII Corps attack to come, and they apparently mistook the 1st Cavalry's feint to be the main U.S. attack — which they believed they had successfully repulsed.[131] In response to these developments, the general staff ordered two brigades of the 12th Armored Division to move out to al-Busayyah to intercept the French force reported in the area. Meanwhile, General Hammash concentrated his primary armored reserve — the 52d Armored Division — closer to the wadi in expectation of a renewed U.S. attack there in the morning, and General Mahmud, still commanding the Iraqi III Corps in southeastern Kuwait, readied the 5th Mechanized Division to counterattack the U.S. Marines.

DAY TWO

The second day of the ground war began with Mahmud's counterattack, employing the 5th Mechanized Division, against the advancing U.S. Marines. Although this was a preplanned and rehearsed counterattack, the Iraqis were thrown off-balance by the rapid maneuvering of the Marine units, and Mahmud's attack was soon halted with heavy losses to his units. The Iraqis fought hard, making repeated attacks against the Marine forces, but they showed little skill, relied only on frontal assaults, refused to maneuver to secure tactical advantages, and showed poor marksmanship. Overall, the Marines saw the counterattack as a frightening and exhausting — but not very damaging — experience.[132] The 5th Mechanized Division was wiped out at little cost to the Americans.

When this counterattack failed, the general staff apparently concluded that its position in southeastern Kuwait was untenable, and it ordered the III Corps and the Khalij forces defending the Kuwaiti coast from al-Ahmadiyah to al-Jahrah to fall back to a new defensive line at the Matlah

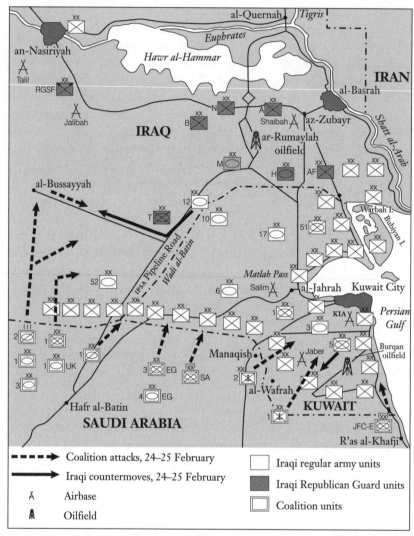

Map 20. Initial Coalition Ground Attacks, 24–25 February 1991

Pass. The 3d Armored Division was ordered to stand and screen this with-drawal. By late morning on 25 February, U.S. Joint Surveillance Target Attack Reconnaissance Systems aircraft detected the Iraqi forces in south-eastern Kuwait redeploying northward.[133]

In the west the U.S. VII and XVIII Corps continued to roll, smashing several Iraqi formations. The U.S. 1st Mechanized Division overran the Iraqi 48th Infantry Division, deployed to the east of the former 26th Infan-try Division positions along the so-called Saddam line. The U.S. 1st Ar-mored Division assaulted the last brigade of the 26th Infantry Division, defending al-Bussayyah, deep behind the Iraqi frontlines. The U.S. 2d Armored Cavalry Regiment (ACR) destroyed about half of the two-brigade force from the Iraqi 12th Armored Division dispatched to al-Bussayyah the night before, and other elements of this force were destroyed en route by U.S. A-10 attack aircraft.[134] Finally, the U.S. 101st Air Assault Division reached the Euphrates River near the Iraqi city of as-Samawah and skir-mished with some local Iraqi Popular Army units.[135]

These various contacts with U.S. forces so far up the western edge of the KTO apparently alerted Iraq's general staff to the threat from the deep Coalition maneuver around their right flank, and they reacted immediately. Baghdad ordered five divisions of the Republican Guard, the 17th Armored Division, and the remnants of the 12th Armored Division to form a screen-ing force to the west to try to hold back the U.S. VII Corps. Concerned with the safety of its key cities, the general staff also began repositioning three other RGFC units to defend against a Coalition attack — the Special Forces Division and the Baghdad Infantry Division were pulled out of their positions in the northern KTO and moved to defend the capital, while the al-Faw Infantry Division was ordered to pull back to al-Basrah to begin pre-paring its defenses.[136] They also ordered the 6th Armored, 1st Mechanized, and 3d Armored Divisions in southern Kuwait to form a similar screen facing southward to cover the withdrawal of Iraqi forces against the U.S. Marine attack threatening to bisect Kuwait at al-Jahrah. Finally, when these units had begun moving, Baghdad announced a general retreat of all forces in the KTO to try to save as much of its army from the Coalition juggernaut as they could.[137]

Many Iraqi soldiers felt the order to retreat was long overdue, and they seized the opportunity to flee before Coalition units caught them or Bagh-dad changed its mind. Iraqi units streamed north, desperate to reach the safety of al-Basrah and paying little heed to how they escaped or what they left behind. Demoralized Iraqi troops ignored security procedures, tactical doctrine, and even the orders of their officers in their determination to get out of the KTO as quickly as they could. Many Iraqi units abandoned any equipment that might have slowed them down (including tanks and artillery), piled into trucks, and headed north.

THE STAND OF THE REPUBLICAN GUARD

On 26 and 27 February, combat centered on the Coalition assaults against Iraq's hastily formed defensive lines. In central Kuwait elements of the Iraqi 1st Mechanized Division fought several half-hearted engagements against the U.S. Tiger Brigade but did not slow it significantly as the Americans drove to cut off the Iraqi retreat from Kuwait by taking the Matlah Pass. In southern Kuwait scattered elements of the Iraqi 3d Armored Division fought a holding action around Kuwait International Airport. Most of the division seems to have bolted despite its orders to stay and screen the retreat, and the isolated forces who obeyed orders and fought (several dozen tanks and a few companies of infantry) did so very ineffectively. The 3d Armored Division elements never pulled together sufficient strength to give the Marines much of a fight, instead dispersing in small units of platoon size that were easily dispatched by the Americans. The most resistance the Iraqis offered was to remain in their defensive positions, firing sporadically and ineffectively at the Marines even after their positions had been outflanked. All told, the Iraqi 3d Armored Division lost 30–40 of its T-72s around the airport while causing "only minimal casualties and equipment losses."[138]

The fight with the RGFC was considerably harder. The U.S. VII Corps first encountered the Tawakalnah 'alla Allah Mechanized Division deployed to the west of the Wadi al-Batin, protecting the Iraqi troops fleeing north along the IPSA pipeline road. The U.S. 2d ACR, 3d and 1st Armored Divisions, and 1st Mechanized Division struck the Tawakalnah's lines during the afternoon of 26 February and fought the Republican Guards all afternoon and night in the battle of the Wadi al-Batin.[139] The Tawakalnah, along with the remnants of the 12th Armored Division, were deployed in a British-style reverse-slope position with mines emplaced along the crest of the ridge. The Tawakalnah was badly outnumbered — U.S. forces deployed over 1,000 tanks, while the Tawakalnah could muster only about 200. They were also badly outgunned because the armor-piercing rounds from the U.S. M1A1 tanks could easily destroy the Iraqis' T-72M1s at over 4,000 meters, while the T-72M1's rounds could not penetrate the frontal armor of the M1A1 even at bore-sight range.[140] Despite these disadvantages, the Republican Guard fought tenaciously, and many veteran U.S. servicemen remarked afterward that the battle had been more ferocious than any they

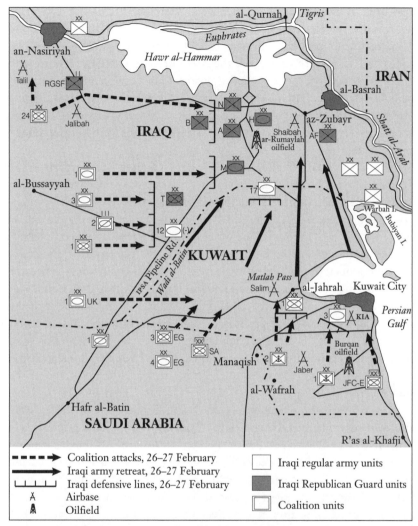

Map 21. Final Battles of the Gulf War, 26–27 February 1991

had been in before, including combat in Vietnam.[141] Unlike the regular-army units, the Republican Guards fought and died almost to a man, and U.S. forces captured few Tawakalnah soldiers and officers. When the Iraqi tanks and APCs were destroyed, their infantrymen charged forward with small arms and rocket-propelled grenades. The Tawakalnah maintained remarkable unit cohesion, with remnants attempting to conduct a fighting withdrawal long after the division had been virtually wiped out. By the morning of 27 February, 177 Iraqi tanks and 107 APCs were burning on the battlefield.[142]

The Tawakalnah fought measurably better than its counterparts in the regular army, although it still performed far below Western standards. In particular, its men destroyed and damaged more U.S. M-2 and M-3 infantry fighting vehicles than any other Iraqi division and actually put out of action four U.S. M1A1s, a feat no other Iraqi unit was able to accomplish.[143] Unlike their compatriots in the regular army, the remnants of the Tawakalnah conducted a fighting retreat to the Wadi al-Batin when it became clear that the battle was lost and tried to employ British-style bounding-overwatch tactics as they fell back. Furthermore, the deployment of the division in a reverse-slope position demonstrated good operational thinking on the part of the division commander and his staff, although this good idea was undermined by poor execution as some Iraqi battalions deployed too close to the military crest of the ridge to take full advantage of the position.

Nevertheless, the Republican Guards still displayed many of the same problems that plagued the rest of the Iraqi army. RGFC tank gunnery was only slightly better than that of the regular-army units. Although a handful of Tawakalnah tanks did get out and "stalk" Coalition armor to get flank shots at them — the primary reason for the division's higher tally of armored vehicles — the vast majority remained in their hastily prepared defensive positions even long after it was clear that their tank rounds could not penetrate the frontal armor of the M1A1s and, therefore, they would *have* to maneuver to get a flank shot if they were to have any success. Moreover, most Tawakalnah units remained in their defensive positions even when Coalition forces had penetrated their line and were rolling up their positions from the flanks. The RGFC division clung tenaciously to its defenses but launched only a handful of counterattacks, and these were made by pitifully small units and conducted as frontal attacks that were wiped out before they gained any momentum. Despite considerable gaps between the American units (a fact that so unnerved the Americans that they constantly imagined Iraqi penetrations into these gaps), the Iraqis never counterattacked into any of these seams to try to take one of the U.S. units in the flank and disrupt the assault.[144] Finally, although the Tawakalnah apparently had at least three or four battalions of artillery still operational, these guns did little damage to Coalition forces. Once again, Iraqi artillery could not shift its fire to hit the fast-moving U.S. forces and were quickly silenced in counterbattery duels.

The major engagements of the last full day of the ground war were fought in and around the ar-Rumaylah oilfield as the Coalition continued to assault Iraq's western defensive line to complete the encirclement of the KTO. Four RGFC divisions were deployed in hasty defensive positions against this attack. At the northern end of the Iraqi defensive line, the Nebuchadnezzar Infantry Division straddled Highway 8, connecting al-Basrah and an-Nasiriyah. At the southern end, the Madinah Munawrah Armored Division defended the IPSA pipeline road as it turned east into the ar-Rumaylah oilfields. In the gap between these two divisions, the Adnan Infantry Division had taken up positions, while the Hammurabi Armored Division waited in reserve behind the Nebuchadnezzar and the Adnan.

The Nebuchadnezzar Division resisted the advance of the U.S. 24th Mechanized Division throughout the day but suffered crippling losses in the process. The division fought by falling back from one defensive line to the next, and the U.S. division spent virtually the entire day pushing through the Nebuchadnezzar's positions. Once again, Iraqi artillery proved virtually useless. Rolling down Highway 8, the 24th Mechanized came under heavy artillery fire from the Nebuchadnezzar. However, the Americans quickly realized that the Iraqis had placed 55-gallon drums in the area and had preregistered their guns on these drums. As soon as the Americans learned to avoid them, they were no longer hindered by the artillery because the Iraqis could not shift their fire and just kept shelling the drums.[145] In the end, the Nebuchadnezzar Division was virtually wiped out in the fighting while inflicting only very slight casualties on the 24th Mechanized.

In the early afternoon of 27 February, the U.S. 1st Armored Division struck the 2d Armored Brigade of the RGFC Madinah Division in the flank and obliterated the unit in the battle of Madinah Ridge. The 2d Brigade was deployed along a north-south ridgeline in expectation of a Coalition attack from the west. Although the Iraqis were well aware that the U.S. VII Corps was bearing down on them from that direction, they did not properly man their vehicles, failed to deploy adequate security and observation screens, and mostly relaxed, and the U.S. forces caught them by surprise. This, plus good visibility allowing the U.S. M1A1 tanks to pick off the Iraqi armor from as far as 3,500 meters away—well beyond the range of the Iraqi

T-72s—led to a complete rout. Nearly 100 Iraqi tanks and APCs were destroyed in the first ten minutes of the battle. The Republican Guards fought back, but again poor marksmanship, the unwillingness of Iraqi tankers to leave their defensive positions to maneuver (or even to change firing positions), and the inability of Iraqi artillery to shift fire from its predesignated fire missions prevented them from having any significant success. Indeed, one anecdote from a meeting between the U.S. VII Corps commander, Lt. Gen. Frederick Franks, and the U.S. 1st Armored Division commander, Maj. Gen. Ronald Griffith, recorded in the official U.S. Army history concisely displays the problems of Iraq's artillery batteries: "Griffith was briefing his commander [Franks] when one of many Iraqi artillery concentrations hit nearby, causing some concern to VII Corps staff officers, one of whom turned quizzically to Griffith's aide and asked, 'What's that, some short rounds from our artillery?' Robinson shook his head and offered, 'Nah, that's Iraqi artillery.' He smiled at the officer's confused expression and said, 'Don't worry, that's about the fifth barrage they've fired, but they don't move it. It just goes into the same place every time.' "[146] A small force from the Madinah Division tried to mount a fighting withdrawal but were quickly dispatched by Coalition armor and helicopters. In all, 93 tanks and 73 APCs of the Madinah were destroyed in the engagement.[147]

The battle of Madinah Ridge and other fighting in the ar-Rumaylah oilfields were the last significant combat of the Gulf War. By the end of 27 February, Coalition forces controlled four-fifths of Kuwait's territory and had cut off virtually all routes of escape to al-Basrah. That night the Hammurabi Armored Division (which had so far been unengaged during the ground war) and the remaining brigades of the Madinah Armored Division pulled back to the az-Zubayr area and began forming a new defensive line. The Iraqis no doubt expected to have to fight to defend al-Basrah, and these Republican Guard divisions would have served as the key elements in such a contest.[148] The Iraqis, however, were spared from having to defend their second city by the Coalition decision to suspend combat operations at 8:00 A.M. on 28 February.

General Observations on Iraqi Military Performance during the Gulf War, 1990–91

The forty-three days of Operation Desert Storm constituted one of the most lopsided defeats in modern military history. A wide range of factors contributed to Iraq's demise. While most are highlighted above, several others bear inclusion. One important factor was that the Iraqis expected a slow-moving battlefield on which armored forces might advance quickly

for brief spurts, though generally the armies would maneuver at an in-
fantryman's pace. The Iraqis expected that the fighting would be characterized by brief, sharp clashes followed by long periods of regrouping and
reorganization. Although Baghdad clearly recognized the Coalition would
be able to rely on air power to a greater extent than had Iran, the Iraqis
nevertheless expected that combat would be limited to the front lines and
that rear areas would generally be as quiet as in the Iran-Iraq War. In
particular, they expected to be able to reposition their forces, commit reserves, bring up reinforcements, and concentrate for counterattacks. The
fact that the Coalition did not play by these rules was a big problem for the
Iraqis. The pace of Coalition operations, particularly those of American
and British forces, kept the Iraqis off-balance and desperately trying to keep
up. Many of their planned operations were rendered moot because they
could not be implemented before the Americans were on top of them.

Another area of difficulty for the Iraqis was maintenance. Iraq had low
operational readiness rates even before the war began. For example, at least
20 percent of the Iraqi Air Force was grounded because of maintenance
problems. In part, this was due to the loss of Iraq's contingent of foreign technicians, most of whom left soon after the invasion of Kuwait. Of
course, the Coalition air campaign was also disastrous for Iraqi maintenance practices. Iraqi vehicle crews learned quickly that Coalition aircraft
were targeting their vehicles and weapons but rarely went after personnel
bunkers. Consequently, few of them were willing to go near their vehicles,
and upkeep was virtually forgotten. Moreover, broken or damaged equipment could not be sent back to rear-area repair depots because Coalition
aircraft prevented movement along the roads. The Iraqis also were unable
to bring replacement vehicles or equipment into the theater to make up for
losses. As a result, by the beginning of the air campaign, a great many Iraqi
weapons and vehicles were inoperable because of inadequate service.

Air defense was still another problem. In particular, the Iraqis failed
to provide adequate air defense of the main roads throughout the KTO.
This neglect almost certainly reflected the experience of the Iran-Iraq War,
when the Iranian air force was incapable of sustaining an interdiction campaign against the Iraqis. With the roads unprotected, the Coalition air
forces had little difficulty shutting down Iraq's logistical distribution system
in the theater. Ultimately, Iraqi logistics should have been more than adequate because Baghdad had moved enormous amounts of supplies into the
theater well ahead of hostilities. Before the air campaign started, the Iraqis
were able to keep their troops supplied, with the exception of a few infantry
divisions deployed in the far west of the KTO, where roads were few and

poor. However, all of this collapsed under Coalition interdiction because the Iraqis did not deploy air defenses along the main supply routes.

Information was a problem at every level. First, there was the poverty of Iraqi intelligence, which could not provide any information of value to anyone in the Iraqi military hierarchy. Prior to the Gulf War, the general staff had concluded that Iraqi tactical intelligence was so bad that they stripped the reconnaissance units from all tactical formations and consolidated them at division level. However, this does not seem to have helped much because the problems persisted. For example, on 2 March, after the ceasefire, the Hammurabi Division failed to reconnoiter the road it was taking to move out of the KTO and was unaware that it was occupied by the U.S. 24th Mechanized Division, which hammered a brigade of the division when it tried to pass through. Iraqi commanders rarely sent out patrols, and most officers were reduced to listening to foreign radio broadcasts for information on their adversary. Moreover, what little information was gleaned from intelligence was regularly abused at all levels of the chain of command. Probably the most important example of this was on 24 February, when Iraqi units misinformed the general staff about the threat in the western KTO, claiming that the main U.S. VII Corps attack was a small force of twelve French tanks and APCs. Because of this mistake, the general staff did not realize until twenty-four hours later where the main Coalition effort was. As the U.S. Air Force's *Gulf War Air Power Survey* notes: "Whatever information was available to the General Staff was not shared with tactical commanders. Each corps daily disseminated a general daily [*sic*] situation report but provided little else in the way of detailed intelligence, and division commanders likewise rarely shared information with their subordinates. . . . Commanders frequently misreported the condition of their units — particularly readiness and maintenance problems, low morale, and widespread desertions."[149]

TACTICAL LEADERSHIP

Without doubt, however, Iraq's greatest liability remained the limited capabilities of its tactical formations. Setting aside the superior performance of Western equipment over Iraq's largely Soviet arsenal, Iraqi units simply could not fight at the same levels of effectiveness as the British, French, and especially American soldiers and officers who made up the core of the Coalition's military forces. Iraqi tactical commanders were inflexible and incapable of adequately responding to the constant maneuvering, deception, and speed of their adversary. Time and again, the response of Iraqi units to being surprised or outflanked was either to do nothing, to keep doing what they were already doing, or to flee. Only rarely did Iraqi junior officers try to devise quick responses to unforeseen developments. For example, the 52d Armored Brigade was deployed with the rest of the 52d Armored Division as the operational reserve of the Iraqi VII Corps and, therefore, its primary mission was to counterattack a Coalition attack against one of the VII Corps infantry divisions. Late on 24 February, the commander of the 52d Brigade received a frantic message from the headquarters of the 48th Infantry Division — directly in front of his unit — that they were being overrun by American armored forces. Nevertheless, because he had not received orders from divisional command, the officer did nothing: he did not execute his primary mission by moving to support the embattled 48th Division; he did not ready his brigade to move or fight; he did not even contact divisional headquarters to report the message and ask if he should counterattack. As a result, the 48th Infantry Division was overwhelmed by the U.S. 1st Mechanized Division, and the 52d Brigade was later overrun by the British 1st Armored Division without much of a fight.[150]

Combined arms at tactical levels was similarly poor. While the initial deployment schemes of Iraqi units did a good job of weaving together infantry, armor, antitank units, artillery, and other supporting arms into a cohesive pattern, this was the product of the five months Iraqi division and corps commanders had to plan and inspect the dispositions of their subordinates. On every other occasion, Iraqi combined-arms cooperation was almost nonexistent. For example, the 5th Mechanized Division counterattack out of the Burqan oilfields featured large concentrations of armor, infantry, and artillery support — but none of them together. Most of their attacks consisted of armored charges without either infantry or artillery support. Likewise, when the Republican Guard's Madinah and Tawakalnah Divisions redeployed to the west to meet the U.S. VII Corps attack, their new defensive positions displayed only very haphazard integration of infantry and armor. The dispositions of the two divisions along their defensive lines showed little interspersing of tanks and APCs.[151] While both the armor and the infantry of the Tawakalnah were active against the U.S. forces, it was generally the case that in any given sector, U.S. forces had to worry about T-72s *or* mechanized infantry, rarely both.

OPERATIONAL AND STRATEGIC LEADERSHIP

Iraqi corps and division commanders performed unevenly. On the one hand, some senior field commanders stood out as quite competent, such as the III Corps commander, General Mahmud, and the commander of the Tawakalnah Mechanized Division of the Republican Guard. With the exception of the inattention of the Tawakalnah commander to proper combined-arms coordination noted above, both of these generals appear to have handled their forces as well as they could have under the circumstances. Mahmud came up with a commendable plan of attack for the R'as al-Khafji operation; recognized quickly that his command was being shredded during implementation and ordered a retreat; and during the coalition ground offensive, set up a well-devised counterattack out of the Burqan oilfields that employed operational-level maneuver to catch the U.S. Marines in the flank. Similarly, the Tawakalnah deployed to meet the U.S. VII Corps attack in a reverse-slope position; it had ample observation posts in front of its positions; the division fought ferociously in combat against vastly superior forces; and—like few other Iraqi units—its formations correctly employed bounding-overwatch tactics. However, there were seven other Iraqi corps commanders and fifty other division commanders in the KTO, and at this point, there is little information about them on which to reach a judgment. Many probably did not have the chance to prove their worth because their units cracked under the strain of the Coalition air campaign. Some seem to have performed competently in their tasks, such as the commanders of the RGFC's Nebuchadnezzar, Adnan, and Madinah Divisions, all of whom devised reasonably good hasty defenses when their units repositioned to meet the Coalition attack. Others seem to have done little to mitigate the factors working against their troops and may have done much to exacerbate them.

By comparison, Iraq's high command, led once again by General Husayn Rashid (now chief of staff of the armed forces), turned in a very creditable performance, considering what they had to work with. Iraq's greatest mistake was to fight the Coalition rather than finding a way to negotiate its way out of Kuwait. This was a political decision, not a military one, and ultimately made by Saddam, not the Iraqi General Staff. Saddam's decision to fight clearly reflected a misunderstanding of the balance of forces between the United States and Iraq. We have too little information at this time about Iraqi decision making to know if the general staff was even asked its advice on the issue; however, even if they were, and even if they shared Saddam's misunderstanding of the balance of power, this would be a mark against their judgment, not necessarily a sign of bad generalship. The Iraqis did not understand what Coalition air power could do to their ground forces in the KTO. The Iraqis did not understand the Coalition's ability to supply its forces and navigate in the trackless desert of southern Iraq and so left their western flank unguarded. The Iraqis did not understand how

Coalition air power could savage Iraqi heavy divisions when they left their protective revetments and consequently had two of their best divisions badly beaten up at R'as al-Khafji. The Iraqis did not understand that their T-72s simply could not stand up to the U.S. MIAIs. Indeed, like Hannibal, Napoleon, and many of Germany's best World War II generals, the Iraqi high command failed to understand the power of their enemy, which led to their defeat. This is not to claim that the Iraqi generals were in the same league as these great commanders, only to point out that misjudging the balance of power is not necessarily a sign of incompetence.

Once one gets beyond Iraq's gross underestimation of its adversary, the Iraqi General Staff's performance actually looks pretty good. Specifically, given the limitations of the forces at their disposal, their strategic choices must be considered quite creditable. For instance, a major criticism often leveled at Iraq's plan is that the Iraqis should have realized that a set-piece defense-in-depth would not work against the powerful armored forces of the Coalition. Many critics have argued that Iraq should have employed a mobile defense instead. But the Iraqi army could not have effectively prosecuted any other kind of defensive scheme — particularly not a mobile defense. The dearth of tactical aggressiveness and independence of action among junior officers; the inability of their tactical units to maneuver, to react to unforeseen events, and to conduct ad hoc operations efficiently; the inability of Iraqi tactical commanders to cope with unstructured engagements; and the constant disintegration of combined-arms cooperation all meant that Iraqi forces simply could not have fought with any degree of skill in a mobile defense.

Instead, the Iraqis relied on a strategy based on what their troops were capable of doing. Their engineers could build first-rate fortifications. The infantry could defend tenaciously when well dug in and when not expected to maneuver. Iraq's armor could mass devastating firepower and smash into enemy formations when they knew where the enemy was located — and if he was located right in front of them. This approach was not just Iraq's best strategy, *it was their only possible strategy*. Asking their tactical forces to do anything more than this would have been a very poor strategic decision. This assertion is borne out by the actual history of the war, for the Iraqi forces did reasonably well when they stuck to these missions but became helpless when they had to fight in fluid, maneuver battles.

If the Coalition had played into Iraq's hands, the Iraqis almost certainly would have done better. There is no question that the Coalition still would have won handily because its advantages over Iraqi forces in numbers, equipment, and tactical skill were overwhelming. However, if the Iraqis had been able to implement their strategy and thus fight in the manner that suited their strengths, they almost certainly would have been able to inflict significantly more casualties than was actually the case. The Coalition prevailed at so little cost largely because it would not let the Iraqis fight setpiece operations, instead making them fight maneuver battles, which the Iraqis were simply incapable of doing.

Most of Iraq's strategic decisions during the war were also quite sound. When the Iraqis realized that the air war was starting to cause too much damage, they tried to get the ground war started the only way they could: they launched a ground offensive. When this failed and revealed that more such operations would severely degrade Iraq's armored forces, they called off their attack and dug in deeper. Some analysts have criticized the Iraqi high command for not changing its strategy after R'as al-Khafji when the devastation wrought by Coalition air power demonstrated that Iraqi heavy divisions would not be able to move and concentrate to counterattack as envisioned in their defensive scheme. It is hard to see how the Iraqis could have changed their strategy at this point. Other than withdrawing from Kuwait, a political decision that was not the military's to make (and which Saddam appears to have been trying to do two weeks later), there was nothing the general staff could do. They could hardly reconfigure their defenses in the midst of constant Coalition air attacks and, as noted above, they already were using the one strategy their forces were actually capable of executing. After R'as al-Khafji, the only thing the Iraqis might have done was deploy more tactical air defenses with their heavy divisions to try to minimize the damage Coalition airstrikes could do to them.

Failing to deploy air defenses to protect the roads in the KTO was a significant mistake, as mentioned earlier, but this is counterbalanced by other Iraqi strategic decisions, such as the way the general staff handled the discovery of the VII Corps flanking attack in the west. The U.S. Army history records that as soon as the Iraqi high command became aware of the threat in the western KTO, "GHQ [the general staff] directed General [Iyad Futah] ar-Rawi, commander of the Republican Guard, to establish blocking positions to the southwest, facing the open desert. In a matter of hours and with great speed and efficiency, al-Rawi had six heavy brigades from at least four divisions moving west."[152] The general staff recognized that the U.S. VII Corps was the greatest threat and moved to place its strongest forces — the RGFC — against it.

A critical feature of this move was the decision to use the best Iraqi units to conduct the rear guard while the mass of less-capable units escaped from the KTO. Under different circumstances, Baghdad almost certainly would have preferred to use mediocre units to screen the retreat and allow the better units to escape. In this case, however, the general staff recognized that this was impossible. The U.S. and Western forces of the Coalition had demonstrated an ability to destroy Iraqi units extremely quickly and efficiently, and the high command recognized that only their best units — the Republican Guard and the better heavy divisions of the regular army — had the skill, strength, and mobility to successfully delay the Coalition forces and have a chance of disengaging and withdrawing when their mission was completed. Baghdad apparently calculated that if it used any but its best troops to screen the withdrawal, Coalition forces would simply roll over the rear guard and catch the retreating units from behind. Therefore, if *any* Iraqi units were to escape from the KTO, Baghdad would have to risk the destruction of its best units by committing them to the rear guard.

Despite the enormity of Iraq's military defeat, the manner in which Baghdad's military leadership was able to conduct the retreat from the KTO enabled them to snatch a small victory from the jaws of total defeat. Despite all of their mistaken assumptions about the war, at the crucial moment, the Iraqi General Staff quickly put together an effective operation to save as much of their military as was possible. The determined stand by several Iraqi units — mostly RGFC divisions — on 26 and 27 February allowed a larger number of other — albeit, mostly inferior — Iraqi units to escape destruction. The sacrifice of the Tawakalnah, Adnan, and Nebuchadnezzar Divisions, the 2d Armored Brigade of the Madinah Division, and a handful of other units allowed the survival of the forces Baghdad relied on to suppress the Shi'ah and the Kurds when they revolted against Saddam's rule after the war. Moreover, the escape of other Republican Guard units left Saddam with a core of competent, relatively powerful, formations to spearhead the campaigns against the internal insurrection. To some extent, then, Baghdad's victory over the Iraqi *Intifadah* of 1991 can be said to have been won on the battlefields of the Wadi al-Batin and Madinah Ridge.

The performance of Iraq's junior officers — and the skill of their American and British adversaries — was the most important cause of Baghdad's defeat, not Iraqi generalship. As military analyst Murray Hammick observed, "[Iraqi] tactical incompetence would almost certainly have put paid to the best laid strategic plans."[153] A close second was the severe imbalance in the weapons wielded by each side and the inability of the Iraqis to take full advantage of many of the more sophisticated weapons they possessed. For instance, many U.S. fighter pilots reported that their fear of Iraq's advanced MiG-29 fighters abated considerably when they realized that most of Iraq's MiG-29 pilots barely knew how to fly the plane, let alone employ its avionics. Nevertheless, as veterans of the Gulf War unanimously aver, Iraqi tactical incompetence was ultimately more important than the technological balance between the two sides.[154] This is perhaps best illustrated by comparing the success of the U.S. Marine Corps advance with that of the U.S. Army's VII Corps. Although the U.S. Army units had considerably more advanced weapons (for example, M1A1 tanks against M60A1 tanks and Bradley Infantry Fighting Vehicles against M-113 APCS or AAV7 amphibious vehicles), the Marines fought and defeated Iraqi units just as easily as their army compatriots. Indeed, in many ways the Marines had the tougher task—punching into heavily fortified southeastern Kuwait as opposed to working around the end of the Iraqi line and catching the Republican Guard in the flank—but they seem to have had a comparatively easier fight. The crucial difference here was that the army faced the more capable units of the RGFC, who were more dedicated and (somewhat) more tactically competent than the Iraqi army units facing the Marines. Thus, the better-equipped VII Corps had a much tougher fight against the Tawakalnah than the 1st Marine Division had against the Iraqi 3d Armored Division (which was equipped almost identically to the Tawakalnah) because the RGFC officers were slightly more willing to maneuver in battle, slightly more aggressive, and had a slightly better understanding of armor tactics than their Iraqi army counterparts.[155]

Iraqi Military Effectiveness, 1948–91

Iraqi military effectiveness between 1948 and 1991 closely parallels the Egyptian experience. Both countries enjoyed mixed success at the strategic level but were constantly plagued by extremely poor tactical capabilities. In most cases Iraqi generals were prevented from obtaining all that they might have with the resources at their disposal because of the limitations of Iraqi field units. In addition, Iraqi and Egyptian forces shared almost identical patterns of strength and weakness among their tactical units, demonstrating a reasonably good ability to perform set-piece offensives and static defensive operations but almost entirely incapable of fighting fluid, maneuver battles.

With regard to Iraqi generalship, no clear pattern emerges. In some cases Iraqi strategic leadership was quite good, such as in the latter half of the Iran-Iraq War. Likewise, during the latter half of the First Kurdish War, the entire Second Kurdish War, and the Gulf War, Iraqi generals performed adequately, if not well. Of greatest importance, in each of these conflicts Iraq's generals came up with what was probably the best strategy available to them. At other times, its leadership was miserable. In the October War, the War of Israeli Independence, and the beginning of the Iran-Iraq War, Iraqi generalship compounded the tactical failings of the forces under their command.

By contrast, Iraqi tactical performance remained constant. Regardless of the opponent or the situation, Baghdad's junior officers performed very poorly. Iraqi commanders from platoon to brigade (and often division) level repeatedly showed little aggressive initiative, little willingness to innovate or improvise, little ability to adapt to unforeseen circumstances, and little ability to act independently. Iraqi forces were virtually oblivious to tactical maneuver and reacted poorly to enemy maneuvers, often failing to do anything at all in response. Intelligence gathering and information flows throughout the chain of command were perverse, and most Iraqi units fought their battles in a haze of misinformation. Iraqi forces used their tanks like moveable artillery; their artillery was incapable of anything but preplanned, preregistered bombardment missions; and combined arms usually could only be engineered by the direct intervention of the general staff. The Iraqi Air Force generally was even worse than the ground forces, with the one exception being the small number of Mirage F-1 pilots who, during the latter half of the Iran-Iraq War, developed a modest air-to-air capability and some real air-to-ground ability. This exception was noteworthy because there were so few Mirage F-1 pilots (the vast majority having been rejected by the French) and, even with advanced equipment and Western training, this cream of the Iraqi crop achieved only a marginal improvement in effectiveness over their compatriots.

Iraqi forces consistently had problems because of a dearth of technical skills and a limited exposure to machinery. As a result, Iraqi troops were never able to realize the full capabilities of the sophisticated equipment they fielded. Maintenance and repair was almost nonexistent; Iraqi forces took extremely long periods of time to learn to handle new weaponry (even simple Soviet weapons); and, with the exception of a few high-priority projects that received lavish resources and Iraq's best scientific minds, the Iraqi arms industry was a sham.

Nevertheless, like the Egyptians, there were also areas of real Iraqi strength and other important areas where the results were consistently mixed. Two strong categories for the Iraqis were logistics and combat engineering. Some of Iraq's logistical accomplishments were impressive by any standards, such as their ability to sustain an armored corps on the Golan Heights in 1973 and their ability to move corps-sized formations the length and breadth of the country in a matter of days by the end of the Iran-Iraq War. Similarly, its soldiers fought bravely in every one of Baghdad's wars.

This is not to say that there were not instances of cowardly behavior, even of entire units surrendering. But on balance, Iraqi personnel fought hard even in difficult situations. For example, what is noteworthy about the Gulf War is not that 150,000–250,000 men deserted during the forty-two-day Coalition air campaign or that another 80,000 surrendered largely without a fight during the Coalition ground campaign, but rather that another 250,000–275,000 did not flee, and some of them fought hard. After six weeks of constant pounding, with their logistical network destroyed, and facing a vastly superior enemy, the Iraqi soldiers (mostly Republican Guards) who fought and died at the battles of the Burqan oilfields, Wadi al-Batin, and Madinah Ridge deserve considerable credit. Similarly, while Iraqi unit cohesion varied throughout the postwar period, on balance it was probably better than worse. Even in their worst defeats at the hands of the Kurds in the 1960s, the Israelis in 1973, the Iranians in 1982, and the American-led coalition in 1991, many Iraqi units hung together in extremely difficult circumstances. Iraqi military performance throughout this period was hardly a model to be emulated, but it was not without its bright spots.

3

JORDAN

After taking over the region called Transjordan after World War I, Great Britain found it necessary to create a local military force to defend the territory against both internal and external threats. In October 1920 the British created a unit of 150 men, called the Mobile Force, under Capt. Frederick G. Peake. Transjordan was in a state of relative anarchy at that time, having experienced many centuries of benign neglect under the Turks. Thus, when Amir 'Abdallah ibn Husayn, descendant of the Prophet and the son of the Hashimite Shaykh of Mecca, arrived in 1921 with the intent of making himself king (with British approval), he was not universally welcomed despite his lofty pedigree. Almost immediately, 'Abdallah was forced to suppress a series of tribal challenges to his rule. His security problems forced him to turn to the British for help in late 1921, and London agreed to expand the Mobile Force under Peake to meet 'Abdallah's military needs. Between 1921 and 1923, the British built up the Mobile Force — renamed the Arab Legion — to a reinforced battalion in strength and used it to crush a series of tribal revolts throughout the country. Nevertheless, beginning in 1922, Arabian Ikhwan warriors under 'Abd al-Aziz Ibn Sa'ud began raiding Transjordan, eager to expand the areas they had conquered for their Wahhabi interpretation of Islam. Royal Air Force (RAF) aircraft and armored cars were dispatched to Transjordan and, together with the new Arab Legion, succeeded in stopping the tide of Saudi expansion.

By 1926, Peake's Arab Legion had accomplished a great deal. The force had grown to about 1,500 men and officers. A small number of the officers were British, but the rest, and all the enlisted, had been recruited from the settled villages of Transjordan. (The Transjordanian towns supported 'Abdallah's centralized rule and the security from Bedouin raiding it promised.) The legion had decisively defeated several of the more aggressive

Arabian tribes, which had prompted Ibn Sa'ud to rein in his forces from further attacks on Transjordan. Finally, by crushing the various tribal revolts, the legion had forcefully asserted the strength of the monarchy and demonstrated its ability to rule the Bedouin tribes.

Between 1926 and the outbreak of the Second World War, the British decided to exert greater control over the Arab Legion and to rationalize their own force structure in the Middle East to reduce the costs of empire. The legion was reduced in strength, placed under the command of the British high commissioner in Jerusalem, and relegated to internal-security duties. The RAF presence in Transjordan was also greatly reduced. Finally, a new force, called the Transjordan Frontier Force (TJFF) was created to take over the external-security responsibilities previously handled by the legion and the RAF. The TJFF was created in the image of the British Indian Army, with all billets above the rank of major held by British officers. But the TJFF proved less successful in policing the borders against raids by Saudi and Iraqi tribes than had the Arab Legion. In response, Capt. John Bagot Glubb was made Peake's second in command in 1930 and ordered to raise a "Desert Mobile Force" to deal with the raiding tribes. Glubb enjoyed great success recruiting Bedouin tribesmen to serve in the new force, which he employed more in the manner of a nomadic warrior band (albeit one with trucks and armored cars) than a conventional Western military force. Glubb's outfit succeeded in once again pacifying Transjordan's borders.

World War II saw the Arab Legion grow into a professional military. The small size of the British army at the start of the war forced London to scrounge ground forces wherever it could to meet the wide-ranging Axis challenges. The Arab Legion became one of the beneficiaries of Britain's desperation. Both the Desert Mobile Force and the TJFF were amalgamated into the legion, which by the end of the war had grown to a force of nearly 8,000 men and officers. The heart of the army was a 3,000-strong mechanized brigade (built from the core of Glubb's Desert Mobile Force) and the Desert Patrol Force of 500 men.[1] The legion was then commanded by Glubb and officered largely by British regulars, seconded from the British army. In addition, the legion had gained some combat experience during the war. Elements of the legion, including the Desert Mobile Force, participated in the British campaigns to overturn the anti-British Rashid 'Ali government in Iraq as well as the conquest of Syria from Vichy France. Other units of the legion were posted to garrisons throughout the Middle East to free up British regulars and other Commonwealth troops for combat duties, and the Arab Legion briefly trained for duty in Egypt, where they were to have been deployed had the Germans not been turned back at El Alamein.

The War of Israeli Independence, 1948

In 1948, when the Arab Legion marched into Palestine, it was the most professional indigenous military in the Middle East. Jordan's army was trained and led entirely by British officers or Jordanian officers trained in the British manner. In fact, all but five of the officers of the rank of major or higher were British, including Glubb, who remained its commander.[2] The British saw to it that the legion was well prepared for conventional military operations. During the first twenty-four years of its existence, the Jordanian army was responsible for both internal and external-security duties, but regardless of other priorities, Jordanian soldiers and officers constantly practiced for combat operations against organized militaries. Moreover, during the Second World War, internal-security duties and even combat against Arabian tribes had taken a backseat to the need to prepare the legion for combat with the Iraqi army, the Vichy French, and the Germans.

Ultimately, the British built the Jordanian army in their own image – or at least in the cherished image of Britain's vanished colonial forces. Just as Britain traditionally relied on a small, long-term-service professional army, so too did Jordan. Just as Britain traditionally relied on a purely volunteer force, so too did Jordan. Just as the British emphasized the quality of their manpower rather than its quantity, so too did Jordan. Just as the British stressed the skills of the individual soldier honed in constant practice over many years, so too did Jordan. In Nadav Safran's words, "excellently drilled and ably commanded by British officers it was then [1948] a model of the level of effectiveness that could be achieved with Arab soldiers through careful training and organization."[3]

The Jordanian Armed Forces on the Eve of War

As a result of this British tutelage, the Arab Legion in 1948 was a highly motivated elite body of long-term-service professionals. Glubb purposely insisted that the legion remain all volunteer so that it could retain its carefully nurtured esprit de corps. In 1948, Jordan was one of the most backward regions of the Arab world, and the pay of an enlisted man was almost a princely sum. In addition, the military was considered a prestigious career among the Bedouin. The combination of the legion's prestige, economic benefits, and esprit contributed to a very high retention rate, with many personnel serving for decades and many sons of legionaries following their fathers into the king's service. Moreover, by keeping the force small, the legion had its pick of new recruits and was able to man its ranks largely from Transjordan's minority Bedouin population, whom the British believed made better and more loyal soldiers. Last, the small size of the army allowed Jordan to continue to provide high-quality training for its troops.

Nevertheless, the Arab Legion did have its problems, mostly related to the economic backwardness of the country. Because Glubb favored the Bedouin over the Hadari townsmen, the tribesmen made up at least 50 percent of legion strength (although they represented no more than 30 percent of the larger Jordanian population). Unfortunately, the Bedouin rarely had an education, so literacy was almost nonexistent among legion recruits. Even fewer had any technical background. Most had never owned anything more complicated than an ancient bolt-action rifle. Of course, the Hadari had had greater exposure to machinery than the Bedouin, and so they were heavily represented in the mechanical-support branches, but this advantage was entirely relative, and few had any true technical training. Moreover, the legion suffered from friction between the Bedouin and the Hadari, and the British were forced to mostly segregate the two groups into separate units to prevent them from feuding.[4]

At the outbreak of war in May 1948, the Arab Legion had 8,000 men, fifty British armored cars, and about twenty artillery pieces. As paltry as this arsenal may seem, it greatly exceeded that of the Israeli Haganah units they faced. For example, in the initial battles around Jerusalem, to which the legion committed nearly half its strength, the heaviest weapons the Israelis possessed were two medium machine guns and two Piat shoulder-fired antitank weapons.[5] For the war, Glubb formed the legion into a single divisional command with two brigades, each of which had two battalions of infantry, as well as a number of independent infantry companies. An armored-car company was attached to each infantry battalion. The artillery was organized as a separate battalion with three batteries. Finally, a third brigade was organized as a "dummy" formation to fool the Israelis into believing that another brigade was in reserve to deter them from launching a counteroffensive against Transjordan itself. The most significant material problem the legion faced was a shortage of ammunition. Before the outbreak of fighting, Glubb estimated that he had only enough rounds for one short battle if it involved the entire division.[6] Against this force, the Israeli Haganah could field 50,000 poorly armed and mostly untrained troops. No more than half of this force was organized into the nine Palmach and Haganah field brigades ready for deployment anywhere in Palestine. The rest were regional militia that could only be used to defend their town or settlement.[7] At the start of the war, the Israelis had no real armor, artillery, aircraft, or even heavy crew-served weapons to speak of. Moreover, the Jews had to spread these forces to fend off five other Arab armies in addition to the legion.

Jordanian Goals and Strategy

There is considerable uncertainty regarding King 'Abdallah's intentions when he ordered the invasion of Palestine in May 1948. It is clear that he did *not* hope to eradicate the Jewish state altogether, unlike his Palestinian, Syrian, Egyptian, and Iraqi allies. At least initially, in 1947, it appears that 'Abdallah hoped only to occupy the parts of Palestine reserved by the UN commission to the native Palestinians and annex them to his own state. At that time, the monarch opened secret negotiations with the Israelis intended to reach an accommodation that would allow him to divide the territory with the Jews without bloodshed. As time went by, however, his ambitions appear to have grown. He apparently began to desire that the new Jewish state be reduced to an autonomous region of Jordan. Barring that, 'Abdallah hoped to increase the amount of territory under Jordanian control and, in particular, he seems to have wanted to control Jerusalem rather than leaving it an international city as specified by the UN partition plan. It might be most accurate to say that 'Abdallah intended to conquer the West Bank territories and then take whatever else he could if the opportunity arose.[8]

'Abdallah's intentions were complicated by the limited military forces at his disposal and by the divided loyalties of his British officers. On the one hand, the Arab Legion simply was not large enough to occupy all of Palestine; it was not even large enough to conquer the various parts assigned to the Palestinians by the UN. On the other hand, the Israelis could be expected to fight tooth and nail, and Jordan could not be sure how its ostensible Arab allies would react to blatantly self-serving moves. Beyond this, 'Abdallah was completely dependent on Glubb and the other British officers, whose loyalties were divided between Amman and London. The British government made it clear that, although they had little love for their erstwhile Jewish subjects in Palestine, they would not tolerate actions in contravention of the UN settlement. London specifically ordered all of the British officers seconded to the Arab Legion "to abandon their units if these invaded Jewish territory."[9]

In the end, Jordanian strategy attempted to straddle these competing positions. Glubb intended to push into the West Bank immediately and occupy it up to the international borders declared by the UN. The legion

would then shift to the defensive as quickly as possible to avoid unnecessarily provoking the Jews and to secure the Palestinian territories as soon as
they had been taken. One final consideration in Glubb's approach was the
need to minimize his own casualties. A problem with having a small, long-
term-service professional army was that casualties were not easily replaced.
Consequently, Glubb wanted to avoid bloody battles at all costs, particularly in the streets of Jerusalem, where the training of his troops would be
discounted and many might be killed in house-to-house fighting.

Course of Operations

The first Jordanian combat operations actually occurred before the outbreak of war on 14 May 1948. Israelis from the four Etzioni settlements
outside Jerusalem began harassing Arab military movements during April
1948. The British considered these actions intolerable and had sent British
regulars with tanks and backed by a reinforced company of the Arab Legion
plus Arab irregulars to attack these settlements in early May. Remarkably,
the Jews held their positions against the assault, but the British still decided
that they had taught the Jews enough of a lesson and withdrew their own
forces. The Arab Legion company and the Palestinian irregulars remained,
however, hoping to receive orders from Amman to resume the attack.

A week passed, and on 11 May the company commander, Col. Abdallah
at-Tel, took matters into his own hands and ordered an attack on the settlements. The Jews had about 500 able-bodied settlers (men and women) in
the four settlements but had only small arms. While the Arab force was
somewhat smaller, it was centered on the legion company and was backed
by a squadron of armored cars as well as considerable artillery and mortar
support. In three days of fighting, the Arabs succeeded in isolating the four
settlements, and then the legion company assaulted the main settlement of
Kfar Etzion with heavy-fire support. The Arabs used part of their force to
pin the Israeli defenders along their main line of defenses, and then sent
another portion with the armored cars to outflank the primary Jewish positions. On 13 May the legion was able to take Kfar Etzion, prompting the
other three settlements to surrender.

The main body of the Arab Legion crossed over the Jordan River into
Palestine on the morning of 14 May 1948. There they linked up with the
Jordanian troops already operating south of Jerusalem and quickly oc-
cupied the superb defensive terrain of the Samarian hills. Glubb deployed
one of his brigades to cover the entire area from Janin to just north of
Ramallah, which allowed him to concentrate his other brigade, plus a num-

ber of independent infantry companies, in and around Jerusalem and establish brigade headquarters at Ramallah.

THE BATTLE OF JERUSALEM

On 17 May King 'Abdallah ordered Glubb to attack Jewish Jerusalem in strength. This was a clear contravention of both the UN plan and the orders of the British government. Nonetheless, Glubb reluctantly complied, rationalizing it simply as intervention to end the confused fighting that had been raging in the city for the last three days. He detached one of the battalions sent initially to Samaria, the 3d Infantry, from its parent brigade and ordered it back south to Jerusalem to take part in the attack on the city. The Jordanians then launched a coordinated attack from both north and south of town with a supporting thrust against the Jewish Quarter of the Old City. From the north, Glubb sent the 3d Infantry — supported by armored cars, artillery, and mortar batteries — into the Shaykh Jarrah area of northeastern Jerusalem. In the center, several companies of the legion bolstered by Palestinian irregulars were ordered to assault the isolated Jewish Quarter and either overrun it or besiege it. Meanwhile, the Jordanian units that had come up from the Etzioni Bloc (since reinforced to about a battalion in strength), tried to envelop Jerusalem from the south by attacking the settlement of Ramat Rachel on the road to Bethlehem.

The legion's northern thrust met initial success but then was brought to a halt by fierce Jewish resistance. The Israelis had only seventy members of the Irgun Zvi Leumi, the freelance militia–terrorist group headed by Menachem Begin, in Shaykh Jarrah. This small force was easily overpowered by the legionaries, thereby cutting off the Jewish garrison on Mount Scopus. The Jordanians then attempted to drive westward, from what would later be known as the Mandlebaum Gate, to surround the Old City and cut it off from Jewish territory. Although the Arab Legion had a huge advantage in firepower — the defenders had only a pair of light machine guns and two antitank weapons — they could not break through the Israeli positions. After their initial rebuffs in this sector, the Jordanians shifted their effort closer to the Old City. The legionaries employed excellent combined-arms tactics, moving in teams of infantry and armor supported by mortar fire and, occasionally, artillery when practical. Nevertheless, they found the going very tough against the underarmed, but resourceful, Israelis. Eventually, the course of the fighting centered on the Israeli-held monastery of Notre Dame de France at the northwest corner of the Old City. Although it was defended by no more than a handful of Israelis with only one Piat antitank weapon and a handful of rounds, the Jordanians could not take the position. They lost several armored cars to Israeli Piat rounds and Molotov cocktails, and their battalion suffered nearly 50 percent casualties.[10] Late on 24 May, Glubb called off the attack, fearing additional losses. The legion effort north of the Old City then slacked off considerably until the first UN-brokered ceasefire halted fighting altogether on 10 June.

The southern thrust of the initial Jordanian offensive, against Ramat Rachel, was conducted in conjunction with Egyptian units and was even less successful than the northern assault. Elements of the Egyptian invasion force had marched across the Negev Desert to Beersheba and then on to Jerusalem, where they linked up with the units of the Arab Legion south of the city. On 21 May the two Arab armies launched a combined assault against the small Israeli force defending the village on the hills south of Jerusalem, driving out the defenders by sheer weight of numbers. However, later that day, a company of the Haganah's Etzioni Brigade reinforced the Israelis, who counterattacked and retook the village. Over the next three days, the Arabs attacked the settlement over and over again, recapturing it several times only to lose it to Israeli counterattacks each night. On 24 May reinforcements dispatched by Glubb arrived at Ramat Rachel to restart the flagging offensive. In the ensuing battle, the legionaries and Egyptians once again managed to storm the kibbutz, but the Israelis also brought up reinforcements and retook it early the next day. In that counterattack the Israelis also succeeded in taking a nearby monastery that dominated the surrounding terrain and that had served as a jumping-off point for the Arab attacks on Ramat Rachel. With the loss of this key base of operations, the Egyptians and Jordanians called off their attack and dug in, ending their joint effort to envelop Jerusalem from the south.

Only in the center, against the Old City, was the Arab Legion able to secure its objectives. The Jewish Quarter had the disadvantage of being surrounded by Arab-controlled territory and cut off from the Jewish section of the new city. However, it had the advantage of being an ancient Middle Eastern *madinah*, overbuilt with adjoining houses and cut by narrow winding streets that were easy to block or defend. While the British were in Palestine, the Israelis had smuggled a small amount of supplies and some Haganah and Irgun soldiers into the Old City so that it could withstand the inevitable assaults and likely siege they expected would follow the British withdrawal. The Arab Legion attacked the Old City on all sides on 16 May, slowly overpowering the small number of defenders and forcing them to give ground. The Israelis attempted a relief operation during the night of 17–18 May. This effort was badly bungled and turned into a frontal

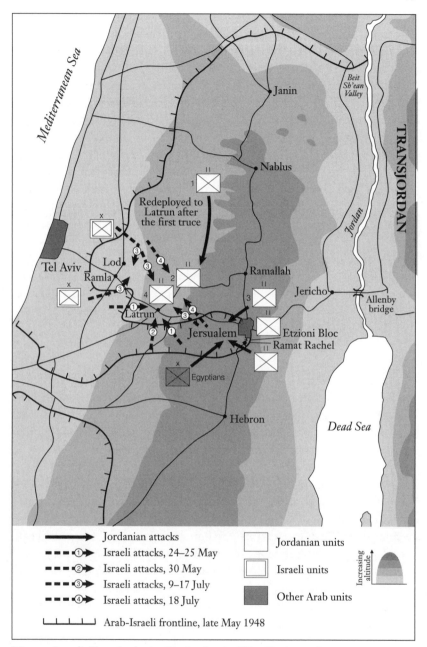

Map 22. Israeli-Transjordanian Battles for the West Bank, 1948

assault on Arab Legion positions. The Jordanians proved to be excellent marksmen and inflicted heavy casualties on the Israelis. Nevertheless, the main attack so diverted the legionaries that another force was able to surprise and overpower the Arab irregulars guarding Mount Zion and then breach the Zion Gate into the Jewish Quarter. Although the legion was surprised by the operation, they quickly regrouped and counterattacked the Israeli forces holding open the Zion Gate. In a brief, fierce fight during the day, the Jordanians defeated the Israelis and again shut off the Old City from the Jewish-held sector. For the next ten days, the Israelis tried to open a corridor to the besieged Jewish Quarter, but all of their attacks failed. The legion devised a very effective tactic of allowing the Israeli soldiers and sappers to penetrate through the Zion Gate and then trap them in a kill sack in the small courtyard on the Arab side of the gate. Meanwhile, inside the Old City, the legion conducted a highly effective clearing operation. The Jordanians did an excellent job, using armored cars in conjunction with small infantry teams and support from mortars and direct-fire weapons on the city walls. They pushed deeper and deeper into the Jewish Quarter, defeated several more Israeli relief efforts, and finally compelled the defenders of that sector to surrender on 28 May.

THE FIRST BATTLE OF LATRUN

In conjunction with his efforts to conquer Jerusalem outright, Glubb also moved to impose a siege on the city by cutting the narrow corridor that ran from the Jewish cities along the coast to Jerusalem. The winding roads that crawled over the hills to Jerusalem had been the center of constant fighting long before the end of the British mandate, but in late May the Arab Legion made a determined effort to fully cut these links. Glubb ordered his 2d Infantry Battalion, then deployed north and west of Jerusalem, to move south and take up positions around Radar Hill, from which it could interdict Israeli traffic on the Tel Aviv-Jerusalem road.[11] Farther west, the commander of the legion's 4th Infantry Battalion, Lt. Col. Habas al-Majali, seized an opportunity to block the Tel Aviv–Jerusalem road at the critical Latrun police fort. The Israelis had initially driven out a small force of Arab irregulars from this position but then had to draw down its own garrison to send reinforcements to deal with the combined Egyptian-Jordanian assault on Ramat Rachel. On his own authority, al-Majali moved forward and retook the post on 20 May, blocking the road to Jerusalem where it could not easily be bypassed.

The legion's occupation of Latrun placed Israel's hold on Jerusalem in real jeopardy, and Tel Aviv resolved to launch an immediate counterattack to retake the position. The offensive was to be conducted by the newly created 7th Brigade. The 7th comprised three battalions. The 79th Battalion was Israel's first mechanized infantry unit, formed with the first shipment of M-3 halftracks and filled out with soldiers and officers hastily transferred from other Israeli brigades. The other two battalions, the 71st and 72d, were "leg" infantry comprised entirely of European immigrants, refugees from the Holocaust literally right off the boat. The men in these units spoke at least eight different languages, almost none of which were understood by their Israeli-born officers. So bad was the resulting confusion that these units were called the "Tower of Babel" battalions by the rest of the Haganah. Moreover, the Israeli top leadership was so anxious to take Latrun that the entire brigade was given less than a week of training before being sent off to battle. Nevertheless, the Israeli plan was for the veteran 32d Battalion of the Alexandroni Brigade to attack the western face of the Latrun salient while the 7th Brigade made a supporting attack against the eastern face of the position.

The Latrun police fort, built on a rock promontory that juts out to the southwest from the Samarian hills behind it, was a formidable position. Al-Majali had deployed his battalion in the fort itself and dug in along the promontory with his main strength facing west, where the incline was slightly gentler. Thus, he was well prepared for the main attack against this flank. The Israeli assault itself was awful. It began at midnight of 24–25 May with a short bombardment from a handful of old 65-mm field guns but immediately ran into problems. Some units were four to six hours late moving into position, delaying the ground assault commensurately. Consequently, the initial bombardment merely alerted the Jordanians, and the sun was rising in the midst of the Alexandronis' advance. The immigrant battalions blundered around in the darkness and then managed to get themselves pinned down by Jordanian fire once the sun rose. The feeble efforts of the 7th Brigade allowed al-Majali to concentrate his efforts on the Alexandronis attacking his right flank. The legionaries were protected by the walls of the police fort and were well fortified on the flanks of the hill. Their fire was very heavy and very accurate against the exposed and clumsy Israelis, and the battle turned into a slaughter. The Jordanians broke the attack by noon, inflicting as many as 2,000 killed on the Israelis.[12]

On 30 May the Israelis attempted another equally ill-conceived attack against Latrun. They attacked with only two battalions: the armored infantry battalion of the 7th Brigade and a battalion of the Givati Brigade, which had replaced the badly mauled Alexandroni battalion. This time the Israelis attacked from the south, and although the Givati troops were able to take the village of Dayr Ayub at the foot of the Latrun position, they were subsequently disrupted by Jordanian fire, and their attack repulsed. Once again, the rapid defeat of the Israeli supporting attack allowed al-Majali to concentrate his forces against the main effort, in this case the armored infantry of the 79th Battalion. The Israelis bravely attacked into the teeth of the Jordanian defenses, but the legionaries again held their ground and put up a murderous fire. In particular, al-Majali found that by reinforcing his troops along the parapets of the police fortress, his well-trained marksmen could pour fire down into the Israeli halftracks and armored cars, which had no protection from above. Again the Jordanians beat back the Israelis with heavy losses.

The two defeats at Latrun were so decisive that the Israelis decided to build a bypass around Latrun to allow vehicular movement between Tel Aviv and Jerusalem without having to use the main road in that area. However, the Israeli leadership had become fixated on Latrun and so decided to try once more to take the position. During the night of 8–9 June, veteran battalions of the Harel and Yiftach Brigades were to assault the Latrun position on both sides of the promontory but farther to the northeast, along the "neck" of the promontory rather than at its tip. The Israelis were unaware that Glubb had reinforced the Latrun position with the 2d Infantry Battalion and additional artillery. While the 4th Battalion continued to hold the fort and its flanks, the 2d dug in along both sides of the neck of the position. Thus, what the Israelis thought would be a double envelopment to get behind the 4th Battalion's positions, turn both its flanks, and cut it off from Samaria turned into a pair of frontal assaults against the 2d Battalion's positions. As in the past, the Jordanian soldiers concentrated a heavy volume of fire on both Israeli columns. The Israeli units fought with tremendous determination in the face of Jordanian fire, and they were able to break into the legion's lines on both sides. However, by that point they had suffered such heavy casualties from Jordanian marksmanship that they were thrown back by aggressive, well-timed Jordanian counterattacks. The Israelis tried again the next night, but one of the battalions got lost in the darkness, while the other took heavy casualties from Jordanian fire during the advance and was forced to retreat before coming to grips with the legionaries.

THE ISRAELI TEN DAYS OFFENSIVES AND THE SECOND BATTLE OF LATRUN

On 11 June the first ceasefire put an end to combat around Latrun. During this truce, both the Israelis and the Jordanians (and the other Arab armies) reorganized themselves for battle. The Israelis raised and trained new for-mations, while most of the Arab armies reinforced their contingents in Palestine. The Arab Legion, however, suffered a devastating loss when London demanded the return of all British officers seconded to the legion because of 'Abdallah's clear violation of the UN partition plan by attacking into Jewish Jerusalem and the Jerusalem corridor. Although those British officers under contract to the Arab Legion remained, including Glubb, London's edict suddenly deprived him of both brigade commanders, three of his four battalion commanders, and many of his other officers. Re-placements — most of whom were also British — were quickly promoted and assigned the vacant commands, but it took some time to work out new command-and-control arrangements.

Nevertheless, the truce gave the legion a breathing space to regroup, reorganize, and improve its defenses. The various independent infantry companies were integrated into two new battalions, the 5th and 6th. The Jordanians continued to fortify their positions around Latrun. They also used the ceasefire to repair and perform overdue maintenance on their vehicles, especially their armored cars. Of particular importance, King 'Abdallah was able to secure large stocks of arms and ammunition to re-plenish Glubb's magazines. As far as strategy was concerned, Glubb con-cluded that his troops were spread very thin and so decided to confine future legion operations to small-scale offensives intended mainly to im-prove his defensive position. The prospects for a successful defense also improved during this period with the arrival of a large Iraqi expeditionary force in northern Samaria, enabling Glubb to withdraw the remaining legion battalion from the Nablus area and send it south to Latrun, upon which he suspected the Israelis would continue to fixate. Consequently, by the end of the first truce, the Jordanians had three battalions supported by a considerable number of artillery pieces, armored cars, and mortars well fortified in and around Latrun.[13]

When the ceasefire expired on 9 July, the Israelis launched a major offensive against the Jordanian forces defending both Jerusalem and the corridor. In the city itself, the Israelis mounted drives southward to secure their right flank, into the Old City, and northeastward to try to retake the Shaykh Jarrah area and reestablish contact with the garrison on Mount Scopus. The southern Israeli effort was the most successful, driving a small force of Arab irregulars and legionaries off of Mount Herzl, which strengthened the position of their right flank. In the center the Israeli attack against the Old City was clumsy, and accurate fire from Legionaries along the city walls stopped it quickly, inflicting heavy losses. Against Shaykh

Jarrah, not only did the legion halt the Israeli assault but also pushed it back and launched a counterattack of their own, which succeeded in taking a few minor strips of territory previously held by the Israelis.

The heaviest fighting, however, came once again in the Latrun area. The Israelis remained determined to recapture the fort and reopen the main Tel Aviv–Jerusalem road. Their plan was to conduct a division-sized operation to reduce the salient around the towns of Lod and Ramla north of Latrun, which would both reduce a major potential threat to Tel Aviv and would allow the Haganah to then mount an operation against Latrun from the north. (Lod and Ramla were only about ten kilometers from downtown Tel Aviv and today are suburbs of the city.) Glubb had consciously decided to forego the defense of Lod and Ramla to allow for greater concentration around Latrun. Those towns were too far forward and thus too exposed to Israeli flanking attacks from north or south to be defensible by anything but a very large force. Moreover, the terrain made it difficult for the Israelis to develop a successful conquest of Lod and Ramla into a drive into Samaria itself without first taking Latrun. Thus, Latrun remained the key position and that was where Glubb concentrated his forces, leaving the rest to irregulars of Fawzi al-Kaukji's Arab Liberation Army (ALA) backed only by tiny detachments from the Arab Legion.

During the night of 9–10 July just as the ceasefire expired, the Israeli offensive against Lod and Ramla began. It involved three brigades, including Israel's new 8th Armored Brigade, which included a collection of thirteen American, British, and French early-model World War II tanks. The Israeli attack was a well-orchestrated double envelopment that pushed the Arabs back to the Samarian hills. The ALA forces put up little resistance, and the only time the Israelis were delayed at all was when a small Arab Legion force briefly held up the 8th Armored at Dayr Tarif before being overwhelmed. By 12 July, the Israelis had eliminated the Arab salient and driven a salient of their own into the Jordanian lines north of Latrun. Glubb ordered his forces around the police fort to brace themselves for another Israeli attack.

The Israelis launched their assault during the night of 14–15 July. They sent a battalion from the Harel Brigade to make a diversionary attack against the legion force at Radar Hill. Meanwhile, the main body of the Harel Brigade would assault the Latrun salient from the southeast and the Yiftach Brigade would assault Latrun from the northwest. The Israelis were unaware of the extent of Jordanian reinforcements or that Glubb had again extended his lines both north and east to guard the shoulders of the salient. Thus, the Israelis again believed they were bringing overwhelming force to bear against the undefended flanks of the Jordanian positions but were actually attacking dug-in Jordanian units head on. Once again, the odds were fairly even (three dug-in Jordanian battalions supported by considerable artillery and armored cars against five Israeli battalions with only a handful of guns and armored cars); the Jordanians were entrenched in good defensive terrain; and the Israelis were conducting what amounted to frontal assaults against the Jordanian lines.

For three days there was ferocious fighting around Latrun. The Israelis were surprised to find the Jordanians waiting for them on the supposedly unoccupied ridges north and east of the post, and their first attacks were repulsed with heavy losses. In particular, the Jordanians counterattacked with armored cars and badly mauled several Israeli units that had not expected to face armor and so had few antitank weapons. In a few areas the Jordanians were surprised by Israeli units that stealthily approached their positions at night and then attacked suddenly out of the darkness. However, the legionaries recovered quickly and counterattacked with "unparalleled fury," in the words of one Israeli, Lt. Col. Netanel Lorch.[14] The battles were fierce and seesawed back and forth between the two sides. At one point, the Israelis forced the Jordanians to relinquish a key village by outflanking their positions and rolling up their line, but the Jordanians mounted a sudden counterattack with armored cars and infantry supported by mortars that drove the Israelis out of another important village. By 17 July, the legion's dogged resistance and counterattacks finally brought the two Israeli pincer thrusts to a halt — although they had come within three kilometers of linking up and cutting off Latrun altogether.

On 18 July the Israelis tried one last attack, this time launching a frontal assault against the main Latrun position itself in the hope that the previous fighting had so weakened the garrison that it would fall if given one last push. The Israelis pulled together a company from the exhausted Yiftach Brigade with mechanized infantry and a small number of tanks from the 8th Armored Brigade. The Jordanians were equally exhausted, and apparently much of their strength had been drawn away from the police fort to block the thrusts against the shoulders. Nevertheless, Jordanian artillery laid down a heavy barrage against the Israeli armor as they approached the legion positions. The Israeli tanks still made good progress at first until a communications problem caused the entire unit to mistakenly retreat. The abrupt departure of his tanks caused the Israeli commander to pull back his infantry for fear that they would be slaughtered without armored support . At that point, the second truce intervened, preventing further combat. Nevertheless, the Israelis had penetrated so deeply into the Jordanian lines that their troops could fire down onto the one remaining road in Jordanian hands that linked Latrun to Samaria. Had there not been a ceasefire, the Israelis almost certainly could have starved Latrun into submission by blocking any resupply columns with their fire.

When this second truce ended in late August, neither Tel Aviv nor Amman had any desire to keep fighting each other. Glubb recognized that the military situation had degenerated into a stalemate with neither side able to make much of an impression on the other's lines. Any additional territory he might capture could only come at an exorbitant cost in casualties. In addition, the heavy fighting at Latrun had depleted the legion's stock of artillery and mortar shells, antitank rounds, and hand grenades. For his part, King 'Abdallah, while no doubt disappointed in not having secured Jerusalem, had other pressing concerns. In particular, the monarch wanted to make sure that he secured control of all the West Bank territories. The Iraqis still occupied northern Samaria, and the Egyptians were still in much of Judaea. He wanted to focus his efforts on gaining control over these areas rather than continuing pointless attrition battles with the Israelis. As a result of this convergence of interests, fighting gradually halted along the Israeli–Arab Legion lines. Local commanders on both sides continued to encourage sniping and raids against their opponents, but neither military command undertook any large operations. By November, 'Abdallah had distanced himself from the Arab League and unilaterally opened up truce negotiations with the Israelis. These talks resulted in a full ceasefire on 1 December 1948.

Jordanian Military Effectiveness in the War of Israeli Independence

The conduct of the Arab Legion against the nascent Israeli army in 1948 was, without doubt, the best performance of any Arab military against any foe of the modern era. Alone among the Arab armies, the legion acted and fought like a modern, professional military. Its units demonstrated remarkable cohesiveness, sticking together and clinging to their positions even under the most severe pressure, such as in the second battle of Latrun. The soldiers themselves regularly displayed a high level of personal courage, and there are any number of stories from both the Israeli and Jordanian sides to attest to this.[15] The Jordanians demonstrated a good grasp of combined-arms operations, regularly integrating infantry, armored cars, and artillery better than the Israelis. Their marksmanship was very high, and their counterattacks were usually well timed and aggressive. Jordanian units covered their flanks well and were not paralyzed when the Israelis did succeed in turning them. The legion patrolled constantly, often precluding

Israeli surprises and even surprising the Israelis on several occasions. Jordanian junior officers showed real initiative, seizing fleeting opportunities — such as attacking the Latrun police fort when the Israelis had left it dangerously undermanned — that proved to be critical to their war effort. Jordan's tactical leaders led well-timed and effective counterattacks that frequently were the decisive factor in combat. Finally, legion officers regularly employed operational maneuver to gain an advantage in combat, although at the tactical level, many Jordanian attacks were simple frontal assaults.

Nevertheless, at least two qualifiers must be kept in mind when considering Jordanian performance during this conflict. First, while the Jordanians unquestionably fought better than any of the other Arab armies, and in many ways they fought as well as or better than the Israelis, their performance does not exactly rank as one of the great campaigns of military history. The Jordanians did not face a very capable adversary, and they had several important advantages in their favor. Myths of Israeli invincibility aside, the Haganah of 1948 was a very mediocre force. Its unit capabilities were uneven, with some brigades performing well and others giving a rather poor account of themselves. The Israelis were inadequately armed and trained and suffered from political infighting. They had all kinds of problems with personnel and languages and with the incompatibility of their hodge-podge of weaponry. Some Haganah units paid too little attention to reconnaissance and so were surprised by Jordanian actions that might easily have been discovered and averted. The Jordanians were able to defend the superb terrain of Judaea and Samaria, while the Israelis were mostly forced to attack from the coastal plain up into the central hills. Finally, the Israelis also had to fight five other Arab armies, which prevented them from concentrating decisive force against the Jordanians.

Despite all of these advantages, Jordan's forces only succeeded in fighting the Israelis to a draw. The Jordanians consistently defeated Israeli attacks against their prepared defensive positions. Most of the successful Israeli offensives in the Jerusalem area (such as at Lod, Ramla, and Mount Zion) were conducted against small Arab Legion forces, while larger Jordanian units in the Old City and Latrun held their ground against numerous determined Israeli assaults. Of course, in virtually all of these cases, the Israeli attacks were clumsy frontal assaults that played right into Jordanian hands. Although the legion defeated most Israeli attacks, they fared little better in their own offensives. The only significant gains the Jordanians were able to make against Israeli resistance were the conquests of the Etzioni bloc, the Jewish Quarter of the Old City, and the Shaykh Jarrah area. All of these successes came in the first weeks of the war, before the first truce, and were all modest achievements. In none of these battles did the Jordanians face a large, well-armed, and adequately trained force. For example, in Shaykh Jarrah, a legion infantry battalion supported by artillery and armored cars defeated seventy infantrymen from the Irgun. Even with the advantage of urban terrain on the Israeli side, this was a mismatch, and the legion's victory cannot be taken as a sign of real prowess on the part of the Jordanians. Conversely, the moment that they ran into better-trained or larger Israeli units — such as in the Mandlebaum Gate area and at Notre Dame — their attacks went nowhere.

An additional qualifier that must be attached to Jordanian performance is the contribution of the Arab Legion's British officers. There is a consensus among experts on the Jordanian military and the 1948 war that it was the British influence and presence that was the single most important element of Jordanian military effectiveness. For instance, Brig. Gen. S. A. El-Edroos, an unabashed admirer of the Jordanian military, remarked, "The credit for the excellence of the Arab Legion's performance during the war of 1948 and later, during the border wars of 1951–1956, must in all fairness be given to Glubb Pasha and the contingent of British officers who served with the Arab Legion from its formation in 1921 to the exodus of 1956."[16] Col. Trevor Dupuy has similarly noted that the principal source of Jordanian military effectiveness was "decades of British leadership and military tradition."[17]

There is a great deal of validity to this assessment. Most of the successes the Jordanians enjoyed and most of the competent military practices they demonstrated were attributable to their officer corps, which was comprised entirely of British and Jordanians with long years of British schooling and military training. The aggressive counterattacks, battlefield maneuvers, flexible operations, and acts of opportunistic initiative were all exercised by the (British-dominated) officer corps. Likewise, the high level of individual soldiering skills found in the Arab Legion, such as its excellent marksmanship, is directly attributable to the British emphasis on long-term-service professionals, who thereby benefited from iron discipline and lengthy training. The very competent strategic direction of the war, itself another element of Jordan's praiseworthy showing in this conflict, was entirely the product of British officering. It is hard to discount the pervasive British influence as a source of the various skills displayed by the Arab Legion in 1948.

Jordanian-Israeli Clashes, 1949–66

Almost immediately after the conclusion of the war in Palestine, Amman inaugurated plans to enhance its military capabilities both quantitatively and qualitatively. Although 'Abdallah and his British military chiefs had generally been pleased with the performance of the Arab Legion against the Israelis, they recognized that it was too small a force to adequately defend the new nation against the variety of threats it now confronted. In the years after the Arab defeat in 1948, Arab nationalists overthrew several of the Arab monarchies and narrowly failed to unseat many others. The new regimes in Egypt, Syria, Iraq, Yemen, and elsewhere bore little love for the remaining monarchs like 'Abdallah and mounted both clandestine and overt challenges to their rule. In the face of these threats, Amman began a major campaign to augment the Arab Legion.

This expansion, however, did not imply a move to a mass army. The British officers in particular were adamantly opposed to diluting the caliber of manpower by adopting large-scale conscription. Instead, they chose to retain the same long terms of service and rigorous discipline and training but accept more volunteers. In addition, as another important way of increasing the overall combat power at its disposal, Amman began pursuing newer and heavier weapons, particularly tanks and combat aircraft, to improve the firepower and mobility of the legion.

The war in Palestine had also pointed out other shortcomings that Jordan attempted to address in the years thereafter. The legion combat-support and combat-service-support branches had proven to be weak links. Prior to 1948, the Arab Legion had relied on British military forces in the Middle East to take care of its various logistical and support functions as well as provide air cover, signals, and combat-engineer units. When the British pulled out of Palestine in 1948, they took these support personnel with them, forcing the legion to improvise during the war with Israel. In particular, the Jordanians had suffered from a dearth of technically competent personnel to man signals, artillery, combat engineering, logistics, and maintenance billets.

Across the board, Jordan and its British officers tried to remedy these problems and to expand and modernize the legion. In 1950, Amman established an officer cadet training school followed by training programs for technical and logistics personnel, the Royal Military College, and the Command Staff College. In 1951 King 'Abdallah created the Royal Jordanian Air Force (RJAF) with a small number of older British aircraft. In addition, the Arab Legion began accepting large numbers of new volunteers. Throughout the 1950s and 1960s, the legion remained an extremely popular career. Its prestige was enormous and its economic benefits excellent. Indeed, by the mid-1960s, there was a long waiting list for volunteers, and many applicants resorted to bribery simply to be able to serve as enlisted men. Consequently, the legion's strength rose from 12,000 men in nine infantry battalions and several independent infantry companies in 1949 to 55,000 men in nine infantry brigades, two armored brigades, and five independent tank and infantry battalions in 1967.[18]

These efforts also produced some unintended problems, however. First, as part of the effort to improve Jordan's ability to operate and maintain technical equipment, Glubb encouraged the recruitment of more technically qualified personnel, including many who simply had a passing exposure to modern machinery and electronics. The segment of Jordan's population that most possessed these traits were the Hadaris, particularly the new Palestinian refugees. The Palestinians mostly came from the big coastal towns like Jaffa and Haifa and so had been around cars, telephones, and other mundane technology. They also possessed the largest number of young men trained in technical fields such as engineering and the physical sciences. But the Hashimites had developed a very strong relationship with the Bedouin population during the 1930s and 1940s and felt less comfortable relying on the Jordanian Hadaris; they did not trust the Palestinians at all. Most of the Palestinians looked down on the Hashimites and their Bedouin supporters as unsophisticated "bumpkins." Furthermore, the Palestinians were intent on reconquering their homeland, a goal about which the Jordanian monarchy was ambivalent at best. Thus, Glubb's efforts to recruit technically skilled Palestinians and Hadaris was regarded with misgiving in Amman, and such recruits were strictly segregated within the military. Ultimately, "West Bankers" were relegated to the technical services — engineering, supply and transport, maintenance and repair, medical services, and signals — and to four of the infantry brigades. The other five infantry brigades, the two armored brigades, and the independent armor battalions were all kept strictly Bedouin. Moreover, the four "Palestinian" brigades were deployed to the West Bank, while both armored brigades and up to four of the "Bedouin" infantry brigades were kept on the East Bank, between the West Bank units and the capital. Amman kept a close watch on its handful of Palestinian officers, and few were allowed to rise even as high as battalion commander (and then usually only in support units). Command in the combat units was reserved for Bedouin officers.[19]

The second problem the Jordanians encountered derived from the manning of their new officer billets. The dramatic expansion of the Arab Legion demanded a corresponding increase in the size of the Jordanian officer corps. Amman's response was to secure large numbers of additional British officers seconded from the British military. By 1955, British officers accounted for over half of all the officer billets in the Jordanian army, more than at any previous time. This influx proved crucial in training the hordes of new recruits being brought in to fill out the expanded-force structure. Simply put, there existed no readily available pool of trained officers in Jordan that could have been drawn upon to provide adequate training to such a large number of new personnel inducted in such a short amount of time. Had the Jordanians not been able to obtain the services of these British officers, their expansion program would have been less successful and might have failed altogether, producing a larger but far less capable force. However, the addition of more British officers created resentment among the Jordanian junior officers, who believed that they should have been given first preference for the new command assignments that opened up as a result of the expansion.[20]

This disgruntlement eventually contributed to the dismissal of the British from Jordanian service. In March 1956 the new Jordanian king, Hussein ibn Talal, grandson of 'Abdallah, dismissed Glubb and the other British officers from the Arab Legion and officially renamed the force the Jordan Arab Army (al-Jaysh al-Arabiyyah al-Urduniyyah). Although the young king and Glubb had some differences regarding the future course of the Jordanian armed forces, the real causes of the rupture were Arab nationalism and the ambitions of Jordan's junior-officer corps. Many Jordanians saw the continuing British presence in the military as a lingering vestige of imperial control over the country. At best, the British officers had divided loyalties, and their conduct in the war with Israel served as proof that their first allegiance was to London. Finally, ambitious young Jordanian officers realized that their future advancement depended on removing the obstacle of the British officers. Consequently, they agitated for Glubb's dismissal under the guise of nationalism, though really for their own self-interest.

The sudden departure of the British officers from the former Arab Legion not only created considerable "headroom" for aspiring Jordanian officers but also ushered in new headaches for the regime. In particular, the Jordanians found that few among their officer candidates were really qualified for tactical command assignments. Amman was able to find enough competent officers to fill the relatively small number of senior slots opened up by the British exodus but ran into difficulties adequately filling the much larger number of lower-ranking commands. As Brig. Peter Young, a highly decorated British commando and the commander of the Jordanian 9th Infantry Battalion until 1956, succinctly noted, "there was a distinct shortage of potential battalion and company commanders."[21] Ultimately, the

Jordanians were forced to make do with a number of officers who would not have passed muster under the British because they were the only men available.[22]

Combat Operations

Adding to the tumult caused by these changes, the Jordanians had to be constantly on their guard against Israel. Combat never fully ceased along the Israeli-Jordanian border even after the December 1948 ceasefire. Palestinians, Jordanians, and Israelis found reasons to snipe at each other across the ceasefire lines, raid each others' villages, and kidnap each others' soldiers. Israeli forces performed poorly in these operations at first, prompting Tel Aviv to set up a special elite force, Unit 101, under the leadership of Maj. Ariel Sharon, specifically for crossborder raids. In 1954 the Israelis expanded this elite force by merging Unit 101 with their paratrooper battalion to form the 202d Paratroop Brigade, again under Sharon's leadership. Sharon's troops dramatically altered the balance along the Israeli-Jordanian border. He proved to be a brilliant tactician, his men were superb fighters, and they regularly defeated much larger Jordanian and Palestinian forces. This string of defeats, and the increasing ferocity of Sharon's raids, forced the Jordanians to beef up the army's presence on the West Bank, escalating the scale of combat even further. The largest and most important clash between Sharon's force and the Arab Legion was at the West Bank village of Qalqilyah in October 1956.

THE BATTLE OF QALQILYAH

In September and October 1956, a group of Palestinian *fedayeen* guerrillas conducted a series of attacks on Israel from the Qalqilyah area that left nine Israeli civilians dead. Tel Aviv decided to mount a reprisal raid using Sharon's 202d Paratroop Brigade. The target of the strike would be the Jordanian military headquarters at Qalqilyah for sanctioning, or at least not preventing, the operations of this Palestinian group. Qalqilyah is about twenty kilometers northeast of Tel Aviv at the western tip of a salient that sticks out into Israel from the West Bank territories to create the narrowest point of Israel's narrow waist. The town was defended by elements of the Jordanian 9th Infantry Battalion. At least another company of the battalion was in reserve at Azzun, several miles to the east, waiting to counterattack any Israeli reprisal raid.

On 10 October Sharon led elements of his brigade against Qalqilyah. Israel's political leadership placed several unusual constraints on his operation so as not to jeopardize the ongoing negotiations with Britain and

France for a combined military campaign against Egypt. Sharon's plan had been to deploy a blocking force along the Qalqilyah-Azzun road; another force would seize the Zuffin Hill, which overlooked the Azzun road; a third force would clear the Jordanian strongpoints south of Qalqilyah; and another force would actually seize and demolish the military headquarters. However, Tel Aviv vetoed the capture of Zuffin Hill, and the attack against the strongpoints south of the town, they feared, would make the operation seem too large.[23]

As a result of these changes, the raid turned into a pitched battle. When Sharon's units drove eastward into Qalqilyah, the Jordanian company in the strongpoint south of town opened fire on them. Although these troops did not get out of their positions and counterattack the Israelis to prevent them from reaching the military headquarters, their fire was accurate, and since it came at the Israelis from the flank, it slowed down their operation. Meanwhile, the reserve elements of the 9th Battalion came racing down the Azzun-Qalqilyah road as soon as they received radio reports of the Israeli attack only to blunder into the Israeli blocking force, which threw them back with heavy losses. The Jordanian reinforcements were considerably larger than the Israeli blocking force, however, and their size prompted the Israelis to fall back to another ambush position. The Jordanians regrouped and attacked down the road again, and again they were surprised and mauled in an Israeli ambush. Once more they fell back in disarray, regrouped, attacked again, and were again ambushed. After this third bloody nose, the Jordanian commander deployed a part of his force to move north of the road into a flanking position. It is unclear whether he intended to mount a flanking attack on the Israeli blocking force or had given up and was simply deploying to prevent the Israelis from driving farther east into Jordan.

Regardless of its purpose, this move suddenly turned things in favor of the 9th Battalion. By this time, the Israeli main body had completed demolishing the headquarters compound in Qalqilyah and were ready to withdraw back to Israel. As part of the withdrawal, the small Israeli blocking force was ordered to pull back, not west, but north to the Israeli kibbutz of Eyal, which caused them to run into the Jordanian flanking position. The Jordanians surprised the Israelis and inflicted a fair number of casualties on them. At that point, the Jordanian commander realized he had caught a small Israeli unit in a bad position and threw all of his forces against them. He attacked the pinned-down Israelis but sent part of his force west to occupy Zuffin Hill to cut their escape route west to Qalqilyah. The Israelis did try to escape westward and were then caught in an ambush by the

Jordanians on the hill. Sharon eventually was forced to call in artillery and to dispatch a small force of APCs he had been holding in reserve, which cut their way through the Jordanian lines and extracted the trapped unit at the cost of one of the APCs lost to antitank fire. All told, the Israelis suffered 18 dead and 60 wounded, while the Jordanians suffered between 120 and 300 casualties.[24]

THE BATTLE OF AS-SAMU'

The constant raiding back and forth from Jordan and Israel continued throughout the 1950s and into the 1960s. The Palestinian attacks were a constant frustration for Israel, and the Israeli retaliatory raids were a constant embarrassment for Jordan. Indeed, in 1964, with the formation of the Palestine Liberation Organization (PLO), Palestinian attacks on Israel actually increased, and the Israeli responses escalated as well. By the mid-1960s, Amman was determined to try to catch and destroy the Israeli raiding forces and deployed significant ground forces to the West Bank for this purpose.

On 12 November 1966, a truck carrying an Israeli patrol hit a mine near the Jordanian border, killing three and wounding six others. The next day before dawn, the Israelis launched a major reprisal raid against the nearby Jordanian town of as-Samu'.[25] The Israelis sent a parachute battalion in halftracks with a company of AMX-13s to demolish the Jordanian police station there as well as facilities of the Jordanian government and the Palestinian fedayeen.[26] Part of the force — a paratrooper company and a light-tank platoon — set up a blocking position along the main road to Hebron, where the Arab Legion's 29th "Hittin" Infantry Brigade was deployed. When the Jordanians were alerted to the raid, they dispatched nearly a battalion of the Hittin brigade to smash the Israelis.

The Jordanian counterattack turned into a fiasco, however. First, reports coming back from as-Samu' were hopelessly confused and led the 29th Brigade's commander to believe that the Israeli force was not at as-Samu' but closer to the border, near the (Israeli) village of Yattir. Next, the Jordanian battalion commander failed to scout his route of advance. As a result of these two mistakes, the entire Jordanian battalion (mounted in trucks) blundered into the Israeli ambush outside of as-Samu' along the road to Hebron. The Israelis destroyed the first 15 of the 28 trucks in the Jordanian column before the rest could escape. Nevertheless, the survivors regrouped and launched an attack on the Israeli blocking force in conjunction with an airstrike by four RJAF Hawker Hunters. Despite their numerical advantage, the Jordanians failed to mount a proper antitank effort and charged straight at the Israeli position. Their attack failed quickly and unceremoniously. Nevertheless, the Israelis were not interested in pursuing the battered battalion, allowing it to retreat without further loss. In all, the Jordanians suffered twenty-one killed and thirty-seven wounded, while the Israelis lost one killed (the battalion commander) and ten wounded.[27]

Meanwhile, Tel Aviv had dispatched a pair of Israeli Mirages, which intercepted the Jordanian Hunters. Two of the Hunters probably fled when the Mirages arrived on the scene, but the other two engaged the two Israeli fighters. One of the Jordanian pilots quickly got on the tail of one of the Mirages, but just as quickly the Israeli reversed the situation and got in behind the Hunter. For eight minutes the Jordanian tried to shake the Mirage before he was finally shot down.[28] This was the longest single dogfight in Israeli Air Force (IAF) history and was twice as long as most previous Israeli air battles. Afterward, the Israelis opined that these Jordanian pilots had proven far more capable than either the Egyptians or the Syrians.[29]

Jordanian Military Effectiveness in the Battles of Qalqilyah and as-Samu'

It would be unwise to draw too many lessons from two small battles fought ten years apart. Nevertheless, they do establish a pattern subsequently borne out in the Six Day War.

The Jordanians fought well, albeit not brilliantly, at Qalqilyah. On the one hand, they responded quickly to the Israeli attack; the company in place took the Israelis under accurate, long-range fire to harass and delay the attackers, while the reserve force rushed forward for a counterattack. All competent actions. On the other hand, the company south of town failed to counterattack into the exposed Israeli flank or to otherwise get out of their positions and engage the attackers to prevent them from carrying out their mission. This was a failure on the part of the local commander to take the initiative or to improvise a response to the Israeli move. Similarly, the commander of the reserve force (probably the battalion commander) failed to scout his route of advance and so fell prey to an Israeli ambush. Not only did he fail to correct this mistake by probing the road ahead before sending his main body down it, but twice he simply regrouped and rushed forward along the same route—making no effort to outflank the Israeli blocking force or even to deploy flank guards. As a result, he was ambushed again and again. Finally, after having his column surprised three times by a smaller Israeli force (a reconnaissance company of about 50 men, compared to the 200–300 men of the Jordanian reserve), he deployed a flanking force, although it is unclear what his intentions were for it. Fortune shone on the

Jordanians when the Israeli blocking force stumbled into this flanking unit and got mauled. At that point, the Jordanian commander showed real initiative by seizing the opportunity to crush the Israelis by attacking with his main body and sending another force around to cut the Israeli escape route. While these deft moves at the end of the battle allowed the Jordanians to inflict some losses on this smaller Israeli force (heavy losses by Israeli standards), the passivity of the company at Qalqilyah and the inept initial conduct of the reserve force allowed the Israeli main body to complete their mission and inflict heavier losses on the Jordanians.

As-Samu' was an even briefer battle, but the Jordanians clearly performed worse than they did at Qalqilyah. In this case the Jordanian reaction was hampered from the start by the misleading reports coming back from those on the spot as to what was going on and where it was happening. As at Qalqilyah, the troops piled into their trucks and went roaring off down the road, without adequate scouts or advance guards, only to smack into an Israeli ambush. Although the Jordanians showed real courage and a remarkable degree of cohesiveness in regrouping and counterattacking, they displayed little skill in the conduct of their assault. Even taking into account the presence of a platoon of Israeli light tanks, given the Jordanians' advantage in size (a battalion against an Israeli paratroop company — which are smaller than line-infantry companies — plus 3–4 AMX-13s), they should have been able to overwhelm this roadblock or at least force the Israelis back by lapping around their flanks. Jordanian antitank teams should have been able to handle such a small number of light tanks: even shoulder-fired weapons were deadly against the lightly armored AMX-13. Instead, the attack was inept and a failure, inflicting only minor casualties to the Israelis. The only impressive element of the Jordanian effort was the performance of the Hunter pilots, whom the Israelis described as very capable.

These battles suggest a decline in Jordanian military capabilities between 1948 (or 1956) and 1967. Once again, these examples are weak reeds upon which to base an entire argument, but they conform closely to a larger pattern. At Qalqilyah, the Jordanians did fine: some aspects of their operations were quite good, others quite poor. Averaging the strengths and weaknesses, they seem to have done about as well as they had in 1948, perhaps a bit worse, though not by much. At as-Samu', they did not do well at all. There were some mitigating circumstances: the Israelis had tanks, were on the defensive, and held the initiative. In addition, it was a small Jordanian force and may have been a poor one. Indeed, in the fighting in 1967, the Hittin Brigade proved to be one of the worst brigades in the Jordanian army. Nevertheless, the Jordanian performance at as-Samu' was far worse than even their most inept performances in 1948. One cannot point to a single occasion when Glubb's troops fumbled a military operation as badly as this battalion did. Consequently, even making allowances for mitigating circumstances, as-Samu' indicates a change — a decline in Jordanian performance that would more fully manifest itself in 1967.

The Six Day War, 1967

When war broke out between the Arabs and Israel in 1967, the British had been gone from Jordan for eleven years. That break was hardly total — many Jordanian officers still received training in Great Britain, while London sent frequent military missions to Amman for advice and planning — but it was still important. It removed the British from the day-to-day training and command of the Arab Legion. Although the long terms of military service meant that there was still a good percentage of men who had trained, and even fought, under the British, there were many more who had not. The army had expanded dramatically after the departure of the British, from 20,000 men in 1955 to 55,000 men in 1967.[30] Consequently, the majority of enlisted personnel and junior officers had not had the benefit of British tutelage. At most, some of the junior officers may have attended Sandhurst or possibly Camberly or had taken courses in Britain on armored combat, artillery operations, or other specialized military disciplines.

The British legacy, however, lingered on. The Jordanian armed forces still had much of the feel of a British colonial army. Its officers' messes clung to the trappings of British regimental messes, and most traditions of the Arab Legion established under Peake and Glubb were carefully preserved in the post-British army. Jordanian ground and air forces still relied exclusively on British doctrine and organization. The army was equipped largely with British arms, although Amman had begun purchasing American equipment such as 155-mm howitzers and M-47 and M-48 Patton tanks. Moreover, the Arab Legion continued to be modeled on the ideal of a small, elite, long-term-service army of professionals as originally conceived by Peake and Glubb.

The Balance of Forces

Although the entire Israel Defense Forces (IDF) outnumbered and out-gunned the Jordanian armed forces in 1967, because Israel was fighting Egypt and Syria as well, in terms of actual forces engaged, the two sides were about even both in manpower and equipment. The Jordanians had roughly 45,000 troops, 270 tanks, and 200 artillery pieces in the West Bank.

These forces were organized into nine brigades (seven infantry and two armored) and several independent battalions. The tiny RJAF consisted of just 24 Hawker Hunters and 5 U.S. F-104 Starfighters, but the F-104s had not been turned over to the Jordanians yet, and their American pilots flew them to Turkey at the start of hostilities. Against this, the Israelis deployed eight brigades (one armored, two mechanized and five infantry) with about 40,000 men and roughly 200 tanks.[31] The Israeli Air Force had a bit more than 200 combat aircraft, of which 72 were sophisticated French Mirages and the rest were much older Mysteres, Super-Mysteres, Ouragons, and Vautours.[32] However, the IAF also had to deal with Syria, Egypt, and Iraq, whereas the RJAF was free to concentrate fully against Israel.

Jordanian equipment was, on average, slightly better than Israeli equipment. Jordanian tanks were clearly superior to that of their Israeli opponents. Of the 270 Jordanian tanks on the West Bank, 170 were M-47 and M-48 Pattons and the other 100 were British Centurions. Against them, the IDF deployed 50–60 Centurions, 50 M-4 Shermans (which carried only a 76-mm gun rather than the French 105-mm gun carried by the M-51 Super Shermans, which were mostly sent to the Sinai), and nearly 100 French-built M-50 Shermans, armed with high-velocity 75-mm guns. The Jordanians had modern U.S. M-113 APCs, while the Israelis were still using World War II–vintage M-3 halftracks. Amman's artillery was primarily American 105-mm howitzers and even some old British 25-pounders, although it also boasted several batteries of U.S. 155-mm guns, while Israel was equipped almost entirely with old French 105-mm howitzers. The Mirage and the Hawker Hunter, the mainstays of the IAF and the RJAF respectively, were essentially on a par, according to the Israelis, because the Mirage was faster and had more advanced avionics, but the Hawker was more maneuverable in a dogfight.[33]

The Jordanians had several other advantages. First, they had had nineteen years to establish themselves on the West Bank. Although they had not made the same effort as the Syrians to fortify their positions along the entire border, in places, the Jordanians had built elaborate fixed defenses; this was especially the case in Jerusalem and along the Jerusalem corridor. Geography also was in Amman's favor. Jerusalem lay at the end of a narrow salient bracketed on three sides by high ground held by the Jordanians. Similarly, their forces in Samaria could threaten to attack Tel Aviv, which was less than twenty kilometers from the border, or drive fifteen to twenty-five kilometers to the sea and cut Israel in half. Israel had the added disadvantage of having to fight three enemies simultaneously, forcing Tel Aviv to divide up the IDF rather than concentrate it against any one foe. Ultimately, Syria's quiescence during the first four days of the war allowed the Israelis to draw off forces from Galilee to fight Jordan, but the bulk of the Israeli army was deployed opposite Egypt throughout the fighting with Jordan. Similarly, the IAF had other responsibilities and was largely unavailable for the Jordanian front on the first day of the war, except to destroy the small RJAF.

Jordan had at least one important weakness, its command and control arrangements. The Jordanians had no divisional or corps formations because King Hussein feared that such positions would be too powerful as bases from which to overthrow the monarchy. Consequently, Jordanian brigades on the West Bank had difficulty coordinating their actions since communications had to go through Amman. The commander of Jordan's Western Command had direct control of all nine brigades on the West Bank plus several independent battalions, various General Headquarters (the General Staff) reserve assets (mostly additional artillery and anti-aircraft defense units), and all of the combat-service-support units for the Jordanian army in the West Bank. In addition, Jordan had a very weak general staff—both institutionally and in terms of personalities—in which numerous top military commanders had ambiguous and overlapping responsibilities. Consequently, all major decisions had to be approved by the king, and the high command was not in a position to ease the burden on the Western Command.

Finally, to add to the command and control mess, King Hussein joined the United Arab Command (UAC) established by Egypt and Syria immediately before the outbreak of war. As a condition for Jordanian admission, Nasser demanded that it accept an Egyptian general as the new commander in chief of its forces. The Jordanians were fortunate enough to get Lt. Gen. 'Abd al-Mun'im Riyad, a superb officer who had distinguished himself in Yemen and was considered one of Egypt's best operational minds.[34] However, neither the UAC nor the Jordanians had sorted out exactly how he was to fit into the command structure by the time war broke out. Riyad tended to take his orders from Egypt's Field Marshal 'Abd al-Hakim 'Amr in consultation with King Hussein, but from there Riyad's orders were transmitted via the Jordanian General Staff down the normal Jordanian chain of command. Riyad's authority over GHQ in operational matters was left unclear.[35]

Goals and Plans

Amman's major objective during the Six Day War was simply to survive intact. Jordan had no particular interest in acquiring any Israeli territory, with the possible exception of the tiny Mount Scopus enclave in Jerusalem. Consequently, its strategic goal was essentially defensive. The Jordanian General Staff recognized that they lacked the manpower to defend the entire expanse of the West Bank—as well as Jordan's East Bank borders with Israel to the north and south of that region—and wanted to concentrate their forces along shorter defensive lines in the mountainous terrain of central Samaria. But the king felt that politically he could not afford to be seen as surrendering any of the West Bank to the Israelis without a fight, so he overruled his generals' expert advice and ordered a forward defense of the West Bank.

There was a critical offensive element of the Jordanian plan. Operation Tariq ("Victory") called for a strike against Jerusalem to take the Jewish part of the city. Amman expected the Israelis to conquer vast swathes of territory in Samaria and Judaea, and their intent was to use Jewish Jerusalem as a bargaining chip to get back their lost territories when the fighting ended. Thus, GHQ planned attacks from northwest and southwest of Jerusalem to sever the roads in the Jerusalem corridor, surrounding the city. An important element of this operation was the seizure of Israel's Mount Scopus enclave in the northeastern section of Arab Jerusalem. The Jordanians felt that they had to eliminate this pocket of resistance lest it tie down forces needed for the enveloping attack or serve as a base for an Israeli offensive into northeastern Jerusalem.

The Jordanians correctly predicted Israel's strategy for an invasion of the West Bank. They deduced that the IDF would conduct two major pincer attacks—one at Jerusalem and the other farther north against the Janin-Nablus axis—coupled with a "defensive" attack around Qalqilyah-Tulkarm to push the Jordanians back from the coastal plain. This accurate reading of enemy intentions allowed the Jordanians to concentrate their forces against the IDF's expected thrusts, which, along with the requirements of Operation Tariq, largely dictated the deployment of Jordanian forces. The general staff deployed five infantry brigades along Jordan's borders: one at Janin, one covering the area from Tulkarm to Qalqilyah, one along the corridor from Latrun to Jerusalem, one in and around Jerusalem, and one in Judaea mostly between Jerusalem and Hebron. Another infantry brigade and the elite 60th Armored Brigade were bivouacked in the Jordan Valley between Jerusalem and Jericho, from where they were to move toward Jerusalem to take part in Operation Tariq. Similarly, an infantry brigade and the elite 40th Armored Brigade were held back in the Jordan Valley near the Damiyah bridge to support the brigade at Janin and parry the expected Israeli thrust toward Nablus. Finally two independent armored battalions — the 10th and 12th — were deployed forward to provide support for some of the frontline infantry brigades, the 12th near Janin and the 10th near Hebron. This deployment scheme left the Jordanian infantry stretched thin at some points, especially in Judaea, but succeeded in concentrating division-sized forces in the two main Israeli breakthrough sectors: Jerusalem and Janin. Indeed, the Jordanians were confident that they could defend the West Bank against an Israeli offensive of eight to twelve brigades for two or three weeks.[36]

For its part, Israel was desperate to avoid a war with Jordan. It wanted only to fight Egypt and, before the outbreak of hostilities, made several secret overtures to Jordan.[37] Although both the Israeli GHQ and Gen. Uzi Narkiss, in charge of Israel's Central Command, recognized the possibility of war with Jordan, the political context prevented them from developing elaborate plans; Narkiss really did not know what forces would be available to him. Tel Aviv wanted to maximize the number of brigades deployed against Egypt, and this front would have first priority for all Israeli forces. In addition, there were also the Syrians to consider. If the Israeli victory over the Egyptians was swift and the Syrians stayed out, Narkiss could expect some reinforcements from the Southern Command, facing Egypt, and the Northern Command, facing Syria. However, just how much he could expect and when he might get them were questions still very much up in the air. Consequently, the Israelis could only draw up very sketchy plans for a drive south toward Janin and Nablus, a push from the coastal plan against Qalqilyah and Tulkarm, a limited offensive in Jerusalem to link up with the Mount Scopus enclave, and another limited offensive to take Latrun — exactly as Amman surmised.

Initial Moves

Jordan was well prepared for the Israeli attack when it finally materialized on 5 June. Jordanian intelligence learned of the impending Israeli offensive against Egypt on 3 June, and Amman passed this information to Cairo immediately. In addition, King Hussein claims in his memoirs that he believed war with Israel had become inevitable as early as 23 May, with Nasser's closing of the Straits of Tiran.[38] Consequently, Jordan spent this time deploying its forces to their wartime positions, building and repairing fortifications, stockpiling provisions, and otherwise bracing for the coming onslaught. The one area in which the Jordanians appear to have failed to take adequate preparations was the deployment of their air force. The RJAF had no hardened shelters and was left concentrated at Mafraq Airbase rather than dispersing around the country.

Early on 5 June Nasser and the Egyptian General Staff told King Hussein and the Jordanian General Staff that the Egyptian Air Force had destroyed the IAF and the Egyptian army was already driving into southern Israel. Based on this, they asked Jordan to launch an armored attack into the Negev to link up with the (mythical) Egyptian attack. General Riyad and King Hussein complied with Cairo in full. Although the Egyptian request went well beyond what Jordan originally had intended to undertake in its prewar planning, the information from Egypt indicating that the IAF had been destroyed — eliminating it as a threat to Jordan and freeing up the EAF to provide air support to the Jordanians — and that Egyptian armor was threatening to cut Israel in half, caused the king and Riyad to agree to the more ambitious strategy. Despite protests from some members of the Jordanian General Staff, they apparently saw this as too good an opportunity to squander and ordered a considerably larger operation than they had previously believed prudent.[39]

Orders quickly came down from Amman for the armed forces to begin implementing their preplanned operations. All across the front, Jordanian units began opening fire on whatever was opposite them, often without any particular rhyme or reason. Jordanian artillery began bombarding Israeli cities and military installations near the border. The 12th Armored Battalion was ordered to attack an Israeli armored formation deployed near the border, but it could not get organized and moving in time before the Israelis launched their own offensive. As the Egyptians had requested, but not as envisioned in Jordanian planning, the 60th Armored Brigade was sent south to the Hebron area to develop an attack into the Negev to link up with the (mythical) Egyptian drive from the Sinai. In addition, the 40th Armored Brigade was ordered south to take over the 60th's part in Operation Tariq.

The Israelis tried even as late as the morning of 5 June to convince Jordan to remain on the sidelines, but King Hussein had already committed himself and rejected their entreaties. The Jordanian attacks did little but provoke the Israelis. Amman sent sixteen of its Hawker Hunters probably to attack Tel Aviv and Ben Gurion Airport. However, because Jordanian military intelligence did not have one shred of information about Israeli airbases, the pilots were forced to improvise the entire operation. The Jordanians appear to have gotten lost because they ended up attacking the Israeli beach resort of Netanyah and the nearby (abandoned) airfield at Kfar Sirkin instead. Even in these attacks they did poorly, causing only light damage to some of the structures at the airfield and destroying one Noratlas transport that had been dispersed there.[40] Nevertheless, this raid, coupled with the Jordanian artillery bombardment and small-arms fire in Jerusalem, were enough to warrant Israeli retaliation. At about 1:00 P.M., while the Hunters were being refueled and rearmed for their next mission, eight IAF Mirages struck Amman International Airfield and Mafraq Airbase, destroying sixteen of twenty-two Hunters there and badly damaging another four. The remaining two Hunters were late returning from Israel and tried to engage a pair of the attacking Mirages. Despite their sudden appearance and the greater maneuverability of the Hunters, the Israelis quickly gained the advantage, and one Hunter was shot down immediately. The second Jordanian pilot was fairly good, and so it took the other Israeli Mirage several minutes to destroy his aircraft.[41]

Israel Decides on War

It was the Jordanian threat to Jerusalem, however, that finally provoked Tel Aviv to launch a general offensive to seize the West Bank. Around noon on 5 June, General Riyad ordered a battalion of the 27th "Imam 'Ali" Infantry Brigade deployed in Jerusalem to seize the hill of Jebel Mukhaber and Government House south of the Old City. Riyad wanted to secure these positions to prevent Israeli forces in Jerusalem from striking south against his planned thrust to link up with the Egyptians in the Negev.[42] Since Government House was considered neutral territory, it was undefended, and the Jordanians occupied both the compound and the hill without trouble. They then continued their attack westward against the Israeli settlement of Ramat Rachel. This time the Israelis brought up several companies of infantry to hold the area. The Jordanians did not expect resistance, launched a frontal assault on the kibbutz, and were driven back quickly and easily by the IDF. Several hours earlier, Radio Amman had announced the fall of Jebel Mukhaber, which the Israelis had dismissed as Jordanian propaganda. However, when Radio Amman then announced the fall of Mount Scopus after Jebel Mukhaber had actually been taken, Tel Aviv saw this as a preview of things to come.

After the various Jordanian attacks and the radio claims regarding Mount Scopus, Israel finally abandoned its hope of keeping Jordan out of the war and ordered a full-scale offensive against the West Bank. For this operation, Tel Aviv reassigned an ugdah commanded by Brig. Gen. Elad Peled, comprising one armored brigade, one mechanized brigade, and one paratroop brigade from the northern front facing Syria, to mount the drive on Janin and Nablus. Later, the Israeli General Staff also transferred the 55th Paratroop Brigade from the Southern Command to the Central Command for use in Jerusalem. General Narkiss intended to conduct a double envelopment of Jerusalem, using the paratroopers to attack northeast into Shaykh Jarrah to link up with the enclave on Mount Scopus and then swing south along the Augusta-Victoria Ridge on the eastern outskirts of the city. The 16th "Etzioni" Brigade would be responsible for retaking Jebel Mukhaber and Government House in the south and then pushing east and north around the southern wall of the Old City. Other elements of the oversized 16th Brigade would hold the line elsewhere in Jerusalem. Meanwhile, the 10th "Harel" Mechanized Brigade would attack from the Jerusalem corridor north toward Ramallah and then east to link up with Mount Scopus and possibly envelop Jerusalem from the north. An Israeli infantry brigade would be responsible for attacking Latrun as well as driving the Jordanians back from the Tulkarm-Qalqilyah area. Finally, another infantry brigade would watch the Jordanian forces in Judaea and the east bank area south of the Dead Sea.

Battles on the Outskirts of Jerusalem

The struggle for Jerusalem began during the afternoon of 5 June, when an Israeli infantry battalion from the 16th Brigade, reinforced with a company of ancient and mechanically unreliable Sherman tanks, counterattacked the Jordanians at Government House. The Jordanians fought poorly. They had failed to deploy in proper defensive positions to defend the compound and could put up only token resistance. Throughout the battle, Jordanian artillery fire was highly inaccurate, with shells falling on both sides indiscriminately. The Israeli attack initially got hung up on the difficult terrain, with the result that all but three of the Shermans got stuck, and the Israeli infantry battalion attacked piecemeal. Still, the Jordanians could not keep even such a clumsy assault out, and once the Israelis had penetrated into the Government House compound, the Jordanian soldiers fought in place without reorienting themselves to face the Israelis now inside the compound. Their battalion commander bolted when it became clear the battle had turned in the IDF's favor, and, although most of his troops stayed on to continue the fight, because they would neither counterattack to throw the Israelis off the hill nor reform their lines to contain the Israeli breakthrough, it was simply a matter of time before they were defeated.

The attack on Government House went so well that the Israeli battalion went on to clear "the Sausage" and "the Bell," two elaborate Jordanian trench-and-bunker systems guarding the southern approaches to Jebel Mukhaber. The Sausage faced west and had been designed to have the neutral Government House compound as the anchor for its right (northern) flank, with the Bell at its southern end facing south and guarding its left

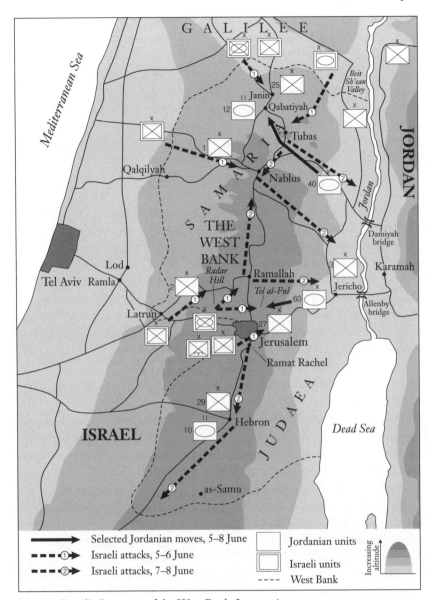

Map 23. Israel's Conquest of the West Bank, June 1967

flank. With Government House in their hands, the Israelis were able to move east and then south down Jebel Mukhaber, rolling up the Sausage from its right flank and then falling on the Bell from the rear. Here as well, the Jordanians stayed in their positions and fought on, often to the death, but without counterattacking or otherwise reorienting to meet the Israeli flanking attack. Consequently, they too were systematically overpowered by Israeli infantry without doing much damage to the attackers. The Israeli commander who led the operation could only say: "In the Sausage and the Bell they fought stupidly. The Jordanian firing positions were badly planned. They expected us only from one direction. Therefore, we were always fighting one against one. We came down the Sausage and attacked the Bell from the rear, and they were not smart enough to reorganize themselves to stop us."[43] In the end, the entire Jordanian battalion was destroyed while inflicting only minimal casualties on the Israelis.

At the beginning of the war, Jordan had seven battalions of infantry in and around Jerusalem. Late in the afternoon of 5 June, another battalion of the 27th Infantry Brigade was ordered to reinforce the units already there. Initially, few of these units could coordinate their actions, though, because they belonged to at least four different brigades and there was no division command to direct operations. In response to this chaos, Amman gave Brig. Gen. Ata 'Ali Haza'ah, commander of the 3d Infantry Brigade, overall command of all Jordanian forces in Jerusalem. Haza'ah's chief concern was an Israeli attack into Shaykh Jarrah to try to relieve Mount Scopus, so he ordered a battalion of his own 3d Brigade, positioned north of Jerusalem, to redeploy farther south to link up with the units defending Shaykh Jarrah. He then ordered the newly arrived battalion from the 27th Infantry Brigade to replace the battalion of the 3d Brigade north of Jerusalem. By this time, Amman had finally realized that the Egyptian claims of destroying the IAF and mounting an offensive into Israel were lies. In particular, the increasing number of Israeli aircraft appearing over Jordanian airspace and the absence of any Egyptian aircraft convinced them that it was instead the EAF that had been destroyed. Realizing that there was no Egyptian armored column driving into the Negev and also that East Jerusalem was already under attack, General Riyad ordered both Jordanian armored brigades in the south to reverse direction: the 40th was sent north to reinforce Janin, while the 60th was ordered back to Jerusalem to implement Operation Tariq.

OPERATIONS ALONG THE JERUSALEM CORRIDOR

The next Israeli attack hit the Jordanian positions northwest of Jerusalem along the formidable ridges overlooking the Jerusalem corridor. General

Narkiss ordered his 10th Mechanized Brigade to drive north to take the Jordanian positions on Radar Hill and then turn east to swing around the right flank of the enemy defensive lines in Jerusalem. The ridgeline near Radar Hill where the Israelis attacked was held by a battalion of the 2d "Hashimi" Infantry Brigade and the newly arrived battalion of the 27th Infantry Brigade. The Jordanians had built extensive fortifications on these heights, recognizing them as key positions either for an outflanking attack against Jerusalem or as the base for a drive on Ramallah. However, in some places they had concluded that the cliff faces were too steep to climb and so had left them only lightly defended.

The Israelis attacked at five points along the Jordanian lines. In some places they attacked into the teeth of the Jordanian positions, at others they attacked sectors left undefended because of the terrain. While the Israelis encountered some severe problems climbing the escarpment — the 10th Mechanized Brigade lost all ten of its Centurions and many of its M-50 Shermans to boulders and mechanical failures — they eventually made it to the top at every point. Initially, the Jordanians poured fire, including artillery, onto the Israelis. Still, this bombardment was not very accurate, so it did not cause many casualties and only slightly slowed their breaching operations. Both Jordanian battalions put up heavy resistance against the initial Israeli thrust, but the IDF units were able to employ accurate fire and deft maneuver to punch through or outflank each of the Jordanian positions. In many cases, when the Israelis penetrated their lines (or when the Israelis simply got close), the Jordanian officers fled. The Israelis reported afterward that they did not find one Jordanian above the rank of sergeant among the dead and captured from the battle. The desertion of their officers produced mixed results: some units disintegrated and fled too, while others remained in place and fought on. Nevertheless, just as had been the case at Jebel Mukhaber, the Jordanians would not reorient their positions or counterattack to meet the Israeli penetrations and flanking maneuvers, and so the entire ridgeline was taken quickly and rather easily. Indeed, the Jordanian fortifications on Radar Hill itself fell in under twenty minutes.

A showdown was brewing between the Israeli 10th Mechanized Brigade and the Jordanian 60th Armored Brigade. Once the Israelis had punched through the line of Jordanian defenses along the Jerusalem corridor, both sides recognized the hill of Tel al-Ful as a critical height north of Jerusalem from which the Jordanians could block any further Israeli advance north and east of the city. Consequently, Amman ordered the M-48 battalion of the 60th Armored Brigade to get there as quickly as it could, while Tel Aviv ordered the tank battalion of the 10th Mechanized Brigade to do the same.

Because of breakdowns in the rough terrain, the Israelis arrived in the early morning hours of 6 June with just six M-50 Shermans and ten halftracks. The Israelis had been aware of the 60th Armored Brigade's movement toward Tel al-Ful and had hit the Jordanian armor with airstrikes twice during the night. These attacks only destroyed a couple of tanks and some other vehicles, but they delayed and disrupted the battalion's movement so that it did not reach Tel al-Ful until after dawn on 6 June.[44]

The Jordanians had every advantage at Tel al-Ful — equipment, numbers, terrain — but were still defeated. The lead M-48 Patton company of the 60th Armored arrived shortly after dawn and opened fire on the Israelis from a higher elevation, knocking out several of the halftracks and forcing the rest to fall back. The Israeli Shermans returned fire, but at the relatively long range, the rounds from their 75-mm guns simply bounced off the Pattons' armor.[45] The Jordanians pressed their attack slowly and destroyed one of the Shermans. An Israeli tank commander whose main gun had jammed noticed that the Jordanians had attached extra fuel tanks to the rear deck of their tanks, and he began firing at these with his heavy machine gun, setting one ablaze. He eventually succeeded in destroying another of the Pattons in this way, prompting the others to turn back. Other elements of the Jordanian tank battalion had since arrived in the area, and these forces took up positions in a village at the foot of Tel al-Ful. But the Israelis too had received reinforcements, and with a reinforced company of Shermans and mechanized infantry, they attacked the Jordanian armor at Tel al-Ful. Most of the Jordanian M-48 battalion was well deployed, with infantry support among the buildings at the foot of the hill, but the Israelis used part of their force to provide a base of fire while the rest swung around and hit the Jordanian positions from the flank. In a brief firefight, the Jordanians lost another four to six Pattons (reports vary) and then fled the battlefield. The Jordanian forces — both tanks and infantry — had remained static in their defensive positions rather than attempting to maneuver against the Israelis or to reform their lines to meet the flanking attack. In addition, their marksmanship was poor, with the result that they caused only minor damage to the Israelis.[46]

LATRUN

The Israelis massed a reinforced brigade to take the Latrun position that had proven so troublesome in 1948. The Jordanians had an infantry battalion in the position itself and a second battalion guarding its flanks. The Israelis intended to launch a diversionary attack with the brigade's reconnaissance company against the southern flank of the Latrun promontory, while the main effort fell against the northern flank. A battalion of artillery began pounding the Jordanian positions around 3:00 A.M. on 6 June, and about an hour later the Israelis launched their diversionary attack. Although the Israeli unit was very light and did not press its attack very hard, the Jordanian units throughout Latrun disintegrated. Many surrendered and the rest fled. Very few of the Jordanians offered any resistance, and within two hours the entire position was in Israeli hands almost without a fight.[47]

The Battle for Jerusalem

During the night of 5–6 June, the Israelis attacked Ammunition Hill in the Shaykh Jarrah area to try to link up with their enclave at Mount Scopus. During the nineteen years they had held East Jerusalem, the Jordanians had turned Ammunition Hill into a fortress, with concentric trench lines circling the hill, dozens of superbly camouflaged bunkers, concertina wire, and minefields. They employed a British-style all-around defense, and all of the bunkers and firing positions provided overlapping fields of fire. The Jordanians had a reinforced battalion of the 3d Brigade defending Shaykh Jarrah and Ammunition Hill, supported by artillery and mortars. The Israelis attacked at 2:00 A.M. with the 55th Paratroop Brigade and a company of Sherman tanks, also supported by artillery and mortars. The attack was hastily planned and suffered both from its lack of preparations and from indecisiveness among its commanders, who kept the paratroopers exposed to accurate Jordanian fire in their jump-off positions while they debated whether to launch the attack that night or the next morning.

Finally, the paratroopers received permission to attack and launched a frontal assault on Ammunition Hill and Shaykh Jarrah. The Jordanians were well prepared for the Israeli attack and fought back fiercely. Their fire was accurate and inflicted numerous casualties on the Israelis as they crossed the barren no-man's land and then worked their way through the Jordanian minefields and wire. Eventually, the Israelis pushed through and reached the southern base of the hill, where they turned north and began driving into the trench system itself. The Jordanian soldiers fought extremely bravely, refusing to give up an inch to the Israelis. Because of their determination, their marksmanship, and the superb design of their defenses, they inflicted very heavy losses on the attackers. However, once again, they would not reorient their forces to reinforce their lines facing the main Israeli thrust nor would they counterattack as the Israelis worked their way up the hill. Instead, the Jordanians clung tenaciously to their firing positions — even when these faced the wrong way, given the actual direction of the Israeli attack. Moreover, their artillery batteries could only effectively execute preplanned fire missions, with the result that they had little influence on the battle once the Israelis were through the minefields. But Jordanian mortar teams demonstrated good flexibility and accuracy throughout the battle, though their efforts had little effect because the infantry did not take any action other than to defend in place. Only when the end was clearly approaching did the Jordanian company commander mount a counterattack with his remaining reserve. This modest effort stopped the Israelis just long enough to allow that officer to make good his escape before the Israelis enveloped and massacred the counterattacking force. By morning, Jordan had lost Ammunition Hill. All told, the Israelis suffered 50 dead and 150 wounded, while the Jordanians had 106 dead and about 100 wounded.[48]

The fall of Ammunition Hill led to the disintegration of the Jordanian positions north of the Old City. The units holding Shaykh Jarrah mostly fell apart and fled when they were attacked by Israeli paratroopers. They put up some sporadic resistance as the Israelis breached their minefields and wire but then largely abandoned their positions before the Israelis could close with them. The Israelis rushed through the gap and pressed on into East Jerusalem, trying to work their way east to encircle the Old City and secure its gates. Some Jordanian soldiers took up positions alone or in groups in this area while the rest fled. The Israelis were forced to move slowly and to carefully clear their way of Jordanian snipers, roadblocks, and other defensive positions, but the Jordanians offered no coordinated defense and so could only delay the Israelis, not stop them.

By the morning of 6 June, initiative was entirely in the hands of the Israelis in and around Jerusalem, and the Jordanian units in the city could do little more than try to parry each Israeli thrust. Most of the Jordanian artillery deployed in the hills east of the city had been silenced by IAF airstrikes. Israeli paratroopers began working their way east along the north wall of the Old City. Jordanian snipers on the wall proved to be excellent marksmen and caused a number of casualties among the Israelis but also could not stop their advance. South of the Old City, the Israeli 16th Brigade attacked the Jordanian positions on Abu Tor, northeast of Jebel Mukhaber. They mounted a very poor frontal assault that hit the Jordanians piecemeal, and the defenders inflicted heavy casualties on them with small-arms and artillery fire. Nevertheless, the Jordanians again failed to reorganize once the Israelis had penetrated the defensive lines in a sector. Their only counterattack consisted of just four men, who, though brave, could not stop the Israelis from clearing the fortifications and capturing the hill. The Israelis then turned northwest and attacked the Jordanian defenses on Mount Zion from the rear. The defending unit there simply collapsed and fled in the face of the Israeli flanking maneuver.

Later in the day, the Israeli paratroopers north of the city were joined by Shermans from the 10th Mechanized Brigade, which had secured Tel al-Ful and then sent a mechanized battalion task force off to capture Ramallah and its tank battalion east to join in the envelopment of Jerusalem. The Jordanian units north of Jerusalem could not hold back the Israeli armor, and by midmorning, the 10th Mechanized was within a kilometer of Ammunition Hill. A Jordanian battalion from the 3d Infantry Brigade deployed on Mivtar Hill, north of Ammunition Hill, caught the Israeli armor in an antitank ambush and — with the aid of a mistaken strike by IAF Mysteres — destroyed two Shermans and two halftracks and damaged another tank. As on Ammunition Hill, the Jordanian company was deployed in British-style 360-degree "hedgehog" defenses along the southern face of the elevation. The Israelis set out a covering force to pin the Jordanians in their trenches and then sent an infantry unit backed by tanks around to the north side of the hill, which they climbed, and then attacked back down the southern face. Despite their all-around defenses and plentiful antitank weapons, the Jordanians were no match for the Israelis. Some Jordanians fought fiercely — many had to be rooted out of their positions in close fighting — but as was the case elsewhere, they failed to redeploy or counterattack to block the Israeli clearing operation. Thus, the Israelis were once again able to systematically work their way through the trench system, reducing each area of resistance in turn.

By the late afternoon of 6 June, the Old City was virtually surrounded by Israeli forces, and only the Augusta-Victoria Ridge directly east remained in Jordanian hands. Brigadier Haza'ah had a battalion in the Old City, and he concentrated the remnants of other units, amounting to about another battalion, to defend Augusta-Victoria. Although Haza'ah believed the city was lost, King Hussein asked him to try to hang on to the Old City and the ridge until reinforcements could be sent. Meanwhile, in the early evening, the Israelis dispatched a combined force of paratroopers and Shermans from the 10th Mechanized Brigade to take Augusta-Victoria and complete the encirclement of Jerusalem. In the darkness the Israelis lost their way and, rather than climbing the ridge, found themselves descending into the Kidron Valley between it and the Old City and were taken in a crossfire by Jordanians on the ridge and the city walls. The Jordanians destroyed two Shermans and several jeeps before the Israelis could pull back and regroup. That same evening, Amman ordered the remaining elements of the 27th

Infantry Brigade to reinforce Jerusalem, as the king had promised Haza'ah. Meanwhile, the second battalion of the 60th Armored Brigade also was finally approaching East Jerusalem after having been ordered to the Ramat Rachel area the day before. However, both Jordanian units were caught by Israeli airstrikes on the narrow roads through the Judaean hills. The armored battalion lost several tanks, and both columns were scattered and spent the night licking their wounds and regrouping.

Battles in Northern Samaria

In the northern West Bank, Jordanian plans and deployments were entirely defensive. Samaria was too large to be adequately defended by the three infantry brigades, one armored brigade, one armored battalion, and one infantry battalion assigned to it. The Jordanians hoped only to minimize the amount of territory Israel might take and to prevent the IDF from mounting a major drive either down the Jordan River Valley or along the Janin-Nablus-Ramallah axis. Consequently, Jordanian forces were deployed with the 25th Infantry Brigade and the main body of the 12th Independent Armored Battalion around Janin, the 1st Infantry Brigade defending Tulkarm and Qalqilyah, and the 6th Infantry and 40th Armored Brigades at the Damiyah bridge in the Jordan Valley.

The Jordanians had read Israeli intentions well. The Israelis planned to use an infantry brigade to demonstrate in the Bayt She'an Valley as if preparing to drive down the Jordan Valley. Meanwhile, another infantry brigade would attack from the coastal plain to drive the Jordanians back from Tulkarm and Qalqilyah. Finally, the main attack, comprising General Elad Peled's ugdah of an armored brigade, a mechanized brigade, and an infantry brigade from Israel's Northern Command, would drive south through Janin and on to Nablus. Thus, despite the size of the area to be covered, the Jordanian force was roughly equal to its Israeli counterpart and was perfectly deployed along the Israelis' primary axes of advance.

JANIN

At 5:00 P.M., the Israelis began their offensive against Janin. The IAF conducted airstrikes against Jordanian artillery positions in the Dotan Valley where Peled's three brigades crossed over into the West Bank. Peled positioned his armored brigade to the east of Janin and sent it southwest to hit the Janin-Tubas road well to the south. Meanwhile, the other two IDF brigades conducted a double envelopment of the town. Peled's infantry brigade deployed northeast of Janin and attacked southwestward, while his mechanized brigade burst through the thin Jordanian screening force northwest of town and began pushing southeast toward the main road in two battle groups. The commander of the Jordanian 25th Infantry Brigade at Janin, Brig. Gen. Awad Muhammad Khalidi, responded by forming up two battle groups of his own, each with infantry, antitank teams, and a company of M-47 Pattons, to block the two Israeli columns. Khalidi probably realized that his force was too small to hold the town against a determined Israeli assault. However, the elite 40th Armored Brigade was headed back north to Janin after spending the morning driving south to Jericho, and Khalidi probably hoped to delay the Israelis in the excellent defensive terrain north and west of town until the 40th Armored could arrive. Thus, both Jordanian task forces took up positions on ridges blocking the routes of advance of the two Israeli columns.

A battle group of the Israeli mechanized brigade hit one of the blocking forces at the northern end of the Dotan Valley. The Jordanians were deployed across the gap in three reinforcing lines, with their Pattons in the last line. Because there was no way to outflank these positions, the Israelis launched two frontal assaults, which the Jordanians beat back with losses both times. In addition to their strong defenses, Khalidi's men had an important advantage in that the Israelis had no weapons available that could defeat the dug-in Pattons. But the Israelis came up with a clever ruse and, at dawn on 6 June, began pulling back from their positions as if retreating. As the Israelis had hoped, the Jordanian commander assumed that the Israelis were running and seized the opportunity to finish them off. The Pattons charged without infantry support, only to have the Israelis turn and open fire. With the Jordanian tanks now out and in the open, the Israelis were able to maneuver for shots against their more vulnerable flanks and sides. As a result, the Jordanians lost eight of thirteen Pattons before pulling back.[49] The Israelis then retreated again, and the Jordanians again followed, only to have the Israelis turn on them once more and finish off the remaining tanks. With the Pattons gone, the Israeli Shermans and mechanized infantry resumed their attack on the Jordanian lines. Khalidi's infantry and antitank teams continued to fight back hard and were able to repulse the initial assault. However, the Israelis kept up the attack, and without armor support, the Jordanians could not hold back the Israeli combined-arms team.

The Israeli breakout in the Dotan Valley undermined the Jordanian defense of Janin. General Khalidi had only a small force left in the town itself, and the 40th Armored Brigade had not yet arrived. During the night of 5–6 June, Khalidi ordered his other task force to abandon its blocking position and pull back to Janin. This allowed the two Israeli mechanized task forces to link up again and assault the town from the south during the morning of 6 June. Meanwhile, the Israeli infantry brigade had pushed southeast, at which point it wheeled northwest and joined the assault on the rear of the Jordanian defenses. The Jordanian defenders fought back, and their infantry units gave the Israelis some trouble, but the complement of Pattons in the town were quickly dispatched by the more skillful Israeli Sherman crews. As a result, in less than thirty minutes, the Israelis had effectively taken the city. Just then, like the cavalry in a Hollywood Western, the main body of the 40th Armored Brigade arrived south of Janin.

THE BATTLE OF QABATIYAH CROSSROADS

The commander of the 40th Armored Brigade, Brig. Gen. Rakan al-Jazi, had been urging on his men all day so as to be able to counterattack the Israelis before they had penetrated too deeply into northern Samaria. Counterattacking an Israeli offensive against Janin had been al-Jazi's primary mission at the start of the war, his men had practiced and planned for it constantly, and he was determined to make it work. As the 40th Brigade drove back north on 5 June after its pointless detour to Jericho, al-Jazi detached two companies of tanks that, along with a company task force from the 12th Independent Armored Battalion, were to establish a blocking position on the Janin-Tubas road. Meanwhile, the bulk of the 40th Armored Brigade continued on to Janin.

Southeast of town, the 40th Armored Brigade ran into the reconnaissance company of the Israeli mechanized brigade. This force of AMX-13s, jeeps, and halftracks had been ordered to push on south of Janin and take up a blocking position at the Qabatiyah crossroads, where the Janin-Nablus and Janin-Tubas roads joined, while the rest of Peled's ugdah cleared the town. General al-Jazi sent part of his force directly against the Israeli unit and had another element loop around through the hills to the east to flank its positions. The Israelis were outnumbered, outgunned by the Jordanian M-48s, and outflanked. They lost several vehicles but were able to retreat back into a good defensive position from which they were able to hold off the Jordanians. Again al-Jazi divided his force, leaving part to finish off the Israeli reconnaissance company and taking the main body north against Janin. However, General Peled was aware of what was happening to the south, and he dispatched the Super Sherman battalion of his mechanized brigade down to aid the trapped company. Hearing the sounds of battle from the south and seeing the Israeli armor depart, the surviving Jordanian forces in Janin rallied and counterattacked. Although this was not much of a threat, it kept the Israeli infantry tied down there and prevented them from aiding their armor.

General al-Jazi learned from his scouts of the approach of the Israeli armor and ordered his force into hull-down positions along a ridge overlooking the road. The Israeli Super Shermans were low on fuel and ammunition but were determined to reach their trapped comrades. They came barreling down the road only to be hit full force by fifty to sixty Jordanian Pattons. In the battle that followed, the Israelis lost seventeen Super Shermans while knocking out only a handful of Pattons. The Shermans began to pull back, and al-Jazi ordered his forces to go after the Israelis and finish them off. But the Israelis called in artillery, which kept the Jordanians pinned to the ridge and allowed the Israelis to pull back and regroup. The Super Shermans tried another thrust down the road several hours later but were again mauled by the Jordanians and again had to call in artillery to prevent a pursuit. Late in the afternoon, the Israelis arranged for airstrikes against the main force of the 40th Armored Brigade. These attacks did not kill many Jordanian tanks, but they kept them pinned down and allowed a force of Super Shermans to get around al-Jazi's position and fight its way down to where the Israeli reconnaissance force was still holding out. The Israelis tanks surprised the Jordanians there and were able to get the remnants of the company out before falling back on Janin.[50]

Early the next morning, 7 June, the Israelis resumed their attack on the 40th Armored Brigade at Qabatiyah crossroads.[51] With the support of heavy airstrikes, the Israelis employed part of what was left of their mechanized brigade in a holding attack to pin the Jordanian armor to the ridgeline while another force, mostly from the Israeli infantry brigade, swung around the left flank of the Jordanian positions. In the daylight the Israeli airstrikes began to inflict heavier casualties on the Jordanians than they had the night before. In addition, al-Jazi's flank guard detected the Israeli maneuver, and the general decided to fall back rather than risk being enveloped. When the Jordanians pulled out of their dug-in positions and began to retreat, Israeli armor attacked, and IAF airstrikes were able to catch many Jordanian tanks in the open. Under the combined air and armor attacks, the 40th took heavy casualties and fell apart, with squads and platoons fleeing down the Nablus-Tubas road as best they could. The brigade seems to have lost about half its effective strength in the retreat from Qabatiyah crossroads.[52]

THE JANIN-TUBAS ROAD

As planned, during the night of 5 June, Peled's armored brigade struck out through the hills east of Janin and reached the Janin-Tubas road well south of town.[53] Remarkably, the Israeli armor hit the road only a short while after the main body of the 40th Armored Brigade had passed heading north to its encounter at Qabatiyah. The Israelis, however, turned south and headed for Tubas, and Nablus beyond. North of Tubas, the Israelis ran into a Jordanian antitank ambush, which inflicted some damage on their reconnaissance force probing ahead of the main column. The Jordanians failed to retreat once their ambush was tripped, so the Israelis pinned them down with artillery, called in airstrikes, and worked a combined force of tanks and dismounted infantry around their flank, routing the small force by this deft operation. Shortly thereafter, the Israelis ran into the battalion task force from the 40th Armored Brigade and the 12th Armored Battalion which al-Jazi had ordered to guard the Janin-Tubas road. The Jordanians had found an outstanding blocking position, where the road passed between dominating heights, that prevented any off-road movement. Unable to mount a flanking attack, the Israeli armor attempted a frontal assault. The Jordanians were well camouflaged and dug in on the overlooking hills, and their fire stopped the advance. However, because of the heavy armor of the Israeli Centurion tanks, the Jordanians destroyed only three of the IDF tanks. The Israelis fell back to regroup and then tried again late in the day, this time with air support. The airstrikes did little damage to the Jordanian tanks and again, the Pattons beat back the Israeli charge with some minor losses.

The Israeli commander recognized that he was never going to bull his way through the Jordanian roadblock—the terrain was too difficult and the Jordanians were not going to be scared off. So instead he waited until 1:00 A.M. on 7 June and then made a sudden rush with his Centurions at the same moment his artillery battalion let loose on the Jordanian positions. As the Israelis had hoped, many of the enemy crewmen were asleep and were jolted by the sudden onslaught. Some of the crews fled, while others had difficulty reacting to the sudden Israeli assault, allowing the lead Centurions to get in among the Pattons and bust them up before they could effectively fight back. Surprised, disoriented, and with the Israelis seemingly all around them, the Jordanians mostly bolted; the few tanks and infantry units that remained were quickly dispatched. After regrouping on the objective, the Israelis set out in pursuit of the fleeing Jordanians, but the superior road speed of the Patton over the Centurion allowed them to outrun their pursuers. Close to dawn, however, the IAF caught the Jordanian units fleeing down the Tubas-Nablus road and destroyed a number of Pattons and M-113s on the road.[54]

The Jordanians made their last stand in Nablus. There, remnants of the 12th Independent Armored Battalion, the 40th Armored Brigade, and tanks and infantry from various other formations throughout the West

Bank regrouped after having lost their original positions or having had their parent formations scattered by air attacks. The Jordanians established a blocking position east of Nablus to guard the way into the Jordan Valley and the Damiyah and Allenby bridges. The Israelis took Nablus unopposed and then sent the reconnaissance company of Peled's armored brigade east to scout the descent to the Jordan. There, the Israeli AMX-13s ran into the Jordanian blocking force of roughly twenty-five Pattons. Seeing that he had an advantage in both numbers and tank quality, the Jordanian commander attacked. The Israelis did not panic or run but coolly took up hull-down positions from which they were able to hold back the Pattons. Then they called in airstrikes. The IAF arrived quickly and routed the Jordanians, who were exhausted and demoralized from their previous battles. The Israeli light tanks gave chase and were able to get excellent shots on the vulnerable rears of the Pattons as they retreated. Between the airstrikes and the tank fire, nearly the entire Jordanian force was obliterated.

The Jordanians Retreat

As early as the afternoon of 6 June, the situation looked bleak to Amman. The Jordanian air force lay in ruins. Latrun had fallen quickly and easily. The 1st "Princess Aliyah" Infantry Brigade holding Qalqilyah and Tulkarm had collapsed when it was attacked earlier that day by an Israeli infantry brigade. In Jerusalem the fortified positions at Ammunition Hill, Shaykh Jarrah, and Mivtar Hill had all fallen to Israeli armor and paratroopers, while in the southern part of the city, Abu Tor and Mount Zion had been captured by the Etzioni Brigade. The Old City was nearly surrounded, and its only link to the Jordanian rear was east over the Augusta-Victoria Ridge to the Jericho road. Janin had fallen, and (at that moment) only the 40th Armored Brigade, entrenched at Qabatiyah crossroads, was having any success in holding back the Israelis. Moreover, the IAF was making a coordinated defense of the West Bank impossible. Israeli aircraft roamed across the Jordan Valley, destroying military traffic on both banks. They had disrupted and decimated elements of the 27th Infantry Brigade as well as a battalion of the 60th Armored Brigade as that unit moved to reinforce Jerusalem. Likewise, the IAF had beaten up the 6th "Qadisiyah" Infantry Brigade as it moved south toward Jerusalem. Thus, while the Jerusalem-Jericho road was still in Jordanian hands, in effect, it had been cut by Israeli air power.

Moreover, the Jordanian General Staff in Amman believed the West Bank situation was even worse than was actually the case because of exaggerations and misreporting by their tactical commanders in the field.[55]

Almost across the board, Jordanian officers exaggerated the size of the Israeli forces that were attacking them, the size and number of airstrikes they were facing, and the losses they were taking. No less an authority than Samir Mutawi has observed: "Another element that helped create this sense of defeat were the exaggerated reports sent to the GHQ by Jordanian commanders at the front. These emphasized the tremendous losses the Jordanians were sustaining and the odds against which they fought. This resulted in an inflated assessment of Jordanian losses and was one of the factors which led the GHQ command to conclude that they stood no chance of maintaining control of the area and that they faced the stark choice of putting up a hopeless defence or a retreat in which no more lives would be lost than necessary."[56] Based on these reports, the Jordanian high command had begun to believe as early as the evening of 5 June that the West Bank was lost. Indeed, reports from Jordanian field commanders were so alarmist that the general staff concluded the army was losing strength at the rate of one tank every ten minutes.[57]

Nor was help from other Arab states forthcoming. Before the beginning of the conflict, Egypt, Syria, Saudi Arabia, and Iraq had promised Jordan reinforcements in the event of war. The Egyptians had sent only two commando battalions, which tried to infiltrate into Israel to sabotage roads, airports, and military facilities, but their attacks fizzled, and they were nearly all rounded up by the Israelis. Iraq had dispatched the 8th Motorized Infantry Brigade, probably as the vanguard of a larger force, but the IAF had caught it on the open road in eastern Jordan and had hammered it for most of an afternoon. The Saudi brigade was late in arriving, and from Syria there was nothing except encouragement.

The straw that broke the camel's back for the Jordanians was the final realization during the afternoon of 6 June that the Egyptian military had been destroyed and, therefore, no help could be expected from that quarter. King Hussein and General Riyad then agreed to order a general retreat from the West Bank to try to regroup their forces on the east side of the Jordan and mount a defense of Amman. The king issued this retreat order around 10:00 P.M. on 6 June. However, within minutes, the United Nations issued its own call for a ceasefire. Reasoning that a UN ceasefire would be observed along the lines of currently occupied territory, the king instructed General Riyad to rescind the retreat and instead order Jordanian troops to return to their positions and hang on until the ceasefire took effect. But the Israelis had no interest in a ceasefire and ignored it. This proved to be the nail in the coffin for Jordan's defense of the West Bank. Some Jordanian units did not receive Riyad's countermanding order at all.

Others had long since been routed by the Israelis and were fleeing back to the Jordan River bridges. A number of other units, however, had begun to retreat on the king's initial order only to be told to return to their positions an hour or two later. By that point the Israelis had overrun their former positions, and several Jordanian units were badly bloodied launching frontal assaults to try to retake the trenches they had just abandoned.

By the morning of 7 June, the West Bank was lost. Jordanian units were in full retreat everywhere as a result either of defeat at the hands of the Israelis or the king's announcement. The only exceptions were the various units in northern Samaria under General al-Jazi's control, which were only defeated and destroyed by Israeli armor and air forces later that day. Jordanian units streamed down to the Jordan River bridges with Israeli units close on their heels. In addition, the IAF constantly pounded the retreating units. Some Jordanian formations, such as the remnants of the 3d Brigade in Jerusalem, retreated skillfully, while others, such as the 1st and 29th Infantry Brigades and the 10th Independent Armored Battalion, fell all over themselves and abandoned most of their heavy weapons in a mad dash to get across the river. At noon, the king ordered an unequivocal withdrawal of all Jordanian forces from the West Bank. Finally at 8:00 P.M., he agreed to a UN-sponsored ceasefire, which Tel Aviv also accepted.

In the final reckoning, the Jordanians lost heavily, but the Israelis did not go unscathed in their victory. Jordan suffered 6,000–7,000 soldiers killed and probably another 12,000–20,000 wounded. In addition, Amman lost at least 200 tanks — more than 50 of which were simply abandoned during the retreat — and at least 150 artillery pieces. The Israelis had 302 men killed and 1,453 wounded and lost about 100 tanks — although unlike the Jordanians, the Israelis were able to repair many of these and return them to battle.[58]

Jordanian Military Effectiveness during the Six Day War

The Jordan Arab Army probably fought best of all the Arab armies that participated in the Six Day War, but not by much. Despite a roughly equal balance of forces in manpower and equipment, the Jordanians still suffered ten times more casualties than the Israelis. In general, Jordanian combat performance was uneven, perhaps even odd. A handful of units fought extremely well, but the vast majority fought poorly. In addition, some aspects of military operations the entire army performed poorly, but the army handled others rather well.

The comparison with Jordanian performance in 1948 is striking. At one level, the Israelis had certain advantages in 1967 that they did not have in

1948 and that mitigate the extent of the Jordanian failures in 1967. In particular, Israel did not have undisputed air superiority and an extremely capable air force in 1948. However, an equal number of factors were essentially equivalent in both wars, and other differences should have aided the Jordanians in 1967. The numerical balance was about even in both conflicts and, if anything, Israel's numerical superiority was greater in 1948 than in 1967. Jordan was defending the excellent defensive terrain of the West Bank both times. Israel was forced to divide its troops among several fronts in both conflicts, but in 1967 the Sinai was clearly Israel's highest priority, while in 1948 the Arab Legion was probably considered Israel's greatest opponent and therefore commanded the lion's share of Israeli assets. The quality of equipment on the two sides still favored Jordan in 1967, perhaps to a lesser extent than in 1948, though even then the gap in arsenals was not so great as to have been decisive.

Weighing all of these factors, Jordanian forces still performed significantly worse in 1967 than in 1948. In the Six Day War, its generalship was probably adequate, but at a tactical level, only a few Jordanian units were even in the same league as the Israelis. Ultimately, in 1948 a small British colonial army defending excellent terrain succeeded in holding off the attacks of a poorly trained, poorly armed, and poorly organized militia army for several months. In 1967, when that same Jordanian army in the same terrain, but without its British officers, met a well-trained, well-organized, and adequately armed professional military, they were blown away in less than three days.

STRATEGIC PERFORMANCE

Jordanian strategic leadership was decent in most areas but suffered from a few crucial flaws. Jordan's plan for the defense of the West Bank had some strengths and some weaknesses, but the positives probably outnumbered the negatives. On the one hand, Amman presciently recognized it could not hold the whole West Bank against a major Israeli offensive. The idea of trading off West Jerusalem for any Israeli gains was at least a reasonable approach, and Operation Tariq — the plan to realize that strategy — appears plausible on paper. More important than this, however, the Jordanian General Staff correctly anticipated the broad outlines of what an Israeli invasion would look like, allowing them to plan against this attack. Consequently, Jordanian forces were well deployed to counter Israel's strategy.

On the other hand, with the exception of Jerusalem and the adjacent corridor, the Jordanians had not bothered to build fixed fortifications across anticipated key axes of advance. To throw up one's hands and claim that there were too many of them — as the Jordanians apparently did — is not only irresponsible but wrong.[59] If the general staff could correctly identify the likely Israeli attack corridors and deploy forces there, why not fortify them as well? Moreover, in some places the defenses the Jordanians did build were haphazard and did not prove to be very formidable, suggesting a lack of attention on the part of the high command.[60] Although it is unfair to hold the general staff responsible for the decision to employ a forward defense of the entire perimeter of the West Bank, for this was a political decision, even within this framework some of Jordan's deployments were questionable and led to problems during the war. In particular, since the 27th Infantry Brigade was intended to be used in Operation Tariq — which was supposed to kick off before Israel could attack — why was the brigade not stationed closer to Jerusalem? By positioning it near Jericho, Amman had to get the brigade moving early and, thus, left it vulnerable to Israeli air interdiction, which was exactly what happened: when the 27th Infantry Brigade was ordered to reinforce Jerusalem, it was battered by airstrikes, and some elements never reached the city. Such problems would have been eliminated by garrisoning it there from the start. Nor was there another mission for which the brigade would have been better deployed in reserve: it was to participate in Operation Tariq or else defend Jerusalem if the Israelis were able to attack first. It seems likely that the Jordanians kept the 27th back for other reasons — possibly related to internal security. If this were the case, they still could have started moving it forward during the crisis period before the outbreak of hostilities. King Hussein had committed himself to war with Israel, thus there should have been no diplomatic reason to hold it back at that time. Finally, one must add that Jordanian air force planning for war with Israel was inexcusable. Intelligence and targeting information for the raids the RJAF conducted on 5 June were nonexistent, and even though the Jordanians attacked first, they made no effort to disperse their planes, suggesting Amman's air force commanders had never seriously thought through a war with Israel.

It is hard to make a judgment one way or another regarding the strategic direction of Jordanian operations during the course of the fighting itself, although the common wisdom is that it was poor. In particular, many commentators, especially Jordanian military officers, have criticized the decision to redeploy the two armored brigades at the beginning of the war. I am not convinced that this was such a mistake. The problem was that the Jordanians had only one force available to execute Operation Tariq — the 60th Armored Brigade — which was also the only unit that could mount a rapid advance into the Negev to link up with an Egyptian offensive. With

20/20 hindsight, there was no Egyptian drive into Israel; thus executing Operation Tariq would have been the better move for the Jordanians. However, no one in Amman knew that at the time, and there was no reason to suspect it was untrue. The Egyptian army was very large and considered by the Arabs to be very formidable, and it was reasonable at the time to believe that it could have repulsed an Israeli attack and then mounted a counteroffensive into the Negev.

This being the case, the real question is whether the Jordanians should have executed Operation Tariq and left the Egyptians to fend for themselves or sacrificed their own plans in an attempt to win a more convincing victory in conjunction with their allies. This question is a toss-up. Operation Tariq essentially was a "go-it-alone" strategy in which Jordan attempted to solve its own strategic problems in the belief that it would get no outside help. Clearly, seizing West Jerusalem in the hope they could trade it for whatever the Israelis conquered was not an ideal strategy, and the Jordanians only opted for it because they believed they could not prevent the Israelis from making *some* gains. In short, Operation Tariq was not Amman's preferred strategy — it was the only course of action the Jordanians felt had any chance of working. If there had been an Egyptian drive into the Sinai, it seems reasonable for the Jordanians to have jettisoned Operation Tariq and instead bet on a war-winning strategy by cooperating with Egypt. Had there been an Egyptian invasion, and had Jordan contributed a drive southwest toward Bethlehem to complement it, the Arabs would have put Israel in an extremely tight situation and might have defeated the IDF altogether. This seems ludicrous now, but it was not so hard to believe on 5 June 1967. Ultimately, to judge between the two options is nearly impossible, and so one should not find fault with the decision to commit 60th Armored Brigade to the Negev attack.

Once Amman had decided to redeploy the two armored brigades to aid the mythical Egyptian offensive, most of its moves were quite good. Thereafter, most of the actions the GHQ ordered were designed to block the major Israeli thrusts against Jerusalem and Janin. First, they ordered the attacks on Jebel Mukhaber and Mount Scopus to improve the army's tactical position within the city. When it became clear that the Egyptian drive into the Negev was a lie, they ordered both armored brigades to return to their positions in reserve. When the Israeli attack began, the generals ordered the 60th Armored Brigade and the 27th Infantry Brigade to reinforce Jerusalem. Specifically, to counter the Israeli attacks both south (at Jebel Mukhaber, really an Israeli counterattack) and north (along the Jerusalem corridor) of the city, they ordered the 60th Armored brigade to detach a battalion to aid the units to the south, while the main body hit the Israeli mechanized force to the north. After that, the GHQ tried to move the 6th Infantry Brigade south from northern Samaria to reinforce Jerusalem. When it became clear that the absence of a division-level command was hindering this defense, they made Brigadier General Haza'ah overall commander of the forces in and around the city. When the Israelis attacked Janin, Amman ordered the 40th Armored Brigade to counterattack to seal the breach. Finally, when the defense of the West Bank clearly was doomed, they ordered a retreat. In every one of these decisions, the Jordanian General Staff made a reasonable, or even a very good, move.

One problem was that these orders usually came just a bit too late. Overall, the Jordanian high command mostly reacted to Israeli moves, often too late, rather than anticipating them. Consequently, reinforcements always arrived — if they arrived — *after* the crucial issue had already been decided. In general, Jordan's command-and-control system proved slow and inflexible, unable to keep pace with the rapidity of the Israeli thrusts.[61] In addition, there were several actions taken by the general staff during the war that should have been made before the outbreak of fighting. In particular, divisional formations should have been established before war began. If King Hussein was afraid of permanent division commanders, then why not have provisional ones ordered to coordinate operations only in wartime? Also, the preparatory moves for Operation Tariq should have begun on 3 or 4 June, when Jordan received warning of the imminent Israeli attack on Egypt. This was pure negligence on the part of Amman: one cannot argue that the Jordanians were trying to avoid provoking Israel because, in the preceding weeks, the Jordanians had already redeployed four brigades to the West Bank in anticipation of a conflict with Israel, and redeploying two from Jericho to Jerusalem would have been less provocative than this substantial reinforcement.

Of course, the Jordanian high command cannot take all the blame for this sluggishness. A large part of the problem was the inadequacy and inaccuracy of the information available to them. Jordanian intelligence had done a very poor job before the war of gaining information on Israel's order of battle, military facilities, doctrine, and concept of operations.[62] In addition, between the utter lies passed on by the Egyptians, disinformation from Israeli electronic warfare operations, and the barrage of obfuscation and deception from Jordanian field commanders, Amman never really understood its situation until it was too late. For the most part, the general staff fought the war in a fog. Only occasionally did they get a glimpse of reality when one of their own sources could observe part of the battlefield or, in those rare instances, when a field commander actually sent back an objective report. Finally, Amman also suffered from its inefficient command-and-control system. Because the western-front commander had direct responsibility for nine brigades and three to four independent battalions plus all of the support assets on the West Bank, his staff was overburdened with reports and requests for orders. Consequently, it was often the case that he and his staff had to neglect one sector to deal with another problem, which only created a problem in the first sector because of their inattention.

One last issue that needs to be addressed regarding Jordanian strategic leadership is the role of General Riyad. Many Jordanians and their apologists have made General Riyad the scapegoat for the entire war.[63] They claim that he was incompetent and rigid in his thinking, that he disregarded the advice of the Jordanian high command, that he failed to have the king approve his actions, and that he slavishly followed the orders of General 'Amr in Cairo, who had no idea what was happening on the West Bank and only cared about Egypt. By all evidence, only the last point regarding 'Amr's priorities is a valid criticism. First, all Egyptian, Western, and Israeli appraisals of General Riyad give him high marks, and the changes Riyad set in motion when he was made chief of staff of the Egyptian armed forces after the Six Day War were excellent and laid the groundwork for Egypt's success in the canal-crossing operation of October 1973.[64] In fact, the Egyptians believed Riyad to be their best field commander, and Nasser had chosen him to plan and lead the war effort that eventually became the October War, although Riyad was killed by Israeli artillery before he could play his appointed role.[65] Gen. Yitzahk Rabin, chief of staff of the IDF during the Six Day War, said of Riyad, "he was very good, one of the best the Egyptians had."[66] Second, both Trevor Dupuy and King Hussein argue that while Riyad had final say in most strategic debates, he did not ignore the advice of Jordanian generals. Indeed, based on his interviews in Jordan after the war, Dupuy contends that it was Riyad who was "out of the loop" and that the Jordanian hierarchy functioned as before, "with only perfunctory consultation with the Egyptian General."[67] According to King Hussein himself, Riyad conferred with him on all major decisions, and there is no instance when any author has been able to point to a decision regarding Jordanian actions during the war with which the king disagreed.[68] Whether it was Riyad who made the decisions or the Jordanian generals as Dupuy concludes, the king approved all key decisions — in his own words: "It's quite true that I was present at all Riad's [sic] decisions. I even helped with some of them. Riad wanted my approval of those he considered most important."[69]

While it may have been the case that Riyad paid more attention to Cairo than his Jordanian subordinates did, this is not necessarily a fault. Riyad was sent to Amman as the eastern-front commander of the UAC. In other words, his brief was specifically to ensure the coordination of the Arab forces, and whether he put Egypt first or not, he seems to have done this. As noted above, his decision to send 60th Armored Brigade south — the order that seems to have most angered Jordan's generals — might have been the best move for all of the Arab states had it been the case that the Egyptian army was driving into the Negev as 'Amr claimed, and Riyad had no reason to believe that 'Amr was deliberately lying to him. If the Egyptian army really had been driving into the Negev, then sticking to the "Jordan first" strategy embodied in Operation Tariq might have allowed Israel to scrape together enough forces to defeat the Egyptians and then turn on the Jordanians. In that case, today it would be the Egyptians chastising the Jordanians for losing the war for the entire Arab cause — and the Egyptians would be right to say so. Again, the point is that Riyad's decision was a reasonable move: it was an honest mistake, not an unconscionable blunder. While this decision clearly was detrimental to Jordan's fight against Israel, it was not necessarily a sign of incompetent generalship.

TACTICAL PERFORMANCE

In contrast to their strategic leadership, the tactical proficiency of Jordanian forces showed a marked decline from 1948. Their tactical performance, however, was not *uniformly* poor. Some aspects of military operations the entire Jordanian armed forces continued to demonstrate a high degree of competence across the board. In addition, a small number of units were reasonably effective in a wide range of combat operations.

On the positive side, Jordanian forces continued to demonstrate first-rate soldiering skills. As individual soldiers and pilots, the Jordanians remained quite good and generally did everything that could be expected of them. The soldiers were mostly brave and well disciplined, despite certain important exceptions such as the panicky retreat of the company of Pattons from the 60th Armored Brigade at Tel al-Ful and the disintegration of the Jordanian units holding Radar Hill and the surrounding ridgeline. Jordanian marksmanship was generally quite good, although there was variance: the infantrymen were superb with their small arms and mortars, but Jordanian tank and artillery crews were not as good with their weapons.

Likewise, based on the very limited information available, Jordanian pilots seem to have been fairly proficient in handling their aircraft in air-to-air engagements but did not demonstrate much skill in their lone air-to-ground operation.[70]

Jordanian unit cohesion ran the gamut. In some cases their units hung together and continued to fight on in tremendously difficult, even hopeless, situations. The 40th Armored Brigade and the Jordanian infantry units defending Ammunition Hill, Mivtar Hill, Abu Tor, and Janin, stand out in particular. But a number of Jordanian formations fell apart after only slight pressure from the Israelis. For instance, the 1st and 2d Infantry Brigades, defending Tulkarm-Qalqilyah and Latrun respectively, both collapsed and ran or surrendered en masse long before their battles had been decided. And while the 40th Armored Brigade and other units conducted a first-rate fighting withdrawal after Amman ordered a general retreat from the West Bank, the 29th Infantry Brigade and the 10th Armored Battalion in Judaea, among others, fell apart and bolted, abandoning much of their heavy weaponry when they received the retreat order. Although in some cases Jordanian officers deserted their units, this did not correlate with poor unit cohesion: as many Jordanian units appear to have stuck together and fought on after their officers fled as disintegrated. Although it is impossible to be certain, there appears to be some correlation between unit cohesion and whether the unit was Bedouin or Hadari. The 40th Armored Brigade and the 3d Infantry Brigade were both Bedouin units, and they showed excellent unit cohesion, while the 1st Infantry Brigade was Hadari, and it disintegrated with the first Israeli probes. Unfortunately, it is hard to push this correlation much further because little information exists as to the composition of other Jordanian brigades.

Jordanian tactical performance really fell down at the unit level. Once Jordanian formations got beyond squad or maybe platoon level, their problems suddenly became overwhelming. As Abraham Rabinovich has observed: "The bravery of the Jordanian soldiers on Ammunition Hill and elsewhere along the city line would save Jordanian honor, but not the reputation of its arms. Bereft of its British officers and with its tough Bedouin core of regulars diluted with urban elements and reserves, the once-formidable Arab Legion had become an army much like the other Arab armies Israel knew. Fratkin's report to Gen. Mordechai Gur from Nablus road that the enemy seemed incapable of executing even platoon movements summarized the situation in most sectors. Only in their deadly accurate mortar fire and in squad-level infantry encounters did the Jordanians prove effective."[71]

For the most part, these problems were failures in leadership. It was not necessarily that Jordanian soldiers were unable to work together, but rather their officers had difficulty coordinating and directing the action of the forces under their command. Jordan's junior officers showed little imagination, adaptability, or initiative. The quintessential pattern of Jordanian combat performance was for a unit to put up a hail of deadly fire against an Israeli frontal assault, but as soon as the enemy had penetrated their lines and began clearing their fortified positions, the Jordanians would be unable to respond. On occasion, the Jordanians organized small counterattacks that were launched much too late to make a difference. More often than not, their officers failed to counterattack altogether. Instead, they remained in their defensive positions, making no move to reorient their forces or otherwise counter the Israeli penetrations. Thus, even at battles such as Ammunition Hill, the Jordanians decimated the Israeli paratroopers as they made their frontal assault against the defensive lines, but once the Israelis had broken through and could begin to work their way down the trench-lines from the flanks, the battle was effectively over because the Jordanians would not shift their forces or counterattack to block or seal the Israeli penetration. Similarly, the official U.S. survey team found that the over-whelming majority of Jordanian tanks destroyed by the Israelis were killed by flank shots rather than frontal shots, indicating that the Israelis successfully outmaneuvered the Jordanians time and again.[72]

The kingdom's forces experienced all sorts of problems whenever presented with unexpected situations or fluid battles. According to Samir Mutawi, Jordanian operations on the West Bank in 1967 were characterized by "confusion and panic" largely because the Jordanians were surprised by the speed and strength of the Israeli advance and were forced to try to conduct operations for which they were unprepared.[73] Combined-arms coordination was fine as long as the Jordanians were defending established positions, but when the battle turned fluid, this too fell apart. For example, in the Dotan Valley, while the IDF was attacking the prepared defensive lines, Jordanian infantry, antitank teams, artillery, and armor worked well together and stopped the Israelis cold. As soon as the Israelis feigned a retreat, however, the Pattons dashed off after them unsupported, giving the Super Shermans the chance to butcher them in tank duels and then turn on the Jordanian infantry. The army's artillery support was unable to keep up with the rapid Israeli advance through the West Bank. Even in Jerusalem, where the Jordanians had had nineteen years to preplan fire missions, their artillery could not provide timely support when the Israelis took unorthodox or unforeseen actions. Jordanian armor performed adequately at best. Israeli

Super Shermans and even Shermans consistently outfought Jordanian Pattons in battle. The 60th Armored Brigade should have demolished the Israeli 10th Mechanized Brigade based solely on numbers and types of equipment, but instead it was outfought and driven off rather easily. Likewise, once the Israeli mechanized force near Janin had duped the 12th Armored Battalion's tanks out of their defensive positions and could engage them in a "fair" fight in the Dotan Valley, the Israelis smashed them.

One major exception to these patterns of tactical performance was the 40th Armored Brigade. This unit fought far better than any other Jordanian formation. Two qualifiers must be added to this statement, however. First, the 40th appears to have fought no better than average Israeli units and probably somewhat worse. After all, at Qabatiyah crossroads they outnumbered the Israelis by at least two to one, had M-48s against the Israeli Super Shermans, and were defending excellent terrain. The Israelis launched two frontal assaults and were stopped cold, which is exactly what should have happened, given the various Jordanian advantages. On the Janin-Tubas road, the 40th Armored Brigade elements were defending an almost impregnable position. Again the Israelis conducted two frontal assaults, and in this case the Jordanians actually did very little damage to the Israelis mostly because the Israeli force was about equal in tank strength to the Jordanian detachment (although the narrow roadway constrained their ability to employ their entire force) and they were using more-heavily-armored Centurions.

The second qualifier is that the 40th Armored Brigade was the exception that proved the rule. General al-Jazi was an exceptional officer: every Jordanian, Western, and Israeli account notes that he was head and shoulders above other Jordanian commanders in his aggressiveness and tactical skills. The 40th performed well when it was under his direct control. At Qabatiyah crossroads, the Jordanians used fire and maneuver to envelop the Israeli reconnaissance force. When this force had been cornered, al-Jazi broke off the main body of the brigade and sent it north to deal with the major task, defending Janin. He deployed an advance guard that warned of the approaching Israeli tanks, at which point he quickly deployed his forces in hull-down positions on a wooded ridge perfectly sited to hold the road. When the Israelis attacked, the 40th Brigade beat them back, and then al-Jazi attempted to pursue and finish off the fleeing Super Shermans only to be halted by Israeli artillery. Finally, when it was clear that his forces were being outflanked and their position was untenable, he retreated rather than be surrounded and destroyed. Compare this first-rate performance to that turned in by the battalion of the 40th on the Tubas-Janin road, where it was surprised by the Israelis at night and then quickly outfought and driven off by the Israeli Centurions despite the strength of its position. Thus, without al-Jazi's direct control, even units of the 40th Armored Brigade did poorly. The other Jordanian brigades could not even approach this performance.

ISRAELI LOSSES AND JORDANIAN PROWESS

Many authors, both Jordanian and Israeli, have cited Israeli casualty figures as a means of demonstrating the clear superiority of the Arab Legion over other Arab armies during the Six Day War. While the discussion above should make it clear that the Jordanians *were* better than other Arab armies in a number of important respects, this is not necessarily demonstrated by the casualty figures. Moreover, Jordan's proficiency over its allies was not as a great as the casualty figures suggest. Israeli losses on the Jordanian front primarily reflect the prevalence of infantry combat in built-up terrain in this theater — as well as some questionable tactical decisions by the Israelis — rather than a high-degree of Jordanian skill.

During the Six Day War, the Israelis took almost half of all their casualties fighting Jordan. They suffered 812 killed and 3,053 wounded during the war, of which 302 of the dead and 1,453 of the wounded fell to Jordanian forces.[74] However, most of these losses came in the fighting in and around Jerusalem, where the Israelis had 195 killed and 1,131 wounded.[75] House-to-house combat in urban terrain is inherently very difficult and very costly in terms of casualties. It does not take skilled troops to hide in doorways, in windows, and on rooftops and snipe at attacking forces. Indeed, the best armies try to avoid combat in cities because the built-up terrain is seen as an equalizing factor, eliminating the advantages of greater proficiency. Moreover, the fighting in Jerusalem was particularly bloody for the Israelis because they conducted a number of frontal assaults against heavily fortified Jordanian positions. These attacks were extremely costly. For example, at Ammunition Hill alone, one Israeli paratrooper company of 80 men had 17 killed and 42 wounded, while another company had 35 dead.[76] Conversely, in the battles elsewhere in the West Bank during 1967, Jordanian forces actually inflicted relatively few casualties on the Israelis.[77]

THE CONTRIBUTION OF ISRAELI AIR POWER

The Israeli Air Force had an important role in the fighting in the West Bank during the Six Day War. Nevertheless, the IAF influence on the campaign has still been exaggerated. Many Jordanians have tended to blame their loss in 1967 almost solely on the destruction of the RJAF on 5 June and the subsequent Israeli airstrikes on Jordanian ground forces. For example, immediately after the war, King Hussein himself claimed, "The battle was waged against us almost exclusively from the air with overwhelming strength and continual, sustained air attacks on every single unit of our armed forces, day and night."[78] In Jordanian accounts of the war, the IAF has grown into a *deus ex machina* — sometimes even including broad hints that the Israelis were actively aided by the United States — thus absolving the army for its defeat.[79] These sources frequently assert that Israeli airstrikes decided particular battles when Israeli and Western sources convincingly demonstrate that the IAF did not participate at all. For example, even Samir Mutawi, Jordan's most insightful and objective commentator on the war, claims that one reason the Israelis eventually prevailed at Ammunition Hill was because of airstrikes. However, all of the Israeli accounts, including those of Generals Narkiss (the front commander) and Gur (the commander of the 55th Paratroop Brigade), point out that there was a major debate among the Israeli commanders as to whether to launch the attack at night without air cover or wait until morning when the IAF could participate. Ultimately, Narkiss and Gur decided to launch the attack at night, against the judgment of the Israeli General Staff, and therefore, no IAF aircraft participated in the battle at all.[80]

There are many other instances of this phenomenon, particularly for battles on 5 June, when Jordanian sources claim their troops "were subjected to [air] attack almost every time they moved."[81] Yet the Israelis conducted only 95 ground-attack sorties against Jordan on 5 June.[82] Of these, 42 struck targets in the Jordan Valley, while only 32 struck targets in the key combat zones around Jerusalem and Janin.[83] An army of 45,000 men should have been able to shrug off even 95 highly proficient air-to-ground sorties with little strain. And since the bulk of Jordanian combat power was deployed around Jerusalem and Janin, it is almost unimaginable that 32 ground-attack sorties could have somehow proven decisive against them (see chap. 1, table 1).

Indeed, the IAF actually conducted relatively few ground-attack sorties against the Jordanians. Altogether, the air force flew only 549 ground-attack sorties against the Arab Legion during the entire war. This is fewer than the sorties flown against either Egypt or Syria. On no day during the war did the Israelis devote the bulk of their air-to-ground effort against Jordanian forces. Moreover, the greatest number of ground-attack sorties were flown on 7 June, when the battle for the West Bank had already been decided.[84] Thus, the contention is that the 316 ground-attack sorties the IAF flew on 5 and 6 June were decisive, constituting the "continual, sustained air attacks on every single unit of our armed forces, day and night," that won the war for Israel. This seems far-fetched to say the least.

The damage inflicted by these airstrikes has also been overstated. The official U.S. military survey team sent to Israel after the Six Day War to collect data for U.S. planners concluded that the role of the IAF in the Israeli victory had been greatly exaggerated. After examining in detail a sample of 40 percent of all the tanks (Israeli and all Arab armies) destroyed in the fighting, they concluded that airstrikes had been only a minor cause of damage to armor. They found that the 20- and 30-mm cannons that were the primary ground-attack weapon on Israeli aircraft did "uniformly slight damage" to Arab armor. Only 8 percent of the Arab tanks were even hit by aerial munitions of any kind, and less than 3 percent were actually destroyed by Israeli aerial munitions. The survey team concluded, "This type of data tends to refute the contention that the Israeli Air Force was directly responsible for the damage to the majority of the Arab tanks and shows conclusively that ground weapons were, in fact, responsible for practically all damage to tanks under the strategical, tactical, terrain, and weather conditions of the June 1967 war."[85]

Although the IAF made an important contribution to Israel's campaign on the West Bank, it was not the decisive factor in the conflict. Had the IAF not been able to participate in the campaign against Jordan, Israeli casualties would undoubtedly have been higher and it would have taken Israel longer to complete the operation, but the available evidence indicates the Israelis still would have won, probably quite handily. Jordanian tactical performance was sufficiently poor so that there is little reason to believe they could have defeated the Israelis even without IAF participation. At Latrun, Radar Hill, and throughout Jerusalem, Jordanian units were only capable of fighting from their fixed defenses, and once the course of battle changed, they were incapable of adapting. Thus, as soon as the Israelis had penetrated Jordanian lines, the fight was effectively over because the Jordanians would not shift their forces or counterattack to prevent the Israelis from clearing their positions. In his memoirs, General Narkiss notes that the 10th Mechanized Brigade's attack up the ridge of the Jerusalem corridor should have been suicidal, but because Jordanian resistance was incompetent, it turned into an Israeli victory.[86] Jordan's armored formations did little better than the infantry: The M-48 battalion of the 60th Armored Brigade was easily defeated by a smaller force of Shermans (not even Super Shermans). The 12th Armored Battalion was beaten up by Israeli armor whenever the odds were close to even and the unit was not defending an impregnable position.

Even the 40th Armored Brigade only performed competently when under the direct control of its outstanding brigade commander.[87]

Given these problems, it is hard to believe that the absence of the IAF would have somehow transformed the situation. There were several instances where IAF intervention had a major *and direct* effect on the course of operations, but in each of these cases, had the air force not intervened, there is no reason to believe the Israelis would not still have won the war — just not as quickly or easily. In particular, the IAF interdicted many Jordanian attempts to reinforce Jerusalem, preventing elements of 60th Armored Brigade and 27th Infantry Brigade and the entire 6th Infantry Brigade, from reaching the city on 6 June. However, had those units been able to join that battle, there is nothing to suggest they would have dramatically altered the outcome of the fighting. Even if they had been able to arrive around midday on 6 June, Abu Tor, Tel al-Ful, and Ammunition Hill– Shaykh Jarrah all would have fallen already and the Jordanian defense of the city would have already been unhinged. Nor is there reason to believe that these units would have fought better than the Jordanian forces that actually were there and thus been able to counterattack, drive back the Israelis, and reform a coherent defense of East Jerusalem. Obviously, the additional forces would have delayed Israel's advance, if only because it might have taken a day or more to defeat them, but this probably would not have made much difference in the end. Israel consistently rejected UN and superpower pressure for a ceasefire, further suggesting that an extra day or two to complete the conquest of the West Bank would not have radically altered the outcome of the war.

Similarly, while the absence of the IAF might have allowed the 40th Armored Brigade either to hold its position at Qabatiyah crossroads or to fall back to a more defensible position farther south, this likely would still have proven irrelevant. One capable Jordanian brigade was not going to stop the Israeli conquest of the West Bank. Moreover, Peled's armored brigade had already bypassed the 40th and was in the Jordanian rear on its way to Tubas. Had the 40th not been forced back and then mauled by the combination of Israeli armor and airstrikes, Tel Aviv could just as easily have brought Peled's armored brigade back north along the Janin-Tubas road and crushed the Jordanian brigade between it and the Israeli units around Janin.

Overall, the IAF played a major role in the conquest of the West Bank but was not the decisive element in the defeat of the Jordanian army. Israeli air power eliminated the RJAF, thus allowing Israeli ground forces to conduct operations without fear of air attack. Israeli air power also mauled Jordanian units as they retreated from the frontlines, causing many of the casualties the Jordanians suffered in the Six Day War. And Israeli air power was an important element in cracking some Jordanian defenses and in preventing Jordan from reinforcing its forward defense lines. To this extent, the IAF may have had a greater effect against Jordan in 1967 than in any of Israel's other campaigns against the Arabs. However, the inability of Jordanian units entrenched in superb terrain to hold off equal- or smaller-sized Israeli units was ultimately the crucial factor in Jordan's defeat, and the IAF essentially played a supporting role. In the words of General Narkiss: "The IAF was very important . . . but not so much for the ground battles. Mostly for morale and for the absence of Arab air strikes that they gave us."[88]

WHY JORDAN LOST THE SIX DAY WAR

Jordan suffered a crushing defeat between 5 and 7 June 1967, and as with any such catastrophic failure, a large number of factors produced this outcome. The most obvious problem from which Jordan suffered was the mistaken command decision to send the 60th Armored Brigade south to Hebron and the 40th Armored Brigade south to Jericho on 5 June. Although this was understandable, it still clearly contributed to Jordan's defeat since it took Amman's only armored reserves out of the picture for six to twelve hours and exposed them to air attack.[89] As a direct contributor to this and other mistakes, one must also cite the constant stream of inaccurate information fed to Jordan's senior commanders by the Egyptians, by Jordanian field officers, and probably by the Israelis. Jordanian command-and-control problems, specifically the rigidity of the Jordanian command system and the lack of intermediate formations between the brigades and the theater command, also impeded their army and prevented it from keeping pace with the rapid Israeli moves. Israeli air power also must be credited with playing an important role in the campaign, for it prevented Amman from shifting its forces as it would have liked and broke up Jordanian concentrations whenever the Israeli advance threatened to bog down. However, although each of these factors was important, they were not decisive. Mostly, they affected the timing and the cost of the Israeli victory, but they did not determine which side would win and which would lose.

The decisive factor in the Israeli invasion of the West Bank in 1967 was the tremendous imbalance between Israeli and Jordanian ground forces at the tactical level. Jordanian units were not as capable as they had been in 1948, manifesting many pathologies found in other Arab armies from which Jordan had seemed immune before 1956. In particular, they reacted poorly to Israeli moves, often failing to react at all. By the same token,

Israeli military effectiveness grew tremendously between 1948 and 1967. The bunch of poorly armed and fractious amateurs who had made up the Haganah ranks in 1948 had been transformed by 1967 into an aggressive, well-trained, and highly capable army. It was this gap in tactical capabilities that lost the West Bank for Jordan. With only a few exceptions, Jordanian units simply could not stand up to Israeli forces even when they had the advantages of terrain, superior technology, and superior numbers. Indeed, although publicly they blamed Egyptian general Riyad for their defeat, according to authorities like Samir Mutawi, most Jordanian officers privately admit that their forces were so inferior to those of Israel that the outcome of the Six Day War was a foregone conclusion regardless of the commander or his orders. In tactical engagements the Israelis so consistently outfought the Jordanians, and by such a wide margin, that poor generalship could only have been an exacerbating factor, not a primary cause.[90] In the words of Brig. Peter Young: "To those of us who knew and loved the Arab Legion there can be only regret that given the chance to display its prowess in modern warfare, the Jordan Arab Army should have met with shattering defeat in a bare three days. . . . It is easy to say 'this would never have happened if King Hussein had not sacked his British officers.' And it is true that not all the 'reforms' that followed the events of March 1956 seem to the present writer to have been well-judged, but the essential truth of the matter is very simple . . . : the forces of Jordan . . . were not strong enough to try conclusions with Israel."[91]

Jordanian performance during the Six Day War was not the equal of their showing in 1948.[92] While a few units showed some real competence, most proved to be only slightly better than their Syrian and Egyptian counterparts. In particular, more than ever before, the Jordanians manifested many of the same debilitating patterns of performance common to the other Arab militaries.

The Battle of al-Karamah, 1968

After the catastrophe of June 1967, the leaders of the Jordanian armed forces recognized that they needed to take stock of what had happened to correct their past problems. One of the first and most important conclusions reached was that Jordan suffered from a "cultural tendency toward self-delusion."[93] To try to correct this problem, the general staff attempted to revamp Jordanian training to stress objective reporting above all else. Perhaps because they recognized this tendency and feared that they were unlikely to get an objective appraisal from their own people, Amman brought in a team of Pakistani military officers to conduct the after-action report on their performance in the Six Day War and to recommend a comprehensive reform program for the Arab Legion.

As a result of this outside review, Jordan made a number of changes to its armed forces. Divisions were established, the top ranks were thinned by abolishing redundant command positions, and the general staff's authority was strengthened. A fourth company was added to all battalions and a fourth battalion added to brigades to give tactical units greater staying power. Jordanian training was revamped to stress initiative, independent action, and combined-arms coordination. Plans were made to build a larger, more modern RJAF that would concentrate on counterair and ground-attack operations.

The Course of the Battle

The Jordanians were not the only ones who learned lessons from the 1967 debacle. After the defeat of the Arab armies in the Six Day War, the Palestinians concluded that they had to take matters into their own hands if they were going to regain their lost lands. Palestinian fedayeen once again began attacking Israel, only with a greater frequency and ruthlessness than before the war. Egypt and Syria, still smarting from the drubbing they had taken at the hands of the Israelis, forbade the Palestinians from conducting attacks from their nations' territory. With a huge Palestinian population, Jordan was in no position to do the same, and so the fedayeen congregated there and made it their base of operations against Israel. For their part, the Israelis reacted by returning to their policy of reprisals against the Palestinians — and against Jordan for not preventing the attacks. In response, the Jordanian military regrouped, reorganized, and rearmed as best it could and deployed to try to prevent the Israeli violations of their sovereignty.

Much of the Palestinian activity originated from a base they had established at al-Karamah, just across the Jordan River near the Allenby bridge. As early as 14 March 1968, Jordanian intelligence began to detect signs of an impending Israeli operation against that town. IDF units began to concentrate in the area of the Allenby and Damiyah bridges, and the Jordanians noted two conferences involving high-ranking Israeli military officers in this area. In response Amman alerted the 1st Infantry Division and ordered it to take up defensive positions at the two bridges and around the Palestinian camp at al-Karamah. By 20 March, Jordanian intelligence had identified elements of the Israeli 7th Armored Brigade, 60th Armored Brigade, 35th Paratroop Brigade, 80th Infantry Brigade, a combat-engineer battalion, and five battalions of artillery along the west bank of the Jordan between the Damiyah and Allenby bridges. Given this substantial concentration of firepower and the weakened state of their own army, the Jordanians feared that the Israelis were actually gearing up for a drive on Amman.

The Jordanian 1st Infantry Division took up positions at the two bridges, in the various towns of the Jordan Valley, and on the steep ridges that formed the eastern wall of the river valley. The reconstituted but understrength 60th Armored Brigade was attached to the 1st Infantry Division for the coming battle, and some of its elements were parceled out among the infantry to provide armor support. Amman also added most of its remaining armored car, antitank, and artillery units to the 1st Infantry Division to bolster its firepower, bringing its total strength up to 105 Patton tanks and eighty-eight artillery pieces. Infantry brigades of the division were deployed opposite the Allenby, Damiyah, and King 'Abdallah (south of the Allenby) bridges, each with an attached tank company. Most of the artillery and the remaining armor was concentrated on the Jordan Valley ridge overlooking al-Karamah itself, where these forces could fire down into the valley.[94]

The Israelis were indeed preparing for an attack on al-Karamah, but their forces and their ambitions were not nearly as imposing as Amman feared. Israel had less than a brigade's worth of armor, an infantry brigade, a paratroop battalion, an engineering battalion, and five battalions of artillery. The Israeli units were divided up into four task forces. The largest was to cross the Allenby bridge and drive on al-Karamah from the south. A second group would ford the Jordan near the Damiyah bridge and drive on the town from the north, thereby catching the Palestinians in a pincer move. Meanwhile, elements of the paratroop battalion would be helicopter-lifted into al-Karamah itself. The last force would make a diversionary attack at the King 'Abdallah bridge both to draw off strength from al-Karamah and to cover the right flank of the main thrust. Tel Aviv's ultimate objectives even now remain somewhat unclear. That they wanted to destroy the Palestinian camp and capture or kill as many of the fedayeen is certain, but what is not known is to what extent the Israelis were hoping to clash with the Jordanians — to rough them up a little in hopes of convincing Amman to rein in the Palestinians. The Israelis almost certainly were aware that the 1st Infantry Division was dug in around al-Karamah, suggesting they may have been looking for a fight with Jordanian forces.

At dawn on 21 March, all four Israeli forces began their assaults simultaneously, without any prior artillery or aerial bombardment. In the north the Israelis were able to ford the Jordan, and their engineers built a pontoon bridge. When they turned south to drive on al-Karamah, however, they ran into one of the Jordanian infantry brigades, fortified and supported by armor, artillery, and plentiful antitank weapons. The Israelis called in air-strikes against these positions, but the IAF could not inflict much damage on the entrenched Jordanians, who hung tough. Although they did not venture out of their defensive positions to try to maneuver for an advantage against the Israelis, the Jordanians succeeded in stopping several Israeli frontal assaults. In the far south the Israeli diversionary effort against the King 'Abdallah bridge failed to even establish a foothold across the bridge despite repeated efforts with considerable air support. There the Jordanian positions were well sited to bring tremendous firepower on the bridge area itself, and the Israelis were repeatedly driven back by the volume of fire they encountered.

The most successful Israeli drive was the main attack on al-Karamah. The paratroopers landed first and began clearing the Palestinian training camp. The Israeli main body was able to break through the Jordanian defenses at the Allenby bridge and then spread out. The rest of the paratroop battalion, along with some armor, drove north to participate in the operations at the Palestinian camp itself. The fedayeen fought back hard and were joined by Jordanian regulars supported by artillery fire from the surrounding hills. Nevertheless, they were unable to prevent the Israelis from demolishing much of the camp, forcing Palestinian leader Yasir Arafat to flee and killing or capturing most of the Palestinian defenders. A small force of Israeli infantry and armor took up blocking positions to the south to protect the right flank of the Israeli thrust from an attack by the Jordanian brigade deployed opposite the King 'Abdallah bridge. The Jordanians threw some armor against this Israeli unit, but neither side pushed too hard, and the engagement turned into a stalemate. A larger force of Israeli armor and infantry drove east to block the road from as-Salt to the Allenby bridge. The main body of the Jordanian 60th Armored Brigade was deployed in reserve along the as-Salt road, and a firefight developed when this force attempted to join the defense of al-Karamah. In a fierce tank battle, the Jordanians lost eight Pattons without knocking out any Israeli tanks and pulled back into the hills, where they dug-in and continued to fire down on the Israeli forces in the valley below. The Israelis countered with airstrikes against the tanks and artillery along the ridge, but this had little effect on the accuracy or volume of Jordanian fire.

By the end of the day, both sides had had enough. The Israelis retreated back across the river with their Palestinian prisoners, and the Jordanians did not follow. Nevertheless, both sides declared victory. The Israelis claimed to have accomplished their stated objectives of destroying the al-Karamah fedayeen camp, while the Jordanians claimed to have badly bloodied the

Israelis and prevented them from mounting a drive on Amman. The Israelis had 28 killed and 69 wounded in addition to losing four tanks, three half-tracks, two armored cars, and an airplane shot down by Jordanian AAA. Another twenty-four Israeli tanks were damaged but brought back across the river and repaired. The Palestinians had about 100 fedayeen killed, another 100 wounded, and 120–150 captured. The Jordanians suffered 61 dead, 108 wounded, thirteen tanks destroyed, twenty tanks damaged, and thirty-nine other vehicles damaged or destroyed.[95]

Jordanian Performance at the Battle of al-Karamah

A few important points came out of this fight. First, while there is little doubt that the Israelis never had any intention of pushing on to the Jordanian capital, it seems the Jordanians did better than the Israelis had expected. The Israelis almost certainly did not expect to find the scale or intensity of resistance from the army that they encountered. While they did succeed in destroying the Palestinian camp and capturing or killing most of the fedayeen there, they had a tougher time than they expected and probably did not do as much damage to the Jordanians as they had hoped. If they had intended to push the Jordanians around, they had been disappointed.

Jordan's strategic leadership in this incident was quite good, probably reflecting the various changes Amman made in the wake of the Six Day War. At the strategic level, military intelligence did a creditable job in detecting and monitoring the Israeli buildup and identifying al-Karamah as the likely target. If their supposition that the Israelis might drive on to Amman was farfetched, it was the best kind of intelligence mistake because it prompted the military to be overprepared rather than underprepared. Amman's high command also did well in quickly concentrating the 1st Infantry Division around al-Karamah and reinforcing it with armor, artillery, antitank weapons, and everything else they could get their hands on to resist the Israelis. Finally, Jordanian deployments and fortifications around al-Karamah were quite good, showing a real improvement over 1967. Their forces were well sited to block all major axes of advance, to cover all chokepoints with heavy firepower, and to be able to reinforce threatened sectors. For the most part, the general staff was careful to ensure that Jordanian units had the advantages of excellent fortifications, superior firepower, and formidable terrain wherever they took on the IDF.

At the tactical level, al-Karamah did not reflect much on Jordanian reforms, but what it did demonstrate was not encouraging. The artillery was accurate but almost exclusively conducted preplanned, preregistered fire missions and, therefore, did not demonstrate any real improvement over

1967. Whenever Jordanian armor encountered Israeli armor — and these were mostly even fights in both numbers and types of tanks engaged — the Jordanians either lost or, at best, gained a draw, which still favored the Israelis because it kept the Jordanians away from the paratroopers at al-Karamah. In their main armored counterattack on the as-Salt road, the Jordanians were thrown back fairly easily by the Israelis. Army units also continued to remain passive. With the exception of the armor attack along the as-Salt road, the Jordanians failed to conduct any substantial counter-attacks or even many smaller ones. The vast majority of Jordanian units were content to sit in the hills or behind their fortifications and fire at the Israelis from a distance rather than attempting to close with the attackers and destroy them or drive them off.

Black September and the Syrian Invasion of Jordan, 1970–71

Relations between the Palestinian fedayeen and their Jordanian hosts were never good, and they deteriorated rapidly after the Six Day War. The growing intensity of PLO attacks on Israel provoked IDF retaliation — such as the raid on al-Karamah — exacerbating the friction between Amman and its Palestinian guests. Moreover, the humiliating defeat of the Arab Legion on the West Bank in 1967 made the Palestinians more willing to flout Jordanian authority. By 1969, the Palestinians were attempting to establish a state within a state that would give their organizations complete control over Palestinian actions both within Jordan and in the outside world. This situation was anathema to King Hussein, and so in the fall of 1970, Amman moved to reassert its authority over the Palestinians.

The Balance of Forces

Three years after the Six Day War, the Jordanian army had replenished its strength and had even expanded. In 1970 it boasted 70,000 men, of whom two-thirds were Jordanian Bedouin and the remainder either Palestinians or other Hadari. As always, the Bedouin dominated the armored forma-tions, several infantry brigades, and most of the officer billets in the combat units, while the Palestinians manned the technical-support branches and the enlisted ranks of the other infantry brigades. The army had replenished its tank strength with 300 of the latest American M-60s and improved British Centurions (equipped with new engines and the outstanding L7 105-mm gun) in three armored brigades and a mechanized brigade. Like-wise, Amman had rebuilt its air force by purchasing thirty-two Hawker Hunters and eighteen F-104s.[96]

The growing tension between the Hashimite monarchy and the Palestinian fedayeen groups began to have repercussions within the army. Bedouin officers and enlisted men increasingly clashed with Palestinian personnel, straining relations and eroding morale in many mixed-ethnic-group units. These problems led to a growing undercurrent among the Bedouin officers that favored a general move to crush the Palestinian fedayeen groups. These problems also prompted Amman to begin watching — and even redeploying — some of its Palestinian-manned units for fear they would try to stage a coup.

On the other side, the fedayeen were a fractious gaggle of groups and organizations. On paper, the various bands numbered 25,000 full-time guerrillas and 76,000 part-time militiamen.[97] This strength may have been greatly exaggerated and, at any rate, was not as impressive as it seemed. The PLO units were lightly armed, possessing no armor or other weapons heavier than light mortars and shoulder-launched antitank weapons. They had little or no military training, a rudimentary organization, and even less discipline. In addition, the Palestinians were divided up into countless groups, factions, fronts, subfactions, and parties with overlapping and constantly shifting loyalties that further hampered their ability to act in concert.

Initial Moves against the PLO

The Jordanian General Staff had nothing but contempt for the PLO guerrillas, and this sentiment played a major role in their planning. The high command did not expect the Palestinians to be able to offer any significant resistance and anticipated that they would fold quickly under direct pressure from the army. Another ingredient in Amman's plans was the need for a quick campaign to preclude Syrian intervention. The Syrians were active supporters of the PLO and vociferous enemies of the Hashimite monarchy. Consequently, Amman wanted to crush the Palestinians quickly before the Syrians could get involved. Based on their concern for Syrian intentions and disregard for Palestinian capabilities, the Jordanian plan was, in the words of Brig. Gen. S. A. El-Edroos, designed to be a "48-hour blitzkrieg mopping-up operation."[98] The army would begin by sweeping Amman and Jordan's other major cities of fedayeen on 17 September and then would isolate and dispatch any remaining concentrations in the countryside. Because the operation was mounted quickly, and because the Jordanian generals were certain of the great imbalance between their forces and the fedayeen, the general staff's planning was superficial and haphazard, and the operation suffered from it.[99]

In Amman the Jordanians divided operations in the city between the 4th Mechanized Division, reinforced with the 60th Armored Brigade, and the

1st Infantry Division. For some reason, the Jordanians assigned the more open southern suburbs to the 1st Infantry, while the armored elements of the 4th Mechanized and 60th Armored were to advance into Amman's Old City. The Old City was a typical Middle Eastern *madinah*, with narrow streets, abutting houses, unexpected alleys, and frequent dead ends. In short, it was the worst place imaginable to operate with tanks and APCs. To make matters worse, many of the Jordanian units sent their tanks forward with little or no infantry support. Consequently, the Palestinians, many armed with shoulder-launched antitank weapons, wrought havoc with the armor. By the second day, 18 September, the reinforced 4th Mechanized was bogged down on the outskirts of the Old City after having taken unexpectedly high losses. Similarly, the 1st Infantry had enjoyed some success clearing the open and only lightly defended southern suburbs, but they were then halted in their tracks by fedayeen defenses along the southern edge of Amman's central commercial district. At the end of the forty-eight hours the general staff had told the king they would need to crush the Palestinians, the heart of Amman remained in PLO hands, the Jordanians had taken unexpectedly heavy casualties, and the army was stuck in its tracks with little idea of when they might be able to get moving again.

The situation in northern Jordan was even worse. There the GHQ had deployed the 2d Infantry Division, the 40th Armored Brigade, and other supporting units. These forces were to clear the towns of Irbid, ar-Ramtha, and Ajlun, where there were major fedayeen concentrations—albeit smaller than PLO strength in Amman. Although the offensive in the north was to coincide with the push into Amman, Jordanian forces there moved too slowly and allowed the PLO to strike first. The fedayeen established defensive positions around their camps, turned back the initial strikes, and took control of Irbid and most of northern Jordan.

To add to Amman's problems, the operation against the PLO caused some of the frictions within the army to surface. About 5,000 Palestinian soldiers and officers deserted to join the PLO, in some cases bringing badly needed heavy weapons with them. Although it would later become clear that the vast majority of Palestinians in the army remained loyal to the king and that none of the larger Palestinian-dominated formations deserted as a whole, at the time the defections seemed like a virtual hemorrhage to the army high command. Some key Jordanian military personnel also disagreed with the king's policy and either resigned or refused to participate. In particular, the commander of the 2d Infantry Division resigned his command on the third day of the operation, probably because he sympathized with the PLO.

The Syrian Invasion

As if these various problems were not bad enough for the Jordanians, on the second day of the campaign the Syrian government decided to intervene on behalf of the Palestinians. Initially, the Syrians sent a reinforced armored brigade to aid the forces around Irbid. A number of small detachments from the Arab Legion attempted to hold up the Syrian advance, but they were brushed aside. On 20 September Damascus escalated its involvement by sending into Jordan the 5th Infantry Division, reinforced with two armored brigades to bring its tank strength to nearly 300 T-55s and its manpower to over 16,000.[100] The Syrians drove into Jordan and smashed a company of Centurion tanks at the ar-Ramtha police post. They then pushed on toward the critical intersection of the Irbid-Mafraq and ar-Ramtha–Amman roads, which was the most direct route to Amman itself.

At first, the Jordanians had made no direct move in response to the Syrian invasion. King Hussein and his generals were most concerned with gaining control over the capital, which required all their attention. In addition, having one Syrian brigade at Irbid was maddening but not really a threat, for the 2d Infantry Division and 40th Armored Brigade could prevent it from causing real harm. Amman believed it could deal with this relatively small Syrian force later, after it had finished off the Palestinians. Consequently, the Jordanians actually drew off the mechanized infantry battalion of the 40th and sent it south to add more infantry to the efforts of the 4th Mechanized Division in the capital. However, when the Syrians then committed the reinforced 5th Infantry Division on a drive toward Amman itself, the Jordanians suddenly became alarmed. They reacted by shifting the 25th "Khalid ibn al-Walid" Infantry Brigade of the 2d Infantry Division and the two armored battalions (100 improved Centurions) of the 40th Armored Brigade northeast to stop the advance.

The Jordanian forces deployed in two lines south of ar-Ramtha. The 25th Infantry Brigade dug in along the dominating Kitim–an-Nu'aymah escarpment that forms the southern wall of the Vale of ar-Ramtha, blocking the Syrians' egress from the valley south or southwest. Meanwhile, the 40th Armored Brigade took up defensive positions farther forward on another ridgeline along the main road to Amman and just south of ar-Ramtha. The Syrian division first attacked the 40th Armored on 21 September. In a fierce battle that raged all day, the Jordanians were slowly pushed off the ridgeline by the Syrian armor. The Jordanian commander then decided to abandon the valley and pull back to the 25th Infantry Brigade positions along the Kitim–an-Nu'aymah ridge, thereby abandoning the vital ar-Ramtha crossroads to the Syrians. With this intersection in their control, the 5th Division was able to link up with the Syrian forces in Irbid.

Neither force fought terrible well on 21 September. The Syrians essentially blundered into the Jordanian armor and then launched repeated frontal assaults to try to drive the Centurions off the ridge. They employed no stratagems or sophisticated tactics but simply bludgeoned their way through the Jordanian lines with their superior numbers and firepower. Although the Jordanians were determined to stop the Syrians, they made little effort to counterattack into the flanks of the clumsy attacks nor did they otherwise try to outmaneuver the Syrian units. The Jordanian tankers were content to try to pick off Syrian tanks from their hull-down positions along the ridgeline, relying on the greater range and killing power of their 105-mm guns. In fact, most reports suggest that the Jordanian tanks rarely ever even changed their firing positions during the battle. Nevertheless, despite their advantages in equipment and position, the Jordanian gunners appear to have done particularly poorly, for they were only able to destroy ten Syrian T-55s while losing nineteen Centurions. Although both sides had artillery support available, either it was not employed or, more likely, failed to have any appreciable effect on the fighting. Moreover, the Jordanians were helped by the fact that the Syrians did not use their infantry to drive off the unsupported Centurions with antitank weapons. By late afternoon, the poor showing of the Jordanian tankers, plus the Syrians' numerical advantage of at least two to one, began to take their toll, and the Jordanians retreated.

The defeat of the 40th Armored Brigade sent King Hussein into a near panic, and his biographer reports that he did not believe his forces would be able to keep the Syrians from overrunning Amman.[101] On 22 September Amman pulled out all the stops to throw the Syrians back. In particular, they decided to commit the RJAF in full force against the Syrian armor. Prior to that point, the air force had been providing support to the army units battling the Palestinians, primarily those around Amman. In addition, the Jordanians apparently had been concerned that if they committed their rather small air force, the Syrians would do the same, and they would again lose the entire RJAF. However, the situation on the ground appeared so dire to Amman that the king and the general staff felt the regime's survival was at stake, and the air force might have to be sacrificed to save the monarchy.

Thus, on 22 September, when the Syrian 5th Infantry Division attacked the Jordanian forces on the Kitim–an-Nu'aymah ridge, the RJAF threw everything it had into the battle. They reportedly generated about 200–250 ground-attack sorties against the division during the course of the day. Much to the Jordanian's relief, the Syrians did not commit their air force to the fighting, giving the RJAF complete freedom of the skies. In addition, because the 5th Division had only paltry air defense assets, the Jordanian aircraft faced little opposition and did not lose a single plane.

The Syrian armor was badly battered by the airstrikes. Jordanian tanks did little, preferring to remain in their defensive positions and snipe from long range. Consequently, it fell to the RJAF to take out the Syrians. The air force rose to the occasion, flying possibly as many as four or eight sorties per aircraft and maintaining a constant presence over the Syrian division for nearly sixteen hours.[102] The airstrikes destroyed twenty to thirty Syrian tanks and probably an equal number of APCs.[103] These losses certainly were not crippling by themselves, but the constant attacks broke the will of the Syrian armored forces. In the late afternoon the 5th Division began retreating in the face of the Jordanian aerial bombardment after having advanced only a short distance. The next day the Syrians aborted their invasion of Jordan and began pulling out their forces. In all, they lost sixty-two tanks, sixty APCs, and suffered about 600 casualties in the two days of fighting.[104]

Finishing off the Palestinians

With the Syrians in full retreat, the Jordanians were able to turn their attention back to the Palestinians. The Syrian defeat had an important influence on the fighting. The fedayeen had initially gotten a real morale boost from the invasion, while the Arab Legion suffered a corresponding drop. The defeat of the Syrians reversed this, undermining PLO morale and giving the Jordanians a huge lift. Although the Palestinians continued to fight on, they lacked the zeal that had allowed them to rebuff the initial attacks.

Nevertheless, the Jordanians could not dispatch the fedayeen quickly. PLO forces in Amman continued to hold the Jordanian armor and infantry at bay, forcing the army to cordon off the center of the city and besiege the Palestinians there. After leaving a force to watch the Syrian border, the 40th Armored Brigade and 2d Infantry Division again concentrated around Irbid. In a week of brutal house-to-house combat, they were able to overpower the demoralized Palestinians. Nevertheless, by the end of September, the Jordanians needed to regroup. King Hussein agreed to a ceasefire brokered by Egyptian president Nasser on 27 September (the day before Nasser died), and by early October, both sides were generally observing it. Of course, both used the ceasefire as a cover to prepare for the next round.

By late November 1970, the Jordanians had reformed and reinforced the army and were ready to resume their campaign against the Palestinians. The king had put Brig. Gen. Sharif Zayid bin Shakir, his cousin and the deputy chief of staff for operations, in charge of the operation, and he proved to be an able commander. Under his direction, the general staff learned from some of their previous mistakes and carefully planned their future operations. Jordan also received new American M-60 tanks to make good their losses to the PLO and the Syrians.

With their new armor and their new leadership in place, Jordanian armed forces proceeded to conduct a systematic, meticulous campaign against the Palestinians. In the first stage, lasting from November 1970 until April 1971, the army concentrated on regaining control of the major towns still under Palestinian control, including Amman, Ajlun, and Jarash. In the second stage the army forced the PLO into the mountains of Ajlun in north-central Jordan, where they were isolated from the civilian population. This strategy was slow but effective. The Jordanians moved from town to town and from refugee camp to refugee camp rooting out all PLO forces. They isolated each area of resistance and then slowly reduced it by employing massive firepower and indiscriminate killing, slaughtering many Palestinian civilians in the process. On 14 April the last 5,000 Palestinian guerrillas finally agreed to pull out of Amman, leaving the center of the city in Jordanian hands.

In late April 1971 most Jordanian towns were back in the hands of the army, and the Palestinian guerrillas had been forced back into a pocket around R'as al-Aqrah between Ajlun and Jarash. For two months, the Jordanians besieged the fedayeen there, preparing for battle, bringing in reinforcements, whittling away at the Palestinian perimeter, and preventing them from receiving supplies from the outside. On 13 July they launched their final offensive to destroy the Palestinians. Amman sent the 99th Armored Brigade, reinforced with a battalion of infantry, up the eastern face of the mountain, while the 4th "Hussein bin 'Ali" Infantry Brigade assaulted the southern face. Both columns had heavy air and artillery support, and engineer companies were attached to help overcome the difficult terrain. Finally, the 36th "Yarmuk" Infantry Brigade was deployed to the north and west of the mountain to block all routes of escape through the hills of Gilead. In a grueling, four-day pitched battle, the Jordanians eventually overcame Palestinian resistance, taking their strongpoints one by one and wearing down their combat strength. On 18 July the last fedayeen surrendered to the army. In this battle the Jordanians suffered 120 killed and wounded, and for the entire campaign from September 1970 through July 1971, lost 600 killed and 1,500 wounded.[105]

Jordanian Military Effectiveness during
Black September and the Syrian Invasion

The Jordanian armed forces eventually got the job done in this conflict, but their performance left much to be desired. The operation was supposed to have been a forty-eight-hour blitzkrieg, but it turned into a ten-month siege. The effort was poorly directed at the strategic level at first, although it improved dramatically beginning in November. In addition, at the tactical level, Jordanian units compounded the mistakes made by their senior leaders and hindered their better decisions. The one real source of pride was the RJAF, which performed well in stopping the Syrian drive on Amman in September 1970.

STRATEGIC PERFORMANCE

Jordanian generalship during the crucial battles in September was mediocre at best. The planning for the initial moves against the PLO was disgraceful in its superficiality and sloppiness. Most orders were vague and issued only at the last minute with few preparations for logistics and other support. Overall, the general staff either did not understand what was required for such an operation or else paid little attention to its planning. For example, Amman appears to have underestimated the size of the force required to simultaneously clear all of Jordan's main urban centers. In trying to sweep all the major cities at once, they dispersed their limited strength and wound up losing most of the northern towns to the Palestinians. Only in Amman itself did they muster sufficient forces to take the city, and there they made the poor decision to rely primarily on armor without adequate infantry support in the old section of the city. If Jordanian tactical formations had performed better, there is every reason to believe that two reinforced Jordanian *infantry* divisions backed by armor and airpower could have overcome the Palestinians in Amman. However, the decision to send armor into the Old City could only have been a disaster, regardless of how well they fought.

Against the Syrians, the Jordanian high command did reasonably well. The failure of their initial assaults against the Palestinians, plus the realization of their worst nightmare in the Syrian invasion, appear to have served as a wake-up call for these generals. They reacted swiftly to the Syrian moves, choosing a good location to make their stand and scraping together everything they reasonably could to stop the invaders. This amounted to only two brigades at first because they needed to keep the 4th and 1st Divisions and the 60th Armored Brigade around Amman for fear of losing control of the capital to the Palestinians. The other two brigades of 2d

Infantry Division were heavily engaged against the Palestinians throughout northern Jordan—and were also needed to keep an eye on the Syrian armored brigade around Irbid. Finally, the last armored brigade of the 3d Armored Division—the 99th—was watching the Iraqi 3d Armored Division, which had been garrisoned in northeast Jordan since 1967. The Iraqis sympathized with the Palestinians, and it was unclear whether Baghdad would order the division to intervene on behalf of the PLO. In other words, Jordan did not have anything other than the 25th Infantry and 40th Armored Brigades left to send to deal with the Syrians. Moreover, although the Jordanians had purposely refrained from committing their air force to battle before 22 September, when it became clear that their ground forces around ar-Ramtha probably would not be able to hold back the Syrians, Amman overcame its previous hesitance and ordered an all-out air campaign, which won the day.

Jordanian strategic performance improved considerably after November 1970. Once Brigadier General bin Shakir was given control of the direction of the campaign, Jordanian planning improved rapidly. In contrast to the half-baked, country-wide effort the high command had initially attempted, the Jordanians now concentrated their forces on one city or camp and reduced it before moving on to the next. Only the most minimal forces were employed to watch the Syrians and hold the Palestinians elsewhere so that the maximum force could be brought to bear against each fedayeen stronghold in turn. While these clearing operations were slow and brutal, they also were very successful. Moreover, bin Shakir appears to have carefully tailored operations to the capabilities of Jordanian forces, whereas the campaigns of September appeared to assume a much greater gap in capabilities between the Palestinians and the Jordanians than was actually the case.

TACTICAL PERFORMANCE

At the tactical level, Jordanian forces performed poorly, especially against the Syrians. During the initial battles in September against the PLO, the army appeared to disappoint its commanders in terms of its tactical prowess. Specifically, the general staff's plans seemed to assume that Jordanian formations would be able to dispatch Palestinian forces of equal or greater size without much trouble. However, this did not prove to be the case. In all of these battles, the Jordanians possessed overwhelming superiority in firepower as well as the advantages of discipline, organization, and the coordination of being a true army. The Palestinians were mostly unorganized, barely trained, and poorly armed, but they did have the advantages of defending excellent terrain and often outnumbered the Jordanians. Ultimately, these various factors appeared to cancel one another out, resulting in a bloody stalemate and indicating that, given the army's other advantages, the skill of its tactical formations did not count for much in the balance. Indeed, the little bits of evidence we have regarding Jordanian performance against the PLO tends to confirm this. Jordanian combined-arms operations were poor and, on several occasions, the legion took so long to get organized and moving that the Palestinians were able to steal a march.

If most of the evidence suggesting a continued decline in Jordanian tactical capabilities is circumstantial for combat against the fedayeen, it is far more certain in the battles with the Syrians. Jordanian ground forces performed poorly against Syrian armor. The 40th Armored Brigade — the elite unit of the Jordanian army — deployed in hull-down positions along a ridgeline could not hold back the Syrian 5th Infantry Division for even one day. While it may not have been a bad idea to cling to the ridge and allow the more numerous Syrian tanks to beat their heads against such defensive positions, the fact that Jordanian armor apparently did not even change positions to prevent the Syrians from zeroing in on their hiding spots is inexcusable. Furthermore, despite their advantage in equipment and their superior defensive position, the Jordanian Centurions were likely out-shot by the Syrian T-55s, judging by tank kills.

To place the performance of the 40th Armored Brigade against the Syrian 5th Infantry Division in proper perspective, two comparisons are helpful. First, there is the performance of this same unit in 1967 against the Israelis at Qabatiyah crossroads. The 40th faced about the same combat power in each of these battles. In 1967 the Jordanians significantly outnumbered the Israeli Super Shermans they faced, whereas in 1970 they were outnumbered by the Syrians by virtually the same ratio, but the Israeli tankers of 1967 were far superior to the Syrians of 1970, making the net "combat power" of the two attacking forces roughly equal. Yet in 1967 the Jordanians beat the Israelis back with heavy losses twice and only retreated when they were hit by a combination of IAF airstrikes and a flanking maneuver. In 1970 the Syrians could not even bring artillery fire to bear, let alone airstrikes, and they never tried to outflank the Jordanian positions but instead kept making frontal assaults. Yet the Jordanians were still defeated. As a second comparison, in 1973 the Israeli 7th Armored Brigade — the elite armored force of the IDF — faced the reinforced Syrian 7th Infantry Division in the "Valley of Tears." In 1973 the equipment, organization, training, tactics, and operations of the Syrian 7th Infantry Division were virtually identical to those of the 5th Infantry Division in 1970. In 1973 the Israeli 7th Armored Brigade was dug in along a ridgeline, were equipped with Centurions, and had little artillery, infantry, or air support, just like the Jordanian 40th Armored Brigade in 1970. However, the outcome of the two battles was completely different. While the Israeli 7th Armored fought the Syrians to a standstill for four days, and destroyed six of the finest brigades in the Syrian army in the process, the Jordanian 40th Armored was forced back after less than a day and suffered heavier casualties than the Syrians. Clearly then, the 40th was not in the same league as the Israeli 7th, nor was it even as good as it had been in 1967.

The Jordanian air force, however, performed quite well against the Syrians. The sortie rate they managed on 22 September, four to eight sorties per plane in sixteen hours, was extremely impressive and rivaled the Israeli sortie rates at the start of the Six Day War. To some extent, the Jordanians were aided by the absence of any substantial antiaircraft weapons on the Syrian side as well as the extremely short distance between the Jordanian bases and the battlefield in the Vale of ar-Ramtha. Nevertheless, no other Arab air force was ever able to generate a sortie rate such as this, even for just one day. Although the amount of Syrian armor the airstrikes destroyed was at best average, the determination the Jordanian pilots displayed merits real praise.[106] Regardless of the amount of physical damage inflicted, the relentless attacks of the RJAF turned back the Syrians, and probably saved the Hashimite regime.

The October War, 1973

When Egypt and Syria launched their combined surprise attack on Israel on 6 October 1973, Jordan found itself in an awkward position. On the one hand, Amman had no desire to unnecessarily provoke the Israelis. The Jordanians recognized Israel's military superiority and had no desire to repeat the experience of 1967. In addition, since 1970, Israel and Jordan had developed a kind of symbiotic relationship that neither side wished to disrupt. The Israelis had supported King Hussein during Black September by threatening to intervene if the Syrians did not back down, and this played an important role in Syria's decision not to press their invasion after 22 September. The peaceful relationship between the two countries benefited them both once the PLO had been driven out of Jordan, and Amman did not want a new Arab-Israeli conflict to destroy this harmony. On the other hand, the king felt pressure to join the Arab effort from his subjects and his Arab allies — some of whom provided him with considerable financial subsidies. Ultimately, the king agreed to commit forces to defend Syria but not to attack Israel. In addition, he went so far as to secretly ask Israel's permission to send forces to participate in the defense of Syria and to assure Tel Aviv that he had no intention of opening general hostilities with Israel.[107]

With a kind of absolution from Tel Aviv, Jordan dispatched the elite 40th Armored Brigade, under the command of Col. Khalid Hajhaj al-Majali, to Syria on 13 October. By then, the Syrian attack on the Golan Heights had failed, and the Syrian armies had been driven off the plateau completely (see chapter 6). Indeed, on 11 October the Israelis had launched a counteroffensive toward Damascus, but on 12 October the newly arrived Iraqi 3d Armored Division accidentally blundered into the exposed right flank of the Israeli strike, prompting IDF commanders to rein in their tanks and take up defensive positions. Consequently, when the Jordanians arrived in southern Syria on 13–14 October, the front had stabilized: there was no Syrian threat to the Golan, and the Israeli threat to Damascus had mostly abated.

Initially, the Jordanians were placed under the command of the Iraqi armored division, which in turn was under the control of the Syrian General Staff. Over the next several days, the Syrians employed this combined force in several badly planned, badly supported, and badly executed attacks against the southern flank of the Israeli salient. It is unclear whether the Syrians actually hoped the Iraqis and Jordanians would be able to drive the Israelis back or if they simply wanted to keep pressure on the Israelis while they regrouped their disorganized and demoralized units. Although the attacks were all lopsided defeats for the Arabs, the Israelis did not renew their drive on Damascus, and the Syrians were able to reform and reequip some of their battered formations with new weapons rushed in by the Soviets.

The first joint Iraqi-Jordanian attack came on 16 October. The plan was for the 40th Armored Brigade and the Iraqi 6th Armored Brigade to attack in conjunction against the southern flank of the Israeli salient. The Israelis had an understrength ugdah of four armored brigades with about 130 tanks deployed around a series of tels — volcanic hills — east of al-Qunaytarah. The Jordanians were to drive the Israelis off of Tel al-Mal, one of the westernmost hills, and then to push northwest to cut the main Damascus–al-Qunaytarah road. The attack was scheduled for dawn, but the Iraqis could not organize their assault force by this time. Rather than wait for the Iraqis and launch a combined assault as planned, Colonel al-Majali kept to the schedule and attacked alone. The 40th Armored, with about 80 Cen-

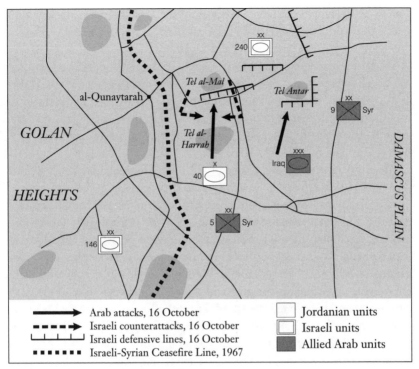

Map 24. Jordanian Operations, 16 October 1973

turions and 40–50 M-113s, launched a frontal assault backed by Syrian and Iraqi artillery and multiple-rocket launchers against the positions of the Israeli 17th Armored Brigade (which was down to about 30 tanks) on Tel al-Mal. Although the Israelis detected the Iraqi forces massing to the east of the Jordanians, and this kept most of the Israeli ugdah pinned to its positions, because the Jordanians were attacking alone, the Israeli commander was able to commit another of his (understrength) brigades to aid the threatened sector. The Jordanians drove slowly at the Israeli positions on the tel, and the Israelis responded by pinning the Jordanians with long-range tank and artillery fire (as well as some friendly fire from the Iraqi artillery batteries that landed among the Jordanians). Then, elements of the two Israeli armored brigades conducted a double envelopment of the attacking force. With the 40th Armored boxed in on three sides by 60–70 Israeli Centurions, the Jordanians began taking heavy losses. The Jordanian tanks fought well as individual crews, but their infantry contributed little to the battle and their armored units were unable to coordinate their actions or develop a coherent response to the Israeli pincer attack. Eventually, the Jordanians simply fled the battlefield, losing 28 tanks, without doing any significant damage to the Israelis.[108]

When the Iraqis did finally attack later in the morning of 16 October, the Israelis were able to concentrate their entire ugdah against them. Without the threat of the Jordanians to the west, the Israeli division commander brought the 17th Armored Brigade south and then swung it east, into the right flank of the Iraqi attack. The Iraqis were severely mauled in this battle, losing 60 of 130 tanks.[109]

After the fighting on 16 October, the Jordanians pulled back to lick their wounds. They were left in relative peace throughout 17 and 18 October because Iraqi and Syrian probes and artillery exchanges kept the Israelis busy. The Jordanians repaired damage to their armored vehicles and brought up replacements for dead and wounded personnel. In addition, they demanded to be resubordinated to another division, for they no longer wanted to be under Iraqi command. Between the inability of the Iraqis to get moving according to the plan and their accidental shelling of the 40th Armored as it approached the Israeli lines, the Jordanians wanted nothing more to do with the Iraqi army. After Amman weighed in with Damascus, they succeeded in forcing the Syrian General Staff to place them under the command of the Syrian 5th Infantry Division, deployed on the Jordanians' left (southwest). Finally, after the disaster of 16 October, the king apparently decided to reinforce his contingent in Syria and ordered the 92d Armored Brigade to join the 40th.

The Jordanians went into battle again on 19 October.[110] The Syrians had planned another large-scale attack in which the 40th Brigade would form the left flank and attack northwest into the "corner" of the Israeli lines, where they turned south just east of al-Qunaytarah. The Iraqis again would be the right flank of the offensive and would attack northward to the east of the Jordanians, while a weak Syrian infantry division waited to serve as an exploitation force. The 92d Armored Brigade had not arrived yet, so the 40th, with its previous losses only partially made up (the brigade had 60 tanks), again would be the entire Jordanian effort.[111]

This Arab offensive failed as well, although not as badly as on the sixteenth. Once again, the attack was scheduled to begin at first light, but this time the Jordanians did not attack on schedule.[112] Their failure exposed the Iraqis to the full attention of the Israelis, who sent them reeling with heavy losses. When the 40th Brigade finally did get moving at about 9:00 A.M., the Israelis were still dealing with the Iraqis, so the Jordanians faced only the understrength Israeli 19th Armored Brigade (30–40 tanks). Colonel al-

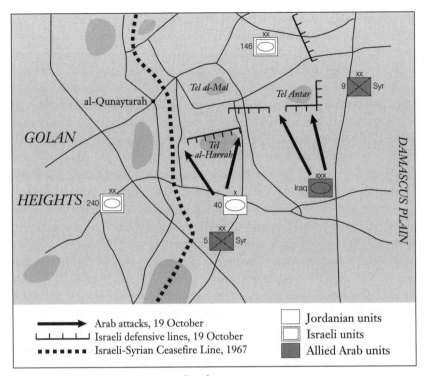

Map 25. Jordanian Operations, 19 October 1973

Majali split his two tank battalions, sending one northeast around the dominating height of Tel al-Harrah and the other to the northwest of this hill, keeping his mechanized brigade in reserve. At this point, al-Majali delegated operational authority to his battalion commanders, leaving them to "act on their own judgment and initiative," and mostly failed to provide more than rudimentary guidance.[113]

Both Jordanian armored battalions fared poorly, but because they had learned caution after their experience on 16 October, they were not beaten up as badly this time. The western armored battalion was able to penetrate all the way to the important Umm Batinah–Jabah road because the Israeli battalion at Umm Batinah mistook them for Israelis (the Jordanians had the exact same equipment as the Israelis: Centurion tanks and M-113 APCs). Nevertheless, when the Israelis realized their mistake, they opened fire. The Jordanian tank crews again fought well as individual crews, but they were not as good as the Israelis nor could they coordinate their actions to mount a coherent scheme of battle. They quickly began losing more tanks than the Israelis, prompting them to disengage and retreat. Meanwhile, the eastern armored battalion probed forward very carefully, moving slowly and keeping both an advance guard and flank guards to prevent the Israelis from enveloping them as they had on 16 October. However, when the western armored battalion was forced to pull back, this allowed the Israelis to concentrate their entire brigade on the eastern battalion. They pinned down the Jordanians with fire from the front and then performed a double envelopment just as the Jordanians had feared. Nevertheless, this time, because the Jordanians were so nervous about the Israelis doing exactly this, they began to retreat as soon as they recognized the flanking maneuvers. During this entire attack, the 40th's mechanized infantry battalion occupied itself with minor tasks like evacuating the wounded but never went into battle to aid their armor. Overall, the Jordanians lost seventeen to twenty tanks in exchange for four or five Israeli tanks.[114]

Although the Iraqis would make two more sallies against the Israelis that day — and would fail both times — after 19 October, the front in southern Syria settled into a desultory stalemate. Both sides sniped at each other and occasionally jockeyed for tactical positions, but there were no major efforts. The Syrians were content to continue to reconstitute their forces. Likewise, the Iraqis had been badly butchered between 12 and 19 October, and they needed time to regroup and repair their damage. The 92d Armored Brigade arrived in Syria, but the Jordanians felt that they had fulfilled their obligations, and after the losses sustained by the 40th Brigade, they had no desire to mix it up with the Israelis again. Consequently, there was little resistance from Jordan when a ceasefire ended the war on 24 October. Altogether, Jordan had fifty-four tanks destroyed and suffered at least eighty casualties.[115]

Jordanian Military Effectiveness during the October War

In 1973, Jordan sent only a token force to participate in the Arab conflict with Israel, and then only to aid in the defense of Syria. Jordanian forces were there mostly to "show the flag," and so their efforts were somewhat half-hearted. Consequently, one must once again be cautious in drawing too many conclusions from Jordanian performance. For the most part, they performed better than the other Arab armies but still did not perform terribly effectively, and the Israelis had little trouble defeating them. To the extent that it is possible to generalize from this limited participation, it is further indication of the gradual decline of Jordanian combat effectiveness since the departure of the British in 1956.

Colonel al-Majali and his battalion commanders were mediocre leaders.

First, al-Majali does not seem to have understood his government's intentions when they sent his unit to Syria. Amman did not want its best brigade destroyed by the Israelis; instead, they wanted the 40th to participate—defend Syrian territory—but to avoid serious losses at all costs. However, al-Majali's decision to go ahead with the attack against the Israelis on 16 October *without the Iraqis* was not just foolish, it contradicted Amman's wishes. By charging alone, the Jordanians gave the Israelis a perfect opportunity to maul the brigade, which is exactly what they did, destroying twenty-eight of eighty Jordanian Centurions. It seems reasonable to surmise that al-Majali probably was upbraided by the general staff afterward, and so on 19 October, he waited until he was certain the Iraqis had attacked before he committed his own units. However, in this battle as well, the colonel performed poorly. He divided his brigade into three forces and then left them on their own, providing inadequate guidance and failing to coordinate the operations of his battalions so that they could support one another. His battalion commanders were incapable of coordinating their efforts on their own and wandered off in different directions and were unable to come to each other's aid when the Israelis engaged each in turn. Finally, the mechanized infantry battalion was allowed to sit back during the entire battle and do essentially nothing, even while both of the armored battalions were being hammered by the IDF.

These mistakes point to some of the other problems the Jordanians experienced. While the Israelis consistently commented that Jordanian tank crews were very professional, they still were not as good as the Israelis and were regularly beaten whenever they came to grips with IDF armor. Of greater importance still, Jordanian formations had serious problems fighting as complete units. As individual tanks they were alright, but they could not coordinate their actions in battle. Just as they had in the Six Day War and at al-Karamah, when they faced an Israeli flanking maneuver, the Jordanians fought back fiercely as individuals but could not react as units to reorient themselves against a new threat. With the exception of the right-hand (eastern) armored battalion on 19 October, the Jordanians failed to employ flank guards or advance guards despite the Israeli predilection for envelopments. Their units also generally did not try to maneuver against the Israelis' flanks. They mostly attacked straight into the Israeli positions and then retreated when the Israelis got on their flanks.

Jordanian combined-arms coordination was awful. Initially, the Jordanians did not deploy with any tube artillery (just two batteries of multiple-rocket launchers) and so had to rely on the Iraqis and Syrians. Even when they sent a battalion of 105-mm howitzers to Syria, these guns had little effect on the Israelis. Worst of all, the Jordanians never employed their infantry in conjunction with their armor. The Israeli units were mostly all-tank with little infantry support and thus were quite vulnerable to a true combined-arms team of artillery, armor, and infantry with antitank weapons. Additionally, in some cases the Jordanians were battered by a few small Israeli antitank teams but never brought up their own infantry to disperse them. Altogether, Jordan's tactical prowess left much to be desired.

Jordanian Military Effectiveness since 1973

The Jordanian armed forces have not seen combat since 1973. Consequently, it is difficult to discern their military effectiveness between the October War and the present. However, some observations are possible. Western contact with the Arab Legion has remained extensive, and in the last two-and-a-half decades, American ties to the Jordanian military have continued to expand. As a result, accounts of Jordanian training, doctrine, and exercises are available from which to try to gauge the capabilities of Amman's military since 1973.

In general, these sources describe a continuing slow erosion of Jordanian capabilities. To some extent, this is a result of financial difficulties that began to affect that nation's defense beginning in the mid-1980s. The overall decline in global oil prices from their high in the 1970s, plus policies that alienated some of the oil-rich Persian Gulf states, resulted in a decline in Jordanian income. Meanwhile, the cost of the American and European weapons Amman has desired continued to rise, forcing the military to forgo additional expansion and to slow down modernization programs. However, earlier Jordanian economic and educational policies began to pay off, with a significant increase in Jordan's socioeconomic development such that, by 1990, Jordan had surpassed most of the other Arab states in terms of its level of development. In particular, the education and health of Jordan's soldiery have increased significantly across the board, although they have not yet reached Western levels.[116]

Lingering Strengths

The Jordanian army still has a number of advantages it relies on to produce higher military effectiveness than other Arab armies. Although the late King Hussein had to introduce a measure of conscription to fill out specific areas of the force structure (principally disciplines requiring technical skills), draftees generally make up less than 15 percent of the entire armed forces. The other 85 percent of servicemen are volunteers who still typically serve for many years, even decades, at all ranks. Army service is still considered very prestigious, especially among the East Bankers, although it is no longer as economically rewarding as it once was because of the decline in Amman's defense budgets and the simultaneous growth of the Jordanian economy. Finally, the military's British origins remain an important, if fading, influence on Jordanian traditions and practices.[117]

These features have helped the kingdom's military retain a number of important strengths. First, because the majority of personnel are volunteers who serve for extended tours, training is very tough, and Jordanian soldiers can be constantly retrained for many years. In the British tradition, the Jordanians use these advantages to concentrate their efforts on creating the highest quality soldiers available, and as individuals, they remain quite good. Jordanian personnel stress individual military skills, discipline, and the care and maintenance of one's weaponry in a manner foreign to most Arab militaries. Their units emphasize the combat skills, discipline, and readiness of individual soldiers that are a hallmark of the British military system. Jordanian training emphasizes the development of its personnel as professional soldiers, and it is frequent and strenuous. Finally, Jordanian instruction stresses the objective communication of information, inculcating the notion that the honor of a Jordanian soldier demands accuracy in reporting to his superiors.

Growing Problems

Nevertheless, the areas of difficulty increasingly outnumber and outweigh the army's strengths. These problems generally exist where the advantages of the small, professional force and those of the lingering British traditions have the least effect. Jordanian exercises and training have become increasingly scripted, and officers are loathe to deviate from their training scripts, even when exercising with Western military personnel. As in other Arab armies, Jordanian troops and officers fear being criticized, and their preferred course of action is usually to conform to their plans and wait for orders from higher headquarters. Despite efforts to ingrain notions of accuracy in reporting, one U.S. military officer who has trained extensively with Jordanian armed forces observed, "Bad news is not something they like to deliver, . . . [while] minor successes are wildly exaggerated and a minor breakthrough gets reported as 'the war is won.'"[118] Jordanian forces are best when performing as small, self-contained units but experience increasing difficulty with larger operations requiring coordinated action. Although higher-level Jordanian officers recognize the importance of combined-arms operations, the same recognition is not as prevalent among junior officers, nor are those who do recognize the importance of combined arms able to put it into practice. Subelements of Jordanian combined-arms units do not regularly train together, nor are they provided with the necessary communications to help ensure good cooperation.

U.S. military officers report that even the best Jordanian junior officers are often considered mediocre by American standards. In exercises in Jordan and at training courses in the United States, most Jordanian tactical commanders show few of the leadership skills prized by modern militaries. They do not take initiative, adapt to fluid battle conditions, or act flexibly or creatively in operational situations, preferring to rely on "school solutions." Jordanian line officers have difficulty integrating combined-arms teams and are mostly poor at synchronizing operations, both vertically up and down the chain of command and horizontally across different units. Instructors generally consider them "very mediocre tacticians" in U.S. training courses, and in wargames they are not allowed to take higher command roles because American instructors do not believe they can handle the responsibility, even in simulation. Jordanian officers generally cannot grasp the mission-type orders employed by modern Western and Israeli forces. When issued such instructions during exercises in U.S. training courses, Jordanian officers often have no idea how to act and have difficulty giving similar orders to their subordinates.[119]

One also can render several broader judgments on Jordanian abilities since 1973. First, while Jordanian soldiers remain quite good as individuals and even in very small units such as sections or squads, their forces really cannot operate above the brigade level. Even from platoon to battalion level, Jordanian units are generally inflexible, slow to react, uncoordinated, and unimaginative, especially when attacking. Another U.S. military officer who trained with them observed that, beyond individual combat, military concepts "get lost" by Jordanian units, indicative of "an inability to grasp the larger concepts of modern war."[120] Second, while Jordanian units remain very skillful and determined when fighting a set-piece defense, they rarely show the same skill in fluid maneuver battles. They generally try to avoid such situations and do not practice unstructured assaults or meeting engagements. Even El-Edroos admits that Jordanian units have performed much better in static defense operations than in maneuver warfare.[121]

The Jordanians also have problems in various technical disciplines despite the considerable improvement in their country's socioeconomic levels and the increasing recruitment of the more urban and technologically skilled Palestinians. Between 1970 and 1990, the armed forces increasingly turned to its Palestinian population in recognition of the growing need for technical skills on the battlefield as military technology grew ever more sophisticated. Nevertheless, Jordanian maintenance practices are not much better than those of other Arab militaries. Although Jordanian soldiers tend to keep their personal weapons well maintained, Western military analysts fear their vehicles and heavy weapons will break down after a few days of fighting.[122] Moreover, U.S. military personnel generally have concluded that Jordanian trainees routinely require longer than specifications normally allow to master technically demanding tasks.[123] These difficulties with technology have placed limits on Jordan's force structure. For example, Western and Israeli analysts have estimated that Jordan lacks the technical base to operate more than a handful of sophisticated helicopters and probably cannot adequately operate and support the 2,000 armored vehicles and over 100 combat aircraft currently in its arsenal.[124]

Jordanian Military Effectiveness 1948–91

The combat performance of Jordanian armed forces changed markedly after 1956. From 1948 to 1956, the Arab Legion was far superior to any of the other Arab militaries. In battle it generally gave as good as it got, and the Israelis considered it their most dangerous adversary. However, after 1956, Jordanian capabilities began to decline. In 1967 they performed worse than in 1948, although the exceptional performance of the elite 40th Armored Brigade and a number of Israeli mistakes helped disguise this deterioration somewhat. Thereafter, Jordanian capabilities continued to gradually erode. By the 1990s, Amman's military still retained a number of advantages over other Arab militaries, but they were fewer in number and of less magnitude than ever before.

Changing Patterns

In a number of important areas, Jordanian forces displayed considerably greater capabilities before 1956 than afterward. While under British tutelage, the Arab Legion demonstrated excellent combined-arms coordination, its junior officers were aggressive and independent minded (even to a fault), and they counterattacked in force and with determination. Jordanian units often employed maneuver at tactical levels, frequently attempting to take an objective or defeat an opponent by outflanking them or otherwise trying to place them in a disadvantageous spatial or geographic position. Jordanian artillery fire was accurate and could shift to provide support in response to battlefield developments. Their units conducted aggressive reconnaissance operations and had few problems handling information in the chain of command. Operational authority was highly decentralized, with local commanders having responsibility and making decisions for the vast majority of events in their sectors.

By the Six Day War, each of these patterns had faded, if not disappeared altogether. With a few notable exceptions, Jordanian commanders were mostly passive, unimaginative, and unwilling to exercise independent judgment. In particular, the kingdom's forces consistently proved unable or unwilling to adapt to changing circumstances. They often failed to counterattack or even reorient their defenses in reaction to a successful enemy attack, with the result that they were destroyed piecemeal. Jordanian attacks increasingly took the form of frontal assaults, showing little creativity or subterfuge. Their artillery fire became less able to shift fire or perform more sophisticated missions such as counterbattery fire. It became a rarity for Jordanian commanders to pay adequate attention to reconnaissance, to scout the route ahead, or to employ flank guards when necessary. As a result, their units increasingly fell prey to ambushes or surprise flanking moves. At least between 1956 and 1967 (and especially during the Six Day War), the Jordanians experienced new problems with misinformation being passed throughout the command structure. Command-and-control procedures grew ever more centralized, with the general staff responsible for ever greater numbers of decisions.

Consistent Patterns

Nevertheless, there were also patterns of combat effectiveness that the Jordanians manifested both before and after 1956 with little apparent change. First, one must credit the abilities of the individual soldiers, whose bravery, discipline, and individual soldiering skills remained at a high level throughout the postwar period. This proficiency was manifested in excellent marksmanship with small arms, good fire discipline, frequent acts of courage, and good hand-to-hand combat abilities. In addition, the limited evidence available indicates that Jordanian air force pilots maintained a degree of competence in air-to-air and air-to-ground operations well after 1956. Jordanian forces experienced some problems with unit cohesion in all of their conflicts, especially the Six Day War, but more often than not Jordanian formations hung together in difficult situations. The quartermaster corps and combat engineers never demonstrated any particular brilliance, but neither were they ever a significant impediment to operations. In general, one can say they did what was asked of them, although they were never asked to perform miracles. Finally, Jordanian generalship remained mostly adequate throughout this entire period. Amman's strategic leadership was occasionally quite good, such as from November 1970 to September 1971, and also occasionally quite bad, such as in September 1970. But overall, the high command performed competently. The generals may never have seized victory from the jaws of defeat, but they were never more than a small part of Jordan's military problems.

4

LIBYA

Unlike most of the Arab militaries, the modern Libyan armed forces were not created by their colonial suzerain. Instead, Libya's army was created by the British to fight the Italians, who ruled Libya from 1912 to 1942. In 1911 the Italians invaded the Ottoman provinces of Cyrenaica and Tripolitania in North Africa. However, the Italians were opposed by local Bedouin tribesmen and, especially after the First World War, were forced into a long, bloody counterinsurgency campaign. Eventually, they secured the Libyan coast, but the interior, the Fezzan, remained mostly beyond their control. Because of these difficulties with the locals, the Italians generally chose not to form indigenous Libyan forces and instead policed the territory with their own troops and soldiers from their other African province, Ethiopia. When war broke out again in Europe in 1939, the British organized a small army of 600 Libyans from the Bedouin of the Sanussi order of Cyrenaica to fight the Italians in Libya. The Sanussi army, or Libyan Arab Forces, grew to five battalions of indigenous soldiers with a healthy leavening of British officers. These units saw little action during the campaigns against the Italians and Germans in North Africa because the British felt the Libyans lacked the technical skills to handle the modern vehicles and weapons that were so crucial to desert warfare. Consequently, the Libyan Arab Forces were relegated to guarding military installations and Axis prisoners of war — although one battalion did participate in the recapture of Tobruk in 1942.

After the war, the British disbanded the Libyan Arab Forces. However, nearly all of its soldiers transferred immediately to the newly formed Cyrenaican Police Force, a paramilitary formation London created to help control its new Libyan protectorate. When Libya proclaimed its independence in 1951, many of these same men then transferred into the new Royal

Libyan Army of Sayyid 'Amr Muhammad Idris, the leader of the Sanussi order and Libya's new king. Despite the Sanussi pedigree of the new army, the king very quickly came to distrust these men. In particular, after the Free Officer's coup in Egypt in 1952, many Libyan officers became deeply enamored of Gamal 'Abd al-Nasser and equally disenchanted with King Idris. Indeed, the British officers kept on by Idris to train and advise his forces considered the army entirely untrustworthy. Many of the British indicated that they felt their job was primarily to watch the army rather than to train it. Meanwhile, Libya's Western benefactors, the United States and Great Britain — both of whom maintained military bases in the country — pressed the king to modernize his armed forces so they could more effectively confront the new revolutionary regimes of the Middle East. In response, Idris formed a navy in 1962 and an air force the following year. The resulting need for technically skilled personnel to man more-sophisticated equipment forced Tripoli to recruit more of Libya's alienated city dwellers and fewer of the loyal Bedouin.

Idris attempted to handle his gnawing doubts about the loyalty of his army by emasculating it. He placed loyal but often unqualified Cyrenaicans in all senior command slots, limited the armed forces to 6,500 men, kept his soldiers lightly armed, and counterbalanced the army with two paramilitary units: the National Security Force and the Cyrenaican Defense Force (CDF), which was recruited entirely from Cyrenaican Bedouins loyal to the Sanussi order. Together, these units fielded 14,000 men armed with helicopters, armored cars, antitank weapons, and artillery.[1]

Despite Idris's efforts, the army did turn out to be the bane of his regime. On 1 September 1969, a cabal of junior officers under the leadership of Nasserist Capt. Muammar al-Qadhafi overthrew the monarchy. The catastrophic Arab defeat by Israel in 1967, which stunned and united the Arab world, was an important spark to the coup. Qadhafi and many other officers believed that Libya should have committed forces to aid Egypt, Syria, and Jordan, and they were enraged when Idris continued to maintain close ties to Israel's Western supporters, Britain and America. The king had also tried to reform the military, but these half-hearted efforts went nowhere, further frustrating young Libyan officers. Finally, although Libya began to produce and export large quantities of oil in 1962, by the late 1960s most of its oil wealth had been sucked up in graft, while the population remained destitute. As a result, when the coup finally came, the army and virtually the entire population supported it. Indeed, not even Idris's paramilitary forces made much of an effort to thwart the conspirators.

The Libyan Armed Forces under Qadhafi

Immediately after the coup, Qadhafi and his compatriots set out to remake the Libyan military as they wished. Their first priority was, naturally enough, to ensure its loyalty to the "Revolution" and prevent someone else from seizing power in turn.[2] Qadhafi dismissed, arrested, or executed every officer above the rank of colonel in the Libyan armed forces as well as a number of lower-ranking officers closely tied to the monarchy. The Sanussi were largely dismissed, and the police forces were disarmed.

The next step was to reform and rebuild the Libyan military in line with its new role in Qadhafi's grand scheme. In the early 1970s Qadhafi had three driving foreign policy ambitions. First was the goal of Arab unification, of which a crucial component was the eradication of the State of Israel from the "Arab" Middle East. Second was the support and strengthening of Islamic states and Muslim minorities throughout the world. Last was the battle against "Imperialism" (that is, the West, particularly the United States and Great Britain). Qadhafi saw military power as a crucial component of each of these objectives. Libya's armed forces therefore had to become both the "arsenal of Islam," stockpiling arms and equipment for the poorer Arab and Islamic states that could not afford them, and a force in their own right, capable of projecting power throughout the Middle East and North Africa.[3]

At the time of the coup, the Libyan armed forces were a paltry organization, virtually incapable of conventional military operations. The army had 6,500 men, and another 14,000 were in the National Defense Force and CDF. The air force had 400 men, and the only jet fighters it owned were ten U.S.–made F-5 Tigers.[4] Qadhafi almost immediately began to remedy this situation. First, Tripoli merged the National Security Force and the CDF into the army (with those men still loyal to the king dismissed) and kicked off a major recruiting drive. By 1970, the Libyan army boasted nearly 20,000 men. That same year Qadhafi scored a major coup by signing a deal with France for the sale of 110 Mirage fighters—the very fighters that Israel had employed with devastating results against the Arabs since 1967.[5] In 1972 the new regime created the Popular Resistance Forces, a militia that was to change its name several times but remained a key element of Qadhafi's vision for the Libyan armed forces. Moreover, throughout this period, Qadhafi and his fellow officers encouraged training, education, and the development of technical skills among Libyan military personnel to improve their fighting power.

The October War of 1973

Qadhafi's first chance to put into practice his foreign policy and national security goals came with the surprise Egyptian and Syrian attack on Israel in October 1973. Since the revolution, Qadhafi had badgered Egypt's rulers to unite the two countries as a first step toward Arab unity. Qadhafi was even willing to accept the leadership of Nasser or Anwar as-Sadat, his successor, but both Egyptian rulers concluded that Libya and its young dictator were too much trouble to become intimately bound to, even taking into consideration Libya's oil wealth. Despite these painful snubs, Qadhafi nonetheless deployed about 30 of his new Mirages to Egypt. These planes were placed under Cairo's command and, since the Libyans could scrape together only twenty-five pilots capable of flying their 110 Mirages, the planes were mostly flown by Egyptian pilots trained by the French specifically to fly the Libyan aircraft. When the war began on 6 October, the Libyan Mirages were committed to the fray along with the rest of the Egyptian Air Force (EAF) and a number of Algerian aircraft. The Israelis could not distinguish between the flying skills of the Libyan and Egyptian pilots, nor did they find the Libyan Mirages any more dangerous in combat than the MiGs flown by the other Arab air forces. Although exact numbers are difficult to find, at least one-third and probably more like half of the Libyan Mirages were shot down, almost entirely in dogfights with Israeli fighters.[6]

The most important effect of the October War on the Libyan military was the rift it created between Tripoli and Cairo. Qadhafi was personally insulted that Sadat and Syrian dictator Hafiz al-Asad had not included him in their secret preparations, nor had they even personally informed him of the outbreak of hostilities. Instead, he heard about it on the radio like the rest of the world. However, Sadat's unexpected proclamation after the war that the Egyptian offensive had been purposely designed as a limited operation intended to pave the way for a negotiated settlement between Egypt and Israel stunned Qadhafi. In his zealously anti-Zionist *Weltanschauung*, this was literally heresy. With Egypt no longer a member of the Arab confrontation against Israel — and possibly even an enemy of the pan-Arab cause — Qadhafi determined that Libya would have to greatly expand its own armed forces to compensate for Egypt's defection.

Thus, after the October War, Libya embarked on an arms buying spree that dwarfed its pre-1973 buildup. In the words of Gwynne Dyer, until 1973, Libya's military expansion had aimed to create "modern, well-balanced forces of a size that Libya could reasonably expect to operate with its limited resources of skilled manpower, although even then there were severe shortages of pilots and skilled technicians."[7] After 1973, Libya's buildup far outstripped the ability of its population or its armed forces to handle such weapons. Its arms purchases soared from $60 million in 1970 to $2.3 billion in 1979 (both figures in 1979 dollars).[8] Between 1973 and 1983, Libya invested $28 billion (calculated in current dollars) into arms purchases. In 1978 Qadhafi was forced to introduce conscription simply to find enough young bodies to man all of the weapons he was buying. By 1983, the air force had 4,000 men and 555 combat aircraft, including 60 Mirages, 175 MiG-23s, and the first MiG-25s sold outside the Warsaw Pact. Meanwhile, the Libyan army bought nearly 3,000 tanks — although it could not find crews for more than a fraction of them — and beefed up its ranks to 55,000 men.[9]

Initially, Tripoli had hoped to secure large numbers of French arms. The 1970 Mirage deal offered hope, and the Libyans preferred Western arms to Soviet-bloc equipment. But after Libya contributed its Mirages to the Arab-Israeli conflict in 1973, the European governments found it politically difficult (albeit not impossible) to continue to sell weapons to Tripoli. Libya instead turned to the USSR and in 1974 signed a deal with Moscow worth over $500 million for 2,000 tanks, Tu-22 bombers, and at least 40 of the Soviet air force's top-of-the-line MiG-23 fighters.[10] Nevertheless, in Lisa Anderson's understated phrasing, the Libyan-Soviet relationship "was never one of great confidence," and Libya's oil wealth allowed Qadhafi to diversify his arms purchases to some extent to reduce his dependence on Moscow.[11] Thus, although the Soviets always remained their primary arms supplier (accounting for at least two-thirds of Libyan arms expenditures), the Libyans were still eventually able to purchase AMX-30 tanks, Crotale surface-to-air missiles (SAMs), and Mirage F-1 fighters from France; Otomat antiship missiles from Italy; and (Soviet-made) T-62 tanks, MiG fighters, and SA-6 SAMs from Syria.

Border Clashes with Egypt, 1977

Relations between Egypt and Libya continued to deteriorate in the years after the October War. As Sadat's Egypt continued to slowly, but determinedly, feel its way toward peace with Israel, Qadhafi's Libya became one of its most vocal critics. The Libyans accused Sadat of betraying the Arab cause, and the Egyptians branded Qadhafi a mad man. Libya began to covertly support opposition groups in Egypt — including Islamic fundamentalists — and tried to incite popular opinion against Sadat. Eventually, both sides traded accusations that each was trying to assassinate the other's leader (almost certainly an accurate charge against the Libyans and possibly against the Egyptians as well). By the mid-1970s, the Libyans had begun harassing Egyptian border guards along their mutual border, prompting the Egyptians to respond in kind.

In the summer of 1976, the two countries nearly went to war. In response to Libya's provocations along the border, Sadat redeployed two mechanized divisions from the Suez Canal and Nile Delta areas to Egypt's border with Libya. Cairo also added 80 combat aircraft, including its newest MiG-23s, to Marsa Matruh Airbase, its westernmost airfield. Previously, Egypt had had only lightly armed border guards along its western boundary, and this sudden buildup greatly alarmed the Libyans; the redeploying Egyptian forces were roughly the size of the entire Libyan military at the time. In response, Qadhafi dispatched 3,000–5,000 of his own troops with 150 tanks to the Egyptian border. Tensions quickly dissipated, however, when it became clear that Egypt would not invade Libya. Speculation at the time attributed Sadat's restraint to Egypt's economic difficulties and to Cairo's unwillingness to antagonize the Soviet Union (which publicly backed Libya) and the Persian Gulf oil shaykhdoms (which were unhappy over Egypt's negotiations with Israel).[12] However, in retrospect, it appears equally likely, perhaps even more so, that Sadat refrained from attacking Libya because the Egyptian military was unprepared for war. His armed forces had neither planned nor rehearsed a major military operation against Libya, and they lacked the logistical, transportation, and communications infrastructure in the western desert to support large-scale offensive operations. Nevertheless, the Egyptian General Staff apparently began work on contingency plans for a full-scale assault into Libya.

The scare of the sudden Egyptian buildup did not appear to inject any caution into Tripoli's behavior. If anything, Qadhafi further ratcheted up the pressure on Cairo, perhaps seeing Sadat's unwillingness to attack as a sign of weakness. Tripoli continued to train Egyptian dissidents as terrorists at several camps in Libya and regularly dispatched them across the border to stir up unrest against Sadat's regime. Border skirmishes grew in frequency and intensity, and the Egyptians continued to increase their combat forces and logistical stockpiles in the area. In May 1977 the Soviets warned Libya and other Arab governments that they had reliable evidence that the Egyptians were planning a major invasion of Libya. The Libyans ignored these warnings, leaving most of their armed forces at low levels of readiness while continuing crossborder raids and artillery duels with the

Egyptians. Intense skirmishes occurred on 12 and 16 July 1977, leading to a four-hour firefight between battalion-sized forces on the nineteenth. Two days later, Egypt attacked.

The State of the Libyan Military

Qadhafi's post–October War buildup notwithstanding, the Libyan military was in no shape to fight a major battle with a veteran army the size of Egypt's. First, the Libyan armed forces were still suffering from considerable political problems. Qadhafi had recently weathered a series of coup attempts from elements in the military, all of which backfired against the entire armed forces. In 1975 there were three major efforts to oust him: in March by thirty-nine senior military officers and the minister of planning; in July by the chief of military transport; and in August by the commander of the regime's palace guard—the Jamahiriyyah Guard—and several members of the ruling Revolutionary Command Council. Qadhafi responded by conducting widespread purges of the armed forces to weed out any officers, especially senior officers, suspected of disloyalty.[13] Moreover, he took a number of other measures to try to hinder the ability of the military to move against him. Most were harmful to Libyan military effectiveness. Qadhafi would not allow standing formations larger than battalions, he placed loyalists in key command billets regardless of their actual qualifications, he frequently and suddenly rotated senior officers to prevent them from developing a rapport with the troops under their command, and he inserted informants and "people's commissars" into the military to keep an eye on the army.[14] However, other actions Qadhafi took to minimize the threat of a military coup may actually have helped Libyan military effectiveness. For instance, he largely relieved the armed forces of their internal-security responsibilities, turning this mission over to a number of overlapping intelligence and paramilitary organizations. Instead, the military was focused entirely on preparing for conventional operations in support of Qadhafi's foreign policy goals.[15]

One of Libya's greatest problems was its dearth of technically competent personnel to handle the rapidly expanding arsenal of modern weapons Qadhafi was buying. Libyan soldiers were often illiterate and rarely had significant exposure to sophisticated machinery. Even fewer had any actual training or education in technical subjects. Consequently, in 1977 Libya had only 200–300 trained crews for the 2,500 tanks it then possessed and no more than 150 trained pilots for its 550 combat aircraft. Libyan maintenance practices were appalling. Routine upkeep was regularly neglected, contributing to extremely low operational readiness rates, probably well below 50 percent for ground vehicles. Complex ground weapons and jet fighters were parked in the desert for months on end with no protection from sand, sun, or wind. Armored vehicles were left in the sun for weeks without any attention, allowing lubricants to evaporate and delicate machinery to deteriorate. Indeed, so great were Libya's problems operating and maintaining advanced weaponry that Tripoli brought in large numbers of skilled foreign personnel to handle these responsibilities. Russians, Eastern Europeans, and Cubans were imported to serve as technicians and maintenance personnel. Close to 2,000 Soviets manned Libya's radar and SAM defenses, while Soviet, Cuban, Syrian, Pakistani, and North Korean pilots flew many of Libya's fighters. Indeed, most of its Mirages were still flown by Pakistani pilots—even though the best Libyan pilots had been sent to France for training on that aircraft—and Tripoli's fleet of advanced MiG-25 interceptor-reconnaissance aircraft were wholly manned by Russians.[16]

The balance of forces was also weighted against the Libyans. The Egyptians had continued to reinforce their western border after the war scare of the previous summer, and during the 1977 clashes, they were able to expand their ground strength facing the Libyans to over 40,000 troops in three heavy divisions and twelve commando battalions; at that time, the entire Libyan army consisted of only 32,000 men. Moreover, because Tripoli had apparently underestimated the threat from Egypt, it had only seven or eight battalions (roughly 5,000 troops) organized into three brigade-sized formations to defend against an Egyptian attack.[17] Perhaps the one thing the Libyan military had going for it was that morale among its forces was high, for the troops believed that the Egyptians had betrayed the Arab cause by seeking peace with Israel.

Course of Operations

On 21 July Libyan forces conducted another battalion-sized harassing raid against the Egyptian border town of as-Sallum, near the Mediterranean Sea, similar to the previous operation on 19 July. This time, however, the Egyptians used the Libyan raid to unleash a much larger operation. Rather than trading fire with the Egyptians for several hours before retiring as they had expected, the Libyan 9th Tank Battalion stumbled into a well-concealed ambush at as-Sallum and was then counterattacked by a much larger Egyptian mechanized force—possibly as much as two entire divisions. The 9th Battalion suffered 50 percent casualties before it could retreat back across the border. A small number of Libyan Mirages also took part in the raid, bombing several nearby Egyptians villages, but they did

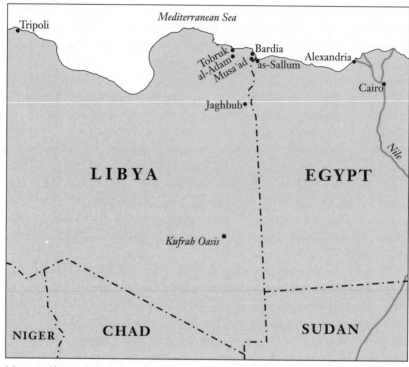

Map 26. Skirmish Sites between Egypt and Libya, 1977

little damage, and the Egyptians claim to have shot down two with anti-aircraft artillery (AAA).[18]

Later that same day, the Egyptians launched their counterattack. They began with airstrikes by Su-20s and MiG-21s against Gamal 'Abd al-Nasser Airbase at al-Adam, the main interceptor field in eastern Libya. The Egyptians caught the Libyans by surprise, with all of their Mirages and MiGs parked out in the open. But the EAF planes botched the raid, doing almost no damage to the prostrate Libyans. They hit a few radars but inflicted only minor damage on a few of the idle jets. Then, an Egyptian mechanized force, probably of division strength, drove into Libya along the coast toward the town of Musa'ad. Libyan forces mostly fled in front of the Egyptians, although there were some desultory tank battles involving a small number of vehicles. The operation seems to have been little more than a reconnaissance-in-force to determine the extent of the Libyan defenses, and at the end of the day, the Egyptians retired back across the border after penetrating fifteen miles into Libya and destroying roughly sixty Libyan tanks and armored personnel carriers (APCS) in the battles around as-Sallum and Musa'ad.[19]

The next two days saw heavy exchanges of fire across the border but little decisive action. Libyan and Egyptian artillery batteries traded salvos without causing much damage. The Libyan air force conducted very modest raids (probably no more than ten to twenty sorties total) against the Egyptian mechanized formations continuing to mass around as-Sallum. The Egyptians claimed to have shot down two Libyan fighters, while Tripoli admitted to the loss of the jets but insisted that one had been shot down by Libyan AAA gunners and the other had crashed during a reconnaissance mission. Meanwhile, the EAF again struck at Nasser Airbase as well as al-Kufrah Airbase and other Libyan towns and military installations in the border area. Against Nasser, the Egyptians conducted much larger strikes (at least three squadrons of Su-20s and MiGs took part) than before but again succeeded in doing only light damage to Libyan aircraft, radars, and ground installations. Egyptian jets also conducted low-level, high-speed passes over villages throughout eastern Libya as a display of their freedom to operate in Libyan airspace. Meanwhile, twelve battalions of Egyptian commandos conducted airborne raids against Libyan radar sites, terrorist camps, and military facilities at al-Kufrah Oasis, al-Jaghbub Oasis, al-Adam, Tobruk, and other locations along the border.

On 24 July the Egyptians again appeared to escalate the fighting. First, they launched the largest raid to date against Nasser Airbase. Egyptian aircraft attacked in concert with Egyptian commandos landed by helicopter. Despite the constant attacks over the last three days, the Libyans had still not dispersed, removed, concealed, or otherwise protected the aircraft at the base. This time the Egyptians were somewhat more successful, cratering the runway, destroying several armored vehicles and six to twelve Libyan Mirages on the ground, obliterating several early warning radars, and damaging several SAM sites. However, the Libyans did shoot down at least two Su-20s.[20] The Egyptians also struck al-Kufrah Airbase once again but did little significant damage. Helicopter-borne raids by Egyptian commandos also inflicted heavy damage on Libyan forward logistics depots at al-Jaghbub and al-Adam. Despite the wider scope and greater success of Egyptian operations on 24 July, at the end of the day—while Egyptian commandos were still in action at al-Jaghbub—President Sadat unexpectedly announced a ceasefire.

Some residual fighting between Egyptian commandos and Libyan forces continued over the next two days as the Egyptians pulled back across the border, but Sadat's declaration essentially ended the clashes as suddenly as they had begun. Although there was never a formal conclusion, the two sides informally kept to the truce and all combat operations halted. Eventually, both sides reduced their military forces along the border, for the limited infrastructure in the area made it difficult for either to maintain large formations there for long periods of time. All told, the Libyans lost at least ten and possibly as many as twenty Mirages — nearly all of which were destroyed on the ground — in addition to thirty tanks, forty APCs, and 400 dead and wounded. The Libyans had also sustained minor damage to some of their main eastern airfields and more substantial damage to their defense network along the Egyptian border. The Egyptians probably lost no more than four aircraft and about 100 casualties.[21]

Intervention in Uganda, 1979

During the 1970s, Libya grew close to the radical regime of Idi Amin Dada in Uganda. Qadhafi saw in Amin a fellow Muslim ruler, an ally in his bid to expand Libyan influence into sub-Saharan Africa, and another staunch adversary of Israel in Africa. In 1972 Qadhafi had dispatched 400 Libyan soldiers to Uganda to bolster Amin's regime after his successful coup. This token force had little military value but signaled Qadhafi's commitment to Amin. Four years later, Qadhafi replaced the eleven Ugandan MiG-21s destroyed by the Israelis in their rescue mission to Entebbe gratis. Given the strength of Qadhafi's commitment to the Ugandan dictator, it was no surprise that Libya came to Amin's aid when his regime was threatened by a Tanzanian invasion in 1979.

In the fall of 1978, Amin had ordered an invasion of Tanzania to seize the West Lake region bordering Uganda. Ugandan formations performed incompetently, but because the Tanzanians had only one light infantry battalion in the area, the Ugandans were able to conquer the small chunk of Tanzanian territory north of the Kagera River before their invasion ground to a halt. The Tanzanians quickly mustered a significant portion of their army in the area and launched a counterattack that retook the Kagera salient. This presented the Tanzanian government with a golden opportunity to realize its longstanding goal of ousting Amin. There had been considerable animosity between Uganda and Tanzania throughout Amin's reign, and each side had covertly supported dissident elements working to destabilize the other's regime. Thus, even though the Tanzanian People's Defense Force (TPDF) was in a very sorry state of readiness, Pres. Julius Kambarage Nyerere decided that he needed to solve the problem of Idi Amin once and for all, ordering a counterinvasion of Uganda. On 20 January 1979, Tanzanian forces crossed into Uganda in strength, smashing

Amin's forces defending the border and taking the key defensive positions in the Simba Hills and Lukoma Airstrip by 13 February.

The Tanzanian invasion of Uganda and its threat to Amin's regime provoked a Libyan reaction. Qadhafi was determined to help his ally and in February began moving military forces south to defend Uganda. Libya staged a major airlift of combat forces to Kampala and Entebbe, sending 2,500 troops with T-54 and T-55 tanks, BTR APCS, BM-21 "Katyusha" multiple-rocket launchers (MRLS), artillery, MiG-21s, and a Tu-22 bomber.[22] The Libyan force was a hodgepodge of regular units, People's Militia, and members of the Islamic Pan-African Legion — a force of sub-Saharan Africans equipped and trained by the Libyans (and reinforced with a number of mercenaries) to serve as an expeditionary force in precisely this sort of operation. Nevertheless, the firepower of the Libyan expeditionary force, particularly its armor and airpower, were well beyond anything that the Tanzanians could field.

The Battle of Lukuya

Libyan forces first saw combat in Uganda in mid-March 1979. The Tanzanians, along with several battalions of Ugandan dissidents, drove north toward Kampala but were stopped by a vast, deep-water swamp north of Lukuya. A twenty-kilometer-long causeway stretched across this swamp northward from the town and could be easily defended from the solid ground at its northern terminus. Given the pitiful performance of the Ugandans to that point, the TPDF decided to try crossing by sending its 201st Brigade directly across the causeway, in hope that the Ugandans would fail to properly destroy or defend the road, while sending the elite 208th Brigade to skirt the western edge of the swamp in case the Ugandans were able to block the causeway. Meanwhile, unbeknown to the Tanzanians, a brigade-sized force of Libyan infantry with fifteen T-55s, over a dozen APCS, land rovers with 106-mm recoilless rifles, and a battery of BM-21 MRLS was assembling north of the swamp. The Libyans did not realize how close the TPDF forces were, for their orders were to launch a counteroffensive to retake the major town of Masaka, south of Lukuya. Consequently, the two forces wandered into each other in a confused meeting engagement.

During the morning of 10 March, the Tanzanians attacked Lukuya to secure the southern end of the causeway. The Ugandans had mostly abandoned the town the night before, and the TPDF's 201st Brigade moved in easily against minimal resistance. As the Tanzanians readied themselves for the next push up the causeway that afternoon, the Libyans (without

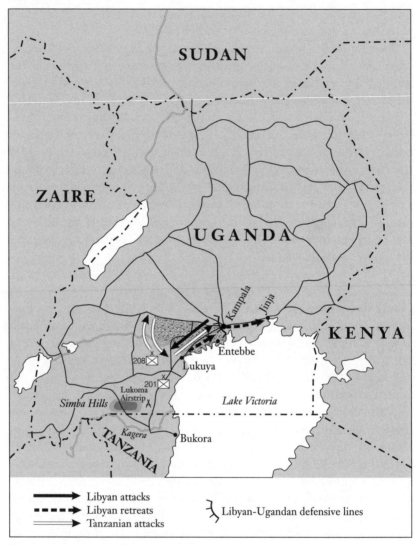

Map 27. Libyan Operations in Uganda, 1979

bothering to secure their route of escape) launched their own offensive toward Masaka. The Libyans, reinforced with several units from Amin's army, charged down the causeway and into Lukuya, fortuitously catching the Tanzanians by surprise as they regrouped. The moment the Libyans spotted the TPDF troops in Lukuya, they stopped and began to shower those units with fire from their BM-21s. The Tanzanians had never faced multiple-rocket launchers before, and many bolted from the town in terror. When the Libyans finally moved in, they encountered little resistance and occupied Lukuya without a man killed on either side.

At this moment, the Tanzanian 201st Brigade — the only force standing between the Libyans and Masaka — was in complete disarray, but the Libyans did nothing to exploit their victory. Despite orders to push on to Masaka, they stopped at Lukuya and made camp; they did not even send reconnaissance units south along the road to determine the TPDF presence between themselves and Masaka. Instead, the Libyans milled around in Lukuya, setting up some defensive positions but not digging in. Meanwhile, the Tanzanians hurriedly regrouped the 201st Brigade, while the elite 208th Brigade raced back east to reinforce it. The Tanzanians counterattacked Lukuya during the night of 11–12 March and caught the Libyans unprepared for a fight. The TPDF launched a double envelopment of the town, with the reorganized 201st Brigade attacking the main defensive lines from the south, while the 208th Brigade — having completed a grueling sixty-kilometer march back to Lukuya and quietly taking up positions northwest of the town — drove east to the Lukuya-Kampala road and then turned south and smashed into the Libyan rear. The Libyans were surprised and unable to react to the Tanzanian flanking attack. TPDF artillery support was very accurate, while the speed and direction of their attacks prevented the Libyans from employing their MRLS and artillery with any effect. Many Libyan units, especially the Islamic Legionnaires and militiamen, broke and ran, and the town was lost to the Tanzanians in a few hours. The Libyans left behind 200 dead plus another 200 dead Ugandan soldiers who had been fighting with them.[23] After the battle, Tanzanian commanders admitted that their initial set-back at Lukuya could have been a disaster and that only the incompetence of the Libyans had saved them.[24]

Entebbe and Kampala

After the defeat at Lukuya, Qadhafi increased his aid to Amin, sending large shipments of weapons and dispatching an additional 2,000 members of the People's Militia. Remarkably, many of the militiamen were not even told they were being sent into combat but instead were told that they were participating in joint-training exercises with the Ugandans. A regular shuttle of Libyan transports began to set down at Entebbe to deliver these troops and supplies, but much of the Libyan equipment piled up around the airport because Amin lacked the manpower or transportation capacity to distribute more than small amounts to his troops. Meanwhile, Libyan troops and armor began to take up positions at key crossroads south and west of Kampala and Entebbe as the Tanzanians closed in on the capital. In their panic to get out of Lukuya, the Libyans there had not bothered to try to block the causeway, with the result that the Tanzanians were able to cross three brigades over the swamp close on the Libyans' heels. In a bid to force Dar es Salaam to call off the invasion, Qadhafi ordered an airstrike against the Tanzanian city of Mwanza with the lone Libyan Tu-22 operating out of Kampala. The aircraft managed to miss the entire city, and its bombs killed a large number of antelope when they landed in a nearby game preserve.

In early April the Tanzanians began to reduce the Ugandan defenses around Kampala. They began by attacking Entebbe, recognizing that in doing so they could cut off the main source of Libyan reinforcements to Amin as well as placing themselves advantageously on the southern flank of Kampala. A large force of Libyans was dug in around Entebbe, along with smaller units of Ugandans, to defend the airfield. The Tanzanians set up 130-mm M-46 artillery pieces around the airfield and began a light bombardment that lasted for three days. Although the artillery fire was limited to a few rounds a day, it was enough to scare off Amin himself, who relocated from the State House at Entebbe to Jinja farther east. Amin's departure caused many of the Ugandan troops to flee. Although the Libyan units remained at their posts, when the Tanzanians finally began their assault on the airport — a slow, methodical operation by the 208th Brigade — the Libyans cracked. Their units fell apart and ran helter-skelter back to the airfield, where they hoped to be airlifted home. However, when the first Libyan C-130 tried to fly out of Entebbe carrying Libyan soldiers, it was destroyed on takeoff by a rocket-propelled grenade fired by advance units of the TPDF. This ended the Libyan airlift efforts, and ever more Libyan units began to throw down their weapons and either surrender or flee. A small force of about company strength attempted to fight its way to Kampala, but they did not post flank or advance guards as they moved and were caught in a Tanzanian ambush and destroyed. In all, 300 Libyans were killed at Entebbe, with many others wounded and taken prisoner, while much of Libya's sophisticated equipment (including three brand new BM-21s) fell into the hands of the Tanzanians.[25]

The remaining Libyan forces gathered with most of the remaining intact Ugandan formations for the defense of Kampala. However, there was little fight left in this combined army. Morale among both the Libyans and Ugandans was very low after their various defeats. Before the Tanzanian attack on the capital, President Nyerere sent a message to Qadhafi informing him that Tanzanian forces had orders not to block the eastern exits from the city, specifically to allow a cordon through which the Libyan units could retreat safely to Jinja, where Libyan aircraft could pick them up and fly them home. Tanzanian units began to push forward against Kampala on 8 April, smashing Libyan and Ugandan forces in blocking positions along the roads south of the city. On 10 April TPDF reconnaissance and forward elements recognized that the defenses of the city were weak and poorly manned and, even though most units were not in their jumping-off positions, the Tanzanians began their assault on the city. The TPDF attacked from three sides, with the 208th Brigade driving north from Entebbe, the 207th Brigade moving east along the Lukuya-Kampala road, and the 201st attacking from the north. The battle for Kampala was entirely anticlimactic, for few Ugandan and Libyan units offered any resistance, and the greatest problem for the Tanzanians was their own lack of maps of the city. The Libyans suffered only a few casualties in the battle, for most took Nyerere's offer and retreated eastward through Jinja and then overland to Kenya and Ethiopia where they were finally repatriated. Over the entire course of the campaign, at least 600 Libyan troops were killed and at least three times that number wounded.[26]

Observations on Libyan Military Performance in Uganda

There were a number of mitigating factors working against the Libyans in Uganda. First, the force sent was considerably smaller than its adversary. By the end of the war, Tanzania had as many as 45,000 men in Uganda facing 4,500 Libyans and — after many of Amin's units disintegrated during the first days after the invasion — an even smaller number of Ugandans.[27] Libyan morale was awful: few wanted to be in Uganda, let alone fight and die for the odious regime of Idi Amin. The Libyans were operating several thousand kilometers from their bases and normal theater of operations and were in an alien climate. Finally, there was the burden of the poorly trained and prepared militia units sent into combat without any warning.

Nevertheless, even taking into account these circumstances, "Libya's performance was disastrous," in the words of former national intelligence officer for Africa William Foltz. The numerical advantage of the Tanzanians was not an issue until the final battle of Kampala, as the battles at Lukuya, Entebbe, and for the approaches to Kampala had been fought by a combined Libyan-Ugandan force against TPDF units of essentially equal strength. What's more, any slight numerical advantage on the Tanzanian side should have been more than compensated for by Libya's massive advantage in firepower. To a great extent, Libya's morale problems were of its own making. Sending the half-trained troops of the People's Militia and the Islamic Legion was clearly a mistake, for their lack of professionalism left them unsure of themselves right from the start. Tripoli failed to properly prepare its troops for combat, and its decision to conceal from many of them the fact that they were being sent into combat was frankly stupid, to say the least. These problems became decisive at the battle for Entebbe, where Libyan firepower and air support should have allowed its dug-in troops to hold the airfield almost indefinitely against the lightly armed Tanzanians. Instead, the Libyans broke under the first TPDF infantry assaults.

To some extent, the inadequate training and poor morale of the Libyan troops were so deleterious that all other problems must, to some extent, be considered outgrowths of these liabilities. However, a number of deficiencies did manifest themselves that cannot be wholly explained as the products of poor morale or improper training. First, Libyan forces made little or no effort to gather intelligence on their adversary. These units almost never sent out patrols, nor did their commanders direct aerial reconnaissance missions to compensate. Consequently, most Libyan forces blundered around Uganda blind, a problem that their commanders compounded by moving without proper advance or flank guards. Second, the Libyans were never able to use their tremendous advantage in firepower, except for their initial assault at Lukuya. Indeed, the success they achieved with their MRLS in this case makes clear how badly they failed in every engagement thereafter. The Tanzanians simply had nothing to handle Libya's armor, artillery, and airpower, but the Libyans proved so incompetent in bringing their assets to bear against the relatively agile TPDF that the Tanzanians had little difficulty defeating them. In addition, Libyan field commanders demonstrated a crucial shortage of initiative, aggressiveness, and adaptability. This was most clearly on display at Lukuya, where they failed to exploit the rout of the Tanzanian 201st Brigade to move on Masaka and then proved incapable of organizing any sort of counterattack or coordinated defense against the Tanzanian assault during the night of 11–12 March.

The expedition was not a *total* fiasco, however. Libyan logistics proved to be a success. Tripoli put together and moved to Uganda by airlift a force of 4,500 men with armor, artillery, and all of the other accoutrements of a modern army. They then kept those forces supplied in difficult subtropical African terrain for several months. Indeed, Libyan forces never suffered from inadequate supplies. In the end, the Tanzanians captured huge quantities of weapons and combat consumables that the Libyans had stockpiled in Kampala, Entebbe, and other locations. This would have been an impressive operation for any country, let alone a resource-poor nation desperate for technically competent personnel such as Libya.

The War for Chad, 1978–87

Libyan involvement in Chad dates back to before the 1969 revolution. In 1965 a group of Chadian dissidents, calling themselves the Front de Libération National Tchadien (Frolinat), declared an open revolt against the inept and increasingly isolated dictatorship of François Tombalbaye. At that time, there was already considerable interaction between the two states as many Saharan tribes migrated back and forth between them, and Libya had irredentist claims to the northernmost portion of Chad dating back to the Italian occupation. Consequently, King Idris felt almost compelled to support the Frolinat against Tombalbaye. However, the king had no particular desire for a confrontation with the French-backed regime in N'djamena, and his support for the dissidents was low-key and limited. In particular, Idris would not provide the Frolinat with arms, essentially giving them only nonlethal supplies and sanctuary in Libyan territory.

As with so many other things, all of this changed with the revolution and Qadhafi's rise to power. Qadhafi had more ambitious designs on Chad. In particular, he claimed the Aouzou Strip, the northernmost one-sixth of the country, based on an unratified treaty from the Italian colonial period.[28] Almost immediately, Qadhafi abandoned the camouflages employed by Idris and increased aid to the Frolinat, providing them with weapons and funding. In 1971 Qadhafi went so far as to back a coup attempt against Tombalbaye that narrowly failed.[29]

Libya's support for the Frolinat, the increasing erosion of his domestic support, and the close call of the 1971 coup attempt convinced Tombalbaye that he needed to reach an accommodation with Qadhafi. In December 1972 the Chadian leader accepted Libyan occupation of the Aouzou Strip in return for Qadhafi's agreement to cease backing the Frolinat. Six months later, Libyan troops moved into the disputed region, occupying the major towns and building an airbase just north of the Aouzou Oasis. Qadhafi, in turn, renounced his support for the Frolinat. However, rapprochement between Libya and Chad did not last long. In 1975 Tombalbaye was overthrown by the army and replaced by Gen. Felix Malloum. One of the principal motivating factors in the coup had been Tombalbaye's humiliating accord with Qadhafi, which Malloum immediately repudiated and resumed supporting Libyan insurrectionists operating from Chad. In response, Qadhafi resumed his aid to the Chadian insurgents, now organized into the First Liberation Army of Ahmed Acyl (comprised mainly of Chadian Arabs) and the Second Liberation Army led by Goukouni Oueddei and Hissène Habré (consisting of African Toubou tribesmen from northern Chad). The Second Liberation Army later split over personal differences between Goukouni and Habré as well as the question of Libyan support, with the vehemently anti-Libyan Habré pulling out of the Frolinat and operating independently against the Malloum regime. In 1976 Qadhafi began hinting publicly that he might annex the Aouzou Strip, and Libyan units began making forays into central Chad along with Frolinat forces. As a result of these widening incursions, by the end of the year, the northern third of Chad was essentially in the hands of the Frolinat and their Libyan allies.

The First Libyan Intervention, 1978

In 1978 Libyan aid allowed the Frolinat to transition from an insurgency to a conventional military campaign against the Malloum government. In their first offensive in January of that year, Goukouni's forces overran the mountainous Tibesti in extreme northwestern Chad, capturing the Toubou towns of Bardai, Zouar, and Ouri. Next, the Frolinat turned south, this time with the active participation of Libyan combat units. As would largely remain the pattern over the next eight years, the Frolinat provided the infantry — which did the bulk of the scouting and fighting — while the Libyans provided armor, artillery, and air support. In February an army of 2,500 Frolinat fighters, with possibly as many as 4,000 Libyans providing fire support, attacked the key town of Faya Largeau in north-central Chad. The 5,000-man army garrison there lacked the weaponry to contend with Libyan firepower, particularly Libyan tanks and airstrikes, and they collapsed after a brief battle, with 1,500 ending up as prisoners of war.[30]

After garrisoning Faya Largeau with 800 Libyans, the combined forces resumed their drive south in April, smashing small government units with Libyan armor and airpower and heading directly for N'djamena. This threat to the capital prompted Malloum to ask France, Chad's former colonial master, to rescue the country from the Libyans. Paris agreed, dispatching a force of 1,000 men and twenty Jaguar fighter-bombers. The Jaguars, in particular, turned the tide because the Libyan MiGs and Mirages would not fight them. As a result, the government suddenly possessed the complete air superiority that the Frolinat previously had enjoyed, and the results were equally decisive. In a pair of battles along the northern approaches to N'djamena at Ati in May and Djedaa in June, the government and French forces routed the Frolinat and Libyans, driving them back to the Aouzou Strip.

The Second Libyan Intervention, 1979

These military reverses led to a series of political realignments that left Libya out in the cold by early 1979. First, Habré built a force of 2,000 disciplined, well-armed, and loyal Toubou warriors, and his virulent opposition to the Libyan presence convinced Malloum that a deal could be struck. So in late 1978 Malloum and Habré announced the formation of a government of national unity, pooling their forces against the Libyans and the Frolinat. Second, the defeats at Ati and Djedaa reopened the issue of Libyan support within the Frolinat. Acyl and the Arabs of the First Liberation Army (now also known as the Volcan Army) were adamantly in favor of maintaining the close cooperation, but at Ati, the Volcans had proven to be the weakest military link in the alliance because they had neither the firepower of the Libyans nor the tactical skill of the Toubous. In contrast, Goukouni and his Toubous had always been uncomfortable with the Libyans, chafed under the Libyan occupation of the Aouzou Strip, and regarded their partnership with Tripoli as nothing more than a temporary alliance to get rid of the Malloum government. These divisions in the Frolinat came to the fore in February 1979 when Habré ousted Malloum, defeated the national army, and gained control of N'djamena. Before Habré could consolidate his control, Goukouni hurried south with his Second Liberation Army to contest power. Rather than fight a mutually destructive battle in the capital, the two Toubou armies (along with the remnants of the national army led by former Chadian army colonel Wadal Kamougue) were able to strike a deal based, to a considerable extent, on a common desire to see Libya out of Chad. The result was a new government of national unity known as the Government d'Union Nationale de Transition (GUNT).

The Libyans were incensed that the new GUNT did not include any of the leaders of the Volcan Army nor recognize Libyan claims on the Aouzou Strip. Qadhafi reacted by ordering a Libyan invasion of north-central Chad in November 1979 to compel the new government to recognize his influence in northern Chad. He sent a force of several thousand Libyan troops with armor and air support along with elements of the Volcan Army to retake Faya Largeau. This time, however, the Libyans were opposed by Goukouni's forces. Without the superb Toubous to provide infantry and reconnaissance, the Libyans' firepower proved mostly useless. The Libyans

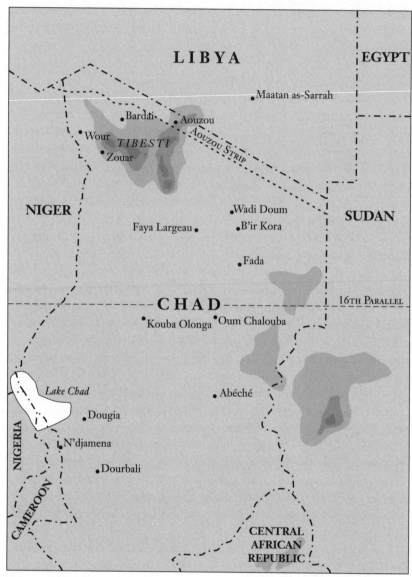

Map 28. Important Locations in the Chad-Libya Fighting, 1986–87

and Volcans again proved their incompetence in combat and were smashed by Goukouni's forces — backed by French airpower — in a series of clashes around Faya Largeau from April to August 1979.

The Third Libyan Intervention, 1980–81
Nevertheless, events in Chad quickly transpired to bring the Libyans back in after their ignominious retreat in the late summer of 1979. After the Libyans were ousted, Habré chafed in his position in the new government under Goukouni, and on 16 March 1980, he expelled the GUNT from N'djamena. Habré and his forces, now called the Forces Armée du Nord (FAN), then set out to gain control of the rest of the country. The FAN was rebuffed by Goukouni's GUNT at Bokoro and Mongo, north of the capital, but regrouped and was able to drive the GUNT out of north-central Chad, seizing the major towns of Faya Largeau and Ounianga Kebir as well as much of the northern Toubou plains. Then on 1 April, Habré's FAN smashed Colonel Kamougue's army at the Chari River south of N'djamena, destroying Goukouni's only real ally. With Kamougue's forces eliminated and the FAN victorious everywhere, Goukouni was forced to turn once more to Tripoli for aid.

Qadhafi was eager for the opportunity to regain his position in Chad, although he also was determined to put it on a firmer footing than before, having recognized that Goukouni would never be more than an ally of convenience. The GUNT forces regrouped in southern Libya, where they rested and were reequipped by the Libyans. Indeed, at that point Goukouni even accepted a Libyan officer, Mansur 'Abd al-Aziz, as commander of the GUNT forces. Starting in August 1980, Tripoli also mustered an army of Libyan regulars and Islamic Legionnaires at Sabha in southern Libya. Then, in October 1980, before Habré had had the opportunity to consolidate his rule, the Libyans, the Volcans, and the GUNT invaded Chad. Qadhafi sent 7,000 Libyan regulars with 300 T-55s and several batteries of BM-21s, all backed by much of the Libyan Air Force (LAF), along with 7,000 members of the Islamic Legion into Chad. The Libyans apparently were wary of French intervention this time and brought large numbers of anti-aircraft systems — including SA-6 SAMs and ZSU-23-4 AAA systems — to try to keep the French at bay. The GUNT and Volcan armies added another 6,000–7,000 soldiers to the invasion force, while Habré had only 4,000 men with no armor, aircraft, or even heavy infantry weapons to resist the onslaught.[31]

The Libyans began the invasion by airlifting large numbers of troops into the Aouzou Strip and then striking directly at Faya Largeau while

Habré's forces were still scattered and preoccupied with consolidating their control over the country. The FAN soldiers were terrified of the tremendous firepower the Libyans were able to bring to bear. Starting at Faya Largeau in late October, the Libyan-GUNT advances developed into a predictable routine. Seasoned GUNT warriors would probe ahead of the main columns looking for FAN concentrations. When these were located, the Libyans would bring up their armor and artillery, dig-in in front of the defenders, and then unleash a barrage from their tanks, artillery, and rocket launchers, accompanied by heavy airstrikes for good measure. The Libyan bombardments were usually very inaccurate, but because Habré's men had never encountered such intense firepower before nor have any answer for the Libyan armor and fighter-bombers, they completely unnerved the FAN defenders. On most occasions FAN soldiers fled during the initial Libyan bombardment. Libyan airpower, free to roam the skies without fear of French fighters or surface-to-air missiles, proved particularly devastating to the FAN, winning numerous engagements single-handed by scattering the defenders before the ground units even came to grips. On those rare occasions when Habré's defenders were not driven off by the initial bombardment, Libyan armor occasionally charged straight at the main FAN positions. Although these tank attacks were clumsy affairs, because Habré's men lacked any antitank weapons, they usually succeeded in breaking FAN resistance. Otherwise, the GUNT infantry would conduct a determined assault, which usually resulted in their overwhelming the disoriented FAN units by sheer weight of numbers in bloody hand-to-hand fighting.

Using these inelegant but effective tactics, the Libyans swept all resistance before them. By early November, Tripoli's army had driven the FAN from Faya Largeau. The Libyans quickly turned the town into a staging base, airlifting vast quantities of supplies, replacement troops, and equipment in to make good their losses. In late November the Libyans and GUNT resumed their advance south toward N'djamena. Habré's men really did not stand a chance: outgunned and outnumbered, they fled back to the capital to try to make a stand. At the end of the month, the Libyans and the GUNT conquered Dougia, just sixty kilometers north of N'djamena. Here they paused to set up another forward logistics depot and airbase and again built up supplies for the impending offensive against the capital. With all troops and logistical support in place, the assault on the defenses of the city began on 8 December and was conducted largely by the GUNT. However, the Libyans committed about 3,000–5,000 troops and nearly all of their heavy weapons (including 200 T-55s and all of their artillery and MRLs) in support of the attack. The fighting was ferocious between Goukouni and

Habré's men, and the Libyans kept up a steady barrage, lobbing 10,000 artillery rounds into the city in the last three days of fighting alone.[32] As before, because the FAN units were outnumbered, had no air defense weapons, and had only a handful of rocket-propelled grenades (RPGS) captured from the Libyans for antitank weapons, they were slowly beaten down under the weight of GUNT numbers and Libyan firepower. N'djamena fell to the Libyans and the GUNT on 15 December.

Qadhafi had finally achieved his goals: N'djamena and the government were in the hands of Goukouni, who was not only beholden to Qadhafi for helping him retake the country but also effectively hostage to the nearly 15,000 Libyan soldiers deployed across Chad. What's more, the Libyan offensive had been a stunning accomplishment, if only as a logistical operation. A Libyan army operating over 2,000 kilometers from its principal bases along the Mediterranean had conducted a sustained armored advance over 900 kilometers through hostile territory in a victorious seven-week campaign. However, this victory was hardly cost-free for Tripoli. As many as 1,500 Libyan soldiers were killed in the fighting, and probably another 4,000–6,000 were wounded.

The Fourth Libyan Intervention, 1983–86

In January 1981 Qadhafi overstepped himself in Chad. He attempted to put Libya's control of Chad on a more permanent and more legitimate basis by almost literally putting a gun to Goukouni's head and forcing him to agree to a merger of the two countries at a meeting in Tripoli on 6 January.[33] Upon returning safely to N'djamena, Goukouni denounced the merger, setting off a firestorm of criticism against Libya in the Organization of African Unity (OAU). Goukouni was emboldened by the vociferous support of the OAU, and GUNT forces clashed with Libyan troops near Abéché in eastern Chad in April 1981. Realizing that he had overplayed his hand, Qadhafi agreed to rescind the merger and withdraw all Libyan troops from Chad in October 1981. The Libyan withdrawal was another remarkable logistical feat, equal to its efforts during the invasion the previous fall. The entire Libyan force pulled back to the Aouzou Strip and southern Libya in just three weeks with a minimum of problems.

Goukouni's rule over Chad did not last long. While the Libyans licked their wounds in the Aouzou Strip, Habré and the FAN retreated to Sudan, where they regrouped, retrained, and recruited new soldiers. With covert aid from Sudan, Egypt, France, the United States, and a number of other countries that all opposed Libya for one reason or another, Habré was able to rebuild the FAN into an efficient fighting force by early 1982. In May of that year, he invaded Chad from Sudan. On 5 June the GUNT and FAN armies met at Massaguet, fifty miles north of N'djamena on the Abéché-N'djamena road. Habré again proved his skill as a commander and routed Goukouni's forces. The GUNT army disintegrated and headed for their homeland in the Tibesti. Two days later, on 7 June 1982, Habré reentered N'djamena and proclaimed himself president of Chad.

The Libyans took no action throughout this brief fight. Qadhafi had been burned by his experience the year before. Moreover, at that moment, he apparently felt it important to maintain the support of the OAU and probably was loathe to sustain heavy casualties as he had in 1981 for ephemeral political gains. Nevertheless, Libya once again welcomed Goukouni and his GUNT fighters, providing them sanctuary, arms, and assistance. Qadhafi also began to prepare to intervene once again in Chad in the near future, renegotiating an alliance with Goukouni and building up Libyan forces in the Aouzou Strip.

In 1983 Qadhafi believed his forces ready and again invaded Chad along with the GUNT and Volcan armies. Although the Libyans had roughly 11,000 men in the Aouzou Strip — the vast majority of whom were Libyan regulars, the Islamic Legionnaires having fought poorly and taken heavy casualties in 1981 — Tripoli committed only a few thousand to the invasion. Moreover, most of these were artillery and logistics units. Qadhafi intended to try to minimize Libyan losses this time by further relegating Libyan troops to pure support roles, forcing the GUNT units to shoulder an even greater share of the burden of actual combat. At Dourbali in April 1983, the GUNT-Libyan force defeated a small government garrison; out of a force of 1,700 men, Habré's troops had 142 dead and 252 taken prisoner.[34] On 25 June the GUNT took Faya Largeau, then overran Abéché, and then marched on N'djamena. However, Habré responded quickly, rallying the rest of his army (now called the Force Armée Nationale Tchadien, or FANT) and marching north to meet the GUNT and Libyans outside Abéché in early July. Once again, Habré proved to be the better general with the better army, smashing Goukouni's forces at Abéché and then launching a counter-offensive of his own. On 30 July Habré hit the GUNT-Libyan army at Faya Largeau and routed them, retaking the town and threatening to drive north on the Tibesti and the Aouzou Strip.

Goukouni's defeat prompted Qadhafi to reenter the Chadian fray in force. The string of defeats in the late spring and early summer had demonstrated that without Libyan armor and airpower, the GUNT could not register more than minor successes against Habré's FANT. Moreover, Libya could not allow Goukouni to be defeated; not only would this be an intolerable blow to Libyan prestige, but also it would leave Chad in the hands of the rabidly anti-Libyan Habré, who could be expected to support all manner of opposition to Qadhafi from Chadian territory. So in August 1983 Qadhafi ordered another general Libyan invasion of Chad, with the regrouped GUNT leading the way.

This time the Libyans committed 11,000 troops, most of them regulars, to the operation and airlifted virtually the entire force—complete with tanks and artillery—directly into the Aouzou Strip. Although Tripoli again dispatched large numbers of tanks and APCs as well as roughly eighty combat aircraft (a considerable portion of the operational LAF) for the offensive, Libyan forces still played their traditional role of providing fire support (and the occasional headlong tank charge) for GUNT assaults. The GUNT probably contributed 3,000–4,000 men to the invasion force. Meanwhile, Habré had dug in a sizable FANT army—perhaps as many as 5,000 men—at Faya Largeau to await the inevitable Libyan-GUNT assault along the traditional invasion route.[35] The GUNT and Libyans attacked on 10 August, battering the FANT with MRL, artillery, and tank fire as well as almost continuous airstrikes by Libyan Su-22s and Mirages operating from Aouzou and Tu-16 bombers flying from Sabha. Although the FANT troops mostly held their positions, by the time the GUNT launched its main infantry assault, supported by slow-moving Libyan armor, the heavily outnumbered government forces were in no shape to put up a fight. Without antitank or antiaircraft weapons, their main line of defense crumbled. At that point, the battle was clearly lost, and Habré retreated south, having had 700 men killed. Despite their crushing victory, the Libyans failed to pursue the FANT, allowing Habré's forces to escape to N'djamena.

This proved to be a crucial mistake. While the Libyans milled around and took their time regrouping at Faya Largeau, Habré pulled his troops back to N'djamena to regroup and rearm. Of greater importance still, the size and firepower of the Libyan intervention caused Habré to recognize that the FANT could not hold N'djamena without assistance. Like Malloum before him, Habré appealed to Paris to save him from the Libyan threat. Due largely to pressure from the United States (heavily engaged in its own miniwar with Qadhafi) and the African outcry against the renewed Libyan intervention, the French acceded to Habré's request and began Operation Manta, deploying 3,500 troops and several squadrons of Jaguar fighter-bombers to Chad. By the time the Libyans and Chadians resumed their march south, the French had established a defensive line along the sixteenth parallel from Salal in the west to Abéché in the east, effectively bisecting the country.

Habré was able to use the French line as a secure fall-back position from which to mount a counteroffensive against the GUNT and the Libyans. In early September he attacked Oum Chalouba in central Chad, southeast of Faya Largeau. Although no French ground troops participated, French aircraft flew defensive counterair missions to keep the LAF at bay. Moreover, Habré had had the time to rally his forces once again, and with the assurance that French Jaguars would keep the Libyan Mirages and Sukhois off their backs, the FANT troops rose to the challenge. On 6 September they drove the GUNT and Libyans out of Oum Chalouba and a few weeks later retook Faya Largeau. Tripoli responded to these reverses with airstrikes using napalm and white phosphorus against both towns that caused extensive damage and killed large numbers of Chadian civilians. In turn, Habré launched another offensive northward against the Aouzou Strip. However, the French refused to fly combat air patrols for this offensive. In addition, the FANT was tired and its ranks depleted from the constant campaigning. Habré tried to make up for his losses by securing a force of roughly 2,000 Zairian soldiers, but the new army consequently lacked the cohesiveness it had enjoyed in the past. In addition, the Libyans had had a chance to regroup, resupply, and establish positions in familiar territory. As a result of these complimentary factors, Habré's offensive quickly ground to a halt in a few small, desultory battles that revealed that the FANT had shot its bolt, while the morale of the Libyan soldiers improved dramatically by defending the Aouzou Strip — territory they considered Libyan.

The final chapter in the fourth Libyan intervention in Chad was played out from the fall of 1984 through the start of 1986. In April 1984, with the war in Chad having bogged down into stalemate, the French proposed a mutual withdrawal to the Libyans. Tripoli accepted, and in September an accord was struck in which both sides pledged to pull all of their forces out of the country immediately. Although the FANT protested vehemently and warned Paris that the Libyans would not abide by the agreement, French president François Miterrand was adamant, and his troops were out of Chad by 10 November. The Libyans did pull out some forces, but they kept roughly 6,000 troops camouflaged in the north.[36] In fact, far from evacuating, the Libyans built new roads from their country into northern Chad and a major new airbase at Wadi Doum, northeast of Faya Largeau, to better support operations beyond the Aouzou Strip. The French continued to maintain that Qadhafi had withdrawn even while evidence mounted to the contrary, and in December 1984 the Libyans resumed offensive operations in Chad.

Perhaps so as not to spark a French redeployment, the Libyans and their

GUNT allies moved more cautiously this time, pushing into northern Chad in measured advances and keeping north of the sixteenth parallel. By mid-1985, the Libyans had built up their forces in Chad to approximately 7,000 troops with 300 tanks and sixty combat aircraft. Like the FANT, the GUNT had taken heavy losses in the battles from 1980 to 1983 and was reduced to no more than 2,000–3,000 fulltime soldiers.[37] As a result, the Libyans shouldered more of the burden than in the past and tended to rely even more heavily on sheer firepower to dislodge FANT units from their positions. The Libyans found that Habré had essentially decided not to seriously contest northern Chad. Without French airpower and still lacking any weapons that would enable his troops to defeat Libyan tanks and jets, Habré chose to conserve his forces and concentrate on defending N'djamena and southern Chad. Consequently, the Libyans had little difficulty reasserting their control over the northern half of the country in 1985 and 1986.

Libya's Defeat, 1986–87

As the Libyan armed forces slowly expanded their control over northern Chad, events in Libya itself led to important changes in their structure, missions, and composition. Qadhafi's regime continued to be buffeted by coup attempts in the late 1970s and early 1980s. The regime faced serious threats from its military in 1980, 1981, 1983, 1984, and 1985. A coup attempt in January 1983 led to the execution of five senior Libyan officers, including the deputy commander of the People's Militia. In May 1984 another coup launched from the military led to bloody fighting in front of the al-Azzizyyah Barracks in Tripoli where Qadhafi often slept. As a result of this failed bid, 5,000 people were arrested, many tortured, and roughly 100 executed. In March 1985 a plot was uncovered within the military, which led to the arrest of 60 mostly senior Libyan officers. Finally, in November 1985 Col. Hassan Ishkal, the governor of Qadhafi's home province of Surt, was executed for differing with the dictator on military and foreign policy, and it was suspected that he may have been preparing to move against the regime.

In response to these threats, Qadhafi stripped the Libyan armed forces of their ability to overthrow him and, in so doing, further hamstrung their organization and functioning. Tripoli proliferated its intelligence and internal-security services and divorced the military from regime-security functions almost completely. Qadhafi also created new institutions designed to allow him to better control the military. First, he extended the regime's "Revolutionary Committees" — somewhat similar to communist party "cells" — to the military to both inspire loyalty to his rule and to monitor the conduct of military personnel. Second, he created the Jama-hiriyyah Guard, a force of several thousand troops hand-picked from his tribe and well armed with tanks, APCS, MRLS, and even their own advanced SA-8 SAMS. (The Jamahiriyyah Guard serves to this day as the key regime protection force, and it was this force and the revolutionary committees that ultimately blocked the May 1984 coup attempt in a series of street battles with army units.) Despite the growth of the Libyan armed forces, Qadhafi would not permit the formation of division-level commands, and all formations larger than brigades had to be created on an ad hoc basis in the field. He also deepened the surveillance of the military by the intel-ligence services and continued to rotate key command billets frequently and unexpectedly. Militia and reserve units were regularly attached to regu-lar formations as "loyalty support." To prevent units from coordinating their activities (and so hinder their ability to conduct an effective coup), Qadhafi created overlapping chains of command. Indeed, he went so far as to limit the size and scope of field-training exercises and to virtually pro-hibit live-fire exercises for fear that the troops would use the ammunition to overthrow the regime.[38]

One important countervailing pressure on these trends was the need for some degree of efficiency among the forces actually involved in combat operations in Chad. Consequently, despite his fears of the military, Qadhafi was forced to place well-regarded and experienced officers in command of his forces in Chad. This may have been easier for Qadhafi to accept be-cause, in faraway Chad, it was difficult for these men to threaten his reign. However, even this consideration had its limitations, and there were still numerous command-and-control eccentricities that probably stemmed from his fear of a military coup. For example, Libyan garrisons in Chad were sometimes manned by battalions from different brigades, all of which were left under the command of their parent brigades, making it nearly impossible for the garrison to act in a concerted manner.[39]

THE CHANGE IN THE BALANCE OF FORCES

In 1985 and 1986 there was a crucial, but initially undetectable, shift in the military balance in Chad. Although the increasing political shackles on the Libyan armed forces were part of this change, in truth, they were only a minor aspect of it. Libyan tactics — relying on massive doses of firepower coupled with the occasional, slow-moving frontal assault — were not terri-bly demanding, and therefore a great deal of inefficiency could be tolerated without "diminishing" Libya's ability to conduct such simplistic operations. Moreover, the Libyans generally executed these tactics so poorly throughout their involvement in Chad that it is difficult to detect any significant further decrease in their abilities as a result of the increased politicization of the early 1980s. Instead, the key changes were in the capabilities of the FANT.

Probably the most important development of the mid-1980s for the Libya-Chad conflict was the evolving attitude of the United States toward Libya. Throughout the early 1980s, the Reagan administration had grown increasingly bellicose toward Libya and increasingly willing to support Habré's FANT as Libya's enemy. In 1985 the United States increased its aid to the FANT, providing arms, money, intelligence, supplies, and diplomatic support. The United States and France (in large part thanks to U.S. pressure) provided the FANT with more-powerful weaponry, increased training, and extensive logistical support. To their credit, Habré and his subordinates recognized which equipment would be useful to them and which would simply be a hindrance. They declined offers of tanks, APCs, and heavy artillery and instead requested light armored cars, trucks, automatic weapons, grenade launchers, recoilless rifles, mortars, antitank weapons, and antiaircraft weapons. In particular, the FANT asked for large numbers of U.S.-made Redeye shoulder-launched SAMs and French Milan antitank guided missiles (ATGMS).

These new weapons made possible new tactics for Habré's forces. With the Milan ATGM and Redeye SAM, the FANT finally had weapons that could take on Libya's tanks and fighter-bombers. This knowledge gave FANT soldiers the courage to stand and fight the Libyans. From that point, the fighting ceased to be a one-sided contest in which the Libyans could simply stand back and frighten off FANT soldiers with their firepower. Suddenly, the Chadians had the means to fight back. Moreover, one serious problem experienced by the FANT (and the GUNT) in the past was that its tribal warriors had great difficulty modifying their traditional desert-warfare tactics to apply to massed infantry operations. The new equipment supplied by the Americans and French, particularly the large numbers of Toyota four-wheel-drive trucks purchased by the Chadians and equipped with crew-served weapons, allowed the FANT to return to the traditional tactics with which they were most comfortable — and with the added benefit of modern firepower and mobility.

The key tactical change that the new weapons made possible was to reintroduce the rapid movement and concentration that were the hallmark of traditional Toubou desert-warfare tactics. The armored cars and Toyota trucks restored to the Chadians the strategic mobility and tactical maneuverability they had lost when they had adopted modern infantry weapons, organization, and tactics. With their new mobility, the FANT's Toubou and Zaghawa warriors were now able to employ their traditional tactics in a way that they had not been able to before. In battle Chadian forces employed "swarming" tactics. They used the speed of their armored cars and Toyotas to dart around the battlefield, hitting Libyan armored vehicles in the flanks and often from several angles simultaneously. The Chadians maintained a very high pace of operations, relying on the speed and flexibility of their units to confuse the slow-moving and slow-to-react Libyans, isolate them in smaller units, and then crush them suddenly with attacks from all sides. The Chadians maneuvered constantly on the battlefield to prevent the Libyans from bringing their heavier firepower to bear and to get flank shots at Libyan armor and fortifications. Indeed, the Chadians moved so quickly that Libyan tank crews often had difficulty moving the turrets on their T-55 tanks fast enough to accurately target FANT Toyotas.

In addition to the new weapons, the change in U.S. attitudes toward the war in Chad also brought other important benefits. In particular, although the Chadians did not employ Western soldiers or even advisers in their campaigns in 1986–87, they benefited from Western personnel (mostly French) manning their logistical system. Inadequate logistics had hamstrung previous FANT offensives, and the added burden of large numbers of motor vehicles further increased their supply difficulties. By taking over the FANT's logistical system and seeing to its effective functioning, Western personnel greatly enhanced the speed and range of Habré's forces.[40]

The last element in the improvement of FANT military capabilities was the development of a cadre of outstanding battlefield commanders whom Habré had found to lead the FANT against Libya and the GUNT. Over the course of the campaigns in 1983–86, Habré picked a number of leaders from among his forces and increasingly used them to command key units. By 1986, Habré had a corps of aggressive, flexible, seasoned commanders such as Idris Deby, Ahmed Gorou, Muhammad Nouri, and Hassan Djamous commanding FANT forces in the field, which enabled him to spend his time overseeing the larger conduct of the campaign and attending to logistical, diplomatic, and administrative matters. Hassan Djamous, in particular, proved to be an outstanding commander, practicing maneuver warfare with a skill that led several Western observers to compare him to Erwin Rommel.[41] In 1986 Habré made Djamous the commander of the FANT's main field army.

THE 1986 CAMPAIGNS

Of course, none of these developments were readily apparent to the Libyans at the beginning of 1986. The FANT and its Western allies worked covertly, and the new weapons were mostly just heavy infantry weapons that did not appear on the surface to constitute a significant improvement in FANT strength. Indeed, because the most important changes were in the tactics and operations enabled by the new weapons and not any advantage inherent in the weapons themselves, Tripoli believed that a renewed offensive to bring still more of Chad under Libyan control would meet the same easy successes they had enjoyed over the last two years. Consequently, it was a shock to Qadhafi's regime when in early 1986 the Libyans were stopped cold by the FANT without French airpower or other direct military intervention.

At the beginning of February 1986, the Libyans and the GUNT attacked south from their positions in north-central Chad. This offensive was far larger and more ambitious than Libyan-GUNT operations over the past two years and may well have been another bid to conquer the entire country. The Libyans committed 5,000 troops, with large formations of armor and artillery backed by considerable airpower, and 5,000 GUNT and Volcan Army soldiers. On 10 February the Libyan-GUNT forces attacked Kouba Olonga, Kalait, and Oum Chalouba. The next day they were able to take Oum Chalouba and Kalait despite fierce resistance by the FANT. However, FANT patrols had long before detected the Libyan buildup, and so Habré had forces already in place to meet the attack. On 13 February the FANT counterattacked, retaking Oum Chalouba and Kalait the next day and crushing the Libyans and the GUNT with their new weapons and tactics. The Libyans were beaten so badly that they were forced to pull back to the Aouzou Strip to regroup and were unable to resume the offensive until March. By then, Habré had concentrated considerable forces in the Oum Chalouba area, and the Libyans were repulsed with heavy losses. Moreover, Habré used the size and power of the initial Libyan thrusts (as well as Mitterand's humiliation from Qadhafi's false withdrawal in 1984) to convince the French to redeploy 2,000 troops and several squadrons of Jaguars to Chad. Although the French still refused to join the FANT in a counteroffensive, they began conducting airstrikes against Libyan airbases in Chad, ostensibly to suppress the LAF while French troops and supplies were airlifted into the country. The unexpected reversals on the ground at the hands of the FANT plus the French airstrikes prompted the Libyans to call off the invasion and retreat back to their positions in the north.

These defeats only convinced Qadhafi to redouble his efforts. Immediately after the March offensive, Libya began a massive reinforcement of its army in Chad, quickly making up the losses sustained in February and March and boosting its overall strength until nearly on a par with the 1983 invasion force. Moreover, by late 1986, the Libyan forces in Chad were equipped with more-powerful weapons than ever before, including T-62 tanks and BMP-1 infantry fighting vehicles. Tripoli did not recognize that the FANT's new Western arms and the new tactics that they made possible were the cause of their defeat and instead blamed inadequate numbers. Qadhafi concluded that the 1986 invasion force had been too small: with only 5,000 Libyan troops it had been unable to accomplish the same objectives as the much larger forces that had overrun Chad in 1980 and 1983. Consequently, he doubled the size of his force in Chad, principally augmenting its armor, artillery, and air components, in expectation of resuming the offensive in the fall.

But events in Chad intervened to preclude an autumn Libyan offensive. In August 1986, before the Libyans had completed preparations for a new campaign, Goukouni's GUNT and Qadhafi's Libya had a final falling out.[42] The GUNT could muster only about 2,000 soldiers at that time, and these men deserted the Libyans and retreated to their traditional strongholds in the Tibesti, ousting Libyan garrisons from Bardai, Wour, and Zouar. In early December 1986 the Libyans sent a brigade task force of 2,000 men with T-62 tanks and heavy air support to smash the GUNT and retake the Tibesti. Because of this firepower, to which the GUNT had no answer, the Libyans were able to force its former allies out of Bardai, Wour, and Zouar once again. However, Habré recognized this moment as his opportunity to unite all of Chad behind him and drive the Libyans from the country. He sent 2,000 FANT troops to the Tibesti to link up with Goukouni's forces.[43] The infusion of these newly equipped and trained troops allowed the Chadians to stop the Libyan advance, but they found it difficult to pry the Libyans out of the mountains. Libyan units proved tenacious when conducting simple, static defensive operations in the difficult terrain of the Tibesti. Moreover, the channeling effect of the mountains minimized the extent to which the Chadians could employ flanking maneuvers against Libyan defensive positions while maximizing the Libyan advantage in firepower. Consequently, the fighting in the Tibesti turned into a slugging match. Although the Chadians retook Zouar and Wour by January 1987, the Libyans were really only forced to pull out of the region altogether in March because of the decisive Chadian victories in the east.

Despite the limited Libyan successes in the Tibesti against the GUNT in December 1986, the split between Goukouni and Qadhafi was very important for the local military equation. For the previous nine years, the GUNT had provided the main infantry formations and all of the reconnaissance for the combined Libyan-GUNT-Volcan armies. The GUNT soldiers found the enemy forces and then closed on them for the kill, while the Libyans stood back and provided fire support with their tanks, artillery, and airstrikes. Without the GUNT soldiers, Libyan formations lacked adequate infantry and reconnaissance elements. Libyan infantry and reconnaissance units were brought in as replacements, but they were very poor compared to the GUNT's Toubous. Libyan formations were forced to scout for themselves — which they rarely did — and in combat they could no longer stand back and blast away while the GUNT soldiers did all the dirty work. Now the Libyans had to engage the tough FANT warriors themselves, and the Chadians, relying on their traditional swarming tactics, proved to be much better in combat than the slow, inflexible Libyans.

THE CHADIAN OFFENSIVE OF 1987

By the beginning of 1987, Libya had completed its buildup in northern Chad. Tripoli had massed nearly 8,000 regulars with 300 tanks, large numbers of artillery and MRLS, Mi-24 helicopters, and sixty combat aircraft.[44] Roughly 2,500 of these troops were engaged in the Tibesti as part of a task force known as Operational Group South (Qadhafi continued to refuse to allow his commanders to establish divisions). The rest of the expeditionary force was concentrated in Operational Group East, with its headquarters at Faya Largeau. The theater headquarters for all Libyan forces in Chad was located at Wadi Doum. Despite the size of Libyan forces in Chad, the need to divert part of it to the Tibesti to deal with the GUNT probably delayed the start of their well-prepared offensive. As a result, the Libyans were preempted by the Chadians.

By 1986, Habré had built an army of 10,000 regulars backed by another 20,000 tribal irregulars who could be called up for short periods of time to conduct operations in their native regions. However, the Chadian offensive was largely conducted by a force of 4,000–5,000 regulars led by Hassan Djamous and Ahmed Gorou. These troops fielded seventy French Panhard and American V-150 armored cars plus about 400 Toyota trucks equipped with machine guns, recoilless rifles, mortars, grenade launchers, and Milan ATGMS.[45] With Tripoli distracted by its battle with the GUNT, Habré sent this army north to evict the Libyans from Chad.

The Chadian offensive began with an attack on the Libyan garrison at Fada, which the FANT captured on 2 January 1987. Although there were 1,200 Libyan troops with armor and artillery in fortified positions, the

Chadians conducted a series of swift pincer movements, enveloping the Libyan positions and crushing them with sudden attacks from all sides. Fada fell in just eight hours, costing the Libyans 784 dead, 81 captured, and 100 destroyed tanks. By contrast, the FANT had only 50 killed and 100 wounded in the battle.[46] The French, still deployed in southern Chad and flying combat air patrols along the sixteenth parallel, took no part in the operation, but under pressure from Habré, they conducted an airstrike against the main Libyan airbase at Wadi Doum, which prevented the LAF from playing much of a role in the battle.

The defeat at Fada stunned the Libyans. They had assumed that their heavy weapons and fortifications, which they had built since 1984, made their garrisons virtually invulnerable to attack by the lightly armed Chadians. In response, Qadhafi ordered still more Libyan units southward. Tripoli dispatched several battalions immediately — including units from the Jamahiriyyah Guard — to shore up its positions around Faya Largeau and Wadi Doum, while the Libyan high command put together more substantial reinforcements and the logistical support to move them south to deal decisively with the unexpectedly puissant Chadian army. By March, the Libyans had roughly 11,000 troops in northern Chad.

After the fall of Fada, the Chadians were forced to pause for a period of time. Because of the difficulty of supplying large mechanized forces in the desert, they had to "hop" from one inhabited place to the next. To the northwest of Fada, the next major inhabited place was the town of Faya Largeau, heavily fortified and garrisoned by several thousand Libyans. But north of Fada, and a bit closer than Faya Largeau, was the even more heavily garrisoned and fortified Libyan base at Wadi Doum. Habré and his commanders reasoned that if they could take Wadi Doum, Faya Largeau would be in an untenable position and would fall without a fight, whereas if they took Faya Largeau, Wadi Doum would still need to be reduced before they continued moving north. Consequently, despite its more formidable defenses, they opted to strike directly at Wadi Doum rather than fight through Faya Largeau first.

In March 1987 Wadi Doum was garrisoned by 6,000–7,000 Libyan troops with 200–300 tanks and APCs. Moreover, it had all-around defenses as much as six kilometers wide at some points and an airbase with several squadrons of fighter-bombers and attack helicopters inside the perimeter. The Libyans believed it impregnable, and the Chadians felt it necessary to weaken the garrison both numerically and psychologically before attacking. Thus, after they had consolidated their position at Fada, the FANT began harassing the Libyans in and around Wadi Doum to try to goad them into launching a counterattack against Fada. In mid-March, the Libyans took the bait and dispatched an armored-battalion task force of about 1,500 men to retake Fada. Chadian scouts trailed them all the way. On the evening of 18 March, the Libyans stopped their day's march and went into laager near B'ir Kora. Djamous immediately brought up a unit of FANT regulars and surrounded the Libyans during the night. At dawn on 19 March, the Chadians attacked. They began by launching a diversionary strike on one side of the Libyan position, which panicked the task-force commander, prompting him to shift all of his reserves to bolster the threatened sector. At that point, the Chadians unleashed their main assault against the other side. This attack caved in a large area of the defensive perimeter, and the Libyans proved too slow and inflexible to shift forces back to cover the gap or counterattack to blunt the Chadian penetration. As a result, the Chadian main force fanned out and struck the rest of the Libyan positions from the rear in conjunction with frontal assaults by the Chadian diversionary force. The Libyans were butchered in the fighting, but their pleas for help caused the Operational Group East commander to dispatch a second battalion task force from Wadi Doum late that day to aid the trapped unit. It took so long for the Libyans to get organized and move south, however, that the battle at B'ir Kora was already decided before the relief force even set out. During the night of 19 March, the Chadians caught the Libyan relief force twelve miles north of B'ir Kora, surrounded it, and demolished it in identical fashion the next morning. Altogether, the Libyans suffered 800 dead and lost eighty-six destroyed and thirteen captured T-55s in the battles.[47]

Wadi Doum was now ripe for attack. Although the garrison still boasted 4,000–5,000 men with ample armor and air support, the Libyans were badly demoralized by the annihilation of their comrades at B'ir Kora. The Chadians decided to capitalize on this advantage by striking quickly. Toward the end of March, Habré sent a force of about 2,000–3,000 men under Djamous to attack the stronghold. Although the Libyans were on alert and became aware that a Chadian army had surrounded the base, they did not scout the FANT deployment and so had no idea from which direction to expect the attack. By contrast, the Chadians carefully reconnoitered the Libyan position and, in so doing, uncovered all of their weak points, including pathways through the extensive minefields. On 22 March Djamous attacked. The hardest part of the fight was breaching the outer ring of Libyan defenses, but the Chadians attacked simultaneously at two opposing points and blasted their way through these lines. The Libyans were slow to commit their reserves, allowing the Chadians to penetrate their forward defenses and fan out before the breakthroughs could be sealed. Indeed, despite their extensive armored reserve, the Libyans failed to counterattack at all — allowing Chadian forces to roam at will once they were inside the Libyan perimeter. According to Lt. Gen. Bernard Trainor, who served as a military correspondent with the FANT, between the unexpected routes taken by the Chadians and the speed of their advance, the Libyans were incapable of reacting, not even firing one artillery round during the battle.[48] Four hours after the attack began, the Libyans had lost the entire base.

Qadhafi's forces regrouped to some extent that night and launched a sloppy, slow-moving, and uncoordinated — yet very determined — counterattack the next day. However, since the Libyans had lost or abandoned most of their equipment in fleeing the base, this counterattack was smashed by the FANT, leaving Wadi Doum firmly in their hands. Libyan airpower had little effect on the fighting because the Chadian Redeyes forced them to remain above 10,000 feet, from which they could do little against the dispersed formations of fast-moving Chadian trucks. Nevertheless, after the battle the LAF mounted numerous airstrikes from Maatan as-Sarrah Airbase against the Chadians at Wadi Doum that, although inaccurate, prevented the FANT from pursuing the retreating Libyans. In all, the Libyans suffered 1,269 dead and 438 taken prisoner (including Col. Khalifa Haftar, the Operational Group East commander) while losing over 300 tanks and APCs, twenty Czech-made L-29 light aircraft, four Mi-24s, and several batteries of SA-13 and SA-6 SAMs. In addition, many of the Libyan casualties were among units of the Jamahiriyyah Guard that had been brought down to stiffen Libyan resistance. Against these losses, the Chadians had only 29 dead and 58 wounded.[49]

The loss of Wadi Doum and its garrison were a major blow to Tripoli. First, the Libyans were forced to abandon central Chad. The fall of Wadi Doum and Fada made it effectively impossible for Libya to supply Faya Largeau and other, smaller Libyan bases in the vicinity because of Chadian forces operating out of the captured strongholds to the northeast and the Tibesti to the northwest. Consequently, the Libyans retreated from central Chad and fell back to their strongholds in the Aouzou Strip. Second, Qadhafi sped up the flow of reinforcements, sending troops and equipment south to try to stop the offensive. The Libyan high command hurried south both the units they had already earmarked for deployment to Chad along with large numbers of additional forces to try to find some level of mass and firepower that would halt the Chadians. By the spring of 1987, Tripoli had rebuilt its forces in the Aouzou Strip to 12,000–13,000 troops — over one-third of the entire Libyan army. Moreover, to make up for the loss of Wadi Doum, the Libyans began a major engineering effort to turn Maatan as-Sarrah Airfield in southern Libya into an airbase capable of supporting large-scale air operations to defend the Aouzou Strip.

The battle for the Aouzou Strip began in late July 1987, when the FANT retook several Libyan-held positions in the Tibesti to secure its western flank for the main offensive in the center. In early August, however, the Libyans put together a counteroffensive of reinforced-brigade strength (3,000 men) to try to reestablish their hold on the Tibesti. On 8 August the Libyans drove toward Bardai but were intercepted by a FANT cohort of roughly equal size at Oumchi, eighty kilometers south of Aouzou. As they had at B'ir Kora and Wadi Doum, the Chadians located the Libyan force, surrounded it, and then attacked on multiple axes. And as *they* had at B'ir Kora and Wadi Doum, the Libyans could not act as quickly as the Chadians nor did they counterattack or commit reserves in time to prevent FANT units from penetrating their lines and then hitting the remaining forces simultaneously from front and rear. The result was predictable: the Chadians demolished the Libyan force. Moreover, Hassan Djamous urged on his forces, aggressively pursuing the defeated Libyans. As the beaten and demoralized forces fell back in disarray, they caused other Libyan units to flee positions they passed through, turning the retreat into a rout. The pursuing Chadians were able to occupy the town of Aouzou on 8 August without much of a fight. Between Oumchi and Aouzou, the Libyans suffered 650 killed, 147 taken prisoner, 111 military vehicles captured, and at least thirty tanks and APCs destroyed.[50]

Qadhafi would not abide the loss of Aouzou and ordered its recapture. He continued to feed reinforcements into Chad until there were nearly 15,000 Libyan troops pitted against the FANT. In addition, he sent 'Ali ash-Sharif, widely considered Libya's most capable general, to organize a counteroffensive to retake Aouzou. Libya began a preliminary bombardment by artillery and airstrikes to soften up the Chadian positions there days before the counterattack. Nevertheless, despite all this firepower, when the Libyans attacked on 14 August, they were soundly beaten, suffering over 200 dead and captured. Ash-Sharif regrouped and attacked again, only to be defeated once more. In both cases, the Libyans conducted simple, slow-moving frontal assaults that were easily broken by fast, enveloping Chadian counterattacks. After these reversals, ash-Sharif concentrated even greater firepower against the town and brought in a number of Libyan commando units and formations from the Jamahiriyyah Guard. He then used these forces as shock troops in a set-piece assault featuring tremendous firepower that finally succeeded in forcing the Chadians out of Aouzou on

28 August. In this final attack, the Libyans greatly benefited from the fact that Djamous, Gorou, and other key Chadian commanders — along with most of their troops — had pulled out of the town in preparation for another operation. This left a garrison of only about 400 FANT soldiers led by a novice commander who deployed his force poorly and was overwhelmed by Libyan numbers and firepower. Still, the fighting for the Aouzou Strip in August cost Libya 1,225 dead and 262 wounded.[51]

Habré too was determined to regain the Aouzou Strip. He had withdrawn Djamous and most of his veteran troops from Aouzou to rest and refit them for the next offensive, which Habré hoped would allow him to secure the strip against further Libyan attacks. This he hoped to accomplish by smashing the major bases in southern Libya from which Tripoli was supporting its operations in northern Chad. Habré and his generals concluded that Libya's greatest advantage, and the key to the FANT's eventual defeat at Aouzou, was Tripoli's ability to conduct incessant airstrikes. Although they rarely caused any real casualties, they were very frightening to the troops and imposed crucial delays as units repeatedly had to disperse for cover and then regroup to move or fight. To remove the threat of Libyan airpower before they renewed their offensive against the Aouzou Strip, the Chadians decided to first eliminate the main Libyan airbase at Maatan as-Sarrah.

Meanwhile, the Libyans hoped to follow up on the limited success of their victory at Aouzou. In early September they sent a brigade-sized force to attack Ounianga Kebir. Simultaneously, Habré dispatched Djamous with several thousand FANT soldiers to drive 200 kilometers into Libya and wreck Maatan as-Sarrah. The Libyans moved noisily through the desert, launched a frontal assault on Ounianga Kebir on 5 September, and were quickly defeated by rapid Chadian counterattacks. Djamous's force, by contrast, carefully followed the wadis to stay undercover while Tripoli's forces in southern Libya made little effort at security or patrolling, allowing the FANT to sneak up on the base undetected. On 5 September, the same day the Libyans were being smashed at Ounianga Kebir, the Chadians attacked Maatan as-Sarrah, taking its defenders completely by surprise. Although the airbase had a 2,500 man garrison, including a brigade of tanks, artillery, and extensive fortifications, the Chadians quickly crushed the slow-reacting defenders. They took control of the airbase, demolished it and all of the equipment they could not carry back with them, and then departed on 6 September. It was a stunning defeat for the Libyans. The Chadians killed over 1,700 defenders, captured another 300, destroyed twenty-six aircraft, seventy tanks, thirty APCS, and numerous SAMS, radars, and electronic equipment. The FANT suffered 65 dead and 112 wounded.[52]

Fortunately for Qadhafi, the Chadian raid on Maatan as-Sarrah proved to be *too* successful. The French became very suspicious of Chadian intentions and became concerned the raid was the first stage of a general Chadian offensive into Libya proper, something Paris did not want to see. Thus, immediately after the attack on Maatan as-Sarrah, Paris forced Habré to agree to a ceasefire before he could set in motion his planned counteroffensive to retake the Aouzou Strip. Over the entire course of the 1987 campaign, the Libyans suffered at least 7,500 dead and nearly 1,000 captured soldiers in addition to losing nearly $1.5 billion worth of equipment, including twenty-eight aircraft and over 800 tanks and APCS. In all of these battles combined, the Libyans killed fewer than 1,000 FANT soldiers.[53]

Observations on Libyan Military Effectiveness in Chad

Although Libya's military fortunes in Chad rose and fell in dramatic fashion over the nine years of its involvement there, the performance of its military forces remained remarkably consistent. By and large, Libyan tactical forces performed extremely poorly from start to finish. Libya's generals proved to be a varied but essentially adequate lot: their qualities as strategists ranged from fairly impressive to middling, and their qualities as leaders of men ranged from uninspiring to reasonably effective. In contrast, Libya's logistics operations were consistently excellent—at times outstanding— throughout the course of its wars in Chad. Thus, the principal causes of Tripoli's varying fortunes in Chad were not the performance of Libyan arms at all, but the changing political alignments on either side and the eventual development of Chadian military forces that were able to exploit the limitations of Libyan tactical forces.

STRATEGIC PERFORMANCE

Libya's generals were rarely spectacular and must bear part of the blame for certain important defeats, but they also deserve credit for many of Libya's victories, and overall they can hardly be considered a principal element of Libya's eventual failure. In general, the various Libyan invasions of Chad were well directed, if simple. The strategy in each offensive was principally to move from one population center to the next on the most direct route from southern Libya to N'djamena: Aouzou, Faya Largeau, Oum Chalouba, Abéché, N'djamena. This route was determined largely by logistical considerations and the need to secure each population center (and its crucial water supplies, road crossings, and airfields) before moving on to the next. Moreover, the directness and predictability of this route proved to be an advantage for the Libyans insofar as their main operational goal was to bring the Chadian army to battle in open terrain outside of N'djamena where it could be smashed by superior firepower. Thus, the fact that the Chadians could anticipate the Libyan route of advance and would often send their main army out to try halt the invasion force frequently meant that the FAN was right where the Libyans wanted them.

For the better part of their involvement, this strategic approach worked well for the Libyans. By carefully securing each population center before moving on to the next, they ensured their logistical and communications lines and frequently were able to draw out sizable Chadian formations and fight them in the open, where Libyan armor and airpower inevitably proved decisive. In 1980–81 Libyan forces successfully conquered Chad, and only Qadhafi's mishandling of the postceasefire political arrangements forced the Libyans out again. Likewise, in 1978 and 1983 there is every reason to believe the Libyans would also have overrun the country had it not been for the sudden French interventions, which blocked their further advance. In 1984–86 the Libyans solved the problem of French intervention by first deceiving them into withdrawing and then moving slowly, cautiously, and with a minimum of force so as not to give the French sufficient provocation to return.

Ultimately, the key limitation on Libyan operations was not poor generalship but the incompetence of Tripoli's tactical formations. Libyan units had such limited effectiveness in combat that only under perfect circumstances could this strategic approach succeed. Specifically, only when Libyan forces were called on to provide almost nothing other than stand-off fire support, airstrikes, and the occasional tank charge could they prevail over their Chadian adversaries. Thus, only when the Libyans had sufficient numbers of Goukouni's Toubous to serve as reconnaissance and assault infantry, only when the French Air Force did not ground the LAF, and only when the Chadian forces had limited tactical mobility and no antitank or antiaircraft weapons could they prevail in tactical engagements. Any time that any of these conditions were not met, the Libyans lost badly. Thus, the 1979 invasion failed because Qadhafi's forces were opposed by Goukouni's Toubous. Likewise, the 1978 and 1983 invasions were halted by French intervention, particularly French air power. And finally, the Libyans were crushed in 1986–87 when they were stripped of all three of these tactical necessities. Consequently, it is hard to fault Libya's generals, at least, for its inability to secure its objectives up until 1986. During that period of time, it was reasonable for Tripoli's strategic commanders to believe that they could create the right conditions under which their forces could defeat the Chadians in battle, and indeed they were frequently proven correct in this belief.

However, after 1986, it is more difficult to make a case for Libyan strategic leadership. Specifically, the high command must bear at least part of the blame for the inability of Libyan armed forces to recognize or adapt to the change in the balance of power on the battlefield. To some extent, the inability of these generals to properly react to the dramatic improvement in FANT capabilities can be attributed to surprise. Beyond that, the high command at least appears guilty of arrogance, inertia, or both: they almost certainly had become either so contemptuous of FANT capabilities or so accustomed to their limitations that Libyan leaders could not accept that the FANT was beating them. By the same token, it is difficult to imagine what Libya's generals might have done differently had they been less stubborn and more willing to adapt. Like the Iraqis in the Gulf War, the "right" military answer to the problem created by the FANT's new capabilities was probably to have evacuated northern Chad, but this was a political decision that Qadhafi almost certainly would have forbidden even if his generals had recommended it. Once their new weapons and motor transport allowed the FANT to return to their traditional swarming tactics, Libyan forces were simply incapable of defeating them in battle. Only when the terrain essentially precluded the free-wheeling maneuver battles at which the Chadians excelled (as in the Tibesti) could the Libyans even slow down Chadian advances. Given that most of Chad was ideal for the FANT's style of warfare, the Libyans were effectively doomed. Again, like the Iraqis in 1991, the Libyans could not have adopted a mobile defense and tried to match Chadian maneuver-warfare techniques because Tripoli's tactical formations simply could not execute them. Thus, the only strategy practicable for the Libyans was to dig in deep at key population centers to force the Chadians to attack heavily fortified positions defended with tremendous firepower and hope to bleed the FANT white. Ultimately, Libyan tactical forces proved unable to accomplish even this objective, and they were routed from Chad.

Nevertheless, even recognizing that the options open to Libyan generals were extremely limited, the direction of the defense of northern Chad in 1987 was hardly faultless. For example, after the destruction of repeated Libyan offensives in February, March, and December 1986, it probably was a foolish decision to try to retake Fada with 2,000 men in March 1987. The Libyans by then should have recognized the new skills of the FANT, and more importantly, they should have recognized that if 1,200 Libyans defending fortified positions could not hold Fada, it was unlikely that a force only slightly larger would be able to retake it.

The decision to send a relief column after the initial force was destroyed at B'ir Kora was a terrible mistake. First, the Libyans should have dispatched combat aircraft to aid the units at B'ir Kora *before* they were destroyed rather than sending out a slow-moving armored column *afterward*. If they were unable to do so, this would underline the inflexibility and limitations of the LAF; if no one thought to do so, it would reflect poor strategic leadership. Moreover, Col. Khalifa Haftar, the commander of Operations Group East, must be faulted for failing to properly reconnoiter the route of advance of the relief column. Even though it was probably the fault of the task-force commander that the Libyans did not send out adequate ground reconnaissance ahead of the column, Haftar must be held responsible for not using aerial reconnaissance (of which the Libyans had plenty at Wadi Doum, Aouzou, and Maatan as-Sarrah) to cover the advance of the relief column and to discover that the original task force had been destroyed and alert the relief force to return to Wadi Doum.

Although Libya's generals cannot really be blamed for responding to the FANT offensive with a static defense of key Chadian population centers, they must be faulted for the numerous counteroffensives they conducted during 1987, which clearly ran counter to the logic that made the static defensive posture a reasonable option. Static defense was the appropriate strategy for the Libyans in 1986 because they lacked the ability to defeat the Chadians in meeting engagements and maneuver battles, and therefore, it made some sense to try to wear down the FANT by forcing it to repeatedly assault heavily fortified positions defended with massive firepower. This logic should have essentially ruled out large-scale counteroffensive operations such as those the Libyans conducted in 1987 at B'ir Kora, the Tibesti, and Oumchi. Sending large forces out of the Libyan fortified bases to try to assault Chadian positions exposed them to the risk of ambush and massacre by FANT units en route. Moreover, even if the Libyan formations made it to their destination, there was no reason to believe that the FANT would not be able to use its swarming tactics to defeat the clumsy, set-piece assaults that were the only kind of attack Libyan forces were able to conduct. Thus, at Aouzou in April, the first two Libyan assaults were butchered by Chadian counterattacks, and the final assault succeeded only because the Chadian forces there were too small and too inexperienced to stand up to the massive onslaught the Libyans unleashed on them. One must admire the aggressiveness of Libya's generals, who kept counterattacking to try to regain the initiative and unbalance the relentless Chadian offensive. But one must also fault them for not recognizing that such counterattacks were fruitless and could only undermine their defensive strategy.

Libyan tactical forces performed extremely poorly in Chad throughout Tripoli's involvement there. This tactical incompetence was the greatest Achilles' heel of the Libyan war effort and the key vulnerability that the FANT was ultimately able to exploit. Libyan tactical forces were so limited in their capabilities that they squandered the opportunities offered by Tripoli's superb logistical efforts and severely constrained the strategic choices available to their generals.

Without doubt, the greatest failure of Libyan tactical forces was their rigidity. They parroted Soviet tactics in the most stereotyped manner and without taking advantage of even the limited flexibility inherent in Soviet doctrine. For example, Libyan mechanized infantry always fought mounted — regardless of the terrain, mission, or other conditions. As a result, they usually did not dig in on defense nor would they dismount to clear out entrenched Chadian infantry or antitank teams. Any number of Libyan APCs were incinerated by the Chadians with full infantry squads inside them (fifty-four such APCs were found at Wadi Doum). The Libyans used tanks like moveable pill-boxes: digging them in on defense and advancing in column or line-abreast in the assault. Libyan tanks rarely maneuvered or attempted to flank an enemy: when defending they sat immobile in their holes, and when attacking they simply rolled straight ahead, in both cases firing almost indiscriminately until the enemy ran away or they were themselves destroyed. The artillery proved quite adept at conducting preregistered, preplanned barrages, but that was the extent of their capabilities. Thus, if the initial bombardment did not shatter the Chadian defense, Libyan artillery could contribute little more to the effort, and so the battle was turned over either to the armor to launch a charge or to the GUNT infantry (when available) to push forward and dislodge the FANT defenders. Moreover, in defense, especially in 1986–87 when the FANT's new mobility allowed them to attack suddenly from any angle, Libyan artillery proved virtually useless since it could not accurately shift its fire around the battlefield.

In addition to the individual failings of each of Libya's combat arms, its junior officers could not integrate these forces into concerted combined-arms operations. In every case, the infantry, artillery, armor, engineers, and other units were left to fight separate battles. About the best they achieved was to coordinate tank, artillery, and rocket-launcher fire with airstrikes in indiscriminate bombardments of fixed targets. They could not provide fire support to actively maneuvering forces. Indeed, Libyan support units really could not even conduct rolling barrages in support of armor or GUNT infantry advances; either they bombarded or they assaulted but not both simultaneously.

As this suggests, the majority of Libya's problems can be traced to ineffective tactical leadership. Junior officers proved inflexible and unaggressive and, therefore, had little ability to cope with either the rapid-maneuver tactics of FANT units at the end of the Libyan involvement or even the slower, more ponderous infantry tactics of Habré's forces before 1986. In contrast to the fairly aggressive leadership displayed by the senior levels of the Libyan command structure — who insisted on counterattacking all through 1987 despite considerable evidence that such operations could not succeed — tactical forces almost never counterattacked except when ordered to do so by higher authority. Indeed, in written accounts of the fighting in Chad, there is not a single mention of Libyan forces conducting a tactical counterattack, and in interviews with Westerners who either accompanied Chadian forces or who closely followed the war in their respective capitals, none could recall a single instance of such a counterattack. There were any number of occasions when the Libyans had ample forces and opportunity to conduct a counterattack and failed to make any effort to do so. Moreover, in most battles they fought, Libyan defenders did not even shift forces to plug breakthroughs, shore up sectors under pressure, or meet a flanking attack. In those few instances when local commanders did make such an effort, their forces did so too slowly and rigidly to make the action worthwhile. Nor did Libyan units attempt to maneuver for an advantageous position in battle. They really tried not to move at all, instead preferring to knock Chadian units out of their positions with firepower when on the offensive. On those occasions when Libyan forces did finally resort to an assault (and when they lacked GUNT infantry to conduct it for them), they launched sluggish, rigidly prescribed frontal attacks directly at the main Chadian positions. Finally, when the Libyans were successful, they rarely pursued defeated FANT units, with the result that they never scored as great a tactical success as was possible and never exterminated Habré's forces, allowing them to regroup and fight again another day.

The Libyans also experienced debilitating problems managing information throughout their command structure, but again, these lapses were greatest at tactical levels. Senior commanders rarely provided adequate information either about Libyan operations or enemy deployment and capabilities to their subordinates. However, they generally recognized the need for accurate assessments of Chadian forces and so employed either GUNT scouts or LAF reconnaissance planes to gather such information. The Libyans were not very thorough even when they did make the effort to find out where Chadian forces were and what they were up to. Libyan strategic intelligence often left significant gaps in their coverage and seldom kept abreast of developments in Chadian politics and military affairs. Junior officers did not even perform up to this level. Libyan tactical units simply did not conduct reconnaissance. The most obvious example of this was at B'ir Kora, where neither Libyan column commander bothered to scout his route of advance or deploy forces to screen his flanks. However, this was a constant of Libyan operations in Chad. Tripoli's forces were notorious for failing to even keep an alert watch around their fortified bases and field encampments. To make matters worse, tactical commanders regularly misled their superiors for fear of bringing shame on themselves, their men, their colleagues, or their superiors; they overstated the scale of victories, failed to report defeats, and exaggerated the size of enemy forces. As a result, Libyan strategic commanders frequently had little idea of what really was happening on the battlefield.

Of course, some of the problems at the tactical levels must be attributed to poor morale. In many of their campaigns, Libyan forces had little desire to be in Chad and so put in half-hearted efforts. Throughout the nine years of direct Libyan involvement in Chad, Qadhafi's legions suffered high rates of desertion among units deployed there, while large numbers of reservists refused to answer mobilization calls if it meant service in Chad.[54] Indeed, especially after the frustrations of 1980–81, it became clear that even Qadhafi wanted to minimize the effort his forces had to make to conquer Chad and essentially left all of the difficult tasks to the GUNT, with Libyan units in supporting roles. At times, morale sunk to dangerous levels, such as in the immediate aftermath of the defeats at Faya Largeau in 1979 and Wadi Doum in 1987. Thus, in a number of cases, the negligence and general inactivity of Libyan forces must, at least in part, be attributed to a lack of motivation.

However, this influence was clearly a limited one, for there were also numerous instances when Libyan morale was high — or else there were other reasons for them to have been highly motivated — and yet there was little or no discernible improvement in their performance. For example, in the various invasions of 1978–80, their battlefield triumphs and rapid advances made Libyan troops euphoric. Likewise, whenever Libyan forces defended the Aouzou Strip itself, their morale improved markedly because the officers and troops felt that they were defending territory that was rightfully Libyan. Finally, on a number of occasions (especially in 1987), Libyan forces were placed in clear life-or-death situations that gave them the motivation to fight for their own survival. What is noteworthy is that in all of these circumstances, Libyan forces fought considerably *harder*, but not any *better*. That is, the soldiers and officers displayed greater courage and determination, but they did not prove any better able to maneuver in battle, to react to Chadian moves, to counterattack, to coordinate their operations, or even to pay greater attention to reconnaissance, security, and intelligence.

As this suggests, the cohesion of Libyan formations in Chad and the degree of commitment and bravery evinced by soldiers fluctuated considerably over the course of the Libyan intervention, correlating to a certain extent with the highs and lows of morale. When morale was high, unit cohesion was stronger and more soldiers were willing to risk their lives for their comrades and their missions. But when they were dispirited, units broke under less pressure, and fewer troops were willing to sacrifice for their mission or one another. Nevertheless, there were other patterns of unit cohesion and individual commitment that did not fit the oscillations in morale. For example, Libyan forces invariably displayed better unit cohesion when defending fixed positions than in any offensive operations or meeting engagements. When they had a chance to dig in and fight from fortified lines, Libyan units from squad to battalion level hung together, fought hard, and clung to their trench lines. This was equally true of Libyan forces battling in N'djamena when riding the crest of their victorious advance in 1980 as it was when they were desperately trying to hold on to the Tibesti after the crushing defeats of 1986 and early 1987. Moreover, it was generally a rarity when Libyan regular units simply collapsed in battle; although the militia and Islamic Pan-African Legionnaires might run at the first sign of combat, Libyan line formations usually had to be beaten before they cracked.

Of course, it should be kept in mind that unit cohesion—even at its best—had little effect on the success of Libyan forces in combat. Although poor unit cohesion often contributed to Libyan setbacks, it was never a singular cause of defeat. Nor was it ever the case that good unit cohesion alone led to a Libyan victory. The limitations of the junior officers left their tactical formations so inutile that this dwarfed other considerations like unit cohesion. Because Libyan forces almost never maneuvered, rarely conducted tactical counterattacks, and were incapable of adapting or responding to unexpected Chadian moves, the ability of these formations to stick together in a tough fight was rarely relevant. When attacking, all that mattered was how much firepower the Libyans could bring to bear and whether the Chadians would sit and take it—because if the Chadians were able to either limit Libyan firepower or maneuver against them, the Libyans were doomed to defeat. Similarly, when defending, all that mattered was whether the Chadians were forced to conduct a slow-moving frontal assault or could conduct quick flanking maneuvers—because if the Chadians could maneuver, the Libyans were going to lose the battle. In these cases, the cohesion of Libyan units determined only how long it would take the FANT to smash their forces. And only when the Libyans were conducting static defensive operations against a Chadian frontal assault did it become at all relevant whether they would stand and fight or break and run.

One factor that clearly was a major influence on Libyan tactical ineffectiveness was the inadequacy of Libyan training practices. Tripoli's units trained very little, and when they did, their drills and exercises were unrealistic, incomplete, and perfunctory. They had no regular training cycle, the extent of their practice being determined largely by unit commanders who saw little value in exerting the effort to teach their troops how to fight (and often did not know themselves). The regular units rarely trained in formations larger than company or battalion size and almost never were allowed live ammunition with which to exercise. Libyan militia and reservists, especially in the late 1970s, were given even less training, often being sent to Chad with only the barest instruction in small-arms handling.

COMBAT SERVICE SUPPORT

The Libyans had a strangely mixed record in terms of supporting their forces in Chad. On the one hand, their maintenance was mostly awful. Libyan soldiers and junior officers seemed to have no understanding of the need for regular preventive maintenance on major weapons systems, nor did they have the desire or the skills to perform repairs to broken equipment. Tripoli apparently concluded that, given the limited education and cultural biases against technical education prevalent in Libyan society, it was not possible to train their soldiers and officers to maintain and repair their equipment in the field. Consequently, they attempted to work around the problem by importing large numbers of Cuban and Eastern European technicians, who were assigned to large, centralized workshops that deployed forward with the Libyan combat forces to Chad. Thus at Wadi Doum, a number of Cubans, North Koreans, and East Germans were captured by the Chadians. These personnel had been assigned to the maintenance crews of the airbase and the major refit facility the Libyans had established there for armored vehicles. Nevertheless, because the Libyans never had enough Warsaw Pact technicians to attach to every field formation down to battalion or company level, and because the Libyan vehicle crews were unwilling and unable to perform basic maintenance, Libyan operational readiness rates remained poor. For example, even though over half of Libya's combat aircraft were kept in storage because they had inadequate numbers of trained pilots to fly them, Libyan line squadrons rarely were able to achieve operational readiness rates of better than 50 percent.[55]

On the other hand, Libyan logistics were first rate throughout the history of their intervention in Chad. In every campaign, Tripoli's forces were kept well supplied. They never were defeated — or even hindered — by shortages of ammunition, food, fuel, water, or other combat consumables. Instead, Libyan forces invariably had ample supplies of everything they needed to prosecute combat operations, no matter how difficult the conditions.[56] Indeed, Libyan maintenance problems cannot be blamed on logistical shortcomings; in 1987, when Chadian forces overran major Libyan forward bases at Faya Largeau, Wadi Doum, and Aouzou Oasis, they discovered vast warehouses full of spare parts, repair tools, repair manuals, and replacement equipment. Similarly, the low morale of Libyan forces cannot be blamed on neglect or inadequate provisioning because Qadhafi's quartermasters took superb care of the combat forces, lavishing them with all variety of creature comforts. For instance, in 1980 the garrison at Abéché was provided with piped-in music, sports facilities, air conditioning, an irrigated wheat field, and even a Guernsey cow for the commander's milk.[57] Libyan forces deploying south to Chad moved quickly and efficiently, arriving where they were supposed to when they were supposed to. On several occasions, the LAF demonstrated the extraordinary ability to airlift vast mechanized forces into Chad at the start of an offensive. The best examples of this were in 1980 and 1983, when Qadhafi began his invasions by airlifting thousands of troops complete with T-55 tanks, BTR APCS, D-30 and M-46 artillery pieces, and BM-21 MRLS into the Aouzou Strip. On both occasions these operations were conducted quickly and skillfully and allowed the Libyans to steal a march on Habré.

Libyan logistical accomplishments appear even more impressive when the circumstances are taken into account. It is over 1,100 kilometers from N'djamena to the Aouzou Oasis on the Libyan border. Moreover, it is a further 900–1,100 kilometers from Aouzou to the main Libyan military bases along the Mediterranean coast. Thus, Libya's most successful campaigns were waged over 2,000 kilometers from its main depots. Moreover, although Chadian terrain is ideal for armored and air operations, it constitutes an extremely forbidding logistical environment. Much of the northern two-thirds of the country is desert, scrubland, or dry savannah with little water, cultivated lands, or population. At the time (and even today), the Chadian infrastructure was primitive. There were few roads or airfields and essentially no rail lines for the movement of large military forces. The Libyans overcame all of these obstacles both in sustaining immediate requirements in the short term and in making their presence in Chad sustainable over the long term. Their engineers and logisticians built roads, airfields, and all manner of logistical bases, slowly developing a considerable transportation network from the Mediterranean coast south into north-central Chad. When the Libyans were finally evicted from Chad, it was not because they lacked the capacity to sustain their forces in battle.

Moreover, in all of their major offensive campaigns, Libyan quartermasters displayed an outstanding capacity to plan and execute very sophisticated support operations for their combat forces. The 1980 campaign is the best example. The Libyans built up as many forces in the Aouzou Strip as the area's infrastructure could support on a sustained basis and then, right before the start of the offensive, they flew in additional forces to ensure they had overwhelming force ratios. When Libyan ground troops had taken Faya Largeau, Tripoli's quartermaster corps quickly improved the airbase there and then pushed huge quantities of military supplies into the facility so that it could serve as a forward logistics base, at which point the Libyan advance continued. As the armor columns continued to roll southward, the quartermasters kept a steady stream of supplies moving forward, employing a Soviet-style "push system" to ensure that resupply operations did not slow the offensive and establishing advance fueling points where needed along the route of attack. Then, when the Libyans had pushed to within striking distance of N'djamena and were anticipating a protracted battle for control of the capital, Libyan logisticians set up a new forward supply base at Dougia. In less than ten days, they had flown in sufficient combat consumables to allow the invasion force (equivalent to a reinforced armored division) to assault and conquer the city without any significant logistical problems.

Although it is true that Libyan combat formations did not advance at a particularly torrid pace, it is nonetheless remarkable that their combat service support elements were able to conduct these operations as smoothly and quickly as they did, displaying a skill in sustainment capabilities that most third-world armies (indeed, that many *first-world* armies) lack. Indeed, so efficient were Libyan logistical operations, especially compared to the utter incompetence of their tactical formations, that some experts have wondered whether Tripoli's quartermaster corps was manned by foreigners in the same way that its maintenance arm was.[58] Although there can be no doubt that the Libyans did employ some Cubans, North Koreans, and Eastern Europeans in their logistical services, it does not appear to be the case that their logistical success can be written off as the product of foreign involvement. First, there appears to have been only relatively small numbers of foreign personnel in the Libyan quartermaster corps, especially compared to the numbers of technicians manning maintenance and repair facilities and flying Libyan combat aircraft. Logistical operations are far more complex and manpower intensive than maintenance and repair, and there would have had to have been an even greater number of foreigners in the quartermaster corps for them to have had a significant effect. Second, even though Soviet-bloc personnel made up a sizable proportion of the Libyan maintenance corps, maintenance remained very mediocre. Libyan logistical operations were not just better than their maintenance and repair performance, they were good by any standard. Thus, it seems unlikely that a smaller number of foreigners in the larger and more demanding realm of logistical operations could have been responsible for the impressive performance of Libyan logisticians. We can only conclude that in this narrow, but important, aspect of military effectiveness, the Libyans were quite good.

LIBYAN AIR FORCE PERFORMANCE

For roughly seven years, the Libyan Air Force was probably the most important arrow in Tripoli's quiver in Chad. When free to participate in combat operations, its aircraft often proved the decisive element in any battle. Nevertheless, the actual combat performance of the LAF was just as dismal as that of the Libyan army. Although its aircraft were able to conduct reconnaissance missions essentially unhindered, the LAF and the Libyan high command had little ability to gather, analyze, and act on information from such flights. Indeed, unless the Libyans had GUNT scouts to provide them with accurate assessments of where Habré's forces were and what they were doing, they usually had no clue as to FANT deployments and missions. Libyan airstrikes, no matter how heavy or protracted, rarely caused any physical damage to the target. Troops of the FAN or FANT suffered few casualties from these attacks, nor did they lose many pieces of equipment. In particular, in 1986–87 the LAF could not destroy or impede the fleet of Toyotas that were instrumental to the Chadian victory. The one exception to this rule were Libyan airstrikes on Chadian villages, which did cause large numbers of civilian casualties but were counterproductive because they incited large elements of the population against Tripoli.

The incompetence of Libyan pilots was the single greatest problem of the LAF in Chad. Because the Chadians had no air force — and the French never sent more than a couple of squadrons of Jaguars, while the Libyans regularly committed five to ten squadrons of Mirages, Su-22s, MiG-23s, and MiG-21s — the LAF invariably had the edge in terms of numbers, firepower, and equipment. But its pilots squandered these advantages, even when unopposed in the air. Tripoli's Eastern-bloc pilots would only defend Libyan airspace and would not fly offensive missions into Chad. These missions were left to the Libyans — and they proved unequal to the task. In Anthony Cordesman's words, the Libyans had "a serious shortage of even mediocre pilots."[59] One U.S. government expert on the Libyan military estimated that no more than about 10 percent of Libyan pilots would have been considered adequate flyers by Western standards.[60] Libyan airstrikes rarely ever caused any physical damage because few pilots actually understood their planes and munitions well enough to put ordnance accurately on target.

One important reason that Libyan fighters never challenged the French Jaguars whenever they were in-country and covering Habré's forces is that they knew they would get blown out of the sky. Libyan pilots were dependent on ground-controlled intercept guidance to the point of being helpless without it. Even still, Libyan fighters had great difficulty finding and identifying aircraft they were vectored out to intercept. This problem was compounded by the fact that many Libyan air defense radars were off-line at any given time because of poor maintenance. On the rare occasions when the Libyans tussled with French fighters (usually by accident), LAF planes were defeated quickly and effortlessly, and their pilots displayed virtually no air-to-air combat skills.

As was the case for Libyan ground forces, the one bright spot in LAF performance was in the logistics. Tripoli's quartermasters and Eastern-bloc technicians were usually able to sustain a reasonable sortie rate for Libyan fighter-bombers. In key battles this meant that Libyan aircraft were over the battlefield for long periods of time and that Chadian troops were under some form of air attack almost continuously.

It was this constant presence, coupled with the inherent terror created by air attacks on ground troops, that allowed the LAF to win victories for Tripoli almost single-handed. Before 1986, Habré's troops had no way of defending themselves against Libyan strike aircraft, possessing little more than light machine guns in the way of antiaircraft weaponry. The knowledge that they could not effectively fight back against the LAF, and the relentless airstrikes, no matter how inaccurate, caused many FAN/FANT units to disintegrate under sustained air attack. The frequently decisive role of Libyan airpower is proof of the tremendous psychological effect of air-strikes on ground forces, regardless of any actual damage inflicted.

By contrast, the turnaround in Libyan fortunes after 1986 provides additional evidence of the limited abilities of the LAF. The key to this reversal was the Redeye shoulder-launched SAM, which the United States provided to the FANT in some numbers. This weapon finally gave the FANT a way of fighting back against Libyan aircraft. However, just as the Libyan advantage before 1986 was almost entirely psychological, so too was the Chadian advantage after 1986. The Redeye was already obsolete in 1986: it was extremely difficult to operate and not very accurate. Moreover, the Chadians were very bad at operating it. As a result, although FANT soldiers fired hundreds of Redeyes at Libyan aircraft, they shot down no more than four planes and helicopters. Yet Libyan pilots were still terrified of the Redeye and often attempted to stay above the missile's maximum altitude or aborted their mission when a Redeye was launched near their target. The SAM frightened the LAF away without actually doing any real damage, just as the LAF had previously frightened away FANT ground forces.

Finally, the command and control of LAF operations were characterized by a tremendous degree of amateurism. The Libyans had a lot of planes, which they used frequently, but had little appreciation of how to employ them in a systematic fashion to achieve the maximum effect. In most cases the LAF did not bother to fly reconnaissance missions over a target before striking it. It also neglected proper air planning, often sending out strike missions with minimal information about the target to be struck, its location, and its air defenses. The Libyans regularly dispatched inadequate numbers of planes to targets and then provided them with improper ordinance for the mission. When allocating strike assets, they made no allowance for the poor skills of their pilots, nor were Libyan strikes accompanied by appropriate measures to suppress enemy air defenses (with more serious consequences after 1986). Finally, the Libyans rarely conducted poststrike reconnaissance to assess damage and whether additional strikes were required to destroy the target. By and large, Libyan pilots reported that the target was destroyed, and the chain of command accepted their word.

EXPLAINING THE RISE AND FALL OF
LIBYAN MILITARY DOMINANCE IN CHAD

Although Libyan performance in Chad remained a relative constant, Tripoli's fortunes there oscillated markedly. Throughout their campaigns, Libyan generalship and unit cohesion were mostly adequate, and Tripoli's logistical capabilities were well above average. But tactical leadership, morale, maintenance, and air power were poor, if not miserable, from start to finish. Thus, Libyan prowess — or the lack thereof — cannot be the principal explanation of the rise and fall of their power in Chad.

To some extent, the sporadic French intervention can be blamed for the variance in Libyan fortunes. Essentially, whenever the French sent military forces to Chad, the Libyans were stopped cold. In 1978, 1979, 1983, and 1986, the French intervened in force, and the Libyans were defeated. By contrast, in 1980 the French did not intervene, and the Libyans overran the country. Thus, there is at least some correlation between French intervention and Libyan victory or defeat. However, although this certainly is one element of the explanation, it is hardly the only factor at work. First, in nearly every one of these instances, the French only committed airpower, and then often only in a counterair role to prevent the LAF from exerting a decisive influence on the ground battles. Although the Libyans were rarely engaged by the French on the ground, Tripoli could not turn its advantages in numbers, firepower, and advanced weaponry into victory on the battlefield without their air force. Second, in 1986–87 the Libyan armed forces were demolished in Chad even though the French barely participated — limiting their involvement to defending the sixteenth parallel, while nearly all of the fighting took place to the north. Thus, the Libyans suffered their worst defeat when the French did not participate at all.

Another important aspect of Libyan military fortunes was Tripoli's alliance with Goukouni's GUNT. The GUNT was crucial to the Libyan army because it provided the high-quality infantry and ground reconnaissance for their combined armies. Although the Libyans could almost always count on the participation of Chadian Arabs from the Volcan Army, these proved to be no more capable fighters than the Libyans themselves and certainly were not in the same league as the Toubous of the GUNT (or the FANT). Indeed, whenever the Libyans had to fight without GUNT contingents, they lost: in 1979 the Libyans were beaten by Goukouni's forces around Faya Largeau, and in 1987 they were crushed by the FANT. Likewise, Libya's greatest victories came when they had firm alliances with the GUNT, most notably in 1980. However, it is not the case that the Libyans were victorious whenever they could count on GUNT forces for support: in February and March 1986, combined Libyan-GUNT armies were smashed by Habré's forces at Oum Chalouba and Kalait.

This evidence indicates that while the episodic participation of the French on one side and the fairly constant GUNT partnership on the other were both important elements in the rise and fall of Libyan military fortunes in Chad, they do not explain the entire story and were not the most important factor in the final Libyan defeat in 1987. Instead, the most important factor was the dramatic reversal in the tactical balance of power in 1985–86. Before the FANT received the Toyotas and heavy infantry weapons (especially the Milans and Redeyes) from the French and Americans in 1986, they were incapable of standing up to Libyan armor and airpower. In these instances even the extremely limited tactical abilities of the Libyans were sufficient to allow them to prevail over the FAN/FANT. However, when the new weapons allowed the Chadians to return to their traditional desert tactics, suddenly the same Libyan tactical capabilities proved woefully inadequate.

Moreover, it was not the weapons provided to the Chadians per se that led to Libyan defeat, but the tactical possibilities that these weapons opened up for the FANT. All that the new weapons did was to "level the playing field" between the two sides. Once the Chadians had a counter to Libyan armor and airpower, they were able to employ their superior tactical abilities to beat Qadhafi's forces in battle. Ultimately, it was the superiority of FANT tactical leadership over Libyan tactical leadership, rather than Chadian weaponry or the ability of Chadian solders to handle that weaponry, that defeated the Libyans. Chadian technical skills were atrocious, and FANT troops rarely employed their weapons properly. These troops were so limited in their ability to handle and support modern military equipment that Habré and his generals had to find the simplest systems that would still allow their men to get the job done. Against Libya, getting the job done meant being able to destroy tanks and jets, and the simplest systems available were the Milans and Redeyes. Thus, Habré turned down offers of tanks, APCs, and aircraft of his own choosing because he recognized his troops would never be able to employ them. Instead of making the FANT more powerful, they would make it weaker. Even with the heavy infantry weapons they acquired, Chadian troops demonstrated very limited competence, firing off huge numbers of antitank and antiaircraft missiles for every hit they scored. Thus, the Libyan defeat had little to do with the size or sophistication of the FANT's arsenal or with the FANT's ability to employ these weapons. Instead, it stemmed from the tactical opportunities these weapons provided the Chadians and the inability of Libyan forces to compete with them in fast-paced maneuver battles.

Skirmishes with the United States, 1981–89

The same ideas that inspired Qadhafi to overthrow the monarchy in 1969 led, perhaps inevitably, to clashes between Libya and the United States. Qadhafi's ferocious anti-Western, anti-imperialist bent led him to back radical dictatorships, sponsor would-be revolutionaries, and arm and encourage the entire panoply of Palestinian and other antiestablishment terrorist groups who dominated the international landscape of the 1970s and early 1980s. As if this were not enough, Libya's massive arms purchases from the USSR and its provision of basing rights to Soviet air and naval forces convinced many Americans that Qadhafi was not merely a major force for instability in the region but also a cat's paw of the Soviet Union. As a result, when the fervently anticommunist Reagan administration took office in Washington in 1981, confronting Libya became a top priority for the United States. Over the course of the next decade, the United States imposed economic, political, social, and military pressures on Qadhafi's regime, ranging from an embargo on Libyan oil to support for the FANT in Chad. Not to be outdone, Qadhafi increased his support to Abu Nidal, Abu Abbas, and a rogue's gallery of international terrorists.[61]

One key arena of conflict between the United States and Libya was the Gulf of Sirte (the Gulf of Sidra to most Americans). Qadhafi claimed the entire 300-mile-wide gulf, stretching from Tripoli in the west to Benghazi in the east, even though this clearly contravened even the most liberal interpretations of the International Law of the Sea. Although the United States had long made it a point of national policy to challenge such infringements on freedom of navigation, once the Reagan administration came to power, it explicitly saw the issue as a pressure point to provoke Qadhafi. The Gulf of Sirte was tailor made for the United States: Libya was in the wrong according to international law, while militarily the United States could employ its unparalleled air and naval power to hit Libya with minimal risk of American casualties.

Despite the political and military advantages the United States enjoyed in this forum, Qadhafi repeatedly took the bait. Between 1981 and 1989, the two nations skirmished in the Gulf of Sirte at least four times. Unfortunately, little information is available in the unclassified literature as to Qadhafi's motives or rationale on any of these occasions. However, in each case, because of the way in which Libyan forces conducted themselves — suddenly opening fire and then trying to flee — it appears that Qadhafi hoped to inflict a few quick losses on the United States, show his people and the world that he would not be bullied by Washington, and then count on America's intolerance for casualties or international pressure to prevent the United States from retaliating. Assuming this was Qadhafi's thinking, he was disappointed every time. Indeed, having had his nose bloodied each time, one wonders why Qadhafi believed things might turn out differently the next.

The First Round, August 1981

On 18 August 1981, the United States dispatched the lion's share of its Sixth Fleet to the Gulf of Sirte for a freedom-of-navigation exercise specifically designed to try to provoke a reaction from Qadhafi. It deployed two carrier battle groups (CVBGS) — the USS *Nimitz* and USS *Forrestal* groups — consisting of fifteen ships with over 150 aircraft for two days of live-fire exercises in the international waters of the gulf. Although the *Forrestal* was one of the older carriers in the U.S. fleet, the *Nimitz* was then the most advanced carrier in the world and boasted state-of-the-art F-14 Tomcat fighters. Libya had over 550 combat aircraft, most of which it concentrated around the Gulf of Sirte to meet the Americans; however, in reality, fewer than 200 were fully operational, and its most advanced aircraft — the 1970s-vintage Mirage IIIs and Mirage Vs and Soviet MiG-23s and MiG-25s — were not in the same league as the F-14. Moreover, Tripoli could not scrounge more than 150 trained pilots, few of whom had the skills or flying experience of the U.S. carrier pilots.[62]

Nevertheless, the Libyans decided to take a shot at the Americans. During the first day of the U.S. exercises, the LAF flew seventy-two sorties (most by Mirages and MiGs), shadowing U.S. warplanes and probing the defenses of the U.S. fleet. No Libyan plane opened fire, however. Early on the second day, 19 August, Tripoli sent up two Su-22 Fitter strike aircraft, which were vectored by their ground controllers directly out to intercept two F-14s flying routine combat air patrols about thirty miles off the Libyan coast. The F-14s were flying a simple race-track pattern, watching for any Libyan planes that might try to attack the U.S. fleet. There was nothing vaguely threatening about these aircraft: they were flying in the same manner and the same position that other F-14s had flown the day before, and there were other U.S. aircraft conducting far more provocative flight profiles that day. The Fitters flew straight out at the F-14s, and at a distance of 1,000 feet, the lead Su-22 fired an AA-2 Atoll heat-seeking missile at the lead F-14.

This was an absurd attack. The AA-2 was an early generation Soviet air-to-air missile and was not particularly capable even when fired under the best of circumstances — directly into the tail of the target aircraft. It did not have an "all-aspect" capability, and since it was not fired at the tail of the F-14, the missile was essentially useless.[63] It could not even acquire the F-14 as a target and simply burned out and fell into the sea. But the U.S. pilots had permissive rules of engagement and were not about to allow the Libyans to get a second shot. The two F-14s immediately engaged the two Fitters, prompting one of the Libyans to turn tail and run. The moment it presented its rear to the F-14s, it was shot down by the wingman of the two Tomcats. The other Fitter continued flying out to sea. The lead F-14 got on its tail and, almost effortlessly, shot it down as well. Remarkably, neither Libyan pilot even tried to maneuver to shake their pursuers.

Operation Attain Document III, March 1986

Five years later, history repeated itself. In response to a series of bloody terrorist attacks conducted with Libyan support and encouragement, the United States decided to conduct a series of provocative freedom-of-navigation exercises in the Gulf of Sirte. Washington hoped to provoke the Libyans to open fire, which would in turn provide the pretext for a series of devastating military strikes against Libya. So in January 1986, the United States again deployed two CVBGS of the Sixth Fleet—the USS *Saratoga* and USS *Coral Sea* groups—to the Gulf of Sirte. For thirty-two days in January and February, the U.S. Navy conducted exercises (known as Operations Attain Document I and II) across the Gulf of Sirte. U.S. aircraft conducted mock dogfights, reconnaissance missions, and mock airstrikes, many of which entailed high-speed dashes directly at Libyan targets, with the U.S. jets veering off only at the last minute.

The Libyans were better prepared to meet the Americans this time, but again, only in theory. They had amassed 700 combat aircraft, and far more of them were newer model MiG-23s and Mirage F-1s. The Libyans had also received advanced Soviet-made SA-5 SAMs and had deployed one battery at Sirte, on the southern coast of the gulf. The SA-5 was the follow-up system to the SA-2 and was a clear improvement over this obsolete design. However, the SA-5 was designed to shoot down high-flying bombers and reconnaissance aircraft and, actually, was not very useful against more maneuverable and lower-flying fighters and attack jets. Libyan SAMs and AAA sites were not integrated into a single command scheme, nor could Tripoli coordinate interceptor aircraft with its ground-based air defenses, so the SAMs and AAA were given certain parts of the sky to defend, and fighters would patrol the other sectors. Moreover, because of their dearth of technically competent personnel, the Libyan air defense system was rarely manned above 60 percent of its actual requirements and was largely shut down at night. Finally, they had done nothing to improve either the operational readiness of their aircraft, the numbers of their trained pilots, or the skills of those pilots available. Indeed, because of the greater sophistication of the aircraft then in its arsenal, Tripoli may have had as few as 100 trained *Libyan* pilots available.[64]

Despite these various handicaps, the Libyans would not back down from the challenge and conducted several hundred sorties, watching and frequently "shadow boxing" with the Americans. In these sparring matches, the U.S. pilots were bewildered by the lack of skills displayed by their adversaries, who flew simplistic and predictable maneuvers and were stiff and inflexible, slow to react. As a result, U.S. fighters repeatedly intercepted the Libyan aircraft and maneuvered into a firing position (albeit without firing), often before the Libyans even realized they had been engaged. In the words of the air group commander on the uss *Saratoga:* "These guys [the Libyans] were grapes. It was incredible how poor they were at what they were doing."[65]

In March 1986 the United States decided to ratchet up the pressure on Qadhafi even further since he stubbornly would not oblige the Americans by firing first. A third cvbg, centered on the uss *America*, deployed to the Gulf of Sirte and began a series of exercises code named Operation Attain Document III.[66] For these exercises, the United States by then had an armada consisting of the three carriers with 250 aircraft plus twenty-three other warships, including several nuclear-powered attack submarines in the area.[67] The most provocative part of Attain Document III was the movement of a three-ship surface-action group (sag) led by the brand new, ultrasophisticated aegis cruiser uss *Ticonderoga*.[68] In January and February the United States had sent aircraft over the gulf but had kept its ships out. At 1:00 p.m. on 24 March, the second day of the exercise, the *Ticonderoga* sag crossed the line of thirty-two degrees, thirty minutes north latitude, marking the northern border of the Gulf of Sirte and the boundary Qadhafi had proclaimed his "Line of Death." Tripoli responded by sending five Soviet-built Nanutchka-type patrol boats out into the gulf to counter the American ships. The Nanutchkas were equipped with early model Soviet antiship cruise missiles and were hopelessly outclassed by the *Ticonderoga* and its escorts.

Inexplicably, the Libyans suddenly decided to start shooting at the Americans. At about 2:00 p.m., two U.S. F-14s flying combat air patrol were targeted by a fire-control radar from the Libyan coast. When the planes were roughly sixty miles away, the Libyan sa-5 battery at Sirte launched two missiles at them. The F-14s were able to outmaneuver the missiles, but the Sixth Fleet began to prepare to retaliate. Several hours later, the Libyans launched three more sa-5s and an sa-2 at other U.S. aircraft, all of which missed. That night, at about nine o'clock, one of the Nanutchkas located the *Ticonderoga* sag and began a high-speed attack run against the cruiser. Since the Libyans had already opened fire, the Americans decided to take no chances, and four A-6 attack jets shadowing the

Nanutchka were ordered to prevent it from closing to within firing range of the *Ticonderoga*. Two of the A-6s fired Harpoon antiship missiles — both of which hit the Libyan vessel — while the other two aircraft finished it off with cluster bombs.

Despite the fireworks earlier in the day, the Libyans do not seem to have further alerted their forces, prepared for additional combat, or even called back the remaining Nanutchkas. As a result, Libyan forces in and around the Gulf of Sirte were hammered by the U.S. forces during the night of 24–25 March. Libyan air defenses were defeated by tactics even less complicated than those the Israelis had used against Syria four years earlier, as the United States simply flew a pair of A-7 attack jets high along the Libyan coast, prompting the Sirte missile battery to switch on its fire-control radar. Two other A-7s, which had flown in low to sneak beneath Libyan radar coverage, then fired two Shrike antiradiation missiles, which homed in on the Libyan radar signals. Although the Shrikes did not destroy the radar, they hit close enough to scare the Libyans into shutting down the SA-5 site. Four hours later, the Americans attempted the same maneuver, and again the Libyans fell for it by switching on their fire-control radar. This time the Shrikes destroyed the radar, shutting down the SAM battery. Finally, U.S. warplanes located three of the remaining four Libyan Nanutchkas, which continued to search the Gulf of Sirte for the U.S. SAG. American A-6 and A-7 attack jets struck the Libyan ships with Harpoons and cluster bombs, sinking one and damaging the other two. Although the Libyans suffered at least 72 dead in these clashes, and possibly many more, the Americans did not have a single casualty.[69]

El Dorado Canyon, April 1986

After the mauling his forces took during Operation Attain Document III, Qadhafi realized that further direct confrontation with the U.S. Navy would not be to Libya's advantage. He reined in his military forces and instead decided to retaliate in an arena in which he held the advantage. He chose to strike back through terrorism, working with well-established terrorist groups to conduct several attacks in the weeks after the clash in the Gulf of Sirte. This campaign culminated in the 4 April bombing of the La Belle Discotheque, a nightclub frequented by U.S. military personnel in Italy. The Libyans did not cover their tracks well, and American intelligence was able to establish that the attack had been ordered by Tripoli. The United States decided to respond to Qadhafi's retaliation with a series of airstrikes against key Libyan military facilities.

Operation El Dorado Canyon, the codename for these airstrikes, was launched during the night of 14–15 April 1986 and involved attacks on five targets. In Tripolitania, a package of eighteen F-111 bombers accompanied by four EF-111 electronic warfare planes attacked the Libyan Frogman School at Sidi Bilal, the military area of Tripoli International Airport, and al-Azziziyyah Barracks, where Qadhafi was sleeping that night. Meanwhile, fifteen U.S. Navy A-6 attack jets, escorted by several dozen F-14 and F-18 fighters, A-7 strike aircraft (whose mission was to suppress Libyan air defenses), EA-6B electronic warfare aircraft, and E-2C command-and-control aircraft, struck at Benina Airfield and the Jamahiriyyah Barracks in Benghazi.

From the Libyan perspective, there was not much to the strikes. After the terrorist attack on La Belle Discotheque, American officials began averring that the United States was convinced Libya was behind the attack, prompting widespread speculation in the Western media that Washington intended to conduct a military retaliation for the bombing. Moreover, despite the extensive precautions taken by U.S. military forces to keep the raid secret, the Italians detected the F-111s flying from bases in Great Britain through the Strait of Gibraltar and across the Mediterranean Sea. Rome passed this information on to Malta, which in turn flashed it to Tripoli. These warnings — both the strategic warning of U.S. rhetoric fingering Libya as the culprit behind the La Belle Discotheque bombing and the tactical warning from Italy and Malta — had no effect on the Libyans. Whether these were simply ignored, never made it to the right levels of the Libyan chain of command, or arrived too late for the Libyans to react is unknown. However, when the U.S. jets began to roar into Libyan airspace, the Libyans were unprepared; their military facilities had all of their lights on and their air and air defense forces were not even on alert.

Consequently, there was little to impede the Americans. In Lisa Anderson's concise judgment, "Libyan defenses proved embarrassingly porous."[70] The airstrikes took them completely by surprise and threw the entire military command into a state of utter confusion. Many soldiers and airmen panicked and fled their posts, while their officers did little to resist the attack unless specifically directed by higher authority. Libyan SAM and AAA batteries were slow to respond. The SA-5 battery at Sirte — which was closest to Tripoli — either was unable to respond until after the raid or, after their experience in March, chose not to. Other sites, however, fired salvoes of SA-2, SA-3, SA-5, SA-6, and SA-8 surface-to-air missiles into the air. Because the U.S. planes flew in at under 150 meters, below the missiles' minimum engagement altitude, the SAM launches had no effect on the U.S. aircraft. Moreover, around Benghazi, the U.S. Navy again flew several decoy aircraft that caused the Libyans to activate their fire-control radars, which were then hit by a hail of forty-eight Shrike and High-speed Anti-radiation Missiles (HARMS). The Shrikes and HARMS wiped out several Libyan radars and convinced other radar operators to turn off their equipment lest they too "eat" a HARM. The batteries continued to fire off SAMS, but without radar guidance, the effort was futile. Most Libyan AAA batteries did not open fire until after the first U.S. bombs began exploding. When the antiaircraft guns did join in, they did prove more of a hindrance to the Americans than the SAMS and may have even shot down one F-111 or caused it to crash into the sea. Other than this lone possible kill, even the AAA did little to actually impede the airstrikes, which went largely as planned. Finally, the LAF did not show at all. Not one interceptor was launched during the raid.

Fortunately for the Libyans, the American pilots were constrained by strict rules of engagement that kept six of the F-111s and three of the A-6s from dropping their bombloads. In addition, the U.S. precision-guided ordnance proved less than precise, and several landed well off-target. Still, the raid was a painful experience for Qadhafi and his regime. At Tripoli International, the F-111s destroyed at least three and possibly five of Libya's thirteen Il-76 transports, the mainstay of Libya's military airlift capability, and damaged several others. At Benina Airfield, as many as fourteen MiG-23s and a pair of helicopters were destroyed. American anti-radiation missiles destroyed and damaged several Libyan air defense radars and control facilities.[71] Finally, and probably of greatest importance, the bombs that landed at al-Azzizyyah Barracks did considerable damage to several structures and appeared to have shaken Qadhafi personally, particularly when afterward U.S. military and diplomatic personnel made it clear that no tears would have been shed in Washington if he had been killed in the attack.

A Final Encounter, January 1989

The April 1986 air raids appear to have had an effect on Qadhafi's thinking regarding the United States and its willingness to strike at his regime and at him personally. By and large, he lowered his international profile after the raids (and after the humiliation of the Libyan defeat in Chad in 1987) and seemed to try to stay clear of the United States generally. Nevertheless, in January 1989 the Libyans again provoked U.S. naval aircraft into a duel in which Tripoli again came out the loser.

Toward the end of 1988, the Reagan administration began to warn that U.S. intelligence had evidence that Qadhafi was building a plant at ar-Rabta (thirty-five kilometers south of Tripoli) to produce chemical warfare weapons. In early January 1989 the United States moved elements of the Sixth Fleet, centered on the USS *John F. Kennedy* battle group, into the southern Mediterranean and began to conduct operations off the Libyan coast. These exercises were designed specifically "to make [Libya] feel uncomfortable," in the words of U.S. Secretary of State George Schultz.[72] Qadhafi apparently feared that the United States was again putting its forces in place for an attack—this time against the chemical-warfare facility at ar-Rabta—and so Libyan planes closely shadowed U.S. forces operating off Libya's coast.

On 4 January 1989, after several days of such interaction without incident, the Libyans provoked an incident with a pair of U.S. warplanes. Two F-14s from the *Kennedy* were flying combat air patrol over the carrier roughly one hundred kilometers from the Libyan coast when they were attacked by two Libyan MiG-23s. The MiGs took off from al-Bumbah Airfield and flew directly out at the *Kennedy* and the two F-14s. The flight path suggested to the U.S. pilots and their superiors on board the *Kennedy* that the Libyans might be on an attack run (real or mock) against the carrier, and the F-14s moved to intercept them. Rather than turn away, the Libyans accelerated and changed course with the Americans, following them maneuver for maneuver. Roughly sixty kilometers from the coast, the two F-14s split, and the MiGs turned quickly toward the trailing fighter. Fearing that the Libyans were about to open fire, the American aircraft instead launched their own air-to-air missiles, shooting down both MiGs. Whether the Libyans had intended to attack the Americans or simply wanted to harass the F-14s or the carrier remains unclear, but immediately thereafter, the Libyans grounded their air force and kept their distance for the remainder of the American exercises.

Observations on Libyan Military Effectiveness against the United States, 1981–89

Although it is difficult to draw too many conclusions from four brief skirmishes spread out over eight years, there is nothing about Libyan performance in any of these encounters that differs from their other experiences in combat. Against the Americans, the Libyans remained true to form. Overall, the air and air defense forces further demonstrated their drastically limited capabilities. Libyan fighter pilots manifested the same rigidity, simplistic tactics, lack of imagination or aggressiveness, poor situational awareness, and meager flying skills as had been repeatedly demonstrated in flight operations over Chad. Likewise, the Libyan air defense system performed very poorly: they were slow to react both to simulated and actual U.S. strike missions in January–April 1986, and when they did react, their fire was inaccurate and uncoordinated.

LAF planners again proved incompetent and amateurish. In 1981, March 1986, and again in 1989, the Libyans deliberately chose to attack the U.S. forces in the Gulf of Sirte, but Tripoli made no preparations to handle the likely response. In 1981 and 1989 they essentially just sacrificed their planes. Especially in 1981, it was absurd for the Libyans to believe that two Su-22s could shoot down two F-14s without assistance. The Libyans could have set up a more sophisticated ambush involving multiple planes. Such an operation would have had a better chance of shooting down one of the F-14s, and at least would have given the Libyan aircraft a better chance of escaping. Likewise, in March 1986 it is stunning that the Libyans would fire off a handful of SAMs and send out a few Nanutchkas to try to attack the U.S. fleet without taking additional preparations, such as dispersing their aircraft and their other naval ships and readying additional fighters and ground-based air defenses for the inevitable American retaliation. Instead, the Libyans woke the proverbial sleeping giant and then sat passively while they got hammered.

Perhaps the most noteworthy lesson of these encounters was the detrimental influence of Qadhafi himself on Libyan military operations. As the absence of planning and preparation makes clear, the strategic thinking behind Libya's moves against the United States appear at best misguided if not irrational or simply foolish. It is uncertain what benefit Qadhafi thought he might derive from presenting the United States with the opportunity to humiliate him by repeatedly opening fire on U.S. warplanes. Nor can a motive be deduced from the context of the three instances when he lashed out: there were other occasions when the United States conducted freedom-of-navigation exercises in the Gulf of Sirte and the Libyans did nothing. However, no Western expert has been able to suggest a motive — derived either from internal or external circumstances — that Qadhafi might have believed would be served by standing up to the United States on those occasions when he did so. In fact, the Libyan decisions to open fire do not, in retrospect, appear to have been terribly well thought out. At least in 1981 and March 1986, the Libyans attacked only on the second day of the U.S. exercises, although they had plenty of opportunities to do so on the first day. It is possible that they were using the first day of the exercise to get a feel for U.S. deployments to plan their strike, but the bizarre and uncoordinated fashion in which these attacks were conducted suggests that very little serious planning was done at all. Instead, it appears that Qadhafi suddenly ordered his forces to open fire on the United States despite the fact that his military had not had the opportunity to adequately prepare itself for such an action or the inevitable U.S. retaliation that it would provoke.

Libyan Military Effectiveness, 1948–91

In many ways, Libya's performance in combat since the Second World War has mimicked that of Egypt, Iraq, and other Arab states, especially its deficiencies in military effectiveness. Like Egypt and Iraq, Libya experienced persistent, debilitating problems in tactical leadership. Junior officers — the commanders of platoons, companies, and battalions — demonstrated little initiative, creativity, flexibility, or adaptability in battle. They rarely thought to employ maneuver in battle, could not make combined-arms operations work properly, and regularly failed to scout or adequately secure their positions. Indeed, intelligence and the handling of information were problems throughout the Libyan chain of command. Information did not flow evenly across the Libyan hierarchy either vertically or horizontally, with the result that few had the requisite information to adequately perform their assigned missions. As a complement to the inabilities of the junior officers, Libyan decision making was rigidly centralized, creating a vicious circle in which senior commanders did not trust their subordinates to make decisions, and junior officers did not demonstrate any abilities that would merit increasing their authority. These problems also greatly affected air operations, which were simplistic and ineffective. Like its tactical commanders on the ground, Tripoli's pilots were unskilled, dogmatic, uncreative, unresponsive, unaggressive, and dependent on their (very mediocre) ground-controlled intercept officers. Libyan air campaigns were amateurish and further limited the ability of Tripoli to get full value out of the billions of dollars it invested in sophisticated warplanes.

Another area in which Libyan military performance conformed closely to that of the other Arab armed forces was in the maintenance and handling of military equipment. Because they were ill-trained and had little technical proficiency, Libyan troops were never able to make full use of the equipment at their disposal. Qadhafi provided his forces with some very powerful weapons, but time and again, his troops used them in simplistic fashion, failing to take advantage of any of the more-sophisticated capabilities of the systems. Likewise, Libyan troops mostly could not, and almost always would not, properly maintain their weapons and vehicles. Preventive maintenance was the exception rather than the rule, and most repairs were left to Tripoli's foreign technicians in rear-area field depots. As a result, Libyan equipment was frequently off-line, and when it was operational, troops made poor use of it.

The Libyans also shared the same uneven, but mostly above-average, patterns of unit cohesion and individual bravery as the Egyptians, Iraqis, and other Arab militaries. Here an important distinction must be made between regular Libyan army formations and the units of the Islamic Pan-African Legion and the People's Militia. These latter forces were hardly a professional military, having been manned largely through forced conscription and press-ganging techniques. Moreover, they were given little training and fewer incentives that would make them want to stick together in a tight situation. Consequently, like Iraq's Popular Army units during the early part of the Iran-Iraq War, they broke and ran whenever there was trouble (or, as often as not, whenever they could get away with it). But Libyan line formations demonstrated reasonably good unit cohesion, hanging together in difficult situations like Lukuya and Entebbe in 1979, the Tibesti in 1986–87, and Wadi Doum and Aouzou in 1987. Indeed, particularly at Wadi Doum, credit must be given to the Libyan forces for being able to regroup after their catastrophic defeat on the first day and try to counterattack—virtually without heavy weapons—on the second day.

Despite these many areas of similarity with the other Arab armies, the Libyan military also demonstrated certain unique patterns of behavior. For instance, the strategic direction of Libyan forces was measurably worse than for many of the other states, and much of this resulted from Muammar al-Qadhafi himself. At least in Chad, Libyan generalship displayed the same fluctuations that marked Iraqi and Egyptian experiences. In some instances their strategic leadership was quite good, while at other times it was quite poor, and on the whole it probably averaged out to an adequate performance. However, Libyan political-military decisions at the highest level frequently were poorly conceived. Picking a fight with Sadat and then failing to adequately prepare a response to an Egyptian invasion was foolish. Repeatedly rising up to the bait offered by the United States in the Gulf of Sirte was even more so. Likewise, dispatching a few thousand militiamen to support Idi Amin could hardly be considered a well-conceived strategy. In Chad as well, Libyan political-military strategy always had the feel of a policy cooked in a geopolitical vacuum and then executed in an impulsive fashion. In particular, Tripoli never properly laid the diplomatic groundwork to be able to sustain an invasion of Chad politically. All of these failings were Qadhafi's, who was a constant hindrance to his own diplomatic and military operations.

Another way that Qadhafi's own pathologies affected the Libyan armed forces derived from his intense fear of a military coup and his resultant determination to emasculate the army to prevent such an occurrence. Consequently, Libya experienced the effects of military politicization more deeply than any of the other Arab states — more so even than Syria under Asad or Iraq under Saddam. For instance, unlike either of those two states, Qadhafi forbade training with live ammunition, prevented the creation of division- and corps-level formations, and effectively discouraged training in his armed forces. In addition, like Asad and Saddam (at least at times), Qadhafi also created overlapping chains of command, frequently and arbitrarily rotated key commanders, and favored loyal incompetents over capable, independent-minded officers for senior command slots.

Just as Libya's problems were similar to those of other Arab states, yet more intense, so too the areas of Libyan strength were similar to those of other Arab states but also more pronounced. Here Libyan logistics stands out. The Egyptians and, to an even greater extent, the Iraqis demonstrated very impressive logistical capabilities. While their military operations were very different and therefore the tasks required of them, Tripoli's quartermasters probably performed even better than either their Iraqi or Egyptian counterparts. As impressive as was Iraq's ability to move and sustain a corps on the Golan Heights in 1973, Libya's ability to sustain a force equivalent to a reinforced division in southern Chad in 1980 and again in 1983 was probably more impressive still. So too was Qadhafi's intervention in Uganda a highly impressive operation from a logistical perspective. Tripoli's quartermasters turned in a remarkable performance, given the enormous distances involved; the primitive state of the Ugandan, Chadian, and Libyan transportation networks; and the efficiency of the Libyan operations. Moreover, they excelled repeatedly, despite the incompetence and confusion that permeated every other aspect of Libyan military operations.

Moreover, unlike the other Arab armies, it is difficult to discern which were Libya's greatest failings. Certainly, its problems with tactical leadership, information management, and weapons handling were just as crippling as for any of the other Arab armies. However, morale problems, poor maintenance, inadequate training, command-and-control dysfunctions, and poor strategic decision-making were far more pernicious than they were for their brother countries. Consequently, in any particular Libyan military operation, it is difficult to argue that any particular problem was worse than another: ultimately, the Libyan armed forces had so many crippling problems that each probably could have cost Tripoli any campaign by itself.

5

SAUDI ARABIA

The modern Saudi military was conceived in war. 'Abd al-Aziz Ibn Sa'ud, the founder of the state of Saudi Arabia, ruled a tribe that had held sway over much of the Arabian Peninsula during the eighteenth and nineteenth centuries when it adopted a fundamentalist brand of Islam known as Wahhabism.[1] At the turn of the twentieth century, Ibn Sa'ud drew upon the religious fervor of his Wahhabi tribesmen to once again conquer most of the peninsula. His Bedouin warriors, called the Ikhwan, or brethren, first defeated the Rashidis of the powerful Shammar tribe to secure the Najd (central Arabia) and al-Hasa (the eastern province), took the Hijaz (western Arabia) — including the holy cities of Mecca and Madinah — from the Hashim clan, and then wrested the southern province of Asir from the Yemenis. By 1926, Ibn Sa'ud was master of three-fourths of the Arabian Peninsula, having been prevented from further expansion only by the mountains of Yemen in the south and in the east and north by the British, who ruled Transjordan and Iraq and were the protectors of Kuwait, the Trucial States (later the UAE and Qatar), Oman, and Aden.

Although Ibn Sa'ud was motivated by the material desire to expand his kingdom, his followers fought to spread the true religion. They saw themselves as successors to the armies that first conquered the Middle East, North Africa, and central Asia for Islam. Thus, when Ibn Sa'ud pragmatically recognized that he could not defeat the British and so curtailed his military campaigns, he came into conflict with the Ikhwan. The Ikhwan were interested only in furthering the true way of Islam and revolted against Ibn Sa'ud when he stopped leading them against foreign foes. Relying on the tribal levies from his homeland in the Najd, and bolstered by some modern weaponry (including several machine guns and a few armored cars) from the British, Ibn Sa'ud crushed the Ikhwan at as-Sibilah in

1929. The end of the Ikhwan revolts left Ibn Sa'ud the undisputed ruler of the kingdom he named Saudi Arabia (Al-Arabiyat As-Sa'udiyyah, or "Arabia of the Sa'ud").

For the next thirty years, the structure and role of the Saudi military, such as it was, grew in fits and starts and overall made little progress. Throughout this period, the dominant influence on Saudi military development was the ambivalence of the royal family toward the mission and importance of its armed forces. From his capital in Riyadh, the king vacillated between fearing the army as a potential threat to the monarchy and relying on it to defend the kingdom against foreign foes. Consequently, Saudi military fortunes fluctuated markedly depending on the royal family's changing perception of its greatest threat.

During the period immediately before and after World War II, the Saudi armed forces languished. For two decades after as-Sibilah, Ibn Sa'ud, by then reigning as King 'Abd al-Aziz ibn Sa'ud, refused to maintain a strong standing army. Only the Royal Guard Regiment was provided the weaponry and training to give them any real military capability, while the small Saudi army was mostly neglected. However, after witnessing the power of modern European armies during the Second World War, the king realized that he could not rely on tribal levies to fight on a modern battlefield and grudgingly created the Royal Saudi Land Forces (RSLF). The Saudis purchased some modern equipment, especially as their oil revenues began to grow in the 1950s and 1960s. They also invited British and then American military officers to help train their forces and plan the defense of their realm. However, much of the kingdom's military strength continued to lie with tribal levies, and Saudi military methods remained largely based on the traditional form of warfare Ibn Sa'ud had employed to conquer Arabia. For the most part, the royal family's principal military concern was maintaining the unity and obedience of their realm against potential revolts by rival Arabian tribes. There were few foreign threats to the kingdom, thus there was little reason to make a determined effort to turn the Saudi army into a modern military force.

Saudi Military Modernization

Events in the Middle East during the 1950s and 1960s brought external-security considerations back to the fore in Riyadh. A series of incidents beginning in the mid-1950s spurred the Saudis to greater interest in enhanced conventional military capabilities. In 1954, Nasser's accession to power in Egypt and his support of revolutionary movements throughout the region made the royal family (the As-Sa'ud) very nervous, especially after several pro-Nasser cabals were uncovered in the kingdom. These fears were exacerbated by Egypt's intervention in Yemen against the imam of Sanaa and its attacks on Saudi bases from which Riyadh was supplying the royalists. The astonishing Israeli victory over the Arabs in the Six Day War then created fears of Israeli expansionism, while the 1971 British announcement that they were withdrawing from all lands "East of Suez" deprived the Saudis of their longtime European protector. The Marxist takeover in South Yemen (Aden), the resulting Soviet presence there, and Aden's subsequent support for the quasi-Marxist rebels in the Dhofar Province of Oman further alarmed the Saudis. Finally, the 1978 Islamic revolution in Iran and the subsequent outbreak of the Iran-Iraq War completed Riyadh's sense of vulnerability and encirclement. Although the United States eventually stepped in to fill the gap left by the British withdrawal and the Saudis began to assiduously develop strong security ties with Washington, Riyadh still felt it had to take a greater role in providing for its own security than in the past.

Beginning in the early 1960s, Saudi Arabia slowly began to try to build a modern military capable of withstanding foreign attack. The most obvious sign of this shift in priorities was the tremendous increase in Saudi defense spending, which peaked in the 1980s. Between 1980 and 1991, the Saudi military accounted for 27–39 percent of Riyadh's budget every year. Starting in about 1970, the Saudis had the highest per-capita defense spending in the world every year and generally spent four times as much as Israel on defense on an annual basis.[2] Saudi military spending was highly rational, largely as a result of the heavy involvement of Western military advisers. Rather than spending the money frivolously on shiploads of expensive hardware, the bulk of Saudi defense spending went to infrastructure development, training, maintenance, and logistical support. Weapons purchases constituted only about 5–15 percent of annual defense spending during the 1980s.[3] In particular, the Saudis were careful to import weapons in smaller, more easily digested chunks rather than buying fleets of fighters and tanks that would have swamped their slowly modernizing military.

The Saudis brought in foreigners both to cover their short-term vulnerability and to build their long-term strength. To bolster Saudi defenses immediately, Riyadh hired British and Pakistani pilots, who formed the backbone of the Royal Saudi Air Force (RSAF) in the 1960s and 1970s. In 1964 the Saudis brought in a team of 150 Jordanian military officers (along with their British military advisers) to help them organize and discipline the Saudi Arabian National Guard (SANG), formed eight years earlier. In the spring of 1973, Riyadh signed an agreement with the United States to provide comprehensive assistance in modernizing the SANG. Indeed, in 1980 the Saudis went so far as to hire 10,000 Pakistani troops to serve in the Saudi armed forces; about half of this contingent manned the Saudi 10th Armored Brigade in its entirety. Large numbers of American and European civilian and military personnel were brought in to run Riyadh's maintenance and logistics networks, while the menial jobs connected with these functions were filled by impoverished workers from south and east Asia.[4] Meanwhile, especially after the relationship with the SANG began to show positive results, the Saudis invited additional foreign advisers, mostly Americans, to train their soldiers to fight like a modern army. By the mid-1980s, there were roughly 30,000 Americans, 4,000–5,000 French, 2,000–3,000 British, and the 10,000 Pakistanis supporting a Saudi military of 50,000 men.[5]

The Saudi military modernization program heavily favored the air and air defense forces. There were a variety of reasons for this emphasis. First, only air forces could be employed against hostile forces attacking by air, land, or sea. Second, airpower could be based centrally and then deployed quickly anywhere in their vast realm, allowing the Saudis maximum flexibility in shifting their strength to meet a threat. Third, many of the direct threats with which Riyadh had to contend with during this period were air threats rather than ground threats—Egyptian bombings in the 1960s, Israeli "touch-and-go" passes at Saudi airfields in the 1970s and 1980s,[6] and an Iranian-Saudi dogfight over the Persian Gulf in 1984. Fourth, a small air force could, in theory, offset a much larger enemy army, thereby reducing the strain on the small Saudi army. Fifth, the desert terrain of Saudi Arabia is ideal for airstrikes against ground forces, making control of the skies crucial to offensive or defensive operations. Sixth, the RSAF quickly became the playground of princes, who saw piloting a modern jet fighter as fun and a source of prestige. Last, the As-Sa'ud were more willing to build a small, competent air force—whose loyalty could more easily be assured—than a large ground force.

For all of these reasons, Riyadh made its air and air defense forces its highest priority. The RSAF probably had the largest number of U.S. advisers relative to its size and the greatest access to U.S. training programs of all the Saudi services. By the 1980s, virtually every Saudi pilot had had some training in the United States. The Saudis pushed hard for the most advanced and powerful weaponry for their air force, and despite the frequent opposition of the Israel lobby in the United States, they eventually were able to get most of what they wanted, including F-15 Eagle fighters and E-3A Sentry Airborne Warning and Control System (AWACS) aircraft. In

1985 the United States and the Saudis began a program called Peace Shield, intended to build an advanced, integrated air defense system for the kingdom second only to that defending NATO. This design included the provision of new radars, surface-to-air missiles (SAMs), battle-management facilities, and communications links.

Politicization

The extent of Riyadh's commitment to military effectiveness implied by a twenty-year modernization and expansion effort should not be overstated. The Saudis cultivated the belief that, in time of dire need, their great Western protector — first Britain, and then America — would come to their rescue. Moreover, the Saudis remained wary of their military. Consequently, Riyadh took numerous steps to ensure the loyalty of the military and prevent it from mounting a successful coup. Military units were generally deployed along the periphery, facing the kingdom's greatest threats, with only trusted units of the SANG near the capital and the oilfields. While this was important for strategic reasons, it was enforced as much to keep Saudi military units away from the seat of government and the kingdom's greatest asset as it was to keep them near potential trouble spots. Communications among Saudi units was purposely hamstrung: the ground forces were incapable of communicating with the air force without going through the armed forces high command, while up until the mid-1980s, Saudi combat units generally could not communicate with each other except via higher echelons. For many years, the Saudis insisted on arming certain units wholly with French and British equipment and other units entirely with American equipment. One reason for this practice was that it allowed the Saudis to diversify their arms purchases. Of equal importance, however, this incompatibility made it difficult for these units to coordinate their operations, thereby limiting their ability to defeat the regime's internal-security forces and take over the government.

Perhaps the most obvious symbol of the As-Sa'ud's fears was the SANG. After the first Nasserist plots were discovered in the 1950s, King Sa'ud ibn 'Abd al-Aziz (the son of Ibn Sa'ud) created both the Royal Guard Regiment and what was then called the White Army, which later became the SANG. Although a militia organization comprising volunteers from the five original tribes of the Ikhwan had been in existence since the 1930s, in 1955 the As-Sa'ud decreed the creation of a modern National Guard to serve as a counterbalance to the army. The new SANG would augment the Royal Guard Regiment, literally a palace guard, which had previously furnished the household troops for the king and borne most of the responsibility for defending the regime against an army coup. The SANG was deployed around Riyadh and at other key locations around the country such as in the oilfields of the eastern province. The SANG chain of command was kept completely separate from that of the other armed forces, culminating in its own ministry headed first by Prince Khalid and eventually by Crown Prince Abdallah. Because of their regime protection responsibilities, senior officers in the SANG were chosen largely for their loyalty to the As-Sa'ud family, and even as the SANG expanded to keep pace with the increase in size of the other services, personnel were still recruited nearly exclusively from loyal Najdi tribes.[7]

This tribal, or regional, preference also affected the other armed services. The As-Sa'ud were most comfortable with Najdi tribesmen, believing them to be the most devoted to the royal family. Riyadh was least enthusiastic about the large Shi'ah population of al-Hasa, who were mostly excluded from the armed forces because they were considered politically unreliable. In addition, the As-Sa'ud disliked accepting Hijazis, many of whom still chafed at Saudi rule, into the armed forces. The Hijazis generally considered themselves more urbane and sophisticated than the Najdi tribes upon whom the As-Sa'ud based their rule, and some Hijazis still felt that they should rule instead. Thus, despite the fact that as a group the Hijazis were probably the best-educated people in the country, Riyadh tried to minimize their presence in the military. Nevertheless, the drive to expand and modernize the armed forces, coupled with general problems in recruiting adequate numbers of fit manpower, forced the Saudis to accept larger numbers of Hijazis. Because Najdis were given greater preference in the RSAF and SANG, the Hijazis were very well represented in the army — the RSLF — and dominated its technical and support branches.[8]

Another manifestation of politicization affecting the Saudi military was the rampant nepotism and prevalence of royal family members throughout the military. To some extent, Saudi princes were assigned to key positions to ensure that all important posts were in the hands of men loyal to the As-Sa'ud. However, the ubiquity of Saudi princes was mostly a result of favoritism: many Saudi princes wanted important jobs commensurate with their station, and being a military officer — a warrior — was one of the more desirable occupations for members of the royal family. Since there were several thousand princes by the late 1980s, it was very easy to populate the senior military ranks with members of the royal family.[9] The presence of so many princes in the senior command echelons was a mixed blessing for the armed forces. On the one hand, it meant that subordinates within the chain of command were willing to act independently because, being princes, they knew that they would be indulged. On the other hand, this same independence greatly complicated the smooth functioning of the Saudi military hierarchy; on many occasions Saudi princes defied the orders of their superiors and, when challenged, successfully appealed to senior members of the royal family.

Manpower Problems

Another problem the Saudis had to contend with in the two decades preceding the Gulf War was a shortage of fit men for the armed services. Many Western military experts have argued since the 1980s that the Saudi force structure required 25–50 percent more men than were actually on hand in the military. In particular, the Saudis had great difficulty finding enough technically competent personnel to operate and maintain their burgeoning arsenal of sophisticated military hardware.

A wide variety of factors contributed to this problem. The Saudi military was all volunteer, meaning Riyadh had to try to persuade skilled personnel to join the armed forces instead of starting a career elsewhere. This proved difficult because of the strong allure of the Saudi financial and oil industries. Young men could make a fortune quickly and easily by taking a job in the oil sector or a related field. Opportunities to get rich either honestly or dishonestly were plentiful in other industries (including arms imports), and the lifestyle of a Saudi businessman was more appealing to potential recruits than was the life of a soldier. Beyond this, Saudi Arabia's oil wealth and the corresponding largesse distributed by the government to its people meant that many Saudis did not feel the responsibility to choose *any* career. Thus in 1990, Saudis constituted only 33 percent of their nation's workforce and only 10 percent of the private-sector workforce. Overall, only 54 percent of Saudi men were employed.[10]

The Saudis also had difficulty finding adequate personnel for their military because few who were interested in joining were fit to serve. Even into the late 1980s, illiteracy remained at around 50 percent among the Saudi populace, and these numbers were highest among the tribesmen who were the most interested in serving in the armed forces (especially the SANG). Those who could read often had only the most rudimentary education and little or no exposure to machinery or electronics. The Saudis also were limited by the fact that very few of their people were willing to take on a job that they considered menial labor — hence the support services suffered — and relatively few Saudi students studied technical subjects — hence there were few available personnel qualified to handle advanced military technology. The Saudi educational system did not teach much in the way of science and engineering because of the low demand, and even those who joined the military were often reluctant to learn the technical skills needed for their jobs.

Manpower problems became a kind of catch-22 for the Saudis in the years preceding the Gulf War. Because they could not recruit enough personnel to field a large army to defend the kingdom, they opted for a smaller, high-tech, high-firepower force that would not require high staffing levels. However, this approach immediately ran up against the dearth of technically competent people, limiting Riyadh's ability to man such a force. For example, the Saudi emphasis on their air force was one manifestation of their strategy of a small, high-technology force to compensate for manpower deficiencies. However, because of the shortage of trained, technically skilled personnel, the Saudis had great difficulty operating more than about 200 combat aircraft.[11] Better pilots had to be shifted onto more advanced planes, with the result that the pilots flying some of Riyadh's older jets had limited competence.

The Gulf War, 1990–91

The Iraqi invasion of Kuwait in early August 1990 caught the Saudi armed forces completely off-guard. They were still in the midst of their seemingly permanent military modernization program and had made only limited progress toward fielding a deterrent force able to meet the security needs of the kingdom. Nevertheless, it was galling to the Saudi people to discover that after spending roughly $300 billion on defense between 1965 and 1990, their military was still virtually impotent.[12]

The Saudi Military in 1990

Saudi armed forces at the outset of the war were no match for the Iraqis and were fortunate to be able to fight alongside a modern Western army and sizable contingents from other Arab countries. In 1990 the RSLF comprised two armored brigades, four mechanized infantry brigades, one infantry brigade, and one airborne brigade, totaling about 45,000 men and 550 tanks. In addition, the SANG added another two mechanized brigades (with a third forming),[13] five infantry (tribal militia) brigades posted at sensitive facilities throughout the kingdom, and the Royal Guard Regiment — all told, another 56,000 personnel and about 400 armored fighting vehicles. The RSAF had fifteen squadrons with 250 combat aircraft, including 60 F-15s and 70 Tornado fighter-bombers.[14]

The Saudis had some factors in their favor. Their forces had the benefit of a long tutelage under the Americans as well as weapons that were at least as good as those of the Iraqis, if not far better. For example, Saudi M-60A3 and AMX-30 tanks were about on a par with Iraq's T-72s and T-62s, but Saudi F-15s were clearly superior to anything in the Iraqi inventory, including their MiG-29s and Mirage F-1s. Moreover, both sides suffered equally from having a wide range of military equipment from a variety of arms makers. Thus, while the Saudis had some units equipped with British and French gear and other units equipped with American gear, the Iraqi forces had a mélange of Soviet, European, Chinese, and South American equipment. In addition, the Saudis were able to overcome their manpower problems to some extent through wartime volunteers. In August 1990 the kingdom asked for volunteers to fill out their ranks for the war, and although they expected only about 25,000 men, they ended up with over 200,000.[15]

The one advantage the Iraqis did have over the Saudis was their mostly veteran (albeit war-weary) army. Saudi forces, in contrast, had seen little combat since the days of Ibn Sa'ud; some Saudi units had participated in the Green Mountain Revolt in Oman in the late 1950s. Riyadh had actually pulled back the armored brigade at Tabuk near Israel during the Six Day War to make sure they did not get mauled by the Israelis. The Saudis clashed with Yemeni forces along their borders on several occasions during the 1960s and 1970s, but these were rarely more than minor incidents involving platoons or companies of troops. The kingdom sent a battalion to join the Arab effort against Israel in 1973, but this unit saw little action and clearly was meant only to "show the flag." Finally, the RSAF had had a few run-ins with Iranian attack aircraft during the 1980s, culminating in the downing of at least one and probably two Iranian F-4s by a pair of Saudi F-15s in 1984. These incidents constituted the sum total of Saudi combat experience to 1990, whereas the Iraqis had had eight years of combat against Iran to hone their military skills. While the Iraqi army never reached a high level of military competence (see chapter 3), the conflict with Iran did provide Iraqi commanders valuable experience in planning and leading their forces in combat and gave their troops a taste of battle.

The Course of Operations

When the Iraqis invaded Kuwait on 2 August 1990, the Saudis had to scramble to get forces in place to meet a possible Iraqi drive into the kingdom. They had only two combat formations in the northeast: the 20th Mechanized Brigade at Hafr al-Batin and the SANG's 2d "King 'Abd al-Aziz" Mechanized Brigade at Dhahran. It took a long time for the Saudis to prepare these forces and other units around the country for redeployment, as most were disorganized, unready, and took inordinately long to move. As late as 20 August, there were only two combat-ready Saudi battalions in the entire eastern province. The Saudis had never really thought through such a contingency, and their moves suffered at every level. Thus, when U.S. forces began arriving as part of Operation Desert Shield in mid-August, they found the 20th Mechanized and 2d SANG Brigades deployed in the open desert, in positions from which they could not adequately defend the main invasion routes into Saudi Arabia and were highly vulnerable to being outflanked. Saudi units had failed to dig-in properly, to site their weapons' positions to provide overlapping fields of fire, or to place their units where they could easily support one another. In short, Riyadh was very fortunate that the Iraqis did not continue their attack into Saudi Arabia. Indeed, after the fact, the Saudi high command estimated that during the first week of August, the Iraqi Republican Guard could have overrun the entire eastern province in as little as six hours, perhaps as many as twelve if U.S. airpower intervened.[16]

U.S. military personnel placed little faith in Saudi combat capabilities. Based on the experience many had had with them in training or on joint operations, the Americans largely assessed that the Saudis could contribute little to the Coalition campaign against Iraq. Many, including high-ranking U.S. officers, expected the Saudis to run away en masse when the first shots were fired. In addition, experienced U.S. officers noted the Saudi tendency to dissemble and obfuscate rather than admit a mistake. As a result, U.S. military commanders carefully structured Coalition operations to minimize the role of the Saudis and to make sure that they only went into battle under optimal conditions. U.S. air and artillery forces were assigned to provide fire support to Saudi units, which were given only supporting missions in less critical sectors of the front, and U.S. military personnel were attached to Saudi forces to provide advice and to make sure that their reporting was accurate.[17]

SAUDI PERFORMANCE DURING THE COALITION AIR CAMPAIGN

Saudi Arabia's greatest contribution to the Coalition war effort came during the air campaign. U.S. military planners considered the RSAF, and particularly its F-15 pilots, to be the most competent element of the Saudi military. Because of the favor in which the RSAF was held (and the high number of princes flying F-15s), Saudi pilots were lavished with funds for training, and as a result, they often had more time in the air than their NATO counterparts; U.S. pilots who had flown with them unanimously averred (both before and after the war) that Saudi F-15 pilots were very good at dogfighting. Coalition military commanders assigned them a somewhat more demanding mission during the air campaign than they did during the ground campaign.[18] The Saudis flew 6,852 sorties during Operation Desert Storm, including roughly 2,000 over Iraq and the Kuwaiti Theater of Operations.[19] Over one-third of these sorties (nearly 2,400) were counterair missions flown by F-15s and Tornado interceptors. Saudi fighters primarily flew defensive combat air patrol duties over Saudi Arabia: 93 percent of all Saudi F-15 sorties and 100 percent of all Tornado interceptor sorties were defensive counterair missions.[20]

Despite the large number of sorties flown, because the Saudi fighters mostly flew defensive combat air patrol, they had only one opportunity to engage in air-to-air combat. On 24 January 1991, a Saudi F-15 shot down two Iraqi fighters probably trying to attack Coalition ships in the Persian Gulf. Although the result was perfect, the actual engagement was not. The Saudi pilot initially panicked when he was vectored out to intercept the Iraqis. U.S. AWACS air controllers had to carefully position his aircraft so he could get a shot on the two Iraqi planes and then had to talk him through the operation. Fortunately, the Iraqis demonstrated little situational awareness, flew a simplistic flight profile, and made only a minimal effort to shake the F-15 and so were shot down relatively easily. In this and other engagements, Saudi fighters demonstrated a particular inability to operate in formations larger than pairs as well as difficulty acting on information provided by AWACS.

Saudi pilots flew fewer strike missions as part of the Coalition air campaign than counterair missions, reflecting both U.S. military planners' lower confidence in Saudi attack proficiency and their poor showing in the initial missions they flew. According to the U.S. Air Force's *Gulf War Air Power Survey*, Saudi aircraft flew 1,656 strike sorties during the Gulf War.[21] The airstrikes they conducted were poor and added little to the overall Coalition effort. For example, on the first night of the Coalition attack, a flight of Saudi Tornado attack aircraft failed to link up with a tanker for refueling, and their mission had to be aborted. Another Tornado got separated from the rest of its flight, lost its way to the target, and was nearly shot down by a U.S. F-15. After the war, U.S. forces had the opportunity to closely inspect Safwan Airfield, one of the targets left to the Saudis, and found that it had sustained almost no damage in repeated airstrikes by Saudi Tornados. In general, Saudi pilots were only able to fly strike missions against fixed, lightly defended targets with U.S. planning and support. They could not locate moving targets, and Iraqi ground-based air defenses regularly caused their pilots either to abort their mission or to miss their targets. The Saudis could not plan or control their own operations, they could not operate in formations larger than squadron level, and they had no real strategy or concept of operations as to how to attack enemy targets.

Finally, RSAF reconnaissance was infrequent and of little value. The RSAF was asked to fly only 118 reconnaissance sorties during the entire course of the war.[22] In Anthony Cordesman's words, "The Saudi RF-5 force proved largely useless in seeking out targets and rapidly processing information."[23] Consequently, the Saudis were forced to rely on the United States for all reconnaissance and intelligence for their strike missions.

THE BATTLE OF R'AS AL-KHAFJI

Saudi Arabia's most significant ground combat occurred in the battle of R'as al-Khafji. During the night of 29 January 1991, the Iraqis launched a series of probing attacks into northern Saudi Arabia by battalion-sized task forces from the 5th Mechanized Division. Three of these ran into U.S. Marine covering forces and were driven back with heavy losses. A fourth column, a mechanized infantry battalion from the 15th Mechanized Brigade of the Iraqi 5th Mechanized Division — reinforced with a company of tanks — blundered into a Saudi screening force north of the Saudi coastal city of R'as al-Khafji. The Saudis put up a very brief resistance and then fled. The Saudi 5th Combined Arms (Mechanized) Battalion of the SANG's 2d King 'Abd al-Aziz Mechanized Brigade, screening the Kuwaiti border in the area, retreated back south of R'as al-Khafji when the U.S. Marines began reporting contact with Iraqi armor. Moreover, a battalion of Saudi marines guarding the beaches north of the city fled all the way to al-Mishab, nearly sixty kilometers to the rear. The panic of Saudi forces in this area allowed the Iraqis to occupy R'as al-Khafji. However, a small forward detachment of U.S. Marines in the city called in air support from Cobra attack helicopters, which kept up a continuous fire on the Iraqi armor.[24]

The Saudi government and military high command were incensed by the Iraqi occupation of R'as al-Khafji. While of no military significance, it was a humiliating blow to Saudi pride, and they became obsessed with retaking the town — and retaking it themselves. As a result, U.S. Marine Corps forces that had moved to reinforce the threatened sector and were in position to assault and retake the town the next morning were ordered to stand down and allow the Saudis to conduct the operation. Meanwhile, the Iraqis were massing two of their better heavy divisions — the 3d Armored and the 5th Mechanized — for a major offensive designed to trap and maul the Saudi units congregating around R'as al-Khafji. This attack never came off, however, because U.S. airpower located the two divisions in southern Kuwait as they were mustering for the assault and cut them to pieces. The

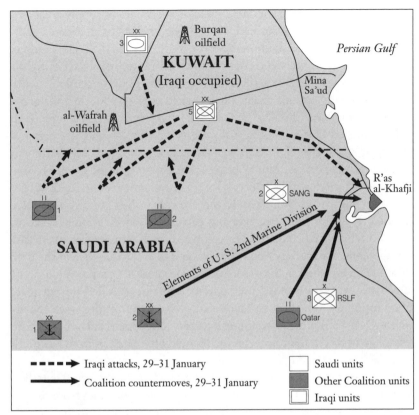

Burqan
oilfield

KUWAIT
(Iraqi occupied)

Persian Gulf

al-Wafrah
oilfield

Mina
Sa'ud

R'as
al-Khafji

SANG

SAUDI ARABIA

Elements of U. S. 2nd Marine Division

RSLF

Qatar

- - - ▶ Iraqi attacks, 29–31 January

───────▶ Coalition countermoves, 29–31 January

☐ Saudi units

■ Other Coalition units

☐ Iraqi units

Map 29. The Battle of R'as al-Khafji, 29–31 January 1991

relentless pummeling from Coalition attack aircraft and helicopter gunships convinced the Iraqis to call off their offensive, leaving the battalion in
R'as al-Khafji to its fate.

With the main Iraqi offensive aborted, the local odds at R'as al-Khafji
heavily favored the Saudis. Riyadh massed the SANG 2d Brigade, reinforced
by a battalion of Qatari AMX-30 tanks, for the operation. The Saudis also
had their RSLF 8th Mechanized Brigade standing by to join the attack if
needed. In addition, they were provided almost constant fire support from
U.S. Marine artillery battalions, attack helicopters, and strike aircraft. Although the Iraqi troops in the city were veterans of countless battles during the Iran-Iraq War, they were unenthusiastic about this conflict and
their equipment was terrible: obsolete and poorly manufactured Chinese
Type-63 APCs and Type-59 tanks (a bad Chinese copy of the old Soviet

T-55). In addition, the Iraqis were isolated, their lines of supply and communication having been cut by U.S. airpower, which also prevented additional Iraqi forces from reinforcing those units. Finally, the Saudis had the benefit of the U.S. Marine reconnaissance team trapped in the city by the Iraqi attack, who served as artillery spotters throughout the battle.

The first Saudi assault was finally launched at 11:00 P.M. on 30 January. Earlier, throughout the day, Qatari tanks and Saudi antitank units with Tube-launched Optical-tracking Wire-guided, or TOW, missiles harassed the Iraqis while the U.S. Marines maintained a constant bombardment with artillery, airstrikes, and helicopter attacks that kept the Iraqis on edge and slowly wore down their forces. It took some time for the Saudis to get their units in place for the attack, and even then their preparations were terrible: They had not sent out any patrols or other reconnaissance to gather intelligence on the Iraqi forces in R'as al-Khafji; had not made any arrangements for artillery or air support, and only the initiative of the U.S. liaison team attached to the SANG 2d Brigade ensured that the Saudis went into battle with the needed fire support; had not provided for adequate ammunition for their forces; had no way of communicating with the attached Qatari units; had no training in urban combat; and did not even have a strategy to retake the town, simply intending to march in from the south and take it from the dug-in Iraqi veterans in a frontal assault.

The first attack was conducted by the 7th Combined Arms Battalion (CAB) of the SANG 2d Brigade, reinforced with two companies from the 6th CAB and two companies of tanks from the Qatari armored battalion. Although this force was twice as large as the Iraqi task force in the town and was backed by firepower from U.S. Marine air and artillery units, the attack was a fiasco. The Saudi mechanized infantry advanced directly up the main road into R'as al-Khafji from the south — right into the teeth of the Iraqi defenses — and then suddenly the armored cars and APCs deployed for an attack and dashed off at the Iraqis. Neither the U.S. Marine advisory group attached to the Saudi unit nor the Qatari armor had any idea what was going on as the Saudis apparently had issued the order to charge only on their battalion command net. The Qatari armor, at a loss as to what to do, simply stopped while the Saudi mechanized infantry charged headlong at the Iraqis. According to U.S. and British liaison officers accompanying the Saudis, the Iraqis stood their ground and unleashed an awesome amount of firepower at the SANG, and although the Iraqi fire was wildly inaccurate and inflicted almost no harm to the Saudis (one dead, four wounded), it still caused them to turn back and retreat.

To their credit, the Saudis regrouped and attacked again at 8:30 the next morning. This time the 6th and 7th CABs made sure to try to coordinate their plans with the Qatari tanks. In addition, they arranged to have the 5th CAB conduct a flanking attack into the northern quarter of the town; the 8th CAB remained in reserve. Even though the Saudi battalions and the Qatari tanks attacked in unison this time, the results were the same as the night before. First, instead of attacking into R'as al-Khafji, the 5th CAB simply took up a blocking position to the north. In the south the Saudis launched another frontal assault under cover of heavy U.S. Marine fire support, charging straight at the Iraqis with no effort either to outflank their positions or even to use a combination of fire and movement to pin the Iraqis while an assault force closed with them. The Saudis and Qataris simply rushed forward, stopping occasionally to fire but causing little damage. At 10:00 A.M., the Saudis committed the 8th CAB in support of the 6th and 7th, but still made little headway. Despite the weight of numbers and firepower, the attack was stopped in its tracks. Fortunately for the Saudis, Iraqi marksmanship was awful, and the Iraqi commanders remained passive — refusing to counterattack or even maneuver against the Saudis. As a result, neither side suffered many casualties in the attack.[25]

The one successful element of the assault for the Saudis occurred north of town. As part of their effort to hold R'as al-Khafji to use it as bait in their projected offensive, the Iraqis had dispatched a second mechanized-battalion task force from the 15th Mechanized Brigade to reinforce the battalion already in the city. At about 10:00 A.M., this force ran into the SANG 5th CAB, holding north of the town. This time it was the Iraqis who advanced slowly in no apparent order while the Saudis were in defensive positions, and the results were accordingly reversed. With Marine artillery and airstrikes, the Saudis busted up the Iraqi battalion, destroying as many as thirteen tanks and APCs, capturing six others abandoned in the fight, and chasing off the rest. However, the Saudis failed to pursue the Iraqis and so lost the opportunity to smash the battalion.[26]

Again the Saudis pulled back to regroup, but they remained determined to liberate R'as al-Khafji themselves. During the night of 31 January–1 February, the U.S. advisory team gave the SANG units a quick lesson in urban-combat operations and arranged for a massive Marine artillery bombardment to accompany the next attack. Meanwhile, the U.S. Marine shelling of the forces in R'as al-Khafji continued, wearing down the morale and combat strength of the Iraqis. In Riyadh, however, the government was virtually apoplectic over the failure of their forces to recapture the town and restore the kingdom's injured pride. King Fahd reportedly went so far as to ask U.S. military leaders to reduce the city to rubble so that if the Saudis could not retake it, at least the Iraqis would not be able to stay. Cooler heads prevailed, the city was not destroyed, and another Saudi attack was set for the morning of the first.

The third Saudi assault was an even larger effort than the first two. The Saudis concentrated the entire SANG 2d Brigade for the operation, again supported by the Qatari armored battalion. As noted above, U.S. Marine artillery was to provide fire support, and U.S. attack aircraft were brought in to provide close air support. In addition, the Saudis sent two battalions of their RSLF 8th Mechanized Brigade north of the town to take over the blocking positions established by the SANG 5th CAB to prevent the Iraqis from sending reinforcements to aid the units in R'as al-Khafji. By this time, the Iraqis had long since called off their attack and abandoned their units in the city. The Saudi units encountered some company-sized Iraqi for- mations — the paltry elements of the 5th Mechanized Division that had made it past their own lines before the rest of the division retreated in the face of the Coalition airstrikes. These Iraqis were trapped, tired, weak, and completely demoralized from the air assault and were easily overpowered by the Saudis. Nevertheless, the Saudi forces reported that they had en- countered and destroyed a full brigade of Iraqi armor.[27]

The main attack against the Iraqis defending R'as al-Khafji was not much of a contest. The assault began with a heavy artillery barrage by the Marines, behind which the Saudi brigade crept forward, led by the 7th and 8th CABs. U.S. aircraft then began hitting major Iraqi strongpoints while American attack helicopters flew up and down the streets of R'as al-Khafji, knocking out Iraqi tanks and APCs along the way. The Saudis again con- ducted a frontal assault, without maneuver, covering fire, or combined- arms coordination; they just marched forward behind the artillery and air- strikes, stopping occasionally to add their own fire to the attack. When they reached the town itself, the Saudis ran helter-skelter through the streets, firing in all directions and mostly abandoning their formations, rather than conducting a determined, block-by-block clearing operation. The Iraqis fought back at first but were simply overwhelmed by the magnitude of the firepower they faced — "smothered by fire" in the words of one U.S. liaison officer.[28] As a British liaison officer to the SANG put it, after two and a half days of "unrelenting air and artillery strikes, [the Iraqis] began to lose the will to resist."[29] By around 1:00 P.M., the Iraqi defensive lines in the southern portion of the town had collapsed, and many were surrendering to the Saudis. Although snipers and small pockets of Iraqi troops resisted throughout the afternoon, the Saudis reoccupied the city, and by nightfall, the entire Iraqi force had surrendered. All told, the Iraqis had over 50 tanks and APCs captured or destroyed, 60 men killed, and 400 others taken prisoner. Against this, the Saudis lost seven V-150 armored cars and two Qatari tanks in addition to 18 dead and 50 wounded.[30]

THE COALITION GROUND OFFENSIVE

Saudi army forces were mostly kept out of the spotlight during the Coalition ground offensive. For political reasons, the Saudis and the other Arab armies participating in the war against Iraq were made responsible for "liberating" Kuwait City. One Arab force—a division-sized formation called the Joint Forces Command–East (JFC–E)—was assigned the axis of advance up the coastal road from R'as al-Khafji directly to Kuwait City. The JFC–E included the RSLF 10th Mechanized Brigade, the RSLF 8th Mechanized Brigade, and the SANG 2d Mechanized Brigade as well as a Kuwaiti brigade and battalions and companies from most of the other gulf emirate states. Here the Saudis could be supported by naval gunfire from the Coalition armada in the Persian Gulf, including the American battleships USS *Wisconsin* and USS *Missouri*. In addition, if the Saudis ran into trouble, the Coalition military command could give it support from the U.S. Marine divisions driving into the opposite side of southeastern Kuwait. The Saudis also contributed two brigades — the 20th Mechanized and 4th Armored of the RSLF — to the Joint Forces Command–North (JFC–N). The JFC–N was centered around an Egyptian corps-sized formation, which Coalition military commanders expected to be more capable than the Saudis. The Saudi units, along with two Kuwaiti brigades, were banded together under two multibrigade formations called Task Force Khalid and Task Force Muthanna and were assigned the mission of guarding the right flank of the Egyptian advance on al-Jahrah.

The JFC–E had a virtual cakewalk up the Kuwaiti coast. The Saudis attacked early on the morning of 24 February, simultaneous with the Marine attack farther west. The Iraqi 18th Infantry Division, defending this sector, simply collapsed in a swarm of surrenders and desertions. Its troops were sick and tired of living in the desert with inadequate supplies and under constant air attack and were eager to surrender. Later that day, the Iraqis pulled most of their remaining combat formations out of the Saudi sector to try to stop the far more dangerous U.S. Marine advance, leaving the Saudis an open road to Kuwait City. During their advance up the coast, the only serious resistance they faced was from a battery of Iraqi artillery pieces that put up a desultory barrage until Saudi multiple-rocket-launcher units and artillery batteries opened up on them. Although these did little damage to the Iraqi battery, it was enough to convince the unenthusiastic Iraqi crews to abandon their guns and head north for home. For the most part, the only resistance the Saudis faced was the occasional Iraqi soldier who waited to blow-off one magazine of his AK-47 for pride before surrendering.

Nevertheless, the JFC–E advance was slow and lagged behind the Marine advance, which faced much heavier resistance. To some extent, the Saudis were impeded by the huge number of Iraqi prisoners they were taking, but this was not the only problem. Although the SANG units attacked with great determination and moved quickly to secure their objectives, the RSLF formations were slow, plodding, and extremely timid in conducting operations. These units were particularly unaggressive, unwilling to diverge from their set plans, unable to adapt to unforeseen circumstances, and uninterested in exploiting the undefended avenue in front of them. One account of the Gulf War remarks that the RSLF "struggled to stay up with the National Guard and operated like a garrison army, highly dependent on Filipino bottle-washers and Pakistani mechanics."[31] Moreover, whenever there was a change in plan, such as when their U.S. advisers wanted the Saudis to speed up the timetable of their advance, the Saudis insisted on stopping and referring the matter all the way up the chain of command to Prince Khalid bin Sultan, the commander of all Coalition Arab forces.[32]

Saudi units attached to Task Force Khalid of the JFC–N performed even worse than the JFC–E, primarily because of the absence of SANG units in their formation. The JFC–N moved at the slowest pace of all the Coalition forces in Operation Desert Storm. On the second day of the ground war, it had barely breached the Iraqi defensive lines and still had not taken its first day's objectives despite the fact that the Iraqi forces in front of them had offered virtually no resistance and had mostly surrendered or fled.

The lion's share of the blame for this poor showing must go to the Egyptians who commanded the JFC–N and formed the primary assault force, but the Saudis (and the Kuwaitis) did little to ameliorate the Egyptian problems. First, they simply could not advance the timetable for their operations. When the U.S. military command realized that the Iraqi defenses were crumbling, they moved up the start times for the U.S. VII Corps and JFC–N attacks. Originally, both of these formations had been scheduled to attack in the early morning of 25 February, but now they were ordered to attack during the afternoon of 24 February. The Egyptians refused to comply until ordered to do so by Cairo, and even then they were late getting started. But the Saudis simply could not get moving and made only a very minor effort on 24 February. When they did get going on the morning of 25 February, they moved slowly and tentatively, displaying little aggressiveness. They lost contact with the Marines on their right, did a poor job of screening the Egyptian flank, and made no effort to keep up with even the glacial advance of the Egyptian units. There were also friendly fire incidents between the Saudis and the Egyptians, although it is unclear which side was at fault. Ultimately, none of the JFC–N units were able to accomplish their missions. Capturing al-Jahrah and the Matlah Ridge were left to the U.S. 1st Armored "Tiger" Brigade of the 2d Armored Division, and token formations of the JFC–N were hastily transferred east to participate in the "liberation" of Kuwait City.

Saudi Military Effectiveness during the Gulf War

Little was asked of the Saudi military during the Gulf War; little was delivered. In some ways the Saudis did surprise their critics. For example, most Western military personnel expected Saudi units to break and run at the first shots, but many units — and particularly the SANG units — went into battle and fought stoutly. While it is true that Saudi formations were never particularly taxed in combat, they often showed an unexpected degree of bravery and determination. In other ways, however, Saudi units performed even worse than projected. For example, the RSAF, which was expected to be the stand-out service among Arab militaries because of its superb equipment and extensive U.S. training, proved to have significant limitations. Specifically, although Saudi F-15s demonstrated good air-to-air skills under the right conditions, few Saudi pilots showed any real ability to operate in large formations or to handle particularly complex missions. Saudi strike and reconnaissance sorties were of little value and could only be assigned missions of tertiary importance, for Allied planners could not risk giving them more-important assignments.[33]

Little can be said about Saudi performance at the strategic level because all of their military operations were essentially planned by the Americans. Once the U.S. Central Command began deploying to Saudi Arabia on about 7 August 1990, defense of the country effectively fell to the Americans. The hasty Saudi deployment before Central Command's arrival was awful, showing little real understanding of how to conduct a proper defense against a large armored force. Thereafter, the Saudi high command demonstrated little that would suggest they could have planned and executed large-scale combat operations, but they were never asked to do so. In short, the available evidence points to a poor performance by Saudi strategic leadership, but one that had little or no effect on the actual course of the war.

At the tactical level, Saudi forces were mostly terrible. Although the SANG troops were generally very brave and determined fighters, they showed little military acumen despite their long tutelage under the Americans. The Saudis did not patrol and made no effort to conduct reconnaissance before an assault; unless their American advisers provided them with intelligence, they went in blind. Saudi attacks were poorly planned frontal assaults that showed no ability to employ fire and maneuver synergistically. Although Saudi attacks often featured both armor and infantry, and sometimes artillery, there was no effort to actually integrate these elements into a combined-arms team in which each supported the others. Instead, Saudi forces simply rolled forward in an uncoordinated mass. Moreover, Saudi infantry refused to dismount from their APCs, except for the final house-to-house clearing operations by the SANG in R'as al-Khafji. According to a Pakistani officer who had served as an adviser to the Saudi armor corps, Saudi tank crews "were not very conversant with basic tank drills such as those for crossing crests, taking up hull-down positions, or tank jockeying."[34] Planning for both air and ground operations was very haphazard and, at least at R'as al-Khafji, failed to provide for even the most basic elements like synchronization, a communications plan, and fire support. Saudi artillery was so poor it could do little more than conduct preliminary bombardments against fixed targets.

Saudi ground forces were virtually paralyzed by overcentralization and passivity. U.S. military personnel reported that operations were delayed sometimes for days by the necessity of referring all decisions up to the highest levels of command. Because the Saudis generally made little effort to prioritize issues and could only make decisions by communal debate rather than staff work, the process of decision making itself was extremely slow and further delayed operations. Since any change in plans could only be approved by this process, Saudi forces moved at a ponderous pace and were incapable of taking advantage of fleeting opportunities. Both the JFC–E and the JFC–N moved so slowly that gaps opened on both sides of the U.S. Marine Corps advance into southeastern Kuwait, seriously worrying the commanders of the Marine divisions whose flanks the Arabs were supposed to be covering.[35]

The Gulf War also exposed a number of other problems in the Saudi armed forces. For example, the kingdom's modern arsenal proved of little value since few Saudi personnel demonstrated an ability to handle their sophisticated equipment. In general they experienced tremendous difficulty learning to master their weaponry. For instance, of the dozens of militaries all over the globe that purchased the Cadillac Gage V-150 armored fighting vehicle, Saudi troops took longest to learn to operate and maintain it.[36] Indeed, U.S. military personnel concluded that it generally required twice as long to train a Saudi in a technically demanding task than it would take to train a U.S. soldier.[37] Even decades after equipment had been introduced into their military, the Saudis could not operate it properly. For example, by the Gulf War, the Saudis were only just beginning to handle the maintenance of their fleet of old and relatively simple F-5 fighters on their own. Mordechai Abir's 1984 comment, "Reports of U.S. federal agencies, private companies, and military analysts indicate that the training of Saudi operational and maintenance personnel to replace foreigners and to help incorporate systems into the Saudi armed forces, is years behind schedule, and that in some cases there is no solution in sight," continued to ring true in the early 1990s.[38]

Saudi maintenance practices were abysmal but never became a significant problem because they relied heavily on foreign technicians to perform even the most minor services on their equipment. Saudi forces did not know the first thing about keeping their vehicles running. For example, tank crews did not even know to replace the air filters in their tanks. In one battalion, better than two-thirds of its M-60 tanks were inoperable because of clogged air filters only weeks after deploying from garrison to a defensive position in the desert. Rather than properly care for their personal weapons and gear, Saudi soldiers were issued completely new "kits" every six months.[39] RSAF attrition rates, even among the elite F-15 squadrons, were "significantly higher" than for U.S. squadrons with the same aircraft.[40] Nevertheless, the Saudis employed 14,000 foreign technicians to keep their vehicles running. As long as the Saudis could have their vehicles towed back to the rear-area depots where these technicians worked, they were fine — and the peculiar course of the conflict allowed them this luxury. The only Iraqi ground attack was at R'as al-Khafji, which never developed into much of a battle thanks to the intervention of U.S. air power. So the Saudis basically had five months for their foreign contractors to bring their equipment up to peak readiness levels before the start of the Coalition offensive. Moreover, since during the ground war the Saudis faced little resistance, they did not tax their equipment, and since the ground campaign lasted only four days, maintenance problems never became an issue.[41]

Saudi unit cohesion was uneven, but mostly better than worse. Some units did break and run at the first sign of trouble, specifically some of those deployed forward when the Iraqis began their R'as al-Khafji offensive. Other formations, particularly the RSLF, showed little desire to aggressively attack the Iraqis as part of the Coalition ground offensive. However, by and large, Saudi units fought hard and stuck together. Even after the defeat of their inept first counterattack at R'as al-Khafji, Saudi units did not fall apart but regrouped and kept attacking.

In a number of additional areas such as intelligence, logistics, communications, and air defense, it is not possible to assess Saudi performance because they relied entirely on foreigners. For instance, as was the case with maintenance, their logistical system was manned and operated almost exclusively by foreign contractors and expatriates. Although the Saudis showed no particular indication that they would be capable of taking over and efficiently running their logistics system, they never tried, thus it is impossible to conclude for certain the extent of their logistics capabilities. Likewise, the Saudis relied on the United States and other Coalition members to gather and analyze intelligence for them and to direct the defense of Saudi airspace.

Summary

Despite their radically different circumstances, military history, and political context, Saudi forces evinced many of the same patterns of behavior as other Arab armies. Saudi oil wealth and the kingdom's close cooperation with the United States did not prevent its military from developing the same problems as Egypt, Iraq, Jordan, Libya, and Syria. Indeed, in some ways, the Saudis' advantages made these problems more prevalent and more debilitating. Their oil wealth allowed them to indulge certain tendencies, such as their unwillingness to accept jobs they considered menial labor or to acquire technical skills in school. As a result, Saudi personnel often displayed even less familiarity with machinery than their poorer brethren elsewhere in the Arab world. Similarly, because they knew that the United States would be there to save them if things ever got too bad, the Saudis were able to treat military effectiveness in a somewhat cavalier fashion. In the end, they had little to show for their billions of dollars spent on defense since the first oil boom. Saudi troops suffered from all of the same problems as other Arab armies, only worse.

6

SYRIA

The Syrian army was founded by the French after World War I when France obtained its mandate over the northern Levant, organized into the new states of Syria and Lebanon. French rule was highly unpopular and faced constant friction from the general populace, punctuated by several outright revolts. In 1919 France created the Troupes Spéciales du Levant with 8,000 men, which later grew into the Syrian and Lebanese armies. These units were used primarily as auxiliaries alongside its own regulars. Senior officer billets were held by French personnel, although Syrians were allowed to hold commissions below major. The Troupes Spéciales was intended almost exclusively for internal-security responsibilities, while France handled external security.

The small Syrian army that developed during this period was dominated by Syria's minority groups: Druze, Alawis, Christians, Circassians, and Kurds. The French favored the Christians as coreligionists and dispensed commissions liberally throughout their small population. They also encouraged other minorities to join the army, while discouraging the majority Sunni Arabs from doing so, as a means of controlling the country. Paris hoped that the Syrian minorities would feel dependent on the French for their position and security and so would defend its control of the country against the Sunnis. For their part, the more cosmopolitan Sunnis viewed the Syrian army as a mandate tool, and so it was not considered prestigious or fashionable; most considered the army a career only for the incompetent. By contrast, the army offered economic and social advancement to the minorities, who clamored for the opportunity to enlist. By the Second World War, non-Sunni Syrians were significantly overrepresented in the armed forces.

The War of Israeli Independence, 1947–48

The Syrian military's first taste of combat was not particularly auspicious, but neither was it as catastrophic as for some of the other Arab armies. Newly independent Syria contributed most of its fairly meager military power to the Arab war effort against the nascent Israeli state in May 1948. At that time, the army was small, poorly armed, and poorly trained. Paris had relied primarily on French regulars to keep the peace in Syria and had neglected indigenous forces. Consequently, training was lackadaisical, discipline lax, and staff work almost unheard of. In terms of quantitative strength, there were about 12,000 men in the Syrian army. These troops were mostly grouped into three infantry brigades and an armored force of about battalion size. In addition, the Syrians had an air force of about fifty aircraft, of which the ten newest were World War II–generation models. Syrian ammunition stocks were so inadequate that the quartermasters initially could provide only a few hundred rounds for each soldier sent to Palestine.[1]

Syrian Operations with the Arab Liberation Army

Even before the Arab League resolution to attack Israel, Syria intervened in the conflict by sending large numbers of men and considerable arms and provisions to the Arab Liberation Army (ALA), led by the Syrian Fawzi al-Kaukji. Indeed, the Syrians were largely responsible for creating the ALA and soliciting contributions to it from other Arab countries. They also committed 2,500 "volunteers," or about one-third of the ALA and nearly the full strength of its Northern Command, which came under Kaukji's personal control.[2] The other commands — Southern, Eastern, and Western — were manned largely by Iraqis, Palestinians, and Lebanese and were commanded by Kaukji's lieutenants.

In February 1948 the Syrian-dominated Northern Command launched its first offensive in the Bayt She'an Valley against the Israeli settlement of Tirat Zvi. Kaukji's force of over battalion size greatly outnumbered the poorly armed defenders. However, the ALA units launched a frontal assault on the kibbutz's defensive positions in the rain. The Israelis beat back several such charges, and then they sent out a small force that caught the ALA in the flank as they launched their final attack. Surprised by this unexpected counterattack, Kaukji's men fled, leaving 60 dead and a great deal of equipment on the battlefield.[3] Edgar O'Ballance observed of this clash, "The Arabs had shown much individual bravery, but little tactical skill."[4]

By April, Kaukji's army had regrouped and was ready for another try. But he had apparently realized by this time that his original goal of actually "liberating" Palestine was unrealistic and instead set his sights considerably lower: he simply wanted to take one Israeli settlement, which he could then tout for propaganda purposes. This time, the ALA struck at the small Israeli settlement of Mishmar Ha'Emeq, southeast of Haifa. Kaukji assembled over 1,000 troops and a battery of Syrian 75-mm howitzers. The Israeli forces were less than one-fifth this size, and the defenders were armed with only one light machine gun, a few mortars, and not even enough small arms to go around.[5] In the early morning of 4 April, the Syrian artillery began a bombardment that damaged the buildings of the settlement but had little effect on the defenses. Soon after the shelling began, Kaukji launched an infantry assault into the main defensive lines. Despite their dearth of heavy weapons, the Israelis were able to stop the attack short of the settlement's fence. That night, an Israeli company reinforced Mishmar Ha'Emeq. The next day Kaukji contented himself to simply bombard the settlement, hoping this alone would compel the Israelis to surrender, but his shelling was inaccurate and did little damage to the defenders. On the sixth a small British force arrived and imposed a twenty-four-hour ceasefire to allow the Jewish women and children to be evacuated.

During the ceasefire, the Israelis brought up additional reinforcements, the 1st Palmach Battalion, commanded by Maj. Dan Laner. Nevertheless, when fighting resumed, the Israeli commander decided not to use this force to counterattack Kaukji's army because the ALA force was too large and well armed. Instead, the Palmach Battalion set out from En Ha'Shofet, southwest of Mishmar Ha'Emeq, and headed east, outflanking Kaukji's force and occupying several Arab villages on the ridgeline east of Mishmar Ha'Emeq, along which ran the ALA's line of supply. This Israeli move caused Kaukji to panic and turn back to try to retake the captured villages. For the next week, the ALA and the Haganah forces fought for control of these settlements. The Syrians were generally able to bring their superior numbers and firepower to bear during the day to force the Israelis out of a position only to lose it again when the Palmach counterattacked at night. By 12 April, the Israelis had secured their control over most of the ridge. Kaukji then tried to launch one last attack on Mishmar Ha'Emeq to try to draw off Laner's forces, but his units failed to adequately scout their route and were ambushed. Meanwhile, the Israelis had continued to push around the ALA's eastern flank, and after two more villages fell, Kaukji apparently realized that he was virtually encircled. At that point, he was forced to pull out of Galilee altogether, extricating himself from the Israeli noose only with great difficulty.

Thereafter, the ALA Northern Command remained mostly passive. Kaukji was shaken by his near annihilation at Mishmar Ha'Emeq. He retired to Lebanon and sent most of his units, including his artillery, to aid the Arab efforts around Jaffa and Jerusalem. For the rest of the war, Northern Command operations were small and inconsequential. Meanwhile, on 14 May 1948 the main Arab armies invaded Palestine. Many of the "volunteers" previously under ALA control were recalled by their respective governments to fight with their own national armies, including most of Kaukji's Syrian contingent. For the rest of the war, the forces under his command were largely indigenous Palestinians, Lebanese, and non-Arab Muslims. Later in 1948, the Israelis defeated Kaukji's remaining forces in a series of offensives that drove them out of Palestine altogether.

Operations of the Syrian Army in Palestine

On 14 May 1948 the Syrian army invaded Palestine as part of the coordinated Arab League effort to snuff out the State of Israel before it could establish itself. The initial Syrian thrust was directed along the southern shore of the Sea of Galilee (Lake Kinneret). In support of this move, the Syrians set up a logistics depot near the B'nat Ya'acov bridge north of the Sea of Galilee. As they had hoped, the Israelis detected this and took it as a sign that the Syrians were going to make their major thrust in that area. Consequently, the few Israeli mobile units in eastern Galilee were deployed north of the Kinneret to guard against the expected attack from the B'nat Ya'acov bridge, leaving only a few defenders south of the Sea of Galilee to defend against the main Syrian attack.

Nevertheless, the Syrian thrust south of the Kinneret proved to be something less than a blitzkrieg. The 1st Infantry Brigade, supported by Syria's entire armor corps — consisting of a battalion of armored cars and a company of French Renault-35 and 37 tanks — an artillery battalion, and other units, first attacked the Israeli village of Zemach. During the night of 15–16 May, they attacked Zemach with infantry supported by armored cars. The infantry moved south of the town to try to flank its defenses, but the Israelis detected the move and were able to shift forces to block it, after which the Syrians fell back to regroup. In the meantime, the Israelis established hasty defensive positions at Zemach and, more importantly, began work on more-extensive fortifications in the twin Deganyah villages west of Zemach, which guarded the way to the bridge across the Jordan River at Deganyah Alef. On the morning of 18 May, the Syrians renewed their assault on Zemach. They had used the two-day interregnum to carefully plan and rehearse the attack, and as a result, there was a noticeable improvement in execution. This time, the infantry hung back while the tanks

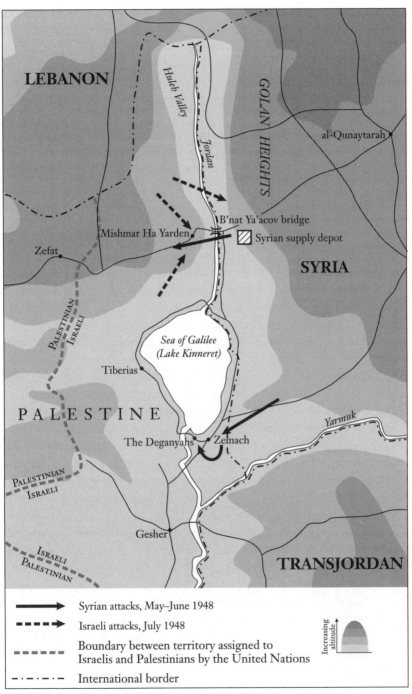

Map 30. Syrian Army Operations in 1948

and armored cars advanced in front of them, all supported by a heavy bombardment. The Syrian artillery had used the two days respite to plot and preregister their fire missions, and so their initial volleys were very accurate. The armor again swung south of the town, and this time the Israelis could not block them, for they had only two 20-mm antitank guns. The Syrians forced the defenders to abandon the town and retreat back to the Deganyah positions.

With the fall of Zemach, the Israelis realized they faced a serious threat south of the Kinneret. They scraped together reinforcements from all over eastern Galilee and sent them to the Deganyahs under the command of Maj. Moshe Dayan, who had grown up there. Dayan attempted a counterattack on Zemach, but the Syrians fought back hard and repulsed the Israelis.

The Syrians began their assault on the Deganyahs before dawn on 20 May. The attack was very poorly coordinated at almost every level. First, the Syrians failed to synchronize the timing of their strikes on the villages, with the result that the attack on Deganyah Alef started hours before that on Deganyah Bet. At Deganyah Alef, they committed an infantry company supported by artillery, armored cars, and half their tank force in a frontal assault against seventy Israeli defenders. Although the Syrian units began moving in tandem, the armor outpaced the infantry and ended up attacking the Israeli lines first. The defenders had only one Piat shoulder-fired antitank weapon and one 81-mm mortar, and so the Syrian tanks and armored cars were able to break into the settlement itself but then were stopped by determined Israeli resistance. The Israelis knocked out four tanks and four armored cars with Molotov cocktails, the Piat, a 20-mm gun, and even the mortar employed as a direct-fire weapon. When the Syrian infantry arrived, their tanks had been defeated and were beginning to retreat. The Israelis were then able to redirect their fire on the soldiers, who, seeing the armor in full retreat, fell back as well.[6]

The attack on Deganyah Bet later that day showed that the Syrians had learned some lessons from their earlier mistakes. In this assault the Syrians were careful to have their armor keep pace with the infantry. Nevertheless, they again conducted a frontal assault, which the Israelis beat back after a short battle. The Syrians were regrouping for another attack when unexpected Israeli reinforcements appeared: two 65-mm field guns that had arrived in Tel Aviv only days before. These guns began firing on the Syrian units around Zemach as they formed up for another attack on the Deganyahs. The Israeli crews had never fired their guns before, and their accuracy suffered. But their mere presence had a disproportionate effect on the Syrians — this sudden appearance of Israeli artillery after having had a total monopoly on heavy weapons for the last week unnerved them. In addition, the Syrian forces around Zemach were low on ammunition, and the resupply they had been promised was diverted to the 2d Brigade, operating north of the Sea of Galilee. In response, the 1st Brigade pulled back.[7] They abandoned their positions in front of the Deganyahs as well as Zemach and retreated back to the foothills of the Golan Heights. Indeed, they even left behind a number of lightly damaged or otherwise inoperable tanks that the Israelis were able to repair. Although the Syrians still outnumbered the Israelis by a wide margin in this area — especially in artillery and armor — they never again mounted another attack south of the Sea of Galilee.

After their defeat at the Deganyahs, the Syrians redirected their attention north to the B'nat Ya'acov bridge. They had planned to launch a supporting attack in this area around 22 May. However, when the Israelis realized that the main strike was coming south of the Sea of Galilee, they sent a company of the Yiftach Brigade across the Jordan, overpowering the Syrian forces protecting the supply depot near the bridge and then destroying their provisions. This loss forced the Syrians to delay their offensive north of the Kinneret until logistical stocks could be rebuilt to support the operation.

On 6 June the Syrians were finally ready to go, and that morning their 2d Infantry Brigade, supported by armor and artillery, attacked across the Jordan River at Mishmar HaYarden. The Israelis had emplaced some automatic weapons along the river and also were able to call in mortar fire, which prevented the Syrian infantry from establishing a bridgehead and prevented their armor from even getting across the river. The Syrians pulled back to regroup while the Israelis brought in reinforcements.

On 10 June the Syrians renewed their assault on Mishmar HaYarden, and this time they turned in a very creditable performance. Damascus had reinforced its units to nearly two brigades in strength. The Syrians began the attack with a determined infantry assault across the river supported by heavy artillery fire from the Golan. In addition, they brought in aircraft to conduct strikes against the defenders in support of the river crossing. The Syrian guns delivered heavy, accurate fire on the Israeli positions, and their infantry were able to establish three bridgeheads on the west bank. The Syrians then crossed an infantry force north of Mishmar HaYarden and an armored unit south of the settlement. These then converged on the settlement while Syrian artillery continued to pound the Israeli fortifications.

This combined attack succeeded in taking the settlement by about noon, although mopping-up operations continued for the rest of the day.

The Syrians had hoped to continue pushing westward into Galilee from Mishmar HaYarden to link up with Lebanese forces to sever the Huleh Valley from the rest of Galilee. Indeed, at that point, the road to Zefat lay wide open because the Israelis had no sizable forces in the area and were desperately trying to rush in reinforcements. After securing the settlement, the Syrians attacked westward toward Mahanayim. However, this attack was slow and tentative, and their careful combined-arms cooperation fell apart. Moreover, they conducted a frontal assault rather than trying to outflank the small Israeli force there and so were easily defeated. This rebuff ended the Syrian offensive into Galilee. They retreated to Mishmar HaYarden, dug in, and did not try to press their advantage to try to drive on to Zefat.

In July the Israelis mounted an operation to try to retake Mishmar HaYarden. They concentrated 2,000 men from the Carmeli and Oded Brigades in the hills surrounding the settlement. The Syrians had built up their forces in Mishmar HaYarden to about 2,500 men behind formidable defenses.[8] The Israeli plan was to launch a diversionary attack against the southern flank of the Syrian positions while the main force crossed the Jordan in strength north of the Syrian bridgehead and drove south along the east bank of the river to cut off the Syrians from the rear. The offensive began during the night of 9 July. The diversionary attack was highly successful, and the Syrians were unable to prevent the capture most of their critical strongpoints defending the southwestern perimeter of the Mishmar HaYarden bridgehead. However, the Israeli main effort failed miserably. Syrian observation posts watching the river recognized that the Israelis were trying to ford it to their north. Artillery then fired preregistered barrages at the Israeli fording operations. This shelling badly disrupted the Israeli operations so that they were only able to cross a small part of their attack force over to the east bank, where they were forced to go to ground.

The next morning the Syrians launched a series of skillful counterattacks. They sent their armored reserves against each of the Israeli penetrations in turn. Supported by fierce artillery fire, the Syrian armor succeeded in driving the Israelis back from the positions they had taken during the night. Meanwhile, most of the Syrian Air Force (SAF) was committed to battlefield air-interdiction (BAI) missions, which prevented the Israelis from shifting forces and allowed Syrian armor to defeat each Israeli formation in detail. The last counterattack was directed against the Israeli forces straddling the Jordan to the north of the Mishmar HaYarden bridgehead and was intended to eliminate this threat and then drive on north to clear the west bank of the river. Syrian armor overwhelmed the Israelis at the river and forced them to liquidate their bridgehead on the east bank, but then the Israelis were able to bring up reinforcements and halt the attack. For the next four days, there was ferocious combat all along the perimeter of the Syrian bridgehead as the Israelis struggled to drive them back across the Jordan and the Syrians fought to maintain their positions. Ultimately, Syrian advantages in armor, artillery, and air power allowed them to successfully fend off the Israeli attacks, and by 15 July the lines had essentially returned to the positions held at the start of the Israeli campaign.

Syrian Military Effectiveness during the War of Israeli Independence

The Syrians turned in a mixed performance during the fighting in 1948. In a number of areas, they fared reasonably well. Syrian forces were extremely brave, repeatedly attacking or counterattacking to take key positions and fighting hard to hold their defensive lines. Unit cohesion also was quite good, as there were few instances of Syrian units disintegrating, even under intense pressure. They fought well on the defensive, particularly at Mishmar HaYarden, where their operations were very skillful by any criteria. In that battle particularly, Syrian reserves reacted promptly and counterattacked hard with good artillery support. Syrian air support at Mishmar HaYarden also was quite impressive, although the absence of any Israeli aircraft made their missions considerably easier.

Combined-arms cooperation was an interesting problem for the Syrians. Their officers seemed to appreciate the need for such operations at all levels: in every Syrian attack there was at least some effort to have the different combat arms support one another. Even in their worst performances, they tried to use armor supported by artillery. However, the success of these operations ranged widely from the excellent coordination displayed on 10 June in the second (successful) attack on Mishmar HaYarden to the awful performances turned in at Deganyah Alef and Mahanayim. To some extent, the critical variable appears to have been whether the Syrians had time to thoroughly prepare their forces for an operation. When they had several days to arrange a set-piece attack, the combined-arms coordination generally came off well, whereas on those occasions when one attack followed close on the heels of the last, forcing them to plan "on the fly" and attack without extensive rehearsals, their coordination never came off.

This pattern strongly suggests that only *senior* Syrian field commanders really understood how to make combined-arms operations work. When

Syrian command staffs could carefully lay out the details of an operation and walk their subordinates through each step of the mission, combined-arms coordination worked well. On those occasions when commanders could only order their troops into battle and improvise the operation as they went, Syrian junior officers seemed to know that they were supposed to try to coordinate with the other combat arms but just could not figure out how to do so. Thus, in hastily planned operations, the Syrians tried to employ combined arms, but it never worked quite right: the armor would leave the infantry behind or would attack on a totally different axis.

As with combined-arms operations, maneuver was another feature that appeared to come and go based on the extent to which senior Syrian officers could plan an operation and conduct it in set-piece fashion. For the most part, when they had several days to think through an operation, the Syrians came up with an outflanking maneuver that frequently brought them victory. However, when forced to commit to an attack without adequate preparation time, they generally utilized a frontal-assault approach that only succeeded when their firepower advantage over the Israelis was huge. For example, in the two attacks on Zemach, the Syrians relied on flanking maneuvers, and in the second attack—which appears to have been the more carefully planned of the two, the first having been more of a probing attack—they succeeded in taking the town. By contrast, in the strike on the two Deganyahs, for which the Syrians had less than a day to regroup and prepare, they conducted a blundering frontal assault that failed despite a huge disparity in numbers and firepower. Moreover, at a tactical level, there was little use of maneuver at all as Syrian infantry and armor simply charged their objectives and rarely, if ever, tried to jockey for a more advantageous spatial position. If nothing else, these patterns indicate the Syrians had a reasonably competent corps of senior field commanders.

The Syrians generally were more successful in defensive than offensive operations. The only offensives that were successful were those in which they had considerable advantages in numbers, firepower, and could conduct a set-piece attack. In all three successful assaults—Zemach, the Deganyahs, and Mishmar HaYarden—victory came only after their initial attacks had failed and they were forced to regroup and conduct a set-piece operation. Syria's limited offensive capability was mostly the product of the sluggishness, inflexibility, passivity, and inability of its tactical forces to coordinate their actions. In particular, their unwillingness or inability to move on Zefat after the fall of Mishmar Hayarden was inexcusable.

Overall, Syrian participation was limited and half-hearted. This prevented them from suffering the same humiliations the Israeli Haganah inflicted on their Iraqi, Egyptian, Lebanese, and ALA allies but also ensured that their accomplishments were negligible. The Syrians aborted their offensive south of the Sea of Galilee as soon as they experienced a setback, even though they still had a huge advantage in men and heavy weapons over the Israelis in this sector. In the north they won a small but impressive victory at Mishmar HaYarden only to give up when their exploitation hit meager Israeli resistance. Thereafter, the Syrians were content to sit on the defensive and conduct a few minor attacks on small, exposed Israeli settlements, none of which had any effect on the course of the fighting. Although it is possible that this tentativeness derived from the fear that a bolder offensive would end in disaster — as befell the Egyptians in the Negev — based on Syrian tactical performance, it seems far more likely that the pervasive confusion and passivity of the officer corps simply precluded a decisive, offensive campaign.

The Six Day War, 1967

Between 1948 and 1967, Syria was wracked by internal turmoil. A seemingly endless series of military coups destroyed the stability of the government and what little professionalism the officer corps had inherited from the French. This constant involvement in domestic politics distracted the armed forces from addressing the serious military shortcomings that had been revealed in the 1948 fighting. In addition, it succeeded in thoroughly politicizing and regularly decimating the officer corps. In short, when Syria blundered into war again in 1967, it was only after two decades of military neglect and abuse.

In March 1949 the chief of staff of the Syrian armed forces, Gen. Husni az-Za'im, overthrew the fragile civilian government and installed himself as president. Thereafter, military dictatorships became the norm in Syria, and a succession of officers passed through the presidential office. Most of these dictators reigned for less than two years, and only a rare few were able to stay in power for as much as four or five years. The army became little more than a ladder to presidential power as military officers quickly shed their professional interests and turned their attention to the pursuit of political power. Indeed, by the 1950s, most young officers were joining the army expressly as a means of gaining political power.[9]

This pattern of constant coups and military dictatorships splintered the armed forces along ethnic lines. The first three Syrian dictators — all of whom took power between March and December 1949 — were of Kurdish descent, reflecting the dominance of minorities within the army. Between 1947 and 1952, however, large numbers of the Sunni urban middle class and the better-off peasantry began joining the military. At first they joined out of nationalist ambitions to help build a Syrian nation, but by the early 1950s, most were joining as a means of acquiring political power. By 1952, 80 percent of new officer candidates were Sunnis, and by 1958 the majority of officers were Sunnis.[10] Meanwhile, Alawis made up a plurality of the rank and file and eventually dominated Syria's corps of noncommissioned officers. The Druze also became actively involved in politics through the army, vying with the Kurds and Sunnis for control of the government.

In the mid-1950s, political ideologies were introduced into this mélange, further confusing the issue and further distracting Syrian officers from military matters. Initially, ideological divisions cut across ethnic and religious lines, fragmenting the armed forces to an even greater extent. However, over time, as family members, fellow tribesmen, and co-religionists aided each other in achieving positions of power both within the respective political parties and within the military and political hierarchies more generally, party affiliations began to correspond more to ethnic and religious backgrounds as one or another ethnic group came to dominate each party's apparatus.

None of this was very good for the development of Syrian military capabilities. Each successful or unsuccessful coup was followed by a purge of the officer corps in which the victor would attempt to extirpate all of the loser's supporters from the ranks. Invariably, these purges fell heaviest on the senior officers, whose ranks were decimated by the end of the 1950s. To a large extent, Syrian officers were too preoccupied with political issues to have time for training, planning, and equipping for war. Although Syria continued to raid and harass Israel — and to retaliate whenever the Israelis provoked them — military operations were low on the list of priorities for most Syrian governments and most members of the officer corps. Discipline in the army broke down across the board as units and their commanders pledged their allegiance to different groups and parties. Indeed, by the late 1950s, the situation had become so bad that Syrian officers regularly disobeyed the orders of superiors who belonged to different ethnic or political groups.

Syria agreed to a merger with Pres. Gamal 'Abd al-Nasser's Egypt, forming the United Arab Republic (UAR) in 1958. This state was dominated by Egypt and headed by Nasser. An important motivating force for Damascus was the constant infighting and plotting within the army. The Syrians turned to Nasser — the only figure they believed who could unite them and patch their fissures — to save them from themselves. But within a year, many Syrians had soured on the Egyptians, who ruled the UAR largely for

Egypt's sake. In 1961 a group of mostly Sunni Syrian officers seized power and evicted the Egyptians. However, the new junta soon fell to fighting among themselves, leading to their rapid demise.

In 1963 the quintumvirate of the Military Committee (essentially a splinter group of the Arab-nationalist Ba'th Party), consisting of Salah Jadid, Muhammad 'Umran, 'Abd al-Karim al-Jundi, Ahmad al-Mir, and Hafiz al-Asad, took power. All five were junior officers in the Syrian military, and so they enlisted the help of several senior officers, mostly other Ba'thists and Nasserists. Since these five were also all Alawis or Isma'ilis, and most of their followers were Alawis, Isma'ilis, and Druze, they brought on board the Sunni general 'Amin al-Hafiz to serve as a front man. Upon taking power, this coalition immediately purged the clique of officers who had overthrown UAR rule, dismissing 700 men (half of whom were replaced by Alawis). With the old regime out of the way, the new rulers quickly fell to scheming against one another. First, the Ba'thists purged the Nasserists, then the minority officers ousted 'Amin al-Hafiz and the Sunnis. Finally, the Alawis purged their Druze and Isma'ili rivals so that by 1967, the Alawis, led by Salah Jadid and Minister of Defense Hafiz al-Asad, had eliminated all rivals.

Enter the Soviets

In addition to the short-lived union with Egypt, 1958 also saw the beginning of Syria's military relationship with the USSR. After Nasser's precedent-setting arms deal with the Soviets in 1955, Damascus joined numerous other Arab states in seeking military assistance from Moscow. Although a deal was struck as early as 1956, the first deliveries of Soviet equipment did not arrive in Syria until 1958. Soon thereafter, Soviet advisers began to trek to Syria to teach its armed forces Soviet tactics and doctrine. Although the advisory group numbered only a few hundreds throughout the early 1960s, they played an important role in Syrian military development. To some extent, they were the only officers in the nation who were serious about teaching Syrian soldiers how to fight. The Russians encouraged Syrian officers to focus on training their troops rather than maneuvering for political position, usually to no avail. In many instances the Soviets were forced to shoulder the entire training burden themselves because Syrian officers were simply uninterested.

The Opposing Forces

Despite these distractions, on paper the Syrians appeared to have the advantage when they again found themselves at war with Israel in 1967.[11]

Their army boasted about 70,000 personnel. They had roughly 550 tanks and assault guns (mostly T-54, T-55s, and Su-100s), 500 APCS (mostly BTRS), nearly 300 artillery pieces, and 136 MiGs (of which 36 were the new MiG-21s). The Syrians were organized into sixteen brigades: twelve infantry, two armored, and two mechanized. Virtually all of these forces were part of Syria's standing army, and so little in the way of mobilization was required to bring the army up to strength, nor were the Syrians burdened with large numbers of half-trained reservists.

Damascus deployed twelve of its sixteen brigades to the Golan, including both armored brigades and one mechanized brigade. In addition, the Syrians attached a battalion of tanks to most of the infantry brigades deployed there. In the north the 12th Brigade Group, with three infantry brigades and an armored brigade, held the sector from the B'nat Ya'acov bridge to the slopes of Mount Hermon. Two of its infantry brigades were deployed forward, entrenched along the western escarpment of the heights, while its third infantry brigade and its armored brigade were deployed farther back at key road junctions where they could move forward quickly to reinforce the forward brigades or counterattack an Israeli penetration. The Syrian 35th Brigade Group held the southern sector of the front, defending the much shorter sector from the B'nat Ya'acov bridge to the Yarmuk River, the border with Jordan. The 35th had three infantry brigades and a mechanized brigade, and like its counterpart to the north, the 35th had two brigades forward (one north of the Sea of Galilee and one south of it) and its last infantry brigade and its mechanized brigade in reserve positions designed to maximize their ability to move forward quickly and counterattack an Israeli thrust. Finally, Damascus held the 42d Brigade Group back in theater reserve southwest of Damascus. The 42d had one armored and three infantry brigades and was to be used in a theater-level counterattack once the main Israeli effort was identified.[12]

In addition to the size and weaponry of their forces, the Syrians also had the advantage of formidable natural positions and extensive fortifications. The Golan is a forbidding obstacle to assault, especially from the west, where it climbs sharply from the Huleh Valley in an escarpment rising 1,000–2,000 feet to the crest in most places. With the help of their Soviet advisers, the Syrians had developed a sophisticated series of fortified positions throughout the depth of the Golan. These generally relied on mutually supporting defensive positions with interlocking fields of fire, reflecting the Soviet linear pattern of defense. (One British officer who later visited the Golan *scoffed* that the Syrians had not built a single all-around defensive position — in the British manner — and that all of its fields of fire were "limited and interlocking.")[13] The Syrians and Soviets had identified most of the key avenues of advance and had carefully sited multiple defensive positions to block and trap an Israeli attack along any of them.

Against the fortified Syrians on the Golan, Tel Aviv mustered a much smaller force. For the first few days of the war, the Israelis had only a few brigades deployed opposite the Golan because everything that could be spared was needed to fight Egypt and Jordan. However, by 9 June, the contests in the Sinai and the West Bank had been decided, and Tel Aviv was able to shift forces to the north to take on the Syrians. Eventually, the Israelis attacked with seven brigades — two armored, one mechanized infantry, two paratrooper, and two infantry — grouped into two ugdot. Four of these brigades had been heavily involved in combat in the Sinai or the West Bank and were rushed north with little rest or refit. In all, the Israelis amounted to no more than about 20,000 troops and 250 tanks. However, one advantage Tel Aviv possessed was that, by the time of their attack on the Golan, the Israeli Air Force (IAF) was free to participate fully against the Syrians, all of its other missions having been completed. Despite its busy week, the IAF could still muster over 150 serviceable combat aircraft.[14]

Of course, the odds were not as lopsided against the Israelis as these simple comparisons would suggest. In fact, the Syrian military was in terrible shape. As a result of the constant purges of the previous nineteen years, Syrian combat formations were generally underofficered, and those who remained frequently knew little about military operations and cared even less. For example, seasonal rains cause heavy topsoil erosion and mud runoff on the Golan so that minefields need to be resown every year. The Israelis carefully maintained their minefields, but the Syrians did not bother, with the result that in some places their minefields were completely washed away.[15] The Syrian military also suffered from debilitating repair and maintenance practices. Preventive maintenance was so infrequent and so haphazard that fully half of Syria's tanks were inoperable because of upkeep and repair problems. At no point were the Syrians able to achieve better than a 65 percent operational readiness rate for the vehicles in any of its mechanized or motorized units.[16]

The Syrian command-and-control system was a disaster. The purges had depleted the senior officer ranks and led to such frequent turnover in operational billets that some officers were unsure of who their superiors were. In addition, the thorough politicization of the armed forces blurred who was in charge of any given operation: in many cases nominal commanders were not as powerful or important as their deputies or subordinates. Syrian forces on the Golan were organized into three "brigade groups" that were not like normal divisional formations — or even Israeli ugdot — but simply administrative entities concerned primarily with supply and personnel matters. They had no actual command authority and so could not coordinate the actions of their subordinate brigades in combat. Moreover, the Syrians failed to provide an adequate communications structure to allow communication among brigades; instead, all messages had to be relayed through the brigade-group headquarters.

Finally, the intelligence balance was heavily against the Syrians. The Israel Defense Force (IDF) had spent years meticulously cataloguing developments on the Golan Heights and within the Syrian armed forces. Israeli cryptologists had broken many of the Syrian military codes and were regularly deciphering their deepest secrets. In addition, the Israelis had an extensive human intelligence operation in Syria. The most famous, and probably the most important, of these Israeli spies was Eli Cohen, who insinuated himself into the highest circles of the Syrian government and provided Tel Aviv with complete descriptions — in one case even photographs — of all Syrian fortifications on the Golan, technical specifications of all Syrian Air Force planes, and an encyclopedic breakdown of SAF plans, training, and tactical doctrine. In contrast, Syrian intelligence knew almost nothing about the Israelis. They had only the most rudimentary knowledge of Israeli orders of battle and never attempted to understand their plans or doctrine.

Syrian Provocations

In the morning of 5 June 1967, the Syrians learned from their Egyptian allies that three-quarters of the IAF had been destroyed and that the Egyptian Air Force was pounding Israeli airbases. Of course, nothing could have been further from the truth, but the Syrians bought the Egyptian claims and dispatched a handful of their own aircraft to join the fray. The Syrian planes arrived over Israel while the IAF was finishing off the Egyptians and so faced no opposition. There was no particular purpose or strategy to the SAF attacks. In the words of a former IAF officer, "they sent a duo here and a trio there in a disorganized fashion, somewhat hysterically and with no real preparation."[17] The Syrian pilots had little idea what was a military target and what was not, but they seemed to concentrate their attacks in the area of the Haifa oil refinery and Megiddo Airfield (which was not in use, suggesting the Syrians mistook it for the nearby Ramat David Airbase). They did no damage to any military targets, but these attacks prompted the IAF to retaliate by striking the Syrian airbases at Damascus, Marj Ruhayyil, Dumayr, Sayqal, and T-4. Syrian aircraft were lined up neatly on the tarmac of each airfield, making them easy prey for the Israelis, who destroyed about half the SAF, including all but four of its MiG-21s. The Syrians also lost four MiG-17s in air-to-air combat with the Israelis, while the IAF lost only one Mystere in the air raids.[18]

For several days thereafter, things were not quiet, but were not really active either, between Israel and Syria. The Syrians opened up an artillery barrage on Israeli settlements in the Huleh Valley, and the Israelis responded in kind. The two sides traded artillery rounds for the next four days. Meanwhile, on 6 June the Syrians staged their only ground offensive of the war. They sent a battalion of infantry with about a dozen old T-34s and supported by the artillery positioned along the Golan escarpment to attack the Israeli settlements of Kibbutz Dan, Dafna, and Shaar Yishuv in the exposed "finger" of Galilee. The Syrian strike was a half-hearted frontal assault in which the officers mostly pointed their men in the direction of the Israeli defenses and ordered them to charge rather than actually leading their troops into battle. The attack was clumsy and slow and was stopped by the Israeli settlers unassisted. Shortly thereafter, a flight of IAF fighter-bombers arrived and scattered the Syrians, sending them reeling back to their fortifications on the Golan. All told, the Syrians lost six tanks and 200 dead for no gain.[19]

Israel Attacks

The Israeli offensive, when it came, was a difficult operation. They sent the stronger of their two ugdot, that under Brig. Gen. Dan Laner, into the northern flank of the Syrian defensive lines. The terrain was exceptionally difficult there, and as a result, the Syrians had fewer forces and fortifications in this sector; the 12th Brigade Group had concentrated most of its forces to defend the better terrain in the southern half of its long stretch of the front. The Israeli plan was to break through the forward defenses in this sector and then turn south, rolling up the rest of the Syrian fortifications from the flank. In the north the Israelis would actually launch a main effort and four supporting attacks to try to confuse the Syrians as to where the main attack was and thereby prevent them from counterattacking it with their theater reserve — the four brigades of the 42d Brigade Group deployed in the al-Qunaytarah area. Finally, the smaller ugdah would demonstrate south of the Sea of Galilee to prevent the Syrians from drawing off forces from the more passable terrain of the southern Golan.

The Israeli offensive began on the morning of 9 June 1967 with a tremendous air assault. With all of their other foes defeated, the IAF directed its full might against the Syrians, while IDF engineers cleared paths through the Syrian minefields. The Israeli air campaign against Syrian ground forces was the most intense of the entire war. The IAF flew 1,077 ground-attack sorties against Syria during the course of the war, more than they flew against either Jordan or Egypt.[20] Although the airstrikes caused little *physical* damage to the Syrians, who were well protected in their emplacements and deep bunkers, it traumatized them, pinned them down, and prevented them from interfering with the work of the sappers. Although in some places the IDF found that Syrian negligence had left few mines to be cleared, the fields were still so deep and numerous that the process took a long time.

At 10:00 A.M., well after their airstrikes had shifted eastward, Israeli armor and infantry began climbing the Golan escarpment. This was not the most elegant breaching operation ever conducted. The terrain was very difficult, and the Israelis lost large numbers of tanks and other vehicles to boulders, ditches, and loose gravel, which caused some to slide down the hillsides. In addition, the limited road network in the area channeled the Israeli movements, causing traffic jams and confusion whenever lead elements hit Syrian resistance or terrain obstacles. Finally, several units took wrong turns and got lost in the winding paths of the Golan.

The Syrians failed to take advantage of any of the opportunities presented by these Israeli miscues. Rather than counterattacking the vulnerable columns as they stumbled through the forward defenses, the Syrians simply sat in their positions. Defending units fought back hard whenever the Israelis came into their fields of fire — indicating that they had recovered from the effects of the earlier aerial bombardment — but they made no effort to hit the Israelis while they were disoriented, constricted, and confused during the initial assault and so throw them off the Golan altogether. This pattern held true at every level of the Syrian hierarchy. The company, battalion, and brigade commanders manning the forward defensive positions failed to order counterattacks against the Israelis as they breached Syrian lines. This greatly eased the burden on the Israelis, for it meant that all they needed to do was silence the defenders immediately in front of them and then clear away minefields and earthworks. At a higher level, the armored brigade and the last infantry brigade of the Syrian 12th Brigade Group — in local reserve behind the front lines — failed to counterattack or even move forward to support their infantry when the Israelis successfully breached the forward lines. Finally, at a higher level still, the Syrian General Staff failed to release the 42d Brigade Group being held in GHQ reserve around al-Qunaytarah to counterattack or reinforce the forward brigades when the Israeli penetration in the northern sector began to threaten to unhinge the entire defensive system on the Golan.

The Israelis only had to contend with Syrian artillery fire during the initial breaching operation, after which it essentially disappeared as a factor. These guns plastered some Israeli units as they scaled the escarpment. However, most of Syria's batteries insisted on continuing to fire on the Huleh Valley settlements even long after the Israelis had begun to breach the Golan defenses and had penetrated deep into the Syrians' operational depth. Moreover, once the Israelis had made it to the top of the escarpment, even those few batteries that had fired at them while they were scaling the escarpment continued to pound the slopes rather than shifting their fire to aid the Syrian infantry positions. Syrian frontline commanders pleaded with their artillery units to stop firing at the Israeli kibbutzim and give them fire support against the IDF assaults, but the battery commanders largely ignored their requests. At one point, members of the Soviet advisory mission interceded to try to get the artillery fire redirected against the attacking Israeli units, but they too failed. Eventually, late in the day, word apparently came down from the general staff to shift fire to the Israeli forces on the Golan. By that point, however, the Israelis had pushed so far onto the Golan that the artillery was unable to adequately target them because the gunners had neither planned fire missions in these areas nor registered their guns against targets so far east. As a result, when Syrian artillery tried to bombard Israeli-held positions during the night of 9–10 June, their fire was highly inaccurate and more of an annoyance than a real threat.[21]

Syrian passivity gave the IDF a crucial grace period, which they used to get their operations back on track. Demonstrating the improvisational abilities the IDF has always nurtured, Israeli units simply kept moving forward, finding new paths east and unplanned routes to outflank and overpower Syrian defensive positions. With the exception of one platoon of T-34s that tried to work its way around the flank of an Israeli armored battalion — only to be quickly destroyed for its efforts — the Syrians remained immobile. They fought back fiercely from their bunkers and trenches, and in some cases Syrian gunners showed fair marksmanship, but they uniformly declined to get out of their trenches to reorient their defenses, counterattack, or actively maneuver to try to halt the offensive. By the end of the day, Israeli forces had worked their way along a number of routes to the east, at which point they began pushing southward in a wide flanking maneuver designed to envelop the entire Golan.

By nightfall on the first day of fighting on the Golan, the war between

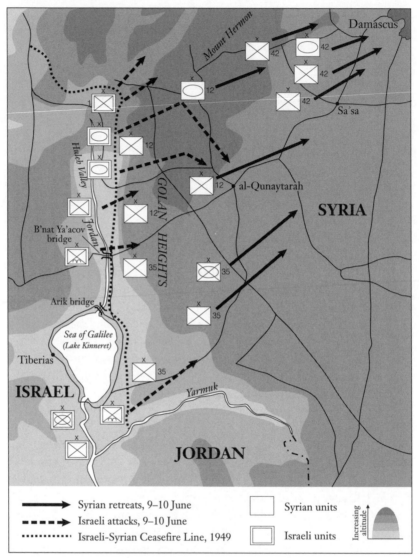

Map 31. The Israeli Conquest of the Golan, June 1967

Israel and Syria had been decided in Israel's favor. Although there were plenty of Syrian units still manning very formidable defensive positions in the southern and central Golan, the entire northern third of the plateau was in Israeli hands, and it was simply a matter of time before the IDF pushed south, rolled up the Syrian lines from their flank or rear, and cut off all enemy forces on the Golan. The Syrian General Staff responded to this situation by moving to secure the position of the regime but made little effort to try to save the rest of the army. The high command pulled most of the 42d Brigade Group back to the capital during the night of 9–10 June to guard the government against a possible Israeli thrust against Damascus, leaving only a small rear guard to cover their withdrawal. At this point, Syria's military leadership appears to have been in a state of chaos and probably left the other forces on the Golan to their own devices. However, given the rigid and unaggressive behavior of Syrian units throughout the day, it is equally possible that Damascus did order its forces still on the Golan to reposition to meet the Israeli threat from the north, only to find that its formations were incapable of such a maneuver.

Denouement

The IDF offensive resumed early in the morning of 10 June. Israeli armor and infantry task forces of all sizes made their way south and east, seizing crucial road junctions and clearing important defensive positions, mostly from the rear. Throughout the Golan, the Syrians fought back bravely, but because they continued to remain immobile in their bunkers, it was only a matter of time before each position was reduced. Because Syrian forces would not counterattack, would not come to the aid of neighboring units, would not reform their defensive lines to present a contiguous bulwark against the Israeli flanking maneuver, and would not try themselves to outflank or ambush enemy units, they were doomed regardless of how bravely they fought. In some areas, particularly on the roads running into al-Qunaytarah, the Syrians were able to delay Israeli forces for some time. Movement was heavily restricted by the terrain along some of these routes, and the Syrians had dug-in infantry and armor in depth along them; it took hours for the Israelis to fight their way through. However, the terrain was never so poor that the IDF could not find some way to send some units to outflank a Syrian position and overpower it from the rear. In this way, the Syrians delayed the Israelis but could not stop them, and they could not even really bloody them in these battles.

At 8:45 A.M. on 10 June, Syria's government-controlled radio announced the fall of al-Qunaytarah to the Israelis.[22] IDF units were still several kilometers from the town and were mystified by the announcements. Most of the Syrian units on the Golan were not as clear about the situation and took this report to mean they were trapped. This led to the general collapse of the Syrian army. Some units remained in place and continued to defend their fortifications because they had not been ordered to do otherwise. These had to be mopped up by Israeli forces in difficult hand-to-hand fights. However, the bulk of what was left of the Syrian army ran. In a number of cases, officers simply jumped into their staff cars and fled, abandoning their troops, who were forced to make their way out on their own as best they could. Because al-Qunaytarah had not fallen to the Israelis and thus many routes east were still open, some Syrian units in the central and southern sectors were able to escape in relatively good shape, while others dropped their weapons and fled pell-mell. By the end of 10 June, the Syrian army had deserted the plateau and the Israelis had accepted a UN-brokered ceasefire.

Actual losses in the fighting are hard to assess, for neither side has issued a full accounting and many of the numbers are in conflict. The Israelis probably took about 750 casualties. The Syrians claim to have knocked out 160 IDF tanks, which seems absurdly high, but there are no Israeli figures available to contradict it. The best estimates of Syrian personnel losses suggest about 7,500 dead and wounded plus nearly 600 taken prisoner. The Syrians admit to the loss of 130 artillery pieces and 86 tanks. In addition, the Israelis claim to have captured at least 40 Syrian tanks intact and simply abandoned by their crews.[23]

Syrian Military Effectiveness in the Six Day War

On the face of it, Syria should have beaten the Israelis in June 1967, and beaten them badly. Syrian forces outnumbered the IDF on the ground in every important category of military power by anywhere from two or four to one. Syria was on the defensive, positioned in superb terrain with very formidable fortifications. Its forces were fully alerted and waiting, hence the Israelis lacked even the advantage of surprise. Moreover, because the Syrian defenses covered the entire western face of the Golan escarpment, the IDF had to conduct a frontal attack somewhere to try to penetrate the Syrian lines; that is, the Israelis could not simply outflank the entire position as they effectively had done to Egypt only days before.[24] The advantages Israel possessed were its complete control of the air, its thorough understanding of the Syrian defenses, and the psychological momentum its soldiers possessed from their stunning victories over Egypt and Jordan earlier that same week. However, most of the Israeli forces that took part in the offensive were tired and understrength from having participated in the earlier campaigns in the Sinai and the West Bank, while the Syrian units were fresh. Even allowing for the Israeli advantages, there is no question that had the Syrians turned in even a reasonably competent performance in battle, they would have prevailed. In short, it required a truly awful combat performance for Syria to have lost the Golan to Israel in less than two days.

Military disasters such as the Syrian collapse on the Golan in June 1967 are rarely the product of a single cause, no matter how powerful. Almost invariably, such defeats are the result of numerous factors, all contributing to an outcome worse than the sum of its parts. The Syrian defeat during the Six Day War was no exception. Syrian forces performed extremely poorly at virtually every level. Perhaps the only Syrian personnel who can be excused for the defeat were the actual soldiers, artillerymen, and tankers who fought with great bravery and determination and did everything asked of them, only to have nearly every rung of their leadership betray them. In addition, one must also give credit to the Israelis for an impressive victory. Given the inherent difficulties of the campaign, they devised a very effective strategy, and their forces executed it brilliantly.

Syrian strategy per se was not part of the problem. The approach Damascus adopted for the defense of the Golan was obvious and entirely appropriate. The Syrians built extensive fortifications across the entire length and breadth of the Golan, taking advantage of the natural strength of their positions to (in theory) force the Israelis to fight to take the entire plateau. These defenses were manned by infantry units supported by armor and plentiful artillery. Behind the forward infantry were two infantry and two armored brigades slated to conduct immediate counterattacks against Israeli assaults and prevent them from penetrating into the operational depth of the plateau. Finally, in the al-Qunaytarah area, the Syrians held the 42d Brigade Group as a theater reserve that could be committed to counterattack the main Israeli thrust when it was identified. All things considered, this plan itself was not bad — in fact, it was quite good. The problem was its execution.

The critical Syrian failing was the unwillingness of any officer in the chain of command to take the initiative and actually execute the counterattacks that were the key to their defensive system. At the brigade-group and GHQ levels, these failures may be excusable: after all, the brigade-group commanders lacked the authority to order counterattacks. Likewise, brigade commanders had great difficulty communicating with one another, and we cannot rule out the possibility that the commanders of the brigades assigned as operational reserves did not want to launch a counterattack because their communications problems could have resulted in friendly fire casualties. Finally, the IAF was flying numerous BAI missions and, although the evidence is murky, it may be that the Syrian reserve brigades, particularly the units of the 42d Brigade Group — which Tel Aviv was watching very carefully — simply could not move to the front because of air interdiction.

Whether or not one accepts these excuses for the inaction of the Syrian operational and theater reserves, there is no excuse for the dearth of local counterattacks. The commanders of the infantry brigades deployed along the front lines were in complete command of their units, and since the IAF concentrated its interdiction campaign farther back to avoid hitting Israeli ground forces, there was no reason for Syrian tactical commanders not to launch counterattacks to throw the Israelis off the escarpment before they could secure footholds on the plateau. Although it is unclear whether such counterattacks could have actually won the day for the Syrians — the imbalance in tactical skills between Israeli and Syrian units was so great that the Israelis might well have defeated such counterattacks — they unquestionably would have made the IDF's breaching operation considerably more difficult, and ultimately, *they were the Syrians' only chance for victory*. By failing to counterattack, to shift forces to cover exposed flanks, to move reserves to help threatened sectors, or to reform their lines to meet the Israeli assault once it had penetrated the forward defenses and were caving in their right flank, the Syrians allowed the IDF to regroup after its difficult breaching operation and then systematically shred the Golan defenses one position at a time. Only a coordinated, aggressive defense — as originally envisioned in Syrian planning — could have defeated the Israelis.

A second major failing of the Syrian military was the general lack of consideration shown by officers at all levels for the troops under their command. After the war, rumors spread quickly throughout Syria and the Middle East that many of the Alawi, Druze, and Isma'ili officers cared little for their (by then) primarily Sunni troops.[25] While there is no evidence to support this specific contention of sectarian problems, there is ample evidence that Syrian officers generally neglected their troops. The sudden departure of many officers during the morning of 10 June is only the most blatant example of this behavior. The unwillingness of most to actually lead their troops in the attack on Kibbutz Dan on 6 June is another. Without their officers to direct them, Syrian troops floundered, and it is testimony to their bravery and discipline that so many continued to fight on from their bunkers after their officers had fled.

Another important element of military effectiveness this question touches on is unit cohesion. Such blatant disregard for their men ought to have produced extremely poor unit cohesion among Syrian forces defending the Golan, but this is not the case. Overall, one can only say that Syrian unit cohesion was uneven, and the behavior of the Syrian officers appears to have been only one element in this pattern, and not necessarily the decisive element. In some instances Syrian units disintegrated at first contact with the Israelis. For example, at Burj Babil, Syrian officers fled after the first Israeli shots were fired, prompting their men to do the same. By contrast, the number of Syrian units that fought on in their positions even long after the Israelis had gained the upper hand was at least as great, and probably greater, than those instances of units breaking at first contact. Indeed, at Tel Aziziyat, the officers tried to surrender their position to the Israelis, but their men would have none of it: they fired on their officers and then fought the Israelis tooth and nail before they were overwhelmed by tank fire and the inevitable flanking attack.

For the most part, the real collapse of Syrian unit cohesion came during the retreat, after the false announcement of the fall of al-Qunaytarah. We know that many officers did flee, abandoning their men, and that many Syrian units then disintegrated. However, we also know that many Syrian units not only hung together but also remained in place, did not retreat, and had to be reduced by the Israelis in close assaults. What we do not know is to what extent the officer desertions — or any other factor — were correlated with instances of unit disintegration.

Nevertheless, the problems with unit cohesion were only a minor element of Syria's defeat. During the crucial first day of fighting, unit cohesion was very good: there were only a few instances of Israeli troops prevailing because the Syrians had abandoned a position, and the rule was that the IDF was forced to clear each and every trench and bunker no matter how badly isolated or otherwise compromised it was. (Indeed, given the pervasive neglect of training or other attention from officers for their men over the preceding twenty years, Syrian unit cohesion must be considered astonishingly good.) The real breakdowns only occurred on 10 June, when the battle had already been decided. By the time Damascus mistakenly announced the fall of al-Qunaytarah, the Israelis were hours away from that goal. They had turned the flank of the entire Golan defensive system and were in the process of rolling up the Syrians from the rear. If Syrian forces had held together, they would have delayed the Israelis in securing the Golan, probably would have inflicted more casualties on the Israelis (though not many more), but would not have been able to *prevent* the Israelis from conquering the heights. In fact, the time they might have bought would not even have been relevant in terms of securing a UN ceasefire that might have deprived the Israelis of part of the Golan: the Syrians already had accepted such a truce even before the Israeli attack on 9 June, but Tel Aviv was determined to have the Golan and ignored the ceasefire until after they had conquered the region completely.

The last major problem that afflicted Syrian forces was their very limited tactical capabilities. At bottom, Syrian units simply could not defeat Israeli units of equal or even lesser size. The Syrians fought with great courage, and between their fortifications and determination, they inflicted a fair number of casualties on the Israelis. But in virtually every firefight on the Golan, the Israelis won handily. Most of the small-unit engagements pitted IDF forces against Syrian units of equal or slightly smaller size but which were well dug in. In some cases the Israelis were able to compensate by calling in airstrikes or artillery support. However, in most instances the Israelis prevailed simply by outmaneuvering and outshooting their Syrian opponents. Time and again, IDF units would stumble onto a Syrian defensive position, at which point they would conduct a holding attack against it or else suppress its fire with long-distance fire of their own while another part of their force would work its way onto an exposed Syrian flank. The flanking force usually could then overpower the Syrian defenders quickly and with a minimum of casualties.

Understanding Syrian Military Ineffectiveness

To better gauge the various factors shaping Syrian military effectiveness in 1967, it is useful to compare Syrian performance with Jordanian performance in the same war. There were both important differences and interesting similarities between these two Arab armies. The greatest differences between the Syrians and the Jordanians were at the highest and lowest levels of the chain of command. Jordanian soldiers were better disciplined, better marksmen, better tank crewmen, and more adept at a wide range of other basic skills. Jordan's senior officers also performed much better than their Syrian counterparts. In particular, Amman did an excellent job identifying the likely Israeli axes of advance, positioning its forces to meet these expected attacks, and shifting its reserves to counterattack or block Israeli offensive thrusts. For example, after the ill-fated decision to shift the two Jordanian armored brigades for an attack into the Negev, the 40th Brigade was dispatched to counterattack the Israeli drive on Janin, while one battalion of the 60th Brigade was sent to reinforce southern Jerusalem and the rest of the brigade was sent to block the Israeli 10th Mechanized Brigade north of Jerusalem. Similarly, as the Israelis slowly gained the upper hand in Jerusalem, the Jordanians hurried more brigades to the defense of the city, dispatching the 27th and 6th Infantry Brigades. The Syrian high command, in contrast, made no effort to shift forces or direct counterattacks anywhere on the Golan.

Syrian and Jordanian forces shared striking similarities at intermediate levels of leadership—the junior officers commanding tactical formations from platoon to brigade level. It is remarkable how both Jordanian and Syrian units rarely ever attempted to maneuver in battle, could not properly integrate the various combat arms into proper combined-arms operations, and mostly refused to counterattack or even reorient their forces to meet an Israeli flanking maneuver. In countless battles on both the West Bank and the Golan, the Israelis faced the same situation: they encountered murderous fire from dug-in Jordanian or Syrian defenders, but once they had penetrated the main line, it was simply a matter of working their way down the Arab trenches because the defenders would not counterattack or shift forces to establish a new defensive line facing the Israeli flanking attack. The course of the battles at Jebel Mukhaber, the Sausage and the Bell, Ammunition Hill, Abu Tor, and numerous other locations on the West Bank were almost identical to those on the Golan Heights. Likewise, Jordanian and Syrian artillery batteries encountered virtually identical problems in terms of their difficulties shifting fire, conducting counterbattery fire, or executing on-call fire-support missions. Although the greater ability of Jordanian tank crews to handle their armored vehicles definitely made them more formidable opponents than the Syrians, the battles against the Jordanian 12th Armored Battalion and 60th Armored Brigade were broadly similar to IDF clashes with Syrian armor on the Golan, particularly in the unwillingness of Arab armor to maneuver and their tendency either to remain in hull-down position or else to charge straight ahead with guns blazing.

To a considerable extent, these tendencies probably illustrate the strengths (and the limitations) of Jordanian professionalism as opposed to Syrian politicization. The professional Jordanian military selected generals for their merit, provided them with a first-class military education, and allowed them to concentrate on learning the art of leading troops and directing battles. In contrast, Syrian armed forces were horribly politicized, generals were chosen for their loyalty (if not their incompetence), and officers were wholly caught up in politics and cared little about military tasks. As a result, in combat Jordan's generals demonstrated the ability to identify Israeli actions, to formulate counters to the Israeli moves, and to have those strategies translated into actual operations. Syria's generals had no idea what to do or how to do it, and the only decision they seem to have made was to pull the 42d Brigade Group back to the capital to save the regime. Likewise, the constant drilling and exercising of Jordanian troops developed superb soldiering skills, while the utter neglect shown by Syrian officers for their troops left Syrian soldiers with little understanding of how to fight.

In the case of tactical leadership, however, the differences between Jordanian professionalism and Syrian politicization do not appear to have been very significant. The rigidity, passivity, and inflexibility displayed time and again by Syrian junior officers was reflected by almost identical behavior in their Jordanian counterparts. Moreover, it is worth noting that the most important element in the catastrophic defeats of both the Jordanians and Syrians were these failings in tactical leadership. Amman's superior generals and enlisted personnel appear to have only slightly mitigated the Jordanian defeat, for it is difficult to make the case that Syria was defeated that much worse than Jordan. Thus, the politicization of the Syrian military clearly had an effect on the proficiency of its soldiers and the abilities of generals, both of whom were elements in Syria's defeat. However, the politicization of the armed forces and the resulting neglect of training and other military preparations can only be made to shoulder so much of the blame. Ultimately, Syrian deficiencies in maneuver warfare — shared not only by the Jordanians but by all of the Arab armies — were significantly more detrimental to Damascus's cause than the disorders of politicization.

Syria's defeat in the Six Day War can be attributed to several factors. First, it resulted from poor leadership at every level of the Syrian armed forces, in particular to the pervasive lack of aggressive initiative and improvisation, certainly among tactical field commanders and almost certainly at senior levels of command as well. Second, the vast gap in capabilities between Israeli and Syrian forces, such that in engagements in which the two sides were roughly evenly matched, IDF forces were able to quickly defeat their opponents, was another ingredient. This too can be traced to failures in leadership since Israeli weaponry was no better (and probably worse) than that of Syria, while man for man, Israeli and Syrian soldiers were probably about even. The difference was that Israeli junior officers were aggressive, motivated, creative, and led their men into battle, while Syrian junior officers were passive, apathetic, unimaginative, and often took the first opportunity to rid themselves of their men. Third was Israel's complete control of the skies, which in part was the product of a superb performance at every level by the IAF but also was a product of the failure of the SAF command to take adequate precautions to prevent the loss of their aircraft after the destruction of the Egyptian Air Force earlier that day. The IAF softened up Syrian defenses for the IDF, impeded movement and coordination of Syrian efforts across the Golan, and may have contributed to the crucial inactivity of Syria's operational reserves. Finally, one must add the Israeli plan itself, which correctly assessed the areas of greatest Syrian weakness and found a way to turn those chinks in the Syrian armor into decisive advantages.

The Syrian Invasion of Jordan, 1970

The defeat of Syria's army and the loss of the Golan Heights had serious repercussions in Damascus. Defense Minister Hafiz al-Asad and the generals of the Syrian General Staff were widely blamed for the defeat. Asad was able to avoid being ousted from the Defense Ministry, but the situation was touch and go for several weeks. The entire experience of the war and its aftermath had two important effects on him. First, he developed an obsession with defeating Israel and avenging the defeat of 1967. Second, he learned that he needed a firmer grip on power to avoid another close call.[26]

Asad moved to address the second of these lessons first by securing his control over the military. He had begun his career as an SAF officer, and after the 1963 Ba'thist coup, he had slowly gained control of the air force and built it into his fiefdom and power base. When he eventually took over the Defense portfolio, he retained his dominance of the air force but could only make limited inroads into the rest of the armed forces. Indeed, during the Six Day War, he had felt that a number of senior officers in key command positions owed their loyalty to other members of the Ba'thist hierarchy or were altogether independent. After 1967, Asad removed these officers and installed men loyal to him throughout the command structure.[27]

Control of the military became increasingly important to Asad because subtle fissures began to open up between him and Salah Jadid, the real power behind the Syrian throne. Before 1967, Asad had been Jadid's most steadfast supporter, and it was this unquestioned loyalty that had prompted Jadid to elevate Asad to the Defense Ministry. However, after 1967, Asad's priorities and even some of his goals began to diverge from those of Jadid and the president of the republic, Dr. Nur ad-Din al-Atasi. Specifically, Asad's determination to attack and defeat Israel led him to begin trying to improve Syrian military capabilities. To this end, he wanted to try to depoliticize the military by taking it out of domestic politics, focus its attention on conventional military operations rather than internal security, and improve its training practices. For Jadid and Atasi, however, the "revolution" took precedence over defeating Israel, and they saw the military as a key instrument in effecting the social changes they hoped to accomplish.

Jadid opposed Asad's efforts to professionalize the military, arguing that the ideological commitment of the army to the "revolution" was more important than its professional skill. By 1970, it was clear that a showdown was brewing, with Asad securing his control over the officer corps and Jadid tightening his grip on the civilian hierarchy. Before they could settle their differences, events in Jordan intruded.

The Course of Operations

On 17 September 1970 King Hussein of Jordan moved to assert his authority over the Palestine Liberation Organization (PLO) and other Palestinian fedayeen groups in Jordan. He ordered his army to crush the Palestinian guerrillas, ushering in what came to be known as "Black September." The Syrian government decided to intervene on behalf of the PLO. The Syrian Ba'thists had never been on particularly good terms with the Hashimite monarchy and were ardent supporters of the Palestinian guerrilla campaign against Israel.

On 18 September the Syrians sent a reinforced armored brigade into northern Jordan to aid the Palestinians. It is unclear what Damascus hoped to achieve by this action. The Syrians may have hoped that this intervention would simply compel the Jordanian army to give up its campaign against the PLO. Alternatively, it may have been designed to create a Palestinian enclave or autonomous region in northern Jordan or it may have been intended to bring about the fall of the Hashimite monarchy and the establishment of a Palestinian government. Syrian military operations give little clue as to their intentions because the armed forces do not seem to have had any kind of plan for their intervention, at least initially. Their objective seems to have been simply to occupy northern Jordan. Thus, their armor crossed the border and pushed south, quickly overrunning the northern city of Irbid with the aid of local Palestinian forces. The Syrians encountered several small Jordanian army detachments, but they brushed these aside with little difficulty.

Nevertheless, the Jordanians refused to call off their campaign against the PLO, nor were there any signs that the king was going to be overthrown. On 20 September Syria escalated its involvement in the conflict by sending in the heavily reinforced 5th Infantry Division. Damascus attached two armored brigades to the division, bringing its tank strength up to nearly 300 T-55s and its manpower to over 16,000. In addition, unlike the initial Syrian invasion force, which confined itself to extreme northern Jordan, the 5th Infantry drove into Jordan at ar-Ramtha, smashed a company of Jordanian Centurions there, and headed directly south toward Amman. Syrian intentions have never been divulged, but it appears likely that they intended to overthrow King Hussein themselves, although it is also possible that they meant only to compel him to call off his army's assault on the PLO.[28]

The Jordanians responded by rushing elements of the 2d Infantry Division and the elite 40th Armored Brigade east from Irbid to stop the Syrians. The 40th Armored deployed along a ridgeline on the main ar-Ramtha–Amman road just south of ar-Ramtha, while the infantry took up positions on another ridge farther to the southwest. On 21 September the Syrian forces ran into the Jordanian tanks. In a fierce battle that raged all day, the Syrians slowly pushed the Jordanians back from their defensive positions, eventually capturing the ar-Ramtha crossroads, which provided a direct link between the 5th Infantry and Syrian forces in Irbid.

This was not an elegant victory. The Syrians failed to properly scout their route and were not aware of the ridgelines ahead of them or of the positioning of Jordanian armored units in this terrain. Thus, they basically just blundered into the 40th's tanks, yet the Jordanians still could not win. Neither side displayed high standards of marksmanship, even though the tank battalions of the 40th Armored fielded Centurion tanks armed with the superb L7 105-mm tank gun. Moreover, neither side showed any desire or ability to maneuver for position. The Jordanians were content to try to pick off Syrian tanks from their hull-down positions along the ridgeline. For their part, the Syrians tried to simply bull their way through the Jordanian positions, launching repeated frontal assaults en echelon against the Jordanian defenses and relying primarily on their superior numbers to prevail. They never really even tried to bring their advantages in infantry and artillery to bear but instead relied exclusively on their tanks. By the end of the day, constant pressure from the larger Syrian units had forced the Jordanians to fall back to another ridgeline farther south after losing nineteen of their own tanks while destroying only ten of the Syrian tanks.[29]

The next morning the Syrians resumed their advance south, this time against new Jordanian positions. Amman pulled out all the stops, committing its small air force in full against the invaders. The Jordanians reportedly generated about 200–250 ground-attack sorties against the 5th Infantry Division. The SAF, however, did not rise to meet the challenge. Asad apparently disagreed with the Syrian invasion, or at least with the commitment of the 5th Infantry and the decision to drive on Amman. Although Atasi and Jadid were able to order the invasion, Asad's firm grip on the air force allowed him to veto employment of Syrian planes to support the ground forces.[30] Neither air force had participated in the invasion up to that point, and when the Jordanians finally committed their planes to the fray, Asad refused to allow the Syrians to do the same.

In the ensuing battle, the Syrian armor was badly mauled by Jordanian airstrikes. The king's armor again did little, preferring to remain in their defensive positions and snipe at the Syrians from long range. It fell to the Royal Jordanian Air Force to fully engage the Syrians. The amount of physical damage the warplanes inflicted on them was not crippling — the pilots destroyed about 40–60 Syrian tanks and APCs over the course of the day.[31] However, the psychological effect of the constant aerial attacks and the complete absence of their own air force caused Syrian units to break contact and to begin retreating late in the afternoon of 22 September. In all the Syrians lost 62 tanks and 60 APCs — most to mechanical breakdowns and abandonment by their crews — and suffered about 600 casualties in the two days of fighting.[32]

Although there was still debate in Damascus about renewing the attack, Asad made it clear that he would not support any additional moves. Of at least equal importance, the Israelis had ominously begun massing armor along the Syrian and Jordanian borders and were making noises to the effect that they would consider the overthrow of King Hussein a threat to their own security. Damascus decided that it would be best not to provoke the Israelis any further. Thereafter, the Syrians mostly withdrew their forces from Jordan, essentially ending their involvement in Black September.

The October War, 1973

In November 1970, in the wake of the humiliation in Jordan, Hafiz al-Asad ousted Salah Jadid and made himself undisputed ruler of Syria. Having previously secured his control over key military units, Asad's putsch required little force. He promptly purged the military, the security services, and many important civilian bureaucracies of Jadid's supporters. Many senior officers were dismissed, while others were simply transferred to less sensitive posts. The junior officers were not seriously affected by this purge, except to the extent that it provided them with room for advancement.[33]

When the dust of the coup and purges had cleared, Asad turned his attention to his number one priority: war with Israel. He was obsessed with the notion of avenging Syria's defeat — his defeat — in 1967. As the new ruler came to see it, this effort required him to not simply rearm and expand the Syrian armed forces but also turn them into a force completely committed to the external-security mission, something they had never been in the past. This realization forced Asad to make two important compromises.

First, he would have to set aside his well-developed sense of paranoia and turn the military into a more professional (and thus less politically reliable) force. Second, he would have to strike a deal with the Soviets — whom he never trusted — for weapons, training, and expertise.

The professionalism of the armed forces and, by association, the priority of war with Israel had been the major causes of Asad's falling out with Jadid. After his successful coup, Asad began to act on his conviction to professionalize the military. First, it was refocused on the external-security mission. Internal security was left to the intelligence and security services, the police, the National Guard, and various specially designated regime protection units. Second, Asad began systematically purging the officer corps of incompetents and political hacks. This culminated in a large-scale dismissal of senior officers in 1972. In these purges Asad concentrated on removing those he considered unfit for command as well as those who still viewed their military career as a path to political power. Finally, Asad began to encourage the promotion of ability over loyalty throughout the officer corps.[34]

Asad's version of depoliticization, however, was far from comprehensive. It fell well short of the real structural changes accomplished by the Egyptians in 1967–73 and the Iraqis in 1982–86. Promotions based on merit became more common among junior officers, but at senior levels, Asad scrupulously chose only those officers whose commitment to him was unquestioned. Similarly, although the military was ordered to concentrate on preparing for conventional combat with Israel and its training became more rigorous and frequent, its internal-security responsibilities were always a high priority. As a result, command and control of the Syrian armed forces remained somewhat dysfunctional. Asad continued to rotate officers among the senior command billets after only brief tours of duty to prevent them from developing a loyal base of support in any particular unit or command. One lesson the Syrians learned from the 1967 war was that they had to have division commands because the brigade groups were simply inadequate. However, Asad would only allow the creation of five division headquarters for fear that the division commands were too powerful and could serve as a springboard for a coup attempt. Consequently, many Syrian units remained independent brigades under GHQ control or temporarily attached to one or another division for a specific mission.

The president's preoccupation with the security of his regime warped military operations during the October War. For example, his fear of a coup led him to veto the Syrian General Staff's plan to insert commando teams by helicopter into Israeli rear areas to seize key terrain ahead of the attacking armored columns. The commando units were elite formations with a high proportion of Alawis and so were considered very loyal to the regime. Asad did not want them to take part in risky operations that might result in their destruction or otherwise prevent them from coming to his rescue if his regime were threatened from within. Similarly, he refused to release the brigades of the Republican Guard to participate in the initial assault against the Israelis on the Golan Heights. These brigades were manned mostly by Alawis with strong ties to Asad and his regime. They also were among the best-armed and best-trained units in the Syrian army, and the General Staff had hoped to employ them in the offensive against Israel. Asad insisted on keeping them under his personal control and told his generals not to count on using them in the coming war.

The Soviet Role

Hafiz al-Asad was never more than a cautious ally of the Soviets. Before 1967, he had favored limiting Syrian contact with the USSR to prevent Moscow from meddling in Syria's internal affairs or limiting its foreign policy options. He recognized the need for the advanced weaponry that, for geopolitical reasons, only the Russians could provide, but he relentlessly campaigned to minimize Soviet influence in his country. Jadid and Atasi were never as suspicious of the relationship with the USSR, but once they were gone from the scene a chill set in between Moscow and Damascus. However, his burning desire to defeat Israel prompted Asad to strike a deal with the Soviets. Syria needed Russia's most advanced weaponry, and lots of it, to retake the Golan. In addition, because for the last twenty-five years the Syrian military had neglected its training and doctrine, the Syrians also needed Soviet expertise to teach them how to fight the Israelis. So Asad struck a pragmatic bargain with Moscow: he would agree to serve Soviet diplomatic efforts in the Middle East in return for Soviet weapons and advisers.

The Russians then began a considerable expansion of their presence in Syria, although they moved slowly at first. Damascus particularly griped that Moscow was slow to ship the weapons it had promised and that Egypt always seemed to get the latest Soviet equipment long before Syria. In truth, the Kremlin doubted to what extent Syria could be of real value to it and so gave Egypt priority in all categories of aid. In addition, the USSR was entering into the period of détente with the United States and did not want an aggressive aid program to Israel's Arab adversaries to derail its improving relationship with Washington. However, after Sadat evicted most of his Soviet advisers in 1972, the Russians quickly turned to Damascus as a more committed partner in the region, and Soviet weapons deliveries to Syria picked up considerably. By 1973, there were as many as 3,000 Soviet advisers in Syria, and Soviet personnel were attached to every Syrian combat formation down to battalion and squadron level.[35]

The Syrian Plan

Given this heavy Soviet influence, it should come as no surprise that the Syrian design for its offensive to retake the Golan closely resembled what a Soviet command staff might have drawn up. The Syrians hoped to break through the Israeli defenses on the Golan at two points: in the area north of al-Qunaytarah and in the south-central region at ar-Rafid. Planners carved out three narrow attack sectors in these areas and hoped to mass enough firepower to blow holes in the Israeli lines. Once Syrian forces had penetrated the defenses, armored reserves would be committed to pass through the breaches and exploit into the Israeli rear. In particular, the exploitation forces were to concentrate on seizing the small number of points of entry onto the Golan from Israel, sealing the plateau to prevent a counterattack by reserve units assembling in Galilee and trapping the Israeli forces defending the Golan.[36]

The Syrians also learned the importance of surprise from the Soviets. Their plan required surprise for two reasons. First, the Syrians needed to launch their offensive before Tel Aviv was able to mobilize its reserves. They intended to rely on overwhelming mass to compensate for Israeli tactical competence, and therefore they needed to make sure that the IDF had as few units on the Golan as possible to maximize their advantage. Second, the Syrians needed to hold the initiative throughout the conflict so they could dictate the terms of battle. They prepared a set-piece offensive. In this respect the operation differed from standard Soviet procedures, which allowed for a higher degree of flexibility, at least at operational levels of command. In contrast, the Syrians had laid out in great detail the course of the entire offensive and intended to stick to that plan fairly rigidly. To be able to accomplish this, they had to seize the initiative and conduct operations in such a way that the Israelis were constantly reacting to Syrian moves and would be limited in their ability to disrupt the offensive. The Syrians would secure that initial advantage by achieving surprise and would maintain it with relentless offensive pressure to keep the Israelis off-balance.

To ensure surprise, the Syrians devised an elaborate deception scheme, similar to the Egyptian effort along the Suez. The Syrians went to great lengths to disguise the buildup of their forces opposite the Golan Heights, camouflaging weaponry and making most preparations in complete secrecy. Their units also began practicing the sudden conduct of offensive operations from a standing start so that they could launch their attack with minimal preparations that could otherwise tip off the Israelis. Like the Egyptians, the Syrians also began conducting frequent maneuvers and large-scale exercises to desensitize the Israelis to their preparations for war. In addition, they conducted a careful reconnaissance and intelligence-gathering campaign to determine Israel's order of battle, the layout of its Golan fortifications, the road network, and Israeli command and control on the plateau.

Although the Syrian plan reflected a considerable Soviet influence, it was not the product of Soviet planning. The Russians were regularly frustrated by Syrian efforts to prevent them from directly influencing operations. In 1972 the Soviet ambassador to Damascus fumed, "These damned Syrians, they will take anything except advice."[37] This blocking started at the top. While Asad was willing, indeed eager, to have Soviet equipment and to have Russian advisers teach his men the art of war, he expected them only to provide the tools — not to actually wield them. In particular, Asad was wary of allowing the Soviets too much access to Syrian planning for fear that they might betray that information in pursuit of their own agenda. Consequently, the Soviets were excluded from the offensive planning and were not even told of its timing until 4 October, just two days beforehand.

Of course, a good plan is meaningless if it cannot be executed properly, and to ensure this the Syrians drew on the lessons of their own combat experience. Like the Egyptians, the Syrians became meticulous planners. The Syrian offensive was scripted in great detail, not quite to the same extent as the Egyptian operation but far more so than was the case for a normal Soviet operation. They also implemented a program of repetitive training for the offensive. Like the Egyptians, Syrian units were assigned individual tasks for each part of the campaign and then made to practice executing that mission again and again on full-size terrain mockups until they had learned it by heart. In particular, Syria planned the initial assault against Israel's defensive lines down to the last detail. Every unit knew exactly what it was supposed to do as part of the breaching operation and practiced this repeatedly to ensure that it could execute its tasks flawlessly when the time came.

The Opposing Armies on the Eve of War

In 1973 the Syrian army totaled 150,000 men with 1,650 tanks (of which 450 were T-62s and the rest nearly all T-55s), 1,000 APCs, and 1,250 artillery pieces. The ground forces deployed opposite the Golan on 6 October 1973 comprised 60,000 men, nearly 1,400 tanks, 800–900 APCs, 600 artillery pieces, 400 antiaircraft artillery (AAA) pieces, and about 65 batteries of SA-2, SA-3, and SA-6 surface-to-air missiles (SAMs). These forces were mostly organized around five divisions: three infantry and two armored. The infantry divisions, which normally possessed two infantry brigades and a mechanized brigade, were each reinforced with an independent armored brigade. Consequently, each division was much "heavier" than normal, disposing of roughly 200 tanks apiece. In addition, Asad grudgingly gave up control of two of Syria's seven commando battalions to the general staff for use in the offensive.[38]

The Syrian Air Force mustered over 350 combat aircraft in 1973, including 200 newer-model MiG-21 fighters as well as 30 Su-20 and 120 MiG-17 fighter-bombers. However, the Syrians intended the SAF to play only a limited role in the offensive. They meant to rely on their SAM and AAA defenses to keep the Israeli Air Force off the backs of their soldiers while relegating their air force to hit-and-run missions — also contrary to normal Soviet doctrine. Like the Egyptians, the Syrians planned to use their aircraft primarily for quick strikes against low-risk targets, which minimized the chances that they would be shot down by ground-based air defenses or IAF fighters. Although this probably had been Damascus's intention all along, it almost certainly was reinforced on 13 September 1973 when a border skirmish led to an air battle in which the Syrians lost 13 MiGs without shooting down a single Israeli plane.[39]

In contrast to this feverish Syrian activity, the Israelis were unprepared for war on 6 October. On the Golan they had three brigades — two armored and one infantry — with perhaps 6,000 men, 170 tanks, and about 60 artillery pieces. During peacetime, the Golan was normally manned by the 188th "Barak" Armored Brigade and elements of the 1st "Golani" Infantry Brigade. The Syrian deception efforts had completely fooled the Israelis, and they had not mobilized their reserves by the morning of the offensive. The Israelis had detected the Syrian buildup opposite the Golan in the first days of October, but their military intelligence concluded that this was only routine Syrian maneuvers, and any anomalies were probably the result of heightened Syrian precautions after the September air battle. Israel's chief of staff, Lt. Gen. David Elazar, was not so easily convinced, and although he was unable to persuade the government to order a mobilization, he was able to shift Israel's elite 7th Armored Brigade to the Golan. The IDF had fortified the heights with antitank obstacles, concertina wire, trenches, firing positions for infantry and tanks, and seventeen fortified strongpoints. But these strongpoints—like those of the Bar-Lev line along the Suez—were platoon positions that could not stop a Syrian attack unless the entire line was adequately defended. Thus, the Golan fortifications were formidable when fully manned, but the Israelis had too few forces on hand on 6 October to adequately defend the entire front. The IAF had 366 combat aircraft—including 280 state-of-the-art American F-4 Phantoms and A-4 Skyhawks—that could rapidly swing into action, but it also had to face Egypt along the Suez front and so could not devote all its attention to the Golan.[40]

In terms of weapons quality, the Syrian-Israeli balance was basically a draw. On the Golan the Israelis generally employed Centurion and Super Sherman tanks, while the Syrians used T-62s and T-55s. The Israelis considered the T-62 a better all-around tank than the Centurion for its cruising range, road speed, simplicity, and 115-mm gun, among other things, but they loved the armor and the highly accurate L-7 gun of the Centurion. Especially in the close combat of the Golan, these were important features. Syrian artillery pieces, like the superb Soviet 130-mm M-46, were generally superior to Israel's handful of Western guns, and Israeli mechanized infantry were still relegated to World War II–vintage M-3 halftracks, while the Syrians had Soviet BTR-50s and BTR-60s and even a number of the new BMP-1 infantry fighting vehicles. But Tel Aviv fielded better electronic-warfare equipment and its air force far outclassed Syria's older-generation MiGs and Sukhois.[41]

Syrian forces were qualitatively better than they had ever been in the past. Asad had strenuously recruited better-educated and technically more-proficient men into the military and had enjoyed a fair degree of success. As a result of his (admittedly modest) efforts at depoliticization, Syrian officers were more committed to the military profession than ever before, most junior officers had been promoted because of demonstrated ability rather than political ties, and morale was very high. In addition, for the first time in their recent history, the Syrians were not suddenly thrown into a conflict after years of neglect of military skills and without having given much thought to how to fight a modern war. Instead, the Syrians would be fighting at a time and place of their own choosing, with a well-thought-out plan, and having spent the preceding years studiously preparing for the upcoming conflict.

The Syrian Offensive

The Syrians began their assault with an airstrike against Israeli targets across the Golan. The Syrians sent over 100 planes to attack command-

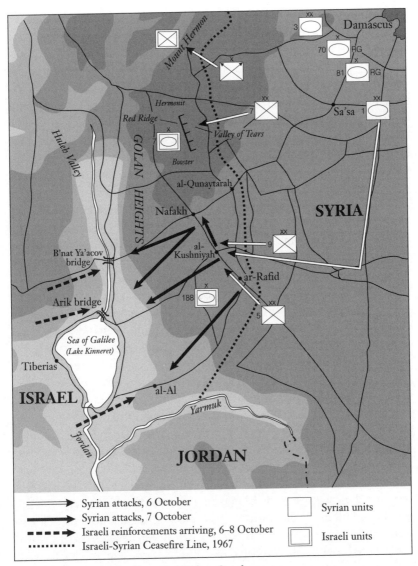

Map 32. The Syrian Attack on the Golan, October 1973

and-control centers, electronic-warfare facilities, military encampments, garrisons, vehicle parks, and key defensive positions. The pilots faced only meager resistance: there were no Israeli fighters in the sky, few ground-based air defenses on the Golan, and even fewer Israeli personnel ready to fight back when they were attacked on the afternoon of 6 October. The Syrians had planned the strikes carefully, their intelligence was excellent, and they struck at what were in fact the crucial military targets on the heights, but their execution left much to be desired. Because of their limited flying skills, Syrian pilots had to rely on predetermined routes of approach as well as predetermined release points, and on numerous occasions pilot error resulted in wide misses. In all, the Syrian airstrikes had little effect on the Israelis. As Jerry Asher has written in his outstanding account of the battle for the Golan: "Considering the numbers of aircraft and the utter surprise they achieved, the Syrians had little to show for their attack. Damage and casualties on the ground were minimal. Not one tank or artillery piece was disabled."[42]

On the ground as well, the initial Syrian assaults failed to live up to the skill of their preparations. The Israelis were taken completely by surprise — "Shocked, not just surprised," in the words of one Israeli division commander.[43] Yet despite their detailed planning and constant rehearsals, the attack immediately went awry. Syrian columns generally advanced with armor and mechanized infantry formations forward, leaving their combat engineers toward the rear. Consequently, Syrian combat units reached the Israeli antitank ditch before the engineering units that were supposed to bridge the trenches for them. They then got hopelessly tangled as their commanders tried to get the bridging equipment to the front. In some cases Syrian tanks and APCs did not stop despite the lack of bridges: they kept rolling forward according to plan and drove straight into the antitank trenches. One aggressive division commander ordered his infantry to dismount and fill in the ditch with shovels rather than wait until his bridging units could come forward. Moreover, when Israeli fire destroyed the lead armored vehicles in some Syrian columns, their tanks kept driving forward, refusing to stop or move off the roads to bypass the destroyed vehicles, causing numerous collisions that only added to the huge traffic jams.

These various problems hamstrung the initial Syrian assault, taking away much of their punch when they were strongest and the Israelis weakest. Although the Israelis had redeployed the 7th Armored Brigade to the Golan, they had decided to hold it in reserve west of al-Qunaytarah. Consequently, on 6 October only two battalions of infantry and the 65 tanks of the Barak Brigade were deployed along the forty-five-kilometer-long border when the three Syrian infantry divisions attacked with 30,000–40,000 men and 800–900 tanks. The force ratios were overwhelmingly in favor of the Syrians, whose various miscues prevented them from fully exploiting these huge advantages. Indeed, the 7th Infantry Division — the northern prong of the offensive — was able to launch only a disorganized attack with part of its force that was easily beaten back by the Israelis because its units got so hopelessly snarled in traffic jams and the Israeli antitank trenches.

THE SOUTHERN ASSAULT SECTOR

The Syrian effort to break through the Israeli lines in the south-central Golan involved three divisions. The 5th Infantry Division attacked up the Trans-Arabian Pipeline (TAPline) road from near ar-Rafid northwestward into the central Golan. Farther north, the 9th Infantry Division attacked in a narrow sector around Kudnah, between al-Qunaytarah and the 5th Infantry's sector. Meanwhile, southwest of Damascus, the 1st Armored Division waited to serve as the exploitation force for a breakthrough. It was to pass through the gap created by the 5th and 9th Infantry and drive west to the crucial Arik and B'nat Ya'acov bridges to seal off the southern Golan from Israel.

The Syrians' quantitative advantages paid off with a successful breakthrough by the end of the first day. The 9th Infantry Division was slowed by the misplacement of its bridging equipment and by traffic problems, suffering heavy losses to Israeli defenders, but by massing its forces, the division eventually was able to blow open a hole in the thin Israeli lines and drive west to al-Kushniyah, where it turned northwest along the TAPline road toward the main Israeli headquarters at Nafakh. Seeing an opportunity to completely unhinge the Israeli defenses in the central Golan, the 9th's commander, Col. Hassan at-Turkmani, detached his 43d Mechanized Brigade and sent it north to try to take the Israeli defenses around al-Qunaytarah from the rear. However, this move was not part of the original Syrian operations order, and the 43d Mechanized acted tentatively and failed to deploy adequate scouts or flank guards, resulting in it being repeatedly ambushed and mauled by a miniscule force of seven Centurions from the Israeli 7th Armored Brigade. Eventually, the brigade suffered such crippling losses — including the destruction of all but five of its forty-five tanks — that it had to pull back and abandon this mission. Meanwhile, the 5th Infantry Division got hung up around ar-Rafid by similarly tiny Israeli armored units that caused it disproportionate damage. However, the division eventually was able to bludgeon its way up the TAPline road to link up with the 9th Infantry at al-Kushniyah.

Early in the morning of 7 October, after much debate, the Syrian GHQ decided to commit the 1st Armored Division to the breach created by the 9th Infantry Division. The 9th was already driving along the TAPline road toward the main IDF headquarters at Nafakh but was being slowed by small Israeli tank and infantry forces that inflicted heavy damage on the Syrians in ambushes and running tank battles. The 5th Infantry Division had turned westward to secure the Jordan River bridges on either side of Lake Kinneret. The 1st Armored arrived on the Golan around midday on 7 October, suffering minor losses to increasingly desperate Israeli airstrikes during its move from the Damascus area. The Israelis, for their part, were sending their reservists to the frontlines in platoons, squads, or even as individuals as soon as they arrived at their mobilization sites without waiting to assemble larger units. When the Syrian 1st Armored finally passed through the 9th Infantry's lines and set out toward Nafakh and the B'nat Ya'acov bridge, they were met by scattered platoons of Israeli tanks and infantry that nevertheless fought with great determination and skill. Elements of these two Syrian divisions were able to force their way up the TAPline road to Nafakh but were stopped there by the Israeli headquarters' personnel together with bits of armor and infantry pulled from elsewhere on the central Golan.

Col. Tawfiq al-Jahani, commander of the Syrian 1st Armored Division, recognized that Nafakh was not the critical objective and instead redirected his main force westward toward the Jordan bridges. He sent the T-62-equipped 91st Armored Brigade westward to take the B'nat Ya'acov bridge and his 2d Mechanized Brigade, together with elements of the 9th Infantry Division, southwest to secure the Arik bridge just north of the Kinneret. Meanwhile, Brig. Gen. 'Ali Aslan, commander of the 5th Infantry Division, sent his 132d Mechanized Brigade south along the al-Al road to seize the Jordan crossings south of the Kinneret and ordered his 47th Armored Brigade westward to aid in the taking of the Arik bridge.

By midafternoon, all four of these powerful Syrian thrusts had built up a head of steam and had only minor Israeli forces between them and the Jordan bridges, yet all four stopped before they reached their objectives. Farthest south, the 132d Mechanized Brigade ploughed down the road to al-Al, where they ran into an understrength battalion of IDF Super Shermans. In a sharp firefight, the Israelis knocked out seventeen T-55s for the loss of only four Shermans, causing the Syrians to retire for the night rather than pushing through the Israelis to the river, even though it was still only late afternoon. This action took place so far south that Jordanian officers (along with Brig. Gen. Syed 'Ali El-Edroos, an observer from the Pakistani army) were able to watch the battle from Jordanian territory and were astounded that so large a Syrian armored force would hunker down for the night early rather than force their way through the much smaller defending force to achieve their crucial objective. Farther to the north, the lead tank battalion of the 47th Armored Brigade was charging toward the Arik bridge when it ran into a company of Israeli Centurions and, in a brief firefight, lost thirty-five tanks while destroying only three. This bloody nose prompted the 47th Brigade's commander to pull in his horns and go into laager for the night. Also pressing toward the Arik bridge, the 2d Mechanized Brigade blundered into a column of IDF infantry reservists heading east to join the fight, completely unaware that the Syrians had penetrated so far west. Although the Syrians quickly dispersed the Israelis with little damage to themselves, for some reason, this skirmish led the Syrian brigade commander to order his men into night laager as well, despite the fact that there was at least an hour of daylight left, the Syrians had superior night-fighting gear, and the brigade had encountered few other Israelis for the last few miles. Finally, the Syrian 91st Armored Brigade made excellent progress along the route to the B'nat Ya'acov bridge, encountering no Israelis until the middle of the afternoon, when they overran four Israeli self-propelled guns. Later, around 5:00 P.M., the brigade vanguard encountered a handful of Golani Brigade infantry who put up only "desultory fire" and were easily broken up by the Syrian armor. However, in response to this clash with Israeli infantry, the 91st Brigade commander inexplicably ordered his men into night laager too rather than pressing on. At that point, the 91st Armored Brigade—with virtually its entire complement of ninety-five T-62s intact—was only three miles (a ten-minute drive) from the B'nat Ya'acov bridge, which was defended by nothing but a platoon of Israeli infantry.[44]

This was the high-water mark of the Syrian offensive. They had penetrated to within a hair's breadth of the key Jordan River bridges and had stopped. Their failure to take these crossings on 7 October allowed the Israelis to continue rushing reserves onto the Golan. Within the next twelve hours, they were able to build up sufficient strength to prevent the Syrians from penetrating any farther and then to begin pushing them back off the plateau.

THE NORTHERN ASSAULT SECTOR

While the southern prong of the giant Syrian pincer movement stopped short when it had victory within its grasp, the northern prong never even penetrated the Israeli forward defenses. The Syrians committed two divisions to this assault sector. The 7th Infantry Division was responsible for breaking through the Israeli lines north of al-Qunaytarah, at which point the 3d Armored Division was to pass through the breach, exploit into the northern Golan, and sweep south to meet the 1st Armored Division around the B'nat Ya'acov bridge to complete the encirclement of Israeli forces on the Golan. However, the 7th Infantry got so badly jammed by poor traffic management, the misplacement of its bridging units in the rear of its columns, and Israeli long-range tank fire that it could launch only a badly disjointed and partial attack on 6 October. This was unfortunate for the Syrians because the Israelis had only an understrength armored battalion from the Barak Brigade strung out north of al-Qunaytarah along with a battalion of Golani infantry manning the strongpoints there. The preliminary Syrian artillery barrage blanketed the Israeli positions but did little damage, and during the night of 6–7 October, as the Syrians struggled across the antitank trench, the Israelis moved up the elite 7th Armored Brigade to hold this sector.

On the morning of 7 October, the Syrians were able to mass the 7th Infantry Division for a full-strength assault on the IDF lines. The Israelis were deployed primarily on two volcanic hills — tels — called by the Israelis "Hermonit" and "Booster" and a ridgeline that ran from north to south between these two hills and known as "Red Ridge." The Syrians charged straight at the Israelis in full divisional strength, were stopped cold, and were forced to retreat with heavy losses. For the next three days, they hammered away at the Israeli 7th Armored Brigade and never broke through. The Syrians launched two to four assaults each day, but with no success. They kept the Israelis under almost constant fire, but their shooting was inaccurate and they regularly received worse than they gave. Each time they attacked, the Syrians added additional forces to the 7th Infantry Division in hopes of finally overpowering the dwindling Israeli defenders. Eventually, they became so desperate to break through that they committed both of the Republican Guard armored brigades to the attack, but these too were beaten back by the handful of remaining Israeli tanks and infantry.

At times the Syrians came close to breaking through the IDF lines, but each time the Israelis fought back skillfully and tenaciously and held their ground. For instance, in their final effort to break through on 9 October, the Syrians reinforced the 7th Infantry Division with additional artillery and even the T-62- and BMP-1-equipped 70th Armored Brigade of the Republican Guard. The division launched a massive attack against Red Ridge and the Hermonit. Before the attack began, the Israeli 7th Armored Brigade was down to less than 30 operational tanks, while the Syrians committed over 200. The Syrians preceded the armor attack with a huge artillery barrage followed by dismounted infantry armed with antitank weapons and a vertical envelopment by a battalion of Syrian commandos who were helicopter-lifted behind the Hermonit position while the armor assaulted that tel and Red Ridge. The attack failed because the Israelis quickly counterattacked north and drove off the commandos, then counterattacked east against the main Syrian assault. When the tiny force of Israeli tanks struck the mass of armored vehicles and infantry, the Syrians were thrown into disarray. Even the elite Republican Guards had no idea what to do or how to react: they stopped and began firing wildly in all directions. Some crews even abandoned undamaged tanks and ran. As a result, the Israelis beat the Syrians back with such severe losses that one brigade from 7th Infantry Division had to be pulled out of action for three days before it could be reorganized *as a battalion.* So great was the damage the Syrians suffered on 6–9 October in trying to take Red Ridge that the valley between the Booster and Hermonit tels came to be known as the "Valley of Tears." In that valley, the Syrians lost over 500 tanks and APCs, while the Israelis lost 60–80 armored vehicles of their own.[45]

MOUNT HERMON

As part of the initial assault on the Golan, the Syrians seized the Israeli observation and listening post high on Mount Hermon, overlooking the Golan and the Damascus plain. The Israeli position there was manned by a platoon from the Golani Infantry Brigade, and the Syrians helicopter-lifted in a battalion of commandos for the operation. The Syrians had gathered detailed information on the layout and manning of the entire Israeli position from espionage and surveillance. Nevertheless, they initially attempted a frontal assault, which the Israelis beat back with heavy casualties. The Syrians regrouped and, in their second assault, approached cautiously in a bounding-overwatch fashion until they could make a quick charge that succeeded in overcoming the Israeli outer defenses. This allowed them to clear the inner defenses, which they secured through sheer weight of numbers, though only after a fierce hand-to-hand fight. Later that day, the Syrians repulsed a clumsy attack by Golani Brigade units trying to retake the Mount Hermon position.

THE ISRAELIS COUNTERATTACK

On the morning of 9 October, the Israelis began to retake the Golan. Initially, they concentrated their efforts in the southern Golan, where the Syrians had been able to drive deep across the plateau. They left the northern Golan to be defended by the remnants of the 7th Armored Brigade,

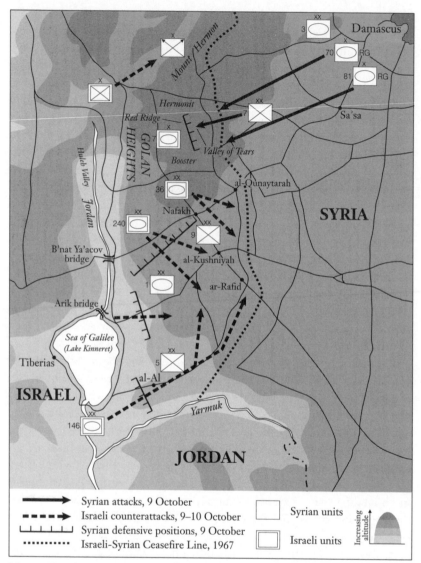

Map 33. Israel's Counterattack on the Golan, October 1973

which continued to hold back repeated Syrian armored assaults. After the various Syrian columns failed to seize the Jordan River bridges on 7 October, the 5th Infantry Division began to establish hasty defensive positions. The division commander, General 'Ali Aslan, reasoned that while his forces were far forward, they had not sealed the Golan at the Jordan and it was unlikely that, after failing to take the bridges the day before, they ever would. He redeployed his units into a defense-in-depth anchored on the al-Al ridgeline to parry the inevitable Israeli counterattack.

In fact, the Israeli counterattack began in 'Ali Aslan's sector. The 146th Reserve Armored Division under Brig. Gen. Moshe "Musa" Peled — an ugdah of three armored brigades and a mechanized infantry brigade with only about 110 operational tanks remaining — attacked up the main al-Al–ar-Rafid road. Meanwhile, another Israeli reserve division, the 240th under Brig. Gen. Dan Laner, conducted a supporting attack into the central Golan against the Syrian 1st Armored and 9th Infantry Divisions. Although the rough terrain prevented the Israelis from deploying their entire force on line, the T-55s of 'Ali Aslan's 47th Armored Brigade could not hold back the lead Super Sherman battalion of Peled's ugdah, and the Syrians were repeatedly mauled and forced to fall back. Later, the Israelis penetrated into terrain that allowed General Peled to employ a second battalion to swing around to the south and cave in the left flank of the 47th, causing the entire unit to collapse. Many Syrian tank crews simply abandoned their vehicles and fled on foot. The disintegration of the 47th Armored unhinged the Syrian position, and the Israelis quickly exploited this breakthrough by pouring all of the tanks and infantry they could scrounge into the gap.

'Ali Aslan realized that the collapse of his brigade, and the resulting Israeli breakthrough, created a dire emergency, and he began trying to shift forces to try to plug the gap. However, his units took an inordinately long time getting moving, and most proved incapable of reorienting themselves or counterattacking to close the breach. When his own efforts failed, 'Ali Aslan tried to convince the Syrian General Staff that they had to send immediate reinforcements to try to shore up his flank or else conduct a general withdrawal to prevent the Israelis from encircling and destroying the entire Syrian army on the southern Golan. But GHQ was unperturbed by his warnings. In the end, 'Ali Aslan's reading of the situation was correct: the Israelis pushed through the breach in his lines and then turned north to hit the Syrian units in the central Golan from the rear. Many Syrian units fought hard against the Israelis, but the combination of attacks from their rear and Israel's superior tactical proficiency led to total defeat. By nightfall on 9 October, the Israelis had reached the TAPline road and had effectively destroyed the 5th Infantry Division.

The virtual destruction of this division led to the disintegration of the entire Syrian front in the central and southern Golan. Israeli units began to penetrate Syrian lines across the front, driving into the flanks of nearby units, while Peled's 146th Division turned the flank of the entire Syrian line and drove north and eastward, smashing Syrian units from behind and cutting their lines of communication back to Damascus. To their credit, the Syrians generally did not crack. Most of their formations stuck together and fought back hard even when outflanked and surrounded by Israeli armor. In many places the Syrians clung to their positions. These units failed to reposition to meet the new threat of the 146th Division on their left flank, but neither did they panic and abandon their sector. The Israelis had to reduce each of these positions one at a time, which they did quickly and with few losses, but only after a sharp fight in every instance. In other cases Syrian units conducted a fairly effective withdrawal from the Golan, deploying rear guards and covering forces that held up the advancing Israelis long enough to let other units get away. Even among those that retreated, only a few formations simply fell apart, abandoning their equipment and fleeing headlong for Damascus.

By the evening of 10 October, the Israelis had driven the Syrians back to the post-1967 ceasefire line, erasing all of their gains over the previous four days. Moreover, the Israelis had devastated the Syrian army in the process. In the battles on the Golan alone, the Syrians lost 867 of the roughly 1,400 tanks they had committed to the fighting, while knocking out only about 200 Israeli tanks.[46] None of the Syrian units that managed to make it back from the Golan were in good enough shape to stop, dig in, and halt the pursuing Israelis. Most were demoralized and disorganized by the retreat and had suffered heavy casualties during the fighting. While the Israeli forces were exhausted from the grueling contest, their morale was high, and they had rebuilt their strength to the point where they could consider an attack into Syria.

The Israeli Counteroffensive

On the morning of 11 October, the IDF launched a counteroffensive into Syria itself. The Israelis hoped to further cripple the already beat-up Syrian army and then drive to within artillery range of Damascus. They reasoned that the further reduction in Syrian military strength, coupled with the threat to the capital, would neutralize Syria as a threat, allowing the transfer of units to the Sinai front. The Israeli forces in the north consisted of three ugdot: the 36th Armored Division under Brig. Gen. Rafael Eitan, the 240th Armored Division under General Laner, and the 146th Armored Division under General Peled. The Israeli offensive plan called for Eitan's and Laner's divisions to drive north toward Damascus with Eitan on the left—attacking the sector north of al-Qunaytarah—and Laner on the right—attacking south of al-Qunaytarah. Meanwhile, Peled's 146th Division would guard Laner's right flank by holding the southern and central Golan all the way to the Jordanian border. All of these units were well below their authorized strengths, but the Syrians had been so badly pummeled on the heights that the Israelis were certain they could make good headway against them.

After the loss of the Golan in 1967, the Syrians had built three lines of fortifications to defend Damascus against an Israeli offensive. These lines were very formidable, having been built with the aid, advice, and materiel assistance of the Soviets. The first was only a few kilometers back from the ceasefire line agreed to at the end of the Six Day War. The second was five to ten kilometers farther northeast, centered on the Syrian town of Sa'sa, and the last was on the outskirts of the capital itself. Syrian forces were so badly disorganized from their defeat on the Golan and subsequent retreat that they were able to offer almost no resistance to the Israelis at their first line of defense. These units mostly fled in front of the Israelis rather than even trying to stop and defend their ground. As a result, the IDF pushed through the first line of fortifications without a fight in most areas. Indeed, in the north, the 36th Armored Division reported very little enemy contact at all early on 11 October. Elsewhere, scattered Syrian units continued to stand and fight as rear guards but were easily outflanked and destroyed, or simply bypassed, by the Israeli armor. One Israeli officer stated, "No [Israeli] tank or APC was hit during the 17 kms of the breakthrough, neither in ours nor the Centurion regiment [the other tank battalion in his brigade]."[47]

The Israeli onslaught panicked the Syrian General Staff. The Syrian army was in poor shape, and although its troops generally were retreating stubbornly and in good order, there were few units capable of turning and actually stopping the Israeli assault. The Syrians apparently were so unnerved that they went to the Soviets for advice. Asad previously had barred the Soviets from any of the planning sessions and had mostly kept the Russians in the dark as to what was going on during the fighting for the Golan. On 10 October his commanders revealed the entire course of the battle and the current situation to their Soviet advisers and asked for help. The Soviets concluded that the Syrians would not be able to make a stand at the first defense line and suggested that they make their stand at the Sa'sa

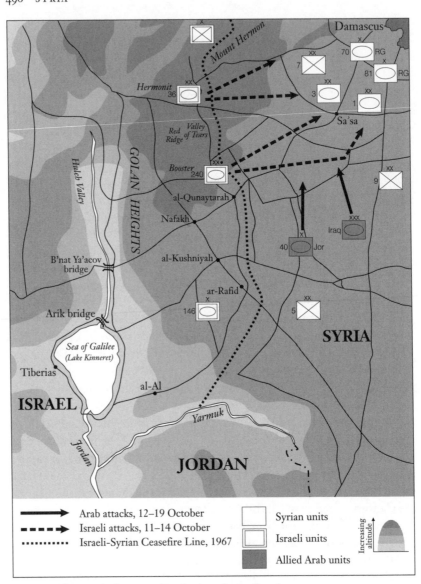

Map 34. The Israeli Counteroffensive into Syria, October 1973

line. The one major combat unit left in the Syrian army that was still relatively intact was the 3d Armored Division. It had never gotten the opportunity to exploit into the northern Golan, and the only combat it had seen was on 10 October, when the GHQ had ordered its 15th Mechanized Brigade to counterattack the Israelis on the Golan to try to relieve the pressure on the retreating Syrian units and possibly break through to relieve several large pockets of trapped Syrian armor. These counterattacks had mostly failed, but the division as a whole was still in good shape. On Soviet advice Damascus ordered the 3d Armored and several other smaller units that had not been committed to the attack on the Golan — including several commando battalions — to man the Sa'sa line. Syrian units retreating from the Golan were told to fall back to that position.[48]

The Israelis began to hit the Sa'sa line later on 11 October and early on 12 October. The fresh Syrian 3d Armored Division fought hard from these positions and was able to throw back the initial Israeli probes in several places. In particular, Syrian commandos with antitank guided missiles (ATGMS) rebuffed several Israeli tank attacks that were conducted without adequate infantry or artillery support. However, the Israelis quickly brought up additional forces, including paratroopers, and began to cut through the Syrian defense lines in key places. The units on the right flank of the Israeli 240th Armored Division later broke into the largely open and undefended terrain southeast of Sa'sa and began threatening to turn the left flank of and envelop the entire defensive line.

Just when things were beginning to look very bleak for Damascus, the Syrians were saved from an unexpected quarter. During the afternoon of 12 October, the Iraqi 3d Armored Division, newly arrived in Syria, blundered into the undefended right flank of Laner's 240th Armored Division. The Iraqis moved slowly and haltingly, but their mere appearance south of the Israeli axis of advance caused General Laner to call off his flanking maneuver against the Sa'sa line and redeploy his ugdah to face south, toward the Iraqis. With the 240th Armored forced onto the defensive, Jerusalem reined in General Eitan's offensive and ordered his 36th Armored Division to take up defensive positions as well. For the next eleven days, the fighting south of Damascus bogged down into a stalemate. The Syrians used the Iraqis (and the Jordanian 40th Armored Brigade, which arrived soon thereafter) to conduct attacks against Laner's ugdah, while their own forces licked their wounds and tried to regroup. The Iraqi attacks were inept, but they kept the Israelis occupied, preventing the IDF from doing much damage to the weak Syrian forces holding the Sa'sa line. Thanks to a huge resupply effort by the Soviets, the Syrians had replaced large amounts of equipment lost on the Golan before the end of the war, and they claimed to have been preparing to launch a major counterattack against the Israelis to push them back from the Golan. However, if such an attack were being contemplated, Damascus apparently had little confidence that it could actually succeed, for it accepted a UN-brokered ceasefire on 23 October without launching any offensive. For their part, by about 14 October, the Israelis—who were within artillery range of southern Damascus— concluded that they had essentially met their objectives, and the appearance of the large, fresh Iraqi and Jordanian forces would preclude further offensive action. They were content to sit on the defensive in the north and began transferring units south to the Sinai front before agreeing to the ceasefire on 23 October. The only other significant military action on the northern front came on 20 October, when a combined Israeli force of paratroopers and Golani Brigade infantry retook the Mount Hermon position against fierce Syrian resistance.

By the end of the war, the Syrians had lost 1,150 tanks, had 3,500 men killed in battle, probably another 10,000–12,000 wounded, and 370 taken prisoner. Israeli losses in the fighting against the Syrians, Iraqis, and Jordanians amounted to only 250 tanks destroyed, 772 personnel dead, 2,453 wounded, and 65 captured (including pilots).[49]

The Air War

Syria's air and air defense forces did not perform particularly well. To some extent, they kept the Israeli Air Force occupied during the first three days of their offensive, but even in this mission they were only partially successful and paid a very high price for their efforts. Ultimately, the Syrians did not do even as well in this regard as the Egyptians on the Sinai front. The Egyptians effectively prevented the IAF from participating in the ground war until Israeli ground forces created a gap in their SAM screen, deterred the Israelis from attacking their SAM network until it had been degraded by the Israeli ground advances, and also prevented or deterred the Israelis from hitting strategic targets elsewhere in Egypt. The Syrians never were able to prevent the IAF from attacking their ground forces to this extent, had much of their ground-based air defense system neutralized by Israeli airstrikes, and could not prevent the IAF from conducting an extensive air campaign against military, political, and economic targets throughout Syria.

From a broad perspective, the air battle on the northern front during the October War was primarily a contest to determine just how long the Syrians could keep the IAF from gaining air superiority and then exerting its influence on the ground fighting. The Syrians conducted their initial 100-sortie air attack on Israeli targets on the Golan, did little damage, and were unable to generate many more sorties for the next twenty-four hours. Meanwhile, the IAF concentrated on the Egyptian front during the first day of the war and were badly bloodied by Egyptian SAMs and AAA. Beginning on 7 October, the second day of the war, Jerusalem shifted its air effort to the Golan. Although a number of IAF aircraft flew close air support (CAS) and battlefield air interdiction missions against Syrian ground forces, the lion's share of the Israeli air effort over the next three days went toward destroying Syrian SAM forces. During the same period, the Syrians flew a fair number of CAS and BAI sorties of their own (sometimes exceeding the Israeli figures in these categories), though with little effect. In addition, Syrian fighters tried to prevent the Israelis from suppressing Syrian ground-based air defenses. These efforts failed, and by 10 October the Syrian air and air defense forces were in disarray, and the Israelis essentially had established air superiority over the Golan. From then on, the IAF increasingly concentrated on attacking Syrian ground forces as they retreated from the Golan and, in response to Syrian Free-Rocket-Over-Ground (FROG) rocket attacks on northern Israel, began bombing strategic targets throughout Syria such as oil storage tanks, power plants, port facilities, airfields, and even the Syrian Defense Ministry. Finally, after 12 October, when the Iraqi intervention forced the Israelis to halt their drive on Damascus — and when the Suez front began to heat up again — the Israelis shifted their air effort back to the southern front.

The Syrians flew roughly 3,000 sorties during the October War, of which about one-sixth were ground-attack sorties of one kind or another. In particular, during the first four days of the war, while the IAF was still recovering from the shock of the surprise attack and the Egyptian SAM and AAA defenses, the Syrians were able to fly a number of ground-attack sorties in support of their offensive. Nevertheless, these missions contributed very little to their war effort. Syria's command system for receiving air-support requests from ground commanders and then allocating and executing air-strikes in response proved rigid and overly compartmentalized. As a result, their CAS and BAI missions were rarely timely. Except when air support was requested well ahead of time to coincide with a ground assault, the Syrians rarely managed to time their air attacks for maximum effect. When Syrian aircraft did arrive on the scene, only occasionally did they do any damage to the Israelis. For example, when a tank battalion of Laner's ugdah was attacked by twenty-four SAF aircraft on 11 October, the Syrians did not score one hit on any of the battalion's vehicles and caused only minor personnel

Table 2. Israeli and Syrian Ground-Attack Sorties on the Northern Front, by Day, during the October War

October	6	7	8	9	10	11	12	13	14	15	16	17	18	19	20	21	22	23
Israeli	25	247	188	168	230	353	197	133	48	62	30	18	0	2	4	55	24	42
Syrian	100	20	NA	85	80	50	NA	NA	NA	NA	20	NA	0	2	NA	24	NA	0

Source: Cordesman and Wagner, *Lessons of Modern War: Volume I, The Arab-Israeli Conflicts, 1973–1989*, 25–28; Nordeen, *Fighters over Israel*, 146. Note: NA = Strike sorties flown, but number not available.

injuries. Although these airstrikes often caused the Israelis to run for cover, because they rarely coincided with a ground assault, even this had no meaningful effect on the battle. On at least two occasions late in the war, Syrian aircraft attacked Jordanian and Iraqi forces as they moved to attack the Israelis, although in these cases as well they did little damage. Finally, the Syrians conducted one strategic air raid into Israel—against the Haifa oil refinery. In this strike the Syrians attacked the wrong facility, missed the one they attacked, and lost one Su-7 to an Israeli Homing-All-the-Way-Killer (HAWK) SAM for their effort.

Syrian fighters fared no better in air-to-air combat with the Israelis. There were sixty-five major dogfights between the SAF and IAF. In these battles the Syrians appear to have shot down 6–10 Israeli aircraft, while losing roughly 162 of their own.[50] The Syrians tried to avoid dogfights with the Israelis, but this was difficult in practice. The IAF intercepted SAF aircraft conducting CAS, BAI, and interdiction missions, provoking dogfights between the Israelis and escorting MiGs. The Syrians also committed their fighters to defend their SAM network when the Israelis went after it on 7–10 October. In addition, the Israelis conducted fighter sweeps over Syria with the specific intent of provoking fighters to come up and get shot down—which mostly accomplished their goal. On 8 October, for example, the IAF was causing such damage to the Syrian SAM network that Damascus committed large numbers of interceptors to try to chase off the Israelis but ended up losing 27 of their own planes for no Israeli losses. Likewise, on 14 October the SAF lost another 21 aircraft in aerial engagements, and although the Israelis lost 4 Phantoms, at least 2, and possibly all or them, were shot down by ground-based air defenses rather than Syrian fighters. Nevertheless, the Israelis remarked that the Syrian pilots, while less skillful even than the Egyptians, were also considerably more aggressive and courageous than their fellow Arabs.[51]

Syria's air defense forces were the most effective element of its overall effort, but they were less successful than their Egyptian counterparts. Initially, the Syrians were able to prevent the IAF from having an undue influence on the ground fighting by shooting down, damaging, or chasing away large numbers of Israeli planes. On 7 October alone, Syrian SAMs and AAA shot down 22 Israeli aircraft. But beginning late on 7 October, the IAF focused its efforts on reasserting Israeli air supremacy. Over the next two to three days, Syrian SAMs continued to preoccupy the IAF, but now as a target set, absorbing most of its sorties, as the Israelis made an all-out effort to suppress Syria's ground-based air defenses. Syrian SAM and AAA crews were extremely poor and had to fire huge salvoes of missiles or projectiles to have any chance of knocking down an enemy plane. Nevertheless, because the Israelis were determined to suppress the Syrian air defenses quickly so that the IAF could fly CAS missions, they pressed home their attacks on Syrian SAMs and took fairly heavy losses. During the entire course of the war, the Israelis lost 33 planes to SAMs and AAA in 5,442 ground-attack sorties against the Egyptians, but 27 aircraft in 1,830 ground-attack sorties against the Syrians. (A loss-per-sortie rate of .006 against the Egyptians and .015 against the Syrians.) However, in the end it was not Israeli bombs that silenced Syria's SAMs but Syrian profligacy. By 9 October, the Syrian SAM batteries had nearly run out of missiles as a result of their poor accuracy and poorer fire discipline. Thus, by about the time of the start of the Israeli counteroffensive, the Syrians had lost their ability to keep the IAF at bay, and thereafter they suffered proportionately greater damage to their ground forces and strategic and economic targets from airstrikes. As a final note, Syrian SAMs and AAA shot down two or three dozen of their own aircraft and at least 4 Iraqi warplanes operating from Syrian bases.[52]

Syrian Military Effectiveness during the October War

The Syrians fought terribly during the October War, yet they still came close to achieving their goals because of the huge advantages they had created for themselves at the start of the conflict through careful preparation. Their breakthrough in the southern Golan on 6–7 October was the most promising Arab opportunity of the war to achieve a meaningful *military* victory. Of course, it is unclear whether the Syrians could have held back an Israeli counterattack from the Galilee had they been able to seize the Jordan River bridges and encircle the Israeli forces on the Golan. However, it is beyond doubt that such a counterattack would have been considerably more difficult for the Israelis than the operation they actually executed. The forbidding terrain of the Golan's western escarpment and the general absence of a military infrastructure for such an operation in Israel's

Huleh Valley would have greatly complicated an Israeli counteroffensive to retake the heights had the Syrian attack been successful.

The measure of just how poorly the Syrians fought is the tremendous advantages they possessed over the Israelis. In particular, they had achieved strategic surprise. The IDF was completely unprepared for their attack, both psychologically and physically. Strategic surprise alone has historically proven to be a decisive advantage that can only be overcome by tremendous skill on the part of the defender — or remarkable ineptitude on the part of the attacker. At the most obvious level, strategic surprise allowed the Syrians to secure an overwhelming material advantage over the Israelis. On 6 October the Syrians had a ten to one advantage in infantry, a twelve to one advantage in tanks, and a twenty to one advantage in artillery. Strategic surprise creates any number of other material problems for the defender, leaving him unready and vulnerable to attack: the defender's units are often out of position, his defenses are not in proper shape for combat, formations are dispersed or disorganized, and his forces are usually conducting administrative activities that render them far more vulnerable than if they had had even a few days warning. All of these problems affected the Israelis for at least the first two to three days of the war.

Finally, one should not discount the enormous psychological importance of this advantage. Strategic surprise means that the defender has not had the opportunity to steel his troops for battle, and thus they are much more likely to panic when the first shots are fired. The defender also has not had the opportunity to check and double check all of the minutiae of war that are the primary source of what Clausewitz called "friction." Israeli officers who fought on the Golan in October 1973 uniformly admit that their forces were virtually paralyzed by the unexpected Syrian onslaught.[53] Given these overwhelming advantages, the salient question is how did the Syrians lose?

STRATEGIC PERFORMANCE

Syria's strategic leadership, its divisional commanders and above, performed very unevenly. In some ways they were quite good and were a principal element of the successes the Syrians enjoyed in the war. In other ways they were miserable and contributed to the overall defeat of Syrian arms. On balance, however, they did as much good as harm and cannot be considered the decisive element in Syria's military failure.

The invasion plan was a good one, and credit for this must go to the Syrian General Staff. Damascus recognized its advantage over the Israelis in standing military forces and the potential of strategic surprise to magnify that advantage, and it built a plan designed to exploit these. The operational concept itself—punching though the Israeli defenses both north and south of al-Qunaytarah by concentrating overwhelming force against narrow attack sectors, then exploiting to the Jordan to prevent Israel from reinforcing the Golan or counterattacking the Syrian columns—was quite good. The fact that the Syrians learned this from the Soviets should not detract from the achievement. The attack sectors they picked for these two breakthroughs were well chosen, and the forces assigned for the campaign should have been adequate. Indeed, the Syrians generally did an impressive job concentrating their units to achieve advantageous force ratios in the crucial breakthrough sectors. Damascus also did a superb job both in working out the details of the offensive, including all support functions, and in gathering information on the Israelis.

Consequently, there are few elements of the Syrian campaign plan that can really be faulted. One obvious exception is the absence of deep helicopter-borne or airborne operations to seize the key chokepoints of the Golan. For example, if units could have been airlifted in to take the Jordan bridges on the first day of the war, the Syrians might have been able to prevent the Israelis from sending their reservists to the Golan in dribs and drabs, forcing them to collect enough combat power to actually clear the Syrian units holding the bridges. Since it was this steady trickle of reinforcements that eventually allowed the Israelis to hold, cutting off this flow for a day, or even a few hours, might have been the difference between victory and defeat. However, even in this case, the Syrian General Staff cannot be criticized, for they had wanted to conduct such operations but decided it was impossible given the very small number of commandos Asad was willing to release to them for the assault. It is unclear whether there were other infantry formations in Syria that could have undertaken such missions; the general staff apparently concluded there were not, and they deserve the benefit of the doubt given their otherwise highly competent preparations.

Nevertheless, beyond the initial invasion plan, the Syrian high command handled itself poorly. They debated for five hours whether to commit the 1st Armored Division after General Turkmani reported that his 9th Infantry Division had broken through late on 6 October. This dithering may or may not have played a role in Syria's defeat, but given the priority of speed to the offensive—that is, securing the entire plateau before the Israelis could mobilize their reserves—it was still an inexcusable delay. After the IDF had thrown Syrian forces off the Golan on 10 October, the general staff panicked and went running to the Soviets for advice. Finally,

Syrian direction of the Iraqi and Jordanian attacks beginning on 12 October was extremely poor. The Syrians could not adequately coordinate the efforts of these forces or their own supporting artillery and airstrikes, resulting in a great deal of friendly fire casualties and attacks that lost their punch because of poor planning. In general, Syrian preparations for these attacks was very careless. At least part of this neglect, and probably a large part, stemmed from the fact that they really did not care whether the Iraqis and Jordanians won or lost but simply wanted them to keep the Israelis occupied.

Probably the worst mistake by the general staff, however, was their failure to shift the effort of the 7th Infantry and 3d Armored Divisions to a different assault axis after it became clear that the Israeli 7th Armored Brigade was not going to be pushed off Red Ridge. Although it is certainly true that Syrian forces should have taken Tel Hermonit, Tel Booster, and Red Ridge given their enormous advantages in men and weapons, after the first attacks failed, Damascus should have recognized that they were banging their heads against a wall in the Valley of Tears and thus wasting precious time. Consequently, it is inexcusable that the Syrian high command did not order the 7th Infantry to redirect its efforts to another attack route. Worse still, they compounded this error first by continuing to hold the 3d Armored in reserve, awaiting a breakthrough by 7th Armored Division, and then committing the two elite Republican Guard armored brigades to the 7th Infantry's attack. This kind of behavior is called "reinforcing failure" by military officers and is a cardinal sin of armored breakthrough operations. By stubbornly committing the 3d Armored and Republican Guards to the floundering attack in the north, Damascus squandered these well-armed formations on what had become, by 8 October, a secondary battle because of the remarkable performance of the Israeli 7th Armored Brigade. But if the 3d Armored and the Republican Guards had been passed through the breach in the south and committed to the fighting in the central Golan, they would have greatly increased the weight of the Syrian forces participating in what was ultimately the decisive battle of the conflict. Indeed, with the added punch of these formations, the Syrians might have been able to prevail over the Israelis on 8 October. As it was, with only the 1st Armored and the 5th and 9th Infantry Divisions engaged in this battle, the Syrians had effectively lost when they failed to seize the Jordan River bridges on 7 October, for this allowed the Israelis to build up enough strength so that the Syrians no longer had the overwhelming numerical advantages they would have needed to resume the offensive on 8 October. With the wildly imbalanced force ratio the Syrians had scrupulously engineered to give them a chance at victory slipping away on 8 October, only the injection of additional large, well-armed forces could have prevented their losing the initiative, and with it the Golan, to the Israeli counteroffensive. There is every reason to believe that the Syrians still would have lost the war in such circumstances because of the equally vast imbalance in tactical proficiency between their own forces and the IDF, but the general staff's pig-headed determination to break through in the Valley of Tears removed powerful forces that might have been the difference between victory and defeat in the decisive battle for the central Golan.

Unlike the uneven performance of the general staff, Syria's division commanders performed quite well. For instance, the 9th Infantry Division commander, Colonel Turkmani, did superbly. Not only did he mass his division so tightly that they were able to overcome skillful Israeli resistance and achieve the crucial breakthrough on 6 October by dint of overwhelming mass, but he also recognized a golden opportunity and took the initiative to redirect one of his brigades north — a move not anticipated by the campaign plan — to try to roll up the Israeli defensive positions in and around al-Qunaytarah. This gambit failed only because his troops could not fight effectively without the detailed guidance of the campaign plan and so were defeated by a tiny, but very skillful, Israeli force. General 'Ali Aslan of the 5th Infantry Division also was able to penetrate the Israeli lines and link up with Turkmani's forces, and he must be given credit for establishing a defense-in-depth to try to hold the southern Golan after it became clear that the Syrians would not take the Jordan River bridges. In his case as well, it was the inability of the units under his command to defeat numerically inferior Israeli forces that doomed his effort. Finally, Colonel al-Jahani of the 1st Armored Division correctly recognized that the bridges, not the Israeli headquarters at Nafakh, were the crucial objective and redirected his best brigades toward them. Nevertheless, Syria's division commanders were not flawless: all failed to organize their march columns properly before the initial assault on the Israeli lines and, to some extent, Turkmani, al-Jahani, and 'Ali Aslan must also be held responsible for the failure of their forces to capture the Jordan River bridges on 7 October.

TACTICAL PERFORMANCE

In contrast, the performance of Syria's tactical forces had little to recommend itself. By and large, Syrian forces performed extremely poorly against the highly skilled Israelis. More than anything else, this huge imbalance between Syrian incompetence and Israeli hypercompetence led inexorably to Syria's defeat. At every turn, the limitations of Syrian tactical performances forced their strategic leadership to work harder to achieve modest successes and turned even minor strategic mistakes into catastrophes.

During the initial assaults against the undermanned Israeli defensive lines, Syrian tactical performance was so poor that what should have resulted in an easy victory became a fifty-fifty proposition, with one attack succeeding and the other failing despite equally overwhelming odds. Their units made little or no use of tactical maneuver to secure advantages over the Israelis. Syrian forces insisted on conducting their attacks as frontal assaults, and in defense they either remained in their prepared positions and blasted away at the Israelis or counterattacked into the teeth of IDF assault forces. According to Israeli armor officers, Syrian tank crews were not bad at handling their vehicles. One of Israel's foremost authorities on armored warfare, Maj. Gen. Musa Peled, commander of the 146th Armored Division on the Golan in 1973 and later commander of the Israeli Armored Corps, rated Syrian tank crews at "8" on a 10-point scale, with Israeli and U.S. tank crews rated at "10." However, this skill was almost irrelevant because Syrian tank units only rarely maneuvered in battle, and on those few occasions when they did, their actions were slow, tentative, and predictable.[54] This consistent failing proved particularly detrimental during the fighting on the Golan, as Israeli tanks constantly darted around the flanks of Syrian columns, destroying armored vehicles and blocking their routes of advance. Because Syrian armor simply surged forward mindlessly, they often created severe traffic jams and "target-rich environments" from which they could not fight back effectively. More than anything else, this disparity between the relentless maneuvering of Israeli units and the near total lack of maneuver among the Syrians allowed tiny IDF units to smash far larger Syrian forces, which proved the difference between victory and defeat.

The best example of these problems was the series of attacks on the Israeli 7th Armored Brigade. Not only was it the case that, at an operational level, the Syrians would not find an alternative axis of advance but also, at the tactical level, Syrian tanks and APCs simply rolled forward, only to be destroyed by Israeli long-range gunnery and flanking maneuvers. In those cases where Syrian tanks did manage to bull through the IDF lines, it was the exception when they turned to hit nearby Israeli forces in the flanks. Instead, they generally just kept driving forward until an Israeli unit could chase them down and destroy them.

At first, Syrian artillery provided reasonably good covering fire for the advancing armor and infantry. This was because they had planned and calibrated these bombardments over the course of six years. However, once the initial attacks were over — and especially where Syrian units had broken through the Israeli lines and the battle became very fluid — the accuracy and timeliness of Syrian artillery support faded precipitously. During the fighting on the Damascus plain, Syrian artillery fire landed so far off the mark that on many occasions it struck allied Jordanian and Iraqi formations. The Syrians demonstrated a fairly good ability to use direction-finding equipment to pinpoint certain Israeli commands, but their batteries consistently failed to hit these targets. Their artillery also generally did poorly in counterbattery duels with Israeli guns, relying on mass fire rather than precision fire and rarely taking out enemy batteries (although they were occasionally able to force them to displace by getting close with their rounds).

These problems with artillery were one element of the virtual absence of combined-arms operations, especially after the first series of attacks. After these initial assaults, Syrian forces rarely employed combat engineers or other specialized support units to aid them in the performance of their mission. Once they were through the Israeli fortification belt, they relied almost exclusively on armor to execute operations. Syrian infantry support to their armor was very limited. They consistently led their attacks with tanks, and if they even bothered to include mechanized infantry formations in the operation, they generally kept their infantry mounted regardless of the situation. There were a few exceptions, most notably the final 7th Infantry Division–Republican Guard assault against Red Ridge on 9 October, but even on these occasions the infantry attacked, like their tanks, walking slowly in line-abreast at the Israelis, who mowed them down with the machine guns on their tanks and APCs. Syrian infantry generally did not even try to take cover or otherwise use the terrain when they attacked dismounted but instead simply marched forward, looking more like British troops at the Somme than a modern army. In particular, the Syrians made no effort to use ATGM-equipped troops to infiltrate forward of the armor and get in among the Israelis to cause havoc before the main attack arrived. Many of the Israeli units on the Golan were pure tank formations, and their greatest fear was of Syrian infantry getting in among their positions (especially at night) and hitting them from behind with antitank weapons.[55] In general, far fewer Israeli tanks were lost to Sagger rounds on the Golan than in the Sinai. The lack of infantry support for their armor also hurt the Syrians when they were defending against Israeli counterthrusts after 9 October. In some places they set up massive antitank positions manned by ATGM-equipped infantry that gave the Israelis real fits. However, in most areas the Syrians had only tanks that sat motionless in their positions. Without the threat of Syrian infantry to concern them, Israeli tankers could do what they did best, moving from position to position, taking flank and rear shots until the Syrian tanks were destroyed or forced to retreat.

These various failings reflected the incompetence of Syrian tactical leadership. Syrian officers from brigade commander on down rarely displayed any initiative, creativity, or independence in executing their missions. The worst case of this phenomenon was the failure of battalion and brigade commanders to seize the Jordan River bridges on 7 October after they had been redirected there and urged on by both the general staff and their division commanders. The bridges were the decisive objectives of the entire campaign, and they were within the grasp of four powerful Syrian formations, all of which failed to keep moving forward to take the crossings even though they were only a few kilometers away and guarded by, in most cases, pitifully small Israeli forces. Whatever their reasons for stopping, there is no question that better commanders with a modicum of initiative would have done anything necessary to secure those bridges.[56]

Syrian junior officers could not properly coordinate their actions with those of neighboring units, nor did they understand how to integrate their various combat arms into unified combined-arms teams. These commanders never thought to change their tactics: even after the Israelis repeatedly pummeled them in combat, Syrian formations kept attacking in exactly the same manner as before. Chaim Herzog has remarked about Syria's tank commanders, "they never departed from the doctrine implanted in them, and when situations for which they were not prepared arose, they proved in general to be at a loss."[57] Their tactical commanders also regularly neglected reconnaissance and patrolling, resulting in their frequent ambush by Israeli units lying in wait in the rough terrain of the Golan.

The failings of Syrian junior officers were thrown into sharper relief as the campaign unfolded. Initially, Syrian operations were fairly deft because they were following the detailed plans of the general staff. As the fighting continued, and especially in the southern and central Golan, where combat became fluid, Syrian command authority was increasingly decentralized as a result of physical dispersion — not as a result of a conscious decision by the high command. The more operational command devolved upon lower levels of the military hierarchy, the worse the Syrians did. For example, all of the successes of Colonel Turkmani's 9th Infantry Division were a result of preplanned and rehearsed operations. However, whenever he tried to improvise — such as his thrust up the ar-Rafid–al-Qunaytarah road to outflank al-Qunaytarah on 6 October — the operation fizzled. Without the detailed guidance of the original operations orders, Turkmani's subordinates were helpless. Likewise, the attack on 9 October by the elite 70th

Armored Brigade against Red Ridge came unglued when Lt. Col. Avigdor Qahalani, commanding the seven remaining tanks of the Israeli 77th Tank Battalion, seized an opportunity to counterattack into the seam between two Syrian tank battalions, causing both units to panic. In the words of one Arab military analyst, commenting on the identical failings of the Egyptian and Syrian armed forces: "In 1973, Egyptian and Syrian operational planning, while initially exploiting to great advantage the combination of infantry borne antitank and anti-aircraft missiles, was unable to cope with the fluidity of the battle and remained to a large extent transfixed by the very meticulous planning which contributed to initial successes. Arab tactical deployment remained basically inflexible and incapable of fully exploiting its own hard won success."[58] It was this tactical incompetence that doomed the Syrian war effort.

Syrian unit cohesion during the October War was not perfect but was quite good overall. Syrian troops were very courageous, making repeated attacks despite the slaughter the Israelis repeatedly inflicted on them. In these attacks they stuck together well, but the real test came when the Israelis went on the offensive. By and large, Syrian formations hung together and fought back fiercely, although there were important exceptions, such as the 47th Armored Brigade of the 5th Infantry Division, which went to pieces under moderate Israeli pressure. Although Syrian divisions and brigades were often shattered by Israeli penetrations and flanking maneuvers, the smaller formations — platoons, companies, and even battalions — maintained their cohesiveness and either stood their ground and fought until overcome or retreated as intact units. Moreover, they generally conducted fighting withdrawals rather than simply fleeing. While many of these units were later caught and destroyed by (frequently smaller) Israeli forces, the fact remains that they maintained their unit integrity and attempted to conduct a good withdrawal.

ADDITIONAL INFLUENCES ON THE COURSE OF THE FIGHTING

A few Syrian problems can be blamed on their reliance on Soviet doctrine, though only in those areas where Soviet methods was clearly wrong. For example, at that time, Soviet doctrine called for infantry to ride into battle buttoned-up in their APCs and to fight from their vehicles, shooting with small arms through the firing ports in the APCs' sides. This was the primary reason that the Syrians, unlike the Egyptians, generally did not have dismounted infantry preceding their armor with antitank weapons. These exceptions aside, the problem largely was not the tactics themselves but the Syrian application of those tactics. For instance, the Soviets never intended for armored formations to plough straight ahead with no tactical maneuver at all. While the Soviets did plan to attack in waves, it was expected that some groups would penetrate enemy lines and would then hit nearby enemy units in the flanks to aid the breakthrough of other units, thereby creating a larger gap into which follow-on forces could pour. Similarly, the Soviets recognized that there were occasions — particularly assaults into bad tank terrain — in which the infantry had to dismount so they could employ their antitank weapons to clear out enemy armor. These variations and subtleties seem to have been lost on Syrian commanders, who rigidly surged forward in an endless series of frontal assaults, succeeding only by weight of numbers and suffering crippling losses in the process.

For their part, the Syrians have tended to blame most of their setbacks in the October War on the Israeli Air Force.[59] While the IAF certainly did play an important role in the combat on the Golan and the Damascus plain, its influence has been exaggerated. In particular, the IAF is often given the lion's share of the credit for halting the Syrian advance on the heights by stopping the armored columns headed for the Jordan River bridges on 7 October. Both of these claims are untrue. The IAF flew comparatively few airstrike missions against Syrian ground forces between 6 and 10 October. (See table 3.) On 6 October the IAF concentrated on attacking the Egyptian bridges across the Suez, flying 197 ground-attack sorties against them and only 25 against the Syrians. Beginning on 7 October, the Israelis did shift air assets to face the more dire Syrian threat, but the lion's share of the ground-attack effort still went to the Sinai front. Between 7 and 9 October, the crucial days of the ground fighting on the Golan, the IAF concentrated primarily on Syria's SAM batteries. Thus, for example, on 7 October, probably the decisive day of the entire campaign, the IAF flew 247 ground-attack sorties against the Syrians, of which only 98 were directed against combat units, the rest going against SAM sites and, to a lesser extent, logistics columns. Moreover, we also know that a considerable number of IAF ground-attack sorties were directed not against the Syrian forces on the Golan but on their second-echelon forces. In particular, the 1st Armored Division received considerable attention from the IAF on its way to the front during the morning of 7 October, but not when it was on the Golan and racing toward the Jordan that afternoon. Thus, the actual number of Israeli ground-attack missions flown against Syrian ground forces on the Golan was actually quite small. Indeed, Israeli armor and Golani Brigade officers unanimously averred that they received little or no air support during the fighting since the IAF was concentrating on interdiction missions to destroy Syrian SAM sites and, later, logistics trains and second-echelon forces.[60]

Table 3. Israeli Ground-Attack Sorties on the Northern and Southern Fronts, by Day, during the October War

October	6	7	8	9	10	11	12	13	14	15	16	17	18	19	20	21	22	23	24
vs. Syria	25	247	188	168	230	353	197	133	48	62	30	18	0	2	4	55	24	42	4
vs. Egypt	197	241	434	442	296	69	172	96	229	246	283	213	265	375	376	327	532	354	315

Sources: Cordesman and Wagner, *Lessons of Modern War: Volume I, The Arab-Israeli Conflicts, 1973–1989,* 25–34; Nordeen, *Fighters over Israel,* 146.

In recent years it also has come to light that the IAF's airstrikes against Syrian ground forces did surprisingly little damage. After the October War, the Israelis came to the conclusion that their ground-attack missions had been very poor. They found that their pilots delivered their munitions inaccurately and the IAF was not responsive to the needs of ground commanders. In addition, they concluded that Syrian air defenses, particularly AAA and the SA-7 shoulder-launched SAMs, had badly degraded IAF strike missions. Trevor Dupuy was able to examine many of the Syrian tanks on the Golan shortly after the war and found no clear evidence that *any* were destroyed by air attack. Likewise, an official U.S. military survey team — allowed by the Israelis to inspect the Golan battlefield in great detail after the war — found less than five Syrian tanks destroyed by airstrikes. While these findings must be balanced against the accounts of several observers, which indicate that Israeli airstrikes, regardless of their meager physical effect, seemed to have a more profound *psychological* effect on the Syrians than on the better-disciplined Egyptians, it is hard to make the case that the IAF was decisive in stopping the Syrian offensive.[61]

As a final point on this issue, regardless of the number of sorties the IAF flew and regardless of the effect of those attacks, the simple fact is that the four Syrian armored columns bearing down on the Jordan River bridges were *not* stopped by airstrikes. Only the southernmost column — the 132d Mechanized Brigade moving south of the Sea of Galilee — was even attacked by Israeli aircraft. The other three columns encountered resistance only from Israeli ground forces, and even the 132d Mechanized was principally stopped by Israeli Super Shermans, not the IAF. Thus, Asher appears to be largely correct in stating, "The Israeli Air Force's initial contributions on the Golan front were minimal."[62]

Later, after the Syrian medium-range SAM threat (the SA-2s, SA-3s, and SA-6s) had been neutralized, the IAF was able to participate to a much greater extent in operations in the north and provided heavy air support to the initial drive into Syria itself. However, since the Syrians were retreating, the IAF was used mostly to harass and pursue their fleeing units. IAF warplanes also played a considerable role in cracking the Syrian Sa'sa line, but after 12 October, when the Iraqi intervention made the drive on Damascus impossible and the Egyptian front began to heat up again, these units were once again redirected south to the Suez front. Thereafter, the IAF conducted relatively few airstrikes in support of the ground forces in the north. Most Israeli air activity against Syria after about 14 October was aimed at economic targets.

SUMMARY JUDGMENTS FROM THE OCTOBER WAR

It is impossible to know how close the Syrians came to victory on the Golan Heights in 1973. Even had they secured the Jordan River from the B'nat Ya'acov bridge south, there were still points of entry on to the plateau to the north—the very routes from the Huleh Valley the Israelis had used in 1967—and the northern prong of the Syrian invasion was never a threat to secure these access points. Even had the Syrians been able to overrun the *entire* Golan, there is reason to believe that the Israelis could still have mounted a successful counterattack from Galilee and once again driven them from the plateau. In short, it is unclear how good or bad Syria's strategic concept actually was.

What is clear is that the Syrians paid a horrendous price for the successes they did achieve, primarily because of the limited capabilities of their forces. According to one estimate, they lost over 200 of the 800 tanks employed in the initial assault during the first twenty-four hours of their offensive, and the actual number may well have been even higher.[63] The Syrian high command correctly appreciated that they would have to rely on mass to defeat the Israelis because they could not improve the proficiency of their forces to the extent necessary to prevail in tactical engagements. Instead, they would have to simply overwhelm the defenders with superior numbers. This approach worked on the southern Golan at first, but only because the numerical imbalance plus the advantages of surprise were so enormous. In the north these advantages were still inadequate because the Syrians were employing only one reinforced division against an Israeli brigade (as opposed to the two reinforced divisions they concentrated in the south) and because of the even greater competence of Israel's elite 7th Armored Brigade compared to the Barak Brigade defending in the south. Yet even in the southern Golan, Syrian losses were so horrific and the Israeli mobilization so rapid that the numerical imbalance quickly diminished after only twenty-four to thirty-six hours. Although the Syrians out-numbered the Israelis in all relevant categories of combat power through-out the war, the problem was that Israeli tactical skills were so far superior to those of Syria that a numerical advantage of only three or four to one was inadequate for the Syrians. Thus, when their armor failed to secure the Jordan River bridges on 7 October, the Syrians forfeited their one chance to possibly prevent the Israelis from building up enough strength to drive them back off the Golan.

Syrian performance at the strategic level was far from perfect, but it is hard to assign them more than a small part of the blame for the 1973 defeat. The initial Syrian plan was well conceived, and with a few problems that may have been the result of political decisions, it could have succeeded in retaking the Golan if their tactical units had proven more capable of execut-ing it. Perhaps the Syrians should have recognized just how badly out-matched they were in terms of tactical effectiveness and so should not have attacked at all. But that was a political decision, and given that Asad was determined to attack Israel, the plan the high command developed was a reasonable approach to the mission. After the initial assault failed, the Syr-ian General Staff did poorly, but by that point the war had already been de-cided. One must also balance this against the very creditable performance of Syria's division commanders, although they are not entirely blameless for the problems on 6 and 7 October.

The Soviets and the IAF have also been made scapegoats for the Syrian defeat. In both cases their role has been greatly exaggerated. While some Soviet practices were flawed, overall the Syrians fought much better than they had in 1967. The USSR had given Syria a full-fledged military doctrine, something the Syrians had never had before. In some ways the Soviet approach was perfectly suited to the Syrians, for it was designed to compen-sate for tactical shortcomings. But Syrian tactical capabilities were so poor that they took good Soviet tactics and made them bad and took bad Soviet tactics and made them worse. Ultimately, even Soviet doctrine could not overcome tactical incompetence as far reaching as that of the Syrians. For its part, the IAF clearly contributed to the Israeli victory, but its role, espe-cially in stopping the initial Syrian ground thrust, has been greatly distorted by the Syrians, some Westerners, and even some members of the IAF. For the most part, its warplanes were far more destructive to Syrian ground forces during the Israeli offensive into Syria than during the Syrian drive into the Golan. For their part, Israeli ground forces played a major role in stopping the offensive, but in the end it was the Syrians themselves who essentially just stopped.

The Syrian Invasion of Lebanon, 1976

It took the Syrian armed forces some time to learn from the painful experiences of the October War. At first, they continued to skirmish with the Israelis along the ceasefire line, and political negotiations dragged on into 1975, preoccupying the Syrian military leadership. In the aftermath of the October War, the Syrians mostly blamed their defeat on their Soviet weaponry and demanded that Moscow provide them with more-modern and more-powerful equipment. By 1976, the only lesson the Syrians had drawn from the 1973 war was that their commandos were the best troops in the army and the only ones with any real combat capabilities. As a result, a major expansion of these units had just gotten underway when Damascus decided to intervene in Lebanon.

In 1975 a long-brewing civil war broke out in Lebanon. Essentially, this conflict pitted the "Rightist," or "Status Quo," coalition mostly centered on the ruling minority Christian community against a "Leftist," or "Revisionist," coalition of mostly Muslims centered on Lebanese Sunnis, Druze, and the PLO, which had relocated to Lebanon after its expulsion from Jordan in 1970.[64] Lebanon had been an integral part of Syria prior to its separation by the French after World War I, and it was still closely tied to Damascus. Consequently, the civil war worried Hafiz al-Asad. In late 1975 he began to actively dabble in Palestinian affairs, surprisingly backing the Maronite Christians rather than the Muslims. Syria began to send detachments of the Palestine Liberation Army — a force of Palestinians trained and mostly officered by Syrians to fight Israel — into Lebanon to aid the Maronites. Still, the Muslims continued to make gains in Lebanon, forcing the Christians back into their mountain enclave northeast of Beirut and nibbling away even at this. By the spring of 1976, the position of the Maronites had become so serious that Asad decided to set aside the fig leaf of the Palestine Liberation Army and openly employ Syrian military forces to prevent the defeat of the Christians.[65]

The First Syrian Offensive

The Syrians underestimated the forces they would require to accomplish their goals. Damascus hoped to drive into Lebanon, push the Muslim forces back from the Christian enclaves, and then occupy the urban centers from which the Muslims mainly drew their strength: West Beirut and the coastal cities of southern Lebanon such as Tyre and Sidon. The Syrians expected that the mere appearance of a conventional army equipped with tanks and artillery and supported by aircraft would overawe most of the Muslim militias, and the rest could be dispatched with little effort. Indeed,

Damascus believed it could overrun Lebanon and scatter the leftist resistance in a few days—if not hours. Thus, the Syrians put together an invasion force of about 6,000 men, roughly a brigade from the 3d Armored Division plus two commando battalions, extra artillery, and other supporting forces. They faced about 20,000 leftists equipped with small arms, mortars, and a few armored cars captured from the Lebanese army. Moreover, the Syrians could count on the aid of about 20,000 rightists, including 8,000 well-armed Maronites of the Phalange militia.[66]

The Syrian invasion of Lebanon began on 1 June 1976 with assaults from both east and north. In the north a force of about 2,000 Syrian troops and sixty T-54 tanks drove down the Lebanese coast toward Tripoli. This detachment faced little resistance, quickly relieved the sieges of the Christian towns of Qubiat and Anarqiat, and then pushed on to Tripoli, where they were halted by Muslim resistance and forced to besiege the city. In the east the main Syrian force of about 4,000 men centered on an armored brigade, equipped with T-62s and BMP-1s, of the 3d Armored Division drove into Lebanon along the Beirut-Damascus highway. The Syrians quickly occupied the Bekaa Valley without much resistance, except in the far south in a Palestinian enclave known as "Fatahland," and then continued their drive on Beirut. As the Syrians began to move through the Lebanon mountain range, they were suddenly confronted with Muslim roadblocks and antitank ambushes that stopped them cold. Damascus was forced to commit another armored-brigade task force from the 3d Armored to get the drive started again, and then only with considerable losses.

Once past the mountains, the central Syrian force split into two columns. Most of the detachment continued west along the Beirut-Damascus highway toward Beirut, while a reinforced armored brigade went south to take Sidon. Neither force did well. The task force heading south faced serious Muslim resistance along the narrow mountain roads of central Lebanon. The Syrians attacked toward Sidon without proper reconnaissance or flank guards and relied mostly on tanks with only a small component of mechanized infantry. This drive ran into an antitank ambush outside the city, and in a firefight that lasted for several days, the Muslims held their ground and inflicted heavy casualties. Although neither side was terribly skillful, without infantry, the Syrians were at the mercy of the Muslims, who were well supplied with ATGMs and rocket-propelled grenades (RPGs). The Syrians then called in airstrikes, but these caused little damage and had no influence on the fighting. Eventually, the Syrians were able to extract their armor from this ambush, but only after losing thirty T-62s and a corresponding number of BMPs.[67]

The Syrians then launched another attack into Sidon, relying on commandos to lead the charge while their tanks and artillery provided fire support from a distance. The commandos were able to advance into the city but were then trapped by larger Muslim forces, compelling the Syrians to employ helicopters to bring in supplies and take out the wounded. The Syrians sent a relief force of armor, which charged into the town to extract the commandos, only to be ambushed by the Muslims and mauled. Eventually, the Syrians were able to pull back from the city, but with painful losses.

The column advancing on Beirut encountered virtually the same problems. There as well, the Syrians led their drive with armor but failed to provide the tanks with adequate infantry, artillery, and helicopter support or to deploy adequate flank guards and patrols. Consequently, the armored vanguards were repeatedly ambushed by Muslim forces equipped with ATGMS and RPGS. As in the south, the Syrians halted, regrouped, and then resumed their advance with commandos in the lead. Here as well, the commandos were able to punch into the city, but without armor or artillery support ,they were set upon by larger leftist forces and trapped. Initially, the Syrians were able to keep the commandos resupplied by helicopter, but they later had to pull them out as casualties began to mount. In addition, the Syrians were experiencing severe logistical problems. The size of their columns were choking the narrow Lebanese roads, causing long traffic jams exacerbated by leftist ambushes. They began using helicopters flying from their headquarters at Rayak in the Bekaa Valley to supply lead formations, but these were too few and suffered too many maintenance problems to adequately supply the combat units. By 10 June, the Syrians had pulled back from both Beirut and Sidon, and on 20 September they were forced to sign a ceasefire in which they agreed to pull back from Tripoli, Beirut, Sidon, and other towns.

The June invasion had been a fiasco for the Syrians, and they spent the summer licking their wounds and planning for a new offensive. By September, they were ready for another try. Damascus had reinforced its contingent in Lebanon so that the entire 3d Armored Division was now present. The Syrians also added the 47th Armored Brigade as well as more commando units and other supporting forces. Altogether, the Syrians probably had 22,000–25,000 troops and 500–600 tanks in Lebanon.[68] In addition, they made an important tactical change after their experience in June, adopting a doctrine of reliance on massive firepower. Thereafter, the Syrians operated by advancing cautiously, and whenever they encountered any opposition, rather than grappling with the enemy, they would stand back and saturate the area with fire from artillery, tanks, mortars, airstrikes, and helicopter gunships.

This new offensive was designed to once again secure Beirut and the southern coastal cities; however, this time it would be conducted in two phases. In phase one the Syrians would clear the area around the Beirut-Damascus highway and gain access for a sustained presence in Beirut. In phase two they would then drive on both Beirut and Sidon, taking the cities and clearing the surrounding areas of leftist forces.

PRELIMINARY OPERATIONS EAST OF BEIRUT

The first phase kicked off on 28 September 1976. An armored-brigade task force drove northwest along the Beirut-Damascus highway itself and linked up with a Maronite force under Bashir Gemayal at R'as al-Matan. Meanwhile, a mechanized-brigade task force drove north from Zahlah and then west toward Qarnil, where it linked up with another Maronite force under Amin Gemayal. The mechanized-brigade task force faced little Muslim opposition, which generally retreated after initial contact. The Muslims harassed the Syrian vanguard but withdrew whenever the Syrians brought up additional forces to concentrate their firepower against the Muslims. In the face of this minor harassment, the Syrians were able to clear the main route north of the Beirut-Damascus highway. Their task force, however, faced stiff resistance along the Beirut-Damascus highway itself. In particular, the commando units that led the advance took heavy casualties because, as in the past, they failed to take adequate precautions and were repeatedly mauled by leftist ambushes that could only be dispersed by bringing up armor and artillery to pound the Muslim positions. Nevertheless, they kept pushing forward, ignoring the casualties among the commando units, and eventually they and the Maronites were able to capture the Muslim stronghold at R'as al-Matan. While this operation was far from elegant, it succeeded in relieving the leftist pressure against the southern perimeter of the Christian enclave and cleared the Beirut-Damascus highway to the eastern outskirts of Beirut, giving the Syrians a firm base of operations for a future drive on the Lebanese capital.

On 12 October the Syrians launched the second phase of their campaign with offensives toward Beirut and Sidon. Another important lesson the Syrians had learned from their defeat in June was that in the mountains it was best to move over multiple, parallel axes so that if any one route was blocked the advance would not stall altogether. Thus, against both cities

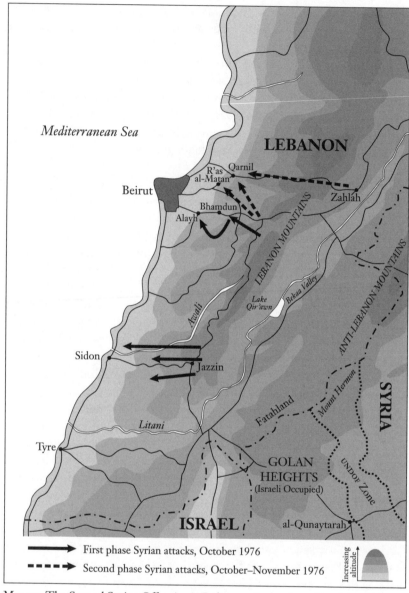

Map 35. The Second Syrian Offensive in Lebanon, September–October 1976

the Syrians advanced on three separate axes: a primary line along the main route westward into the city and then two supporting efforts, one to the north and one to the south.

THE DRIVE ON SIDON

The assault on Sidon began on 12 October with an hour-long artillery bombardment, after which the three Syrian task forces set out. The central force consisted of an armored brigade and a full commando brigade. The southern column was another armored brigade, while the northern column was mainly Christian militiamen reinforced with Syrian commandos. In the center the Syrians immediately hit fierce resistance from the Muslims, and their lead units were once again caught in an ambush. They then brought up a true combined-arms team consisting of tanks, infantry, artillery, and helicopters to break up the Muslim defenses, but they were forced to move extremely slowly to make their coordination work. This ponderous pace and their inability to really integrate the different elements resulted in considerable Syrian casualties and soon brought the entire advance to a halt. The southern thrust was similarly stopped in its tracks by a leftist antitank ambush. The Syrians tried two obvious and poorly executed flanking moves to clear this roadblock, but both failed. In the north the Maronites and Syrian commandos met little resistance but moved frustratingly slowly, in part because of inadequate supply. Indeed, all three thrusts were suffering from a general breakdown in Syrian logistics, which could not keep up with even the glacial pace of the maneuvering units. Their armored formations suffered heavy losses due to vehicle breakdowns caused by inadequate maintenance, and Syrian quartermasters could not properly supply the combat formations. As a result, many units were forced to halt or postpone attacks for lack of fuel, ammunition, food, spare parts, and other necessities.

On 14 October the Syrians were forced to commit additional forces to try to jump-start the drive on Sidon. Even with fresh units, however, the main column in the center could only make slight advances, and each mile was bought with dead soldiers and destroyed tanks. The reinforcements finally allowed the southern column to begin making some headway against the Muslims, but here as well their advance was slow. In the north, however, the slow but steady advance of the Maronites and commandos against minor leftist forces allowed them to reach the mouth of the Awali River north of Sidon late on 15 October. This position put them within artillery range of Sidon, and the Syrians immediately rushed as many guns there as they could scrape together to pound the city into submission. This outcome was good enough for Damascus, and so the embarrassing and painful advances along the central and southern routes were ordered to halt.

THE DRIVE ON BEIRUT

The Syrian offensive against Beirut in October picked up where the September campaign left off. The main advance was to be along the Beirut-Damascus highway, with supporting columns on either side. The push down the highway was mostly an armor assault supported by large numbers of commandos. In the north the Syrians employed infantry along with commandos and Maronite forces. And in the south they relied on a combined armor–mechanized infantry task force. The central attack along the Beirut-Damascus highway was quickly slowed to a crawl by heavy Muslim resistance, while the infantry attack to the north made only slightly better progress. In the south the Syrians had hoped to outflank their first objective, the well-defended town of Bhamdun, but were driven back with heavy losses when they tried to overrun its southern defenses. Moreover, as in the drive on Sidon, poor logistical support proved to be a weight around the neck of Syrian forces, hobbling their progress even where leftist resistance was slight.

The push toward Beirut did not improve very much thereafter. In the north the Syrians were halted with considerable loss by a sizable leftist counterattack. The center column found a way to bypass some of the Muslim positions but could only push a few more miles forward. In the south the Syrians decided to bypass Bhamdun, and instead they moved on and seized the heights overlooking the Muslim stronghold at Alayh. The leftists defeated a Syrian assault on Alayh itself, and Damascus opted to bring up additional artillery and simply shell the town. Meanwhile, the central and northern columns had slowed to a halt, with little hope for additional progress. By 15 October, this second Syrian drive on Beirut had petered out after having advanced only eight to ten kilometers toward the Lebanese capital.

While the Syrian military achievements were paltry, they turned out to be sufficient to serve Damascus's political objectives. Alayh was only about twelve kilometers from the heart of West Beirut, and Asad could threaten to employ artillery against the city as he had at Sidon. While it is unclear to what extent this threat was taken seriously by the leftists, the repeated offensives had demonstrated to them that the Syrians were not going to give up and go home. And the fighting had taken its toll on the Muslim militiamen, who were exhausted and short on antitank rounds. It was unclear to them just how many more Syrian campaigns they could successfully withstand. Finally, the Syrians' ponderous advance appeared to the rest of the Arab world like a deliberate "steamroller" assault to crush the Muslims, and this impression prompted the Arab League to step in and broker a ceasefire arrangement in late October. Because of the misperception of Syrian progress and the leftists' recognition of their precarious military situation, this agreement gave Asad much of what he had sought. It legitimized the Syrian presence in Lebanon and effectively turned over control of much of the eastern and central regions of the country to Damascus in return for Syria's agreement not to drive the PLO out of southern Lebanon and to pull back from the coastal areas.

Syrian Military Effectiveness during the Invasion of Lebanon

Syrian performance in the 1976 invasion of Lebanon showed little improvement since the October War. The first point that must be made is that the Muslim resistance was a small, pathetic, factional group with little combat capability. Most of the Muslim fighters were "militiamen": local recruits taught to fire a Kalashnikov or an RPG and little else. Their command-and-control system was rudimentary and crippled by inadequate communications equipment and ruinous personal animosities. By comparison, the Israelis were able to defeat these same Muslim forces fairly easily when they invaded in 1978 and again in 1982 — although even then many Palestinians fought with great determination. In fact, the Muslims were considerably stronger by the time of the Israeli invasion of 1982 than they were in 1976, having received more military hardware and training from Syria and other Arab states after Damascus flip-flopped and sided with the Muslims in the wake of the Camp David Accords.

Many of Syria's problems must be laid at the doorstep of its senior military and political leadership. First, it is clear that they misunderstood both the size and the nature of the opposition they faced in Lebanon. As a result, they failed to deploy adequate force to accomplish their objectives and, on several occasions, had to send sizable reinforcements to reinvigorate the offensive. Second and closely related to the first point, they had not learned from the October War that their tactical formations had severely limited capabilities, and so their calculus had to change to take into account these limitations. Third, they failed to prepare their forces adequately for combat in the mountains. Syrian units were not trained in mountain warfare and so floundered about trying to apply tactical doctrine designed for flat terrain in the worst tank terrain imaginable. Finally, the Syrian high command failed to recognize a priori that they were facing a guerrilla opposition and so would have to train their troops in counterinsurgency operations and structure their moves accordingly.

Nevertheless, Syrian tactical performance was equally bad. The most obvious problem was their general disregard for combined-arms operations. The initial invasion relied almost exclusively on armor and was dangerously short of infantry to deal with the Muslim antitank ambushes along the mountain roads. Similarly, its commanders never really employed combat engineers to try to clear routes of advance around enemy positions or breach enemy roadblocks. Instead, the Syrians simply tried to bull their way through the Muslim positions with armor, making it relatively easy for the leftists to destroy the tanks with RPGs, mines, recoilless rifles, and Molotov cocktails. Their artillery essentially was used only in preparatory bombardments and then sat silent through the rest of an engagement — although this was as much a product of the inability of Syrian artillery to accurately target Muslim positions as it was a sign of a lack of understanding of combined-arms cooperation. Indeed, in one of the only counterbattery engagements of the campaign, a much larger force of Syrian artillery could not silence a handful of Muslim guns being used to defend the Bhamdun stronghold. During the fall offensives, the Syrians made some effort to integrate infantry, artillery, armor, and helicopters, but this proved so difficult for them to make work properly that it bogged down their advance and evaporated in combat.

These failures with combined-arms operations led the Syrians to rely instead on overwhelming firepower as the solution to their tactical problems. This approach was not much more effective because they generally could not bring to bear the firepower they had available, and the Muslims fled into the mountains whenever the Syrians began to cause damage. One military expert familiar with Syrian operations in Lebanon has commented: "The Syrians lack offensive spirit and a grasp of mobile warfare. Instead, they prefer to fight positional battles of attrition. Targets are pounded for days by heavy artillery before cautious ground thrusts are put in. Their lack of tactical skill is compounded by poor coordination between arms. One Western expert who has witnessed many Syrian operations in Lebanon told me 'they would pound a target all day with artillery then send in the tanks and infantry a day or two later. They didn't seem to be able to organize fire support on the same day, let alone the same hour, as an attack.' "[69]

As a final note, Syrian adherence to Soviet doctrine was not quite so pronounced as in 1973. In particular, they did not rely on Russian mountain-warfare doctrine, which stressed reliance on combined-arms operations, especially the use of infantry and engineers supported by heavy-weapons fire where practicable. Also, the Soviets emphasized employment of flying columns and air-insertion of infantry forces to seize key chokepoints before they could be blocked and fortified. To a great extent, it appears that the reason the Syrians did not use such methods was that they had never learned these tactics. Soviet training of Syrian forces almost certainly focused on armored operations in good terrain (or perhaps rough terrain like that of the Golan) because this was most relevant to Syrian military missions. It is unlikely the Syrians requested specific training for mountain operations for their troops because Damascus did not seem to have recognized the need for a different kind of combat capability for Lebanon's mountainous terrain.

The Israeli Invasion of Lebanon, 1982

In the late 1970s, after the Syrians had settled into their occupation of eastern Lebanon, the military began to make changes in accordance with the lessons it had taken away from its experiences against Israel in 1973 and against the Lebanese Muslim leftists in 1976. First, Damascus concluded that it required even greater mass to defeat the Israelis, still its principal adversary. The Syrians set about increasing the size of their armed forces generally as well as increasing the size and number of its combat formations. For instance, the number of tanks in each tank battalion was increased, and Damascus expanded the Republican Guards into a full armored division and formed another armored division, the 569th, from regime-protection units. To fill out this expanded force structure, they began importing ever larger numbers of weapons and equipment from the USSR. This buying spree received additional impetus from Egypt's "defection" from the Arab cause against Israel after signing the Camp David Accords. With Egypt removed from the balance against Israel, Syria felt it had to shoulder more of the military burden, which meant a bigger, stronger military. By 1982, the Syrian armed forces had expanded to some 250,000 men, 3,600 tanks, 2,700 APCs, 2,300 artillery pieces, eighty SAM batteries, and 500 combat aircraft.[70]

Damascus also began to restructure its army to try to emphasize its areas of strength and diminish areas of weakness. The Syrians concluded that their "leg" infantry units were effectively useless and moved to convert all of them to mechanized infantry and armored formations. The 9th Infantry Division was even converted to an armored division. They also greatly increased the number and mobility of their tactical air defense assets by buying additional SA-6 launchers as well as newer SA-8s. Of particular importance, the Syrians concluded that only their commando units had shown any real skill in combat. In response, they expanded the size of their commando forces from seven to thirty-three battalions by stripping most of the best personnel from their infantry units before they were converted to mechanized formations and diverting many of the most promising new recruits to this branch.[71] After the experience in Lebanon, Syria intended to use its commandos like their Egyptian counterparts, as both special forces teams employed in nonconventional missions and as "shock" troops to spearhead offensives and man key defensive positions. In Lebanon the Syrians began to attach commando units to armored formations and vice versa. While the expansion of the commandos and their new missions gave Syria a small force of quite competent soldiers, it also greatly diminished the skill levels of other units by stripping them of many of their most competent personnel.

Asad continued to encourage the promotion of competent junior officers and tried to keep the military focused on the external-security mission. However, he also continued to ruthlessly purge officers (particularly senior officers) who demonstrated disloyalty to the regime, and in 1978 he cashiered 400 officers who opposed the invasion of Lebanon. The Lebanese involvement corrupted the Syrian military in other ways too. Most Syrian troops in Lebanon performed policing duties and so trained very little for conventional military operations. In addition, many soldiers there became involved in smuggling, narcotics, and other illicit activities that further degraded their operational readiness.

Background to the Israeli Offensive

In June 1982 the Israel Defense Force invaded southern Lebanon. Ever since the Palestinian expulsion from Jordan in 1970–71 and their subsequent resettlement in Lebanon, Israel had been harassed, shelled, attacked, and raided by Palestinian guerrillas based there. The Palestinian presence had been a major contributing factor to the outbreak of the Lebanese civil war in 1975, which had caused the country to decline into chaos and had triggered the Syrian occupation. By the late 1970s, Lebanon's instability had deepened while Palestinian attacks on Israel increased in size and scope. By the early 1980s, key members of the right-wing Israeli cabinet were determined to "solve the Lebanese problem" with military force and began trying to provoke Palestinian actions that could justify a full-scale invasion. In 1982 they found their pretext and sent the IDF and IAF north to conquer southern Lebanon, destroy the PLO, expel the Syrians, and set up a new Lebanese government that would be willing to make peace with Israel and able to keep their northern border safe and quiet.

The Opposing Forces

The Syrian presence in Lebanon in 1982 was primarily an occupation force, unprepared for large-scale combat with the Israeli military. The Syrians had two substantially reinforced heavy brigades in Lebanon at the time of the Israeli invasion. The 62d Armored was bivouacked in the Bekaa Valley and the 85th Mechanized was deployed along the Beirut-Damascus highway east of Beirut. In addition, they had at least ten battalions of commandos operating throughout the country. Altogether, there were about 30,000 Syrian soldiers with 200–300 tanks deployed in eastern and central Lebanon. They also had sixteen batteries of SA-2, SA-3, and SA-6 SAMS deployed in the Bekaa Valley.[72] But, as noted above, these forces' effectiveness had been badly compromised by graft and a general inattention to combat training. Later, the Syrians would commit the 1st Armored Division, additional SAM batteries, and finally the 3d Armored Division to the fighting, but when the Israelis first invaded, these divisions were still deployed around Damascus and the Golan Heights.

The Israelis put together a massive force, including many of the finest units in the Israeli army. For the invasion, the Northern Command deployed nine divisional ugdot plus a variety of smaller formations. These forces totaled 76,000 men, 1,250 tanks, and 1,500 other armored vehicles. In addition, the Israelis would have the entire IAF, 650 combat aircraft, at their disposal.[73] One problem they did face was that many of the units that participated in the operation were reserve units that could only be called up a few days before the start of the offensive and so had very little time to prepare themselves for war.

Several other factors weighed in the balance of forces. Israeli equipment was mostly superior to Syrian weaponry, and in some areas it was literally generations ahead. For example, the Israelis flew state-of-the-art U.S. F-15s and F-16s, while the Syrians had only older Soviet MiG-21s and MiG-23s. Likewise, although few realized it at the time, the new Israeli-designed Merkava tank was years, even decades, ahead of the T-62s and even the T-72s in the Syrian arsenal. However, Israel's greatest advantages were in the areas of command and control, intelligence, and electronic warfare, where they were simply in a different league from Syria. There were a few categories — such as APCs and perhaps artillery — where Syria's Soviet-made weapons were superior to those of the Israelis, but these were the exceptions to the rule. But the Syrians were holding superb defensive terrain. The mountains of Lebanon were tremendous obstacles to an invading force because they channeled movement along narrow ledges, valleys, and wadis. Moreover, they had occupied this terrain for seven years and had generally become accustomed to operating in it, whereas the Israelis had never really planned or trained to fight in the mountains.

The Israeli Plan

Israel's campaign plan for the invasion of Lebanon was very complex and extremely ambitious. The Israeli General Staff, goaded by Defense Minister Ariel Sharon, hoped to accomplish three major tasks in four days. The IDF was expected to, first, occupy Lebanon up to and including the Beirut-Damascus highway and besiege Beirut; second, destroy the Palestinian paramilitary units in Lebanon; and finally, beat up and expel the Syrians from the country. The Israeli plan, an updated version of their "Big Pines" contingency plan, called for multiple penetrations into Lebanon by mechanized columns diverging to isolate Palestinian and Syrian forces and then converging again to envelop and trap them.

In the west the Israelis planned to employ three ugdot to destroy the Palestinians and drive on Beirut. A huge ugdah of one armored brigade, three mechanized infantry brigades, a paratrooper brigade, and an infantry brigade would drive up the coast, its armored brigade serving as a flying column to push north, bypassing populated areas, while the rest of the force invested and later reduced the various Palestinian strongholds in the major coastal cities. Another ugdah would make an amphibious assault to secure the mouth of the Awali River to allow the rapid passage of the armored brigade driving up the coast. Meanwhile, a third ugdah would move into central Lebanon and then at various points detach subunits to drive westward to the coast. These forces would thus be in a position to outflank any opposition that threatened to block the armored brigade moving north along the coastal axis.

The main Israeli forces, however, were located in the east to deal with the Syrians. There the Israelis had put together an intricately timed operation with six different ugdot that was designed to provoke and then destroy the Syrian forces in the Bekaa Valley. The reason for this complexity was political. Simply put, most of the Israeli cabinet was willing to buy in to an invasion to destroy the Palestinian infrastructure in southwestern Lebanon and drive their artillery out of range of Israel — hence the originally stated objective of advancing no more than forty kilometers into Lebanon. However, Sharon, and possibly Prime Minister Menachem Begin, had other ideas. Sharon hoped to completely reorder Lebanese society and create a stable polity dominated by the Maronites that would make peace with Israel. This required the expulsion of the Syrians and the conquest of Lebanon up to Beirut. Since the rest of the cabinet would not sanction an attack on the Syrians in the Bekaa or near Beirut, Sharon had to goad the Syrians into contesting the Israeli invasion so that he could persuade the cabinet that the Syrians were a threat to the IDF and had to be taken care of.[74]

To accomplish this subterfuge, Sharon planned to send a small ugdah, essentially a reinforced brigade of the regular army's 162d Armored Division under Brig. Gen. Menachem Einan, north along the western slope of Mount Lebanon to cut the Beirut-Damascus highway at Ayn Darah. This move would have two effects: first, it would cut off the Syrian forces in and around Beirut from the Bekaa and Syria itself; and second, it would threaten the western flank of the Syrian forces in the Bekaa. The Israelis were certain that once this force was in place, it would be so threatening that the Syrians would have to attack it. Once the Israelis had sufficient provocation, they would then unleash their main assault. The Israelis planned to hurl about a dozen different ground and air systems against the Syrian SAM batteries in the Bekaa Valley to free up the skies over Lebanon for the IAF and prevent the problems the Arab SAMs had created in 1973 from recurring. Then the Israeli army would crush the Syrian forces in the valley.

For this mission, the Israelis created a corps-sized formation — their first ever — called the Bekaa Forces Group (BFG). The BFG was commanded by Maj. Gen. Avigdor Ben Gal, who had commanded the 7th Armored Brigade on the Golan in 1973. Ben Gal's force was centered on the 252d Armored Division and the 90th Reserve Armored Division as well as a slightly smaller armored ugdah called Vardi Force. In addition, he had an ugdah of one paratrooper and one infantry brigade under Brig. Gen. Yossi Peled equipped with large numbers of ATGMs and intended to serve as a tank-killing force in the event the Israelis hit significant Syrian armor concentrations. Finally, Ben Gal had the 88oth Reserve Armored Division as a corps reserve. The BFG was to drive into the Bekaa in a three-pronged assault forming a double envelopment within another double envelopment. In the western Bekaa, Vardi Force would drive west of Lake Qir'awn, while the 90th Reserve Armored Division would swing around the eastern shore of the lake, enveloping the right (western) flank of the Syrian forces in the Bekaa. These forces would link up and then push on to the Beirut-Damascus highway, where they in turn would link up with the 252d Armored Division, driving along the western slope of the Anti-Lebanon range (the eastern border of the Bekaa), creating a second envelopment in which to trap the rest of the Syrian forces in the valley. Peled's ugdah would hang back and wait for a large Syrian armored force to be identified, while the 88oth would remain in corps reserve and serve as an exploitation force if necessary.

The Course of Operations

In the west the Israeli offensive went largely according to plan, though not according to schedule. On 6 June 1982 the Israelis launched their attack only to discover, as the Syrians had six years before, that Lebanon's terrain greatly impeded the movement of large armored forces. Israeli tank columns got jammed up trying to bypass the coastal cities and were further delayed by small groups of Palestinians with RPGs and mines who ambushed Israeli armor as it moved along the narrow roads. While these problems were reminiscent of those experienced by the Syrians in 1976, there were also important differences. First, the Israelis were never actually stopped by the Palestinian guerrillas, and for the most part, ambushes delayed them only hours rather than the days they had cost the Syrians. Second, although the Israelis also began the campaign leading with tanks improperly supported by infantry, within two or three days they had learned their lesson and began employing dismounted infantry and paratroopers to aggressively patrol and picket the hills overlooking the roads. Third, they relied heavily on combat engineers to improve the trafficability of Lebanese roads wherever possible and, in some cases, to cut new paths around pockets of resistance or natural obstacles. Consequently, Israeli forces still made remarkably good time by any standard, suggesting their original timetable was probably unrealistic given the terrain. They reached the outskirts of Beirut by 9 June, where they encountered considerably stiffer resistance, but by 11 June they had fought their way into the suburbs and had besieged the center of the city.

In the east things moved in a more disjointed fashion, reflecting the bizarre political circumstances of the Israeli invasion, the ongoing mobilization of key units, and certain command failures on the part of key IDF officers. During the first three days of the invasion, Ben Gal's BFG pushed into southeastern Lebanon to clear out the Palestinians in the area and to get into position for the expected showdown with the Syrians. The 252d Armored Division penetrated from the Golan Heights and turned east, with Mount Hermon on its right. This division cleared out PLO forces from the foothills of Mount Hermon, the region known as Fatahland, with little resistance. They came under some desultory attacks by PLO antitank teams, but most of the Palestinian guerrillas fled without a fight, abandoning huge caches of arms and provisions. At this point, the 252d Armored purposely refrained from approaching Syrian positions because the cabinet had not yet approved an attack on them, and of greater importance, the BFG was not fully deployed and ready for combat. Indeed, except for the 252d Division, the rest of the BFG remained in Israel on 7 and 8 June because many of its

units, especially the 88oth Reserve Armored Division, had not fully mobilized yet. On the third day, 8 June, the Israeli General Staff finally ordered
the BFG forward into their jumping-off positions for the assault up the
Bekaa Valley, and Ben Gal's divisions hit the forward Syrian screening
positions around Marjayoun. The Syrians put up little resistance and were
easily driven off.

Damascus was surprised and perplexed by the Israeli invasion. The Syrians were not entirely displeased with the idea of the IDF smashing the PLO,
but they did not know whether to believe Israel's (ultimately disingenuous)
claims that it had no desire to fight Syria. Consequently, Asad adopted the
prudent course of cautiously waiting: he would stay out of the Israelis' way
to avoid war if at all possible but would reinforce his positions in Lebanon
in the event the Israelis attacked anyway. Syrian forces in Lebanon were
weak and unprepared for war with the IDF, and Asad did not want to give
the Israelis any pretext to attack his troops. Thus, Damascus ordered its
forces in Lebanon not to fire at the Israelis — even if they were fired upon —
unless they were taking casualties. Syrian troops were forbidden from moving forward in some places to occupy better defensive terrain for fear that
this would appear aggressive to the notoriously paranoid Israelis. Meanwhile, Syria readied its forces in the event the Israelis were looking for a
fight. The Syrians ordered their troops in Lebanon to man defensive positions along many of the major routes from the south into their strongholds
in the Bekaa and along the Beirut-Damascus highway. Asad dispatched
Major General 'Ali Aslan, the deputy chief of staff for operations, to Lebanon to better assess Israeli intentions. Syria also ordered the 1st Armored
Division to move to the Bekaa to bolster the forces already there. This unit
arrived on 7 June and immediately began to prepare defensive positions
based on a typical Soviet defense-in-depth pattern. Damascus also began
moving the 3d Armored Division to Lebanon on 7 June, soon after the 1st's
move was completed and the roads were again free. Finally, they redeployed three more SAM batteries to the Bekaa, bringing the total number of
medium-range SAM batteries there to nineteen.[75]

OPERATIONS IN THE CENTRAL SECTOR

While the Syrians were attempting to decipher Israeli intentions, the
understrength Israeli 162d Armored Division was slowly moving into
south-central Lebanon, making for the western side of the Lebanon range.
This unit was supposed to dash north to reach the Beirut-Damascus highway forty-eight hours after the start of the attack. At first, its route of
advance was largely undefended, though the Syrians had only one company

of tanks and one commando company watching it. However, the Israeli armor got badly jammed up along the narrow roads (less than five meters wide in most places), and their commanders decided not to push ahead during the night. As a result, the force made little progress during the first two days of the invasion. The Syrians detected the division's movement on 7 June and sent several commando companies backed up by a tank battalion to set ambushes along the Israeli route to Jazzin. They also dispatched a multibattalion task force of commandos and armor from the 85th Mechanized Brigade to establish a blocking position farther north at Ayn Zhaltah.

On the third day, pressure from the Israeli General Staff prompted the 162d Armored Division to pick up the pace of its advance. In the morning the 162d ran into several of the small ambushes established by the Syrians the day before. The commando-armor teams fought hard and retreated in good order when they were outflanked and driven off by the IDF. While they did little damage to the Israelis, they delayed them, which proved crucial. Later, the first Syrian helicopter gunships made their appearance, attacking the 162d Division along the narrow, winding mountain paths. The helicopters — French-made Gazelles armed with ATGMS — caused little damage and were easily driven off, but they so unnerved the Israelis that the entire division scrambled for cover and took some time to reassemble and get moving again.

All of these skirmishes, plus additional delays caused by Israeli command problems, bought the Syrians time to establish a very impressive defense at Ayn Zhaltah. Even though the 162d Division covered fifty kilometers through the mountains on 8 June, it was not enough. When the Israelis finally reached the town that evening, they were hammered by Syrian commandos, well dug in, generously armed with RPGS and ATGMS, and covered by tank and other heavy-weapons fire. The Syrians had fortified the high ground around the southern entrance to the town, with their tanks at the far end. The Israelis saw the tanks and drove straight at them, destroying three T-62s before they were themselves caught in a crossfire by Syrian commandos with Saggers and RPGS hiding among the steep ridgelines on both sides of the road. The Syrians destroyed the two lead tanks and several APCS of the Israeli vanguard before the Israelis could halt the column and pull back from the "fire sack." Later, the Syrians beat back an infantry force that tried several times to rescue their wounded. Moreover, when the Israelis pulled back from the village to regroup, Syrian commandos crept forward and again attacked them from several different directions, forcing the Israelis to fight their way back south of the town. Late the next day, the IDF regrouped and conducted a flanking attack under heavy air support that drove the Syrians from the hills overlooking the town; by nightfall on 9 June, Ayn Zhaltah was in their hands. The Syrians did only slight damage to the IDF in these clashes, mostly because their fire was inaccurate and their armor refused to maneuver against the Israelis, but they prevented the 162d Armored Division from cutting the Beirut-Damascus highway and outflanking the Syrian defense lines in the Bekaa. Ultimately, this was one of the most important factors in preventing the complete destruction of the Syrian army in Lebanon.[76]

Farther south on 8 June, an Israeli armored brigade without infantry or artillery support attacked a reinforced brigade of Syrians in the Lebanese town of Jazzin. This site was important because it controlled the intersection of the main road running north-south along the western slope of the Lebanon range (the road the 162d Armored Division was following) with the main east-west route from Sidon to the Bekaa. The Syrians saw Jazzin as the forwardmost position on the right flank of their defensive lines in the Bekaa and had sent a brigade task force to hold the city. The Israelis had been content initially to set up a blocking position at the crossroads — thereby allowing the 162d Armored Division to pass — but not attacking the Syrians in the town. But on 8 June the IDF attacked into the town, where they were met by well-placed antitank ambushes manned by Syrian commandos. The Israelis then sent another part of their brigade in a flanking maneuver to roll up the Syrian positions in the outlying hills. Because the commando units were deployed to fire into the town and could not quickly reorient themselves to deal with this unexpected move, it fell to the Syrian armor to try to stop the Israelis. However, the tanks also had difficulty shifting to face the IDF flanking attack, and the armor battalion was virtually wiped out in a quick firefight, prompting the other Syrian units to pull back.

The events of 7 and 8 June had important ramifications in both Jerusalem and Damascus. For the Syrians, the powerful Israeli attacks on Ayn Zhaltah and Jazzin convinced Asad that the Israelis were lying when they claimed that they intended only to punish the PLO. He recognized that, in reality, they were determined to pick a fight with his forces. In response he sped up the deployment of 3d Armored Division to the Bekaa and sent additional commando battalions to Lebanon. Meanwhile, the fighting at Ayn Zhaltah and Jazzin, along with the movement of the Syrian reinforcements into the Bekaa and the participation of a few Syrian MiGs in combat with IAF jets over Lebanon, were enough for Sharon to persuade the Israeli cabinet to approve the offensive against the Syrians. On the afternoon of 9 June, Ben Gal was ordered to drive the Syrian army out of the Bekaa

Valley. Simultaneously, the IAF was ordered to implement its long-planned contingency operation to knock out the Syrian SAM network there as well.

THE ISRAELI SAM SUPPRESSION CAMPAIGN

Syria's air and air defense forces were crushed by the Israeli air campaign. The Israelis had meticulously studied the lessons of the 1973 war and had developed a comprehensive operation involving over a dozen different ground and air-based systems to suppress and destroy Syria's medium-range SAM units. Although the Syrians had bought considerably more SAMs from the USSR, and in some cases had bought more-advanced models than they had possessed in 1973, they had not kept pace with the development of Israeli SAM suppression techniques. Syrian SAM operations were highly predictable and patterned, allowing the Israelis to develop countermeasures relatively easily. Syrian command and control was primitive, slow, and lacked redundancy, making it susceptible to Israeli attack and incapable of adequately responding to the fast-paced, multifaceted Israeli assault. Their radars, TELS (transporter-erector-launchers), and support equipment rarely moved from their positions, and the radars were left on for long periods of time, making them easy to locate and target. The Syrians also had inadequate early warning radars — they had less than a quarter of the sets called for by Soviet doctrine — and did not recognize that terrain masking from Lebanon's mountains degraded the coverage of the radars they had deployed. All of these problems left them highly vulnerable to attack.

The Israelis began their assault with flights of unmanned drones and electronic spoofing of the Syrian radars to convince the Syrians that large numbers of attack aircraft were overhead. These deceptions prompted Syrian SAM crews to turn on their targeting radars and fire off a huge salvo of missiles against the drones, at which point the Israelis unleashed a swarm of air- and surface-launched antiradiation missiles that homed in on the Syrian fire-control radars and destroyed them. With the Syrian SAM units blinded and "unloaded," Israeli strike aircraft and artillery attacked the early warning radars and TELS themselves, pounding them for several hours with highly accurate strikes. The Syrians mostly panicked during the attack, showing little ability to respond to this unexpected set of Israeli tactics. Some SAM crews tried to fight back as best they could, but few turned off their radars or tried to pack up and move, which were probably the best solutions to their problems. The batteries also had difficulty communicating with each other and with the small number of AAA units supposed to defend them so that they could not coordinate their responses to the Israeli attack. By night on 9 June, the Israelis had destroyed seventeen of nineteen

Syrian SAM batteries in the Bekaa Valley without losing a plane, and by the end of August, subsequent Israeli airstrikes had destroyed another twelve SAM batteries.[77]

When Damascus became aware of the destruction being inflicted on its SAM batteries, it ordered the Syrian Air Force to come to the aid of the air defense forces. The SAF dispatched as many as 100 aircraft, which were met by several score of Israeli fighters. The Syrians labored under several disadvantages. Their command and control was incapable of coordinating the operations of air forces and ground-based air defense units; the result was that these forces could only act either at different times or in different areas, but they could not integrate their efforts. Damascus also had no particular battle plan or operational concept for employing its fighters—they were simply sent to the Bekaa and told to drive off the IAF without much thought to devising a strategy. The Syrians were flying MiG-23s and MiG-21s, and their pilots were heavily dependent on guidance from ground-controlled intercept (GCI) sites, while the Israelis flew more advanced F-15s and F-16s armed with far more capable air-to-air missiles than the Syrians possessed. The Israeli fighters also were supported by E-2C Hawkeye airborne warning and control aircraft, which proved adept in monitoring Syrian air operations and vectoring Israeli aircraft to intercept SAF planes before they could sneak up on Israeli aircraft or flee the battlefield.

Syria's technological disadvantage had some effect on the dogfights but became almost beside the point since Syrian pilot performance was so poor. When the SAF rose to defend the SAMs, the Israelis began a comprehensive electronic-jamming campaign that severed the communications links between the Syrian interceptors and their GCI sites. Deprived of GCI guidance, the pilots "went stupid." Syrian formations immediately dissolved, for their pilots could not handle flying in formations larger than pairs. They were unimaginative and showed no creativity or flare for improvisation and flew into combat mindlessly, making little or no effort to maneuver in dogfights. Some pilots simply flew figure-eights because, without the orders of their GCI operators, they literally had no idea what to do and made no effort to try to think for themselves. Those few pilots who did try at least some air-combat maneuvers employed only simple, predictable tactics and were slow to react to Israeli moves. The result was almost inevitable as 29 MiGs were shot down without killing a single IAF fighter. On 10 and 11 October the same performance was repeated as Syria again sent up large numbers of aircraft to try to provide air cover for its ground forces now that their SAM defenses had been destroyed. On the tenth the Syrians lost 35 aircraft and on the eleventh another 18 aircraft (in only half a day of combat), all without shooting down any Israeli planes. By the end of September, the Syrians still had not shot down a single Israeli plane and had lost 86 MiGs to the IAF.[78]

The performance of the SAF was both hopelessly inept and yet incredibly brave. A senior IAF officer asked to comment on the performance of the MiG-23 replied:

> I can't compare it when a MiG-23 is flown in a tactic that I can't understand or in a situation that I would never get into. The problem is that their pilots didn't do things at the right time or in the right place. . . . [T]he pilots behaved as if they knew they were going to be shot down and then waited for it to happen and not how to prevent it or how to shoot us down. Which was very strange because in the 1973 War the Syrians fought very aggressively. It wasn't the equipment at fault, but their tactics. They could have flown the best fighter in the world, but if they flew it the way they were flying we would have shot them down in exactly the same way. I don't mean they were sitting ducks, but in our view, they acted without tactical sense.[79]

A highly regarded RAND analyst, Ben Lambeth, concluded:

> The Syrians were simply outflown and outfought by vastly superior Israeli opponents. Without question, its sophisticated American hardware figured prominently in helping Israel emerge from the Bekaa Valley fighting with a perfect score. Nevertheless, the outcome would most likely have been heavily weighted in Israel's favor even had the equipment available to each side been reversed. At bottom, the Syrians were not done in by the AIM-9L's expanded launch envelope, the F-15's radar, or any combination of Israeli technical assets, but by the IDF's constant retention of the operational initiative and its clear advantages in leadership, organization, tactical adroitness, and adaptability.[80]

However, by the same token, one Israeli pilot who fought in the June air battles stated that the Syrians "knew they stood no chance against us, yet they kept coming in and coming in as if asking to be shot down. They showed such remarkable dedication and courage, and I have nothing but respect and admiration for them."[81]

THE BATTLE OF THE BEKAA VALLEY

When the Israelis finally launched their ground attack in the east, the Syrians were fairly well prepared for it. The 1st Armored Division, reinforced with additional artillery and commando units, was fully deployed in the valley and had been preparing defensive positions for two days. The

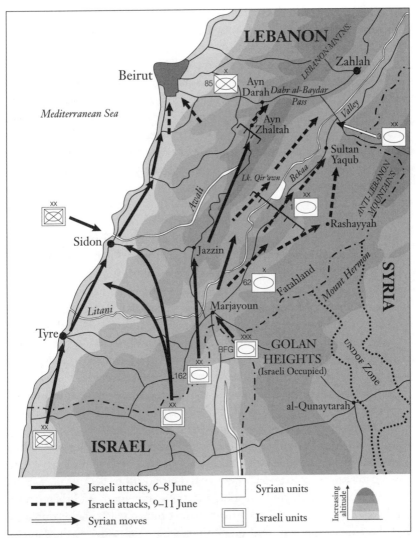

Map 36. The Israeli Invasion of Lebanon, June 1982

Syrians deployed with their 76th and 91st Armored Brigades forward, dug in across the valley floor and anchoring their lines in the mountains on either side. In addition, they were counting on the natural obstacle of Lake Qir'awn in the western Bekaa to strengthen their position and had attempted to work this natural obstacle into their defensive scheme. The 1st Armored Division's mechanized brigade, the 58th, was deployed in depth, dug in behind the two forward armored brigades, where it could serve either as a secondary line of defense or a reserve that could be brought forward. The Syrians also deployed teams of commandos backed with armor in antitank ambushes farther south to delay, disrupt, and attrite the Israeli forces before they hit the main defense line. Meanwhile, the T-72-equipped 3d Armored Division was en route to the Bekaa and was expected to arrive some time on 11 June.

During the afternoon of 9 June, while the IAF was slaughtering Syria's air and air defense forces, the IDF's Bekaa Forces Group slogged their way along the narrow roads of the southern entrance to the valley. On a number of occasions, Syrian helicopter gunships — and occasionally fixed-wing aircraft — attacked the Israeli columns, causing little damage but forcing them to take cover and thus slowing their advance. In addition, the Israelis constantly encountered commando ambushes that further slowed and frustrated them. The Syrian commandos were usually well deployed and tough to root out. Several Israeli units lost armored vehicles and men to these attacks, while all were slowed by the need to move cautiously and clear out the stubborn Syrian defenders whenever they did trip an ambush. The Israelis had learned to use infantry, airstrikes, and armor when possible to clear the surrounding hills when they encountered dug-in antitank teams, but this was a time-consuming process, and the Syrians fought hard and mostly retreated in good order when their positions became untenable. Nevertheless, Syrian aim was poor, and the commandos and their armor rarely tried to get out and maneuver against the Israelis. These problems, and the superb gunnery and quick improvisational skills of the Israelis, tended to minimize the actual damage the commandos were able to inflict, but the loss of time was an important factor. This was especially so since Israel knew that the destruction of the Syrian SAMs would bring immense superpower pressure on them to agree to a ceasefire.

The Israelis finally attacked the main Syrian defense line in the Bekaa in the early morning of 10 June. The Syrians were outnumbered by the Israelis in the assault: the reinforced Syrian 1st Armored Division had 350–400 tanks, 150 artillery pieces, and approximately 150 ATGM-equipped BRDM-2s, while the Israeli ugdot leading the attack had over 650 tanks and about 200 artillery pieces. However, the Syrians had the advantages of their dug-in defenses and the superb terrain of the Bekaa. As planned, two of the Israeli ugdot — the Vardi Force and the 90th Reserve Armored Division — struck the Syrian lines on either side of Lake Qir'awn, while the 252d Armored Division hit the eastern flank of the lines anchored on the Anti-Lebanon range. Although all three IDF attacks were frontal assaults into dug-in Syrian units in excellent defensive terrain that prevented the Israelis from deploying more than a fraction of their forces across the front of their assault, the Israelis broke through along all three axes. In the far west the Syrians deployed only light covering forces, believing the terrain too rough for an Israeli armored drive, with the result that the Vardi Force quickly broke through the lines and began driving deep into the Bekaa along the eastern slope of the Lebanon range. The main battle, however, took place to the east of Lake Qir'awn, where the Israeli 90th Armored Division attacked up the main north-south road in the valley. The Syrians recognized this as a critical threat and fed in ever more reserves to try to stop the IDF. Although the terrain prevented the Israelis from deploying their full force and the Syrians were well dug in along the surrounding hills, the Israelis constantly worked against the flanks and used their gunnery skills to pick off Syrian armored vehicles and grind down the defending forces. By 3:00 P.M., the Syrian lines had buckled and the 90th Division had broken through. In the east the Israeli 252d Armored Division, spearheaded by the elite 7th Armored Brigade, drove through the Syrian lines fairly easily, and by late afternoon, they were threatening to link up with the 90th Division and encircle the remnants of the forward brigades of the 1st Armored Division.[82]

Yet the trap never snapped shut, and much of the 1st Armored Division was able to escape as a result of Israeli mistakes and Syrian successes. Of greatest importance, most of the Israeli units did not aggressively pursue the retreating Syrians and moved at an almost leisurely pace. Despite the urgency in Jerusalem for the BFG to reach the Beirut-Damascus highway before nightfall, Ben Gal's units moved slowly and deliberately. The Syrians for their part retreated well, conducting fighting withdrawals all across the front and maintaining good unit cohesion, except among those formations that had suffered most in the combat with the Israelis earlier in the day. On one occasion, a Syrian commando unit conducted a spoiling attack against an Israeli armored unit near Rashayyah, which only destroyed one APC and killed a few soldiers but still disrupted the Israeli formation and delayed its advance. In addition, the Syrians threw their helicopter gunships into the fray to slow down the advance and to cover the retreat of their ground forces. The Syrian Gazelles and Mi-24 Hinds generally caused only minor damage to the Israelis, but they did further slow their already cautious movement. For the most part, the sluggish pace of the Israeli pursuit appears to have been the product of their experience over the previous four days, during which they had been constantly ambushed by Syrian commandos. This seems to have made the IDF reluctant to engage in any sort of headlong advance through the hills of the Bekaa Valley, even after cracking the main Syrian lines and putting the 1st Armored Division to flight.

This caution was further reinforced when an Israeli battalion accidentally ran into several battalions of the Syrian 58th Mechanized Brigade, plus other elements of the 1st Armored Division, regrouping around the town of Sultan Yaqub during the afternoon of 10 June. Most of the Syrian units were part of the second line of defense, and they were not aware that the Israelis had gotten so far north. The vanguard of an Israeli armored brigade pushed into the town against no resistance and then out the other side only to suddenly find itself in the midst of the Syrian forces. The Syrians apparently did not realize what had happened for some time, probably assuming the Israeli tanks were just another Syrian unit retreating back from the earlier battles. When they did recognize that there was an Israeli battalion among them, they were very tentative in engaging the IDF force, perhaps in response to the devastation to their armor earlier in the day. As the afternoon wore on, however, they realized that the Israelis were trapped and outnumbered and began to attack them more aggressively.

Although the firefights became quite fierce and the Syrians had the advantage of being deployed in hills hemming in the Israelis on three sides, they did remarkably little damage. Syrian armor and APCs remained in the hills and were content to fire down on the Israelis rather than actually coming down and destroying the Israeli armor in a close assault. Twice the Syrians sent small antitank units down to strike the Israelis, but they were driven off by automatic-weapons fire. Finally, at around 9:00 P.M., the Israelis concentrated virtually every artillery piece in the Bekaa on the Syrians around Sultan Yaqub, creating a "box" of fire through which the Israeli battalion was able to withdraw. The Israelis lost only six or eight tanks in this engagement, but it had completely preoccupied Ben Gal's command staff, deprived the rest of his corps of artillery support, and heightened the general Israeli concern over Syrian traps.[83] Thus, by night on 10 June, the Israelis had routed the 1st Armored Division, but they had not finished it off, nor had they reached the Beirut-Damascus highway.

Despite the IDF's problems on 10 June, the defeat of the 1st Armored Division, coming on top of the destruction of Syria's air and air defense forces, threw the Syrian high command into a state of panic. They recognized that the Israelis had powerful forces threatening to cut the Beirut-Damascus highway, which would split the Syrian forces in Lebanon. The general staff also could not be certain that the Israelis did not intend to drive up to the Beirut-Damascus highway, turn right and push into the Damascus plain in conjunction with an assault from the Golan. This fear prompted them to alert their forces around the capital, dispatch two independent armored brigades to block the Beirut-Damascus highway as it debouched into Syria, and order the 3d Armored Division into the Bekaa to reestablish a defensive line south of the Beirut-Damascus highway with the remnants of the 1st Armored Division.

Although one of its brigades suffered heavy losses to IAF airstrikes on 10 and 11 June, by 10:00 A.M. on 11 June, the 3d Armored Division was in the Bekaa Valley and heading south to take up defensive lines forward of the Beirut-Damascus highway before the IDF could get there. The Israelis, meanwhile, had finally gotten going after a late start and were similarly racing north to get to the Beirut-Damascus highway before noon, when a U.S.-brokered ceasefire was due to take effect. Shortly before noon, lead elements of the 82d Armored Brigade of the 3d Armored Division collided with lead elements of the Israeli corps. In the ensuing firefight, the IDF quickly gained the upper hand through superior marksmanship and destroyed at least nine, and possibly as many as thirty, Syrian T-72s before the Syrians, who were unable to knock out any of the Israeli Merkava tanks, pulled back.[84] Nevertheless, the fight was still a sort of victory for Syria since the 3d Armored Division prevented the Israelis from reaching the Beirut-Damascus highway before the noon deadline.

THE ISRAELI OFFENSIVE ALONG THE BEIRUT-DAMASCUS HIGHWAY

The last real combat involving sizable Syrian formations occurred on the Beirut-Damascus highway east of Beirut in the Ayn Darah area on 22–25 June. The Israelis had been sitting on the outskirts of Beirut for two weeks and were trying to draw their noose tighter around the city to impose a real siege. However, their failure to cut the Beirut-Damascus highway in the initial invasion had left that major artery open, and Damascus had gone so far as to deploy additional commandos and some mechanized infantry to the eastern suburbs of Beirut to keep this line open. The IDF decided to mount a drive eastward from Beirut along the highway, supported by a drive from Ayn Darah north to the road, where the Israeli 162d Armored Division had been stopped twelve days before. These forces would link up and then continue east to block the pass over the Lebanon range. The

Syrians had two reinforced heavy brigades in the area, the 85th and the 62d, with about 150 tanks between them. The Israelis brought in elite infantry from the Golani Brigade and paratrooper units supported by armor and the entire IAF. The Syrians were overwhelmed by the Israelis, as the IDF infantry deftly cleared their antitank ambushes, and Israeli armor finally found some room to maneuver against the Syrian tanks. Syrian units could muster little resistance, and some began to collapse and flee. The Israelis took large numbers of prisoners and even began capturing tanks abandoned by their crews. Damascus reacted by quickly assembling a force of commandos and armor in the Bekaa and sending them west along the Beirut-Damascus highway to set up a blocking position at the Dahr al-Baydar pass. This force rebuffed the initial Israeli probes, at which point the IDF decided it was content with its gains and that a further advance was unnecessary. Another ceasefire came into effect on 25 June.

The Syrian armed forces had been defeated in Lebanon, in some areas quite badly, but the campaign had not been a complete fiasco. In particular, they had prevented the Israelis from driving them out of the Bekaa Valley and thereby eliminating them as a factor in Lebanese politics. Although Syrian units had been regularly defeated in battle, their ground forces had stuck together and retreated in good order, allowing them to salvage far more than would otherwise have been the case. In the end, the Syrians lost 1,200 dead, 3,000 wounded, and 296 prisoners in addition to 300–350 tanks, 150 APCs, nearly 100 artillery pieces, twelve helicopters, 86 aircraft, and 29 SAM batteries. Against the Syrians during 6–25 June, the Israelis suffered 195 killed and 872 wounded in addition to 30 tanks lost (with another 100 damaged) and 175 APCs destroyed and damaged.[85]

Syrian Military Effectiveness during the Israeli Invasion of Lebanon

In some respects, Syrian combat performance in Lebanon showed considerable improvement over past wars, while in other ways it showed no improvement whatsoever. Richard Gabriel asserts that their performance in Lebanon was the best of any Arab army the Israelis had ever fought. Moreover, Gabriel's remarks echo the opinion of many IDF personnel. By contrast, Trevor Dupuy and Paul Martell argue that, given the advantage of defending the superb terrain of Lebanon, the Syrians should have done much better and they probably performed worse than they had in 1973. Similarly, Anthony Cordesman and Abraham Wagner conclude that the Syrians only *seemed* more capable to the Israelis because the IDF was constantly hamstrung by the constraining political environment Sharon had created and by command failures among the IDF units in Lebanon. To some extent, all of these assessments are probably correct.[86]

STRATEGIC PERFORMANCE

Given the conditions under which they were forced to operate, Syrian generalship was adequate, though not brilliant. Initially, of course, Asad believed Israeli propaganda about not wanting war with his country, which restricted Syria's efforts. Syrian moves in the first few days of the war were wise, given their desire to avoid provoking Israel while preventing the IDF from securing a decisive advantage and then attacking their forces in Lebanon. Syrian units were placed on alert right away and ordered to begin preparing (and in some cases repairing) defensive positions along key axes of advance. Damascus bolstered its air defenses in the Bekaa Valley and began redeploying two of its armored divisions to reinforce its ground units there, many of which had been on occupation duties for so long they were not combat ready. When the IDF began pushing up the spine of the Lebanon range toward the Beirut-Damascus highway, the Syrians recognized the danger of this move and decided to block it, regardless of the potential for provoking a war with Israel. This too was probably the right move: as bad as the fighting in the Bekaa actually went for Syria, it almost certainly would have been worse had the Israelis been able to move their 162d Armored Division to the Beirut-Damascus highway and then attack into the Bekaa from that position, behind the main Syrian defense lines.

Syria's strategy for fighting the Israelis once it became clear that war was unavoidable also was a reasonable approach. The Syrians deployed their commandos forward, with armor support, in ambushes along the narrow defiles the Israelis had to follow into the Bekaa. Here they were ideally placed to disrupt and delay the Israeli advance. The alternative, deploying all of the commandos with the reinforced 1st Armored Division along the main Syrian defense lines in the Bekaa, would not have taken full advantage of the commandos' capabilities, and their effect would have been much reduced. The Syrian defensive strategy in the Bekaa was straightforward — a standard Soviet-style defense-in-depth with two brigades up and one back — but still an appropriate response to the situation. It may be the case that a truly brilliant general might have found a better approach, perhaps drawing the Israelis in and trapping them in an operational level "fire sack," or perhaps giving up the valley floor to the Israelis only to fall on them in a flanking counterattack out of the mountains on either side. However, the Syrian strategy was not bad, and it is unclear that their tactical forces could have implemented a more sophisticated defensive scheme. For instance, any strategy that relied heavily on large-scale flanking attacks would have given up the enormous advantage of the terrain and handed it to the Israelis. It also would have required Syrian units to prevail over the IDF in fluid armored engagements. Given the drubbing the Syrians took in tank duels when they were defending in place and had all of the advantages of the terrain, it seems likely that such a counteroffensive strategy would have failed miserably.

Finally, although the decision to commit the Syrian Air Force to defend the SAMS and the ground forces in the Bekaa Valley resulted in the destruction of almost one-quarter of the SAF, it too was probably the best move. First, not sending out the SAF to confront the Israelis probably would have been a severe blow to morale throughout the Syrian armed forces. The air force would have felt worthless, while the ground and air defense forces would have felt abandoned. Second, in military terms the SAF succeeded in keeping much of the Israeli Air Force occupied on 9–10 June, the key days of the battle. The IAF was so intent upon killing Syrian MiGs that they concentrated most of their effort on the air battles. As a result, they did not provide very much close air support to Israeli armor in the Bekaa until late on 10 June, when the Syrian lines had already been broken. Before then, those Israeli aircraft assigned to ground-attack missions had mostly aided the stalled drive around Ayn Zhaltah and had flown BAI missions against Syrian reinforcements moving toward the Bekaa. IDF units fighting in the valley generally had to rely on Israel's small number of attack helicopters to provide fire support when needed since the IAF was busy elsewhere. Indeed, Ze'ev Schiff and Ehud Ya'ari comment that the IAF provided only "occasional support" during the critical assault by the 90th Armored Division east of Lake Qir'awn.[87] Of course, what can be faulted in the decision to commit the SAF was the absence of any real strategy or guiding plan that took into account the well-known shortcomings of Syrian planes and pilots and that might have allowed Syrian fighters to accomplish something more than merely serving as a punching bag for the IAF in order to distract them from the ground battles.

There were other problems at the strategic level, but they were not necessarily problems of generalship. For example, Syrian military intelligence performed dismally. They failed to predict the Israeli invasion, nor did they appreciate Israeli objectives toward Syrian forces in Lebanon. At a more technical level, Damascus's intelligence services completely dropped the ball with regard to the development of Israeli military forces and operations. They were entirely unaware of some of the systems the Israelis employed to destroy the SAM systems in the Bekaa Valley and did not even foresee that the Israelis would make a major effort to neutralize Syria's ground-based air defenses.

TACTICAL PERFORMANCE

The real variations in Syrian military effectiveness were at the tactical level. Specifically, there was a very considerable gap between the performance of the commandos and that of the rest of the armed forces. Syria's commando forces consistently performed markedly better than any other units of the military. They chose excellent ambush sites and generally established clever traps to lure the Israelis into prepared kill zones. The commandos showed a good ability to operate in conjunction with tanks and other armored vehicles, integrating them into their own fire schemes and doing a good job of protecting the tanks from Israeli infantry. They also were noticeably more aggressive, creative, and willing to take the initiative and seize fleeting opportunities than other Syrian units. Their surprise counterattacks on Israeli armored columns at Ayn Zhaltah and Rashayyah in the Bekaa particularly stand out. Finally, Syrian commandos did an excellent job disengaging whenever the Israelis began to gain the upper hand in a fight, at which point they usually pulled back to another ambush site farther up the road.

By contrast, the rest of Syria's armed forces performed very poorly, manifesting all of the same problems that had plagued them in their previous wars. In the words of Maj. Gen. Amir Drori, the overall commander of the Israeli invasion, "The Syrians did everything slower and worse than we expected."[88] Without a doubt, the SAF performed worst of all the services (as discussed before), but the Syrian army was certainly disappointing too. In particular, the contrast between the Syrian commandos and their armored forces is striking.

Syria's heavy formations had little to brag about other than their stubborn resistance and orderly retreat. Syrian armor consistently refused to maneuver against the Israelis, with the result that in every tank duel, no matter how much the terrain favored the defenders, it was only a matter of time before the Israelis' superior marksmanship and constant efforts to maneuver for advantage led to a Syrian defeat. Chaim Herzog has echoed this assessment, observing that the Syrian military's greatest problem was its chronic "inflexibility in maneuver."[89] Syrian artillery support was very poor and had little effect on the fighting. Their batteries showed almost no ability to shift fire in response to changing tactical situations or to coordinate fire from geographically dispersed units. While armored and mechanized formations recognized the need to conduct combined-arms operations, they displayed little understanding of how to actually do this. Infantry, armor, and artillery all failed to provide each other with adequate support, allowing the Israelis — who also often failed to integrate the various combat arms into effective teams — to defeat each in detail. In general, the Syrians relied on size to compensate for their tactical shortcomings, but Israeli tactical skill proved so overwhelming that even where Syrian armored and mechanized formations were able to create very favorable odds ratios, they were still easily defeated by the Israelis.

Damascus's ground forces had other problems as well. Syrian units were extremely negligent in gathering information and conducting reconnaissance. Many commanders simply failed to order patrols to keep abreast of Israeli movements in their sector, instead relying on information passed down from higher echelons. Those patrols that were dispatched seemed to have little feel for the purpose of reconnaissance and rarely gathered much valuable information. As a result, many Syrian units blundered around Lebanon with little understanding of where the Israelis were, sometimes with fatal consequences. They showed poor fire discipline, squandering rounds so quickly that many were forced to retreat because they were out of ammunition. Despite extensive training in night combat, their units were almost helpless after dark. According to their Soviet advisers, Syrian personnel at all levels could not night navigate, their units lost all cohesion in the darkness, and morale dropped accordingly. Only some of the commando units showed any ability to actually apply the training they had received and operate after dark, but fortunately for the Syrians, the Israelis generally did not continue their advance at night.

The Syrian Gazelle helicopter gunships were psychologically effective against the Israelis but did little actual damage. Although they employed good Western-style "pop-up" tactics, the Gazelles were not able to manage more than a few armor kills during the war and could only delay the Israelis. Although this was useful in slowing the IDF's advance to the Bekaa and then hindering its pursuit after breaking through the Syrian lines, the Gazelles were unable to prevent Syrian defeats even when committed in large numbers, as in the fighting around Lake Qir'awn. One Israeli officer observed that the helicopters were "not a problem" because the Syrians did not employ them creatively, had bad aim, and operated them only individually or in pairs, making it easy for the IDF to neutralize them.[90] Anthony Cordesman has commented that Syrian helicopter operations in Lebanon suffered from "the same tactical and operational rigidities, training, and command problems that affected its tank, other armor, and artillery performance."[91] Consequently, their contributions were ephemeral.

Syrian combat support was another impediment to their tactical performance. In particular, their logistic support was appalling. Damascus had established huge stockpiles of spare parts and combat consumables in the Bekaa, yet during the course of the fighting many units experienced difficulties in getting resupply (although part of the problem was their wasteful expenditure of ammunition). Graft had riddled the Syrian quartermaster corps to such a degree that a lot of things that were supposed to have been available were not. In addition, the Soviets reported that the Syrians did not understand the Soviet-style "push" logistics, with quartermasters demanding formal requests for provisions rather than simply sending supplies to the front at regular intervals as intended within that system. Maintenance was another problem area. Most Syrian soldiers were incapable and unwilling to perform even basic preventive maintenance on their weapons and vehicles. Instead, these functions had to be performed by specialized technicians attached at brigade and division level, and for most repairs, equipment had to be sent back to a small number of central depots around Damascus. These facilities were manned in part by Cuban technicians who handled the more advanced Soviet weaponry. The Israelis reported capturing a fair number of Syrian armored vehicles abandoned because of minor mechanical problems.

The fact that Syria's commandos performed so much better than its other units ever had in the past should not obscure the fact that, in an absolute sense when compared to the forces of other armies, Syria's commando battalions were still mediocre. In general, Syrian commandos were content to sit in their prepared positions, fire down on Israeli forces that wandered into their ambushes, and then retreat as soon as the enemy recovered and began to bust up the Syrian defensive scheme. Incidents such as the commando counterattacks at Ayn Zhaltah, Rashayyah, and a few other minor engagements were still exceptions to the rule and are noteworthy because they were among the only times that even the commandos tried to get out and aggressively upset Israeli operations. For the most part, though, the commandos established ambushes and then waited passively for the IDF to move into them. They also were not terribly skillful with their weapons: on any number of occasions, Israeli units were completely trapped by commando ambushes; subjected to a hail of gunfire, grenades, and missiles; and emerged having suffered only a handful of casualties.[92] In addition, like other Syrian formations, the commandos frequently neglected to cover their flanks or were too quick to conclude that terrain was impassable. As a result, many ambushes were cleared by Israeli flank guards or bypassed altogether when Israeli combat engineers found a way through terrain the Syrians had deemed impenetrable.

Unit cohesion among Syrian formations in Lebanon, as in earlier conflicts, was actually quite good. For the most part, units stuck together and fought back under all circumstances. With the exception of the combat along the Beirut-Damascus highway on 22–25 June — when Syrian units seem to have cracked under the combined strain of their lengthy combat, the constant Israeli airstrikes, and the clear superiority of Israel's elite infantry formations — few units simply disintegrated in combat. The rule was that they fought hard, remained intact, and retreated well. Although it is true that Israeli pressure was uncharacteristically light on the armored forces withdrawing up the Bekaa after their defeat on 10 June, there were still many instances of Syrian units showing good discipline and retreating in good order under heavy pressure. The commandos in particular showed outstanding unit cohesion. In many fights they clung to their defensive positions until they were overpowered by elite Israeli infantry units, and in several clashes they fought to the last man to hold particularly important positions or when acting as rear guards to allow other forces to escape to safety.

SOURCES OF DEFEAT

The reasons for Syria's defeat in 1982, and for the partial nature of this defeat, are actually quite straightforward. Once again, the crucial factor was the limited capabilities of Syrian forces at the tactical level. In combat — regardless of the odds, the terrain, or any other factor — Syrian units simply could not defeat Israeli units of equal or lesser size. Other factors were largely either irrelevant or washed out in the balance, leaving only the differences in tactical proficiency to decide most of the engagements. For instance, Israel's considerable numerical advantage was more than compensated for by the advantage of defending Lebanon's rugged terrain. The IAF did not participate to a meaningful extent in many of the critical ground battles of the war, especially the defeat of the reinforced 1st Armored Division in the Bekaa Valley. Nor can more than partial blame be ascribed to the low state of readiness of most Syrian forces in Lebanon at the start of the campaign, for most of the real battles against the IDF were fought by Syrian commando battalions and by the 1st and 3d Armored Divisions, which not only were combat-ready units but also considered Damascus's elite formations.

Israel's victory over Syria was not more decisive due to a variety of reasons. First, credit must be given to the Syrian commandos, whose defensive skills allowed them to delay and hinder the Israeli armored columns in every way as they moved through the mountains. The terrain itself was, of course, another major factor. Lebanon's mountains allowed the Syrians to rely on ambushes rather than having to slug it out in maneuver battles with IDF armored divisions. This also greatly enhanced Syrian defensive capabilities, provided countless fall-back positions, and channeled Israeli movement, preventing the IDF from bringing its quantitative advantages to bear and hindering its ability to maneuver off-road and roll up Syrian ambush positions from the flank. Third, the IAF was mostly distracted by their desire to avenge their 1973 losses by annihilating the SAF and Syrian air defenses. In addition, Israeli strike aircraft had difficulty locating and targeting Syrian forces in the Lebanese terrain, and many of their airstrikes had little effect on dug-in Syrian forces in the mountains.

Probably the most important reason that Syria's defeat was not worse, however, was the erratic stop-and-go pace of the Israeli operation. Between the political constraints on the operation, the staggered mobilization and concentration of forces for the offensive, and the failure of IDF commanders to press the attack at key moments, the Israeli offensive was anything but a blitzkrieg. Every time the Israelis got going, they would just as suddenly slow to a halt. IDF units advanced in sudden leaps followed by long pauses. They would move forward, smash a Syrian position, and then halt in their tracks. These constant pauses gave the Syrians the opportunity to regroup, reinforce their positions, and establish new defensive lines that the Israelis then had to break through once more. Clearly, the most important instance of this problem was on 10 June, when the Bekaa Forces Group failed to aggressively pursue and destroy the fleeing 1st Armored Division. Although the Syrians were retreating in good order, there is no question that the Israelis could have caught them and—given the fact that the Syrians had been badly mauled when fighting from prepared positions against Israeli frontal attacks earlier in the day—probably obliterated the entire division. This would have allowed the IDF to seize the Beirut-Damascus highway and seal the route from Syria, thereby preventing the 3d Armored Division from ever making it into the Bekaa.[93]

Had the Israelis been able to conduct an all-out attack right from the start, there can be little doubt that the war would have been a much greater catastrophe for Syria. The ability of Syria's commandos to take advantage of the terrain suggests that the Israeli victory might not have been as lopsided as the defeat of the Egyptians in the Sinai in 1967, but it would have been very considerable.

The Syrian Military since 1982

Between 1982 and 1990, Syrian forces continued to participate in combat operations in Lebanon, occasionally against the Israelis, but mostly against various Lebanese militias as Syria struggled to reassert its dominion over the country. Unfortunately, little detailed information is available regarding the conduct of these engagements or the performance of Syrian troops in them. Similarly, Syria sent the 9th Armored Division and a brigade of commandos to participate in the coalition opposing Iraq in the Gulf War, but they were considered politically unreliable by Coalition military commanders, in part because Asad would not decide until the last minute whether he would allow them to participate in the ground offensive against Iraq. Consequently, they were assigned a reserve role and did not see combat. Still, a number of points can be made about the Syrian armed forces since the Israeli invasion of Lebanon.

The Syrians generally appear to have learned little from their experience against the Israelis. After the war, the Syrians lauded their own performance, in particular citing the courage and prowess of their commandos, while blaming their reverses on poor Soviet equipment and the omnipotent IAF.[94] The Soviets were greatly concerned and embarrassed by the swift Israeli destruction of their SAM systems, and after the ceasefire rebuilt Syria's air defense network, complete with new SA-5 strategic SAMs. In general, the primary Syrian reaction to the war was to acquire more, and more modern, Soviet weaponry like Su-24 strike aircraft, MiG-29 fighters, T-72 tanks, and advanced Soviet air-to-air missiles and ATGMs. Syria also expanded the size of its military establishment, adding seven new divisions and increasing its overall size to 400,000 men, 4,800 tanks, 4,150 APCs, 2,700 artillery pieces, 530 combat aircraft, and 250 SAM batteries.[95]

The Syrians have taken some steps to address their debilitating tactical deficiencies. They have made half-hearted efforts to improve training in combined-arms operations, maneuver warfare, and air-to-air combat. They also have tried, to some extent, to encourage junior officers to show initiative. But little has actually changed since 1982. Syrian exercises and operations are routinely described as "slow moving," "set piece," and "inflexible."[96] Syrian formations at all levels and in all services show little predilection for maneuvering in combat, and their tank crews and pilots are still considered poor and are not getting much better despite efforts to improve their training. Innovation and improvisation among junior officers remains rare.

Considerable difficulties continue for the Syrians in absorbing the masses of equipment they have purchased. Crews and pilots seem no more comfortable with their weapons than they have been in the past. Syria has not been able to train enough personnel to man most of its equipment, and well into the 1990s it had 1,000 tanks that lacked trained crews and a pilot-to-aircraft ratio of less than one to one and probably close to one to two (that is, two planes for every qualified pilot). Syrian maintenance has improved little if at all since 1982. As of the late 1990s, only two-thirds of their tanks were fully operational.[97]

The one positive sign is that, as they began to do after the 1973 war, the Syrians have slowly come to recognize their strengths and weaknesses and to try to emphasize the former and minimize the latter. They continue to concentrate on SAMs and AAA as their primary forms of air defense, recognizing that their poor abilities in dogfighting make it problematic to rely on the SAF for air cover. Damascus has built up a large and imposing arsenal of surface-to-surface missiles as a means of compensating for its inability to penetrate sophisticated air defense barriers (such as Israel's) with fixed-wing aircraft and the difficulties it has experienced in conducting ground-attack missions. The Syrians greatly improved the extent and depth of their defenses in front of Damascus to prevent a repeat of Israel's drive on the capital in 1973. Finally, they continue to try to expand their commando forces as the only really capable units in their army. Damascus now has a Special Forces Division (the 14th) — comprised of commando brigades — as well as seven independent commando brigades.

Summary: Syrian Military Effectiveness, 1948–91

In general, Syrian military effectiveness showed many of the same patterns of behavior as other Arab armed forces. On the positive side, the Syrians consistently demonstrated superb unit cohesion and individual bravery. Indeed, the Israelis always remarked on the ferocity and determination of Syrian soldiers and pilots. Syrian forces fought well in static defense roles and performed adequately when conducting set-piece operations.

On the negative side, Syrian forces regularly displayed problems in tactical leadership that hampered their conduct in freewheeling maneuver warfare. In particular, junior officers showed little initiative, improvisational ability, flexibility, or capability for independent action. Syrian chains of command were rigidly overcentralized, plagued by the compartmentalization of information, and skewed by bizarre command-and-control relationships and the constant reshuffling of senior commanders. Their skills in armored, artillery, air-to-air, and air-to-ground operations were miserable. Syria had tremendous difficulty assimilating new weaponry into its force structure, and its personnel never were able to take full advantage of the capabilities of their equipment. The Syrians also were hindered by poor maintenance and technical support. Their generalship varied significantly, although it was mostly mediocre. The one thing that must be said in defense of Syria's strategic leaders is that they mostly performed better than the forces under their command.

The only anomaly in this otherwise consistent pattern was the better performance of Syria's commandos in 1982 in many categories of tactical operations. In this case the improvement seems to have been a result of the elite nature of the service. The commandos were picked troops, given longer and more-demanding training, and with a strong sense of esprit de corps. As a result, the commandos, still a small force compared to the overall military, were able to develop marginally better skills in a number of important aspects of combat operations.

Syrian forces differed from their Arab brethren in at least two important areas of military effectiveness during the Middle Eastern wars since 1945. First, as noted above, Syrian forces were exceptionally courageous and evinced a tremendous amount of unit cohesion. Although all of the Arab armies could rightfully boast of the bravery of their soldiers, the Syrians stood out. Even in the chaos of their retreats from the Golan in 1967 and again in 1973, numerous Syrian formations gave the Israelis trouble with their stubborn, in many cases suicidal, defense of their strongpoints. While it is true that a fair number of Syrian formations disintegrated in 1967 after the announced fall of al-Qunaytarah, as many if not more hung together and either fought in place until overwhelmed or conducted fighting retreats back to Damascus. Likewise, in every war, Israeli pilots uniformly remarked that while Syrian pilots were usually less skillful than their Jordanian or even Egyptian compatriots, the Syrians were exceptionally tenacious and brave.

The second area of relatively unique Syrian performance was logistics, a military discipline they performed notably worse than the other Arab armies. Syrian forces were constantly hindered by the failures of their own supply trains. In particular, the constant drag on Syrian operations in Lebanon both in 1976 and 1982 from the inability of their logistical units to keep their combat formations supplied significantly influenced the conduct of these campaigns. Moreover, these problems seemed to occur in even the most basic aspects of logistics, such as understanding the central concept of a Soviet "push" system. Syria's logistical incompetence stands in marked contrast to the performance of the Libyans, Iraqis, and Egyptians, whose quartermaster corps always performed ably and on a number of occasions pulled off logistical miracles.

Finally, it is worth noting a dog that did not bark — at least not loudly —

in Syria's military history: politicization and the training, discipline, and command-and-control problems that it created. The Syrian military was — at times equaled by Iraq — often the most politicized and the least-prepared army in the Arab world. Nevertheless, its performance in combat was remarkably consistent with that of the other Arab militaries. The Syrians were often worse than their less-politicized Egyptian, Jordanian, and Iraqi counterparts, but only by a matter of degree. With the exception of Jordanian performance in 1948, none of the Arab armies performed that much better than the Syrians. In 1973 Egyptian forces had been significantly depoliticized and well prepared for war by the draconian policies of Nasser and Sadat, whereas Asad's depoliticization and preparations were a more modest effort. Nevertheless, Egyptian forces still fought only marginally better in the Sinai than the Syrians on the Golan. Moreover, a case can be made that although Syrian forces slipped deeply back into politicization after the October War, their performance in Lebanon in 1982 was somewhat better than their performance on the Golan in 1973. Thus, while politicization may have ebbed and flowed in Syria's armed forces, their performance remained more constant, and even compared to other, less politicized Arab armies, the Syrians did not fare particularly worse.

CONCLUSIONS AND LESSONS

Since 1945, few regions of the world have seen as much war as the Middle East. During this time, the armies and air forces of the Arab states have been involved in almost every type of military situation imaginable, from blitzkrieg offensives, to counterinsurgency campaigns, to wars of attrition and border clashes. This history reveals that the Arabs were not simply mindless buffoons who repeatedly butted their heads against one wall after another. Far from the undifferentiated lumps portrayed by some accounts of Middle Eastern wars, the Arab armed forces evolved in a number of ways in response to various influences. Some armies improved over time, others deteriorated. Some reached a peak of effectiveness — low in comparison to other armies though that may have been — only to lose their edge by over-reaching themselves in war or by neglect in peacetime. Some were forced to improve by ambitious leaders, others were emasculated by fearful ones.

The Arab militaries and their relationship to the larger Arab polities changed constantly throughout this era. Under the pressure of repeated failure, the Egyptian army was forced to become increasingly more professional. At the same time, Egypt's political leadership developed an ever more sophisticated approach to the use of military force in pursuit of its foreign policy goals. The product was Egypt's political victory in the October War and the eventual peace treaty with Israel. This in turn led to the gradual re-erosion of Egyptian military power that followed. The Jordanian army, by contrast, began the post–World War II era at the zenith of its military effectiveness but the next forty-three years it struggled to hang on to its proficiency even as the political leadership in Amman grew less and less inclined to use military force to secure foreign policy objectives. In contrast, the Iraqi armed forces rose from incompetence to become probably the most potent military ever wielded by an Arab government. But the arrogance that came with this strength prompted Baghdad to overreach itself in Kuwait, only to discover that, as much progress as the Iraqi military had made, it was still far from being able to fight a modern war against the United States and its European allies.

Nevertheless, while the Arab armies were far more active in their pursuit of greater success in war than most authors have acknowledged, certain other factors, which remained as constants throughout the modern era, limited the scope of that success. Of greatest importance, the Arabs labored under critical limitations on their combat effectiveness that proved to be insurmountable obstacles to their military operations. In the end, even the most brilliant Arab military leaders were able to do no more than skirt these problems and make political hay from the modest objectives that Arab armed forces were capable of attaining despite their difficulties. It is to the nature of these various weaknesses that we now must return.

Assessing Arab Military Ineffectiveness

In the opening pages of this book I set forth the question, what is it that has consistently hindered Arab militaries over the years and so diminished their fortunes on the battlefield? I then provided a number of explanations that veterans of the Middle East wars and military experts have proposed in answer to this question. So now — after having examined the experiences of the Egyptian, Iraqi, Jordanian, Libyan, Saudi, and Syrian armed forces in combat — the issue is, to what extent did the military history of these Arab states actually conform to the various explanations offered by the experts?

Given that each group of experts contends that their explanation is the "right" one, it is not surprising that many are not supported by the evidence of Arab military history. Several are clearly wrong, others clearly right, while still others appear to have identified a problem that did have some limited influence on Arab fortunes. Perhaps of greatest importance, as could only be expected of a problem as pervasive as Arab military ineffectiveness, history suggests that there is no single right answer but that several different factors combined to produce the general phenomenon.

Unit Cohesion

No ironclad pattern of unit cohesion emerges from the history of the Arab armies since 1948. Instead, the cohesiveness of Arab units has varied to a considerable degree not only from war to war and army to army but even within armies during the same war. There often was no particular way to tell beforehand which Arab formations would flee at the first shot and which would fight to the death. Nor was it always obvious after the fact why some units had fought and others had run. In 1956 a battalion of Egyptian infantry at Qusaymah collapsed when first attacked by the Israelis, while the rest of its brigade fought like lions to hold Abu Ageilah under repeated assaults by larger Israeli forces.

Nevertheless, although the evidence is not entirely consistent, the unit cohesion of Arab armies generally has more often been good than bad, and on many occasions it has been outstanding. The most prevalent pattern has been for Arab tactical formations to remain cohesive and combat effective even when placed in dire situations in which it would have been reasonable to expect the organization of any army to dissolve. The stand of the Iraqi Republican Guard, especially the Tawakalnah 'alla Allah Mechanized Division, against the U.S. VII Corps during the Gulf War; the repeated attacks by the Iraqi 6th Armored Brigade against Tel Antar in 1973; the Egyptian defense of Abu Ageilah and Umm Qatef in 1956 (and again in 1967); the Jordanian defenders of Ammunition Hill and many other positions around Jerusalem in 1967; the tenacious Syrian defense of Ayn Zhaltah, Jizzin, and the Bekaa Valley in 1982; and the determination of Libyan units to hang on in the Tibesti in 1987 all attest to the superb cohesion of Arab formations under extremely adverse conditions. There also have been instances of their units disintegrating under fairly light pressure — the Egyptians at Qusaymah in 1956, the Libyans at Lukuya in 1979, and the Jordanians in Hebron in 1967 come to mind — and while these cannot be written off as mere exceptions to the rule, it is nonetheless the case that this pattern has been considerably less prevalent than instances of Arab units holding up well (or even superbly) in difficult situations.

For the most part, Arab forces tended to fall apart in large numbers and without repeated pummeling only when they were ordered to conduct a general retreat and were faced with aggressive pursuit by their attackers. Thus, Egyptian forces in the Sinai in 1956 and 1967, Jordanian forces on the West Bank in 1967, Syrian forces on the Golan in 1967, Libyan forces at Oumchi and Aouzou in 1987, and Iraqi forces in Iran in 1981–82 began to collapse only after their army had begun to retreat and their escape routes were unexpectedly threatened or cut. By contrast, when Arab units were allowed to retreat without much pressure from an attacking force, and therefore were able to move slowly and deliberately, they tended to remain cohesive and effective. The retreat of Syrian forces in the Bekaa on 10 June 1982 and of Jordanian forces from the Vale of ar-Ramtha in 1970 were both occasions when an attacking force did not aggressively pursue a retreating Arab army, which then was able to fall back in reasonably good order. These patterns strongly suggest that it required the psychological blow of defeat and retreat, coupled with the tremendous difficulties Arab armed forces regularly experienced when attempting to quickly improvise unplanned combat operations, to cause large-scale loss of cohesiveness in Arab armies.

Consequently, one cannot blame poor unit cohesion for the consistent underachievement of Arab armed forces. In fact, quite the contrary is true: unit cohesion was probably more a strength of these armies than a weakness. In combat against an Arab force, an adversary must assume that Arab formations will attack repeatedly despite losses and prior defeats, and that they will defend a position ferociously. The Israelis had their most difficult fight when they assumed the opposite in 1956, and so they were mostly stymied when the Egyptians did not fold under their initial blows. The fact that the Israelis did eventually manage to turn the Egyptian flank, and probably would have eked out a victory even absent Cairo's decision to retreat after the Anglo-French invasion, does not diminish the point that underestimating the unit cohesion of Arab armies is a mistake.

Generalship

For the Arabs between 1945 and 1991, there was no consistent pattern of generalship, good or bad. Some of the men commanding their armies and air forces proved completely incompetent, at times to the ruin of the forces under their authority. But not all Arab generals have been inept political hacks, and even some of the political hacks turned out to be first-rate generals — such as Jordan's Field Marshal Bin Shakir and Iraq's Husayn Rashid Muhammad at-Tikriti. Yet neither have the Arabs produced a string of brilliant generals to rival twentieth-century Germany or any military geniuses of the caliber of Napoleon, Marlborough, and Alexander. Overall, Arab generalship fluctuated and their nations' fortunes, to some extent, fluctuated with it.

It is certainly true that in some Middle East wars Arab militaries were led by incompetent senior commanders who bear much of the responsibility for defeat. Iraq's generals planned and directed the invasion of Iran in 1980 about as poorly as is possible. Its senior commanders directing the war against the Kurds in the early 1960s, and to some extent against Israel in 1973, also turned in performances that were mediocre at best. Jordanian generals achieved a degree of negligence in conducting the initial "Black September" offensive against the PLO in 1970 that nearly cost King Hussein his throne. Saudi leadership after Iraq's invasion of Kuwait showed little understanding of how to plan or conduct military operations, and Riyadh was fortunate that its generals were not called on to block an Iraqi attack. Libyan direction of its air and air defense (and naval) forces against the

United States in the 1980s was comical to anyone but the soldiers, airmen, and sailors who died as a result of its amateurishness. Finally, Cairo's direction of the Egyptian defense of the Sinai during the Six Day War was abysmal, and Field Marshal 'Abd al-Hakim 'Amr's drug- or alcohol-induced behavior was only part of the problem.

In other wars Arab generals performed reasonably well, not necessarily paving the way to victory single handedly, but also not damning their armies to defeat. Syria's high command did a decent job in 1982 against Israel. On the one hand, their handling of the SAM units was fairly poor, but on the other hand, their response to the initial Israeli moves was entirely reasonable and rational. Iraqi and Egyptian generalship in Palestine in 1948 was fine, occasionally performing badly and occasionally well but mostly doing an adequate job. Likewise, by the late 1960s, Baghdad had figured out a strategy to beat the Kurds and developed a number of competent operations that probably could have resulted in victory if the tactical forces at its disposal had been more competent. Libyan generalship in Chad was mostly adequate, displaying sometimes more and sometimes less deftness with the forces at their disposal, though again mostly getting the job done. The one obvious exception was their insistence on conducting major operational-level counterattacks in 1987 even after it had become apparent that their plodding mechanized forces stood no chance in battle against the agile Chadians. The Egyptian high command did all that was asked of them in 1956, and most of their moves were eminently sensible. Jordanian scapegoating of Egyptian general 'Abd al-Mun'im Riyad aside, Amman's direction of the defense of the West Bank in 1967 was also reasonably good, and even those moves that ultimately proved harmful were based on creditable strategic thinking.

Finally, in some of their conflicts, Arab armies have been led by very competent senior commanders, but these generals were able to achieve only modest results because they were hamstrung by the poor performance of the forces under their command. Indeed, in these cases it has been the limited abilities of Arab tactical units that have hindered the achievements of their generals, not vice versa. Iraqi generalship against Iran in 1987–88, and to a slightly lesser extent in the Gulf War, probably deserved the highest praise, while Cairo's planning and direction of the War of Attrition and the October War were very good too. Jordan's generals did an excellent job organizing the defense of al-Karamah in 1968 and conducting the campaign against the PLO after the initial false start in September 1970. Their failure to employ proper counterinsurgency operations aside, Egyptian generals displayed considerable ability in the design and preparation of their conventional offensives in Yemen during the early 1960s. The Ramadan and Haradh offensives employed clever schemes of maneuver, they were well planned, and might have been very effective against a conventional foe. In addition, U.S. military personnel who have had contact with Jordanian, Egyptian, and Iraqi senior officers uniformly have expressed a high degree of respect for their professionalism and skill. In short, Arab generalship has run the gamut of quality, and no particular pattern of competence or incompetence is readily apparent.

Tactical Leadership

In contrast to the mixed performance of the generals over the years, Arab junior officers performed remarkably and consistently poorly between 1948 and 1991. Arab tactical commanders regularly failed to demonstrate initiative, flexibility, creativity, independence of thought, an understanding of combined-arms integration, or an appreciation for the benefits of maneuver in battle. These failings resulted in a dearth of aggressiveness, responsiveness, speed, movement, intelligence gathering, and adaptability in Arab tactical formations that proved crippling in every war they fought. Because this trait applies to all six of the Arab militaries examined in this study, and in virtually every war they fought, I will refrain from listing historical examples but will simply note the broad patterns.

Unimaginative and passive junior officers made it nearly impossible for the formations under their command to engage effectively in maneuver warfare, meeting engagements, ad hoc operations, or other forms of combat in which authority devolved upon the battlefield commanders. Arab forces were unable to adapt quickly to unforeseen events and were rarely able to improvise tactical solutions to unexpected problems. Their formations generally could not maintain a rapid pace of operations, and when on the defensive, their units rarely shifted forces to meet the enemy's thrust or counterattacked to seal off or smash an enemy penetration. On those occasions when they did do so, the units generally moved too slowly, and by the time they acted, the decisive moment had passed. The recurrent pattern among these armies was that once an enemy had broken through their lines and was threatening to roll them up from the flank, the Arab units would fight tenaciously from their existing positions but could not or would not reorient themselves to form a new line to prevent the reduction of their positions in detail. On the offensive, Arab forces usually attacked straight ahead with no thought given to potential threats or opportunities waiting elsewhere on the battlefield.

Arab tactical units were repeatedly defeated by enemy forces of equal or smaller size because they clung to doctrine or orders from above that had been overtaken by events and refused to act in response to the vicissitudes of combat. Junior officers also regularly failed to take advantage of opportunities in battle. All too often, their units remained passive for lack of orders, even when action might have staved off defeat. In addition, Arab militaries consistently centralized decision making at the highest levels of command. This helped create a vicious cycle in which senior officers were unwilling to delegate command authority to their subordinates, concerned that those men would be unable to properly exercise that responsibility, and when Arab junior officers did have command delegated to them — either on purpose or, more often, because of the chaos of battle — they performed so poorly that it confirmed their superiors' lack of confidence. Because few Arab officers at lower levels would move without orders from a higher echelon, their armies tended not to respond to battlefield developments until information had been passed up the chain of command for consideration and a decision had been passed back down in the form of specific orders. Consequently, there was little spontaneity in Arab military operations. Indeed, it was commonplace for even the most minor issues to be referred up the chain of command, overburdening the top leaders and further slowing reaction times. When attacking, this meant that Arab armies almost never were able to turn tactical success into strategic victory, and when defending, they were often just beginning to respond to a breakthrough (or even an initial attack) while the enemy had already transitioned to exploitation, pursuit, or consolidation of their victory.

Units in the field rarely attempted to gain an advantage over an adversary by active maneuvering. Consistently, Arab formations on the defensive stayed in their prepared positions and relied on firepower to defeat an attacker. When attacking, their armies likewise tended to rely solely on firepower and mass, employing either frontal assaults to simply overwhelm a defender or stand-off bombardments in which they attempted to obliterate defensive strongpoints through massive fire support before advancing. In particular, Arab armies employed their armored forces either like battering rams or mobile direct-fire artillery and almost never attempted to maneuver against an opponent for flank or rear shots. Similarly, Arab artillery units generally were only able to conduct preplanned fire missions and proved incapable of rapidly and accurately shifting fire, conducting counterbattery missions, concentrating fire from geographically separate batteries, or providing on-call fire support in a timely or accurate fashion. As a result of these problems, whenever Arab forces became involved in fluid battles—and were most in need of fire support because of their difficulties fighting such actions—their artillery was incapable of delivering.

Arab armies generally displayed very poor combined-arms coordination. Their junior officers generally had little understanding of how to integrate the various combat arms even if they did recognize the need for them to operate in unison. It was regularly the case that Arab armor charged into battle without any infantry support. Likewise, mechanized infantry frequently did not dismount to eliminate antitank units—even in difficult terrain or when they knew they were opposed by dug-in infantry with such weapons—but remained buttoned up in their APCs. Arab artillery could not, and at times would not, support maneuvering units in battle beyond their initial preparatory barrages. Combat engineers and other specialized support troops were often an afterthought to commanders and only rarely integrated into the scheme of an attack. Finally, as limited as combined-arms coordination among Arab ground forces was, it was that much worse between their ground and air forces, which invariably had to fight their own separate wars because they could not fight together.

The same problems plaguing Arab ground forces also hindered the effectiveness of their air forces. In all kinds of missions, most Arab pilots proved to be rigid, unaggressive, unimaginative flyers who could only employ simplistic tactics. They had poor situational awareness, and if they did react to circumstances, they usually did so too slowly to make a difference. Arab fighter pilots mostly demonstrated poor dogfighting skills and fared badly in air-to-air engagements. Arab air force units frequently were defeated by smaller, more competent, adversaries. Even against mediocre opponents, such as those the Iraqis faced in the Iranian air force, Arab air forces were able to prevail in aerial combat only when they enjoyed a heavy advantage in numbers. Pilots often could not react to unexpected moves by their adversaries and instead kept doing what they had been doing even after it became clear that their adversary was moments from converting the kill. They were heavily reliant on ground-controlled intercept guidance, and most could not function without it.

The performance of Arab air forces in air-to-ground missions was as bad as or even worse than their performance in air-to-air combat. At the most basic level, their airstrikes rarely put ordnance on targets. Such attacks were inadequately reconnoitered, often haphazardly planned, simplistic, and dangerous. Arab pilots showed little ability to make last-minute adjustments to bring their weapons on target and had great difficulty adapting to unforeseen developments. They also generally did not employ independent judgment as to the value of different targets, striking only those they were ordered to while leaving higher-value targets untouched. Arab close air-support missions achieved little, taking too long to approve, plan, and execute to be of benefit; remaining under the control of the air force high command rather than the local ground commander, who was best positioned to know against what and where to direct the airstrike; and failing to do much damage to the targets they did attack.

There were a few noteworthy exceptions to these overall tactical patterns. The Egyptian and Iraqi (and to a much lesser extent, Syrian) armed forces learned to conduct limited, set-piece operations employing surprise and overwhelming numbers that were extensively scripted and rehearsed until the participating units could execute their missions by rote. In these operations the Egyptians and Iraqis displayed limited maneuver, a reasonable synchronization of effort, and a crispness of action, not to mention much better combined-arms integration than at any other time. Similarly, the Jordanian armed forces of 1948, and to a decreasing extent since then, demonstrated higher levels of initiative, improvisation, flexibility, alacrity, combined-arms ability, and use of maneuver at tactical levels. The same could be said of Syria's commandos after 1976 and Iraq's Republican Guard after 1986, although neither ever achieved the levels of tactical proficiency of the Arab Legion. Finally, the Royal Jordanian Air Force, Saudi Arabia's F-15 pilots, and Iraq's Mirage F-1 pilots demonstrated better flying skills than their Arab counterparts.

In every one of these cases, however, the exceptions prove the rule. Egyptian and Iraqi success in 1973 and 1986–90 respectively (and Syrian success in 1973) were derived largely from the fact that the extensive scripting and rehearsals of their operations essentially relieved their junior officers of the need to make command decisions — they simply had to execute detailed orders. Cairo's and Baghdad's competent general staffs wrote maneuver, combined arms, and all other necessary combat activities into the operations orders, and as long as the forces under their command were asked only to implement these plans, they were fine. Even then, they required force ratios as great as ten to one in their favor plus the element of surprise to ensure that their operations were successful. The proof, of course, was whenever they either ran out of script or their enemy forced them to deviate from it. For the Egyptians and Syrians in 1973 and the Iraqis in 1988–91, their tactical forces immediately reverted back to the same patterns of ineffectiveness as in the past, with little trace of the efficiency they had demonstrated just days before.

Jordan's Arab Legion of 1948, however, owed its superior performance largely to its British officer corps as well as to intensive British training, the small size of the legion (which allowed them to select only the finest soldiers and officers), and its long terms of service (which allowed them to keep those men and thoroughly train them in the British manner). Some of these same factors were responsible for improving the Syrian commandos and the Iraqi Republican Guard, which comprised the best soldiers in their respective armies — men who had proven their skills in combat — and benefited from being (relatively) small and elite formations with extensive training. Likewise, the pilots of the Royal Jordanian Air Force, Saudi Arabia's F-15 squadrons, and Iraq's Mirage F-1 squadrons were the cream of their societies (standards for fighter pilots were extremely high, and those for the elite units even higher) and were provided with very extensive training in Britain, the United States, and France, respectively. Once again, what is ultimately most interesting is how modest the increased effectiveness of these various forces were over the Arab norm despite the extensive measures taken to try to boost their prowess.

Information Management

All of the Arab militaries suffered from problems in the flow of information all along the chain of command. A tendency to compartmentalize information was in evidence in all of these forces to a greater or lesser extent. Officers often saw knowledge as a form of power, allowing them to enforce their authority over their subordinates and gain leverage over their peers. Consequently, information was often hoarded, and key intelligence frequently was not conveyed to those most in need of it because whoever was responsible for collecting or disseminating it failed to do so.

A constant among Arab armed forces during this period was consistently exaggerated and even falsified reporting by military personnel to higher echelons. Simultaneously, superior officers routinely withheld information about operations from their subordinates. These reinforcing tendencies meant that Arab forces routinely operated in a thick fog of ignorance and half-truths. Lower echelons sent inaccurate reports to strategic commanders, who then made plans based on this misinformation. Since the higher authorities rarely provided all available information to lower formations, many units had to execute operations with little knowledge of the enemy, the terrain, or the larger mission. Field units then either had to try to execute the operation — which often was suicidal because of the limited and inaccurate information available to the planners — or to lie and report that they did perform it when they had not.

Intelligence was another persistent problem of Arab militaries. Intelligence services in these nations frequently made little effort to collect information on their adversaries, even unclassified information that could be gathered from press reports and the military literature. Analysis was frequently skewed or superficial, and distribution of intelligence was badly inadequate, to some extent because of the compartmentalization of information, both formal and informal. Consequently, Arab armies often went into battle with little understanding of the order of battle, organization, infrastructure, plans, or tactical doctrine of their enemy.

At tactical levels, Arab armies did uniformly poorly because junior officers rarely patrolled their defensive sectors or their routes of advance. Indeed, on many occasions Arab tactical commanders even failed to deploy security screens, observation posts, or listening posts in front of their night laagers or defensive lines. Arab commanders at platoon through brigade level generally relied on information passed down from superiors rather than attempting to find out for themselves what was over the next hill. Among the more egregious examples of this problem are the failure of Saudi units to reconnoiter the Iraqi positions at R'as al-Khafji; the dearth of patrols by Iraqi forces in the October War, the Iran-Iraq War, and the Gulf War; the reliance of the Libyans on Toubou scouts for reconnaissance in Chad, and Libya's inability to properly reconnoiter for themselves after Goukouni's men abandoned them in early 1987; the failure of many Iraqi units in the Gulf War and nearly all Libyan units during the wars in Chad to deploy security screens; and the failure of Egyptian forces in October 1973 to patrol their defensive sectors, which allowed the Israelis to split the Second and Third Armies and cross over to the west bank of the Suez Canal.

The paucity of reliable information flowing upward from tactical units was only one liability for Arab strategic intelligence. Arab air forces flew inadequate — and often misdirected — reconnaissance missions and their intelligence services produced little in terms of human reporting. Numerous generals must be faulted for failing to appreciate the importance of proper intelligence. In most cases little was collected because little was requested by the senior planners and operators. For example, before the Six Day War, Field Marshal 'Amr ignored developments in the Israeli military and concentrated Egypt's intelligence services on affairs within the army and the bureaucracy. In addition, intelligence collected by Arab military forces and intelligence services was frequently distorted at the highest levels to conform to the preconceived notions of the regime. Syrian intelligence, in particular, frequently suffered from all of these problems, contributing significantly to the humiliations on the Golan in 1967, in Lebanon in 1976, and in the air over the Bekaa in 1982.

There were several important exceptions to this rule. On a number of occasions, particularly competent Arab generals or command staffs recognized the importance of having adequate information about their adversaries and directed comprehensive efforts to gather and analyze intelligence on the enemy, often producing useful results. The Egyptian intelligence effort prior to the October War was the best example of this, but Syria's intelligence campaign in 1973 and Iraqi preparations for the 1988 offensives against Iran and the 1990 invasion of Kuwait were also quite thorough. Likewise, Jordanian intelligence correctly predicted both the broad outlines of the Israeli invasion of the West Bank in 1967 and their attack on al-Karamah in 1968, while Egyptian intelligence in 1956 had a fairly good understanding of what the original British-French invasion plan would look like — although they were crossed up by the sudden Allied decision to change invasion sites.

In most of these cases, the difference appears to have been largely the product of a political decision to bring in competent generals who then insisted on a more professional intelligence effort. The orders and inspiration for these intelligence campaigns came from the highest echelons and were a dramatic break from past behavior. The general staff essentially had to order its subordinates to conduct these missions and had to order its intelligence services to objectively assess the data being collected. However, it is also true that, in every case, these changes remained concentrated at senior levels and had little or no influence on intelligence gathering at tactical levels. The most successful Arab intelligence campaigns relied primarily on strategic assets: spies, aerial reconnaissance, liaison, and technical collection methods such as signals intelligence. In other words, the military high command employed the intelligence gathering assets at its disposal to collect the needed information rather than relying on their tactical forces to gather it. Perhaps the best example of this was the Iraqi General Staff in the latter half of the Iran-Iraq War, which became heavily dependent on military intelligence provided by the two superpowers for the planning of their operations.

Technical Skills and Weapons Handling

Soldiers and officers of the Arab armed forces experienced persistent and debilitating difficulties employing modern weapons in military operations throughout 1948–91. They required long periods of time to learn how to use the new weapons and other equipment, in many cases longer than other third-world personnel. Even then, with only a few exceptions, Arab armies and air forces were unable to take full advantage of the technology at their disposal. They rarely were able to employ the more advanced capabilities of their weapons and often used sophisticated weapons in unsophisticated fashions. Even when their equipment should have given them a commanding advantage over an adversary, they frequently found themselves beaten in the very area of military operations in which their equipment was so dominant. For example, Jordanian Patton tanks were far superior to the Shermans employed by the IDF on the West Bank in 1967, but with the exception of the 40th Armored Brigade, the Jordanians were repeatedly defeated in armor battles. Indeed, a particularly harmful aspect of this problem was that Arab marksmanship was often poor, and they were frequently outshot by their opponents. Consequently, even when they had a significant advantage in the range, accuracy, or power of their guns, they often lost artillery, armor, rifle, and aircraft duels. For instance, in the Gulf War many Iraqi Republican Guard batteries employed the G-5 or GHN-45 howitzer, probably the finest artillery piece in the world at the time. Although the G-5 had greater range, precision, and firepower than any of the Coalition howitzers, Republican Guard units lost every counterbattery duel they engaged in with U.S. batteries employing the M-109 howitzer.

The general dearth of technical skills among Arab military personnel also limited the number of sophisticated weapons systems their armed forces could effectively field. The best example of this was the poor pilot-to-aircraft ratio of all of the Arab air forces, which limited the number of warplanes that they could muster at any given time. These air forces were rarely able to sustain even a one-to-one pilot-to-aircraft ratio, and there were numerous examples of worse ratios. For instance, the Egyptian Air Force in 1956 had only 30 pilots for its 120 MiGs, a one to four ratio. Libya had only 25 trained pilots for its 110 Mirages in 1973, and four years later had only 150 pilots for the 550 aircraft in its air force. Indeed, the Egyptians essentially accepted after the Six Day War that it was impossible for them to train more than about 30 pilots a year despite their population of 30 million people. These problems were not just limited to the air forces: the Libyans have never been able to train crews for more than about one-third of the tanks in their arsenal, while the Syrians have crews for only two-thirds of their armored vehicles.

The result of these problems was that Arab armies and air forces with advanced — even state-of-the-art — equipment often were defeated by adversaries possessing less-advanced — even primitive — weapons because the

Arab armies got so little out of their equipment. The defeat of heavily armed Libyan forces first by the Tanzanians in Uganda in 1979 and then by the Chadians in 1986–87 are good examples of this, but there were many others. The Israeli Haganah was outgunned by all of the various Arab national armies that invaded Palestine in May 1948. Similarly, Egyptian forces in the Sinai in 1956 were better armed than the IDF, and the same was true to a lesser extent in 1967.[1] By the end of the Iran-Iraq War, the Iraqis held a huge advantage in the sophistication of the weapons at their disposal compared to their Iranian foes but rarely could make this advantage count. The Patton tanks, M-113s, and U.S. and British artillery of the Jordanian army defending the West Bank in 1967 were more advanced and capable than the Sherman tanks, M-3 halftracks, and old French howitzers of the Israeli forces that routed them in just two days. Finally, the Saudi forces that participated in the battle of R'as al-Khafji and Operation Desert Storm got little advantage from their advanced Western M-60A3 tanks, V-150 Commando armored cars, M-113 APCs, and TOW antitank missiles, even though they were fighting Iraqi forces armed with obsolete Soviet and Chinese T-55 and Type-59 tanks, MTLB and Type-63 APCs, BTR-60 armored cars, and Sagger antitank missiles.

Logistics and Maintenance

The Arab capability to sustain forces in battle presented a very mixed picture. On the one hand, most Arab militaries performed quite well in terms of formal logistical tasks like the provisioning and movement of combat units and supplies. On the other hand, Arab armed forces uniformly experienced severe difficulties in terms of maintenance and repair of military equipment. This disjuncture is odd since there is some overlap in the skills needed to perform both properly.[2]

Logistics appears to be a strength of most Arab forces. By and large, Arab armies and air forces did not suffer in combat because they lacked ammunition, food, water, fuel, lubricants, medical supplies, repair tools, spare parts, or other combat consumables. Quartermasters generally did at least an adequate job of assuring that their combat formations got the provisions they needed to do the job. Similarly, it was generally the case that the armed forces did not suffer from inadequate lift. Supply and transportation units performed very competently at moving large combat formations and their necessary support and supplies.

Nevertheless, there was considerable variance among the six nations. The Egyptian, Libyan, and Iraqi armed forces performed well in most aspects of logistical operations. Their forces were never hindered by inadequate or incompetent logistical support, and in a number of wars their combat-service support performed brilliantly. The deployment and provisioning of 70,000 Egyptian troops in Yemen for five years was no mean feat, while the logistical requirements of the 1973 crossing of the Suez were truly daunting — and the fact that Egyptian forces suffered only very minor problems in this operation has to be considered a very impressive achievement. The Libyan armed forces did remarkably well moving and sustaining brigade, division, and larger formations in Uganda and Chad, thousands of miles from the main Libyan military-support infrastructure. Similarly, Iraqi logisticians performed extremely well moving and maintaining a reinforced corps in combat with the Israelis in southwestern Syria in 1973 and in meeting all the sustainment needs of a million-man army for eight years during the war with Iran. Even during the Gulf War, not only were Iraqi logistics more than adequate to sustain a very rapid advance over 150 kilometers to conquer Kuwait but also, prior to the start of the Coalition air campaign, Baghdad had relatively little difficulty moving and sustaining an army in excess of 500,000 men in the challenging logistical conditions of Kuwait and southwestern Iraq.[3] The Iraqi case highlights some of the perplexities of this pattern of behavior. Despite the rigidity, overcentralization, and lack of imagination that pervaded every other aspect of the Iraqi military, Baghdad's quartermasters demonstrated surprising flexibility in manipulating their hybrid logistical system.

Although the quartermasters of the Saudi and Jordanian armed forces never achieved the same kinds of logistical coups as their Egyptian, Iraqi, and Libyan counterparts, neither were Saudi and Jordanian forces impeded by logistical difficulties. With the exception of Glubb's shortage of ammunition at the start of the 1948 fighting — quickly set right during the course of the war — Jordanian armed forces were never fettered by inadequate supplies. Of course, they never really asked much of their logisticians either. The Jordanian army never fought far from home, nor did it engage in high-intensity combat for long periods of time. Essentially the same can be said for the Saudis. Since they left their logistical support to foreigners, it cannot be said that the Saudis themselves have been unable to support their own operations: they have never tried, and so it is impossible to judge for certain the extent of their logistical capabilities. Of course, most outside observers would likely comment that the Jordanians have demonstrated a competence that suggests they would have done just as well as the Iraqis or Libyans if given the opportunity, whereas the Saudis have shown no particular indication they would have been capable of taking over their logistics system had they wanted to.

There were also some Arab services that suffered significant logistical problems. First, the Syrian armed forces consistently suffered from debilitating logistical problems. Syria's war effort in 1948 was hampered by inadequate provisions and the need to decide which of its two thrusts would get the provisions to keep fighting and which would have to dig in and wait. The Syrian invasion of Lebanon was constantly hamstrung by a logistical system that could not keep pace with ground forces moving at a snail's pace. Similarly, some units in Lebanon in 1982 were hampered by inadequate supplies (although reinforcements moved very quickly and efficiently after the start of the Israeli offensive). To a certain extent, these problems can be attributed to the failure of Syrian personnel to understand their Soviet "push" logistical system. To a lesser extent, they can also be tied to the endemic graft that had infected the Syrian army in Lebanon. But the forces that invaded in 1976 had not had the opportunity to delve into Lebanese graft, nor did the army in 1948 employ a Soviet-style system. Consequently, these explanations can only be taken so far.

Second, most of the Arab air forces—even among those countries that otherwise enjoyed good military logistics—suffered from significant support problems. The Egyptian, Iraqi, Libyan, and Syrian air forces all had low sortie rates throughout their history. It took long periods of time for their ground crews to service aircraft for further flight operations. Overall, the sortie rates for these air forces averaged less than one per day per aircraft. At times, armorers sent these aircraft off with the wrong ordnance for the missions they were to perform. Of course, some blame for this must also be accorded to air force planners, who may have specified the wrong type of ordnance in their orders, or to air-unit commanders, who may not have checked to see that the planes were armed with the appropriate munitions. Arab aircraft frequently were not checked out properly and were sent off with serious problems that later forced them to abort their missions. Arab aircraft were routinely "dead-lined" for long periods of time because of rather simple problems. Only Jordan did not suffer from these problems.

A considerable part of the inability of Arab air forces to sustain even average sortie rates has to do with the shoddy maintenance practices found in all of the Arab militaries, except possibly Jordan's. Most of the armed forces had a poor track record of keeping their weapons, vehicles, and other equipment up and running. Most Arab soldiers and officers showed little appreciation for the need to attend to their equipment, with the result that units generally had operational readiness rates of 50–67 percent; rates greater than 70–80 percent were rare in Arab units, while rates as low as 25–30 percent were not. Combat units had too few personnel capable of repair work, requiring them to perform even the most minor repairs at large central depots. In addition, the personnel manning these repair depots were often foreigners: Cubans, Russians, East Germans, Czechs, Americans, Pakistanis, British, and Indians dominated the maintenance and repair facilities of Arab armies and air forces.

One of the significant advantages Israel had over its Arab adversaries was that Israeli tank crews had high levels of technical skill and were able to quickly repair most minor problems themselves. In addition, Israel had a large armored-vehicle recovery and repair capability that allowed it to quickly repair even badly damaged tanks and return them to combat. Arab armies displayed the opposite tendency. Crews abandoned vehicles on the field of battle because of relatively minor problems; few were recovered, and those that were sent to a maintenance base for repair rarely returned to the front in a timely fashion.

An explanation for the contradiction between Arab success in logistics and simultaneous failure at maintenance does not spring readily to mind. Many of the same kinds of skills are required to perform both. The same is also true for the sustainment of ground and air operations, although the finer tolerances and greater sophistication of jet aircraft mean that air forces require even higher levels of maintenance and logistical support than tanks and other ground force equipment. For the most part, a military that can perform at a high level in sustaining ground operations should be able to do at least reasonably well for air operations. It is mysterious that a military such as Iraq's could do so well in supporting its ground forces and so poorly with its air forces. It is stranger still that this would be the case for three of the six Arab states examined. If it were only one, one might write off the discrepancy to peculiarities of the unique national system, but this same trend across half the countries in the survey is odd. More normal are the patterns of Jordan—which generally appears to have performed adequately in both areas—and Syria—which performed poorly in both.

Morale

The morale of Arab armies fluctuated from war to war and army to army. There have been wars in which Arab soldiers and officers had little inclination to fight right from the start. The Iraqi armed forces were apprehensive about fighting the United States well before Operation Desert Storm commenced. Likewise, the Egyptian armed forces at the start of the Egyptian-Israeli War of Attrition were still badly demoralized from their defeat during the Six Day War. To a certain extent, Egyptian soldiers were frustrated, apathetic, and disaffected even before the Six Day War—in part because of the weeks spent wandering around the Sinai while 'Amr and Nasser decided whether they were going to fight Israel, and in part because of the neglect of Egyptian enlisted personnel shown by their officers. Nevertheless, there have been other wars in which the Arab armies were totally committed to their cause. For instance, Egyptian and Syrian forces were extremely motivated for the October War, all of the Arab armies were enthusiastic about going into Palestine in 1948 to reclaim land they believed rightfully belonged to the Arabs, and Libyan troops were motivated to fight for the Aouzou Strip in Chad because they believed it was Libyan territory that had been taken from them years earlier. In addition, there were any number of instances in which Arab morale declined precipitously during the course of a war in response to a bad turn in the fighting.

What emerges from history is that when Arab armies have had poor morale, it has hurt them, and when they have had high morale, it has helped them, though not that much. Egyptian forces in October 1973 were nearly in a frenzy when their offensive finally began, and their motivation was an important factor in their success of 6–10 October. However, their morale was equally high on 14 October — perhaps even higher given the stunning victories they had achieved the previous week — when several of the best units in the Egyptian army put in a remarkably inept performance against the IDF. Likewise, Egyptian forces were thoroughly dispirited in 1968 at the start of the War of Attrition, but this had little effect on the course of that war. Indeed, neither the demoralization from their disastrous defeat in the Six Day War nor their daily drubbings at the hands of Israeli Mirages and Phantoms appears to have weakened the fervor of Egyptian pilots to come to grips with the Israeli Air Force. Even when Arab morale was high, their armies were able to achieve little militarily and remained ineffective as combat forces. For example, the determination of Syrian troops to retake the Golan in 1973 counted for little in terms of their actual combat effectiveness, which remained miserable. Syrian forces were highly motivated for the war, but they were very bad at fighting. Ultimately, the fact that they did not fight well was far more important to the outcome than the fact that they fought so hard.

As a final note, it is interesting that estrangement between officers and enlisted men does not appear to have been as bothersome as many authors have suggested. Problems between officers and their men have the greatest effect on morale, discipline, and unit cohesion. Arab armies that suffered from this personnel stratification did not always suffer from these resultant problems. Moreover, even in those cases where both were present, it was not always the case that poor morale, discipline, and unit cohesion were the product of poor officer-enlisted relations. For example, the Syrian military on the Golan in 1967 suffered from rather severe problems between officers and enlisted personnel: for the last twenty years, Syrian officers had paid little attention to their men, considering the preparation of their units for combat irrelevant to their own professional-political ambitions. However, in combat, Syrian forces showed no lack of commitment, discipline, or cohesiveness. Although there were some units that melted away even before Israeli forces came near them, far more stayed in place and fought hard even when their positions were hopeless and their officers had abandoned them. This is not to suggest that poor officer-enlisted relations were not harmful — imagine how much better the Syrians would have fought if their officers had properly trained their men and stayed with them in the fight — only that the harm appears to have been less than often claimed. Arab armies have suffered from having poor officer-enlisted relations but have not suffered excessively from it, and it never proved the difference between victory or defeat.

Training

There were essentially two questions this study sought to answer about the training of Arab armies. First, did Arab militaries spend their time preparing to fight other armies and air forces, or did they concentrate mainly on preserving internal security so that when they were thrown into a war against a foreign power, each was totally unready for the experience? Second, did they take the task of preparing for war seriously, or was their training lax and haphazard? The first question addresses the explanation offered by some Middle East experts that the Arabs did poorly in battle because their armies mostly concentrated on internal-security matters, preparing little for conventional military operations, and so performed poorly because they were being asked to perform a mission they were never taught to conduct. The second assesses the claim of others that Arab problems in combat stem from the fact that their forces simply did not train diligently or "seriously" for any kinds of military threats — external or internal.

In both cases the historical evidence is somewhat mixed. At some points, in some armies, training was lackadaisical and largely neglected. For instance, until the Gulf War, the Royal Saudi Land Forces never made training a major consideration, and what training they did was infrequent and perfunctory. In some cases Arab militaries trained little because their officers were more interested in maneuvering for political position and were not rewarded for preparing troops for battle. The Syrian army suffered from these sorts of distractions throughout the 1950s and 1960s. However, other Arab militaries were extremely diligent about training and exercises. While their instruction was not always terribly effective, it was rigorous and constant. After 1986, Iraq's Republican Guard trained constantly in mechanized combined-arms operations. Likewise, the incredible rigor of Egyptian training between 1967 and 1973 is attested to by the fact that their armed forces practiced the entire crossing of the Suez thirty-five times, and individual units rehearsed their specific roles hundreds, if not thousands, of times. Even the Syrian military made a conscious effort to be diligent about training for war after Asad took power in 1971 and began to prepare his forces for an offensive against Israel.

Nevertheless, a clear pattern does emerge from Arab military history regarding military training that contradicts both claims regarding its role on Arab fortunes since 1945. Most—the Egyptians, Syrians, Iraqis, and to some extent the Saudis—neglected proper training at first, and what little they did often was directed at internal security. But as time went on, all of them became increasingly diligent and serious about preparation for war with foreign foes. For most Arab armies, defeat in the War of Israeli Independence was a rude awakening, resulting in the overthrow of governments and a determination to rebuild their military power to be able to defeat Israel. Although this process took a decade or more, by the 1970s all of the Arab militaries were very professional in their devotion to rigorous and frequent training for conventional military operations. This shift in the emphasis and focus of military training produced only a very modest improvement in Arab performance, however. The same problems continued to haunt their militaries regardless of the extent to which they concentrated on external, not internal, security operations and no matter how diligent they were about training exercises.

There were two exceptions to this rule. One was the Jordanians who, unlike the other Arab armies, conducted rigorous training right from the start because of the tutelage of Glubb and the other British officers from the mandate era. Similarly, even though one of the original Arab Legion's responsibilities was suppressing tribal dissent against King Abdullah's rule, the British made sure that the legion constantly trained for conventional operations against foreign armies. Indeed, Jordanian training may have deteriorated somewhat after the departure of the British, unlike the other Arab armies, whose attention to training increased over time. The other exception was the Libyans, whose training practices remained moribund from start to finish. Their formations were excessively fixated on internal security, with the exception of the latter 1980s, when the war in Chad forced Tripoli to focus its training practices somewhat more on conventional operations. Similarly, the rampant politicization of the Libyan military meant that training often was neglected by its officers, who had little reason to care whether their units were battle ready.

These patterns strongly indicate that diligent training for conventional war against external adversaries was not one of the more important problems hindering the Arabs in combat. The fact that they learned to concentrate their militaries on training for conventional war and that they trained diligently for these wars, though these labors produced such modest results, indicates that the emphasis and rigor of their training were not the primary problems. The exceptions of Jordan and Libya lend further support to this conclusion. The Jordanians never suffered from these problems to the same extent as the other Arab states, and they did enjoy better military effectiveness than the others. Likewise, the Libyans never improved their training practices and clearly performed even worse than the others in battle. But what is most noteworthy is just how relative these distinctions were. The Jordanians were better than the Egyptians, Iraqis, and Syrians, but not by much. Likewise, the Libyans were worse than the Egyptians, Iraqis, and Syrians, but not by much. In comparing the Jordanian army of 1967, the Iraqi Republican Guard of the late 1980s and early 1990s, and the Libyan army of the 1980s, definite differences emerge: the Jordanians were better than the Iraqis, who were better than the Libyans. However, the Jordanians were still a mediocre military force. The Libyans were incompetent, but not that much more incompetent than the Iraqis. Perhaps of greatest importance, all three forces demonstrated the same crippling problems in the areas of tactical leadership, information management, and technical skills. These problems remained constants for Arab armies no matter how hard they trained. Indeed, even when Arab armies trained specifically to overcome these problems — as the Iraqis did in the late 1980s — they had almost no success. Clearly then, something else was at work among Arab armies and air forces beyond simply inadequate training.

Cowardice

Arab military history demonstrates that of all the problems experienced by the Arabs in combat since 1945, a pervasive cowardice has *not* been among them — it puts the lie to the slanders of those who have dismissed the Arabs as cowardly soldiers. Of course, one can point to any number of incidents in which individual soldiers, officers, or even entire units behaved in a less than valorous manner. However, this is true for every army. Even the Japanese army of World War II had its share of cowards. The key questions are how widespread was such behavior, was it more prevalent than courageous performances, and how much did acts of cowardice affect Arab fortunes? On each count the historical evidence demonstrates that Arab armies performed creditably, if not meritoriously. There are countless anecdotal accounts of soldiers and officers sacrificing their own safety for their comrades or their mission, and their opponents generally credited them with staunch (although not necessarily skillful) resistance.

On the offensive, Arab forces routinely charged into murderous fire and kept up their attacks even when mauled by their adversaries. This was evinced by the Iraqis against the Israelis in southwestern Syria in 1973, by the Syrians at Red Ridge in 1973, by the Syrian Air Force over Lebanon in 1982, by the Libyans at Aouzou in 1987, and by the Saudis at R'as al-Khafji in 1991. On the defensive Arab units often fought ferociously from their positions, even long after they had been outflanked, bypassed, or otherwise effectively neutralized — as was the case with Jordanian defenders of the West Bank in 1967 and at al-Karamah in 1968; Libyan forces in the Tibesti in 1987; Egyptian forces in the Fallujah pocket in 1948, at the Mitla Pass and Abu Ageilah in 1956, at Rafah, Khan Yunis, Abu Ageilah, Umm Qatef, and the Jiradi Pass in 1967, and at the Chinese Farm and Ismailia in 1973; Iraqi forces at al-Basrah in 1982 and again in 1987; and Syrian forces on the Golan in 1967 and in Lebanon in 1982. Arab rear guards, when they were employed, usually fought hardest of all, sacrificing themselves to see that the rest of their armies escape safely. Egyptian forces at Jebel Libni and B'ir Gifgafah in 1967 and the stand of the Republican Guard against the U.S. VII Corps in 1991 attest to the willingness of Arab rear guards to do their duty even when it meant their destruction. Indeed, what is truly noteworthy about the Iraqi performance in the Gulf War is not that 200,000–400,000 deserted or surrendered immediately to Coalition ground forces, but that after thirty-nine days of constant air attack, the destruction of their logistical distribution network, their lack of commitment to the cause, and their clear inferiority to Coalition forces, another 100,000–200,000 Iraqi troops actually stood their ground.

What Were the Most Important Factors Shaping Arab Military Fortunes?
So why did Arab armies and air forces perform relatively poorly in every war they fought since 1948? There are at least three purported explanations — cowardice, poor unit cohesion, and poor logistics — that were simply not problems for the Arab militaries. Although some soldiers and officers were cowardly in battle, the majority of Arab military personnel demonstrated impressive degrees of self-sacrifice and personal bravery. Although there were units that melted under the slightest pressure, it was

more often the case that Arab formations had to be defeated in detail even long after their situation had become hopeless. Similarly, with the exception of the Syrians (and potentially the Saudis), the Arab armies demonstrated a capacity to move and sustain their forces in battle. Ultimately, far from being sources of ineffectiveness, logistics, unit cohesion, and personal bravery would have to be considered among the strengths of the Arab armed forces.

Another set of issues emerged as secondary problems for the Arabs. Poor morale, poor generalship, and inadequate training were clearly contributing factors to the ineffectiveness of their armies and air forces, but these cannot be considered major influences. None of these problems was a constant for the Arabs. There were times when Arab armies began a war thoroughly demoralized, and other times when they began it highly motivated. There were times when Arab armies neglected their training or trained for the wrong missions; but there were also other times when they diligently and rigorously prepared for exactly the sort of missions they were called on to perform when war came. Likewise, there were times when Arab militaries were commanded by incompetent political hacks, and others when they were commanded by highly competent professionals. Every time these problems were present, they did affect Arab fortunes in battle. However, when they were not present, Arab military effectiveness remained quite poor. This indicates that while these issues were part of the overall pattern of postwar Arab military ineffectiveness, they were not the principal driving forces behind it.

Four areas of military effectiveness stand out as consistent and crippling problems for Arab forces: poor tactical leadership, poor information management, poor weapons handling, and poor maintenance. These complications were present in every single Arab army and air force between 1948 and 1991. All had significant and identifiable effects on the performance of Arab armed forces. These were, without question, the principal sources of Arab misfortune in war during this period of history. The lack of initiative, improvisation, adaptability, flexibility, independent judgment, willingness to maneuver, and ability to integrate the various combat arms effectively meant that Arab armies and air forces were regularly outfought by their adversaries. The distortion, compartmentalization, and inattention to information and intelligence meant that Arab units were forced to conduct operations in a fog of war far worse than Clausewitz imagined. The neglect of day-to-day maintenance practices and inability to conduct repair work generally meant that Arab forces could count on far less of their equipment when the balloon went up than could their adversaries. Finally, the inability of Arab pilots and weapons crews to take full advantage of their equipment meant that they fought at a disadvantage against even primitively armed foes.

To some extent, this alone answers the fundamental question of this book: what are the problems afflicting Arab armies and air forces in combat? Given so many Arab armies and air forces fighting in so many wars, it could only be the case that multiple factors were to blame for the broad pattern of military ineffectiveness. Nevertheless, it is still interesting and worthwhile to ask whether this answer can be broken down further to determine which among these four were the most important influences.

POOR TACTICAL LEADERSHIP VS. LIMITED TECHNICAL SKILLS

Ultimately, one can group these four areas into two larger patterns of military ineffectiveness. Problems employing and maintaining sophisticated weaponry both stem from the limited technical skills of most Arab military personnel over the last fifty years. Similarly, problems with information management were most pernicious at lower levels and had their greatest effect on the behavior of Arab junior officers. Thus, one of the most important results of the information-management problems of Arab armed forces were their contribution to problems with tactical leadership. A careful analysis of Arab military history during 1945–91 reveals that the mediocrity of their tactical leaders was more damaging to military effectiveness than the dearth of technical skills among their personnel.

As debilitating as it was that Arab personnel could not employ their weaponry as well as the enemy could handle theirs, it was usually the case that this was almost irrelevant because the failings of Arab junior officers left their units in such precarious situations that defeat was guaranteed no matter how well or how poorly they used their weapons. Perhaps the best illustration of this problem was Jordanian performance on the West Bank in 1967. Jordanian infantry units handled their weapons very well but were defeated quickly by the Israelis because Jordanian officers would not show the initiative, creativity, or flexibility to shift their forces, reorient their lines to meet Israeli flanking attacks, or counterattack Israeli penetrations. Consequently, it did not matter that the Jordanians were quite deadly with their small arms because their tactical leadership was so poor that victory for their adversaries was simply a matter of punching through their defensive lines and then rolling them up from the flank. Similarly, in the tank battles on the West Bank, the problem was not so much that the Jordanians could not handle their Pattons as well as the Israelis could handle their Shermans but that Jordanian junior officers did not know what they were doing. Thus, in the Dotan Valley along the Tubas-Janin road and at Tel al-Ful, Jordanian armor was beaten because of command failures, not poor tank handling. The exception that proves this rule is the 40th Armored Brigade, the only Jordanian unit to actually fight an essentially equal-sized Israeli unit to a draw. The 40th Brigade had greater success not because of better weapons-handling skills, but because its leadership was so far superior to that of other Jordanian armor units.

Syrian military history offers two more examples that support this distinction. First, the personnel of the 77th Tank Battalion of Israel's elite 7th Armored Brigade, defending Red Ridge in October 1973, were incomparably better with their Centurions than the Syrians of the 7th Infantry Division and Republican Guard brigades were with their horde of T-62s, BMPs, and other armored vehicles. However, the Syrians did not lose because they were worse marksmen than the Israelis: their deficiencies in weapons handling were more than compensated by their numeric advantages (generally on the order of five to one or greater in tanks and much higher in all other categories), which made it impossible for even the superb Israeli gunners to destroy enough armored vehicles before the Syrians were on top of them. The Syrians lost because they were outmaneuvered and "out thought" by their Israeli counterparts at every turn. Israeli junior officers showed a tremendous flexibility, creativity, and aggressiveness that allowed them to maul much larger Syrian forces by darting around the lumbering Syrians and smashing them with sudden counterattacks to their flanks and rear.

Second, there is the example of Syrian performance in the air battles over Lebanon in 1982. Although it is certainly true that Syrian pilots could not take full advantage of the capabilities of their MiGs, this is beside the point. Once the Israelis had deprived them of their GCI guidance, Syrian pilots showed so little adaptability or capacity for independent action that their inferior technology and their inferior abilities to use that technology became irrelevant. As the Israelis noted almost incredulously, "They could have flown the best fighter in the world, but if they flew it the way they were flying we would have shot them down in exactly the same way."[4] The problem was not that the MiG-23s were no match for the F-15s or that Israeli pilots made full use of the capabilities of their fighters while the Syrians barely understood how to fly the MiG, it was that no pilot could possibly hope to win — or even live — if he could do nothing but fly figure-eights once he lost contact with the ground. Given such poor performances, it would not have mattered what planes the Syrians flew or how well they knew how to fly them; since they would not maneuver or otherwise adapt to the swirling chaos of a dogfight, they were dead.

In 1981–82, when Iran drove the Iraqi army from Khuzestan, the problem for the Iraqis was not related to their equipment. Iran was so badly outnumbered by Iraq in every category of military hardware that it did not matter how poorly Baghdad's crews handled their T-55s and T-62s because there were simply too few Iranian Chieftains and M-60s to oppose them. Moreover, although the Iranians were slightly better than the Iraqis in employing their weaponry, they were not better by much. But the Iraqis were trounced by the underequipped Iranians, not because they could not handle their equipment, but because their junior officers could not handle their units. They were beaten because their tactical leadership showed a dearth of initiative, adaptability, creativity, maneuver, combined-arms integration, and independent judgment. Iraqi formations generally sat passively while Iranian units punched through weakly held sectors and then enveloped adjacent armored and mechanized formations. Iranian forces moved painfully slowly, but the Iraqis could not shift forces or commit reserves in time to block their penetrations or prevent them from enveloping entire units. Iraqi tactical units rarely counterattacked, and when they did so, it was a straightforward charge into the teeth of the Iranian forces without maneuver or proper combined-arms integration. Given their overwhelming material advantages and their essential equivalence with the Iranians in weapons-handling skills, the Iraqis should have won easily, but they lost because the shortcomings of their tactical leadership outweighed all other considerations.

Egyptian and Libyan experiences provide additional examples. For instance, Egyptian forces in Yemen in the 1960s possessed similarly overwhelming advantages in weaponry over their Royalist adversaries, and they were just as good (or perhaps just as bad) as their enemies in handling crew-served weapons or larger equipment. The Egyptian's advantages mattered little, however, because they could not defeat the Yemenis in small-unit engagements. Egyptian tactical commanders could not act independently of guidance from higher echelons, coordinate their actions with those of other units, or respond quickly or creatively to Royalist ambushes. Finally, Libyan forces in Chad in 1986–87 not only had a far more powerful arsenal than their Chadian foes, they probably were better at handling their weapons too. The Chadians were abysmal when it came to maintaining and operating machines. Consequently, they were incapable of using tanks, armored cars, APCs, jet fighters, and the like and were forced to rely on the simplest heavy-infantry weapons; yet even these the Chadians did not handle particularly well, and their accuracy with antitank and antiaircraft weapons was notoriously bad. Nevertheless, the Chadians not only defeated the

Libyans, they crushed them, and they did so because their tactical commanders could literally run rings around their Libyan counterparts. The Chadians won because their junior commanders were aggressive, resourceful, and flexible, and they constantly maneuvered for advantage against the slow, plodding, and unresponsive Libyans. Whenever they found the weak spot in the Libyan defenses, they struck hard and fast, penetrating and then enveloping enemy positions before the Libyans could react or counterattack. In the end, it was this superiority in tactical combat that allowed the Chadians to overcome their poor weapons-handling skills and win a remarkable victory over Libya.

Arab History and Modern Warfare

As an afterthought, it is worth observing that the history of the Arab militaries since 1948 also has much to teach about modern warfare more generally. If one counts each Arab military's participation in each Middle Eastern conflict, then the six armed forces examined in this study went to war twenty-eight times during the post–World War II era. Countless authors have attempted to glean universal lessons about the nature of war in the twentieth century from the wars in the Middle East. The experiences of the Arabs and their adversaries have gone on to shape the majority of armed forces in one way or another. From the Argentine Air Force pilots taught by the Israelis before the Falklands War; to the United States' military, which learned to obliterate Iraq's air force, air defense forces, and army by watching the Israelis smash Egyptian, Syrian, and Jordanian forces; to the Soviets, who constantly improved their tanks, planes, sAMs, and other hardware based on the results of each effort by their Arab client-states; to the scores of other militaries that have scrutinized the conduct of Middle Eastern wars for methods to defeat their own enemies, there are few countries whose armed forces have not been affected by the experiences of the contemporary Arab armies. With this in mind, I offer several of my own lessons regarding the nature of modern combat as illustrated by the history of the Arabs at war.

Unit Cohesion

As the Arab armies demonstrated time and again, even if an army hangs together and fights like tigers in the worst situations, there is no guarantee that it will be able to defeat its enemies. The experience of the Egyptian, Jordanian, and Syrian armies in the Six Day War proved this point: at least in the initial battles on 5–6 June, each fought very hard and maintained unit cohesion even in dire circumstances. However, all three armies were routed by the IDF because their junior officers were dismal, their commanders had problems managing information, and their personnel were unable to properly employ or maintain equipment. Likewise, Iraq's Republican Guard must be credited with outstanding unit cohesion during the ground offensive of Operation Desert Storm, yet this could not compensate for their inability to conduct maneuver warfare, and so they were destroyed.

This history enriches our understanding of the role of unit cohesion in shaping the effectiveness of modern armies. It indicates that maintaining formations is not synonymous with military effectiveness, as some authors have suggested. It is one component of military effectiveness, potentially an important one, but it is not all important and probably not even pre-eminent. The relative cohesion of Arab tactical formations ran the gamut in the Middle Eastern wars from 1948 to 1991 but tended to be quite good more often than not. Nevertheless, Arab military effectiveness was consistently poor. In those instances when their unit cohesion was poor, their effectiveness was even worse than normal, and this was frequently an important element in their disappointing performances. However, when Arab unit cohesion was good — and even when it was outstanding — it had only a very modest influence on Arab military effectiveness. No matter how good unit integrity was, their military effectiveness was never more than mediocre. Moreover, the best Arab military showings were not always instances of their strongest unit cohesion. The Egyptians in 1948 (especially those trapped in the Fallujah pocket) displayed outstanding unit cohesion but very poor effectiveness. But Egyptian forces were at their most effective in 1973, although their unit cohesion was essentially just average for Arab armies.

Several lessons can be inferred from this pattern. First, they indicate that unit cohesion is primarily a negative factor: it is a necessary but not sufficient aspect of an effective military. An army with poor unit cohesion will find it very difficult to prevail no matter how skillful its soldiers and officers. After all, if the army disintegrates upon contact with the enemy, proficiency will count for little. However, an army with very good unit cohesion is unlikely to emerge victorious unless it is also more proficient than its adversary. Indeed, given a certain level of cohesion, an army is more likely to prevail if it is more proficient than its adversary than if it has better unit cohesion. In other words, given two armies, one with outstanding proficiency but only average unit cohesion and the other with outstanding unit cohesion but only average proficiency, the more proficient army is likely to prevail. Chadian units had relatively poor unit cohesion, certainly worse than the Libyans, but they prevailed over the Libyans because they were more skillful.

It is difficult to specify the minimum level of unit cohesion at which point proficiency becomes the more important factor in battle. The history of the Arab armies suggests that an army needs to be at least cohesive enough so that its formations will only start to disintegrate after they have been placed in untenable positions or worn down by constant combat over the course of several days. Anything less than that would seem to be too little to allow the unit to absorb the punishment inherent in even the most successful combat operations. Beyond this, even tighter unit cohesion is useful, but its effect on overall performance in battle produces diminishing returns. Once an army reaches this level of unit cohesion, then its proficiency relevant to its opponent suddenly takes on far greater significance in determining whether it will prevail. Arab and Israeli units both enjoyed high degrees of cohesion, but the Israelis prevailed again and again. Moreover, the Israelis only failed when their proficiency was poor. This is illustrated by comparing the experiences of the 1956 and 1967 battles at Abu Ageilah–Umm Qatef. In 1956 and 1967 both the Israeli and Egyptian forces engaged enjoyed excellent unit cohesion, at least initially. The Israelis were effectively stalemated by the Egyptians in 1956 but were able to smash them in 1967—even though they enjoyed a better force ratio in 1956—because of the tremendous improvement in Israeli proficiency between 1956 and 1967. There was no apparent improvement in Israeli unit cohesion during this period.

Another important lesson regarding the relationship between unit cohesion and military effectiveness illustrated by Arab military history is that unit cohesion is more important in conducting some missions than others. Ultimately, unit cohesion is extremely important to the conduct of certain missions—such as static defensive operations—and matters much less in other missions—such as fluid armor engagements. In static defense missions, a crucial determinant of whether a unit can successfully execute the mission is whether its men will stick together under attack and hold the sector they have been ordered to defend. It is in situations such as this where unit cohesion is a critical element of victory. But in fluid armor battles, by definition, formations break up into sub-elements (hence the "fluidity"), and maintaining the cohesion of the larger formations is often less important than the aggressiveness, flexibility, and improvisational ability of tactical commanders who must keep fighting and coordinating operations in the midst of chaos. These kinds of battles are decentralized by nature, and so what is crucial is the ability of commanders to compete in this environment, their understanding of the larger goals of the operation when the fog of battle makes it impossible for their superiors to guide them, and their own innate ability to recognize how they can best act to fulfill those larger goals.[5] The generally strong unit cohesion of Arab armies helped them in static defensive operations and partially explains their greater success in such battles as Abu Ageilah in 1956, Syria's defense of the Bekaa in 1982, Libya's stand in the Tibesti in 1987, and Jordan's defense of Latrun in 1948. In contrast, their strong unit cohesion did the Arabs little good whenever they got into fluid engagements.

Strategic vs. Tactical Effectiveness

The history of the Arabs in combat since 1945 also provides some interesting lessons regarding the importance of good generalship as opposed to proficient tactical forces. No one can dispute the influence of generalship on war. The performances of Napoleon, Frederick, Hannibal, and countless other "great captains" attest to what military genius can accomplish. However, tactical proficiency is also an important consideration in a nation's military fortunes. The German Wehrmacht demonstrated throughout the Second World War that superb tactical formations can mitigate the damage wrought by strategic mistakes and at times even allow an army to prevail despite bad generalship. By contrast, the history of the modern Arab armed forces demonstrates that even superb strategic moves may amount to nothing if the nation's tactical formations are incapable of executing them. The Arabs assembled at least two highly competent command staffs: the Egyptian General Staff and senior generals of 1967–73 and the Iraqi General Staff and senior generals of 1986–91. Nevertheless, the achievements of both groups of generals was ultimately very modest in military terms (although quite far reaching in political terms) because of the severely limited capabilities of the tactical formations at their command. One can only wonder what Egypt's Isma'il 'Ali or Iraq's Husayn Rashid—or at lower levels of command, the Jordanian Rakan al-Jazi or the Syrian Hasan at-Turkmani—might have been able to accomplish had they commanded forces with the proficiency of the Wehrmacht or the IDF.

Thus, the history of the Arab armies puts the lie to the contentions of some that there exist strategies so brilliant that they transcend all other liabilities and put the enemy at such a disadvantage that victory is assured. The incompetence of Arab tactical leadership, their severe problems managing information, and the inability of their personnel to properly employ and maintain their military hardware left the Arab states highly vulnerable to most potential adversaries. These extreme limitations of tactical capabilities greatly curtailed the options available to their strategic leadership and badly limited the ability of these nations to employ military force in pursuit of political objectives. Generals of adequate competence had little prospect of successfully achieving any political goal, and even exceptionally competent Arab strategic leaders were able to achieve only the most modest results. Indeed, what is so intriguing about the two greatest Arab triumphs of the last fifty years — Egypt's crossing of the Suez in the October War and the Iraqi victory at the end of the Iran-Iraq War — are the circumstances that allowed Egypt and Iraq to reap such sweeping political gains from such modest military achievements.

A Final Thought

At the end of any study of the recent past, one is inevitably left with the question, what does all of this tell us about the future? This book has much to say about the foreseeable future. The strengths and weaknesses of the Arab armies and air forces have persisted in resilient fashion over the last fifty years, and there is every reason to expect that they will continue to define the performance of the Arabs at war for at least another decade or more. However, beyond that, the future becomes murkier.

One of the main reasons that the strengths and weaknesses of the Arabs have remained constant is that, over the same period of time, warfare in the Middle East has remained largely constant. New types of tanks and planes were introduced and some totally new systems like helicopters and antitank guided-missiles were added to the armies, but ultimately, Middle Eastern wars were dominated by mechanized ground forces and jet fighter–equipped air forces. Infantry, armor, and artillery dominated all of the ground battles from 1945 to 1991 just as fighters and attack aircraft were the key elements of air campaigns. The equipment may have become more advanced, but it was employed in largely the same manner. Unfortunately for the Arabs, their strengths and weaknesses did not mesh well with the demands of this kind of combat. Their problems with tactical leadership, information management, and technical skills were devastating in an age of warfare in which decentralized command, aggressive and innovative tactical leadership, accurate information flows, and advanced weaponry were the keys to victory.

To the extent that warfare in the future continues to require these kinds of skills, the Arab armed forces are likely to remain limited in their ability to pursue political goals through military operations. However, warfare is clearly changing. We are at the beginning (some might say in the middle) of a "revolution in military affairs." There have been numerous such transformations in the past, and each has redefined the requirements of victory.[6] When wars were fought by lines of infantry with smoothbore muskets complemented by horse-mounted cavalry and small numbers of flat-trajectory cannon — as was the case in the seventeenth through nineteenth centuries — discipline, unit cohesion, generalship, and the complete obedience of subordinates to their superiors were the keys to victory in battle. When the latest transformation of warfare is complete, the skills that determine winners and losers on the battlefield might be very different from those of today. In that case the Arabs might suddenly find themselves far better able to wage war. The nature of warfare is constantly changing, and each time it changes, it redistributes military power. The skills fostered by the British regimental system that led to victory at Waterloo were equally responsible for the bloody carnage of the Somme. When warfare changes, the value of armies changes with it, and when this current transformation finally settles into its new form, the Arabs may be even worse off than they are today (though this seems almost unimaginable from the current perspective). However, it is equally possible that they will stand taller than they ever have since their armies swept across the Mediterranean and southern Asia under the banners of Islam in the seventh and eighth centuries. All one can say for certain is that everything will be different and that these changes will have a profound effect on war and politics across the Middle East.

NOTES

Understanding Modern Arab Military Effectiveness

1. Paul Adair, *Hitler's Greatest Defeat: The Collapse of Army Group Centre* (London: Arms and Armour, 1994), 170–71; Alan Clark, *Barbarossa: The Russian-German Confict, 1941–1945*, paperback ed. (New York: Quill, 1965), 436; John Erickson, *The Road to Berlin*, paperback ed. (London: Phoenix Books, 1996), 214; David M. Glantz and Jonathan House, *When Titans Clashed: How the Red Army Stopped Hitler* (Lawrence: University of Kansas Press, 1995), 198, 201, 214–15; Albert Seaton, *The Russo-German War: 1941–1945*, paperback ed. (Novato CA: Presidio Press, 1993), 436.

2. Jerry Asher (with Eric Hammel), *Duel for the Golan* (New York: William Morrow, 1987), 35–44, 52–54; Anthony Cordesman and Abraham Wagner, *The Lessons of Modern War, Volume 1: The Arab Israeli Conflicts, 1973–1989* (Boulder CO: Westview, 1990), 24 [hereafter cited as *LMW: Arab-Israeli Conflicts*]; Col. Trevor N. Dupuy, *Elusive Victory* (New York: Harper and Row, 1978; reprint, Dubuque IA: Kendall Hunt, 1992), 437–44; Chaim Herzog, *The War of Atonement* (London: Weidenfeld and Nicolson, 1975), 61; Chaim Herzog, *The Arab-Israeli Wars* (New York: Random House, 1982), 285; J. M. Moreaux, "The Syrian Army," *Defence Update* 73, July 1986, 40 [hereafter cited as Moreaux, July 1986]; Edgar O'Ballance, *No Victor, No Vanquished: The Yom Kippur War* (London: Barrie and Jenkins, 1979), 121–22, 125.

3. James Brooke, "Chadians Describe Victory in Desert," *The New York Times*, 14 August 1987, A5; George Henderson, "Qaddafy's Waterloo," *Africa Report* (Sept.–Oct. 1987): 25; Franziska James, "Habre's Hour of Glory," *Africa Report* (Sept.–Oct. 1987): 21; Colin Legum, ed., *African Contemporary Record, 1986–87* (New York: Africana, 1988), B181–91, B542 [hereafter cited as *ACR* with appropriate years]; Keith Somerville, *Foreign Military Intervention in Africa* (London: Pinter, 1990), 71–72; Jean R. Tartter, "National Security," in *Chad: A Country Study*, ed. Thomas Collelo (Washington DC: GPO, 1990), 215 [hereafter cited as Tartter

(Chad)]; Lt. Gen. Bernard Trainor, interviews with author, May 1994; U.S. government officials, interviews with author, Sept. 1995.

4. Anthony Cordesman and Abraham Wagner, *The Lessons of Modern War, Volume II: The Iran-Iraq War* (Boulder CO: Westview, 1990), 57–67 [hereafter cited as *LMW: Iran-Iraq War*].

5. Others have used such terms as "combat effectiveness," "military performance," and "fighting power," among others, to denote the same concept. The Soviets used the term *effectivnost*, which John Erickson defines as "efficiency, effectiveness and battlefield performance." See "The Soviet Military System: Doctrine, Technology and 'Style,'" in *Soviet Military Power and Performance*, eds. John Erickson and E. J. Feuchtwanger (Hamden CT: Archon, 1979), 20.

6. For instance, see Cordesman and Wagner, *LMW: Arab-Israeli Conflicts*, 351; Dupuy, *Elusive Victory*, 597–601; Brig. Gen. Syed Ali El-Edroos, *The Hashemite Arab Army, 1908–1979* (Amman: Amman Publishing Committee, 1980), esp. 519–33; Herzog, *Arab-Israeli Wars*, 141, 189–91, 313–23, 362–66; and Anthony Pascal, Michael Kennedy, Steven Rosen, et al., *Men and Arms in the Middle East: The Human Factor in Military Modernization*, RAND R-2460-NA (Santa Monica CA: RAND, 1979).

7. So why is it reasonable to consider explanations that lump all of the Arab armies together and treat them as one? Surely there are differences in the military effectiveness of the various Arab states. Some perform certain military operations better than others. However, there are several reasons that argue in favor of treating them as one for analytic purposes. First, virtually all of the authors, analysts, and military officers who have proposed theories to explain poor Arab military effectiveness have couched their explanations in terms of general statements applicable to all of the Arab armed forces. Consequently, one would be misrepresenting their theories if one did not treat all of the Arab states as similar, if not uniform. Second, in actuality, Arab armies and air forces display a tremendous similarity to one another in terms of their military effectiveness. By and large, the problems they manifest are common to all — so much so that accounts of battles fought by the different armies and air forces often sound like plagiarized versions of one another. Of course, there are aspects of military effectiveness that are not common to all, and these are singled out in the narrative as exceptions. But, in general, Arab militaries display far more similarities of military effectiveness than differences, and for this reason one can feel comfortable considering explanations that consider them as a collective whole.

8. I have chosen to exclude Arab naval forces from this study because there is too little evidence upon which to draw reasonable conclusions. Naval units have participated in a significant way in only a handful of Middle Eastern wars. Moreover, the information available on these battles is too limited to analyze their performance in detail and draw generally applicable conclusions.

9. For a sampling of the literature on the importance of unit cohesion, see Anthony Kellett, "Combat Motivation," in *Brassey's Encyclopedia of Land Forces and Warfare*, ed. Col. Franklin D. Margiotta (London: Brassey's, 1996), 193–200; S. L. A. Marshall, *Men against Fire* (New York: William Morrow, 1946); and W. D. Hender-

son, *Cohesion: The Human Element in Combat Leadership and Societal Influences in the Armies of the USSR, the U.S., North Vietnam, and Israel* (Washington DC: National Defense University, 1979).

10. Yehoshofat Harkabi, "Basic Factors in the Arab Collapse during the Six-Day War," *Orbis* (fall 1967).

11. For Egyptian criticism of 'Amr see, Dupuy, *Elusive Victory*, 343–48; Field Marshal Mohamed Abdel Ghani el-Gamasy, *The October War*, trans. Gilian Potter, Nadra Marcos, and Rosette Frances (Cairo: American University in Cairo Press, 1993), 46–85; Nejla M. Abu Izzedin, *Nasser of the Arabs* (Beirut: Impremerie Catholique, 1975), 133; Lon Nordeen and David Nicole, *Phoenix over the Nile: A History of Egyptian Airpower, 1932–1994* (Washington DC: Smithsonian Institution, 1996), 220. For Jordanian scapegoating of Riyad, see El-Edroos, *Hashemite Arab Army*, 409; Samir Mutawi, *Jordan in the 1967 War* (Cambridge: Cambridge University Press, 1987), 143–47; James Lunt, *Hussein of Jordan* (London: McMillan, 1989), 95, 128–29; and Brig. Peter Young, *The Israeli Campaign, 1967* (London: William Kimber, 1967), 140. On Syrian criticism of Asad, see Patrick Seale, *Asad of Syria: The Struggle for the Middle East* (London: I. B. Tauris, 1988), 142–44.

12. On the 1948 war, see Manfred Halpern, *The Politics of Social Change in the Middle East and North Africa*, 1st paperback ed. (Princeton NJ: Princeton University Press, 1963), 257; Mark A. Heller, "Iraq's Army: Military Weakness, Political Utility," in *Iraq's Road to War*, eds. Amatzia Baram and Barry Rubin (New York: St. Martin's, 1993), 39; and Edgar O'Ballance, *The Arab-Israeli War, 1948* (London: Faber and Faber, 1956), 118. On Saddam's purge of his senior officers after 1982, see Cordesman and Wagner, *LMW: Iran-Iraq War*, 141–42; "Iraq's Army: Lessons from the War with Iran," *The Economist*, 12 Jan. 1991, 36; and Stephen C. Pelletiere, *The Iran-Iraq War: Chaos in a Vacuum* (New York: Praeger, 1992), 65.

13. For purposes of this study, commands at division level or below (wing or regiment level for air forces) are considered "tactical" commands. Although there is no hard and fast rule for dividing forces into strategic, operational, and tactical levels of command, all modern militaries consider formations at or below the Soviet army/Western corps (or numbered air force for both systems) to be tactical commands. See Christopher Donnelly, *Red Banner: The Soviet Military System in Peace and War* (Alexandria VA: Jane's Publishing, 1988), 195–223; Trevor N. Dupuy, "Theory of Combat," in Margiotta, *Brassey's Encyclopedia*, 1075; Headquarters, Department of the Army, *Field Manual 100-5: Operations* (Washington DC: 1993), 6-1– 6-3; Col. Lloyd Matthews, "Thoughts and Second Thoughts: Operationalese Mania," *Army* (Feb. 1987): 19–21; Col. Ghulam Dastagir Wardak, comp. and trans., *The Voroshilov Lectures: Materials from the Soviet General Staff Academy*, vol. 1, *Issues of Operational Art* (Washington DC: NDU Press, 1992), 15–16.

I have generally chosen to distinguish only between the tactical and strategic levels of command in the Arab armed forces. This is because most of them during the Cold War era had no real operational-level commands to speak of. According to both Soviet and Western doctrine, operational-level commands are the largest maneuver formations within a theater of war: army and front level for the Soviets, army and army-group level for NATO. In both Soviet and Western doctrine, it was useful to draw this distinction because it was conceivable to have theater- and army-group-level commands distinct from the strategic decision-making entities. However, in all of the Arab armies from 1945 to 1991, the theater-command and the army-group-command functions were performed by the general staff itself. Instead, in Arab militaries, the division (or the brigade) was the primary unit of maneuver on the ground, and the squadron (occasionally the regiment) was the primary unit of maneuver in the air. A few of the largest Arab armies established Western-style corps or Soviet-style armies; however, these functioned as geographic sector commands rather than maneuver formations. The only real exception to this rule was the Iraqis, who, beginning in 1985–86, began to employ corps as maneuver formations. Because Iraqi corps—and Egyptian armies since 1973—were the largest field commands in their armies, I have treated them as strategic-level commands because they occupied a status comparable to theater commands for Soviet or Western armies. Moreover, only one Arab army ever attempted to create a command formation between the general staff and the corps/army units: the Egyptian Sinai Theater Command in 1967. But this exception proves the rule, for during the course of the Six Day War, this command was completely bypassed by the general staff (see chap. 1).

14. For Western historians who subscribe to this view, see Dupuy, *Elusive Victory*, 597–601, 623–33; Cordesman and Wagner, *LMW: Arab-Israeli Conflicts*, 351–53; Eric Hammel, *Six Days in June* (New York: Scribner's, 1992), 82, 143–46; Insight Team of the *London Sunday Times*, *The Yom Kippur War* (New York: Doubleday, 1974), 164, 231; and O'Ballance, *No Victor, No Vanquished*, 338–39. For a concurring opinion from a non-Western source, see El-Edroos, *Hashemite Arab Army*, 519–33.

15. Avraham "Bren" Adan, *On the Banks of the Suez* (San Francisco: Presidio, 1980), 84–85; Moshe Dayan, *Diary of the Sinai Campaign* (New York: Harper and Row, 1965; reprint, New York: Shocken Books, 1967), 35, 108, 124; Herzog, *Arab-Israeli Wars*, 357, 364–65; O'Ballance, *No Victor, No Vanquished*, 166; Ariel Sharon (with David Chanoff), *Warrior: The Autobiography of Ariel Sharon* (New York: Simon and Schuster, 1989), 119; Martin Van Creveld, "Military Lessons of the Yom Kippur War," *The Jerusalem Quarterly* 5 (fall 1977): 119; senior Israeli military officers, interviews with author, Sept. 1996.

16. For Arabs espousing this view, see Mohammed Heikal editorial, *Al-Ahram*, 28 June 1968, cited in Raymond W. Baker, *Sadat and after: Struggles for Egypt's Political Soul* (Cambridge: Harvard University Press, 1990), 188; Mohammed Heikal, "General Ismail and the War—Interview with Lt. General Ismail," *Journal of Palestine Studies* 3, no. 2 (1974), 217; Insight Team, *Yom Kippur War*, 211; O'Ballance, *No Victor, No Vanquished*, 157; Dupuy, *Elusive Victory*, 346–48. For Israelis and Westerners making the same claim, see Adan, *Banks of the Suez*, 388–91; Dayan, *Diary*, 63; Hammel, *Six Days*, 147; Insight Team, *Yom Kippur War*, 340–44; O'Ballance, *No Victor, No Vanquished*, 339; Ze'ev Schiff, *A History of the Israeli Army* (New York: Macmillan, 1985), 135–36.

17. See, for example, Al-Haytham al-Ayoubi, "The Strategies of the Fourth Campaign," trans. Edmund Ghareeb, in *Middle East Crucible: Studies on the Arab-Israeli War of October, 1973*, ed. Naseer H. Aruri, AAUG Monograph Series, no. 6 (Wilmette IL: Medina University Press, 1975), 71; Anthony Cordesman, *Jordanian Arms and the Middle East Balance* (Washington DC: Middle East Institute, 1983); Cordesman and Wagner, LMW: *Arab-Israeli Conflicts*, 354–55; Efraim Karsh, *The Iran-Iraq War: A Military Analysis*, Adelphi Paper 220 (London: IISS, 1987); and Roger Owen, "The Role of the Army in Middle Eastern Politics: A Critique of Existing Analyses," *Review of Middle East Studies* 3 (1978): 64–71.

18. See, for example, al-Ayoubi, "Fourth Campaign," 70; Ahmed Hashim, "The State, Society, and the Evolution of Warfare in the Middle East: The Rise of Strategic Deterrence," *The Washington Quarterly* (autumn 1995): 61.

19. Lisa Anderson, conversation with author, 25 April 1994; Halpern, *Politics of Social Change*, 257; Hammel, *Six Days*, 423; Owen, "Role of the Army," 74–75.

20. This is an extreme form of the argument, made primarily for analytic purposes to clearly differentiate it from the other explanations. In actuality, most of those who advocate this theory cite other factors in addition to inadequate training that have contributed to the various problems experienced by Arab armies in combat. For arguments along these lines, see Stephen Biddle and Robert Zirkle, "Technology, Civil-Military Relations, and Warfare in the Developing World," *Journal of Strategic Studies* 19, no. 2 (June 1996): 171–212; Hashim, "State, Society, and the Evolution of Warfare," 61; 1st Lt. Matthew M. Hurley, "Saddam Hussein and Iraqi Air Power," *Airpower Journal* (winter 1992): 4–16; and David C. Rapoport, "The Praetorian Army: Insecurity, Venality, and Impotence," in *Soldiers, Peasants, and Bureaucrats: Civil-Military Relations in Communist and Modernizing Societies*, eds. Roman Kolkowicz and Andrej Korbonski (London: George Allen and Unwin, 1982).

21. Quoted in Nordeen and Nicole, *Phoenix over the Nile*, 4.

22. After the Six Day War, numerous jokes made the rounds in Israel (and the United States, for that matter) that had as their punchlines the cowardice of Arab soldiers. In addition, it is worth noting that Moshe Dayan even derived Israel's strategy for the 1956 Kadesh offensive into the Sinai from his belief that Egyptian soldiers would flee when faced by a determined Israeli attack. While based on assumptions regarding the cohesion of Arab combat formations, this understanding also was grounded in a belief that Arab soldiers lacked the mental fortitude to stand and fight a determined adversary. See George W. Gawrych, *Key to the Sinai: The Battles for Abu Ageilah in the 1956 and 1967 Arab-Israeli Wars* (Fort Leavenworth KS: U.S. Army Command and General Staff College, 1989), 30.

23. This, of course, is the inspiration for the famed "3-to-1 Rule," which posits that the attacker must have three times the forces of the defender to prevail. Although this is at best a rule of thumb for military officers and not a very useful analytic tool, the motivation behind it is clearly correct.

24. Carl von Clausewitz, *On War*, ed. and trans. Michael Howard and Peter Paret

(Princeton NJ: Princeton University Press, 1976), 358 (emphasis omitted). Also, see the rest of this chapter, entitled "The Advantages of Defense," 357-59.

1. Egypt

1. O'Ballance, *Arab-Israeli War,* 70-77.

2. Dupuy, *Elusive Victory,* 55; Lon Nordeen, *Fighters over Israel* (London: Greenhill Books, 1991), 11; Nordeen and Nicole, *Phoenix over the Nile,* 67, 72-73, 78, 84-85, 96, 121; O'Ballance, *Arab-Israeli War,* 77.

3. Ahron Bregman, *Israel's Wars, 1947-93* (London: Routledge, 2000), 16; Dupuy, *Elusive Victory,* 43-44; O'Ballance, *Arab-Israeli War,* 70-74.

4. Dupuy, *Elusive Victory,* 57; Lt. Col. Natanel Lorch, *The Edge of the Sword: Israel's War of Independence, 1947-1949* (New York: Putnam, 1961), 209; O'Ballance, *Arab-Israeli War,* 91-92; Donald Robinson, ed., *Under Fire: Israel's Twenty-Year Struggle for Survival* (New York: W. W. Norton, 1968), 65-68; former Israeli Defense Force (IDF) officers, interviews with author, Sept. 1996.

5. Dupuy, *Elusive Victory,* 57-58; Lorch, *Edge of the Sword,* 216-18.

6. Dupuy, *Elusive Victory,* 80-81; O'Ballance, *Arab-Israeli War,* 137; Nordeen and Nicole, *Phoenix over the Nile,* 93.

7. Dupuy, *Elusive Victory,* 81; O'Ballance, *Arab-Israeli War,* 141; Nordeen and Nicole, *Phoenix over the Nile,* 95.

8. Dupuy, *Elusive Victory,* 82-83.

9. Dupuy, *Elusive Victory,* 92; Lorch, *Edge of the Sword,* 335-36.

10. Lorch, *Edge of the Sword,* 351.

11. Dupuy, *Elusive Victory,* 94-99; Lorch, *Edge of the Sword,* 345-55; Nordeen and Nicole, *Phoenix over the Nile,* 104; O'Ballance, *Arab-Israeli War,* 174-79.

12. Sharon, *Warrior,* 96.

13. Senior IDF officer, interview with author, Sept. 1996.

14. Former senior IDF officers, interviews, Sept. 1996.

15. Eliezer Be'eri, *Army Officers in Arab Politics and Society* (New York: Praeger, 1970), 89-108; Nordeen and Nicole, *Phoenix over the Nile,* 136; J. Vatikiotis, *The History of Modern Egypt,* 4th ed. (Baltimore: Johns Hopkins University Press, 1991), 373-84.

16. Michael N. Barnett, *Confronting the Costs of War: Military Power, State, and Society in Egypt and Israel* (Princeton NJ: Princeton University Press, 1992), 87; Eugene K. Keefe, "National Security," in *Egypt: A Country Study,* ed. Richard F. Nyrop (Washington DC: GPO, 1983), 219; Nordeen, *Fighters over Israel,* 35; Nordeen and Nicole, *Phoenix over the Nile,* 6, 131; Nadav Safran, *From War to War* (New York: Pegasus, 1969), 206-7.

17. Barnett, *Costs of War,* 81.

18. Barnett, *Costs of War,* 87.

19. Dayan, *Diary,* 4-5; Nordeen and Nicole, *Phoenix over the Nile,* 145; Safran, *From War to War,* 209.

20. Dayan, *Diary,* 4-5; Safran, *From War to War,* 209.

21. Bernard Fall, "The Two Sides of the War," in Robinson, *Under Fire*, 163; Kennett Love, *Suez: The Twice-Fought War* (New York: McGraw Hill, 1969), 492; Nordeen and Nicole, *Phoenix over the Nile*, 158.

22. Love, *Suez*, 496.

23. Gawrych, *Key to the Sinai*, 14–19; Rechavam Zeevy, "The Military Lessons of the Sinai Campaign," in *The Suez-Sinai Crisis 1956: Retrospective and Reappraisal*, eds. Selwyn I. Tröen and Moshe Shemesh (London: Frank Cass, 1990), 70.

24. Dupuy, *Elusive Victory*, 176; Love, *Suez*, 492; Nordeen and Nicole, *Phoenix over the Nile*, 156–58; J. A. Sellers, "Military Lessons: The British Perspective," in Tröen and Shemesh, *Suez-Sinai Crisis*, 21.

25. Yonah Bandman, "The Egyptian Armed Forces during the Kadesh Campaign," in Tröen and Shemesh, *Suez-Sinai Crisis*, 84; Herzog, *Arab-Israeli Wars*, 118.

26. Bandman, "Egyptian Armed Forces during the Kadesh Campaign," 92; Dayan, *Diary*, 116–20; Dupuy, *Elusive Victory*, 165–68; Gawrych, *Key to the Sinai*, 50–57; Maj. Gen. Avraham "Bren" Adan, interview with author, Sept. 1996.

27. Moshe Shemesh, "Egypt: From Military Defeat to Political Victory," in Tröen and Shemesh, *Suez-Sinai Crisis*, 154.

28. Moshe Shemesh, ed., "'Abd al-Latif Bughdadi's Memoirs," and "Sayyid Mar'i's Political Papers," in Tröen and Shemesh, *Suez-Sinai Crisis*, 345–50, 367.

29. Gawrych, *Key to the Sinai*, 64.

30. Gen. d'Armee André Beaufre, *The Suez Expedition, 1956*, trans. Richard Barry (New York: Praeger, 1969), 90–113; Dupuy, *Elusive Victory*, 205–7; Roy Fullick and Geoffrey Powell, *Suez: The Double War* (London: Hamish Hamilton, 1979), 131–50; Herzog, *Arab-Israeli Wars*, 138–40; Keith Kyle, *Suez* (New York: St. Martin's, 1991), 383–84, 445–63; Love, *Suez*, 601–22.

31. Dupuy, *Elusive Victory*, 212; Nordeen, *Fighters over Israel*, 49.

32. Kyle, *Suez*, 369.

33. Dupuy, *Elusive Victory*, 176; Love, *Suez*, 492; Sellers, "Military Lessons," 21. Nordeen and Nicole claim that "the EAF had a total of 69 MiG-15s and 24 Il-28s assigned to operational squadrons." *Phoenix over the Nile*, 156. Of course, this does not tell us how many of these aircraft were actually operational. It is common for frontline squadrons in any air force to have at least some, and sometimes many, aircraft off-line for maintenance. Moreover, the consistency and level of detail of the accounts in Dupuy, Love, and Sellers is striking. Dupuy also had wide-ranging access to Egyptian sources, and his interviews were conducted soon after the fighting rather than decades later, as was the case for Nordeen and Nicole.

34. Dayan, *Diary*, 109; Dupuy, *Elusive Victory*, 176; Love, *Suez*, 528; Nordeen and Nicole, *Phoenix over the Nile*, 159.

35. Col. Eliezer Cohen, *Israel's Best Defense: The First Full Story of the Israeli Air Force*, trans. Jonathan Cordis (New York: Orion Books, 1993), 122; Dayan, *Diary*, 109; Kyle, *Suez*, 369; Nordeen and Nicole, *Phoenix over the Nile*, 168; Ehud Yonay, *No Margin for Error: The Making of the Israeli Air Force* (New York: Pantheon, 1993), 160–70; Zeevy, "Sinai Campaign," 67.

36. For an excellent analysis of the various problems that afflicted the Israeli military during the 1956 war, see Gawrych, *Key to the Sinai*, esp. 26–30.

37. See Dayan, *Diary*, esp. 35, 106–7, 124.

38. Love, *Suez*, 492.

39. Safran, *From War to War*, 353.

40. Dayan, *Diary*, 63.

41. Former senior IDF officers, interviews, Sept. 1996.

42. Bandman, "Egyptian Armed Forces during the Kadesh Campaign," 86. Indeed, one could argue that Egyptian exaggeration destroyed the Israeli subterfuge. Tel Aviv had hoped that by sending only Sharon's brigade in first, the Egyptians would believe that the attack was merely a deep raid into the Sinai. However, because the initial Egyptian reports so exaggerated the size of Sharon's force, Cairo concluded that the operation was a full-scale invasion.

43. See Shemesh, "Bughdadi's Memoirs," 337–50; and Shemesh, "Mar'i's Political Papers," esp. 367–70.

44. Dayan, *Diary*, 108; Dupuy, *Elusive Victory*, 177–78; Gawrych, *Key to the Sinai*, 41.

45. It is also worth noting that, according to Gawrych, 'Amr opposed the decision to withdraw from the Sinai and Nasser had to overrule him. This does not seem like the actions of a panicked or incompetent general. Rather, it suggests that while he may have been surprised by the initial Israeli invasion, 'Amr concluded (mostly correctly) that Egyptian troops were largely holding in the Sinai and that a major counterattack by the 4th Armored Division would stop the Israelis altogether (an incorrect assumption, but one unproven at that point in time). If, as Gawrych implies, this was the case, then it would appear that 'Amr got over any initial panic fairly quickly and that his confidence in his troops and commanders had resurfaced by the crucial phase of the war.

46. Shemesh, "Egypt," 155.

47. Field Marshal 'Abd al-Ghani al-Gamasy, interview with author, Dec. 1997; former Egyptian generals, interviews with author, Dec. 1997.

48. Gamasy, interview, Dec. 1997.

49. Edward N. Luttwak and Daniel Horowitz, *The Israeli Army, 1948–1973* (New York: Harper and Row, 1975; reprint, Cambridge MA: ABT Books, 1983), 171; Nordeen and Nicole, *Phoenix over the Nile*, 171–74.

50. Saeed M. Badeeb, *The Saudi-Egyptian Conflict over North Yemen, 1962–1970* (Boulder CO; Westview, 1986), 36–37; Be'eri, *Army Officers*, 227; Adeed I. Dawisha, "Intervention in the Yemen: An Analysis of Egyptian Perceptions and Policies," *Middle East Journal* 29 (winter 1975): 49–52; Nordeen and Nicole, *Phoenix over the Nile*, 189; Manfred W. Wenner, *Modern Yemen: 1918–1966* (Baltimore: Johns Hopkins University Press, 1967), 198, 207.

51. Edgar O'Ballance, *The War in the Yemen* (Hamden CT: Archon, 1971), 98; Ali Abdel Rahman Rahmy, *The Egyptian Policy in the Arab World: Intervention in Yemen, 1962–1967* (Washington DC: University Press of America, 1983), 148–49; Dana

Adams Schmidt, *Yemen: The Unknown War* (London: Bodley Head, 1968), 164–65; Wenner, *Modern Yemen*, 206–9.

52. Schmidt, *Yemen*, 164.

53. Barnett, *Costs of War*, 309 n. 91; Lt. Col. Neil McLean, "The War in the Yemen," *Journal of the Royal United Services Institute for Defence Studies* (Feb. 1966): 37.

54. McLean, "War in the Yemen," 28; Schmidt, *Yemen*, 214.

55. McLean, "War in the Yemen," 22, 28; Rahmy, *Egyptian Policy*, 152–53; Schmidt, *Yemen*, 215–22; David Smiley (with Peter Kemp), *Arabian Assignment* (London: Leo Cooper, 1975), 177–78.

56. Smiley, *Arabian Assignment*, 195.

57. Schmidt, *Yemen*, 130–31.

58. Schmidt, *Yemen*, 260–85; Wenner, *Modern Yemen*, 224–25.

59. Dawisha, "Intervention in the Yemen," 59; Nordeen and Nicole, *Phoenix over the Nile*, 191; O'Ballance, *War in the Yemen*, 182; Rahmy, *Egyptian Policy*, 155, 251–52; Schmidt, *Yemen*, 290. See also Edgar O'Ballance, *The Third Arab-Israeli War* (Hamden CT: Archon, 1972), 99; and Safran, *From War to War*, 332.

60. Nordeen and Nicole, *Phoenix over the Nile*, 191; O'Ballance, *War in the Yemen*, 182; Rahmy, *Egyptian Policy*, 251. Similarly, Abdel Magid Farid reports a conversation in which Nasser told Podgorny that only eight brigades were left in Yemen by the time of the Six Day War. See Abdel Magid Farid, *Nasser: The Final Years* (Reading UK: Ithaca Press, 1994).

61. Badeeb, *Saudi-Egyptian Conflict*, 37; Nadav Safran, *Saudi Arabia: The Ceaseless Quest for Security* (Ithaca NY: Cornell University Press, 1988), 122.

62. On U.S. reliance on a conventional-war strategy rather than a COIN approach, see particularly Andrew F. Krepinevich Jr., *The Army in Vietnam* (Baltimore: Johns Hopkins, 1986).

63. Be'eri, *Army Officers*, 108; Gamasy, *October War*, 83; George Gawrych, "The Egyptian High Command in the 1973 War," *Armed Forces and Society* 13 (summer 1987): 542; Edgar O'Ballance, *The Electronic War in the Middle East, 1968–1970* (London: Faber and Faber, 1974), 24; Young, *Israeli Campaign*, 98.

64. For a recent work that sheds much light on the events leading to the outbreak of the Six Day War, see Richard B. Parker, ed., *The Six-Day War: A Retrospective* (Gainesville: University Press of Florida, 1996).

65. After the Six Day War, one excuse the Egyptians offered for their defeat was that large numbers of their troops—and most of their best units—were still in Yemen. Furthermore, many Westerners continue to espouse this excuse, claiming that one-third to one-half of the Egyptian army, or 50,000–70,000 troops, were still in Yemen. However, the various accounts of the Yemeni Civil War—not the accounts of the Six Day War, which often display an ignorance of Egyptian operations in Yemen—all agree that by April–May 1967, that is, *before* the Six Day War, the Egyptians had reduced their forces in Yemen to about 15,000–20,000 men. See Dawisha, "Intervention in the Yemen," 59; Nordeen and Nicole, *Phoenix over the*

Nile, 191; O'Ballance, *War in the Yemen*, 182; Rahmy, *Egyptian Policy*, 251–52; and Schmidt, *Yemen*, 290. See also O'Ballance, *Third Arab-Israeli War*, 99; and Safran, *From War to War*, 332. Indeed, Nasser himself only claimed that eight brigades, or on another occasion two divisions, were left in Yemen before the May crisis and that he redeployed two of those brigades to the Sinai at that time. Even here, Nasser was undoubtedly exaggerating. For example, his statement to Iraqi leader 'Abd al-Rahman Arif that two of Egypt's seven divisions were in Yemen is clearly false, for all seven were in the Sinai for the war. (On these claims, see Farid, *Nasser*, 48, 115. This point was confirmed by Field Marshal Gamasy, who noted that Egypt had only independent brigades in Yemen, and none of its divisions were left there. Gamasy, interview, Dec. 1997.) It is also untrue that the forces remaining in Yemen were the best in the Egyptian army. In fact, largely the opposite was the case. While some paratroopers still garrisoned Sanaa, the better Egyptian line formations had already been withdrawn in response to Nasser's desire to extricate himself from the morass he had helped create there. Indeed, the "cream" of the Egyptian army was deployed in the Sinai — the 4th Armored Division, 6th Mechanized Division, and 2d Infantry Division. (For a concurring opinion regarding Egyptian unit quality, see Hammel, *Six Days*, 144–45.) Indeed, Israeli military intelligence considered the 4th Armored Division to be the single best formation in the Egyptian army and keyed on its movements as a sign of Cairo's intentions. Samuel M. Katz, *Soldier Spies: Israeli Military Intelligence* (Novato CA: Presidio, 1992), 183; Donald Neff, *Warriors for Jerusalem* (New York: Linden Press, 1984) 93. Moreover, Cairo kept up a regular rotation of servicemen through its units in Yemen to keep morale high and ensure that the maximum number of soldiers and officers had some combat experience. Thus, by June 1967, virtually all of Egypt's professional soldiers and many conscripts had served in Yemen. Likewise, at least half of all EAF pilots had flown combat missions there. Nordeen and Nicole, *Phoenix over the Nile*, 190, 193; Rahmy, *Egyptian Policy*, 252. Indeed, there were so many veterans of the Yemeni war among the Egyptian forces in the Sinai that Trevor Dupuy believes Nasser may have been emboldened in his diplomatic moves before the war, believing his "veteran" army to be more capable than it actually was. *Elusive Victory*, 235. (On Nasser's admission to Nikolai Victorovich Podgorny, chairman of the Presidium of the Soviet Central Committee, after the war that he had been overconfident about the military balance before the war, see Farid, *Nasser*, 14.] But Gamasy noted that many of Egypt's career soldiers believed that any experience gained in Yemen was of limited utility because COIN operations were so different from conventional military operations. Gamasy, interview, Dec. 1997.

66. George Gawrych, "The Egyptian Military Defeat of 1967," *Journal of Contemporary History* 26 (1991): 279; Hammel, *Six Days*, 44, 145; Herzog, *Arab-Israeli Wars*, 152; Israeli Ministry of Defense, *The Six-Day War* (Israel: Israel Press, 1967), 52; Neff, *Warriors for Jerusalem*, 193; Nordeen and Nicole, *Phoenix over the Nile*, 193, 199–200; O'Ballance, *Third Arab-Israeli War*, 99; O'Ballance, *Electronic War*, 32.

67. Cohen, *Israel's Best Defense*, 194; Dupuy, *Elusive Victory*, 244; Hammel, *Six*

Days, 149–50; Yonay, *No Margin,* 187; Lt. Gen. Mordechai Hod, interview with author, Sept. 1996.

68. Dupuy, *Elusive Victory,* 238; Samuel M. Katz, *Fire and Steel: Israel's 7th Armored Brigade* (New York: Pocket Books, 1996), 64–65; Katz, *Soldier Spies,* 183; O'Ballance, *Third Arab-Israeli War,* 93; 170–71; Safran, *From War to War,* 318; former senior IDF officers, interviews, Sept. 1996.

69. There is a lingering question as to why 'Amr suddenly introduced this new echelon into the chain of command only weeks before the outbreak of the war but failed to properly define the role he expected it to play. Virtually everyone in the Egyptian high command — including Murtagi — believed it to be superfluous, and Murtagi recommended that it be eliminated, but 'Amr insisted. This decision was probably related to 'Amr's increasing anxiety before the Six Day War. He has left no explanation for this move, but an obvious answer is that in May 1967, faced with the prospect of another war with Israel, the field marshal was attempting to fit Murtagi into the chain of command. Little is known about General Muhsin, but the mere fact that he held a high post under 'Amr strongly suggests he was a political hack. Indeed, General Gamasy criticizes him for abandoning his post at the moment when 'Amr ordered the retreat from the Sinai — the most critical point in the entire war — an action that sounds more like a political appointee trying to save his skin rather than a professional military officer concerned with the well being of his troops. Gamasy, *October War,* 65–66. In contrast, Murtagi had proven himself a highly capable officer time and again in Yemen (notwithstanding his failure to come to grips with guerrilla warfare). It seems most likely that 'Amr hoped to insert Murtagi into the chain of command to ensure that he had a veteran general in charge rather than the at best untried Muhsin without the disruption of sacking Muhsin and installing Murtagi. Gamasy notes that few of the Egyptian generals believed the Israelis would attack at the time 'Amr created this command, thus sacking Muhsin might have unnecessarily made a political enemy for 'Amr in the event that there was no war. Alternatively, 'Amr might have feared that a sudden shake up among the top leadership would disturb the troops in the Sinai — or the Israelis — and instead wanted to preserve a sense of business as usual. Given either of these considerations, creating a temporary command superior to Muhsin's would have been a clever way for 'Amr to have his cake (getting Murtagi, his best veteran commander, into a position where he could control the army in the Sinai) and eat it too (not having to relieve Muhsin). 'Amr's statement to Murtagi that he planned to run the battle with him from Murtagi's headquarters in the western Sinai also suggests that he wanted Murtagi's advice and expertise when making decisions in the event of war. See Gamasy, 45–66.

70. See, for example, Gawrych, *Key to the Sinai,* 77, 86.

71. According to some Egyptian sources, Field Marshal 'Amr wanted to launch an invasion of Israel and issued orders for such an operation, but Nasser wanted only to defend the Sinai and so countermanded him. See the remarks by Egyptian Ambassador Bassiouny in Parker, *Six-Day War,* 67.

72. El-Edroos, *Hashemite Arab Army*, 418–19; Gamasy, *October War*, 46.

73. Farid, *Nasser*, 73; Gamasy, *October War*, 46, 58; Anwar el-Sadat, *In Search of Identity: An Autobiography* (New York: Harper and Row, 1977), 172–74.

74. Gamasy, *October War*, 46; Gawrych, "Egyptian Military Defeat," 285–90.

75. Gamasy, *October War*, 46.

76. Cohen, *Israel's Best Defense*, 193–217; Dupuy, *Elusive Victory*, 245–47; Hammel, *Six Days*, 165–71; Herzog, *Arab-Israeli Wars*, 151–53; Katz, *Soldier Spies*, 191; Neff, *Warriors for Jerusalem*, 32, 202–3; Nordeen, *Fighters over Israel*, 67; Nordeen and Nicole, *Phoenix over the Nile*, 212; Yonay, *No Margin*, 202–13, 231–44.

77. Cited in V. E. Badolato, "A Clash of Cultures: The Expulsion of Soviet Military Advisors from Egypt," *U.S. Naval War College Review* 37, no. 2 (Mar.–Apr. 1984): 70–71. For contrasting accounts of Egyptian pilots who claimed to have tried to get airborne and challenge the Israelis but were prevented by the devastation wrought by the IAF, see Nordeen and Nicole, *Phoenix over the Nile*, 205–11.

78. Sharon, *Warrior*, 95–96, 119, 189–91.

79. Schiff, *Israeli Army*, 135–36.

80. Gamasy, *October War*, 57; Hammel, *Six Days*, 244. Sadat claims that Nasser was told about the destruction of the EAF around noon (*Search*, 175), while Nordeen and Nicole admit only that the EAF commanders were "slow to report the true extent of the defeat" (*Phoenix over the Nile*, 211).

81. King Hussein of Jordan (as told to and with additional material by Vick Vance and Pierre Lauer), *My "War" with Israel*, trans. June P. Wilson and Walter B. Michaels (New York: William Morrow, 1969), 60; Mutawi, *Jordan in the 1967 War*, 96; Neff, *Warriors for Jerusalem*, 205. These actions provoked Israel to destroy the Jordanian Royal Air Force and to launch a full-scale invasion of the West Bank that rapidly overran the forward Jordanian infantry brigades. See chap. 3 below.

82. Gamasy, interview, Dec. 1997. 'Amr is reported to have been an alcoholic, a drug addict, or both. Many accounts suggest he may have been drunk, stoned, or both during the morning of 5 June. However, Gamasy insisted that 'Amr was simply in a state of shock. For claims of Amr's substance abuse, see Dupuy, *Elusive Victory*, 267, n. 1; Farid, *Nasser*, 74; Hammel, *Six Days*, 244; Herzog, *Arab-Israeli Wars*, 160.

83. There is some confusion as to how many tanks the 4th Armored Division lost in this battle, although there is a consensus that it suffered heavily. For instance, Hammel notes one of the two Israeli armored battalions destroyed 28 T-55s on its own and that "many others" were destroyed by airstrikes. Presumably, the other tank battalion also destroyed a fair number of Egyptian armored vehicles. *Six Days*, 226. Sadat claims the entire division was annihilated. *Search*, 177. According to Adan, however, the IAF airstrikes were inaccurate and did not destroy many Egyptian vehicles at all—"maybe two or three." Adan, interview, Sept. 1996. Adan's assertion is supported by the results of several postwar surveys by Israeli, European, and American teams, which found that relatively few Egyptian tanks were actually lost to airstrikes. Adan's recollection was that "probably more than 60 or 70" Egyptian tanks were left burning on the battlefield, nearly all from IDF ground fire.

84. Randolph S. Churchill and Winston S. Churchill, *The Six Day War* (London: Heinemann, 1967), 112; Dayan, *Diary*, 60–62; Dupuy, *Elusive Victory*, 263–64; Hammel, *Six Days*, 223–26; Israeli Ministry of Defense, *Six-Day War*, 67–68; O'Ballance, *Third Arab-Israeli War*, 135–36; Safran, *From War to War*, 342, 346; Emanuel Wald, *The Wald Report: The Decline of Israeli National Security since 1967* (Boulder CO: Westview, 1992), 84; IDF officers, interviews with author, Jan. 1994 and Sept. 1996. Some Egyptian sources claim that the 4th Armored Division was destroyed not in ground combat, but by IAF air attacks as it left B'ir Gifgafah. These claims appear to be specious. First, the Israeli accounts of the engagement at B'ir Lafhan are extremely detailed and there is wide agreement among the participating Israeli officers on the course of the battle. The pilots who participated also largely concur on the course of the battle, although there are discrepancies in the details, mostly related to how effective the airstrikes were. This broad concurrence alone makes it difficult to dispute that some large Egyptian armored force hit the Israelis at B'ir Lafhan. Given the status and deployment of other Egyptian heavy divisions and the constant Israeli air activity over the Sinai, it is difficult to see how this large armored force could have come from any unit other than 4th Division. For example, it is well known that Shazli's armored force did not take part in the fighting, and certainly if it had, Shazli would not have failed to mention this action in his memoirs.

Second, circumstantial evidence from some Egyptian sources seems to support the Israeli version of events. Both Sadat and Gamasy admit in their memoirs that the 4th Armored was ordered to counterattack the Israelis on 6 June. Gamasy claims that it was ordered to Abu Ageilah and then ordered back after the first Israeli airstrikes. Gamasy, *October War*, 62. However, he later stated that he was present when Muhsin gave the order for the 4th to counterattack (via B'ir Lafhan, although the Egyptians did not then realize the Israelis were at B'ir Lafhan) but then said he was told off-hand by another staff officer sometime later that the 4th's attack had been cancelled because Muhsin decided it could not succeed. Gamasy, interview, Dec. 1997. Given that Gamasy attests to the fact that the 4th Armored was ordered to counterattack via B'ir Lafhan and the Israelis uniformly and convincingly assert that they did encounter the division there, this alone suggests that the battle did occur there. Obviously, the off-hand statement of another officer in the fog of the Egyptian retreat is far less damning evidence than Gamasy's testimony that he heard the original order being given. For his part, Sadat admits that the division was destroyed in combat on 6 June but makes no mention of airstrikes. While it is true his memoirs are not without bias, he has a very different axe to grind than do Egyptian *military* authors. Given the extent to which the Egyptians tended to blame their losses in the Sinai on Israeli air superiority, Sadat's failure to make this claim suggests that he means ground combat. See Sadat, *Search*, 177.

A third point bearing on this dispute is the fact that there is no record of IAF airstrikes devastating a large Egyptian armored force near B'ir Gifgafah early on 6 June, only of a CAS effort against the large armored force near B'ir Lafhan. The Egyptian accounts also are extremely vague and impressionistic: while they emphatically assert that the 4th Armored Division never was in contact with Israeli armor, they provide no details concerning the 4th's actual operations nor do they explain what alternate force the Israelis were fighting around B'ir Lafhan. Likewise, both the American and Israeli postwar assessments found very few Egyptian AFVs were destroyed by airstrikes anywhere in the Sinai.

Fourth, most Western experts concur with the Israeli version of events regarding the 4th Armored Division. The only Western author known to support the Egyptian version is George Gawrych. He favors Egyptian accounts over Israeli generally, whereas I have mostly found that the Israeli accounts — especially of the Six Day War — are the more accurate when the two are in conflict and an independent, objective source is available to resolve the dispute.

Finally, even the most revisionist Israeli military experts, such as Emmanuel Wald — who go to great pains to reveal any exaggerations or inaccuracies in Israeli military accounts and who do a far more devastating job exploding the myths of Israeli invincibility than the Arabs ever could — also concur that two brigades of the 4th Armored Division were largely destroyed in a major tank battle at B'ir Lafhan. My sense is that if, after all of their digging, the Israeli revisionists believe the 4th Armored Division was destroyed in combat at B'ir Lafhan, then there is a very high probability that it happened.

85. Dupuy, *Elusive Victory*, 265–67; Gamasy, *October War*, 66–69; Gawrych, "Egyptian Military Defeat," 298; Hammel, *Six Days*, 243–44; Sadat, *Search*, 176; former Egyptian generals, interviews with author, Dec. 1997.

86. Safran, *From War to War*, 351.

87. Dupuy, *Elusive Victory*, 279; Hammel, *Six Days*, 279; Herzog, *Arab-Israeli Wars*, 165; Historical Evaluation and Research Organization, *A Historical Analysis of the Effectiveness of Tactical Air Operations against, and in Support of, Armored Forces* (McLean VA: NOVA, 1980), 35 [hereafter cited as HERO].

88. Dupuy, *Elusive Victory*, 279. Several hundred other tanks suffered battle damage but were repaired, usually within a day or two The 61 tanks the Israelis considered destroyed thus represent catastrophic damage that could not be repaired.

89. Dupuy, *Elusive Victory*, 246; Nordeen and Nicole, *Phoenix over the Nile*, 195, 203; O'Ballance, *Third Arab-Israeli War*, 60.

90. Cohen, *Israel's Best Defense*, 201–2, 206, 215–17, 242–44; Nordeen and Nicole, *Phoenix over the Nile*, 226; Yonay, *No Margin*, 248–49; Young, *Israeli Campaign*, 90; senior IAF officers, interviews with author, Sept. 1996.

91. Cohen, *Israel's Best Defense*, 243, 253; Luttwak and Horowitz, *Israeli Army*, 174; Safran, *From War to War*, 328; Yonay, *No Margin*, 254.

92. Israeli Ministry of Defense, *Six-Day War*, 35–37.

93. Cohen, *Israel's Best Defense*, 242; Nordeen and Nicole, *Phoenix over the Nile*, 212–17.

94. Katz, *Fire and Steel*, 107.

95. G. P. Armstrong, "Egypt: A Fighting Assessment," in *Fighting Armies: Antag-*

onists in the Middle East, ed. Richard Gabriel (Westport CT: Greenwood Press, 1983), 159.

96. On the story of the 125th Mechanized Brigade, see Dupuy, *Elusive Victory,* 275–76; and Hammel, *Six Days,* 268–69.

97. Of course, there were exceptions to this rule. For example, after the commanding general of the 3d Infantry Division, General Nasr, deserted on 6 June, one of his subordinates apparently took command and implemented the general staff's orders to deploy covering forces at Jebel Libni and B'ir Hammah.

98. Quoted in Young, *Israeli Campaign,* 112.

99. Hammel, *Six Days,* 256.

100. For instance, see Sadat, *Search,* 174, 184–85. The Russians came to the same conclusion; see Nordeen and Nicole, *Phoenix over the Nile,* 219.

101. See, for example, Adan, *Banks of the Suez,* 228–29.

102. Schiff, *Israeli Army,* 134.

103. Nordeen and Nicole, *Phoenix over the Nile,* 220; Sadat, *Search,* 185.

104. For example, see Gawrych, "Egyptian Military Defeat," 280–81.

105. Gamasy, *October War,* 47–71; Gamasy, interview, Dec. 1997.

106. History Branch, IAF, correspondence with author, 10 Sept. 1997; HERO, 36.

107. Hod, interview, Sept. 1996.

108. HERO, 36.

109. Hod, interview, Sept. 1996. See also Nordeen, *Fighters over Israel,* 70–80.

110. HERO, 89.

111. HERO, 35–39, 41–42, 56.

112. Joint Technical Coordinating Group for Munitions Effectiveness, *Special Report: Survey of Combat Damage to Tanks,* 3 vols. (Washington DC: Defense Intelligence Agency, 1 Nov. 1970), 1:1–18. [Hereafter cited as JTCGME, *Combat Damage to Tanks.*]

113. HERO, 89.

114. The overall assessment of the U.S. survey team was, "This type of data tends to refute the contention that the Israeli Air Force was directly responsible for the damage to the majority of the Arab tanks and shows conclusively that ground weapons were, in fact, responsible for practically all damage to tanks under the strategical [*sic*], tactical, terrain, and weather conditions of the June 1967 war." JTCGME, *Combat Damage to Tanks,* 1:1.

115. Gawrych, *Key to the Sinai,* 26–30, 123–27.

116. For a concurring assessment that the principal difference between the 1956 and 1967 wars was the improvement in Israeli military effectiveness from a Western author sympathetic to the Egyptians, see Gawrych, *Key to the Sinai,* esp. 123–27.

117. Mark N. Cooper, "The Demilitarization of the Egyptian Cabinet," *International Journal of Middle East Studies* 14 (1982): 204; Richard H. Dekmejian, "Egypt and Turkey: The Military in the Background," in Kolkowicz and Korbonski, *Soldiers, Peasants, and Bureaucrats,* 127; Gamasy, *October War,* 89–90; Gawrych, "Egyp-

tian High Command," 547; Mohamed Heikal, *The Road to Ramadan* (New York: Ballantine Books, 1975), 42; David A. Korn, *Stalemate: The War of Attrition and Great Power Diplomacy in the Middle East, 1967–1970* (Boulder CO: Westview, 1992), 89; O'Ballance, *Electronic War*, 32; O'Ballance, *No Victor, No Vanquished*, 23.

118. Cooper, "Egyptian Cabinet," 217; Dekmejian, "Egypt and Turkey," 34–35; Gawrych, "Egyptian High Command," 547; Heikal, *Road to Ramadan*, 42.

119. Barnett, *Costs of War*, 104; Cooper, "Egyptian Cabinet," 217; Dekmejian, "Egypt and Turkey," 35–39; Gamasy, *October War*, 46, 92.

120. Heikal, *Road to Ramadan*, 186. See also Insight Team, *Yom Kippur War*, 483.

121. Dupuy, *Elusive Victory*, 357; Herzog, *Arab-Israeli Wars*, 200.

122. Nordeen and Nicole, *Phoenix over the Nile*, 234.

123. Cohen, *Israel's Best Defense*, 283–85; Dupuy, *Elusive Victory*, 363–65; Herzog, *Arab-Israeli Wars*, 210, 212; Nordeen and Nicole, *Phoenix over the Nile*, 239–46.

124. Bregman, *Israel's Wars*, 64.

125. Cohen, *Israel's Best Defense*, 296–99; Dupuy, *Elusive Victory*, 366; Herzog, *Arab-Israeli Wars*, 214–17; Nordeen and Nicole, *Phoenix over the Nile*, 248–50; O'Ballance, *Electronic War*, 131; Schiff, *Israeli Army*, 187; Yonay, *No Margin*, 279–91.

126. Cohen, *Israel's Best Defense*, 299–309; Dupuy, *Elusive Victory*, 366–67; Herzog, *Arab-Israeli Wars*, 217–19; Nordeen and Nicole, *Phoenix over the Nile*, 253; Yonay, *No Margin*, 299–302.

127. Sharon, *Warrior*, 264.

128. Cohen, *Israel's Best Defense*, 284; Herzog, *Arab-Israeli Wars*, 212; Yonay, *No Margin*, 274–75.

129. Cohen, *Israel's Best Defense*, 294–96.

130. Korn, *Stalemate*, 92. See also Nordeen and Nicole, 258.

131. Nordeen and Nicole, *Phoenix over the Nile*, 255. Other sources present different figures, but all agree that the Egyptians lost 100–125 aircraft in air-to-air combat with the Israelis during this period, while the Israelis lost 5–15 planes. For various estimates of these losses, see Frank Aker, *October 1973: The Arab-Israeli War* (Hamden CT: Archon, 1985), 46; Dupuy, *Elusive Victory*, 365; Gamasy, *October War*, 113; Herzog, *Arab-Israeli Wars*, 209–17; Luttwak and Horowitz, *Israeli Army*, 302; O'Ballance, *Electronic War*, 127; and Yonay, *No Margin*, 265.

132. Cohen, *Israel's Best Defense*, 284.

133. O'Ballance, *Electronic War*, 12.

134. Heikal, *Road to Ramadan*, 67.

135. Gamasy, interview, Dec. 1997.

136. In particular, Heikal points out that an important reason that Sadat cashiered his first minister of war, General Sadiq, was that Sadiq began trying to influence what Sadat believed were purely political decisions, principally the degree of Egyptian cooperation with the Soviets. *Road to Ramadan*, 183. On Sadat's continued depoliticization, see Cooper, "Egyptian Cabinet," 204, 217; Richard H. Dekmejian, "Government and Politics," in Nyrop, *Egypt*, 201–2; and Robert B. Satloff, *Army*

and Politics in Mubarak's Egypt, Policy Paper no. 10 (Washington DC: Washington Institute for Near East Policy, 1988), 6–7.

137. Gawrych, "Egyptian High Command," 551; Heikal, *Road to Ramadan*, 185; Insight Team, *Yom Kippur War*, 227–28; O'Ballance, *No Victor, No Vanquished*, 21–22; Avraham Sela, "The 1973 Arab War Coalition: Aims, Coherence, and Gain-Distribution," *Israel Affairs* 6, no. 1 (autumn 1999): 47.

138. Hassan El Badri, Taha El Magdoub, Mohammed Dia El Din Zohdy, *The Ramadan War, 1973* (New York: Hippocrene, 1974), 18, 23–24; Dupuy, *Elusive Victory*, 347; El-Edroos, *Hashemite Arab Army*, 490; Herzog, *War of Atonement*, 13–14; Korn, *Stalemate*, 91; O'Ballance, *No Victor, No Vanquished*, 23.

139. Gamasy, *October War*, 157.

140. Mohammed Heikal editorial, *Al-Ahram*, 28 June 1968, cited in Baker, *Sadat and After*, 188.

141. Quoted in Sela, "1973 Arab War Coalition," 47.

142. For a sense of what most Egyptian officers wanted, see "The Suez Crossing: An Interview with Major General Mohamed Abdel Halim Abu Ghazala," *Military Review* 59, no. 11 (Nov. 1979), 2–7. Abu Ghazala went on to become defense minister under Mubarak in the 1980s.

143. Aker, *October 1973*, 97–98; Armstrong, "Egypt," 148; al-Ayoubi, "Fourth Campaign," in Aruri, *Middle East Crucible*, 82 n. 32; Dupuy, *Elusive Victory*, 482; Gamasy, *October War*, 264–72; Heikal, "General Ismail," 219; Insight Team, *Yom Kippur War*, 296; S. L. A. Marshall, "Egypt's Two Week Military Myth," *The New Leader*, 12 Nov. 1973, 11; Donald Neff, *Warriors against Israel* (Brattleboro VT: Amana, 1988), 214; Shazli, 246–47; Sayyid Mar'i, "A Mission to Saudi Arabia and the Gulf States in the Midst of Battle," *Akhir Sa'ah*, 8 Oct. 1980, 16–19; Sela, "1973 Arab War Coalition," 55–58.

144. Lt. Gen. Sa'ad Shazli, *The Crossing of Suez* (San Francisco: American Mideast Research, 1980), 42.

145. Adan, *Banks of the Suez*, 63–64; Armstrong, "Egypt," 164; Badri et al., *Ramadan War*, 18; Gamasy, *October War*, 155–57; Heikal, "General Ismail," 217–19; Herzog, *War of Atonement*, 34–37; Insight Team, *Yom Kippur War*, 224; Ibrahim Karawan, "Egypt's Defense Policy," in *Defense Planning in Less-Industrialized States*, ed. Stephanie Neuman (Lexington MA: Lexington, 1984), 174; Korn, *Stalemate*, 92; Nordeen and Nicole, *Phoenix over the Nile*, 257, 278; O'Ballance, *No Victor, No Vanquished*, 27–30, 338; Shazli, *Crossing of Suez*, 17–47.

146. Herzog, *War of Atonement*, 34–35.

147. Gregory R. Copley, *Defense and Foreign Affairs Handbook of Egypt, 1995* (London: International Media, 1995), 24.

148. Heikal, *Road to Ramadan*, 35. Also see Ahmed S. Khalidi, "The Military Balance," in Aruri, *Middle East Crucible*, 23–24; Mohamed Sadek al Odeimi and Ibrahim Sa'ad el din Moharram, "Some of the Economic and Sociological Repercussions of the October War on Egypt," in *October War: Military, Political, Economic,*

and Psychological Effects (Canberra: Embassy of the Arab Republic of Egypt, Oct. 1976), 89.

149. Satloff, *Army and Politics*, 38–42.

150. Shazli, *Crossing of Suez*, 21. See also Nordeen and Nicole, *Phoenix over the Nile*, 225.

151. Heikal, *Road to Ramadan*, 43–44; Luttwak and Horowitz, *Israeli Army*, 300; Nordeen and Nicole, *Phoenix over the Nile*, 225.

152. Dupuy, *Elusive Victory*, 399–401.

153. For a scathing indictment of this mislearned lesson, see Wald, *Wald Report*, 88–91, 94–97, 107–10.

154. Cordesman and Wagner, LMW: *Arab-Israeli Conflicts*, 24; Dupuy, *Elusive Victory*, 401–3; Herzog, *Arab-Israeli Wars*, 239–41.

155. Aker, *October 1973*, 54; Cordesman and Wagner, LMW: *Arab-Israeli Conflicts*, 24; Dupuy, *Elusive Victory*, 403–5; W. Seth Carus and Hirsh Goodman, *The Future Battlefield and the Arab-Israeli Conflict* (New Brunswick: Transaction, 1990), 54; Herzog, *Arab-Israeli Wars*, 239–41; Nordeen and Nicole, *Phoenix over the Nile*, 273–74.

156. Nordeen and Nicole, *Phoenix over the Nile*, 273.

157. Adan, *Banks of the Suez*, 81; Badri et al., *Ramadan War*, 61; Cohen, *Israel's Best Defense*, 345–46; El-Edroos, *Hashemite Arab Army*, 505; Capt. Robert D. Lewis, "The Ramadan War: Fire Support Egyptian Style," *Field Artillery* 77 (Aug. 1988): 34; Nordeen and Nicole, *Phoenix over the Nile*, 284, 305; Sadat, *Search*, 249; IDF officers, interviews, Jan. 1994 and Sept. 1996.

158. Badri et al., *Ramadan War*, 18–35, 63, 79–82; Cordesman and Wagner, LMW: *Arab-Israeli Conflicts*, 71; Dupuy, *Elusive Victory*, 390–416; Gamasy, *October War*, 210–14; Heikal "General Ismail," 219; Neff, *Warriors against Israel*, 125; O'Ballance, *No Victor, No Vanquished*, 23–30, 96; Shazli, *Crossing of Suez*, 51–62, 233. Of course, the contributions of Egypt's combat engineers began long before 6 October. For example, they built the vast sand ramparts on the western side of the canal that hid Egyptian activity from Israeli observers and allowed tanks and ATGM teams to fire down on Israeli positions to cover the bridgehead on the eastern bank. Likewise, they built the various mockups Egyptian troops used to practice their missions as well as the secret bunkers used to hide men and equipment before the attack.

159. Quoted in Insight Team, *Yom Kippur War*, 147.

160. Badri et al., *Ramadan War*, 61–62; Dupuy, *Elusive Victory*, 411–16; Gamasy, *October War*, 206–9; Shazli, *Crossing of Suez*, 63–68, 233.

161. Heikal, *Road to Ramadan*, 33; Herzog, *War of Atonement*, 155.

162. Cited in Insight Team, *Yom Kippur War*, 221.

163. Adan, *Banks of the Suez*, 25–41, Dupuy, *Elusive Victory*, 419–20; Gamasy, *October War*, 216–18; Herzog, *Arab-Israeli Wars*, 243, 247–51; Lewis, "Ramadan War," 34–35; O'Ballance, *No Victor, No Vanquished*, 94, 115–17; Maj. Gen. Amnon Reshef, interview with author, Sept. 1996.

164. Lewis, "Ramadan War," 34–35.

165. Aker, *October 1973*, 97–98; Armstrong, "Egypt," 148; Bregman, *Israel's Wars*, 81; Dupuy, *Elusive Victory*, 482; Gamasy, *October War*, 264–72; Insight Team, *Yom Kippur War*, 296; Neff, *Warriors against Israel*, 214; Sela, "1973 Arab War Coalition," 55–57; Shazli, *Crossing of Suez*, 246–47. After the war, Isma'il told Mohammed Heikal in an interview that the reason he had not wanted to attack beyond the bridgeheads on 9–13 October was that the Egyptians had not moved their SAM units to the east bank, and so his armor would have had to operate without its protective missile umbrella. Heikal, "General Ismail," 219. Gamasy also notes that Isma'il raised this point in arguments with his staff at the time. But this seems more an excuse than a reason. First, the memoirs of Gamasy, Shazli, and National Security Adviser Hafiz Isma'il all make clear that General Isma'il was opposed to any offensive beyond the bridgeheads and had purposely made no plans for the execution of a phase two offensive to the passes, all the while paying lip service to the idea. (See the sources above.) Bregman notes that both Shazli and Gen. Bahieddin Noufal told him in interviews that the notion of a phase two offensive was never more than a ruse for the Syrians, who desperately wanted the Egyptians to continue the attack beyond the bridgeheads to keep the pressure on Israel and off of them.

Second, Egyptian logistical depots remained largely on the west bank. Supplies for phase two would require transport across the canal, a very awkward and time-consuming process. If Isma'il had ever wanted to even preserve the option of making such an attack, he almost certainly would have begun shifting supplies to the east bank immediately after the combat units were across, around 8 October. See Marshall, "Egypt's Two Week Military Myth," 11.

Finally, the Egyptians never moved large numbers of SAM units across the canal, even though they were fully mobile. A few SA-6 batteries as well as mobile AAA units were transferred to the east bank, but most of the SA-6 units and all of the SA-2 and SA-3 units remained on the west bank. Again, if Isma'il had even considered an offensive to the passes, he would have begun moving those SAM units immediately, again probably around 8 October. (For a Syrian military officer's opinion that the limit of the SAM umbrella was a false excuse, see al-Ayoubi, "Fourth Campaign," 82 n. 32.) Further evidence on this point is provided by Sadat's presidential adviser, Sayyid Mar'i, who was dispatched by Sadat on a diplomatic mission to Saudi Arabia and the other Persian Gulf states on 10 October to ensure their support for Egypt's war effort. Mar'i was accompanied by Maj. Gen. Sa'd al-Qadi of the Egyptian General Staff, who would brief Gulf leaders on the military situation. According to Mar'i, al-Qadi assured King Faysal that Egyptian forces could keep moving eastward with their SAM shield by moving their missile batteries forward so that "Egyptian forces will be constantly and effectively protected from attacks by the Israeli Air Force." So it is clear that the general staff was fully aware of the necessity of moving the SAM batteries across if they were to continue driving beyond the initial ten to fifteen kilometer bridgehead, again indicating that General Isma'il simply did not want to move farther and discrediting the notion that the Egyptians were somehow prevented from doing so by their SAM umbrella. (See part 2 of Mar'i's memoirs about the October War, "Mission to Saudi Arabia," 16–19.)

One additional consideration should be borne in mind regarding the last two points: the fact that the SAMs and logistic support did not begin crossing the canal in large numbers before 10 October (and actually never transferred in large numbers at all) is a clear indication that such moves were not part of the original Egyptian master plan. If Isma'il had wanted the option of a campaign to the passes, he would have included in phase 1 all of the preparations necessary for a rapid continuation. The canal-crossing operation and subsequent attacks were planned in meticulous detail. It defies logic that Isma'il and the general staff simply "forgot" to include in those plans such necessary elements for a phase two offensive if further campaigning had actually been a part of their intended strategy. The fact that they did not include these in the operations order strongly indicates that Isma'il's SAM excuse was a red herring and bolsters the convictions of Gamasy, Shazli, and Hafiz Isma'il that he never intended to go beyond the bridgehead. Indeed, it suggests that General Isma'il may have purposely structured the canal-crossing operation so that it *could not* go beyond the artillery road. It may be that he expected to face heavy pressure for an offensive to the passes if the initial crossing went well (this was obvious — Egyptian military and political leaders were pressing for it even before the October War began), and his plans may have been deliberately designed to head off that pressure. One cannot rule out the possibility that Isma'il hoped that, at some future point, he would be able to conduct another set-piece offensive to the passes. However, the evidence is compelling that he never intended this operation to quickly follow the canal-crossing, that it was at least weeks if not months away in his mind, and that the SAM excuse was just that — an excuse, not a reason.

166. Adan, *Banks of the Suez*, 237; Dupuy, *Elusive Victory*, 486, 490; El-Edroos, *Hashemite Arab Army*, 504–8; Gamasy, *October War*, 277; Herzog, *War of Atonement*, 205; Schiff, *Israeli Army*, 223; Sharon, *Warrior*, 310. Some Egyptian sources claim that no more than four brigades were employed in the offensive. I find this absurd. It seems to be a deliberate effort to downplay the size of the attack and therefore both its importance and the magnitude of the defeat. Several points have convinced me that the attack included nine (or possibly even ten) brigades. First, there are Egyptian accounts that concur with the Israeli and Western versions. For example, Nordeen and Nicole, who interviewed nearly all of the key Egyptian military personnel involved in the war and who are highly sympathetic to the Egyptians, agree that roughly nine heavy brigades participated in the offensive. *Phoenix over the Nile*, 290. Likewise, Gamasy recalled that the attack consisted of six or seven reinforced brigades on four axes of advance. Gamasy, interview, Dec. 1997. Second, all accounts agree on the goals and plan of the attack. Unless Isma'il had temporarily taken leave of his senses, he could never have expected four brigades to be able to defeat four Israeli ugdot dug in on the excellent defensive terrain of the Mitla and B'ir Gifgafah Passes and the hills west of them. While it is true that Isma'il opposed the attack,

Gamasy and Shazli did not and almost certainly would have objected if he had deliberately tried to sabotage it (or simply tried to keep losses to a minimum in what he knew would be a doomed assault) by employing a force so small it could not possibly have succeeded. In addition, detailed accounts of this event, and even his character as a whole, indicate that while Isma'il was not happy about this operation, he fully accepted the notion of civilian control of the military, and it would have been out of character for him to deliberately execute a mission half-heartedly once it had been specifically ordered by Sadat. Moreover, Isma'il's abiding concern for his troops makes it highly unlikely he would have sent four brigades off on an attack that had no chance of succeeding. It seems far more likely that he would have organized the best offensive he could in hope that his forces might pull it off rather than simply sacrificing four brigades because he was ordered to conduct a mission he did not like. Gamasy affirmed that Isma'il did *not* try to undermine the attack once Sadat gave the order but executed it as best he could (interview, Dec. 1997).

In addition, both the Egyptians and Israelis agree that Egypt lost 264–67 tanks in this attack. Four heavy brigades would have mustered about 300–400 tanks, thus 265 tanks would have constituted 66–88 percent losses in a few hours of combat. Such rates are astronomical in modern combat. Even in the worst defeats, it is rare for one side to suffer more than 50 percent casualties in such a short amount of time. Especially in this case, where the Egyptians were not enveloped by an operational-level Israeli maneuver but, in fact, broke off the attack only a few hours after it had begun, it would be very hard to accept such an extraordinary loss rate. For the sake of comparison, in the worst Iraqi attacks against Israeli forces south of Damascus during the October War — attacks in which the Iraqis fought ferociously, launched repeated attacks, and were outflanked and enveloped by operational-level Israeli maneuvers — they still never took more than about 50 percent casualties. And the Iraqis were considered far more inept than the Egyptians.

167. I am indebted to Barry Posen for drawing my attention to this issue. See Dupuy, *Elusive Victory*, 346, 553; and Colonel Dupuy's question to Gen. David Elazar in *International Symposium on the Military Aspects of the Arab-Israeli Conflict*, ed. Louis Williams (Tel Aviv: University Publishers, 1975), 251–60. See also Aker, *October 1973*, 108; O'Ballance, *No Victor, No Vanquished*, 298; and Heikal, "General Ismail," 224.

168. Dupuy, *Elusive Victory*, 488–89; Nordeen and Nicole, *Phoenix over the Nile*, 290; former senior IDF officers, interviews, Sept. 1996.

169. Reshef, interview, Sept. 1996.

170. Adan, interview, Sept. 1996.

171. El-Edroos, *Hashemite Arab Army*, 508.

172. Aker, *October 1973*, 100; Dupuy, *Elusive Victory*, 487; El-Edroos, *Hashemite Arab Army*, 508; Gamasy, *October War*, 277; O'Ballance, *No Victor, No Vanquished*, 165.

173. Dupuy, *Elusive Victory*, 487.

174. This was actually a Japanese experimental farm. However, the Israeli soldiers who captured it in 1967 could not tell Japanese writing from Chinese, hence the name.

175. Adan, *Banks of the Suez*, 290–303; Dupuy, *Elusive Victory*, 506–8, 510–11; Gamasy, *October War*, 288–89; Herzog, *Arab-Israeli Wars*, 272–73; Neff, *Warriors against Israel*, 244; O'Ballance, *No Victor, No Vanquished*, 232–35; former senior IDF officers, interviews, Sept. 1996.

176. Dupuy, *Elusive Victory*, 517–18; Gamasy, *October War*, 290. In the Third Army's sector, the armored brigade withdrawn was from 4th Armored Division. There may already have been one other brigade from the 4th on the west bank. According to Field Marshal Gamasy, part of the division was left on the west bank when the rest moved to the east bank for the 14 October attack. Consequently, between the 4th Armored elements remaining on the west bank and the losses the division suffered on 14 October, the transfer of a brigade back to the west bank probably left the bulk of 4th's remaining combat strength (perhaps as much as 200 tanks) on the west bank. Indeed, General Adan reported facing most of the division on the west bank, not the east bank. Gamasy, interview, Dec. 1997; Adan, interview, Sept. 1996.

177. Adan, *Banks of the Suez*, 388. Both of these anecdotes are from Israeli communications intercepts.

178. Adan, *Banks of the Suez*, 386–87, 391–92; Cordesman and Wagner, LMW: *Arab-Israeli Conflicts*, 93; Dupuy, *Elusive Victory*, 514–15, 552; Gamasy, *October War*, 290; Herzog, *Arab-Israeli Wars*, 276–77; Insight Team, *Yom Kippur War*, 376; Nordeen, *Fighters over Israel*, 139; Nordeen and Nicole, *Phoenix over the Nile*, 296.

179. Cohen, *Israel's Best Defense*, 387–90; Cordesman and Wagner, LMW: *Arab-Israeli Conflicts*, 85–91; Dupuy, *Elusive Victory*, 554; Herzog, *War of Atonement*, 259. Numbers of Israeli aircraft shot down in dogfights remain unclear. Most sources agree that Egypt and Syria *combined* shot down six IAF aircraft. However, as both Dupuy and Cordesman and Wagner note, probably a few of the twenty or so Israeli aircraft lost to "unknown causes" were shot down in air-to-air combat, so the "true" number is closer to ten or fifteen. There seems to be general agreement among the various sources that there were slightly more air-to-air engagements over Syria than over Egypt, although we have no way of knowing how many planes participated in each of these engagements or if dogfights over Syria on average involved the same number of planes as participated on average in the air battles over Egypt. Thus, relying only on the fact that there were slightly more dogfights fought with the Syrians, that the Syrians and Egyptians were about equal in terms of pilot skills, and assuming that on average the engagements involved the same numbers of aircraft, I estimate that the Egyptians probably killed slightly fewer Israeli planes than did the Syrians.

180. Cordesman and Wagner, LMW: *Arab-Israeli Conflicts*, 73, 85–87; Dupuy, *Elusive Victory*, 549–50, 606; Nordeen and Nicole, *Phoenix over the Nile*, 273, 303.

181. I derived the number of Israeli aircraft downed by Egyptian SAMs and AAA as

follows. First, the Israelis flew slightly more than half of all their sorties against Egypt. Second, the Egyptians had a larger and more extensive air defense network than Syria. Third, most sources agree that 40–45 Israeli aircraft were shot down by SAMs during the war and another 30–35 by AAA. Based on the greater number of sorties flown against Egypt and its more extensive SAM network, and assuming that Egyptian and Syrian air defense crews were about equal in terms of skill, I estimated that slightly more than half of all Israeli losses to ground-based air defenses were on the Egyptian front. I did not weight the losses more heavily in Egypt's favor because, on the first two or three days of the war, the Israelis made a determined effort to destroy the Syrian SAM network by airstrikes, which resulted in a significant number of aircraft losses. Note that the U.S. Defense Intelligence Agency also estimated that 40 IAF aircraft were shot down by Egyptian ground-based air defenses (cited in Nordeen and Nicole, *Phoenix over the Nile*, 300).

182. Cohen, *Israel's Best Defense*, 390; Cordesman and Wagner, LMW: *Arab-Israeli Conflicts*, 73–94; Dupuy, *Elusive Victory*, 550–56, 609; Insight Team, *Yom Kippur War*, 188–89; Lt. Gen. Binyamin Peled, interview with author, Sept. 1996.

183. Nordeen, *Fighters over Israel*, 147; Nordeen and Nicole, *Phoenix over the Nile*, 301.

184. Former senior IDF officers, interviews, Sept. 1996.

185. Insight Team, *Yom Kippur War*, 344.

186. Insight Team, *Yom Kippur War*, 340.

187. For instance, see Herzog, *Arab-Israeli Wars*, 317.

188. Dupuy, *Elusive Victory*, 595–605, 632–33.

189. U.S. and Western government officials, interviews with author, May 1992–Mar. 1997.

190. Gwynne Dyer, "Libya," in *World Armies*, ed. John Keegan 2d ed. (London: Macmillan, 1983), 368–73; Milton R. Benjamin and William Schmidt, "Arab vs. Arab," *Newsweek*, 1 Aug. 1977, 29; Dennis Chaplin, "Libya: Military Spearhead against Sadat?" *Military Review* 59 (Nov. 1979): 47; Omar I. El Fathaly and Monte Palmer, "Institutional Development in Qadhafi's Libya," in *Qadhafi's Libya, 1969–1994*, ed. Dirk Vandewalle (New York: St. Martin's, 1995), 173; Smith Hempstone, "Libya: Another Nagging Headache for Sadat," *U.S. News and World Report*, 10 Apr. 1978, 39; Andrew Rathmell, "Libya's Intelligence and Security Services," *International Defence Review* (July 1991): 696; Henry Tanner, "Sadat Orders Halt to Attacks in Libya, Heeding Arab Pleas," *The New York Times*, 25 July 1977, A3; Jean R. Tartter, "National Security," in *Libya: A Country Study*, ed. Helen Chapin Metz (Washington DC: GPO, 1989), 239, 246 [hereafter cited as Tartter (Libya)]; William I. Zartman, "Arms Imports—The Libya Experience," in *World Military Expenditures and Arms Transfers, 1971–1980*, by U.S. Arms Control and Disarmament Agency (Washington DC: ACDA, 1983), 15, 21.

191. David Anable, "Egyptian-Libyan Tensions Rise as Border Clashes Flare," *The Christian Science Monitor*, 22 July 1977, 3; Dyer, "Libya," 371; William J. Foltz, "Libya's Military Power," in *The Green and the Black: Qadhafi's Policies in Africa*, ed.

Rene Lemarchand (Bloomington: Indiana University Press, 1988), 59; Nordeen and Nicole, *Phoenix over the Nile*, 318.

192. Chaplin, "Libya," 50; Henry Tanner, "Libyans Say Egypt Keeps up Air Raids on Widening Front," *The New York Times*, 24 July 1977, A1, A12; Tanner, "Sadat Orders Halt," A1, A3; Henry Tanner, "Egypt Sends Libya List of Conditions for Keeping Truce," *The New York Times*, 26 July 1977, A1, A7.

193. U.S. and Western government officials, interviews with author, May 1992–Mar. 1997.

194. Anable, "Egyptian-Libyan Tensions," 3; Benjamin and Schmidt, "Arab vs. Arab," 29; Dyer, "Libya," 371; Foltz, "Libya's Military Power," 59; Hempstone, "Libya," 39; Don A. Schanche, "Egypt, Libya Seen Approaching Truce," *The Los Angeles Times*, 26 Aug. 1977, 13; Henry Tanner, "List of Conditions," A1, A7.

195. U.S. Department of Defense official, interview with author, Jan. 1992.

196. U.S. Department of Defense personnel and U.S. military officers, interviews with author, Jan.–Mar. 1992, July 1993, Oct.–Dec. 1996, and Feb.–Mar. 1997.

197. U.S. Department of Defense personnel, interviews with author, Jan.–Mar. 1992 and July 1993.

198. Copley, *Handbook of Egypt*, 81; Lt. Col. Joseph Englehardt, *Desert Shield and Desert Storm: A Chronology and Troop List for the 1990–1991 Persian Gulf Crisis* (Carlisle Barracks PA: U.S. Army War College Strategic Studies Institute, March 1991), 8.

199. Col. Daniel M. Ferezan, "Memorandum for Commander, Third U.S. Army, Attn: G-3, APO NY, Subject: Project 5/Liaison Team Golf After Action Report," 31 Mar. 1991, B-1. Col. Ferezan was one of the senior U.S. liaison officers assigned to the Egyptian corps. This letter was obtained via a Freedom of Information Act request.

200. Ferezan, "Memorandum," C-2; Brig. Gen. Robert H. Scales, *Certain Victory* (Washington DC: Office of the Chief of Staff of the U.S. Army, 1993), 222; Bruce W. Watson et al., *Military Lessons of the Gulf War* (London: Greenhill, 1991), 106.

201. Rick Atkinson, *Crusade: The Untold Story of the Persian Gulf War* (New York: Houghton Mifflin, 1993), 248.

202. Ferezan, "Memorandum," C-3–5; U.S. military officers, interviews with author, Oct.–Dec. 1996.

203. Englehardt, *Desert Shield and Desert Storm*, 8.

204. U.S. military officer, interview with author, Nov. 1996.

205. Drew Middleton, "U.S. Aides Say Egypt Lacks Ability to Handle Weapons," *The New York Times*, 21 Feb. 1986, 8.

206. U.S. military officers, interviews with author, Nov. 1996; U.S. Department of Defense personnel, interviews, July 1993.

207. See for example, Steve Rodan, "Report: Western Influence Enhances Egyptian AF Capability," *Defense News*, 27 Jan.–2 Feb. 1997, 9.

208. U.S. Department of Defense personnel and U.S. military officers, inter-

views with author, Jan.–Mar. 1992, July 1993, Oct.–Dec. 1996, and Feb.–Mar. 1997.

209. U.S. Department of Defense personnel, interviews, July 1993.

210. U.S. military officer, interview, Nov. 1996.

211. U.S. military officer, interview, Nov. 1996.

212. U.S. Department of Defense personnel, interviews, July 1993.

213. See for instance, David Ottaway, "For Saudi Military, New Self-Confidence," *The Washington Post*, 20 Apr. 1991, A14.

214. Ferezan, "Memorandum," B-5.

215. U.S. Department of Defense personnel and U.S. military officers, interviews, Jan.–Mar. 1992, July 1993, Oct.–Dec. 1996, and Feb.–Mar. 1997.

216. U.S. Department of Defense personnel, interviews, Jan.–Mar. 1992, July 1993. See also Cordesman, *Jordanian Arms*, 52.

217. U.S. Department of Defense personnel, interviews, Jan.–Mar. 1992, July 1993.

218. U.S. Department of Defense personnel, interviews, Jan. 1992.

219. U.S. military officer familiar with the Egyptian military, interview with author, Feb. 1997.

2. Iraq

1. Mehrdad R. Izady, *The Kurds* (Washington DC: Crane Russak, 1992), 62–65; Phebe Marr, *The Modern History of Iraq* (Boulder CO: Westview, 1985), 57; Reeva S. Simon, *Iraq between the Two World Wars: The Creation and Implementation of a Nationalist Ideology* (New York: Columbia University Press, 1986), 116–19; Marion Farouk-Sluglett and Peter Sluglett, *Iraq since 1958: From Revolution to Dictatorship* (London: Kegan Paul International, 1987), 11; Charles Tripp, *A History of Iraq* (Cambridge: Cambridge University Press, 2000), 47–76.

2. Simon, *Iraq between the Two World Wars*, 116.

3. O'Ballance, *Arab-Israeli War*, 82; Edgar O'Ballance, *The Kurdish Revolt, 1961–1970* (Hamden CT: Archon, 1973), 59.

4. Dupuy, *Elusive Victory*, 18; O'Ballance, *Arab-Israeli War*, 84, 115.

5. Dupuy, *Elusive Victory*, 51; Lorch, *Edge of the Sword*, 169; O'Ballance, *Arab-Israeli War*, 115.

6. O'Ballance, *Arab-Israeli War*, 118.

7. Uri Bar-Joseph, *The Best of Enemies: Israel and Transjordan in the War of 1948* (London: Frank Cass, 1987), 56–57; Dupuy, *Elusive Victory*, 16; El-Edroos, *Hashemite Arab Army*, 250–51; Sir John Bagot Glubb, *The Changing Scenes of Life: An Autobiography* (London: Quartet, 1983), 143; O'Ballance, *Arab-Israeli War*, 79–80.

8. O'Ballance, *Kurdish Revolt*, 59.

9. David McDowall, *A Modern History of the Kurds* (London: I. B. Tauris, 1996), 304–9.

10. McDowall, *History of the Kurds*, 312; O'Ballance, *Kurdish Revolt*, 89–102; Edgar O'Ballance, *The Kurdish Struggle, 1920–1994* (New York: St. Martin's, 1996), 57.

11. Marr, *Modern History of Iraq*, 178–79; O'Ballance, *Kurdish Revolt*, 85–91; Tripp, *History of Iraq*, 164–65.

12. O'Ballance, *Kurdish Revolt*, 104–10; 54, 65–67.

13. Safran, *From War to War*, 239.

14. O'Ballance, *Kurdish Revolt*, 151.

15. O'Ballance, *Kurdish Revolt*, 172–73.

16. O'Ballance, *Kurdish Revolt*, 87.

17. In the Iraqis' defense, the U.S. military would make exactly the same mistake in Vietnam a few years later.

18. Perhaps the Iraqi Air Force's most notable "participation" in the Six Day War occurred in 1966, when an Iraqi pilot defected to Israel with his then state-of-the-art MiG-21. The Israelis used the plane — and the pilot — to learn everything they could about Arab pilot training and the capabilities of the aircraft, knowledge that allowed them to develop effective countermeasures to the MiG-21. Interestingly, the Israelis found that the Iraqi pilot, although one of the elite of the Iraqi Air Force, really did not know how to fly. He had memorized the basic operations of the MiG and so could get it airborne and move around in it, but he had no understanding of the principles of flight or how to take full advantage of the capabilities of the aircraft. As a result, in mock dogfights Israeli pilots defeated him effortlessly again and again. Senior IAF officers, interviews with author, Sept. 1996.

19. Nordeen, *Fighters over Israel*, 77–82, 148.

20. Tzvi Ofer, ed., *The Iraqi Army in the Yom Kippur War*, trans. "Hatzav" (Tel Aviv: Ma'arachot, 1986), 11, 56; John S. Wagner, "Iraq: A Combat Assessment," in *Fighting Armies: Antagonists in the Middle East*, ed. Richard Gabriel (Westport CT: Greenwood Press, 1983), 67.

21. Ofer, *Iraqi Army*, 64.

22. Ofer, *Iraqi Army*, 195–98.

23. Riad Ashkar and Haytham al-Ayyubi, "The Middle East Conflict: The Military Dimension — Interviews with Riad Ashkar and Haytham al-Ayyubi," *Journal of Palestine Studies* 4, no. 4 (1975). Al-Ayyubi was a lieutenant colonel in Syria's combat engineer corps during the October War.

24. The various descriptions of Iraqi operations on the Golan Heights are all highly contradictory. For the most part, whenever there is a discrepancy among the different accounts, I have relied on the descriptions in Ofer, *Iraqi Army*, which is an Israeli General Staff critique of the official Iraqi General Staff analysis of the battle. Consequently, it provides both the authoritative Iraqi and Israeli perspectives on the battle. Unfortunately, I had access only to the unclassified version of this study, which generally uses articles from the Israeli General Staff journal *Ma'arachot* to present the Israeli position. Nevertheless, given the vast number of Israeli accounts of the October War that have been published since 1973, I assume that Ofer selected only the most accurate pieces to make his points. To a lesser extent, I have relied on Herzog, *Arab-Israeli Wars*, and Dupuy, *Elusive Victory*, primarily because their descriptions were close enough to those of Ofer to be confident of their general

accuracy. I relied very little on most other accounts of this combat, for they are too unreliable. In particular, although Edgar O'Ballance presents a very detailed story in his book *No Victor, No Vanquished*, he appears to have based his description primarily on interviews with the various Iraqi brigade commanders, who are inaccurate to the point of bordering on fantasy. In addition, interviews with Gen. Moshe "Musa" Peled — the commander of the 146th Armored Division — and several other IDF officers who took part in these battles generally supported the Ofer study when there was a conflict among the various accounts.

25. By 12 October, Laner's brigades had been in almost continuous combat for six days, having helped drive the invasion force off the Golan before plunging into Syria itself.

26. Dupuy, *Elusive Victory*, 468; Ofer, *Iraqi Army*, 91–111. Dupuy's account is inaccurate on two points: he states that the entire 3d Armored Division attacked and that the attack came on the morning of 13 October. Both Iraqi and Israeli accounts of the battle agree that only the 12th Armored Brigade (minus one tank battalion, though including a mechanized infantry battalion from the 8th Mechanized Brigade) conducted the attack and that it was launched late in the day on 12 October. Herzog claims that the Iraqi attack (he also says it was at full divisional strength) came during the night of 12 October. Herzog, *Arab-Israeli Wars*, 301.

27. Dupuy, *Elusive Victory*, 532–33; Herzog, *Arab-Israeli Wars*, 303; O'Ballance, *No Victor, No Vanquished*, 202–3; Ofer, *Iraqi Army*, 119–20.

28. Dupuy, *Elusive Victory*, 534; Herzog, *Arab-Israeli Wars*, 303–4; Ofer, *Iraqi Army*, 139–48; senior IDF officers, interviews with author, Sept. 1996.

29. Dupuy, *Elusive Victory*, 534; Herzog, *Arab-Israeli Wars*, 303–4; Ofer, *Iraqi Army*, 139–48; senior IDF officers, interviews, Sept. 1996.

30. Dupuy, *Elusive Victory*, 626–32.

31. Ofer, *Iraqi Army*, 14.

32. Ofer, *Iraqi Army*, 96.

33. Despite the lingering distaste for the British colonial period, the Iraqi armed forces kept British military doctrine as their method of operations. However, the Iraqis basically retained the old World War II–version, this being the last period of time that Iraqi troops had been trained by the British. Also, as was evident from their operations in Kurdistan, most of Iraq's tactical commanders at brigade level and below had an extremely poor understanding of exactly how to apply British doctrine, and consequently, many Iraqi operations bore little resemblance to the Sandhurst manuals they sought to emulate. To complicate matters further, the Iraqis had adopted a number of Soviet methods — in particular, they employed Soviet-style ground-control-intercept officers for the direction of air-to-air combat — and in many areas they had not fully integrated these Soviet methods into their overarching British-style doctrine. Many in the West mistakenly assumed that the Iraqis had converted to the Soviet model, and Iraqi tactical ineptitude contributed to this confusion. For example, Iraqi armor proved so bad at implementing British bounding-overwatch tactics that their attacks looked more like Soviet-style eche-

loned assaults, leading observers to conclude that they had adopted Soviet practices. However, this was not the case, for their doctrine remained overwhelmingly British and their execution uniquely Iraqi. Also see Ofer, *Iraqi Army*, 25.

34. Dupuy, *Elusive Victory*, 532–34; Herzog, *Arab-Israeli Wars*, 303–4; O'Ballance, *No Victor, No Vanquished*, 317–18; Ofer, *Iraqi Army*, 128–65.

35. Dupuy, *Elusive Victory*, 532–34; Herzog, *Arab-Israeli Wars*, 303–4; O'Ballance, *No Victor, No Vanquished*, 317–18; Ofer, *Iraqi Army*, 128–65.

36. Ofer, *Iraqi Army*, 207; senior IDF officers, interviews, Sept. 1996.

37. And not just broken promises during these four years: Barzani narrowly escaped an assassination attempt in 1971 probably ordered by Saddam Husayn. Izady, *The Kurds*, 68.

38. Sluglett and Sluglett, *Iraq since 1958*, 169.

39. Marr, *Modern History of Iraq*, 192; Haim Shemesh, *Soviet-Iraqi Relations, 1968–1988* (Boulder CO: Lynne Rienner, 1992), esp. 10, 122–62, and chap. 2; Sluglett and Sluglett, *Iraq since 1958*, 179–81.

40. Sluglett and Sluglett, *Iraq since 1958*, 179–81; William O. Staudenmaier, "A Strategic Analysis of the Gulf War" (Carlisle Barracks PA: Strategic Studies Institute, U.S. Army War College, 1982), 13.

41. Christopher Bellamy, *Expert Witness: A Defence Correspondent's Gulf War, 1990–1991* (London: Brassey's, 1993), 7; Lt. Col. Sergey Ivanovich Belzyudnyy, "Former Soviet Adviser Describes Experiences in Iraq: I Taught Saddam's Aces to Fly" (from *Komsomolskaya Pravda*, 23 Feb. 1991), in JPRS-UMA-91-014, 5 June 1991, 62; Cordesman and Wagner, LMW: *Iran-Iraq War*, 60; Norman Friedman, *Desert Victory* (Annapolis MD: Naval Institute Press, 1991), 270; Ofer, *Iraqi Army*, 25; Scales, *Certain Victory*, 113, 235–36; Staudenmaier, "Strategic Analysis," 6; Wagner, "Iraq," 77; U.S. military personnel, interviews with author, Dec. 1993.

42. Izady, *The Kurds*, 68.

43. Marr, *Modern History of Iraq*, 234.

44. Sluglett and Sluglett, *Iraq since 1958*, 188.

45. On the U.S. experience in Vietnam and the failure of reliance on overwhelming firepower, see Krepinevich, *Army and Vietnam*; and Russell F. Weigley, *The American Way of War* (Bloomington: Indiana University Press, 1973).

46. Cordesman and Wagner, LMW: *Iran-Iraq War*, 56–63; Edgar O'Ballance, *The Gulf War* (London: Brassey's, 1988), 28; Wagner, "Iraq," 63–68.

47. Frederick W. Axelgard, "Iraq and the War with Iran," *Current History* (Feb. 1987), 82; Amatzia Baram, "The Future of Ba'thist Iraq: Power Structure, Challenges, and Prospects," in *The Politics of Change in the Middle East*, ed. Robert Satloff (Boulder CO: Westview, 1993), 36; Cordesman and Wagner, LMW: *Iran-Iraq War*, 43–45; Heller, "Iraq's Army," in Baram and Rubin, *Iraq's Road to War*, 40–45; Christine M. Helms, "The Iraqi Dilemma: Political Objectives vs. Military Strategy," *American-Arab Affairs* 5 (summer 1983): 77–83; Dilip Hiro, *The Longest War: The Iran-Iraq Military Conflict* (New York: Routledge, 1991), 42–47; Andrew Rathmell,

"Iraqi Intelligence and Security Services," *International Defense Review* (May 1991): 394; Sluglett and Sluglett, *Iraq since 1958*, 206–64; Wagner, "Iraq," 68.

48. O'Ballance, *Gulf War*, 49.

49. On Iraq's war aims, see Phebe Marr, "The Iran-Iraq War: The View from Iraq," in *The Persian Gulf War: Lessons for Strategy, Law, and Diplomacy*, ed. Christopher C. Joyner (Westport CT: Greenwood, 1990), 59–74.

50. Former senior Iraqi military officers, interviews with author, Nov. 1998, June 1999, and Sept. 1999.

51. O'Ballance, *Gulf War*, 30–48; Arthur C. Turner, "Nationalism and Religion: Iran and Iraq at War," in *The Regionalization of Warfare*, ed. James Brown and William Snyder (New Brunswick: Transaction, 1990), 157; Wagner, "Iraq," 68.

52. Former senior Iraqi military officers, interviews, Nov. 1998.

53. Cordesman and Wagner, LMW: *Iran-Iraq War*, 70, 84.

54. Dupuy, *Elusive Victory*, 245–47; Yonay, *No Margin*, 254. Yonay notes that 240 Israeli aircraft generated 1,000 sorties on 5 June 1967. However, not only does this include airstrikes against Syria, Jordan, and Iraq, but it also includes combat air patrol, fighter escort, reconnaissance, and other support missions. Lt. Gen. Mordechai Hod, commander of the IAF during the Six Day War, said that he had 207 available aircraft on 5 June 1967, each of which flew four to six sorties. Hod, interview, Sept. 1996.

55. Maj. Ronald E. Bergquist, *The Role of Air Power in the Iran-Iraq War* (Maxwell Air Force Base AL: Air University Press, 1988), 56–58; Cordesman and Wagner, LMW: *Iran-Iraq War*, 81–84, 98–99; Karsh, *Iran-Iraq War*, 36–38; O'Ballance, *Gulf War*, 42–44; Former senior Iraqi military officers, interviews, Nov. 1998 and June 1999.

56. Cordesman and Wagner, LMW: *Iran-Iraq War*, 57–67; former senior Iraqi military officers, interviews, Nov. 1998, June 1999, and Sept. 1999. The estimates of operational Iranian ground forces are Cordesman and Wagner's and are very accurate.

57. Wagner, "Iraq," 70.

58. Cordesman and Wagner, LMW: *Iran-Iraq War*, 92–93; R. D. McLaurin, *Military Operations in the Gulf War: The Battle of Khorramshahr* (Aberdeen Proving Grounds MD: U.S. Army Human Engineering Laboratory, 1982); O'Ballance, *Gulf War*, 37–39.

59. McLaurin, *Military Operations*, 33.

60. Karsh, *Iran-Iraq War*, 45; Shemesh, *Soviet-Iraqi Relations*, 184–88.

61. The terms "push" and "pull" refer to the manner by which supplies reach combat formations. In a "pull" system, the unit must request specific supplies from the quartermaster corps based on actual usage. In a "push" system, preset allotments of supplies are regularly sent forward to combat formations by the logisticians without a specific request. Thus, in a pull system the unit must monitor its stocks and request resupply as the need arises, while in a push system it is up to the rear-

area services to make sure that the frontline formations have a steady stream of supplies. The push system is more wasteful than the pull system but usually is more effective in keeping fast-moving combat units supplied.

62. Former senior Iraqi military officers, interviews with author, Sept.–Nov. 1998, and Sept. 1999.

63. Hiro, *Longest War,* 46–47; O'Ballance, *Gulf War,* 49.

64. Former senior Iraqi military officers, interviews, June 1999 and Sept. 1999.

65. Former senior Iraqi military officers, interviews, Nov. 1998 and Sept. 1999.

66. Cordesman and Wagner, *LMW: Iran-Iraq War,* 115–26, 128–33, 135–43; Hiro, *Longest War,* 52–60; O'Ballance, *Gulf War,* 78–86, 88–89, 93–102.

67. This is not to suggest that Iran did not also suffer horrendous casualties. In many of these battles the Iranians took much heavier losses because of their reliance on human-wave attacks. Nevertheless, given Iraqi advantages in firepower, mobility, and numbers, plus Iran's casualty inducing tactics, such losses were to be expected and should not be seen as mitigating Iraq's defeats.

68. Former senior Iraqi military officers, interviews, Nov. 1998 and Sept. 1999.

69. Cordesman and Wagner, *LMW: Iran-Iraq War,* 123.

70. The importance of this arbitrary constraint can only be pressed so far. Hitler also decreed that German units were not to surrender a single inch of Russian territory, but Manstein, Model, Balck, Heinrici, Guderian, and other German generals responded by holding the forwardmost positions with thin infantry screens, deploying heavier infantry in better defensive terrain behind the frontlines, and then retaining their panzer forces as operational reserves well behind both infantry lines. Hitler's order greatly complicated matters for the Germans, just as Saddam's order did for the Iraqis, but the German generals handled it much better than the Iraqis.

71. Some commentators have blamed the unwillingness of Iraqi forces to reorient themselves to face an attack from an unforeseen direction on Saddam's dictate that Iraqi units not voluntarily relinquish their forward positions. This is not the case. Saddam demanded that the army hold every inch of territory they had gained, but he never specified the axes of advance his troops were to defend nor did he ever forbid units being attacked from the flank or rear to reorient themselves to face the attack. All Saddam had ordered was that the position be held. Once again, the comparison with German forces in Russia is revealing: despite receiving the same orders from Hitler, German units immediately redeployed to meet Soviet attacks from their flank or rear, nor did anyone — including Hitler — see this as contravening the Führer's orders.

72. Former senior Iraqi military officers, interviews, Nov. 1998.

73. Axelgard, "War with Iran," 58.

74. Axelgard, "War with Iran," 82; Cordesman and Wagner, *LMW: Iran-Iraq War,* 141–42; "Iraq's Army," *The Economist,* 12 Jan. 1991, 36.

75. Of course, there were limits to this. Saddam generally preferred to promote Sunni Arabs over Shi'ite Arabs or Kurds, and a competent officer with ties to

Saddam invariably had a better chance than an equally competent officer without the same connections. Indeed, Hanna Batatu has noted that, a number of key Iraqi commanders by the end of the war, including Generals Maher Rashid, Sultan Hashim, Shaban, and al-Barrak (the director of military intelligence) were all members of Saddam's Albu Nasir clan. Batatu, "Political Power and Social Structure in Syria and Iraq," in Sami K. Farsoun, ed., *Arab Society: Continuity and Change* (London: Croom Helm, 1985), 40.

76. Axelgard, "War with Iran," 59, 82; Cordesman and Wagner, *LMW: Iran-Iraq War*, 356; "Iraq's Army," *The Economist*, 36; Heller, "Iraq's Army," 46; Scales, *Certain Victory*, 117; William O. Staudenmaier, "Defense Planning in Iraq: An Alternative Perspective," in *Defense Planning in Less-Industrialized States*, ed. Stephanie Neuman (Lexington MA: Lexington, 1984), 54.

77. Former senior Iraqi military officers, interviews, Sept.–Nov. 1998, and Sept. 1999.

78. On U.S. intelligence-sharing with Iraq, see Capt. Michael Bigelow, "The Faw Peninsula: A Battle Analysis," *Military Intelligence* (Apr.–June 1991): 16; Lawrence Freedman and Efraim Karsh, *The Gulf Conflict, 1990–1991* (Princeton NJ: Princeton University Press, 1993), 25; Lt. Gen. Bernard Trainor and Michael R. Gordon, *The Generals' War: The Inside Story of the Conflict in the Gulf* (Boston: Little, Brown, 1995), 38; Eliot A. Cohen and Thomas A. Keaney, gen. eds., *The Gulf War Air Power Survey*, vol. 2, pt. 1, *Operations* (Washington DC: GPO, 1993), 64; O'Ballance, *Gulf War*, 198 [hereafter cited as *GWAPS, Operations*].

79. Central Intelligence Agency, "Subject: Iraqi Offensive Tactics," Mar. 1995, U.S. Department of Defense "GulfLink," World Wide Web, *http://www.dtic.mil:80/ Gulflink/indexpages/intelligence documents* (10 Nov. 1996).

80. Eliot A. Cohen and Thomas A. Keaney, gen. eds., *The Gulf War Air Power Survey*, vol. 2, pt. 2, *Effects and Effectiveness* (Washington DC: GPO, 1993), 127 [hereafter cited as *GWAPS, Effects and Effectiveness*]; Lt. Gen. Bernard Trainor, interviews with author, June 1994.

81. Political Deputy of the General Command Post, War Studies, and Research, *Battle of Faw* (Tehran, 1988), translated from Persian in FBIS-NES-94-076-S, 20 Apr. 1994, 28–49; Bigelow, "Faw Peninsula," 15–16; Cordesman and Wagner, *LMW: Iran-Iraq War*, 219–21; Hiro, *Longest War*, 167–68; O'Ballance, *Gulf War*, 173–74. It is worth noting that by the time of the Iraqi counterattacks, the Iranian assault had essentially run out of steam and so did not require much of an Iraqi counterattack to halt it.

82. Axelgard, "War with Iran," 58; Political Deputy of the General Command Post, War Studies, and Research, *Battle of Faw*, 49–51; Bigelow, "Faw Peninsula," 16–17; Cordesman and Wagner, *LMW: Iran-Iraq War*, 222–24; Hiro, *Longest War*, 166–70; O'Ballance, *Gulf War*, 173–79.

83. The events of 1991 seem to have largely borne out this assessment of the loyalty of the expanded Republican Guard. After the Gulf War, the RGFC remained loyal to the regime in putting down the Shi'ite and Kurdish revolts in large part

because this was a threat to Sunni control of Iraq. However, after the rebellions had been crushed, there were reports of coup plots having been discovered in the RGFC—and eradicated by units of the Special Republican Guard. Thus while the Guards *have*, on average, appeared to evince greater loyalty to the regime than the regular army, this loyalty is no longer so steadfast as was the case before the expansion of 1986. On this and related points, see Amatzia Baram, "Neo-Tribalism in Iraq: Saddam Hussein's Tribal Policies, 1991–1996," *International Journal of Middle East Studies* 29 (1997): esp. 1–19.

84. The Iraqi solution was almost identical to that devised by the Egyptians prior to the October War. There were considerable numbers of Egyptian military officers attached to the Iraqi armed forces as advisers in the latter part of the Iran-Iraq War, and the Egyptians have claimed that they taught the Iraqis to script their operations. Of course, the Iraqis insist that they hit upon the same method without any input from the Egyptians. Indeed, they claim that Egyptian personnel were only assigned to training commands and so did not have contact with the generals who actually formulated this approach. Unfortunately, at present, there is no way of knowing what, if any, influence the Egyptians did have in this matter.

85. "Fourth Part of Saddam's al-Faw Meeting," in FBIS-NES-93-081, 29 Apr. 1993, 30.

86. Central Intelligence Agency, "Subject: Iran-Iraq Frontline," 23 June 1988, U.S. Department of Defense "GulfLink," World Wide Web, *http://www.dtic.mil:80/Gulflink/indexpages/intelligence documents* (10 Nov. 1996); "Fourth Part of Saddam's al-Faw Meeting," 30–31, 34; "Saddam al-Faw Anniversary Address; Part II," in FBIS-NES-93-075, 21 Apr. 1993, 23–24; Trainor, interviews, June 1994.

87. Cordesman and Wagner, LMW: *Iran-Iraq War,* 247–50; Hiro, *Longest War,* 180–81; O'Ballance, *Gulf War,* 194–95.

88. Cordesman and Wagner, LMW: *Iran-Iraq War,* 250–54; Hiro, *Longest War,* 181–84; O'Ballance, *Gulf War,* 195–96.

89. "Fourth Part of Saddam's al-Faw Meeting," 27–41; "Saddam's al-Faw Anniversary Address; Part II," 23–24.

90. Cordesman and Wagner, LMW: *Iran-Iraq War,* 387–88.

91. Central Intelligence Agency, "Iraqi Offensive in Majnoon Islands Begins," 25 June 1988, U.S. Department of Defense "GulfLink," World Wide Web, *http:www.dtic.mil:80/gulflink/indexpages/intelligence documents* (10 Nov. 1996).

92. Cordesman and Wagner, LMW: *Iran-Iraq War,* 389

93. For concurring opinions that the Iraqi victories on the ground were the most important factor in Iran's grudging decision to accept a ceasefire, see Cordesman and Wagner, LMW: *Iran-Iraq War,* 395–99; and Gary Sick, "Trial by Error: Reflections on the Iran-Iraq War," *Middle East Journal* 43, no. 2, (spring 1989): 242.

94. For a good discussion of the events surrounding the downing of Iran Air Flight 655, see Cordesman and Wagner, LMW: *Iran-Iraq War,* 390–94.

95. Sick, "Trial by Error," 239–41.

96. Army Component, U.S. Central Command (ARCENT), "Battlefield Recon-

struction Study: The 100 Hour Ground War," declassified version, Headquarters, Army Component, U.S. Central Command, 20 Apr. 1991, 30 [hereafter cited as ARCENT, "Battlefield Reconstruction"]; Bigelow, "Faw Peninsula," 16; Cordesman and Wagner, *LMW: Iran-Iraq War*, 414; Freedman and Karsh, *Gulf Conflict*, 25; Trainor and Gordon, *Generals' War*, 38; *GWAPS*, *Operations*, 64; O'Ballance, *Gulf War*, 198.

97. Trainor, interviews, June 1994.

98. Cordesman and Wagner, *LMW: Iran-Iraq War*, 359–60, 363, 389; Hiro, *Longest War*, 195.

99. *GWAPS*, *Operations*, 77.

100. Belzyudnyy, "Former Soviet Adviser," 62–63; *GWAPS*, *Operations*, 75–76.

101. McLaurin, *Military Operations*, 29; Staudenmaier, "Strategic Analysis," 17.

102. Trainor, interviews, June 1994.

103. Some have suggested that Saddam repoliticized his military after the end of the Iran-Iraq War, with the result that the Iraqi armed forces again suffered from many of the problems that had plagued them in 1980 but were largely extirpated as a result of the reforms of the mid-1980s. (For example, see 1st Lt. Matthew Hurley, "Saddam Hussein and Iraqi Air Power," *Air Power Journal* (winter 1992): 4–16.) This claim is inaccurate. On the continued depoliticization of the Iraqi military from the end of the Iran-Iraq War up through Operation Desert Storm, see Kenneth M. Pollack, "The Influence of Arab Culture on Arab Military Effectiveness" (Ph.D. diss., MIT, 1996), 326–55, 662–64.

104. "Talk Questions whether Air Strikes Can Win War," *Baghdad Domestic Service*, 3 Feb. 1991, in FBIS-NES-91-023, 4 Feb. 1991, 45; Norman Cigar, "Iraq's Strategic Mindset and the Gulf War: Blueprint for Defeat," *Journal of Strategic Studies* 15 (Mar. 1992): 14.

105. Iraqi transcript of meeting between U.S. Ambassador April Glaspie and Saddam Husayn, 25 July 1990, in *The New York Times*, 23 Sept. 1990; public statement by Saddam Husayn, 5 Sept. 1990, *Baghdad Domestic Service*; Cigar, "Iraq's Strategic Mindset," 2–5; Friedman, *Desert Victory*, 108–10; Trainor and Gordon, *Generals' War*, 180–81; Eliot A. Cohen and Thomas A. Keaney, gen. eds., *The Gulf War Air Power Survey*, vol. 1, pt. 1, *Planning* (Washington DC: GPO, 1993), 60–64 [hereafter cited as *GWAPS*, *Planning*].

106. "Saddam Says Allies 'Lost War against Iraq,'" *al-Thawra*, 11 Mar. 1992, in FBIS-NES-92-053, 18 Mar. 1992, 15; "Ramadan Interviewed on War, Arab Relations," *al-Sha'b*, 28 May 1991, in FBIS-NES-91-108, 5 June 1991, 10.

107. Trainor and Gordon, *Generals' War*, 180.

108. For the clearest expositions of this belief, see Saddam's "Speech to the Islamic Conference," *Baghdad Voice of the Masses*, 11 Jan. 1991, FBIS-NES 91-009; "Talk Questions whether Air Strikes Can Win War," 45; interview with Yevgenni Primakov, *Paris Europe Number One*, 28 Apr. 1991, in FBIS-SOV-91-083, 11. See also Trainor and Gordon, *Generals' War*, 180; *GWAPS*, *Operations*, 111–13; and *GWAPS*, *Effects and Effectiveness*, 125–26.

109. For a good example of the extent of Iraqi passive defenses, see the photo of Iraq's Tuwaitha Nuclear Facility (the site of the Osirak Reactor) in U.S. Department of Defense, *Conduct of the Persian Gulf War: Final Report to Congress, April 1992* (Washington DC: GPO, 1992), 153.

110. Central Intelligence Agency, "Operation Desert Storm: A Snapshot of the Battlefield" (Washington DC: CIA, Sept. 1993); Barry D. Watts, "Friction in the Gulf War," *Naval War College Review* 48, no. 4, seq. 352 (autumn 1995): 94, 106 n. 5. The Iraqis deployed 500,000–600,000 troops in the KTO only to have this force melt to about 325,000–350,000 as a result of deaths and desertions, mostly during the Coalition air campaign.

111. ARCENT, "Battlefield Reconstruction," 13.

112. The name "Kari" has no particular significance; it is the French spelling of "Iraq" backward.

113. Nor can this be attributed to the possible presence of Iraqi fighters in the vicinity. Because Iraq could never properly coordinate air and air defense operations, Baghdad designated "free-fire" zones for its air defense forces and "free-fly" zones for its air force to minimize friendly fire casualties.

114. GWAPS, *Effects and Effectiveness*, 122.

115. Since the Gulf War, it has become clear that the success of the Patriot against the Scuds was apocryphal, for few, if any, al-Husayns were actually intercepted by Patriots. The best analysis of this subject is Theodore A. Postol, "Lessons of the Gulf War Experience with Patriot," *International Security* 16, no. 3 (winter 1991–92): 119–71.

116. At the time, some believed that the Iraqi pilots headed to Iran of their own volition. This was incorrect. The flight of Iraqi combat aircraft was purposeful and coordinated by Baghdad. See, for example, ARCENT, "Battlefield Reconstruction," 84; "Vice President Discusses Post–Gulf War Affairs," FBIS-NES-91-104, 30 May 1991, 21; GWAPS, *Operations*, 195; interview with Taha Yassin Ramadan, Amman *Sawt Al-Sha'b*, 27 May 1991, in FBIS-NES-91-104, 30 May 1991, 23; and statement by Iraqi Foreign Minister Ahmad Husayn, *Baghdad INA*, 12 Apr. 1991, FBIS-NES-91-072, 15 Apr. 1991.

117. "Number, Type of Planes in Iran Reported," *Iraqi News Agency*, 12 Apr. 1991, in FBIS-NES-91-072, 15 Apr. 1991, 26.

118. Trainor and Gordon, *Generals' War*, 269–71.

119. This story has found its way into the unclassified literature in Trainor and Gordon, *Generals' War*, 286; GWAPS, *Operations*, 273–74; and GWAPS, *Effects and Effectiveness*, 240–41.

120. Lt. Col. Charles H. Cureton, *U.S. Marines in the Persian Gulf, 1990–1991: With the 1st Marine Division in Desert Shield and Desert Storm* (Washington DC: Headquarters, USMC, 1993), 46; Trainor and Gordon, *Generals' War*, 272–88.

121. interview with Yevgenni Primakov, FBIS-SOV-91-083, 11; "INA Reports 'Aziz' Moscow News Conference," *Iraqi News Agency*, 23 Feb. 1991, in FBIS-NES-91-037, 25 Feb. 1991, 35; "Saddam Addresses Nation on Initiative 21 Feb,"

Baghdad Domestic Service, 21 Feb. 1991, in FBIS-NES-91-035, 21 Feb. 1991, 21; Freedman and Karsh, *Gulf Conflict*, 377–81; Hiro, *Longest War*, 368–69. For the text of the various Iraqi initiatives, see Micah L. Sifry and Christopher Cerf eds., *The Gulf War Reader* (New York: Times Books, 1991), 337–45.

122. ARCENT, "Battlefield Reconstruction," 58–59; GWAPS, *Effects and Effectiveness*, 165–69, 220; U.S. Department of Defense, *Conduct*, 159; Watts, "Friction in the Gulf War," 94, 106 n. 5. Watts's article contains the most accurate statistics regarding Iraqi formations, equipment, and manpower in the KTO. As noted by GWAPS, desertion rates varied widely among Iraqi units in the KTO. The frontline infantry divisions were the most heavily depleted by desertions. The regular army armored and mechanized divisions suffered fewer desertions than the infantry. The Republican Guards suffered least and were closest to their authorized strength when the ground war began. For a useful snapshot of desertions from selected Iraqi divisions, see memorandum for record, "The Gulf War: An Iraqi General Officer's Perspective," 11 Mar. 1991, doc. NA-22, declassified 1998. Some of the figures provided are remarkably accurate, others (such as for the Hammurabi Armored Division) are laughably inaccurate, concocted by an officer who spent most of his time trying (unsuccessfully) to desert the army.

123. "The Gulf War: An Iraqi General Officer's Perspective," doc. NA-22.

124. "The Gulf War: An Iraqi General Officer's Perspective," doc. NA-22.

125. Central Intelligence Agency, *Snapshot*; GWAPS, *Effects and Effectiveness*, 207–20. The term "rendered inoperable" refers to vehicles unable to fight against the Coalition forces for any reason, primarily from maintenance problems or destruction by air attack.

126. Central Intelligence Agency, *Snapshot*.

127. GWAPS, *Effects and Effectiveness*, 205–9; U.S. Department of Defense, *Conduct*, 138–39.

128. ARCENT, "Battlefield Reconstruction," 23–24, 30–36; GWAPS, *Planning*, 77; interview with Lt. Gen. William M. Keys, "Rolling with the 2d Marine Division," in Maj. Charles D. Melson, Evelyn A. Englander, and Capt. David A. Dawson, *U.S. Marines in the Persian Gulf: Anthology and Annotated Bibliography* (Washington DC: Headquarters, USMC, 1992), 148.

129. Cureton, *Marines in the Persian Gulf*, 72–88, 265–67; Keys, "Rolling," 153; Lt. Col. Dennis Mroczkowski, *U.S. Marines in the Persian Gulf, 1990–1991: With the 2d Marine Division in Desert Shield and Desert Storm* (Washington DC: Headquarters, USMC, 1993), 52–53; U.S. Department of Defense, *Conduct*, 258; *U.S. News and World Report, Triumph without Victory* (New York: Times, 1992), 294–312, 322–24; Lt. Col. J. G. Zumwalt, "Tanks! Tanks! Direct Front!" *U.S. Naval Institute Proceedings* 118, no. 7 (July 1992): 74–80.

130. ARCENT, "Battlefield Reconstruction," 90–92; Lt. Col. Peter S. Kindsvatter, "VII Corps in the Gulf War," *Military Review* 72 (Feb. 1992): 20–24; Scales, *Certain Victory*, 224–32; Jim Tice, "Coming Through: The Big Red Raid," *Army Times*, 26 Aug. 1991, 20.

131. ARCENT, "Battlefield Reconstruction," 86–87, 90, 95; Kindsvatter, "VII Corps," 24; Richard M. Swain, *"Lucky War": Third Army in Desert Storm* (Fort Leavenworth KS: U.S. Army Command and General Staff College, 1994), 204.

132. Atkinson, *Crusade*, 411–15; Trainor and Gordon, *Generals' War,* 367–68; Lt. Col. John H. Turner, "Counterattack: The Battle of al-Burqan," unpublished manuscript, Mar. 1993, 10–15; *U.S. News and World Report, Triumph without Victory,* 319.

133. Swain, *"Lucky War,"* 250 n. 65.

134. ARCENT, "Battlefield Reconstruction," 109; Central Intelligence Agency, *Snapshot;* Kindsvatter, "VII Corps," 27; U.S. Department of Defense, *Conduct,* 272.

135. For Iraq's discovery on 26 February that the 101st Division was at the Euphrates, see "Spokesman on Allied Landing in Dhi Qar Governorate," *Baghdad Domestic Service,* in FBIS-NES-91-039, 27 Feb. 1991, 20; and "Talk: Dhi Qar 'Will Swallow' Americans," *Baghdad Domestic Service,* FBIS-NES-91-039, 27 Feb. 1991, 20.

136. The Special Forces Division left one battalion of its 3d Special Forces Brigade behind to cover Highway 8.

137. "Official Spokesman Says 'Withdrawal Order' Given," *Baghdad Domestic Service,* 25 Feb. 1991, in FBIS-NES-90-038, 26 Feb. 1991, 16–17; "Saddam Speaks on Withdrawal from Kuwait," *Baghdad Domestic Service,* 26 Feb. 1991, in FBIS-NES-91-038, 26 Feb. 1991, 14.

138. Turner, "Counterattack," 14. Also see "The First Marine Division in the Attack: Interview with Maj. Gen. J. M. Myatt, USMC," in Maj. Charles Melson, Evelyn A. Englander, and Capt. David A. Dawson, comps., *U.S. Marines in the Persian Gulf, 1990–1991: Anthology and Annotated Bibliography* (Washington DC: Headquarters, USMC, 1992), 139–42, Pope, 83; U.S. military personnel, interviews with author, Nov. 1996; Gen. William Keys, interview with author, Feb. 1998.

139. The Tawakalnah Division had deployed in hasty defensive positions on the far side of a wadi that generally paralleled the 73 Easting grid reference line on U.S. military maps, prompting the U.S. 2d ACR to dub its fight with the Tawakalnah "The battle of the 73 Easting." Other U.S. units that participated in the battle had different names for the engagement — the 3d Armored Division called it the "battle of Phase-Line Bullet," and the 1st Mechanized Division referred to its part of the fight as the "battle for Objective Norfolk." Nevertheless, each of these engagements was part of a multidivision assault against the Tawakalnah's lines. Because the nearest major terrain feature was the Wadi al-Batin, and because this roughly paralleled the Tawakalnah defense positions, the official U.S. Army history refers to the fight against the Tawakalnah as "the battle of Wadi al-Batin." Many others have referred to this larger battle as the "battle of 73 Easting," which more properly describes only the 2d ACR's fight against part of the Tawakalnah's 18th Mechanized Brigade. I have chosen to use the name "battle of Wadi al-Batin" because it reflects the key point that the entire U.S. VII Corps attack on the Tawakalnah was part of a single

battle. Employing the name "battle of 73 Easting" or any of the other names used by the individual units conveys the false impression that this was a series of isolated engagements rather than a single, corps-level attack.

140. Ezio Bonsignore, "Gulf Experience Raises Tank Survivability Issues," *Military Technology*, Feb, 1992, 64–70; Central Intelligence Agency, *Snapshot;* Kindsvatter, "VII Corps," 29; Scales, *Certain Victory*, 261–91; Swain, *"Lucky War,"* 259–62; U.S. Department of Defense, *Conduct*, 279–81. Many writers have claimed that Iraq had only T-72MS, the standard export model. This is inaccurate. A significant number of Iraqi T-72s were T-72MIS, a better-armored version known as the "Dolly Parton" for its two prominent bulges on the turret.

141. For accounts of the tenacious resistance of the Republican Guards at the 73 Easting, see ARCENT, "Battlefield Reconstruction," 117–21; Vince Crawley, "Ghost Troop's Battle at the 73 Easting," *Armor* 100 (May–June 1991): 7–12; Col. Gregory Fontenot, "Fright Night: Task Force 2/34 Armor," *Military Review* 73 (Jan. 1993): 38–51; Maj. Gen. Paul Funk, "Keynote Address," in Jesse Orlansky and Col. Jack Thorpe, eds., *73 Easting: Lessons Learned from Desert Storm via Advanced Distributed Simulation Technology* (Proceedings of a conference, 27–29 Aug. 1991) (Alexandria VA: IDA, 1992), I-46; Michael J. Mazarr, Don M. Snider, and James A. Blackwell Jr., *Desert Storm: The Gulf War and What We Learned* (Boulder CO: Westview, 1993), 147; Tice, "Coming Through," 13–20; Steve Vogel, "A Swift Kick: 2nd ACR's Taming of the Guard," *Army Times*, 5 Aug. 1991, 28–61; Steve Vogel, "Metal Rain: 'Old Ironsides' and Iraqis Who Wouldn't Back Down," *Army Times*, 16 Sept. 1991, 16; Steve Vogel, "The Tip of the Spear," *Army Times* 13 Jan. 1992, 13–54; and *U.S. News and World Report, Triumph without Victory*, 336–42, 351–70.

142. Central Intelligence Agency, *Snapshot.*

143. Bonsignore, "Tank Survivability Issues," 64–70; U.S. Department of Defense, *Conduct*, 279–82; *U.S. News and World Report, Triumph without Victory*, 336–42, 351–70; Scales, *Certain Victory*, 269–91 (esp. 269–70).

144. Compare Central Intelligence Agency, *Snapshot*, with Scales, *Certain Victory*, 261–91 (esp. 276). The battle was fought during a sandstorm, and between the swirling sands and the chaos of battle, a number of U.S. units apparently mistook Iraqi units that suddenly opened fire on them from their defensive positions for Iraqi forces that had actually driven at them in a counterattack.

145. Scales, *Certain Victory*, 257.

146. Scales, *Certain Victory*, 298.

147. Central Intelligence Agency, *Snapshot.*

148. Indeed, the Hammurabi Division already had begun to establish defensive positions at the approaches to al-Basrah.

149. GWAPS, *Planning*, 71–72. For a concurring assessment, see ARCENT, "Battlefield Reconstruction," 30–36.

150. ARCENT, "Battlefield Reconstruction," 97.

151. Central Intelligence Agency, *Snapshot.*

152. Scales, *Certain Victory*, 233.

153. Murray Hammick, "Iraqi Obstacles and Defensive Positions," *International Defense Review* (Sept. 1991): 991.

154. U.S. military personnel, interviews with author, 1991–96.

155. For an interesting concurring opinion from an author whose work explores the importance of Iraq's inferior Soviet arsenal, see Bonsignore, "Tank Survivability Issues," 64–70.

3. Jordan

1. Be'eri, *Army Officers*, 343; El-Edroos, *Hashemite Arab Army*, 221–36; Glubb, *Changing Scenes*, 121–28; J. Vatikiotis, *Politics and the Military in Jordan: A Study of the Arab Legion, 1921–1957* (London: Frank Cass, 1967), 73–75.

2. Bar-Joseph, *Best of Enemies*, 57; Be'eri, *Army Officers*, 343–44; Dupuy, *Elusive Victory*, 16; El-Edroos, *Hashemite Arab Army*, 250. Though the country was known as Transjordan until 1949, I have chosen to use "Jordan" and "Jordanian" in my discussion of its participation in the Israeli War for Independence.

3. Safran, *From War to War*, 233.

4. Fouad Ajami, *The Arab Predicament* (Cambridge: Cambridge University Press, 1981), 144; Bar-Joseph, *Best of Enemies*, 56–57; Be'eri, *Army Officers*, 345; Robert B. Satloff, *Troubles on the East Bank* (New York: Praeger, 1986), 63.

5. O'Ballance, *Arab-Israeli War*, 98–99.

6. Bar-Joseph, *Best of Enemies*, 56–57; Dupuy, *Elusive Victory*, 16; El-Edroos, *Hashemite Arab Army*, 250–51; Glubb, *Changing Scenes*, 143; O'Ballance, *Arab-Israeli War*, 79–80.

7. Dupuy, *Elusive Victory*, 43–44; O'Ballance, *Arab-Israeli War*, 70–74.

8. Bar-Joseph, *Best of Enemies*, 4–56; Lorch, *Edge of the Sword*, 142–44. Bar-Joseph's account of Israeli-Jordanian negotiations is highly detailed but also very confusing. At various points he sets out contradictory accounts of 'Abdallah's thinking without indicating whether this reflected an evolution in the king's thought, an alternative approach, or simply a negotiating position. In addition, Bar-Joseph appears predisposed to see a compatibility of interests between Israel and Jordan and consequently downplays events that indicate more aggressive designs on either side.

9. Bar-Joseph, *Best of Enemies*, 15. See also Dupuy, *Elusive Victory*, 29; and Glubb, *Changing Scenes*, 141.

10. Dupuy, *Elusive Victory*, 62–63; El-Edroos, *Hashemite Arab Army*, 254–56; Herzog, *Arab-Israeli Wars*, 59–60; Lorch, *Edge of the Sword*, 179–80.

11. Radar Hill was the former site of a British radar station, hence the name. It dominated the Tel Aviv–Jerusalem road several miles west of Jerusalem.

12. Dupuy, *Elusive Victory*, 63–64; El-Edroos, *Hashemite Arab Army*, 257; Herzog, *Arab-Israeli Wars*, 63–65; Katz, *Fire and Steel*, 31–32, 35; Lorch, *Edge of the Sword*, 189–91; O'Ballance, *Arab-Israeli War*, 106.

13. Dupuy, *Elusive Victory*, 75–77; El-Edroos, *Hashemite Arab Army*, 258–259; Herzog, *Arab-Israeli Wars*, 75; Lorch, *Edge of the Sword*, 249–51, 289–90.

14. Lorch, *Edge of the Sword,* 290.

15. As only one example, see the account in Herzog, *Arab-Israeli Wars,* 83.

16. El-Edroos, *Hashemite Arab Army,* 312.

17. Dupuy, *Elusive Victory,* 627. For British and Israeli authors with concurring views, see Uzi Narkiss, *The Liberation of Jerusalem: The Battle of 1967* (London: Valentine Mitchell, 1983), 52; Safran, *From War to War,* 233; and Young, *Israeli Campaign,* 50–51.

18. Be'eri, *Army Officers,* 342; Dupuy, *Elusive Victory,* 282–84; El-Edroos, *Hashemite Arab Army,* 281.

19. Be'eri, *Army Officers,* 345; Hammel, *Six Days,* 286; Helen Chapin Metz, ed., *Jordan: A Country Study* (Washington DC: GPO, 1991), 234; O'Ballance, *Third Arab-Israeli War,* 172; Edgar O'Ballance, *Arab Guerrilla Power* (Hamden CT: Archon, 1973), 25; Satloff, *Troubles,* 63; Vatikiotis, *Politics and the Military,* 26–29.

20. El-Edroos, *Hashemite Arab Army,* 281; Glubb, *Changing Scenes,* 174–83; Lunt, *Hussein of Jordan,* 12.

21. Young, *Israeli Campaign,* 52.

22. Another problem that quickly arose as a result of the ouster of the British was the threat of a military coup against the regime. The loss of the British broke down the legion's former aloofness from politics. As long as Glubb and his compatriots were in charge of the armed forces, there was no question that the legion would remain apolitical: the British really had no interest in meddling in Jordan's domestic problems, nor did any of the British aspire to political power in Jordan. Thus, for King Hussein, bowing to the pressure of his ambitious, nationalist (mostly Nasserist) officers was like opening Pandora's box. Almost immediately afterward he faced a series of attempted coups and assassinations. In 1960, after narrowly surviving three serious coup attempts in just three years, the king moved to regain control over the military. He dismissed ideologically committed officers and concentrated the command positions in the hands of Bedouin officers with ties to himself and his family. He abolished the divisional organization of the army for fear that the command of the one Jordanian division was too powerful a position and a potential springboard for coup plotters. Meanwhile, he expanded the number of senior staff positions and filled them with family members and loyal senior tribesmen to surround himself with high-ranking men whom he could count on in a crisis. As a result, the king's problems with the military literally vanished, and its loyalty has been essentially unquestioned ever since. See Be'eri, *Army Officers,* 230–33; Cordesman, *Jordanian Arms,* 38; El-Edroos, *Hashemite Arab Army,* 317–19, 321–22, 332–33; and Mutawi, *Jordan in the 1967 War,* 16, 44.

23. Sharon, *Warrior,* 137–38.

24. El-Edroos, *Hashemite Arab Army,* 300; Sharon, *Warrior,* 138–40.

25. In fact, the Israeli raid against as-Samu' was really a retaliation for a fedayeen raid launched from Syria, and the mine incident was only a pretext. For an interesting examination of Israel's motive in attacking Jordan in response to an attack from Syria, see the discussion in Parker, *Six-Day War,* esp. 62–63. Also see El-Edroos,

Hashemite Arab Army, 334; Hammel, *Six Days,* 16–19; and Mutawi, *Jordan in the 1967 War,* 74–78.

26. The Israelis claim to have only demolished the 40 targeted buildings, however, Jordanian sources claim that the Israelis went on to dynamite another 80–100 buildings and homes. Hammel, *Six Days,* 20–21.

27. El-Edroos, *Hashemite Arab Army,* 334; Hammel, *Six Days,* 19–21; King Hussein, *My "War" with Israel,* 26–27; Mutawi, *Jordan in the 1967 War,* 76–79.

28. It is merely a guess that two of the Hunters fled when the Mirages arrived. This is because it is unclear exactly what happened between the other three Hunters and the second Mirage. When the battle started, there were four Hunters and two Mirages. We know that one Mirage immediately locked up with one Hunter, leading to the eight-minute dogfight and the eventual downing of that Jordanian. But this leaves three other Hunters to tackle one Mirage. The Hunter and the Mirage were fairly evenly matched aircraft, so three Hunters should have been able to either shoot down or drive off a single Mirage. If the three Hunters did engage the remaining Mirage but could not convert the kill, it is hard to imagine that the Israelis would have been impressed with their flying skills. Therefore, it seems unlikely that all three engaged. Nevertheless, the fact that the Israelis were full of praise for the Jordanian pilots suggests that someone must have engaged the last Mirage, for it seems unlikely the Israelis would have made such claims if only one of the Jordanian pilots even tried to engage the Israelis when they had a two to one advantage. Consequently, my best guess is that two of the Hunters fled when the Mirages appeared while the wingman of the (eventually downed) Hunter pilot remained and tangled with the other Mirage but was driven off. This would explain both the Israeli praise for Jordanian pilots in general and the fact that the remaining Mirage was not shot down or driven off by three Hunters.

29. Hammel, *Six Days,* 20–21; Yonay, *No Margin,* 220–21.

30. Be'eri, *Army Officers,* 344.

31. Israel's 16th "Etzioni" Brigade, defending Jerusalem, was actually a division-sized formation with eight battalions (four active duty and four reserve) rather than the normal brigade complement of two or three battalions.

32. Cohen, *Israel's Best Defense,* 194; El-Edroos, *Hashemite Arab Army,* 353–55; 373–83; Hammel, *Six Days,* 149–50; 284–87; Yonay, *No Margin,* 187; Young, *Israeli Campaign,* 51.

33. El-Edroos, *Hashemite Arab Army,* 354, 373–83; Dupuy, *Elusive Victory,* 282–85; Hammel, *Six Days,* 118, 286; JTCGME, *Combat Damage to Tanks,* 1:1–18; Mutawi, *Jordan in the 1967 War,* 119–20; Abraham Rabinovich, *The Battle for Jerusalem* (Philadelphia: Jewish Publication Society, 1987), 15, 289; Yonay, *No Margin,* 221; Young, *Israeli Campaign,* 51.

34. For assessments of Riyad's military skills, see Farid, *Nasser,* 173–74; Heikal, *Road to Ramadan,* 42; Gamasy, *October War,* 89–90, 108; and Korn, *Stalemate,* 108.

35. El-Edroos, *Hashemite Arab Army,* 373; Mutawi, *Jordan in the 1967 War,* 108–

14, 117–19; Narkiss, *Liberation of Jerusalem*, 98; O'Ballance, *Third Arab-Israeli War,* 223.

36. El-Edroos, *Hashemite Arab Army,* 373–83; Mutawi, *Jordan in the 1967 War,* 89, 113–17; Narkiss, *Liberation of Jerusalem*, 88–91.

37. Many Arabs, and Jordanians in particular, have spun elaborate conspiracy theories claiming that the Israelis always intended to attack the West Bank and that the entire crisis with Syria and Egypt was merely a ruse to create an opportunity to seize the region. These stories are entirely unconvincing. For a good discussion of these theories that puts them to rest, see Parker, *Six-Day War,* 160–74.

38. King Hussein, *My "War" with Israel,* 11–20, 35–36.

39. King Hussein, *My "War" with Israel,* 60–63, 66, 71, 76–79; Mutawi, *Jordan in the 1967 War,* 144; O'Ballance, *Third Arab-Israeli War,* 68, 142; Parker, *Six-Day War,* 171–72.

40. I assume that the Jordanians were lost because there was no reason for them to have attacked Netanyah and Kfar Sirkin. Netanyah was a resort town of no military value, and was not even a major population center. Similarly, Kfar Sirkin had not been used by the IAF for years, and it was just luck that a transport was present, dispersed there by a cautious Israeli squadron commander. However, Kfar Sirkin in relation to Netanyah approximates the location of Ben Gurion Airport to Tel Aviv, just to the south. Thus, it seems far more likely that the Jordanians were going after Israel's largest city and its largest and best-known airfield, got lost, and mistook Netanyah and Kfar Sirkin for their actual targets.

41. Cohen, *Israel's Best Defense,* 218–20; Dupuy, *Elusive Victory,* 247; King Hussein, *My "War" with Israel,* 66–67; Nordeen, *Fighters over Israel,* 67; O'Ballance, *Third Arab-Israeli War,* 70; Yonay, *No Margin,* 250–53. Nordeen claims that one of the two late-returning Hunters shot down an Israeli Mystere before being shot down by a Mirage.

42. See the comments by Mutawi in Parker, *Six-Day War,* 172.

43. Quoted in Robert Moskin, *Among Lions: The Definitive Account of the 1967 Battle for Jerusalem* (New York: Arbor House, 1982), 158.

44. Hammel, *Six Days,* 305–15; Narkiss, *Liberation of Jerusalem*, 136–37, 159–62; senior IDF officers, interviews with author, Sept. 1996.

45. For confirmation that neither the 75-mm high-velocity gun on the Israeli M-51 nor the 76-mm gun on the Israeli Shermans could effectively penetrate the frontal armor of the Jordanian Pattons, see JTCGME, *Combat Damage to Tanks,* 1:105–21.

46. Dupuy, *Elusive Victory,* 299; Hammel, *Six Days,* 315–20, 335–36; Herzog, *Arab-Israeli Wars,* 176; Moskin, *Among Lions,* 289–90; Narkiss, *Liberation of Jerusalem*, 192–93, 200, 211–13; O'Ballance, *Third Arab-Israeli War,* 192–93; Gen. Uzi Narkiss, interview with author, Sept. 1996. Jordanian accounts of this battle, as for many other battles on the West Bank, claim that most of their losses were to airstrikes. The Israeli accounts, however, make no mention of airstrikes whatsoever.

I favor the Israeli version for two reasons. First, the Israeli accounts are extremely detailed, logical, and generally lack contradictions, while the same cannot be said for the Jordanian versions. In particular, General Narkiss's account of the fighting is very good in terms of its objectivity and attention to detail, and it notes exactly when and where he received airstrikes from the IAF. Second, since the Six Day War, the Jordanians have tended to make the IAF into a kind of deus ex machina against which they were powerless and could not have been expected to prevail, thereby somehow excusing their defeats. (In an extreme example of this kind of obfuscation, El-Edroos claims that "relentless and non-stop" Israeli air strikes prevented the 60th Armored Brigade from getting any farther than al-Ayzariyah — 10 kilometers from Tel al-Ful — and thus he claims that no battle ever took place between that unit and the Israeli 10th Mechanized Brigade. See El-Edroos, *Hashemite Arab Army*, 379–80.) As a result, Israeli airstrikes appear constantly throughout Jordanian accounts of the fighting and invariably are portrayed as the deciding factor in the battle. While IAF strikes were certainly numerous and an important element in the Israeli victory, the reality falls far short of the Jordanian claims. For instance, see the detailed assessment by the American Joint Technical Coordinating Group for Munitions Effectiveness, which concluded that the damage to Arab tanks by Israeli airstrikes had been *vastly* exaggerated and, in reality, was almost negligible. JTCGME, *Combat Damage to Tanks*.

47. Dupuy, *Elusive Victory*, 299; El-Edroos, *Hashemite Arab Army*, 378; Hammel, *Six Days*, 359–61; Herzog, *Arab-Israeli Wars*, 172; Narkiss, *Liberation of Jerusalem*, 195–99. Accounts vary as to what happened at Latrun. I have followed General Narkiss's account as probably being the most accurate. Hammel contends that the Israelis employed a battalion of infantry supported by a company of Shermans against the southern flank, which cut the narrow neck of Latrun, and then hit the Jordanian positions from the rear, leading to their rapid collapse. The official Israeli history notes simply that the Jordanians fought poorly there, and the IDF had little trouble taking it. Neither Herzog nor Dupuy has much to say about Latrun, only that the Israelis overpowered the Jordanians quickly. El-Edroos, however, contends that there was a "savage fight" between the two sides in which the Israelis eventually prevailed. El-Edroos's account is almost certainly nonsense or propaganda, but it is difficult to decide between the differing descriptions of Hammel and Narkiss. I opted for Narkiss's primarily because Hammel's sources are weakest on the fighting in the West Bank, while Narkiss was the commander of the operation, and his account is based on the detailed log kept by his aide during the war. In addition, I have had the opportunity to interview General Narkiss and probe the accuracy and consistency of his account, and I came away convinced of its veracity.

48. Dupuy, *Elusive Victory*, 297–99; El-Edroos, *Hashemite Arab Army*, 378–79; Gur, 58–155; Hammel, *Six Days*, 331–35; Herzog, *Arab-Israeli Wars*, 173–76; Moskin, *Among Lions*, 208–23, 255–74; Mutawi, *Jordan in the 1967 War*, 133; Narkiss, *Liberation of Jerusalem*, 158–59, 162–81; O'Ballance, *Third Arab-Israeli*

War, 197; Rabinovich, *Battle for Jerusalem,* 193–230; senior IDF officers, interviews, Sept. 1996.

49. Dupuy, *Elusive Victory,* 309–10; El-Edroos, *Hashemite Arab Army,* 386; Hammel, *Six Days,* 366–67; Herzog, *Arab-Israeli Wars,* 178–79; Israeli Ministry of Defense, *Six-Day War,* 103; Mutawi, *Jordan in the 1967 War,* 137; O'Ballance, *Third Arab-Israeli War,* 202.

50. Dupuy, *Elusive Victory,* 310–11; El-Edroos, *Hashemite Arab Army,* 387–88; Hammel, *Six Days,* 369–71; Israeli Ministry of Defense, *Six-Day War,* 104; O'Ballance, *Third Arab-Israeli War,* 203–7; senior IDF officers, interviews, Sept. 1996.

51. King Hussein had already ordered a withdrawal and countermanded it By this time. While this caused some severe confusion among other Jordanian units, Brigadier al-Jazi apparently considered the announcements so vague that they were open to interpretation, and his interpretation was to remain in place and keep fighting. Thus, alone among Jordanian formations, the 40th Armored Brigade kept on fighting long after the rest of the army had collapsed. See Dupuy, *Elusive Victory,* 310–11; Hammel, *Six Days,* 374–78; Mutawi, *Jordan in the 1967 War,* 136–38.

52. Dupuy, *Elusive Victory,* 310–11; El-Edroos, *Hashemite Arab Army,* 386–88; Hammel, *Six Days,* 381; Herzog, *Arab-Israeli Wars,* 179; Israeli Ministry of Defense, *Six-Day War,* 112; Mutawi, *Jordan in the 1967 War,* 137; O'Ballance, *Third Arab-Israeli War,* 203–7. This is essentially Dupuy's version of the *denouement* of the battle of Qabatiyah crossroads. Unfortunately, few of the accounts of the fighting agree on why the Israelis eventually were able to get through the Jordanian positions on the morning of 7 June. However, Dupuy's account seems the most likely. Herzog's account is vague but conforms broadly to Dupuy's version. The account in the official Israeli history also squares largely with Dupuy's account of the battle, but I have not relied heavily on this source because of its obvious biases. By contrast, the Jordanian accounts (Mutawi and El-Edroos) state that the 40th was virtually obliterated by the IAF while in place on the ridgeline and that the Israeli ground forces merely swept away its remnants after the battle was essentially over.

I have several reasons for disregarding this version. First, as noted previously, the Jordanian accounts of the Six Day War blame virtually every setback on the IAF, no matter how minor. However, in many of these cases, the Jordanian accounts are gross exaggerations. Second, while it is clear that the IAF was an important element of the Jordanian defeat at Qabatiyah crossroads, the speed of the final Israeli victory suggests that airpower was not the only element of Jordan's defeat. The Israelis allowed only 15–30 minutes (accounts vary) for airstrikes and artillery bombardment prior to their ground assault at dawn on 7 June. Even if the entire IAF had participated in the attack, it is almost inconceivable that 120–150 Jordanian armored vehicles, camouflaged and dug in along a wooded, rocky ridgeline, could have been destroyed by the IAF *in the dark* in just a half hour. In the best of circumstances, against exposed Jordanian columns moving during the day along the narrow roads of the Judaean hills and unable to flee or hide, Israeli airstrikes appear to have achieved an armored vehicle kill-per-sortie ratio of no better than 0.5 (and probably closer to 0.2). It is extremely unlikely that they could have achieved a similar ratio against the 40th Armored Brigade in their positions at Qabatiyah crossroads.

For the sake of argument, however, let us assume the IAF achieved a kill-per-sortie ratio of 0.5 and that it only killed 70 Jordanian tanks and APCs, causing the rest to flee. To accomplish this, the Israelis would have had to have flown 140 attack sorties just against Qabatiyah crossroads. Because thirty minutes is too short a time even for Israeli jets to conduct an attack on dug-in armor, return to base, refuel and rearm, return to the battlefield, and conduct another strike, the Israelis would have had to commit 140 aircraft to this mission. The entire IAF at the start of the war was only 207 aircraft, and by 7 June it was down to about 160–170 operational warplanes. The Israelis only flew 233 ground-attack sorties on 7 June, thus such an effort against Qabatiyah would have constituted over half the air force's entire air-to-ground campaign that day—a day when all sources report heavy air attacks against the Jordanian forces retreating back to the east bank. (History Branch, IAF, correspondence with the author, 10 Sept. 1997.) One would expect that if the Israelis had pulled all of their aircraft off other missions to make a massive attack on Qabatiyah crossroads someone might have mentioned it, but none of the accounts of the Six Day War or the histories of the IAF do. Likewise, if the IAF had committed over half of all of its strike sorties to this battle, it would also be reasonable to expect some source to mention this fact. Instead, by all accounts, the air effort against Qabatiyah, while significant, did not necessarily receive more attention than the constant Israeli air effort against retreating Jordanian forces or those against the Egyptian army retreating from the Sinai.

The Israelis found after the war that, in fact, they generally had achieved an armored vehicle kill-per-sortie ratio of 0.1 — which is also more in tune with historical norms. (See HERO, 36–42.) There is no reason to believe that the IAF strikes on the 40th Armored Brigade achieved better than this average, and given the terrain (wooded hills) and the time of day (before dawn), the IAF probably did worse than average here. Consequently, to have inflicted even 25 percent casualties on this brigade, a far cry from the Jordanian claims, would have required the Israelis to have flown 350–400 sorties if the more accurate kill-per-sortie figure is used—and they only flew 233 against the entire West Bank on the seventh.

Based on this evidence, it seems far more reasonable to assume the Israelis flew 40–50 sorties against Qabatiyah on the seventh. Assuming that the Israelis flew about 50 sorties against this position, we would expect them to have destroyed about five Jordanian armored vehicles. This figure is entirely in keeping with the experience of other Arab armored forces under air attack during the war, and it hardly would constitute the obliteration of the 40th Armored Brigade by the IAF. It also accords well with the official U.S. military survey of damaged tanks after the war, which found that less than 2 percent of Arab tanks lost during the war were destroyed by airstrikes. Consequently, it seems highly unlikely that the IAF alone could have mauled the 40th Brigade given how little evidence there was of armored vehicles being destroyed by airstrikes. (See JTCGME, *Combat Damage to Tanks*, esp. 1:1–17.) As a final note, Nordeen also argues that Israeli ground forces played the key role in defeating the 40th Brigade at Qabatiyah. His book is notoriously sympathetic to the IAF, and so if he claims that the IAF's role was secondary to the ground forces at Qabatiyah, there is good reason to believe him. (See *Fighters over Israel*, 79.)

In Hammel's account of the battle, the Jordanians withdrew during the night—*before the Israeli attack*—as part of the king's order to fall back from the West Bank. However, this version of events seems even less likely than the Jordanian version. First, it does not fit al-Jazi's personality profile: as far as we know, the only withdrawal order issued to the 40th was the king's general announcement during the afternoon of 6 June, which he then countermanded. Al-Jazi disregarded these orders and kept fighting the Israelis. This being the case, why would such a determined soldier as al-Jazi suddenly decide to obey them in the middle of the night? (Hammel himself notes al-Jazi's exceptional aggressiveness on pages 375 and 379). Second, the Jordanian sources agree that al-Jazi did not voluntarily withdraw—he was forced off the ridge by the Israeli assault at dawn on the seventh. Not only is there no reason for them to lie about this, there is every reason for them to have said otherwise if it were true. That is, Jordanian authors are most concerned with preserving the image of Jordanian military prowess, thus a voluntary withdrawal would have suited their objective even better than their claim that the 40th was destroyed by airstrikes, the version they do proffer. Finally, if the brigade retreated voluntarily before the Israeli attack, it should have been cohesive and close to full strength later in the day. Instead, throughout 7 June, Israeli ground and air forces encountered only scattered elements of the 40th, most of which were demoralized and exhausted because the brigade had been mauled and dispersed that morning.

53. In fact, the Israeli armored brigade was understrength, having left its battalion of Super Shermans in the Upper Galilee to deal with any Syrian move. Thus, the brigade attacked Jordan only with its battalion of Centurions, its mechanized infantry battalion, and the AMX-13s of its reconnaissance company.

54. Dupuy, *Elusive Victory*, 312–13; El-Edroos, *Hashemite Arab Army*, 388–89; Hammel, *Six Days*, 379–80; According to Hammel, 16 of about 40 Pattons in this force were destroyed in battle with the Israeli Centurions, and another 19 were destroyed by Israeli airstrikes all along the road. While possible, the number lost to airstrikes appears high.

55. There is reason to believe that Israeli electronic-warfare operations also were contributing to the disinformation in the Jordanian intelligence system, adding to the confusion of Jordanian decision making.

56. Mutawi, *Jordan in the 1967 War*, 138.

57. Mutawi, *Jordan in the 1967 War*, 155, 158. Also see King Hussein, *My "War" with Israel*, 81, 89. On 7 June, the commander of the 60th Armored Brigade reported that he had only six tanks left because of Israeli airstrikes when, in fact, he had almost a battalion's worth of tanks remaining despite losses from combat with Israeli

armor, mechanical breakdowns, and airstrikes. Compare King Hussein, *My "War" with Israel*, 89, with Hammel, *Six Days*, 383.

58. Cordesman, *Jordanian Arms*, 38; Dupuy, *Elusive Victory*, 315, 333; King Hussein, *My "War" with Israel*, 88; Young, *Israeli Campaign*, 166.

59. El-Edroos, *Hashemite Arab Army*, 360–67.

60. Mutawi, *Jordan in the 1967 War*, 166.

61. For a concurring opinion, see El-Edroos, *Hashemite Arab Army*, 366.

62. See, for instance, King Hussein, *My "War" with Israel*, 66–67, 106.

63. See, for example, El-Edroos, *Hashemite Arab Army*, 409; Mutawi, *Jordan in the 1967 War*, 143–47; Lunt, *Hussein of Jordan*, 95; Parker, *Six-Day War*, 160–74; and Young, *Israeli Campaign*, 140. See also the interview with Jordanian Prime Minister Wasfi at-Tell contained in King Hussein, *My "War" with Israel*, 128–29.

64. Heikal, *Road to Ramadan*, 42; King Hussein, *My "War" with Israel*, 54, 106–8; Gamasy, *October War*, 89–90, 108; Korn, *Stalemate*, 108; Moskin, *Among Lions*, 50, 102; Narkiss, *Liberation of Jerusalem*, 96–97; Rabinovich, *Battle for Jerusalem*, 326.

65. Farid, *Nasser*, 173–74.

66. Quoted in Moskin, *Among Lions*, 50.

67. Dupuy, *Elusive Victory*, 235. See also Narkiss, *Liberation of Jerusalem*, 96–97.

68. King Hussein, *My "War" with Israel*, 60–61, 63, 79, 81, 87–89, 106–8.

69. King Hussein, *My "War" with Israel*, 106.

70. Many Israeli pilots reported that Iraqi Hunter pilots were quite skillful, leading them to suspect that Jordanian pilots may have been transferred to Iraq after their own Hunters were destroyed by the IAF on 5 June. However, there is reason to doubt that this is true. For instance, a recent history of the Egyptian Air Force, with no particular interest in this question, noted that many of the Egyptian pilots were very impressed by the Iraqi Hunter pilots with whom they trained after the war. Nordeen and Nicole, *Phoenix over the Nile*, 270.

71. Rabinovich, *Battle for Jerusalem*, 324. Lt. Col. Yosef Fratkin was the commander of the Israeli 28th Parachute Battalion of the 55th Parachute Brigade and Col. (later lieutenant general) Mordechai "Motta" Gur was his commanding officer.

72. JTCGME, *Combat Damage to Tanks*, 1:105–21.

73. Mutawi, *Jordan in the 1967 War*, 151.

74. Hammel, *Six Days*, 279, 383, 424. Unfortunately, there is no agreement on casualty numbers. I have used Hammel's numbers as being the most recent and therefore probably the most accurate. The Israelis are scrupulously honest about casualty figures, reflecting the society's obsession with losses. Thus, it seems likely that Hammel's numbers reflect the revised Israeli totals. For comparison, Dupuy states that Israel lost 983 killed and 4,517 wounded, of whom 553 killed and 2,442 wounded came against Jordan. *Elusive Victory*, 333. Herzog asserts that Israel had 764 dead in the war, of whom 285 came against Jordan. *Arab-Israeli Wars*, 183.

75. Hammel, *Six Days*, 383. Rabinovich's numbers, for comparison, are 179 dead and 1,000 wounded. Rabinovich, *Battle for Jerusalem*, 387.

76. Hammel, *Six Days*, 329–34.

77. Dupuy, *Elusive Victory*, 283–318; El-Edroos, *Hashemite Arab Army*, 360–412; Herzog, *Arab-Israeli Wars*, 183; Metz, *Jordan*, 237.

78. Neff, *Warriors for Jerusalem*, 246.

79. For other examples, see El-Edroos, *Hashemite Arab Army*, 269; Lunt, *Hussein of Jordan*, 99–100; and Mutawi, *Jordan in the 1967 War*, 142.

80. Compare Mutawi, *Jordan in the 1967 War*, 133, with Lt. Gen. Mordechai Gur, *The Battle for Jerusalem*, trans. Phillip Gillon (New York: Popular Library, 1974), 56, 60–155; and Narkiss, *Liberation of Jerusalem*, 158–59, 164. Elsewhere, Mutawi argues, "Most Arab and Western commentators believe that Israeli air supremacy was the most important military factor which led to the defeat of the Arabs." *Jordan in the 1967 War*, 128. In the footnote to this statement, Mutawi cites two Arab authors and two Western authors, one of whom — Col. Trevor Dupuy — makes no such claim on the pages cited by Mutawi. (The pages in question are Dupuy, *Elusive Victory*, 246–47.) The other source cited is the Churchills' book, *The Six Day War*, which does claim that air supremacy was vital to Israel's victory over Jordan. However, the Churchills note that Israeli airstrikes "were not particularly effective against the Jordanian armour" and helped mainly by interdicting Jordanian movements through the hills of the West Bank. It is also worth noting that this work is among the least reliable accounts of the fighting and is prone to considerable hyperbole, such as claiming that the Jordanians had to fight "in open country for several days on end under constant aerial bombardment and strafing, both night and day." *Six Day War*, 144–46.

81. Lunt, *Hussein of Jordan*, 99–100.

82. History Branch, IAF, correspondence with the author, 10 Sept. 1997.

83. History Branch, IAF, correspondence with the author, 10 Sept. 1997.

84. History Branch, IAF, correspondence with the author, 10 Sept. 1997.

85. JTCGME, *Combat Damage to Tanks*, 1:1.

86. Narkiss, *Liberation of Jerusalem*, 113.

87. Some might be willing to attribute the poor performance of the 60th Armored Brigade to the effects of Israeli air strikes as it moved to Jerusalem. While it is true that the 60th was hit by Israeli airstrikes twice while it moved from Jericho to Hebron and then back to Jerusalem, these attacks should not have been a major factor in the fight at Tel al-Ful. First, the brigade lost only a small number of tanks and other vehicles in these attacks. (O'Ballance, *Third Arab-Israeli War*, 182–83, 190, 220.) Second, although the psychological effects of air attack often greatly exceed the physical harm, evidence from the Second World War and the Gulf War indicates that only prolonged, continuous bombing has lasting psychological results, and the effects of even very heavy aerial bombardment fade quickly if they are not constantly repeated over the course of many days or even weeks. For instance, S. L. A. Marshall observed that the psychological effects of airstrikes tend to fade within ten minutes of the attack unless repeatedly reinforced. "The Devil and the Sea," in Robinson, *Under Fire*, 148. Consequently, there is no reason to believe that the 60th should have been significantly handicapped on 6 June by the two air raids

the Israelis conducted against it the previous day. On the psychological and physical effects of airstrikes on ground forces, see Ian Gooderson, "Allied Fighter-Bombers Versus German Armour in North-West Europe, 1944–1945: Myths and Realities," *Journal of Strategic Studies* 14, no. 2 (June 1991): 210–31; Ian Gooderson, "Heavy and Medium Bombers: How Successful Were They in the Tactical Close Air Support Role during World War II?" *Journal of Strategic Studies* 15, no. 3 (Sept. 1992): 367–99; and GWAPS, *Effects and Effectiveness*, 202–5, 221–26.

88. Gen. Uzi Narkiss, interview, Sept. 1996.

89. Just so there is no confusion in the reader's mind, let me reiterate my assessment of the decision to send the two armored brigades south on 5 June. I believe Riyad's decision was an entirely reasonable choice to make. This is important because it indicates that the Jordanians did not necessarily suffer because some political hack from Egypt directed their forces, as many have maintained. Riyad was a competent general who made a reasonable command decision. However, given that the Egyptian drive into the Negev was pure fantasy from Cairo, this move turned out to be detrimental to the Jordanians, for it hindered them from meeting the Israeli thrusts against Jerusalem and Janin more quickly and did not gain them any advantage.

90. Mutawi, *Jordan in the 1967 War*, 148.

91. Young, *Israeli Campaign*, 50–51.

92. This assessment was unanimously shared by Israeli officers who took part in the fighting on the West Bank in both 1948 and 1967. Senior IDF officers, interviews, Sept. 1996.

93. Dupuy, *Elusive Victory*, 346. See also Cordesman, *Jordanian Arms*, 128. Cordesman likewise notes that an important conclusion of Jordan's military postmortem was that it possessed culturally driven problems that had hindered the army's performance in battle.

94. Dupuy, *Elusive Victory*, 351; El-Edroos, *Hashemite Arab Army*, 438–39; Herzog, *Arab-Israeli Wars*, 203; Katz, *Fire and Steel*, 109.

95. Dupuy, *Elusive Victory*, 354; Herzog, *Arab-Israeli Wars*, 205; Katz, *Fire and Steel*, 120.

96. El-Edroos, *Hashemite Arab Army*, 330; O'Ballance, *Arab Guerrilla Power*, 144–45; Metz, *Jordan*, 240.

97. El-Edroos, *Hashemite Arab Army*, 449.

98. El-Edroos, *Hashemite Arab Army*, 449.

99. El-Edroos, *Hashemite Arab Army*, 449–55; Lunt, *Hussein of Jordan*, 138; O'Ballance, *Arab Guerrilla Power*, 144.

100. Neville Brown, "Jordanian Civil War," *Military Review* 51 (Sept. 1971): 44; Arthur R. Day, *East Bank/West Bank* (New York: Council on Foreign Relations, 1986), 77; Dupuy, *Elusive Victory*, 380; El-Edroos, *Hashemite Arab Army*, 455; Lunt, *Hussein of Jordan*, 139; Neff, *Warriors against Israel*, 40; O'Ballance, *Arab Guerilla Power*, 150; Seale, *Asad*, 158.

101. Lunt, *Hussein of Jordan*, 141.

102. The wide range in the number of sorties per plane reflects my uncertainty as to how many Jordanian aircraft participated in this campaign. Specifically, if the Jordanians employed their 20 F-104s, this would place the likely number of sorties per plane at about four. However, the F-104 was one of the worst aircraft imaginable to conduct ground attacks, and I find it hard to believe they were used in this role by the Jordanians, even in their dire straits. If, as seems likely, the RJAF committed only its 32 Hawker Hunters to this battle, the number of sorties per plane was likely closer to eight.

103. Brown, "Jordanian Civil War," 46.

104. Day, *East Bank/West Bank*, 77; El-Edroos, *Hashemite Arab Army*, 455; Lunt, *Hussein of Jordan*, 140–41; O'Ballance, *Arab Guerilla Power*, 152–53; Seale, *Asad*, 158–59. Unfortunately, no figures for Jordanian casualties against the Syrians are available.

105. Dupuy, *Elusive Victory*, 383; El-Edroos, *Hashemite Arab Army*, 459, 462; O'Ballance, *Arab Guerilla Power*, 182.

106. Regarding the amount of damage the RJAF inflicted on the Syrians, since it flew about 200–250 ground-attack sorties on 22 September and destroyed 40–60 armored vehicles, its pilots achieved an armored vehicle kill-per-sortie rate of anywhere from 0.3 to 0.04 An analysis of the effectiveness of airstrikes against armored forces in major wars from World War II to Vietnam performed by Trevor Dupuy's Historical Evaluation and Research Organization (HERO) found that the average number of armored vehicle kills-per-sortie historically has been about 0.25. Thus, the Jordanian performance was anywhere from slightly above average to well below average, depending on which end of the range the actual numbers fell. However, in most of the cases examined by the HERO study, the air forces under consideration faced very significant opposition from enemy air forces and ground-based air defenses, whereas the Syrian units in 1970 had no air cover and little in the way of ground-based air defenses. Thus, even the most favorable kill-per-sortie ratio looks poorer than the historical norm because the Jordanians did not have to deal with such problems. See HERO, esp. 59.

107. Dupuy, *Elusive Victory*, 537; Herzog, *War of Atonement*, 200–201; O'Ballance, *No Victor, No Vanquished*, 218.

108. Dupuy, *Elusive Victory*, 533; El-Edroos, *Hashemite Arab Army*, 519–20, 523–24; Herzog, *Arab-Israeli Wars*, 302–3; O'Ballance, *No Victor, No Vanquished*, 201–7; Ofer, *Iraqi Army*, 125–30, 223–24.

109. Dupuy, *Elusive Victory*, 532–33; Herzog, *Arab-Israeli Wars*, 303; O'Ballance, *No Victor, No Vanquished*, 202–3; Ofer, *Iraqi Army*, 119–20.

110. Many accounts of the October War mistakenly claim this attack took place on 18 October. However, the various Iraqi and Israeli accounts in the Ofer study all state that the battle took place on 19 October. The Ofer version is the most authoritative because it was prepared for the Israeli General Staff using a translation of the official Iraqi General Staff study of their operations during the war. See Ofer, *Iraqi Army*.

111. Dupuy, *Elusive Victory*, 534; Herzog, *Arab-Israeli Wars*, 304; O'Ballance, *No Victor, No Vanquished*, 203–7; Ofer, *Iraqi Army*, 226–28.

112. For a list of possible reasons as to why the Jordanians started late on 19 October, see Ofer, *Iraqi Army*, 227.

113. Herzog, *War of Atonement*, 142; O'Ballance, *No Victor, No Vanquished*, 209; Ofer, *Iraqi Army*, 142–43, 226–28.

114. Herzog, *Arab-Israeli Wars*, 304; Herzog, *War of Atonement*, 142; O'Ballance, *No Victor, No Vanquished*, 207–10; Ofer, *Iraqi Army*, 226–29.

115. Dupuy, *Elusive Victory*, 608; Herzog, *Arab-Israeli Wars*, 306. The figure of 80 casualties is from Dupuy. No other source, including El-Edroos, even mentions a casualty figure, and Dupuy's number strikes me as low, if only because of the fairly large number of tanks the Israelis destroyed. Although it is true that Jordan failed to employ its infantry along with its tanks, and this probably kept down manpower losses, it seems highly unlikely that the Jordanians could have lost 54 tanks and suffered only 80 dead and wounded. In addition, tanks are the only category of vehicle we have data for on the Jordanian side, and it is a virtual certainty that the Israelis destroyed other Jordanian vehicles such as APCs, trucks, and jeeps. Consequently, my guess is that the actual Jordanian casualty figures were two or three times greater than the number Dupuy gives.

116. Cordesman, *Jordanian Arms*, 1, 13, 21–27, 52; Day, *East Bank/West Bank*, 94–116; Alan Richards and John Waterbury, *A Political Economy of the Middle East* (Boulder CO: Westview, 1990), esp. 208–9; Satloff, *Troubles*, 63.

117. U.S. military personnel, interviews with author, May 1993, Sept. 1996, and Dec. 1996.

118. U.S. military personnel, interviews, Dec. 1996.

119. U.S. military personnel, interviews, Dec. 1996

120. U.S. military personnel, interviews, May 1993. See also Cordesman, *Jordanian Arms*, 46.

121. El-Edroos, *Hashemite Arab Army*, 366, 385, 427, 455.

122. Day, *East Bank/West Bank*, 81.

123. Pascal, Kennedy, and Rosen, *Men and Arms*, 46.

124. Cordesman, *Jordanian Arms*, 68, 77.

4. Libya

1. Dyer, "Libya," 367; Rathmell, "Libya's Intelligence," 696; Tartter (Libya), 241, 245; Zartman, "Arms Imports," 15.

2. This was hardly paranoia. Plotting was rife in the Libyan military, and the king's own chief of staff was on the verge of launching his own coup, only to be preempted by Qadhafi by a couple of days.

3. Dyer, "Libya," 368–71; Foltz, "Libya's Military Power," 52–55.

4. Tartter (Libya), 242–43, 262.

5. Dyer, "Libya," 368; Tartter (Libya), 242–45.

6. Nordeen, *Fighters over Israel*, 135–48; Nordeen and Nicole, *Phoenix over the Nile*, 269–73.

7. Dyer, "Libya," 369.

8. Zartman, "Arms Imports," 15.

9. Dyer, "Libya," 373, 369–70; Chaplin, "Libya," 45; Foltz, "Libya's Military Power," 53; Tartter (Libya), 239–40, 262, 272; Zartman, "Arms Imports," 15–17.

10. Dyer, "Libya," 369; Foltz, "Libya's Military Power," 53; Tartter (Libya), 239, 243, 272; Zartman, "Arms Imports," 15.

11. Lisa Anderson, "Libya's Qaddafi: Still in Command?" *Current History* (Feb. 1987) 87.

12. Dyer, "Libya," 371; Mark Stevens (with William E. Schmidt and Lloyd H. Norman), "Mideast: War of Nerves," *Newsweek*, 13 Sept. 1976, 69.

13. Dyer, "Libya," 374; El Fathaly and Palmer, "Institutional Development," in Vandewalle, *Qadhafi's Libya*, 172–73; Tartter (Libya), 280.

14. El Fathaly and Palmer, "Institutional Development," 173; Tartter (Libya), 239.

15. Dyer, "Libya," 371; Foltz, "Libya's Military Power," 52; Rathmell, "Libya's Intelligence," 696.

16. Benjamin and Schmidt, "Arab vs. Arab," 29; Chaplin, "Libya," 47; Dyer, "Libya," 368–73; Hempstone, "Libya," 39; Rathmell, "Libya's Intelligence," 696; Tartter (Libya), 239, 246; Zartman, "Arms Imports," 15, 21. None of the foreign pilots appear to have participated in combat operations. Perhaps out of sensitivity to the possibility that a foreign pilot might get shot down and captured, Tripoli appears to have relied almost entirely on its small cadre of Libyan pilots for combat missions outside of Libya, reserving the foreigners for the defense of Libya itself.

17. Benjamin and Schmidt, "Arab vs. Arab," 29; Hempstone, "Libya," 39; Tanner, "Sadat Orders Halt," A3.

18. Anable, "Egyptian-Libyan Tensions," 3; Dyer, "Libya," 371; Nordeen and Nicole, *Phoenix over the Nile*, 318; Henry Tanner, "Sadat's Jets Pound an Airbase in Libya; He Assails Qaddafi," *The New York Times*, 23 July 1977, A3.

19. Anable, "Egyptian-Libyan Tensions," 3; Dyer, "Libya," 371; Foltz, "Libya's Military Power," 59; Nordeen and Nicole, *Phoenix over the Nile*, 318; Tanner, "Sadat Orders Halt," A3.

20. Chaplin, "Libya," 46; Dyer, "Libya," 371; Foltz, "Libya's Military Power," 59; "Maxi-plots Behind a Strange Mini-War," 8 Aug. 1977, *Time*, 33; Nordeen and Nicole, *Phoenix over the Nile*, 318; Tanner, "Sadat Orders Halt," A3; Tartter (Libya), 262.

21. Anable, "Egyptian-Libyan Tensions," 3; Benjamin and Schmidt, "Arab vs. Arab," 29; Dyer, "Libya," 371; Foltz, "Libya's Military Power," 59; Hempstone, "Libya," 39; Schanche, "Approaching Truce," 13; Tanner, "List of Conditions," A1, A7.

22. Tony Avirgan and Martha Honey, *War in Uganda: The Legacy of Idi Amin*

(Westport CT: Lawrence Hill, 1982), 93; Foltz, "Libya's Military Power," 62; Rathmell, 'Libya's Intelligence," 697; Dirk Vandewalle, "The Libyan Arab Jamahiriyya since 1969," in Vandewalle, *Qadhafi's Libya*, 171.

23. Avirgan and Honey, *War in Uganda*, 91–92; Foltz, "Libya's Military Power," 62.

24. Avirgan and Honey, *War in Uganda*, 92.

25. Avirgan and Honey, *War in Uganda*, 121–23; Tartter (Libya), 248.

26. Avirgan and Honey, *War in Uganda*, 196; Tartter (Libya), 248.

27. Foltz, "Libya's Military Power," 62.

28. On Qadhafi's various motives for coveting the Aouzou Strip and intervening in Chad, see Colin Legum, "Libya's Intervention in Chad," in *Crisis and Conflicts in the Middle East*, ed. Colin Legum (New York: Holmes and Meier, 1981), 53; Mary Jane Deeb, *Libya's Foreign Policy in North Africa* (Boulder CO: Westview, 1990), 132; and John Wright, *Libya, Chad, and the Central Sahara* (Totowa NJ: Barnes and Noble, 1989), 144. Rene Lemarchand notes that Qadhafi also had reason to fear Libyan dissidents operating from Chad and the large Israeli presence there in the early 1970s. "The Case of Chad," in Lemarchand, *Green and The Black*, 109–10.

29. Virginia Thompson and Richard Adloff, *Conflict in Chad* (Berkeley: University of California Press, 1981), 55, 120–23; Wright, *Libya, Chad, and the Central Sahara*, 129.

30. Jonathan Bearman, *Qadhafi's Libya* (London: Zed Books, 1986), 212–13; Deeb, *Libya's Foreign Policy*, 129; Dyer, "Libya," 372; Thompson and Adloff, *Conflict in Chad*, 75.

31. Bearman, *Qadhafi's Libya*, 217; Raymond W. Copson, *Africa's Wars and Prospects for Peace* (Armonk NY: M. E. Sharpe, 1994), 62–63; Colin Legum, "The Crisis over Chad: Colonel Gaddafy's Sahelian Dream," in Legum, *ACR, 1981* (New York: Africana, 1982), A39; Mark A. Lorell, "Airpower in Peripheral Conflict: The French Experience in Africa," RAND R-3660-AF (Santa Monica CA: RAND, 1989), 38–39; Benyamin Neuberger, *Involvement, Invasion, and Withdrawal: Qadhafi's Libya and Chad, 1969–1981* (Tel Aviv: Shiloah Center, Tel Aviv University, 1982), 48–50; Somerville, *Foreign Intervention in Africa*, 67–68; Wright, *Libya, Chad, and the Central Sahara*, 132.

32. Bearman, *Qadhafi's Libya*, 217–18; Foltz, "Libya's Military Power," 64; Legum, "Libya's Intervention," 56; Neuberger, *Involvement, Invasion, and Withdrawal*, 50; Tartter (Libya), 250; Thompson and Adloff, *Conflict in Chad*, 137; U.S. government officials, interviews with author, Sept. 1995.

33. Shortly after the fall of N'djamena, Qadhafi asked Goukouni to come to Tripoli for consultations. A preoccupied (and perhaps wary) Goukouni sent two of his senior military officers instead. These generals were murdered by the Libyans — although Qadhafi claimed that Chadian dissidents had somehow assassinated them under Libyan guard in Tripoli — and Qadhafi insisted that Goukouni come to Tripoli. Goukouni very reluctantly made the trip, although only after making arrangements with President Shagari of Nigeria to try to ensure that Qadhafi would not kill

him too. In Tripoli Goukouni was presented with the merger agreement and had it made clear to him that he would receive the same treatment as his generals if he did not sign. Legum, "Libya's Intervention," 57; Legum, "Crisis over Chad," A40–41; Neuberger, *Involvement, Invasion, and Withdrawal*, 51.

34. Bearman, *Qadhafi's Libya*, 221–22; Deeb, *Libya's Foreign Policy*, 154; Lorell, "Airpower," 41; Somerville, *Foreign Intervention in Africa*, 69; Tartter (Libya), 250; Wright, *Libya, Chad, and the Central Sahara*, 133.

35. Bearman, *Qadhafi's Libya*, 222–23; Foltz, "Libya's Military Power," 64–65; Lorell, "Airpower," 41–45; Somerville, *Foreign Intervention in Africa*, 69–70; Tartter (Libya), 250–51; Tartter (Chad), 192; Wright, *Libya, Chad, and the Central Sahara*, 133; U.S. government officials, interviews, Sept. 1995.

36. Deeb, *Libya's Foreign Policy*, 157; Foltz, "Libya's Military Power," 65; Colin Legum, "Chad: Fatigue Setting in as Stalemate Continues," in Legum, *ACR, 1985–86*, B201; Lorell, "Airpower," 49; Somerville, *Foreign Intervention in Africa*, 71; Tartter (Libya), 251.

37. Cordesman, *Jordanian Arms*, 133; Lorell, "Airpower," 49–50; Somerville, *Foreign Intervention in Africa*, 71–72; Wright, *Libya, Chad, and the Central Sahara*, 133.

38. Foltz, "Libya's Military Power," 57–58; Tartter (Libya), 256–58.

39. U.S. government officials, interviews, Sept. 1995.

40. James Brooke, "Modern Arms a Key Factor in Chadian Gains," *The New York Times*, 2 Apr. 1987, A8; "Chad: End of the GUNT as Hissene Habre Consolidates Power," in Legum, *ACR, 1986–87* (New York: Africana, 1988), B190; Paul Lewis, "Libyans Said to Begin Retreating from Last Major Foothold in Chad," *The New York Times*, 26 Mar. 1987, A1; Lt. Gen. Bernard Trainor, "Chad's Anti-Libya Offensive: Surprising Successes," *The New York Times*, 12 Jan. 1987, A3; Lt. Gen. Bernard Trainor, "Desert Tactics of Chadians: Like Old West," *The New York Times*, 5 Apr. 1987, A4; Lt. Gen. Bernard Trainor, interviews with author, June 1994; U.S. government officials, interviews, Sept. 1995.

41. Brooke, "Modern Arms," A8; Foltz, "Libya's Military Power," 65; James, "Habré's Hour of Glory," 21; Legum, *ACR, 1986–87*, B190; U.S. government officials, interviews, Sept. 1995.

42. After the February and March defeats, Goukouni began to consider the possibility of abandoning the Libyans and striking a deal with Habré. The Libyans got wind of this from their informants among the Chadian rebels and called Goukouni to Tripoli, where he was put under house arrest. At some point soon thereafter, possibly during an escape attempt, Goukouni was shot and wounded by his Libyan captors in a scuffle. When word of this incident reached GUNT forces in Chad, they abrogated the alliance. Geoff Simons, *Libya: The Struggle for Survival* (New York: St. Martin's, 1996)293.

43. Deeb, *Libya's Foreign Policy*, 181; Foltz, "Libya's Military Power," 65; Colin Legum, "End of the GUNT," in Legum, *ACR, 1986–87*, B188; Lorell, "Airpower," 57–59; Somerville, *Foreign Intervention in Africa*, 73; Tartter (Libya), 251; Lt. Gen.

Bernard Trainor, "Victories Shore up Chadians," *The New York Times*, 18 Jan. 1987, A14.

44. James, "Habré's Hour of Glory," 21; "Chad: End of the GUNT," B190–91, B542; Somerville, *Foreign Intervention in Africa*, 71–72; Trainor, "Victories," A14.

45. James, "Habré's Hour of Glory," 21; "Chad: End of the GUNT," B190–91, B542; Somerville, *Foreign Intervention in Africa*, 71–72; Tartter (Chad), 215.

46. Western diplomats and military personnel in Chad unanimously averred that the Chadians — upon whom they largely relied for casualty reports — reported Libyan losses very accurately, although they had a tendency to downplay their own casualties. Brooke, "Chadians Describe Victory," A5; Foltz, "Libya's Military Power," 66.

47. Brooke, "Modern Arms," A8; James, "Habré's Hour of Glory," 21; Legum, "End of the GUNT," B189–90; Lewis, "Libyans Said to Begin Retreating," A5; Lorell, "Airpower," 60; Somerville, *Foreign Intervention in Africa*, 75; Tartter (Chad), 196; Trainor, "Desert Tactics," A4; Lt. Gen. Bernard Trainor, "In the Desert, Chad Exhibits Spoils of War," *The New York Times*, 13 Apr. 1987, A12.

48. Trainor, interviews, June 1994.

49. Brooke, "Modern Arms," A8; Henderson, "Qaddafy's Waterloo," 25; James, "Habré's Hour of Glory," 21; Douglas Kraft, "Chad's Civil War Turns into a Battle with Libya," *The Los Angeles Times*, 9 Mar. 1987, 1; "Chad: End of the GUNT," B190; Legum, *ACR, 1987–88*, (New York: Africana, 1989), B181; Lemarchand, "Case of Chad," 121–22; Elaine Sciolino, "Chad Takes Another Key Libya Base," *The New York Times*, 28 Mar. 1987, A3; Lt. Gen. Bernard Trainor, "France and U.S. Aiding Chadians with Intelligence to out Libyans," *The New York Times*, 3 Apr. 1987, A5; Trainor, "Desert Tactics," A4; Trainor, "Chad Exhibits Spoils of War," A1, A12; Trainor, interviews, June 1994; U.S. government officials, interviews, Sept. 1995.

50. Brooke, "Chadians Describe Victory," A5; "Chad: Peace Seems on the Horizon," in Legum, *ACR, 1987–88*, B181; Lorell, "Airpower," 61; Tartter (Chad), 197.

51. James Brooke, "Chad Reports New Libyan Attack," *The New York Times*, 15 Aug. 1987, A3; James Brooke, "Libya Reported to Retake Key Chad Town," *The New York Times*, 30 Aug. 1987, A4; "Chad: Peace Seems on the Horizon," B181–82; Lorell, "Airpower," 61; Somerville, *Foreign Intervention in Africa*, 78; Tartter (Chad), 197; U.S. government officials, interviews, Sept. 1995.

52. Steven Greenhouse, "Chad Says Troops Are Razing Base Captured in Libya," *The New York Times*, 7 Sept. 1987, A1, A3; Legum *ACR, 1987–88*, B182–83.

53. Cordesman, *Jordanian Arms*, 134; Foltz, "Libya's Military Power," 66; International Institute for Strategic Studies, "Chad: Libya Heading North," in *Strategic Survey, 1987–1988* (London: IISS, 1987), 187; James, "Habré's Hour of Glory," 21.

54. Foltz, "Libya's Military Power," 58.

55. Cordesman, *Jordanian Arms*, 145; Tartter (Libya), 262.

56. Many commentators have claimed that the vast array of types of weapons possessed by the Libyans greatly complicated supply operations. Given that the

Libyans did not suffer from logistical problems, this is further testimony to the skills of Tripoli's quartermasters.

57. Foltz, "Libya's Military Power," 58.

58. Foltz, "Libya's Military Power," 67.

59. Anthony Cordesman, *After the Storm: The Changing Military Balance in the Middle East* (Boulder CO: Westview, 1993), 146.

60. U.S. government officials, interviews, Sept. 1995.

61. On increased Libyan support for terrorism in the 1980s, see Charles G. Cogan, "The Response of the Strong to the Weak: The American Raid on Libya, 1986," *Intelligence and National Security* 6, no. 3 (1991): 611–14; Brian L. Davis, *Qaddafi, Terrorism, and the Origins of the U.S. Attack on Libya* (Westport CT: Praeger, 1990), 65–91; and David C. Martin and John Walcott, *Best Laid Plans: The Inside Story of America's War against Terrorism* (New York: Harper and Row, 1988), esp. 65–73.

62. Dyer, "Libya," 373; Martin and Walcott, *Best Laid Plans*, 67–68; Tartter (Libya), 252.

63. The lead F-14 had begun to turn left to escort the Libyan planes away from the carriers as the Fitter fired. Nevertheless, given the limitations of the AA-2, this was not the proper position to launch the missile. Lt. Cdr. Joseph T. Stanik, *"Swift and Effective Retribution": The U.S. Sixth Fleet and the Confrontation with Qaddafi* (Washington: GPO, 1996), 11.

64. Joseph S. Bermudez Jr., "Libyan SAMs and Air Defences," *Jane's Defence Weekly*, 17 May 1986, 881; Foltz, "Libya's Military Power," 56; "Libya: Defiant Qadhafi Renames the Country 'Great Ja'mahiriya,'" in Legum, *ACR, 1986–1987*, B540–41; Martin and Walcott, *Best Laid Plans*, 269–77.

65. Martin and Walcott, *Best Laid Plans*, 279.

66. Other sources, notably Martin and Walcott, ascribe the operational name "Prairie Fire" to these exercises. Stanik repeatedly calls them "Attain Document III." A career naval officer, Stanik apparently served in the operation. Consequently, I have assumed he is correct regarding the operational code name.

67. Stanik, *"Swift and Effective,"* 23.

68. The AEGIS system is a state-of-the-art air defense system combining powerful phased-array radars, data links, and massive data-processing capabilities to allow AEGIS-equipped ships to detect incoming aircraft and missiles, track them, assign them threat priorities for destruction, and then direct a wide variety of weapons on the ship itself or other ships or planes in its task force to destroy them.

69. Bermudez, "Libyan SAMs," 881.

70. Anderson, "Libya's Qaddafi," 86.

71. Cogan, " Response," 615–16; Davis, *Qaddafi, Terrorism*, 137–41; Martin and Walcott, *Best Laid Plans*, 309–11; Stanik, *"Swift and Effective,"* 40–45.

72. R. Jeffrey Smith and David Ottaway, "U.S. Aims to Pressure Gadhafi on Plant," *The Washington Post*, 5 Jan. 1989, 1.

5. Saudi Arabia

1. The term "Wahhabism" derives from the religious leader who began the movement, Muhammad al-Wahhab. Within the kingdom, the Saudi version of Islam is generally referred to by a term best translated into English as "Unitarianism" when it is differentiated from other interpretations of Islam.

2. Mordechai Abir, "Saudi Security and Military Endeavor," *The Jerusalem Quarterly* 33 (fall 1984): 84; Cordesman, *After the Storm*, 566; Peter W. Wilson and Douglas F. Graham, *Saudi Arabia: The Coming Storm* (Armonk NY: M. E. Sharpe, 1994), 147–48.

3. Cordesman, *After the Storm*, 566–69; Safran, *Saudi Arabia*, 180–96, 420–30.

4. Cordesman, *After the Storm*, 570; F. Gregory Gause III, *Oil Monarchies: Domestic and Security Challenges in the Arab Gulf States* (New York: Council on Foreign Relations, 1994), 125; Thomas McNaugher, "Arms and Allies on the Arabian Peninsula," *Orbis* 28, no. 3 (fall 1984): 502; Richard F. Nyrop, ed., *Saudi Arabia: A Country Study* 4th ed. (Washington DC: GPO, 1984), xxvi; Safran, *Saudi Arabia*, 130, 431, 440; James D. Smith, "Report on Saudi Arabian National Guard Modernization" (Riyadh: Office of the Project Manager, Saudi Arabian National Guard, Aug. 1975), 2–4; Wilson and Graham, *Saudi Arabia*, 157, 167. The Pakistanis of the 10th Armored Brigade were sent home in 1987 when some refused to fight in a border clash with Yemen, claiming that they were there to fight the infidel (the Israelis), not brother Muslims. The Saudis then attempted to hire Bangladeshis to replace the Pakistanis but the deal fell through.

5. Abir, "Saudi Security," 89; Ze'ev Eytan and Aharon Levran, *The Middle East Military Balance, 1987–1988*, Jaffee Center for Strategic Studies (Boulder CO: Westview, 1988), 175; McNaugher, "Arms and Allies," 502; Safran, *Saudi Arabia*, 440.

6. A "touch and go" is when a pilot puts down his landing gear, touches down on the runway as if to land, and then takes off again and races away. The Israelis made it a practice of conducting these stunts at Saudi airfields from time to time to remind the Saudis of their vulnerability to Israeli airpower.

7. Abir, "Saudi Security," 81–83; Cordesman, *After the Storm*, 582–83; Anthony Cordesman, *Saudi Arabia: Guarding the Desert Kingdom* (Boulder CO: Westview, 1997), 139; Adeed Dawisha, "Saudi Arabia's Search for Security," in *Regional Security in the Middle East*, ed. Charles Tripp (New York: St. Martin's, 1984), 7, 16; Gause, *Oil Monarchies*, 124–25; Daniel J. Kelleher, "Security Assistance for Force Modernization—the Saudi Arabian National Guard," student essay, 15 Apr. 1985, U.S. Army War College, Carlisle Barracks PA, 3–20; McNaugher, "Arms and Allies," 497, 503; Nyrop, *Saudi Arabia*, 265; Wilson and Graham, *Saudi Arabia*, 146–47, 156–58; Sarah Yizraeli, *The Remaking of Saudi Arabia*, Dayan Center Papers, no. 121 (Tel Aviv: Moshe Dayan Center, 1997), 153–57; U.S. military officers, interviews with author, Apr. 1991–May 1997.

8. Abir, "Saudi Security," 88–89; Cordesman, *After the Storm*, 570; Gause, *Oil Monarchies*, 124; Safran, *Saudi Arabia*, 439; Yizraeli, *Remaking of Saudi Arabia*, 150–51.

9. Abir, "Saudi Security," 82; Lincoln P. Bloomfield Jr., "Commentary: Saudi Arabia's Security Problems in the 1980s," in *Defense Planning in Less-Industrialized States*, ed. Stephanie Neuman (Lexington MA: Lexington, 1984), 104; Cordesman, *After the Storm*, 565; Wilson and Graham, *Saudi Arabia*, 151.

10. Anthony Cordesman, *The Gulf and the West: Strategic Relations and Military Realities* (Boulder: Westview, 1988), 200; Nyrop, *Saudi Arabia*, 265; Pascal, Kennedy, and Rosen, *Men and Arms*, 44; David E. Long, *The Kingdom of Saudi Arabia* (Gainesville: University Press of Florida, 1997), 18–77, 115–20; Wilson and Graham, *Saudi Arabia*, 254.

11. Cordesman, *The Gulf and the West*, 211, 239; J. E. Peterson, *Defending Arabia* (New York: St. Martin's, 1986), 197.

12. Wilson and Graham, *Saudi Arabia*, 140.

13. These brigades are sometimes referred to as "Motorized" rather than "Mechanized" formations. Their primary vehicle was the Cadillac Gage V-150 Commando armored car, which they had in a wide variety of configurations. Since an armored car is not a tracked vehicle, some authors do not consider the SANG brigades to be fully "Mechanized." I consider the distinction largely academic.

14. Cordesman, *After the Storm*, 572, 582; Cordesman, *Saudi Arabia*, 98–119; "Expanding Saudi's Elite Fighting Force," *Jane's Defence Weekly*, 24 Jan. 1996, 17; Lt. Col. D. P. Hughes, "Battle for Khafji: 29 Jan–1 Feb 1991," *Army Quarterly and Defense Journal* (UK) 124, no. 1 (Jan 1994): 13; Andrew Rathmell, "Saudi Arabia's Military Build-up—An Extravagant Error?" *Jane's Intelligence Review*, Nov. 1994, 503; Wilson and Graham, *Saudi Arabia*, 156–57.

15. Cordesman, *After the Storm*, 571; Rathmell, "Saudi Arabia's Military Build-up," 503.

16. Jacob Goldberg, "Saudi Arabia and the Gulf Crisis," paper prepared for the Center for National Security Studies, Los Alamos National Laboratory, Mar. 1992, 4–5; Trainor and Gordon, *Generals' War*, 73; Lt. Col. Martin N. Stanton, "The Saudi Arabian National Guard Motorized Brigades," *Armor* 55 (Mar.–Apr. 1996), 8; HRH Gen. Khaled bin Sultan, *Desert Warrior: A Personal View of the Gulf War by the Joint Forces Commander* (New York: Harper Collins, 1995), 9–14.

17. Atkinson, *Crusade*, 205; Molly Moore, *A Woman at War: Storming Kuwait with the U.S. Marines* (New York: Charles Scribner's Sons, 1993), 17, 49; Friedman, *Desert Victory*, 232; Trainor and Gordon, *Generals' War*, 170–72, 190–91, 265.

18. Cordesman, *The Gulf and the West*, 203; Cordesman, *Saudi Arabia*, 151–55; Trainor and Gordon, *Generals' War*, 265; U.S. military personnel, interviews with author, Apr.–July 1991.

19. GWAPS, *Operations*, 185; Cordesman, *After the Storm*, 596.

20. Eliot A. Cohen and Thomas A. Keaney, gen. eds., *The Gulf War Air Power Survey*, vol. 5, pt. 1, *A Statistical Compendium* (Washington DC: GPO, 1993), 232, 335, 343 [hereafter cited as GWAPS, *Statistical Compendium*].

21. GWAPS, *Statistical Compendium*, 232.

22. GWAPS, *Statistical Compendium*, 232.

23. Cordesman, *After the Storm*, 597.

24. Atkinson, *Crusade*, 202–8; Trainor and Gordon, *Generals' War*, 275, 277; Hughes, "Battle for Khafji," 13–16; Office of the Program Manager, Saudi Arabian National Guard Modernization, "Letter to Colonel Richard Swain," 6 Oct. 1991 (letter obtained by Freedom of Information Act Request), 4 [hereafter cited as OPM/SANG Letter]; Stanton, "Motorized Brigades," 6–8; Dennis Steele, "Down in the Sand: The First Brushes," *Army* 41 (Mar. 1991): 34.

25. Atkinson, *Crusade*, 209; Bellamy, *Expert Witness*, 93; Trainor and Gordon, *Generals' War*, 282; Hughes, "Battle for Khafji," 20; OPM/SANG Letter, 2–3; Stanton, "Motorized Brigades," 9; Steele, "Down in the Sand," 35.

26. Hughes, "Battle for Khafji," 21; Stanton, "Motorized Brigades," 9.

27. Trainor and Gordon, *Generals' War*, 284–85; Khaled, *Desert Warrior*, 383.

28. Stanton, "Motorized Brigades," 9.

29. Hughes, "Battle for Khafji," 21.

30. Hughes, "Battle for Khafji," 15, 22; OPM/SANG Letter, 5; Stanton, "Motorized Brigades," 9.

31. Watson et al., *Military Lessons*, 98.

32. Freedman and Karsh, *Gulf Conflict*, 395; Khaled, *Desert Warrior*, 405; U.S. Department of Defense, *Conduct*, 513; Wilson and Graham, *Saudi Arabia*, 162; U.S. military personnel, interviews, Apr.–July 1991.

33. No information is available from which to assess Saudi performance in supporting air missions such as airlift, aerial refueling, and aerial surveillance. However, they are notorious for being unable to handle their AWACS aircraft properly. For example, in 1982 an Iranian pilot defected to Saudi Arabia in his F-4 Phantom but was not detected by the Saudis until he landed on the runway at Dhahran. Later that year, another Iranian pilot defected to Egypt in a Boeing 707, flew all the way across Saudi Arabia, and landed in Cairo without ever being detected by the Saudis. See Safran, *Saudi Arabia*, 446; Wilson and Graham, *Saudi Arabia*, 153.

34. M. B. Khan, "Saudi Arabia's Armoured Corps: A Ground-Level Appreciation," *International Defence Review* (Sept. 1990): 966.

35. Cordesman, *Saudi Arabia*, 135; U.S. military personnel, interviews with author, Apr.–July 1991.

36. Cordesman, *The Gulf and the West*, 207.

37. Pascal, Kennedy, and Rosen, *Men and Arms*, 46; Safran, *Saudi Arabia*, 442.

38. Abir, "Saudi Security," 87.

39. Khan, "Armoured Corps," 966.

40. Cordesman, *After the Storm*, 588.

41. Cordesman, *Saudi Arabia*, 98, 123, 155; Khan, "Armoured Corps," 965–66; Nyrop, *Saudi Arabia*, 266; Rathmell, "Saudi Arabia's Military Build-up," 501, 504; Wilson and Graham, *Saudi Arabia*, 166. This is not a new problem for the Saudis. Of 60 U.S. tanks delivered to them in 1959–60, not one was operational by 1962. (Safran, *Saudi Arabia*, 104, 200.) In 1979, when tensions with Yemen prompted a limited Saudi mobilization, virtually all of the SANG's 400 armored cars were non-

operational due to maintenance problems. Moreover, the Saudis became angered when the Vinnell Corporation (the U.S. contractor hired to modernize the SANG) tried to get them to conduct regular maintenance on their vehicles. Abir, "Saudi Security," 91–92.

6. Syria

1. Dupuy, *Elusive Victory*, 17; Rudolph, 195; Patrick Seale, *The Struggle for Syria: A Study of Post-War Arab Politics, 1945–1958* (1965; reprint, London: I. B. Tauris,1986), 33.

2. Dupuy, *Elusive Victory*, 13–14, 41; Lorch, *Edge of the Sword*, 80; O'Ballance, *Arab-Israeli War,* 36–39, 84.

3. Herzog, *Arab-Israeli Wars*, 25; O'Ballance, *Arab-Israeli War,* 39–40.

4. O'Ballance, *Arab-Israeli War,* 40.

5. Dupuy, *Elusive Victory*, 24; Herzog, *Arab-Israeli Wars*, 27; Lorch, *Edge of the Sword*, 93.

6. Dupuy, *Elusive Victory*, 48; Herzog, *Arab-Israeli Wars*, 52–53; Lorch, *Edge of the Sword*, 152–53; O'Ballance, *Arab-Israeli War,* 111; senior IDF officers, interviews with author, Sept. 1996.

7. The Syrian version of the story is that they purposely withdrew from the Zemach-Deganyah area because they already had decided to redirect their efforts north of the Kinneret. In particular, they claim that the diversion of supplies north to the B'nat Ya'acov area reflected this change in priorities. But this version of events is hard to reconcile with the available evidence. First, the Syrians agree that the supply depot set up in the north was to divert Israeli attention from the south, indicating that at least as late as 15 May the Syrian main effort was in the south. Second, the Israelis destroyed this depot on the night of 17–18 May, whereas the preceding day the Syrians succeeded in conquering Zemach, which was considered a major Arab victory and a huge Israeli defeat. Damascus believed that it was on the verge of clearing the western shore of the Sea of Galilee and perhaps cutting off Galilee from the rest of Israel. Thus, it is also highly unlikely that by 19 May (when Zemach had been secured) the Syrians had changed their mind and decided to redirect their effort to north of Galilee: quite the contrary, at that point the Syrians were pushing everything they could to their southern front because of the success they were enjoying there.

The attack on the Deganyahs was conducted the very next day — 20 May — and there is no reason to believe that the Syrians had changed their minds overnight and decided to redirect their efforts north of the Kinneret. Indeed, up until the failure of the attacks on the Deganyahs, the Syrians were confident they would break through and push into Galilee, and the Israelis were afraid they could not stop the Syrians. Another bit of evidence supporting this interpretation is that the supplies redirected to the north were originally intended for the units assaulting the Deganyahs. These provisions were slated to go to the Syrians in this sector all along, and only after the failure of the attacks on the two Deganyahs did the Syrian commander in the south learn that the supplies were being redirected to the north. It was only at this point, according to the Syrians, that they decided to pull back to the Golan in the south and shift their attention to the B'nat Ya'acov area. Based on this evidence, I am persuaded that as late as midday on 20 May, the Syrians intended to continue to attack south of the Kinneret, and only after the failure of the attacks on the Deganyahs and the arrival of the Israeli artillery did they decide to abandon this axis and instead mount an offensive north of the Kinneret. See Dupuy, *Elusive Victory*, 49; and Lorch, *Edge of the Sword*, 153–54.

8. Dupuy, *Elusive Victory*, 83–84; Herzog, *Arab-Israeli Wars*, 76–77; Lorch, *Edge of the Sword*, 265–67; O'Ballance, *Arab-Israeli War*, 152–53; senior IDF officers, interviews, Sept. 1996.

9. Be'eri, *Army Officers*, 55–57; Derek Hopwood, *Syria, 1945–1986: Politics and Society* (London: Unwin Hyman, 1988), 35–36; Tabitha Petran, *Syria* (New York: Praeger, 1972), 96–105; Seale, *Struggle for Syria*, 37–147.

10. Alasdair Drysdale, "The Syrian Armed Forces in National Politics: The Role of the Geographic and Ethnic Periphery," in Kolkowicz and Korbonski, *Soldiers, Peasants, and Bureaucrats*, 59–62.

11. The causes of the 1967 war, and Syria's role in sparking it, are not properly a part of this study. For several discussions of these issues, however, see Fred H. Lawson, *Why Syria Goes to War: Thirty Years of Confrontation* (Ithaca NY: Cornell University Press, 1996), 34–51; Moshe Ma'oz, *Syria and Israel: From War to Peacemaking* (London: Oxford University Press, 1995), 88–101; Parker, *Six-Day War*, 29–33, 127–40, 153–61, 290–91.

12. David Dayan, *Strike First: A Battle History of Israel's Six Day War* (New York: Pitman, 1967), 230; Dupuy, *Elusive Victory*, 318–19; Hammel, *Six Days*, 388–89; Herzog, *Arab-Israeli Wars*, 186; Moreaux, July 1986, 38; Seale, *Asad*, 117.

13. Young, *Israeli Campaign*, 54.

14. Dupuy, *Elusive Victory*, 319; Hammel, *Six Days*, 394–95; Nordeen, *Fighters over Israel*, 83–84; senior IDF officers, interviews, Sept. 1996.

15. In other places this negligence actually worked to the Syrians' advantage as the mines accumulated in such density that they formed shoals that Israeli sappers could not clear, leaving these areas impassable.

16. Hammel, *Six Days*, 390; O'Ballance, *Third Arab-Israeli War*, 238; Seale, *Asad*, 117; Young, *Israeli Campaign*, 54.

17. Cohen, *Israel's Best Defense*, 220.

18. Cohen, *Israel's Best Defense*, 220–21; Dupuy, *Elusive Victory*, 247; Hammel, *Six Days*, 392.

19. Dupuy, *Elusive Victory*, 319–21; Hammel, *Six Days*, 392–93; Herzog, *Arab-Israeli Wars*, 185–86.

20. History Branch, IAF, correspondence with the author, 10 Sept. 1997.

21. Hammel, *Six Days*, 398–99, 416–17; O'Ballance, *Third Arab Israeli War*, 247; senior IDF officers, interviews, Sept. 1996.

22. Exactly why Damascus issued this false, and ultimately self-defeating, report

remains a mystery. Most current speculation seems to focus on the possibility that the Syrians were attempting to get a ceasefire imposed, perhaps by misleading either the superpowers or the Israelis into believing the IDF had secured the Golan.

23. Dupuy, *Elusive Victory*, 326; Hammel, *Six Days*, 424; Seale, *Asad*, 140.

24. See chap. 1.

25. O'Ballance, *No Victor, No Vanquished*, 5.

26. Seale, *Asad*, 142–44.

27. Drysdale, "Syrian Armed Forces in National Politics," 68–69; Hopwood, *Syria*, 50–52; Seale, *Asad*, 144–51; Nikolaos Van Dam, *The Struggle for Power in Syria: Sectarianism, Regionalism, and Tribalism in Politics, 1961–1978* (New York: St. Martin's, 1979), 84–85.

28. For various theories and bits of evidence as to Syrian motives, see Brown, "Jordanian Civil War," 44; Day, *East Bank/West Bank*, 77; Dupuy, *Elusive Victory*, 380; El-Edroos, *Hashemite Arab Army*, 455; Adam M. Garfinkle, "U.S. Decision-Making in the Jordan Crisis: Correcting the Record," *Political Science Quarterly* 100, no. 1 (spring 1985): 124; Lunt, *Hussein of Jordan*, 139; Neff, *Warriors against Israel*, 40; O'Ballance, *Arab Guerrilla Power*, 150; Seale, *Asad*, 158.

29. Brown, "Jordanian Civil War," 44–45; Day, *East Bank/West Bank*, 77; El-Edroos, *Hashemite Arab Army*, 455; Lunt, *Hussein of Jordan*, 140–41; Petran, *Syria*, 247. King Hussein was near panic at this point, and his biographer reports that he did not believe the Jordanians would be able to hold. Lunt, *Hussein of Jordan*, 141.

30. Patrick Seale claims in his biography that Asad did not oppose the invasion but, in fact, had ordered it. *Asad*, 157–59. All other sources contradict this claim, and I find it unpersuasive. See, for example, Brown, "Jordanian Civil War," 45; Drysdale, "Syrian Armed Forces in National Politics," 68–69; Hopwood, *Syria*, 51–52; Lawson, *Why Syria Goes to War*, 68; Moshe Ma'oz, "The Emergence of Modern Syria," in *Syria under Assad: Domestic Constraints and Regional Risks*, ed. Moshe Ma'oz and Avner Yaniv (New York: St. Martin's, 1986), 26; Ma'oz, *Syria and Israel*, 119; Petran, *Syria*, 243–44, 247–48; James Rudolph, "National Security," in *Syria: A Country Study*, ed. Richard F. Nyrop (Washington: GPO, 1979), 199; and Van Dam, *Struggle for Power*, 84–88.

31. Brown, "Jordanian Civil War," 46.

32. Day, *East Bank/West Bank*, 77; El-Edroos, *Hashemite Arab Army*, 455; Henry A. Kissinger, *White House Years* (Boston: Little, Brown, 1979), 628; Lawson, *Why Syria Goes to War*, 53; Lunt, *Hussein of Jordan*, 140–41; O'Ballance, *Arab Guerrilla Power*, 152–53; Seale, *Asad*, 158–59.

33. Dupuy, *Elusive Victory*, 381; Ma'oz, *Syria and Israel*, 116–19; Seale, *Asad*, 171.

34. Asher, *Duel for the Golan*, 52; Drysdale, "Syrian Armed Forces in National Politics," 69–70; Michael Eisenstadt, "Syria's Defense Companies: Profile of a Praetorian Unit," unpublished manuscript, copy in author's possession, 1–5; Insight Team, *Yom Kippur War*, 200; Ma'oz, *Syria and Israel*, 121–23; O'Ballance, *No Victor, No Vanquished*, 35; Seale, *Asad*, 205.

35. Helena Cobban, "The Nature of the Soviet-Syrian Link under Asad and

under Gorbachev," in *Syria: Society, Culture, and Polity*, ed. Richard T. Antoun and Donald Quataert (Albany: SUNY Press, 1991), 112; Michael Eisenstadt, *Arming for Peace? Syria's Elusive Quest for "Strategic Parity"* (Washington DC: Washington Institute for Near East Policy, 1992), 13–15; El-Edroos, *Hashemite Arab Army*, 414; Roger F. Pajak, "The Soviet-Syrian Military Aid Relationship," in *The Syrian Arab Republic: A Handbook*, by Anne Sinai and Allen Pollack (New York: American Academic Association for Peace in the Middle East, 1976), 98; Rudolph, "National Security," 199–200; Seale, *Asad*, 185–201.

36. Asher, *Duel for the Golan*, 55–58; Cordesman and Wagner, LMW: *Arab-Israeli Conflicts*, 44; El-Edroos, *Hashemite Arab Army*, 493–95. Some sources have suggested that the Syrians intended to drive into northern Israel once they secured control of the Golan. For example, El-Edroos asserts that the Syrians planned to take at least the Galilee towns of Zefat, Tiberias, and Nazareth. *Hashemite Arab Army*, 507. The paltry sources available on the Syrian side argue that this is not the case and that, while Asad may have had it in the back of his mind that if the opportunity were available he would continue his offensive into Galilee, his immediate objective was simply to retake the Golan. (See, for example, Seale, *Asad*, 185–201.) I have not been able to reconcile or decide between these two versions. However, because the Syrians never got the chance to put into effect any "phase two" offensive into Israel — and therefore it is not possible to judge the skill of the plan or its implementation — this absence is largely irrelevant to this study. Consequently, for purposes of this analysis, I have considered only the Syrian planning and operations to take the Golan itself.

37. Insight Team, *Yom Kippur War*, 72.

38. Asher, *Duel for the Golan*, 52–54; Cordesman and Wagner, LMW: *Arab-Israeli Conflicts*, 24; Dupuy, *Elusive Victory*, 441; Eisenstadt, *Arming for Peace?* 15–16; Herzog, *Arab-Israeli Wars*, 285; Moreaux, July 1986, 40; O'Ballance, *No Victor, No Vanquished*, 125.

39. Cordesman and Wagner, LMW: *Arab-Israeli Conflicts*, 24, 83; Dupuy, *Elusive Victory*, 441; Eisenstadt, *Arming for Peace?* 15–16; Nordeen, *Fighters over Israel*, 118; O'Ballance, *No Victor, No Vanquished*, 285.

40. Asher, *Duel for the Golan*, 35–44; Dupuy, *Elusive Victory*, 437, 443–44, 606; Herzog, *War of Atonement*, 61; Nordeen, *Fighters over Israel*, 116; O'Ballance, *No Victor, No Vanquished*, 121–22.

41. Cordesman and Wagner, LMW: *Arab-Israeli Conflicts*, 45–102; Dupuy, *Elusive Victory*, 598; Katz, *Fire and Steel*, 183; senior IDF officers, interviews, Sept. 1996.

42. Asher, *Duel for the Golan*, 83.

43. Maj. Gen. Moshe Peled, interview with author, Sept. 1996.

44. Asher, *Duel for the Golan*, 178–84; Dupuy, *Elusive Victory*, 456–57; El-Edroos, *Hashemite Arab Army*, 495; Herzog, *Arab-Israeli Wars*, 289–91; Herzog, *War of Atonement*, 104; Insight Team, *Yom Kippur War*, 159, 177–82; O'Ballance, *No Victor, No Vanquished*, 136–37; Charles Wakebridge, "The Syrian Side of the Hill," *Military Review* 56 (Feb. 1976): 29. O'Ballance claims that the Syrian General Staff

purposely ordered all of its forces on the Golan to stop short of the bridges on 7 October. Indeed, O'Ballance states that General Tlas told him as much in an interview, although Tlas refused to explain the reason for such an action. Asher, Dupuy, the *London Sunday Times*'s Insight Team, and Wakebridge — whose accounts of the Syrian side are far better than O'Ballance's — clearly indicate that the halt of the Syrian divisions on 7 October was *not* ordered by the general staff. In fact, according to Wakebridge, Tlas admitted in an interview with him that the Syrian General Staff were desperate to take the bridges and that the halt was contrary to their desires.

45. Asher, *Duel for the Golan*, 225–40; Dupuy, *Elusive Victory*, 447, 457–59; Herzog, *War of Atonement*, 113; Avigdor Kahalani, *The Heights of Courage: A Tank Leader's War on the Golan*, trans. Louis Williams (New York: Praeger, 1992), 93–123; Katz, *Fire and Steel*, 158–66; Neff, *Warriors against Israel*, 163, 194; O'Ballance, *No Victor, No Vanquished*, 142.

46. The vast majority of the Israeli tanks "knocked out" were repaired and returned to combat within a few days. Asher, *Duel for the Golan*, 272.

47. Ofer, *Iraqi Army*, 93.

48. It was also at this point that Syria began to pressure Egypt to launch a major attack from their bridgeheads to try to relieve some of the pressure on their Golan positions.

49. Asher, *Duel for the Golan*, 272.

50. Cordesman and Wagner, *LMW: Arab-Israeli Conflicts*, 85–91; Herzog, *War of Atonement*, 259; Dupuy, *Elusive Victory*, 554. See chap. 1, note 179, above for a discussion of the number of Israeli aircraft shot down in dogfights over Egypt and Syria.

51. Cohen, *Israel's Best Defense*, 361, 390–91; Cordesman and Wagner, *LMW: Arab-Israeli Conflicts*, 85–90; Insight Team, *Yom Kippur War*, 204; Nordeen, *Fighters over Israel*, 119–21, 132, 136–37, 144–45; Yonay, *No Margin*, 323–51.

52. Dupuy, *Elusive Victory*, 551–53; Brereton Greenhous, "The Israeli Experience," in *Studies in the Development of Close Air Support*, ed. Benjamin F. Cooling (Washington DC: U.S. Air Force, 1990), 515; Herzog, *Arab-Israeli Wars*, 288–91; Insight Team, *Yom Kippur War*, 315; Nordeen, *Fighters over Israel*, 126, 133, 147; O'Ballance, *No Victor, No Vanquished*, 295; Yonay, *No Margin*, 350–51.

53. Author's interviews with IDF officers, May 1991, Jan. 1994, and Sept. 1996.

54. Maj. Gen. Moshe Peled, interview, Sept. 1996; IDF officers, interviews, May 1991, Jan. 1994, and Sept. 1996.

55. Kahalani, *Heights*, 70–71; Katz, *Fire and Steel*, 133–60; IDF officers, interviews, Jan. 1994 and Sept. 1996.

56. Several theories have been offered to explain the Syrian failure to secure the bridges over the Jordan on 7 October when they were within kilometers of the river and faced only meager Israeli defenses. Some have argued that the problem was logistical, claiming that Syrian units were largely out of fuel late in the day and so could not physically reach the bridges. (See, for example, Ashkar and al-Ayyubi, "Middle East Conflict," 6; and J. M. Moreaux, "The Syrian Army," *Defence Update*

69, Mar. 1986, 26 [hereafter cited as "Moreaux, Mar. 1986"].) This explanation is highly dubious and largely appears to have been devised by apologists for the Syrians well after the fact. Although some tanks were found abandoned after the war for lack of fuel, Syrian commanders interviewed soon after the fighting made no mention of logistical difficulties as the cause of their halt. (See, for example, Dupuy, *Elusive Victory*, 456–57; O'Ballance, *No Victor, No Vanquished*, 134–37; and Wakebridge, 26–30. Dupuy, O'Ballance, and Wakebridge all interviewed numerous Syrian officers after the war, and when specifically questioned about this halt, none mentioned supply deficiencies. Indeed, Wakebridge goes to some length to demonstrate that this theory is false.) There is no indication that Syrian units were suddenly refueled during the night, yet they fought vigorously the next day. Finally, there is no question that even if all four Syrian brigades had been desperately short of fuel, each still could have pooled its assets and sent at least a battalion to cover the last few kilometers to take the virtually undefended bridges. Tanks do not all run out of fuel simultaneously, and it is absurd to claim that all 200 armored vehicles in a Syrian heavy brigade suddenly did when they were only three to five kilometers from their ultimate objective—let alone that this happened to several brigades simultaneously.

Others have speculated that the Syrians might have been using a phase-line method for the offensive and that various Syrian units had reached their phase line for the night and so stopped and made camp. (See, for example, El-Edroos, *Hashemite Arab Army*, 495; and Insight Team, *Yom Kippur War*, 159, 177.) The conduct of the Syrian campaign suggests a much less formal approach to timing than this indicates, for during the initial battles, Syrian commanders seemed interested in going as far and as fast as they could—nor were there other instances of units voluntarily stopping short of important objectives. In addition, the various division commanders clearly recognized the importance of securing the bridges as quickly as possible, so much so that Jahani diverted his best brigades from the major battle going on around Nafakh to take the bridges. Moreover, if the Syrians had been using phase lines, it seems highly unlikely that they would have set a stopping point for the end of the second day roughly five kilometers short of the bridges. Standard Soviet doctrine for an armored breakthrough would have insisted that any halt occur only after these key objectives had been seized, and there is nothing in the Syrian General Staff planning that suggests they would have been so incompetent as to place phase lines a few miles before the bridges. Indeed, such a lapse would have been completely at odds with the skill the high command demonstrated in planning the Syrian assault. Furthermore, even if it were the case that they were using phase lines, it should have been clear to every Syrian officer how important it was to take the bridges and, given the fact that both the general staff and their division commanders believed taking the spans had been given the highest priority, Syrian tactical commanders should have pushed the remaining miles to secure them. No battalion or brigade commander with the least bit of initiative would have failed to go the few extra kilometers to secure what were the crucial objectives of the entire Syrian war effort.

Based on the more detailed accounts of the Syrian operations, particularly Asher's descriptions, I suspect that the battalion and brigade commanders leading the drive on the Jordan called off their operations for the night primarily because they had outrun their command and control. It is fairly clear that by the time the Syrians began approaching the bridges, they were so far forward and so dispersed that even their division commanders could not effectively control their operations. Command authority had effectively devolved upon the brigade and battalion commanders. With the loss of guidance from higher authority, Syrian operations became increasingly tentative, and when each column ran into even the slightest Israeli resistance, it caused a disproportionate delay since tactical commanders were unwilling to make important decisions on their own. Eventually, each column got so far out from divisional control that relatively minor Israeli resistance prompted them to call a halt for the night to allow the rest of the division to catch up so that they could receive more detailed guidance from their superiors. Indeed, the *London Sunday Times*'s Insight Team notes that Syrian commanders stopped to await further orders, although they (probably incorrectly) speculate that it was because the Syrians had reached their objectives for that day. See *Yom Kippur War,* 177.

I believe this explanation fits the actual activities of the Syrians on 6–8 October better than the other two theories. My confidence in this explanation was greatly bolstered by conversations in September 1996 with a number of senior Israeli military officers who had fought on the Golan in 1973, all of whom had reached identical conclusions based on their own experiences and subsequent Israeli analysis of the Syrian campaign. However, what is most important in assessing Syrian combat performance is that, regardless of which theory one believes, it is still the case that, at the end of the day on 7 October, the Syrians had the vital Jordan River bridges within their grasp and their tactical commanders squandered this opportunity. Given how close the Syrians were to the bridges and how slight the Israeli resistance was in front of them, good commanders would have *found* a way to take those bridges regardless of any other circumstances. It is worth contrasting the passivity of the Syrians on 7 October with the aggressiveness of German general Heinz Guderian and his panzer commanders in France in 1940 and Russia in 1941 and of the Israeli armor commanders in 1956 and 1967, who all stretched or disobeyed direct orders and found ingenious ways to overcome supply and command problems so they could push the extra kilometers needed to secure objectives they knew were crucial to the success of their campaigns.

57. Herzog, *War of Atonement,* 275.

58. Khalidi, "Military Balance," in Aruri, *Middle East Crucible,* 39.

59. For Syrian claims that the IAF stopped the Golan offensive, see, for example, Seale, *Asad,* 209–10.

60. IDF officers, interviews, May 1991, Jan. 1994, and Sept. 1996.

61. Cordesman and Wagner, LMW: *Arab-Israeli Conflicts*, 90–98; Dupuy, *Elusive Victory*, 456; Nordeen, *Fighters over Israel*, 151–52. Even the most favorable after-action report for Israeli airpower was an informal survey conducted by a former Bundeswehr officer who concluded that less than 20 percent of Syrian armored losses could be attributed to Israeli artillery *or* airstrikes. See HERO, 95.

62. Asher, *Duel for the Golan*, 260.

63. D. K. Palit, *Return to Sinai: The Arab Offensive, October 1973* (New Delhi: Palit and Palit, 1974), 98.

64. On the composition of these various camps, see Itamar Rabinovich, *The War for Lebanon, 1970–1985*, 2d ed. (Ithaca NY: Cornell University Press, 1985), 60–88.

65. I have no intention of trying to wade into the debate over Asad's motivations in invading Lebanon on the side of the Christians. There are any number of theories that purport to explain his thinking, some of which are better than others. However, none has sufficient empirical proof to stake an exclusive claim to the truth. Indeed, my own guess is that a number of different factors probably combined to push Asad toward invasion. On this issue, see Reuven Avi-Ran, *The Syrian Involvement in Lebanon since 1975* (Boulder CO: Westview, 1991), 3–22; Robert Fisk, *Pity the Nation: The Abduction of Lebanon* (New York: Atheneum, 1990), 80–91; Dilip Hiro, *Fire and Embers: A History of the Lebanese Civil War* (New York: St. Martin's, 1992), 33–44; Hopwood, *Syria*, 60–62; Ma'oz, *Syria and Israel*, 160–65; Itamar Rabinovich, "The Changing Prism: Syrian Policy in Lebanon as a Mirror, an Issue, and an Instrument," in Ma'oz and Yaniv, *Syria under Assad*, 179–84; Rabinovich, *War for Lebanon*, 36–37, 47–56, 85–88, 201–36; Rudolph, "National Security," 202–4; Seale, *Asad*, 267–89; and Naomi Joy Weinberger, *Syrian Intervention in Lebanon* (New York: Oxford University Press, 1986), 95–213.

66. Lt. Col. Daniel Asher, "The Syrian Invasion of Lebanon — Military Moves as a Political Tool," trans. Michael Eisenstadt, *Ma'arachot* (June 1977): 3; Avi-Ran, *Syrian Involvement in Lebanon*, 22 n. 14; Lt. Col. David Eshel, *The Lebanon War, 1982* (Hod Hasharon, Israel: Eshel-Dramit, 1983), 28; Rabinovich, *War for Lebanon*, 55. Weinberger, *Syrian Intervention in Lebanon*, 213.

67. Asher, "Syrian Invasion of Lebanon," 5–6; Avi-Ran, *Syrian Involvement in Lebanon*, 23 n. 18; Eshel, *Lebanon War*, 29; Fisk, *Pity the Nation*, 85; Seale, *Asad*, 284; Lawrence Whetten, "The Military Dimension," in *Lebanon in Crisis*, ed. P. Edward Haley and Lewis W. Snider (Syracuse NY: Syracuse University Press, 1979), 80.

68. Asher, "Syrian Invasion of Lebanon," 8–9; Eisenstadt, *Arming for Peace?* 21; Eshel, *Lebanon War*, 29–30; Rudolph, "National Security," 202–3; Whetten, "Military Dimension," 82.

69. Mark Urban, "Fire in the Galilee, Part 2: Syria," *Armed Forces* 5, no. 5 (May 1986): 210.

70. Cordesman and Wagner, LMW: *Arab-Israeli Conflicts*, 109, 118, 277–78; Eisenstadt, *Arming for Peace?* 24–25, 28, 98–99; Eisenstadt, "Syria's Defense Companies," 1, 5.

71. Syrian commando battalions are considerably smaller than normal infantry

battalions, with only about 200–250 men. Consequently, the expansion of Syria's commandos entailed an increase from about 1,500–2,000 to about 10,000–15,000 commandos. Hanna Batatu, "Some Observations on the Social Roots of Syria's Ruling Military Groups and the Causes for its Dominance," *Middle East Journal* 35, no. 3 (summer 1981), 332; Eisenstadt, *Arming for Peace?* 29, Richard Gabriel, *Operation Peace for Galilee* (New York: Hill and Wang, 1984), 119; Moreaux, Mar. 1986, 26, 30; Urban, "Fire in the Galilee, Part 2," 209.

72. Col. Trevor N. Dupuy and Paul Martell, *Flawed Victory: The Arab-Israeli Conflict and the 1982 War in Lebanon* (Fairfax VA: Hero, 1986), 90; Seale, *Asad,* 377; Wald, *Wald Report,* 41–47.

73. Cordesman and Wagner, *LMW: Arab-Israeli Conflicts,* 118; M. Thomas Davis, *40 KM into Lebanon* (Washington DC: National Defense University Press, 1987), 78–84; Dupuy and Martell, *Flawed Victory,* 91–94; Gabriel, *Operation Peace for Galilee,* 75–81; Ze'ev Schiff and Ehud Ya'ari, *Israel's Lebanon War,* ed. and trans. Ina Friedman (New York: Simon and Schuster, 1984), 110–17.

74. The best description (and the original revelations) of the machinations by Sharon and Begin and their influence on the development of Israeli military planning can be found in Schiff and Ya'ari, *Israel's Lebanon War,* 31–108. See also Avi-Ran, *Syrian Involvement in Lebanon,* 132; and Ma'oz, *Syria and Israel,* 170–74.

75. Avi-Ran, *Syrian Involvement in Lebanon,* 132–36; Cordesman and Wagner, *LMW: Arab-Israeli Conflicts,* 83; Ma'oz, *Syria and Israel,* 174–75; Schiff and Ya'ari, *Israel's Lebanon War,* 117–18, 155–56; Seale, *Asad,* 380; Wald, *Wald Report,* 41–42.

76. Cordesman and Wagner, *LMW: Arab-Israeli Conflicts,* 139; Dupuy and Martell, *Flawed Victory,* 112; Schiff and Ya'ari, *Israel's Lebanon War,* 161–62; Seale, *Asad,* 382; Francis Tusa, "Lebanon 1982: Israeli Hubris or Syrian Strength?" *Armed Forces* 6, no. 9 (Sept. 1987): 418; Wald, *Wald Report,* 38; senior IDF officers, interviews, Sept. 1996.

77. Avi-Ran, *Syrian Involvement in Lebanon,* 136; Cohen, *Israel's Best Defense,* 466–72; Cordesman and Wagner, *LMW: Arab-Israeli Conflicts,* 186–93; Dupuy and Martell, *Flawed Victory,* 119–21; Eshel, *Lebanon War,* 46–47; Gabriel, *Operation Peace for Galilee,* 97–99; Katz, *Soldier Spies,* 293; Benjamin S. Lambeth, *Moscow's Lessons from the 1982 Lebanon Air War,* RAND Report R-3000-AF (Santa Monica CA: RAND, 1984), esp. 7–11; Schiff and Ya'ari, *Israel's Lebanon War,* 166–67; Tusa, "Lebanon 1982," 418–19; Yonay, *No Margin,* 358.

78. Cohen, *Israel's Best Defense,* 465–72; Cordesman and Wagner, *LMW: Arab-Israeli Conflicts,* 144,197–203; Eshel, *Lebanon War,* 46–47; Carus and Goodman, *Future Battlefield,* 26; Lambeth, *Moscow's Lessons,* esp. 7–11; Nordeen, *Fighters over Israel,* 168–72; Seale, *Asad,* 381; Tusa, "Lebanon 1982," 418–19; Yonay, *No Margin,* 358.

79. Quoted in Cordesman and Wagner, *LMW: Arab-Israeli Conflicts,* 197.

80. Lambeth, *Moscow's Lessons,* 31.

81. Quoted in Seale, *Asad,* 381. See also Nordeen, *Fighters over Israel,* 179.

82. Cordesman and Wagner, *LMW: Arab-Israeli Conflicts,* 143, 150; Davis, *40 KM*

into Lebanon, 93; Dupuy and Martell, *Flawed Victory,* 123–24; Eshel, *Lebanon War,* 62–64; Gabriel, *Operation Peace for Galilee,* 102–5; Katz, *Fire and Steel,* 249–61; Schiff and Ya'ari, *Israel's Lebanon War,* 171–79; Wald, *Wald Report,* 46–54; senior IDF officers, interviews, Sept. 1996.

83. Cordesman and Wagner, LMW: *Arab-Israeli Conflicts,* 143; Davis, *40 KM into Lebanon,* 93; Dupuy and Martell, *Flawed Victory,* 123–24; Gabriel, *Operation Peace for Galilee,* 102–5; Schiff and Ya'ari, *Israel's Lebanon War,* 171–79; Wald, *Wald Report,* 46–54; senior IDF officers, interviews, Sept. 1996.

84. There is some confusion as to the number of Syrian T-72s destroyed in this clash. Cordesman and Wagner as well as Dupuy and Martell state that Israeli Merkava tanks destroyed nine T-72s. However, other sources (principally Davis, *40 KM into Lebanon*) make it clear that the Syrians were fighting Peled's tank-killing ugdah and that most of the Syrian tank losses were actually to Israeli ATGMS, not to the Merkavas. This last point was confirmed by Maj. Gen. Amir Drori, the overall commander of the Israeli invasion. According to Drori, the majority of T-72s destroyed were knocked out by TOW ATGMS and only a small number were destroyed by tanks. This seems to support Tusa's claim that the Israelis destroyed thirty T-72s in the firefight. Tusa sides heavily with the Syrians in most debates, suggesting that this figure is not an Israeli exaggeration. Gabriel confuses the issue further by claiming that the Syrians only lost nine T-72s to Israeli ATGMS and that the Merkavas did not destroy any. Gabriel's account is almost certainly inaccurate. Maj. Gen. Amir Drori, interview with author, Sept. 1996; Tusa, "Lebanon 1982," 419; Gabriel, *Operation Peace for Galilee,* 105.

85. Cordesman and Wagner, LMW: *Arab-Israeli Conflicts,* 150, 153; Dupuy and Martell, *Flawed Victory,* 140; Gabriel, *Operation Peace for Galilee,* 120–21; Moreaux, Mar. 1986, 28; Seale, *Asad,* 394; Tusa, "Lebanon 1982," 419. The Israeli casualty estimates are those of Cordesman and Wagner, which strike me as pretty accurate. All other casualty figures for Israel fail to distinguish losses between combat with Syrians and those with the Palestinians.

86. Cordesman and Wagner, LMW: *Arab-Israeli Conflicts,* esp. 151–52; Dupuy and Martell, *Flawed Victory,* 218–26; Gabriel, *Operation Peace for Galilee,* 119.

87. Schiff and Ya'ari, *Israel's Lebanon War,* 172.

88. Drori, interview, Sept. 1996.

89. Herzog, *Arab-Israeli Wars,* 357.

90. Senior IDF officers, interviews, Sept. 1996. See also Davis, *40 KM into Lebanon,* 93; Dupuy and Martell, *Flawed Victory,* 123–24; Eshel, *Lebanon War,* 63; Gabriel, *Operation Peace for Galilee,* 102–5; and Katz, *Fire and Steel,* 249.

91. Cordesman, *Jordanian Arms,* 77.

92. Israel's aversion to taking casualties invariably made some of their battles seem like massacres when in fact their losses would be considered negligible by most other militaries.

93. For an emphatic concurring opinion that Syria got off lightly because of Israeli failings rather than Syrian successes, see Wald, *Wald Report,* 21–54.

94. Mark A. Heller, "Israeli and Syrian Military Concepts in Light of the Lebanon War," *IDF Journal* (winter 1989): 42–46.

95. Anthony Cordesman, *The Arab-Israeli Military Balance and the Art of Operations* (Lanham MD: University Free Press, 1987), 45, 113; Cordesman and Wagner, *LMW: Arab-Israeli Conflicts*, 275–78, 285–87; Eisenstadt, *Arming for Peace?* 31–40, 57–76.

96. Cordesman and Wagner, *LMW: Arab-Israeli Conflicts*, 279, 290, 352–54; Ze'ev Eytan and Aharon Levran, *The Middle East Military Balance, 1986*, Jaffee Center for Strategic Studies (Boulder CO: Westview, 1986), 183–85.

97. Cordesman, *Arab-Israeli Military Balance*, 45, 121, 157; Cordesman and Wagner, *LMW: Arab-Israeli Conflicts*, 279–85; Efraim Karsh, "Gulf War Lessons: Syria," unpublished paper prepared for the Center for National Security Studies, Los Alamos National Laboratory, 1992, 4.

7. Conclusions and Lessons

1. Of course, Egyptian forces were much better armed than the Royalists in Yemen, just as the Iraqis were far better armed than the Kurds. However, these were counterinsurgency campaigns in which the relative balance in weaponry actually counts for little. Once again, the U.S. experience in Vietnam and the Soviet experience in Afghanistan make clear this distinction between conventional and counterinsurgency operations.

2. Indeed, maintenance is normally considered a part of logistics by most military authors and armed forces manuals. See J. H. Skinner, "Combat Service Support," and "Logistics," in Margiotta, *Brassey's Encyclopedia*, 200–202, 602–39.

3. As noted previously, most post–Gulf War assessments of Iraqi manpower strength in the KTO are incorrect because they employ an incorrect order of battle for Iraqi forces. See chap. 2, notes 111 and 123, above.

4. Quoted in Cordesman and Wagner, *LMW: Arab-Israeli Conflicts*, 197.

5. It is for precisely the same reasons that unit cohesion is much less important to the effectiveness of air forces than armies. Dogfights and all other air operations are inherently decentralized affairs because of the tremendous difficulty any central authority has exercising constant control in them. For this reason, initiative, adaptability, creativity, independent judgment, and other such attributes are essential for pilots just as they are for tactical commanders in maneuver battles on the ground.

6. For a superb treatment of revolutions in military affairs and the transformations of warfare over the last six centuries, see Andrew A. Krepinevich Jr., "Cavalry to Computer: The Pattern of Military Revolutions," *The National Interest* (fall 1994), 30–42.

SELECTED BIBLIOGRAPHY

Government Documents

Army Component, U.S. Central Command (ARCENT). "Battlefield Reconstruction Study: The 100 Hour Ground War." Declassified version. Headquarters, Army Component, U.S. Central Command, 20 April 1991.

Belzyudnyy, Lt. Col. Sergey. "Former Soviet Adviser Describes Experiences in Iraq: 'I Taught Saddam's Aces to Fly'" (from *Komsomolskaya Pravda*, 23 February 1991). JPRS-UMA-91-014 (5 June 1991).

Central Intelligence Agency. "Operation Desert Storm: A Snapshot of the Battlefield." Washington DC: CIA, September 1993.

Eighteenth Airborne Corps Headquarters. "XVIII Airborne Corps Desert Storm Chronology, 24–28 February 1991: Ground Offensive Combat." *http://www .army.mil/cmh-pg/chronos/28feb91.htm* (visited 27 March 1998).

Englehardt, Lt. Col. Joseph. "Desert Shield and Desert Storm: A Chronology and Troop List for the 1990–1991 Persian Gulf Crisis." Carlisle Barracks PA: U.S. Army War College Strategic Studies Institute, March 1991.

Ferezan, Col. Daniel M. "Memorandum for Commander, Third U.S. Army, Attn: G-3, APO NY, Subject: Project 5/Liaison Team Golf After Action Report." 31 March 1991. (Report obtained through Freedom of Information Act request.)

First Brigade, First Infantry Division Desert Shield/Desert Storm Unit History. N.p., n.d.

Al-Harbi, Col. Bandar O. Nahlil. "Saudi Arabia National Guard." USAWC Military Studies Program Paper, 27 March 1991, U.S. Army War College, Carlisle Barracks PA.

Joint Technical Coordinating Group for Munitions Effectiveness. *Special Report: Survey of Combat Damage to Tanks.* 3 vols. Washington DC: Defense Intelligence Agency, 1 November 1970.

Karsh, Efraim. "Gulf War Lessons: Syria." Unpublished paper prepared for the Center for National Security Studies, Los Alamos National Laboratory, 1992.

Karsh, Efraim, and Inari Rautsi. "Gulf War Lessons: The Case of Iraq." Unpublished paper prepared for the Center for National Security Studies at Los Alamos, 1992.

Memorandum for the record, "The Gulf War: An Iraqi General Officer's Perspective," 11 March 1991. Doc. no: NA-22. (This is a declassified summary of U.S. debriefings of Iraqi generals captured during the Persian Gulf War.)

Office of the Program Manager (AMCPM-NGT-O), U.S. Army Program Manager, Saudi Arabian National Guard Modernization to Col. Richard Swain, 6 October 1991. (Letter obtained through the Freedom of Information Act.)

Political Deputy of the General Command Post, War Studies and Research. *Battle of Faw*. Tehran, 1988. Translated from Persian in FBIS-NES-94-076-S, 20 April 1994.

Smith, James D. "Report on Saudi Arabian National Guard Modernization through Project Manager." Office of the Program Manager, Saudi Arabian National Guard, 20 August 1975.

Staudenmaier, William O. "A Strategic Analysis of the Gulf War." Carlisle Barracks PA: Strategic Studies Institute, U.S. Army War College, 1982.

U.S. Department of Defense. *Conduct of the Persian Gulf War: Final Report to Congress, April 1992*. Washington DC: GPO, 1992.

U.S. Forces Command Intelligence Center. *Handbook of Military Forces (Ground) — Egypt*. Declassified (originally secret). Fort Bragg NC: U.S. Army Forces Command Intelligence Center, February 1975.

Books

Adan, Avraham "Bren." *On the Banks of the Suez*. San Francisco: Presidio, 1980.

Aker, Frank. *October 1973: The Arab-Israeli War*. Hamden CT: Archon, 1985.

Antoun, Richard T., and Donald Quataert, eds. *Syria: Society, Culture, and Polity*. Albany: SUNY Press, 1991.

Aruri, Naseer H., ed. *Middle East Crucible: Studies on the Arab-Israeli War of October, 1973*. AAUG Monograph Series, no. 6. Wilmette IL: Medina University Press International, 1975.

Asher, Lt. Col. Daniel. "The Syrian Invasion of Lebanon — Military Moves as a Political Tool." Translated by Michael Eisenstadt. *Ma'arachot* (June 1977).

Asher, Jerry (with Eric Hammel). *Duel for the Golan*. New York: William Morrow, 1987.

Atkinson, Rick. *Crusade: The Untold Story of the Persian Gulf War*. New York: Houghton Mifflin, 1993.

Avi-Ran, Reuven. *The Syrian Involvement in Lebanon since 1975*. Boulder CO: Westview, 1991.

Avirgan, Tony, and Martha Honey. *War in Uganda: The Legacy of Idi Amin*. Westport CT: Lawrence Hill, 1982.

Badeeb, Saeed M. *The Saudi-Egyptian Conflict over North Yemen, 1962–1970*. Boulder CO: Westview, 1986.

Badri, Hassan El; Taha El Magdoub; and Mohammed Dia El Din Zohdy. *The Ramadan War, 1973.* New York: Hippocrene, 1974.

Bailey, Clinton. *Jordan's Palestinian Challenge, 1948–1983: A Political History.* Boulder CO: Westview, 1984.

Baker, Raymond. *Sadat and After: Struggles for Egypt's Political Soul.* Cambridge: Harvard University Press, 1990.

Ball, Desmond. *The Intelligence War in Gulf.* Canberra: Strategic Studies Centre, Australian National University, 1991.

Baram, Amatzia, and Barry Rubin, eds. *Iraq's Road to War.* New York: St. Martin's, 1993.

Bar-Joseph, Uri. *The Best of Enemies: Israel and Transjordan in the War of 1948.* London: Frank Cass, 1987.

Barnett, Michael N. *Confronting the Costs of War: Military Power, State, and Society in Egypt and Israel.* Princeton NJ: Princeton University Press, 1992.

Bearman, Jonathan. *Qadhafi's Libya.* London: Zed, 1986.

Be'eri, Eliezer. *Army Officers in Arab Politics and Society.* New York: Praeger, 1970.

Bellamy, Christopher. *Expert Witness: A Defence Correspondent's Gulf War 1990–1991.* London: Brassey's, 1993.

Bergquist, Maj. Ronald E. *The Role of Airpower in the Iran-Iraq War.* Maxwell Air Force Base AL: Air University Press, 1988.

Beufre, General d'Armee André. *The Suez Expedition, 1956.* Translated by Richard Barry. New York: Praeger, 1969.

Blackwell, Maj. James, Jr. *Thunder in the Desert.* New York: Bantam, 1991.

Blair, Arthur H. *At War in the Gulf.* College Station: Texas A&M University Press, 1992.

Bregman, Ahron. *Israel's Wars, 1947–93.* London: Routledge, 2000.

Bulloch, John, and Harvey Morris. *The Gulf War.* London: Methuen, 1989.

Carus, Seth W., and Hirsh Goodman. *The Future Battlefield and the Arab-Israeli Conflict.* New Brunswick: Transaction, 1990.

Churchill, Randolph S., and Winston S. Churchill. *The Six Day War.* London: Heinemann, 1967.

Clevenger, Maj. Daniel. *"Battle of Khafji": Air Power Effectiveness in the Desert.* Washington DC: Air Force Studies and Analyses Agency, July 1996.

Cohen, Col. Eliezer. *Israel's Best Defense: The First Full Story of the Israeli Air Force.* Translated by Jonathan Cordis. New York: Orion, 1993.

Cohen, Eliot A., and Thomas A. Keaney, gen. eds. *Gulf War Air Power Survey.* Vol. 1, pt. 1, *Planning.* Washington DC: GPO, 1993.

———. *Gulf War Air Power Survey.* Vol. 2, pt. 1, *Operations.* Washington DC: GPO, 1993.

———. *Gulf War Air Power Survey.* Vol. 2, pt. 2, *Effects and Effectiveness.* Washington DC: GPO, 1993.

Cooley, John K. *Libyan Sandstorm.* New York: Holt, Rinehart, and Winston, 1981.

Copley, Gregory R. *Defense and Foreign Affairs Handbook on Egypt, 1995*. London: International Media, 1995.

Copson, Raymond W. *Africa's Wars and Prospects for Peace*. Armonk NY: M. E. Sharpe, 1994.

Cordesman, Anthony. *Jordanian Arms and the Middle East Balance*. Washington DC: Middle East Institute, 1983.

——. *Western Strategic Interests in Saudi Arabia*. London: Croom Helm, 1987.

—— *The Arab-Israeli Military Balance and the Art of Operations*. Lanham MD: University Free Press, 1987.

——. *After the Storm: The Changing Military Balance in the Middle East*. Boulder CO: Westview, 1993.

Cordesman, Anthony, and Abraham Wagner. *The Lessons of Modern War, Volume 1: The Arab-Israeli Wars, 1973–1989*. Boulder CO: Westview, 1990.

——. *The Lessons of Modern War, Volume 2: The Iran-Iraq War*. Boulder CO: Westview, 1990.

——. *After the Storm: The Changing Military Balance in the Middle East*. Boulder CO: Westview, 1993.

——. *The Lessons of Modern War, Volume 4: The Gulf War*. Boulder CO: Westview, 1996.

——. *Saudi Arabia: Guarding the Desert Kingdom*. Boulder CO: Westview, 1997.

Craft, Douglas W. *An Operational Analysis of the Persian Gulf War*. Carlisle Barracks PA: Strategic Studies Institute, U.S. Army War College, 1992.

Davis, Brian L. *Qaddafi, Terrorism, and the Origins of the U.S. Attack on Libya*. Westport CT: Praeger, 1990.

Davis, M. Thomas. *40 KM into Lebanon*. Washington DC: National Defense University Press, 1987.

Day, Arthur R. *East Bank/West Bank*. New York: Council on Foreign Relations, 1986.

Dayan, David. *Strike First: A Battle History of Israel's Six-Day War*. New York: Pitman, 1967.

Dayan, Moshe. *Diary of the Sinai Campaign*. New York: Harper and Row, 1965. Reprint, New York: Shocken Books, 1967.

——. *The Story of My Life*. New York: William Morrow, 1976.

Deeb, Marius. *The Lebanese Civil War*. New York: Praeger, 1980.

Deeb, Mary-Jane. *Libya's Foreign Policy in North Africa*. Boulder CO: Westview, 1990.

De La Billiere, Gen. Sir Peter. *Storm Command: A Personal Account of the Gulf War*. Dubai, UAE: Motivate, 1992.

Dunnigan, James F., and Austin Bay. *From Shield to Storm*. New York: Morrow, 1992.

Dupuy, Col. Trevor N. *Elusive Victory*. New York: Harper and Row, 1978. Reprint, Dubuque IA: Kendall Hunt, 1992.

Dupuy, Col. Trevor N., and Paul Martell. *Flawed Victory: The Arab-Israeli Conflict and the 1982 War in Lebanon*. Fairfax VA: HERO, 1986.

El-Edroos, Brig. Gen. Syed Ali. *The Hashemite Arab Army, 1908–1979.* Amman: Amman Publishing Committee, 1980.

Eisenstadt, Michael. *The Sword of the Arabs: Iraq's Strategic Weapons.* Washington DC: Washington Institute for Near East Policy, 1990.

———. *Arming for Peace? Syria's Elusive Quest for "Strategic Parity."* Washington DC: Washington Institute for Near East Policy, 1992.

———. *Like a Phoenix from the Ashes: The Future of Iraqi Military Power.* Washington DC: Washington Institute for Near East Policy, 1993.

Eshel, Lt. Col. David. *The Lebanon War, 1982.* Hod Hasharon, Israel: Eshel-Dramit, 1983.

Eytan, Zeev, and Aharon Levran. *The Middle East Military Balance.* Jaffee Center for Strategic Studies. Boulder CO: Westview, 1986–94.

Farid, Abdel Magid. *Nasser: The Final Years.* Reading UK: Ithaca, 1994.

Fisher, Sidney. *The Military in the Middle East: Problems in Society and Government.* Columbus: Ohio State University Press, 1963.

Fisk, Robert. *Pity the Nation: The Abduction of Lebanon.* New York: Atheneum, 1990.

Freedman, Lawrence, and Efraim Karsh. *The Gulf Conflict, 1990–1991.* Princeton NJ: Princeton University Press, 1993.

Friedman, Norman. *Desert Victory.* Annapolis MD: Naval Institute Press, 1991.

Fuldheim, Dorothy. *Where Were the Arabs?* Cleveland: World, 1967.

Fullick, Roy, and Geoffrey Powell. *Suez: The Double War.* London: Hamish Hamilton, 1979.

Gabriel, Richard. *Operation Peace for Galilee.* New York: Hill and Wang, 1984.

El-Gamasy, Field Marshall Mohamed Abdel Ghani. *The October War: Memoirs of Field Marshal El-Gamasy of Egypt.* Translated by Gillian Potter, Nadra Marcos, and Rosette Frances. Cairo: American University in Cairo Press, 1993.

Gause, Gregory F., III. *Oil Monarchies: Domestic and Security Challenges in the Arab Gulf States.* New York: Council on Foreign Relations, 1994.

Gawrych, George W. *Key to the Sinai: The Battles of Abu Ageilah in the 1956 and 1967 Arab-Israeli Wars.* Fort Leavenworth KS: U.S. Army Command and General Staff College, 1990.

Glassman, Jon D. *Arms for the Arabs: The Soviet Union and War in the Middle East.* Baltimore: Johns Hopkins University Press, 1975.

Glubb, Sir John Bagot. *The Story of the Arab Legion.* New York: Da Capo, 1976.

———. *The Changing Scenes of Life: An Autobiography.* London: Quartet, 1983.

Grummon, Stephen R. *The Iran-Iraq War: Islam Embattled.* Washington Papers no. 92. New York: Praeger, 1982.

Gur, Lt. Gen. Mordechai. *The Battle for Jerusalem.* Translated by Phillip Gillon. New York: Popular Library, 1974.

Halion, Richard. *Storm over Iraq.* Washington DC: Smithsonian Institution Press, 1992.

Halpern, Manfred. *The Politics of Social Change in the Middle East and North Africa.* 1st paperback ed. Princeton NJ: Princeton University Press, 1965.

Hammel, Eric. *Six Days in June*. New York: Scribner's, 1992.

Heikal, Mohammed. *The Road to Ramadan*. Paperback ed. New York: Ballantine, 1975.

———. *The Sphinx and the Commissar*. New York: Harper and Row, 1978.

Herzog, Chaim. *The War of Atonement*. London: Weidenfeld and Nicolson, 1975.

———. *The Arab-Israeli Wars*. New York: Random House, 1982.

Hillsman, Roger. *George Bush vs. Saddam Hussein*. Novato CA: Lyford, 1992.

Hiro, Dilip. *The Longest War: The Iran-Iraq Military Conflict*. New York: Routledge, 1991.

———. *Desert Shield to Desert Storm: The Second Gulf War*. New York: Routledge, 1992.

———. *Fire and Embers: A History of the Lebanese Civil War*. New York: St. Martin's Press, 1992.

Historical Evaluations and Research Organization. *A Historical Analysis of the Effectiveness of Tactical Air Operations against, and in Support of, Armored Forces*. McLean VA: NOVA, 1980.

Hopwood, Derek. *Syria, 1945–1986: Politics and Society*. London: Unwin Hyman, 1988.

———. *Egypt: Politics and Society, 1945–90*. London: Harper Collins, 1991.

Hurewitz, J. C. *Middle East Politics: The Military Dimension*. New York: Praeger, 1969.

Insight Team of the *London Sunday Times*. *The Yom Kippur War*. New York: Doubleday, 1974.

Israeli Ministry of Defense. *The Six-Day War*. [Tel Aviv]: Israel Press, 1967.

Izady, Mehrdad R. *The Kurds*. Washington DC: Crane Russak, 1992.

Joarder, Safiuddin. *Syria under the French Mandate, the Early Phase: 1920–1927*. Dacca: Asiatic Society of Bangladesh, 1977.

Joyner, Christopher C., ed. *The Persian Gulf War: Lessons for Strategy, Law, and Diplomacy*. Westport CT: Greenwood, 1990.

Kahalani, Avigdor. *The Heights of Courage: A Tank Leader's War on the Golan*. Translated by Louis Williams. New York: Praeger, 1992.

Kamiya, Maj. Jason J. *A History of the 24th Mechanized Infantry Division Combat Team during Operation Desert Storm*. 3 vols. Fort Stewart GA: U.S. Department of the Army—Headquarters, 24th Mechanized Division, 1992.

Karsh, Efraim. *The Iran-Iraq War: A Military Analysis*. Adelphi Paper 220. London: IISS, 1987.

Karsh, Efraim, and Inari Rautsi. *Saddam Hussein: A Political Biography*. New York: Free Press, 1991.

Katz, Samuel M. *Soldier Spies: Israeli Military Intelligence*. Novato CA: Presidio, 1992.

———. *Fire and Steel: Israel's Seventh Armored Brigade*. New York: Pocket, 1996.

Khaled, HRH Gen. Bin Sultan. *Desert Warrior: A Personal View of the Gulf War by the Joint Forces Commander*. New York: Harper Collins, 1995.

King Hussein of Jordan (as told to and with additional material by Vick Vance and

Pierre Lauer). *My "War" with Israel*. Translated by June P. Wilson and Walter B. Michaels. New York: William Morrow, 1969.

Kolkowicz, Roman, and Andrej Korbonski, eds. *Soldiers, Peasants, and Bureaucrats: Civil-Military Relations in Communist and Modernizing Societies*. London: George Allen and Unwin, 1982.

Korn, David A. *Stalemate: The War of Attrition and Great Power Diplomacy in the Middle East, 1967–1970*. Boulder CO: Westview, 1992.

Kuppersmith, Maj. Douglas A. *The Failure of Third World Air Power: Iraq and the War with Iran*. Maxwell Air Force Base AL: Air University Press, June 1993.

Kyle, Keith. *Suez*. New York: St. Martin's, 1991.

Laffin, John. *War of Desperation*. London: Osprey, 1985.

Lambeth, Benjamin S. *Moscow's Lessons from the 1982 Lebanon War*. RAND Rpt. R-3000-AF. Santa Monica CA: RAND, 1984.

Lawson, Fred H. *Why Syria Goes to War: Thirty Years of Confrontation*. Ithaca NY: Cornell University Press, 1996.

Legum, Colin. *Africa Contemporary Record*. New York: Africana, 1982–88.

Long, David E. *The Kingdom of Saudi Arabia*. Gainesville: University Press of Florida, 1997.

Lorch, Lt. Col. Natanel. *The Edge of the Sword: Israel's War of Independence, 1947–1949*. New York: Putnam, 1961.

Love, Kennett. *Suez: The Twice-Fought War*. New York: McGraw Hill, 1969.

Lunt, James. *Hussein of Jordan*. London: Macmillan, 1989.

Luttwak, Edward N., and Daniel Horowitz. *The Israeli Army, 1948–1973*. New York: Harper and Row, 1975. Reprint, Cambridge MA: ABT Books, 1983.

Makiya, Kanaan [Samir al-Khalil, pseudo.]. *Republic of Fear: The Politics of Modern Iraq*. Berkeley CA: University of California Press, 1989.

Ma'oz, Moshe. *Syria and Israel: From War to Peace-making*. London: Oxford University Press, 1995.

Ma'oz, Moshe, and Avner Yaniv, ed. *Syria under Assad: Domestic Constraints and Regional Risks*. New York: St. Martin's, 1986.

Margiotta, Col. Franklin D., ed. *Brassey's Encyclopedia of Land Forces and Warfare*. London: Brassey's, 1996.

Marr, Phebe. *The Modern History of Iraq*, Boulder CO: Westview, 1985.

Marshall, S. L. A. *Swift Sword: The Historical Record of Israel's Victory, June 1967*. N.p.: American Heritage, 1967.

Martin, David C., and John Walcott. *Best Laid Plans: The Inside Story of America's War against Terrorism*. New York: Harper and Row, 1988.

Mazarr, Michael J., Don M. Snider, and James Blackwell Jr. *Desert Storm: The Gulf War and What We Learned*. Boulder CO: Westview, 1993.

McDowall, David. *A Modern History of the Kurds*. London: I. B. Tauris, 1996.

McLaurin, R. D. *Military Operations in the Gulf War: The Battle of Khorramshahr*. Aberdeen Proving Grounds MD: U.S. Army Human Engineering Laboratory, 1982.

McNaugher, Thomas L. *Arms and Oil: U.S. Military Strategy and the Persian Gulf.* Washington DC: Brookings, 1985.

Metz, Helen Chapin, ed. *Libya: A Country Study.* Washington DC: GPO, 1989.

——. *Iraq: A Country Study.* Washington DC: GPO, 1990.

——. *Jordan: A Country Study.* Washington DC: GPO, 1991.

Moore, Molly. *A Woman at War: Storming Kuwait with the U.S. Marines.* New York: Charles Scribner's Sons, 1993.

Moskin, Robert J. *Among Lions: The Definitive Account of the 1967 Battle for Jerusalem.* New York: Arbor House, 1982.

Mutawi, Samir. *Jordan in the 1967 War.* Cambridge: Cambridge University Press, 1987.

Narkiss, Uzi. *The Liberation of Jerusalem: The Battle of 1967.* London: Valentine Mitchell, 1983.

National Training Center. *The Iraqi Army: Organization and Tactics.* Fort Irwin CA: National Training Center, 1991.

Neff, Donald. *Warriors for Jerusalem.* New York: Linden, 1984.

——. *Warriors against Israel.* Brattleboro VT: Amana, 1988.

Neuberger, Benyamin. *Involvement, Invasion, and Withdrawal: Qahdhafi's Libya and Chad, 1969–1981.* Vol. 83. Occasional Papers of the Shiloah Center for Middle Eastern and African Studies. Tel Aviv: Shiloah Center, Tel Aviv University, 1982.

Niblock, Tim. *State. Society and Economy in Saudi Arabia.* London: Croom Helms, 1982.

Nordeen, Lon. *Fighters over Israel.* London: Greenhill, 1991.

Nordeen, Lon, and David Nicole. *Phoenix over the Nile: A History of Egyptian Airpower, 1932–1994.* Washington DC: Smithsonian Institution, 1996.

Nyrop, Richard F., ed. *Syria: A Country Study.* Washington DC: GPO, 1978.

——. *Egypt: A Country Study.* Washington DC: GPO, 1983.

——. *Saudi Arabia: A Country Study.* 4th ed. Washington DC: GPO, 1984.

O'Ballance, Edgar. *The Arab-Israeli War, 1948.* London: Faber and Faber, 1956.

——. *The War in the Yemen.* Hamden CT: Archon, 1971.

——. *The Third Arab-Israeli War.* Hamden CT: Archon, 1972.

——. *Arab Guerrilla Power, 1967–1972.* Hamden CT: Archon, 1973.

——. *The Kurdish Revolt, 1961–1970.* Hamden CT: Archon, 1973.

——. *The Electronic War in the Middle East, 1968–1970.* London: Faber and Faber, 1974.

——. *No Victor, No Vanquished: The Yom Kippur War.* London: Barrie and Jenkins, 1979.

——. *The Gulf War.* London: Brassey's, 1988.

——. *The Kurdish Struggle.* New York: St. Martin's, 1996.

Ofer, Tzvi, ed. *The Iraqi Army in the Yom Kippur War.* Translated by "Hatzav." Ma'arachot Forum for Military Studies. Tel Aviv: Ma'arachot, 1986.

Orlansky, Jesse, and Col. Jack Thorpe, eds. *73 Easting: Lessons Learned from Desert*

Storm via Advanced Distributed Simulation Technology. (Proceedings of a conference, 27–29 August 1991). Alexandria VA: IDA, 1992.

Palit, D. K. *Return to Sinai: The Arab Offensive, October 1973.* Dehra Dun, India: Palit and Palit, 1974.

Palmer, Michael A. *Guardians of the Gulf.* New York: Free Press, 1992.

Parker, Richard B., ed. *The Six-Day War: A Retrospective.* Gainesville: University Press of Florida, 1996.

Pascal, Anthony; Michael Kennedy; Steven Rosen; et al. *Men and Arms in the Middle East: The Human Factor in Military Modernization.* RAND Report R-2460-NA. Santa Monica CA: RAND, 1979.

Pelletiere, Stephen. *The Iran-Iraq War: Chaos in a Vacuum.* New York: Praeger, 1992.

Pelletiere, Stephen C., and Douglas V. Johnson. *Lessons Learned: The Iran-Iraq War.* Carlisle Barracks PA: Strategic Studies Institute, U.S. Army War College, 1990.

Pelletiere, Stephen C.; Douglas V. Johnson; and Leif R. Rosenberger. *Iraqi Power and U.S. Security in the Middle East.* Carlisle Barracks PA: Strategic Studies Institute, U.S. Army War College, 1990.

Perlmutter, Amos. *Egypt: The Praetorian State.* New Brunswick NJ: Transaction, 1974.

Peterson, J. E. *Defending Arabia.* New York: St. Martin's, 1986.

Petran, Tabitha. *Syria.* New York: Praeger, 1972.

Pimlott, John and Stephen Badsey, eds. *The Gulf War Assessed.* London: Arms and Armour Press, 1992.

Rabin, Yitzhak. *The Rabin Memoirs.* London: Weidenfeld and Nicolson, 1979.

Rabinovich, Abraham. *The Battle for Jerusalem.* Philadelphia: Jewish Publication Society, 1987.

Rabinovich, Itamar. *The War for Lebanon: 1970–1985.* 2d ed. Ithaca NY: Cornell University Press, 1985.

Rabinovich, Itamar, and Haim Sheked, eds. *From June to October.* New Brunswick NJ: Transaction, 1978.

Rahmy, Ali Abdel Rahman. *The Egyptian Policy in the Arab World: Intervention in Yemen, 1962–1967.* Washington DC: University Press of America, 1983.

Rajaee, Farhad, ed. *Iranian Perspectives on the Iran-Iraq War.* Gainesville: University Press of Florida, 1997.

——. *The Iran-Iraq War.* Gainesville: University Press of Florida, 1993.

Record, Jeffrey. *Hollow Victory: A Contrary View of the Gulf War.* Washington DC: Brassey's, 1993.

Robinson, Donald, ed. *Under Fire: Israel's 20-Year Struggle for Survival.* New York: W. W. Norton, 1968.

El-Sadat, Anwar. *In Search of Identity: An Autobiography.* New York: Harper and Row, 1977.

Safran, Nadav. *From War to War.* New York: Pegasus, 1969.

——. *Saudi Arabia: The Ceaseless Quest for Security.* Ithaca NY: Cornell University Press, 1988.

St. John, Ronald Bruce. *Qaddafi's World Design: Libyan Foreign Policy, 1967–1987*. London: Saqi, 1987.

Satloff, Robert B. *Troubles on the East Bank*. New York: Praeger, 1986.

——. *Army and Politics in Mubarak's Egypt*. Policy Paper no. 10. Washington DC: Washington Institute for Near East Policy, 1988.

——. *The Politics of Change in the Middle East*. Boulder CO: Westview, 1993.

Scales, Brig. Gen. Robert H. *Certain Victory*. Washington DC: Office of the Chief of Staff of the U.S. Army, 1993.

Schiff, Ze'ev. *A History of the Israeli Army*. New York: Macmillan, 1985.

Schiff, Ze'ev, and Ehud Ya'ari. *Israel's Lebanon War*. Edited and translated by Ina Friedman. New York: Simon and Schuster, 1984.

Schmidt, Dana Adams. *Yemen: The Unknown War*. London: Bodley Head, 1968.

Schwarzkopf, Gen. Norman, and Peter Petre. *It Doesn't Take a Hero*. New York: Bantam, 1992.

Seale, Patrick. *The Struggle for Syria: A Study of Post-War Arab Politics, 1945–1958*. 1965. Reprint, London: I. B. Tauris, 1986.

——. *Asad of Syria: The Struggle for the Middle East*. London: I. B. Tauris, 1988.

Sella, Amnon. *Soviet Political and Military Conduct in the Middle East*. New York: St. Martin's, 1981.

Sharon, Ariel (with David Chanoff). *Warrior: The Autobiography of Ariel Sharon*. New York: Simon and Schuster, 1989.

Shazli, Lt. Gen. Sa'ad Din. *The Crossing of Suez*. San Francisco: American Mideast Research, 1980.

Shemesh, Haim. *Soviet-Iraqi Relations 1968–1988*. Boulder CO: Lynn Rienner, 1992.

Simon, Reeva S. *Iraq between the Two World Wars*. New York: Columbia University Press, 1986.

Simons, Geoff. *Libya: The Struggle for Survival*. New York: St. Martin's, 1996.

Sinai, Anne, and Allen Pollack. *The Hashemite Kingdom of Jordan and the West Bank: A Handbook*. New York: American Academic Association for Peace in the Middle East, 1976.

——. *The Syrian Arab Republic: A Handbook*. New York: American Academic Association for Peace in the Middle East, 1976.

Sluglett, Marion Farouk, and Peter Sluglett. *Iraq since 1958: From Revolution to Dictatorship*. London: Kegan Paul International, 1987.

Smiley, David, (with Peter Kemp). *Arabian Assignment*. London: Leo Cooper, 1975.

Somerville, Keith. *Foreign Military Intervention in Africa*. London: Pinter, 1990.

Stanik, Joseph T. *"Swift and Effective Retribution": The U.S. Sixth Fleet and the Confrontation with Qaddafi*. Washington: GPO, 1996.

Swain, Richard M. *"Lucky War": Third U.S. Army in Desert Storm*. Ft. Leavenworth KS: U.S. Army Command and General Staff College, 1994.

Tahir-Kheli, Shirin, and Shaheen Ayubi, eds. *The Iran-Iraq War: New Weapons, Old Conflicts*. New York: Praeger, 1983.

Tarbush, Mohammed A. *The Role of the Military in Politics: A Case Study of Iraq to 1941*. London: Kegan Paul International, 1982.

Taylor, Thomas. *Lightning in the Storm: The 101st Air Assault Division in the Gulf War*. New York: Hippocrene, 1994.

Teveth, Shabtai. *The Tanks of Tammuz*. New York: Viking, 1968.

Thompson, Virginia, and Richard Adloff. *Conflict in Chad*. Berkeley: University of California Press, 1981.

Trainor, Lt. Gen. Bernard, and Michael R. Gordon. *The Generals' War: The Inside Story of the Conflict in the Gulf*. Boston: Little, Brown, 1995.

Tripp, Charles. *A History of Iraq*. Cambridge: Cambridge University Press, 2000.

Tröen, Selwyn I., and Moshe Shemesh, eds. *The Suez-Sinai Crisis 1956: Retrospective and Reappraisal*. London: Frank Cass, 1990.

U.S. News and World Report. Triumph without Victory. New York: Times, 1992.

Van Dam, Nikolaos. *The Struggle for Power in Syria: Sectarianism, Regionalism, and Tribalism in Politics, 1961–1978*. New York: St. Martin's, 1979.

Vandewalle, Dirk, ed. *Qadhafi's Libya, 1969–1994*. New York: St. Martin's, 1995.

Various. *The Seventh Day: Soldiers Talk about the Six-Day War*. London: Andre Deutsch, 1970.

Vatikiotis, P. J. *Politics and the Military in Jordan: A Study of the Arab Legion, 1921–1957*. London: Frank Cass, 1967.

——. *The History of Modern Egypt*. 4th ed. Baltimore: Johns Hopkins University Press, 1991.

Wald, Emmanuel. *The Wald Report: The Decline of Israeli National Security since 1967*. Boulder CO: Westview, 1992.

Watson, Bruce W., et al. *The Military Lessons of the Gulf War*. London: Greenhill, 1991.

Weinberger, Naomi. *Syrian Intervention in Lebanon*. New York: Oxford University Press, 1986.

Wenner, Manfred W. *Modern Yemen: 1918–1966*. Baltimore: Johns Hopkins University Press, 1967.

Williams, Louis, ed. *International Symposium on the Military Aspects of the Arab-Israeli Conflict*. Tel Aviv: University Publishers, 1975.

Wilson, Peter W., and Douglas F. Graham. *Saudi Arabia: The Coming Storm*. Armonk NY: M. E. Sharpe, 1994.

Woodward, Bob. *The Commanders*. New York: Simon and Schuster, 1991.

Wright, John. *Libya, Chad, and the Central Sahara*. Totowa NJ: Barnes and Noble, 1989.

Yizraeli, Sarah. *The Remaking of Saudi Arabia*. Dayan Center Papers, no. 121. Tel Aviv: Moshe Dayan Center, 1997.

Yonay, Ehud. *No Margin for Error: The Making of the Israeli Air Force*. New York: Pantheon, 1993.

Young, Brig. Peter. *The Israeli Campaign, 1967*. London: William Kimber, 1967.

Zabhi, Sepehr. *The Iranian Military in Revolution and War*. London: Routledge, 1988.

Articles, Essays, and Reports

Abir, Mordechai. "Saudi Security and Military Endeavor." *The Jerusalem Quarterly* 33 (fall 1984).

Allen, Lt. Col. Larry R., and Maj. Fred W. Bucher. "Modernizing the Saudi Guard." *Soldiers* 50, no. 8 (March 1995).

Anable, David. "Egyptian-Libyan Tensions Rise as Border Clashes Flare." *The Christian Science Monitor,* 22 July 1977.

Anderson, Lisa. "Libya's Qaddafi: Still in Command?" *Current History* (February 1987).

Antal, Maj. John F. "The Iraqi Army Forged in the Other Gulf War." *Military Review* 71 (February 1991).

Armstrong, G. P. "Egypt: A Combat Assessment." In *Fighting Armies: Antagonists in the Middle East*, edited by Richard Gabriel. Westport CT: Greenwood, 1983.

Ashkar, Riad. "The Syrian and Egyptian Campaigns." *Journal of Palestine Studies* 3, no. 2 (1974).

Ashkar, Riad, and Haytham al-Ayyubi. "The Middle East Conflict: The Military Dimension—Interviews with Riad Ashkar and Haytham al-Ayyubi." *Journal of Palestine Studies* 4, no. 4 (1975).

Atkeson, Maj. Gen. Edward B. "Iraq's Arsenal: Tool of Ambition." *Army* 41 (March 1991).

Axelgard, Frederick W. "Iraq and the War with Iran." *Current History* (February 1987).

Badolato, E. V. "A Clash of Cultures: The Expulsion of Soviet Military Advisors from Egypt." *U.S. Naval War College Review* 37, no. 2 (March–April 1984).

Baram, Amatzia. "Neo-Tribalism in Iraq: Saddam Hussein's Tribal Policies 1991–1996." *International Journal of Middle East Studies* 29 (1997).

Barclay, C. N. "Learning the Hard Way: Lessons from the October War." *Army* 24 (March 1974).

Barnett, Michael N., and Jack S. Levy. "Domestic Sources of Alliances and Alignments: The Case of Egypt, 1962–1973." *International Organization* 45, no. 3 (summer 1991).

Batatu, Hanna. "Some Observations on the Social Roots of Syria's Ruling Military Group and the Causes for Its Dominance." *Middle East Journal* 35, no. 3 (summer 1981).

Benjamin, Milton R., and William Schmidt. "Arab vs. Arab." *Newsweek,* 1 August 1977.

Bermudez, Joseph S., Jr. "Libyan SAMs and Air Defences." *Jane's Defence Weekly,* 17 May 1986.

Bigelow, Capt. Michael E. "The Faw Peninsula: A Battle Analysis." *Military Intelligence* (April–June 1991).

Bishop, Patrick. "Egyptians Overcome Determined Defence." *The Daily Telegraph,* 26 February 1991.

Blackwell, Maj. James, Jr.; and William J. Taylor. "The Ground War in the Gulf." *Survival* 33 (May–June 1991).

——. "Georgia Punch: 24th Mech Puts the Squeeze on Iraq." *Army Times*, 2 December 1991.

Blair, William G. "UN Hears Defense in Downing of Jets." *The New York Times*, 7 January 1989.

Bloomfield, Lincoln P., Jr. " Commentary: Saudi Arabia's Security Problems in the 1980s." In *Defense Planning in Less-Industrialized States*, edited by Stephanie Neuman. Lexington MA: Lexington, 1984.

"Both Egypt and Libya Accept Cease-fire, Arafat Says." *The Los Angeles Times*, 26 July 1977.

Brandon, Henry. "Jordan: The Forgotten Crisis." *Foreign Policy* 10 (spring 1973).

Brooke, James. "Libyan Jets Bomb Chadian Units." *The New York Times*, 31 March 1987.

——. "Modern Arms a Key Factor in Chadian Gains." *The New York Times*, 2 April 1987.

——. "Chadians Describe Victory in Desert." *The New York Times*, 14 August 1987.

——. "Chad Reports New Libyan Attack." *The New York Times*, 15 August 1987.

Brower, Kenneth. "The Yom Kippur War." *Military Review* 54 (March 1974).

Brown, Neville. "Jordanian Civil War." *Military Review* 51 (September 1971).

Burgess, Capt. William H., III. "Special Operations in the Iran-Iraq War." *Special Warfare* (winter 1989).

Carus, W. Seth. "The Bekaa Valley Campaign." *The Washington Quarterly* 5, no. 4 (autumn 1982).

——. "Defense Planning in Iraq." In *Defense Planning in Less-Industrialized States*, edited by Stephanie Neuman. Lexington MA: Lexington, 1984.

——. "Military Lessons of the 1982 Israel-Syria Conflict." In *The Lessons of Recent Wars in the Third World*, vol. 1, edited by Robert Harkavy and Stephanie Neuman. Lexington MA: Lexington, 1986.

——. "How Vulnerable is Iraq's Military?" Washington DC: Washington Institute for Near East Policy, 1990.

"Chad: The Battle of Ouadi Doum." *The Economist*, 28 March 1987.

"Chad: Toyota War." *The Economist*, 12 September 1987.

Chaplin, Dennis. "Libya: Military Spearhead against Sadat?" *Military Review* 59 (November 1979).

Cigar, Norman. "Iraq's Strategic Mindset and the Gulf War: Blueprint for Defeat." *Journal of Strategic Studies* 15 (March 1992).

Cogan, Charles G. "The Response of the Strong to the Weak: The American Raid on Libya, 1986." *Intelligence and National Security* 6, no. 3 (1991).

Cohen, Avert. "Cairo, Dimona, and the June 1967 War." *Middle East Journal* 50, no. 2 (spring 1996).

Cooper, Mark N. "The Demilitarization of the Egyptian Cabinet." *International Journal of Middle East Studies* 14 (1982).

Cordesman, Anthony. "Defense Planning in Saudi Arabia." In *Defense Planning in Less-Industrialized States*, edited by Stephanie Neuman. Lexington MA: Lexington, 1984.

Crawley, Vince. "Ghost Troop's Battle at the 73 Easting." *Armor* 100 (May–June 1991).

Danis, Aaron. "Iraqi Army Operations and Doctrine." *Military Intelligence* 17 (April–June 1991).

Dawisha, Adeed I. "Intervention in the Yemen: An Analysis of Egyptian Perceptions and Policies." *Middle East Journal* 29 (winter 1975).

———. "Saudi Arabia's Search for Security." In *Regional Security in the Middle East*, edited by Charles Tripp. New York: St. Martin's, 1984.

Dyer, Gwynne. "Libya." In *World Armies*, edited by John Keegan. 2d ed. London: Macmillan, 1983.

Eaker, Ira C. "The Fourth Arab-Israeli War." *Strategic Review* 2 (January 1974).

Eilts, Hermann Frederick. "Commentary: Defense Planning in Egypt." In *Defense Planning in Less-Industrialized States*, edited by Stephanie Neuman. Lexington MA: Lexington, 1984.

Eisenstadt, Michael. "The Iraqi Armed Forces, Two Years On." *Jane's Intelligence Digest* 5, no. 3 (March 1993).

Eldar, Lt. Col. Nahum, and Lt. Colonel Tzvi. "Combat against the Egyptian Commandos during the Yom Kippur War." *Ma'arachot* (November–December 1992).

Emery, Fred. "North Korean Pilots in Egypt MiGs Open Fire on Israelis." *The Times of London*, 19 October 1973.

"Expanding Saudi's Elite Fighting Force." *Jane's Defence Weekly*, 24 January 1996.

Fahad, A. H. "In Defense of Saudi Arabia: Why Has Such a Rich State Had Such a Weak Military." *Washington Post*, 12 February 1991.

Foltz, William J. "Libyan Military Power." In *The Green and the Black: Qadhafi's Policies in Africa*, edited by Rene Lemarchand. Bloomington: Indiana University Press, 1988.

Fontenot, Col. Gregory. "Fright Night: Task Force 2/34 Armor." *Military Review* 73 (January 1993).

Gabriel, Richard. "Lessons of War: The IDF in Lebanon." *Military Review* 64 (August 1984).

El-Gamasy, Field Marshal Mohamed Abdel Ghani. "The Military Strategy of the October 1973 War." In *October War: Military, Political, Economic and Psychological Effects (Proceedings of the Cairo Symposium on the October War)*. Canberra: Embassy of the Arab Republic of Egypt, October 1976.

Ganz, A. Harding. "Abu Ageila — Two Battles, Part I: 1956." *Armor* 33, no. 3 (May–June 1974).

———. "Abu Ageila—Two Battles, Part II: 1967." *Armor* 33, no. 4 (July–August 1974).

Garfinkle, Adam M. "U.S. Decision-Making in the Jordan Crisis: Correcting the Record." *Political Science Quarterly* 100, no. 1 (spring 1985).

Gause, F. Gregory, III. "Saudi Arabia: Desert Storm and After." In *The Middle East after Iraq's Invasion of Kuwait*, edited by Robert O. Freedman. Gainesville: University Press of Florida, 1993.

Gawrych, George W. "The Egyptian High Command in the 1973 War." *Armed Forces and Society* 13 (summer 1987).

———. "The Egyptian Military Defeat of 1967." *Journal of Contemporary History* 26 (1991).

Ghareeb, Edmund. "The Forgotten War." *American-Arab Affairs* 5 (summer 1983).

Gordon, Shmuel. "The Air Force and the Yom Kippur War: New Lessons." *Israel Affairs* 6, no. 1 (autumn 1999).

Greenhous, Brereton. "The Israeli Experience." In *Case Studies in the Development of Close Air Support*, edited by Benjamin F. Cooling. Washington DC: Office of Air Force History, 1990.

Hammick, Murray. "Aerial Views: USAF Air-to-Air Combat." *International Defense Review* (July 1991).

———. "Iraqi Obstacles and Defensive Positions." *International Defense Review* (September 1991).

Heikal, Mohammed. "General Ismail and the War—Interview with Lt. General Ismail," *Journal of Palestine Studies* 3, no. 2 (1974).

Heller, Mark. "Politics and the Military in Iraq and Jordan, 1920–1958." *Armed Forces and Society* 4, no. 1 (November 1977).

———. "Israeli and Syrian Concepts in Light of the Lebanon War." *IDF Journal* (winter 1989).

Helms, Christine Moss. "The Iraqi Dilemma: Political Objectives vs. Military Strategy." *American-Arab Affairs* 5 (summer 1983).

Hemphill, Paul P. J. "The Formation of the Iraqi Army, 1921–1933." In *The Integration of Modern Iraq*, edited by Abbas Kelidar. New York: St. Martin's, 1979.

Hempstone, Smith. "Libya: Another Nagging Headache for Sadat." *U.S. News and World Report*, 10 April 1978.

Henderson, George. "Qaddafy's Waterloo." *Africa Report* (September–October 1987).

Holthus, Capt. Michael D., and Steven M. Chandler. "Myths and Lessons of Iraqi Artillery." *Field Artillery* 80 (October 1991).

Hotz, Robert. "Egypt Plans Modernized Air Arm." *Aviation Week and Space Technology*, 30 June 1975.

Hughes, Lt. Col. D. P. "Battle for Khafji: 29 Jan–1 Feb 1991." *Army Quarterly and Defense Journal* (UK) 124, no. 1 (January 1994).

International Institute for Strategic Studies. "The Middle East War." In *Strategic Survey, 1973*. London: IISS, 1973.

———. "Chad: Libya on the Run." In *Strategic Survey, 1986–1987*. London: IISS, 1987.

———. "Chad: Libya Heading North." In *Strategic Survey, 1987–1988*. London: IISS, 1988.

"Iraq's Army: Lessons from the War with Iran." *The Economist*, 12 January 1991.

James, Franziska. "Habré's Hour of Glory." *Africa Report* (September–October 1987).

Janowitz, Morris. "Comparative Analysis of Middle Eastern Military Institutions." In *Military Conflict: Essays in the Institutional Analysis of War and Peace*, edited by Morris Janowitz. Beverly Hills CA: Sage, 1975.

Jawdat, Nameer Ali. "Reflections on the Gulf War." *Arab-American Affairs* 5 (summer 1983).

Jupa, Richard, and James Dingemann. "The Republican Guards: Loyal, Aggressive, Able." *Army* 41 (March 1991).

Kam, Ephraim. "Gulf War Lessons Learned by Egypt." Unpublished paper prepared for the Center for National Security Studies at Los Alamos, 1992.

Karawan, Ibrahim A. "Egypt's Defense Policy." In *Defense Planning in Less-Industrialized States*, edited by Stephanie Neuman. Lexington MA: Lexington, 1984.

Khadduri, Majid. "The Role of the Military in Middle Eastern Politics." *American Political Science Review* 47 (1953).

Khan, M. B. "Saudi Arabia's Armoured Corps: A Ground-Level Appreciation." *International Defense Review* (September 1990).

Kindsvatter, Lt. Col. Peter S. "VII Corps in the Gulf War." *Military Review* 72 (February 1992).

Kumrasamy, P. R. "The Arabian Interpretation of Operation Desert Storm: An Analysis of Saudi Military Communiques." *Strategic Analysis* (June 1991).

Legum, Colin. "Libya's Intervention in Chad." In *Crisis and Conflicts in the Middle East*, edited by Colin Legum. New York: Holmes and Meier, 1981.

Lemarchand, Rene. "The Case of Chad." In *The Green and the Black*, edited by Rene Lemarchand. Bloomington: Indiana University Press, 1988.

"Lessons from the Arab-Israeli War: Report of a Seminar at the Royal United Services Institute for Defence Studies, January 30, 1974." *Army Journal* 308 (January 1975).

Lewis, Paul. "Libyans Said to Begin Retreating from Last Major Foothold in Chad." *The New York Times*, 26 March 1987.

Lewis, Capt. Robert D. "The Ramadan War: Fire Support Egyptian Style." *Field Artillery* 77 (August 1988).

MacGregor, Lt. Col. Douglas A. "Closing with the Enemy." *Military Review* 73 (February 1993).

Macris, LCDR Jeffrey R. "Knowing Thy Gulf Partners." *U.S. Naval Institute Proceedings* 124, no. 3 (March 1998).

Marshall, S. L. A. "Egypt's Two Week Military Myth." *The New Leader*, 12 November 1973.

———. "Tank Warrior in the Golan." *Military Review* 56 (January 1976).

Mason, R. A. "The Air War in the Gulf." *Survival* 33, no. 3 (May–June 1991).

"Maxi-Plots behind a Strange Mini-War." *Time*, 8 August 1977.

McIntire, Katherine. "Speed Bumps: The 82d's Shaky line in the Sand." *Army Times*, 21 October 1991.

McLean, Lt. Col. Neil. "The War in the Yemen." *Journal of the Royal United Services Institute for Defence Studies*, February 1966.

McNaugher, Thomas L. "The Iran-Iraq War: Slouching toward Catastrophe?" *Middle East Review* (summer 1987).

———. "Arms and Allies on the Arabian Peninsula." *Orbis* 28, no. 3 (fall 1984).

Middleton, Drew. "U.S. Aides Say Egypt Lacks Ability to Handle Weapons." *The New York Times*, 21 February 1986.

Moodie, Michael. "Six Months of Conflict." *The Washington Quarterly* 5, no. 4 (autumn 1982).

Moore, Molly, and George C. Wilson. "U.S. Navy Jets Shoot Down 2 Libyan Fighters." *The Washington Post*, 5 January 1989.

Moreaux, J. M. "The Syrian Army." *Defence Update* 69 (March 1986).

———. "The Syrian Army." *Defence Update* 73 (July 1986).

Naylor, Sean D. "Flight of Eagles: 101st Airborne Division's Raids into Iraq." *Army Times*, 22 July 1991.

Neff, Donald. "Israel-Syria: Conflict at the Jordan River, 1949–1967." *Journal of Palestine Studies* 23, no. 4 (summer 1994): 26–40.

Nelson, S. S. "Cultural Differences a Factor in Saudi Deployment." *Air Force Times*, 10 September 1990.

Ottaway, David. "For Saudi Military, New Self-Confidence." *The Washington Post*, 20 April 1991.

Owen, Roger. "The Role of the Army in Middle Eastern Politics: A Critique of Existing Analyses." *Review of Middle East Studies* 3 (1978).

Pardew, James W., Jr. "The Iraqi Army's Defeat in Kuwait." *Parameters* (winter 1991–92).

Parker, Richard B. "The June 1967 War: Some Mysteries Explored." *Middle East Journal* 46, no. 2 (spring 1992).

Pengelly, Rupert. "Jordan Hones Its Regional Security Blade." *International Defense Review* (November 1996).

Peterson, J. E. "The GCC States After the Iran-Iraq War." *Journal of Arab-American Affairs* 26 (fall 1988).

Rabinovich, Abraham. "Stemming the Syrian Onslaught." *MHQ: The Quarterly Journal of Military History* 13, no. 3 (spring 2001).

Rabinovich, Itamar. "The Limits of Military Power: Syria's Role." In *Lebanon in Crisis*, edited by Edward P. Haley and Lewis W. Snider. Syracuse NY: Syracuse University Press, 1979.

Rathmell, Andrew. "Iraqi Intelligence and Security Services." *International Defense Review* (May 1991).

——. "Libya's Intelligence and Security Services." *International Defence Review* (July 1991).

——. "Saudi Arabia's Military Build-up — An Extravagant Error?" *Jane's Intelligence Review* (November 1994).

Record, Jeffrey. "The October War: Burying the Blitzkrieg." *Military Review* 56, no. 4 (1976).

"Revenge in the Desert." *Time*, 1 August 1977.

Rodan, Steve. "Report: Western Influence Enhances Egyptian AF Capability." *Defense News*, 27 January–2 February 1997.

Rosenthal, Andrew. "Pentagon Defends Tactics of Pilots off Libya." *The New York Times*, 11 January 1989.

Rottman, Gordon L. "Saddam's Juggernaut or Armed Horde? The Origins of the Iraqi Army." *International Defense Review* (November 1990).

Roumani, Jacques. "From Republic to Jamahiriya: Libya's Search for Political Community." *The Middle East Journal* 37, no. 2 (spring 1983).

"The Royal Jordanian Air Force: The Arab Professionals." *Air International* 9, no. 3 (September 1975).

Scales, Brig. Gen. Robert H. "Accuracy Defeated Range in Artillery Duel." *International Defense Review* (May 1991).

Schanche, Don A. "Egypt, Libya Seen Approaching Truce." *The Los Angeles Times*, 26 August 1977.

Scicchitano, J. Paul. "Eye of the Tiger: Stalking Prey with the Tiger Brigade." *Army Times*, 10 June 1991.

Segal, David. "The Iran-Iraq War: A Military Analysis." *Foreign Affairs* 67, no. 3 (summer 1988).

Sela, Avraham. "The 1973 Arab War Coalition: Aims, Coherence, and Gain-Distribution." *Israel Affairs* 6, no. 1 (autumn 1999).

Shazli, Lt. Gen. Sa'ad Din. "How the Egyptians Crossed the Canal — Interview with Lt. General Shazli." *Journal of Palestine Studies* 3, no. 2 (1974).

Sick, Gary. "Trial by Error: Reflections on the Iran-Iraq War." *Middle East Journal* 43, no. 2 (spring 1989).

Sluglett, Marion Farouk. "Contemporary Iraq: Some Recent Writings Reconsidered." *Review of Middle East Studies* 3 (1978).

Stanhope, Henry. "Text-Book Invaders Dither towards Disaster." *The Times of London*, 26 October 1973.

——. "A Bitter Lesson for the Arabs." *The Times of London*, 22 October 1973.

Stanton, Lt. Col. Martin N. "The Saudi Arabian National Guard Motorized Brigades." *Armor* 55 (March–April 1996).

Starr, Barbara. "Saudis Pause for Thought." *Jane's Defence Weekly* 16, no. 24 (14 October 1991).

——. "Defense Planning in Iraq: An Alternative Perspective." In *Defense Planning in Less-Industrialized States,* edited by Stephanie Neuman. Lexington MA: Lexington, 1984.

——. "The Iran-Iraq War." In *The Lessons of Recent Wars in the Third World,* volume 1, edited by Robert Harkavy and Stephanie Neuman. Lexington MA: Lexington, 1986.

Steele, Dennis. "Down in the Sand: The First Brushes." *Army* 41 (March 1991).

Stevens, Mark (with William E. Schmidt and Lloyd H. Norman). "War of Nerves." *Newsweek,* 13 September 1976.

"The Suez Crossing: An Interview with Major General Mohamed Abdel Halim Abu Ghazala." *Military Review* 59, no. 11 (November 1979).

"Syria and Egypt: Against Iraq." *The Economist,* 5 January 1991.

Tanner, Henry. "Sadat's Jets Pound Air Base in Libya; He Assails Qaddafi." *The New York Times,* 23 July 1977.

——. "Libyans Say Egypt Keeps Up Air Raids on Widening Front." *The New York Times,* 24 July 1977.

——. "Sadat Orders Halt to Attacks in Libya, Heeding Arab Pleas." *The New York Times,* 25 July 1977.

——. "Egypt Sends Libya List of Conditions for Keeping Truce." *The New York Times,* 26 July 1977.

Tartter, Jean R. "National Security." In *Chad: A Country Study,* edited by Thomas Collelo. Washington DC: GPO, 1990.

Terrill, W. Andrew. "The Nature and Value of Commando Operations during the Egyptian-Israeli War of Attrition." *Small Wars and Insurgencies* 8, no. 2 (autumn 1997).

Tice, Jim. "Coming Through: The Big Red Raid." *Army Times,* 26 August 1991.

Trainor, Lt. Gen. Bernard. "Chad's Anti-Libya Offensive: Surprising Successes." *The New York Times,* 12 January 1987.

——. "Victories Shore Up Chadians." *The New York Times,* 18 January 1987.

——. "France and U.S. Aiding Chadians with Intelligence to out Libyans." *The New York Times,* 3 April 1987.

——. "Desert Tactics of Chadians: Like Old West." *The New York Times,* 5 April 1987.

——. "In the Desert, Chad Exhibits Spoils of War." *The New York Times,* 13 April 1987.

——. "Iraqi Offensive: Victory Goes Beyond Battlefield." *The New York Times,* 20 April 1988.

Tripp, Charles. "The Iran-Iraq War and the Iraqi State." In *Iraq: Power and Society,* edited by Derek Hopwood, Habib Ishow, and Thomas Koscinowski. Reading UK: Ithaca, 1993.

Turner, Arthur C. "Nationalism and Religion: Iran and Iraq at War." In *The Regionalization of Warfare,* edited by James Brown and William P. Snyder. New Brunswick NJ: Transaction, 1990.

Tusa, Francis. "Lebanon 1982: Israeli Hubris or Syrian Strength?" *Armed Forces* 6, no. 9 (September 1987).

Urban, Mark. "Fire in the Galilee, Part 2: Syria." *Armed Forces* 5, no. 5 (June 1986).

———. "Fire in the Galilee, Part 3: A Future Conflict." *Armed Forces* 5, no. 6 (May 1986).

Van Creveld, Martin. "Military Lessons of the Yom Kippur War." *The Jerusalem Quarterly* 5 (fall 1977).

Viksne, Lt. Col. J. "The Yom Kippur War in Retrospect, Part II — Technology." *Army Journal* (Australia) 324 (May 1976).

Viorst, Milton. "Iraq at War." *Foreign Affairs* 65, no. 2 (winter 1986–87).

Vogel, Steve. "A Swift Kick: Second ACR's Taming of the Guard." *Army Times*, 5 August 1991.

———. "Metal Rain: 'Old Ironsides' and the Iraqis Who Wouldn't Back Down." *Army Times*, 16 September 1991.

———. "The Tip of the Spear." *Army Times*, 13 January 1992.

Wagner, John S. "Iraq: A Combat Assessment." In *Fighting Armies: Antagonists in the Middle East*, edited by Richard Gabriel. Westport CT: Greenwood, 1983.

Wakebridge, Charles. "The Egyptian Staff Solution." *Military Review* 55 (March 1975).

———. "The Syrian Side of the Hill." *Military Review* 56 (February 1976).

Weller, Jack. "Infantry and the October War." *Army* 24 (August 1974).

Whetten, Lawrence L. "The Military Dimension." In *Lebanon in Crisis*, edited by P. Edward Haley and Lewis W. Snider. Syracuse NY: Syracuse University Press, 1979.

Wickman, Maj. Michael D. "'Hold at All Cost': 24 Hours on the Golan Front during the October War of 1973." *Armor* 60, no. 2 (March–April 2001).

Wilson, George C. "Libyan Sailors, Aviators Reportedly Unskilled." *The Washington Post*, 9 January 1986.

———. "U.S. Dogfight Began without Top-Alert Call." *The Boston Globe*, 10 January 1989.

———. "Secretly Acquired MiGs Aided Navy Pilots in Libya Combat." *The Washington Post*, 13 January 1989.

———. "Despite New Details, Libyan MiG Incident Is Still Puzzling." *The Washington Post*, 26 March 1989.

Zartman, William I. "Arms Imports — The Libya Experience." In *World Military Expenditures and Arms Transfers, 1971–1980*, U.S. Arms Control and Disarmament Agency. Washington DC: ACDA, 1983.

Zumwalt, Lt. Col. J. G. "Tanks! Tanks! Direct Front!" *U.S. Naval Institute Proceedings* 118, no. 7 (July 1992).

Unpublished Works

Bingham, Lt. Col. Price T. "The Battle of Al Khafji and the Future of Surveillance Precision Strike." Unclassified manuscript, 1996.

Dahmy, Talal M. "The Military Organization as an Agent for Modernization in Third World Countries: Case Study—National Guard in Saudi Arabia." Ph.D. diss., Florida State University, 1988.

DePuy, Gen. William E. "Implications of the Middle East War on U.S. Army Tactics, Doctrine, and Systems." Briefing slides for U.S. Army Training and Doctrine Command, 1981.

Eisenstadt, Michael. "Syria's Defense Companies: Profile of a Praetorian Unit." Unpublished manuscript, 1989.

Kelleher, Daniel J. "Security Assistance for Force Modernization—The Saudi Arabian National Guard Program." Student essay, 15 April 1985, U.S. Army War College, Carlisle Barracks PA.

Lorell, Mark A. "Airpower in Peripheral Conflict: The French Experience in Africa." RAND Rpt. R-3660-AF. Santa Monica CA: RAND, 1989.

Moore, James Kennon. "Walking the Line of Death: U.S.-Libyan Relations in the Reagan Decade, 1981–1989." Master's thesis, San Jose State University, 1991.

Titus, James. "The Battle of Khafji: An Overview and Preliminary Analysis." Airpower Research Institute, College of Aerospace Doctrine, Research, and Education, Air University, September 1996.

Turner, Lt. Col. John H. "Counterattack: The Battle of al-Burqan." Unpublished essay, Security Studies Program, Massachusetts Institute of Technology, March 1993.

INDEX

Note on indexing of Arabic names: Many Arabic names take the form of "'Abd al-Something," with the "something" being one of the ninety-nine names of Allah. Translated, these names mean "servant of God." Arabs often employ a shorthand that uses only the last part of such names, which is often how most Westerners know them: hence, Gamal 'Abd an-Nasr is referred to simply as "Nasser." In all cases, these names have been indexed under *A*.

Note on indexing of Arabic tribal names: Other Arabic names, especially those in tribal societies such as Saudi Arabia, Iraq, and Jordan, consist of a string of names in which an individual's first name is joined to that of his father. As a result, there may be no single name by which all ancestors in the same family could be identified. For example, the name Saddam Husayn consists of Saddam's own first name (Saddam) and that of his father (Husayn), and Saddam's sons' full names are Udayy Saddam and Qusayy Saddam. Saddam Husayn's father's full name was Husayn al-Majid; 'Abd al-Majid was Saddam's grandfather's name. In some cases, this relationship is indicated by the use of the Arabic words "ibn" or "bin" (for men), which means "son of" (e.g., Fahd ibn 'Abd al-Aziz). In other cases, no patronymic is used (e.g., Salah Abud Mahmud). In this index, for all of these cases, the names have been indexed according to the first initial of the person's first name; therefore, Saddam Husayn appears under *S*.